THE SPANISH CIVIL WAR

The Spanish Civil War: A Military History takes a new, military approach to the conflict that tore Spain apart from 1936 to 1939.

In many histories, the war has been treated as a primarily political event with the military narrative subsumed into a much broader picture of the Spain of 1936–9 in which the chief themes are revolution and counter-revolution. While remaining conscious of the politics of the struggle, this book looks at the war as above all a military event, and as one in whose outbreak specifically military issues – particularly the split in the armed forces produced by the long struggle in Morocco (1909–27) – were fundamental. Across nine chapters that consider the war from beginning to endgame, Charles J. Esdaile revisits traditional themes from a new perspective, deconstructs many epics and puts received ideas to the test, as well as introducing readers to foreign-language historiography that has previously been largely inaccessible to an anglophone audience.

In taking this new approach, *The Spanish Civil War: A Military History* is essential reading for all students of twentieth-century Spain.

Charles J. Esdaile has been a member of staff in the Department of History at the University of Liverpool since 1989 and was awarded a personal chair in 2004. He is the author of numerous works on Spanish history including *Spain, 1808–1939: From Constitution to Civil War* (Blackwell, 2000).

WARFARE AND HISTORY

General Editor: Jeremy Black
Professor of History, University of Exeter

THE SPANISH CIVIL WAR

A Military History

Charles J. Esdaile

Routledge
Taylor & Francis Group

LONDON AND NEW YORK

First published 2019
by Routledge
2 Park Square, Milton Park, Abingdon, Oxon OX14 4RN

and by Routledge
711 Third Avenue, New York, NY 10017

Routledge is an imprint of the Taylor & Francis Group, an informa business

British Library Cataloguing-in-Publication Data
A catalogue record for this book is available from the British Library

Library of Congress Cataloging-in-Publication Data
Library of Congress Cataloging-in-Publication Data
Names: Esdaile, Charles J., author.
Title: The Spanish Civil War: a military history/Charles J. Esdaile.
Description: Abingdon, Oxon; N.Y., NY: Routledge, [2019]
Identifiers: LCCN 2018021234 | ISBN 9781138311268 (hardback :
alk. paper) | ISBN 9781138311275 (pbk. : alk. paper) |
ISBN 9780429458965 (ebook)
Subjects: LCSH: Spain–History–Civil War, 1936–1939. |
Spain–History–Civil War, 1936–1939–Historiography.
Classification: LCC DP269 E7234 2019 | DDC 946.081/4–dc23
LC record available at https://lccn.loc.gov/2018021234

ISBN: 978-1-138-31126-8 (hbk)
ISBN: 978-1-138-31127-5 (pbk)
ISBN: 978-0-429-45896-5 (ebk)

Typeset in Bembo
by Deanta Global Publishing Services, Chennai, India

MIX
Paper from
responsible sources
FSC
www.fsc.org
FSC™ C013985

Printed in the United Kingdom
by Henry Ling Limited

For Martin Blinkhorn who taught me and
Sukey Elstob who learned with me.

CONTENTS

MAPS

PREFACE

This work is something of an alpha and an omega. Holidaying in the home of my newly married elder brother in the summer of 1972, I happened one evening quite by chance to catch a documentary on the International Brigades on the television. Being of a somewhat naïve and romantic disposition, I was utterly hooked and for most of my teenage years devoured everything that I could find on the Spanish Civil War; the battered copy of Hugh Thomas' seminal work on the subject – incidentally, the work that has probably been the greatest single influence on my writing and, indeed, my general approach as a historian – that I read on the train going to and from sundry university interviews and open days is lying on my desk in front of me even as I write these words. As an undergraduate at Lancaster, then, I very much specialized in the Civil War and ended up writing not one but two dissertations on the subject, whilst my intention was to follow all this up with a Ph.D., probably on the way in which the political militias in Nationalist Spain were incorporated into the regular army, thereby ensuring that the Carlists and Falange alike had little option but to acquiesce in the rise of Franco to power. In the end, various factors, not least the wise and kindly advice of my much esteemed Special-Subject tutor, Martin Blinkhorn, led me down different roads, and this is something that I have never regretted: not only did the Peninsular War prove a field of study rich beyond my wildest imagining, but I do not believe that the youthful idealism of all those years ago would have been of the slightest help in disentangling the complexities of Civil War Spain (at the same time, too, if I have shone at all, I do not believe that I could possibly have done so in the company of such redoubtable practitioners of the historical art as Paul Preston, Helen Graham, Nigel Townson and Mary Vincent). Yet the Civil War has never gone away: very soon after my arrival at Liverpool in 1989, I found myself putting on a Special Subject on the Spanish Republic and Civil War, while my endless journeys to and from Spain brought me into contact with numerous Spaniards whose family histories were intimately (and frequently tragically) bound up with the conflict, the link being further maintained by my publication in 1999 of *Spain in the Liberal Age: from Constitution to Civil War*. As I near the end of my career – I suspect that this will be the last monograph I will ever write – and, more particularly, now that my long war against Bonaparte and his legions of apologists is finally at an end, there is something very natural about turning back to my roots in what has had been a real voyage of rediscovery.

But, even if I am not totally unqualified to embark on such a project, how can yet another history of the Spanish Civil War be justified? To answer this question, let us take a look at the current state of the question, and particularly so with regard to the specific area of military history. Almost eighty years on, the Spanish Civil War remains a source of bitter controversy. Whilst rival sectors of the hard Left continue to excoriate one another over the issue of how the Spanish Republic should have defended itself against the military rising of July 1936, in Spain from 2004 onwards, the consensus that marked the first thirty years of the post-Franco democratization was torn apart by ferocious debates about the question of 'historic memory' (roughly speaking, the issue of how Spain should remember the Franquist regime and offer compensation to its victims). All this has ensured the continuation of the flood of memoirs that the subject had always generated, although the emphasis is now much more on rank-and-file combatants rather than senior officers and political leaders, whilst at the same time persuading numerous anglophone scholars to write monographs on various aspects of its history. Yet this continued activity has barely engaged the reading public in Great Britain and beyond: tackling the memoir literature requires a good grasp of various foreign languages and tackling the scholarly literature a degree of immersion in the period that is beyond the vast majority of casual readers. Even if this last was not the case, meanwhile, there is a serious disjuncture between the interests of the casual reader and those of specialists in the period: whilst the former for the most part want to read military narrative, few of the latter are comfortable with this area of study, and all the more so given the increasing popularity of such foci of activity as gender, culture and memory. Also true, meanwhile, are the facts, first, that most professional historians are not conversant with military affairs, and, second, that most popular writers have neither foreign languages nor access to adequate research libraries. The result of all this is that military history has had a tendency to fall by the wayside: on the one hand, those who are equipped to write it are not willing or able to do so, whilst, on the other, those who are willing and able to write it are not equipped to do so.[1] To the best of my knowledge, then, in the whole period since the Civil War, setting aside assorted offerings from Osprey, only one popular work of military history has appeared on the subject in English, namely George Hill's *The Battle for Madrid* (London: Vantage Books, 1976).[2]

This is not to say, of course, that is impossible to acquire a general understanding of the Spanish Civil War. On the contrary, Hugh Thomas' magisterial *Spanish Civil War* (London, 1961) remains a highly accessible read that offers an introduction to all the main battles and campaigns, while in 2006, Anthony Beevor revisited the same subject in *The Battle for Spain: the Spanish Civil War, 1936–1939*

(London, 2006).[3] And, finally, Paul Preston's *The Spanish Civil War: Reaction, Revolution and Revenge* (London, 2006) may be said to rival Thomas as the standard text. Yet none of these works can be deemed entirely satisfactory if what is wanted is a work focused on military events, as they necessarily spend as much time discussing the politics of the war as they do the fighting. Still worse, with respect to crucial episodes such as the defence of Madrid in November 1936, they retail stories that were in reality nothing more the work of over-enthusiastic journalists or political activists eager to undermine their rivals and build up the prestige of their own movements. To take just one example, if the city of Madrid was successfully defended against a massive Nationalist assault in November 1936, it is generally held that this was the work of the people of Madrid, and this claim is then in turn exploited as a means of contesting the Communist policy of closing down the revolution that broke out in the wake of the military rising and arguing that, instead, every effort should have been made to defend and reinforce the gains that had been made for the working classes.

Such instances could be cited at length, and it therefore follows that a prime goal of this volume is to purge the military history of the war of the sort of baggage that has been alluded to. That said, there is also a second objective, in that it draws very heavily on the immense foreign-language historiography, much of which has never been accessible to anglophone readers, many of whom, if they have any knowledge of the war at all, see it above all through the prism of foreign intervention. With many battles of the Civil War being fought out in the popular mind in terms of the International Brigades on the one hand and the Condor Legion on the other, a second aim of the proposed work may therefore be said to be portray the war for what it was, namely a Spanish conflict fought out in the vast majority by Spaniards about issues that were largely Spanish.

So much for my aims, but what of my acknowledgements? As ever, top of the list must come the staff of the various libraries that have done so much to sustain my studies, the Biblióteca Nacional de España, the British Library and the Sydney Jones Library of the University of Liverpool all coming in for an honourable mention here. Next must come Martin Blinkhorn, a great scholar of the Civil War in his own right, but, above all, the man who made it all possible, and, with him, all the many scholars without whose work I could never have written this book: too numerous to mention here, their writings and their influence have enriched its every page. And, then, there are all the approximately 150 students who between 1992 and 2013 followed my Special Subject, and especially the many who came with me on annual field trips to Madrid: if you ever read these words, know that you are each and every one of you remembered with love and appreciation – truly I have been much blessed. Finally, last but not least, there is, as ever, my devoted family: I do not know what I have done to deserve them, nor, in quite another sense altogether, what they have done to deserve me.

Charles J. Esdaile, Liverpool,
15 February 2018.

Notes

1 A prime example of this last tendency is Ronald Fraser. Thus, in the introduction to the pioneering oral history of the war he published in 1979, he writes as follows: '[This] book does not focus on the war at the front. After the first months, when direct civilian militia participation is all-important, it follows the fighting rather from the rearguard. In the circumstances, this may seem a curious procedure. It is based on the conviction that the civil war was won as much in the rearguard as at the front.' R. Fraser, *Blood of Spain: the Experience of Civil War, 1936–1939* (London, 1979), p. 30.

2 R. Colodny, *The Struggle for Madrid: the Central Epic of the Spanish Conflict, 1936–37* (New York, 1958) could also be mentioned here, but this was the work of a volunteer in the International Brigades and is as much a work of propaganda as it is a work of history.

3 Readers wishing to read Thomas' work should read not the 1961 edition but rather the new edition published by Penguin Books in 1977.

1

BEGINNINGS

On 14 April 1931, for the second time in its history, Spain became a republic. On 18 July 1936, that republic collapsed in a civil war that cost hundreds of thousands of lives, devastated large areas of the country and plunged the country into a dictatorship from which she was not to emerge until 1975. It was a traumatic experience – one, indeed, that continues to cast a long shadow over the country to this day – and as such it is a topic that has understandably tended to dominate the historiography of modern Spain down to the current moment. What is striking about much of this writing, however, is a tendency to imagine that civil war was an inevitable 'given' – that when the red, yellow and purple banner of the republic replaced the red and yellow one of the monarchy, the country was immediately placed on a slippery slope that had only one end, namely the physical division of Spain into two armed camps that could not but fight one another to the finish. Yet, if entirely understandable, this is a line that seems to be dangerously determinist. In the climate of the 1930s, certainly, the advent of a reformist régime in Spain was always likely to produce armed confrontation, even to end in violence, but neither confrontation or violence need in themselves to have led to civil war. Even in Spain, such a development was not anticipated. To quote the writer Manuel de Heredia Lozano, 'We were each and every one of us worried; we were each and every one of us convinced that something was going to happen. However, few of us, very few of us even, foresaw a civil war of the sort that was going to break out on 18 July 1936.'[1]

What happened in Spain was therefore anything but a foregone conclusion. If this is doubted, one only has to cast an eye over inter-war Europe as a whole. All but unrelieved though the gloom may be, civil war is actually a very rare phenomenon, and that despite the fact that there was not a single corner of the continent that did not live in the shadow of the October Revolution, the Great Depression and the rise of violent protest movements that found their most terrible expressions in the regimes of Hitler and Mussolini: indeed, there was scarcely a corner of the continent where democracy did not succumb to dictatorship. There were periods of guerrilla insurrection – Poznania in 1918–19 – shoot-outs between rival factions of revolutionary movements – Ireland in 1922–3 – and armed revolts – Munich and Sofia in 1923, Vienna and Oviedo in 1934 – whilst there were also various occasions when armies stepped in to overthrow reformist governments or impose order on domestic situations threatened by what they, genuinely or otherwise, perceived as a slide into complete chaos – Spain and Bulgaria in 1923, Poland and Portugal in 1926, Yugoslavia in 1929 – but only in Russia in 1918, Greece in 1923 and Spain in 1936 do we see civil wars as such, and, of these, the second was over so briefly as to leave scarcely a trace on the historical record. For a civil war to break out, then, something other was needed than the mere fact of social and political division, and it will be here contended that the crucial factor is the existence of not just two hostile camps, but also two rival military forces that are capable of taking one another on and sustaining an armed conflict. In Russia, then, the enormous army that had fought the First World War was never fully demobilized but rather split into substantial regional forces that could compel the allegiance and support of the local population whilst at the same time garnering thousands of recruits who were sometimes ideologically motivated and sometimes driven to enlist by starvation. In Greece, traumatized by defeat in the war with Turkey, the armed forces turned on one another in a conflict that was, mercifully enough, brought to a rapid end by want of arms and munitions. And, finally, always under strain thanks to a variety of historical factors, in Spain the unity of the officer corps was torpedoed by the impact of the long war waged by the Spaniards in Morocco, it essentially being the two armed camps in which this resulted that formed the basis for civil war. To quote Raymond Carr, indeed, 'The organization of the military conspiracy proved a difficult business, not least because the army itself was divided in a concealed civil war between those who accepted the Republic loyally and those who … believed that the politicians were bent on destroying the army "morally," if not physically.'[2]

To reinforce this point, let us take the various examples offered by the year 1934. On 6 February of that year, after weeks of growing tension occasioned by a major financial scandal, a massive demonstration took place in Paris in which a large force of right-wing demonstrators tried to storm the national assembly. With their ranks at breaking point, the police opened fire, and fourteen demonstrators were killed and another 600 wounded. And then, just six days later, there came the events that one historian at least has dubbed the 'Austrian Civil War.' In brief, having a few months earlier suppressed parliament, the right-wing Austrian chancellor, Döllfuss, announced his decision to suppress the Austrian Socialist Party. At this, the Socialists barricaded themselves into their premises around the country and attempted to stage a revolt. In most places the rebels were crushed very quickly, but in Vienna the working-class district of the city known as Floridsdorf was completely taken over by the Socialists. Fighting raged in the streets for four days, but by 16 February it was all over. Several hundred people had been killed, and the newsreels were full of dramatic images of artillery pieces blasting blocks of flats into heaps of rubble, but in reality, the words 'civil war' do not seem to apply here any more than they do in the case of the disturbances of 6 February in France. What we have in both instances is rather a dramatic clash between the state and the activists of one particular political movement in which actual armed conflict was limited both to very small areas of the countries concerned and to mere street fighting of a very traditional sort: the siege of Floridsdorf, for example, is in some respects a carbon copy of the suppression of the Paris Commune in 1871. Finally, also from 1934 comes the insurrection that took place in Spain in October of that year. We shall say more about this below, but, in brief, convinced, like the Austrian Socialists, that they were about to be suppressed, the Catalan nationalists and large parts of the Left staged a revolt. In most of the country, this was a fiasco and, as in Austria, the rebels were quickly put down, but in the isolated northern region of Asturias a variety of very special circumstances – abnormally high rates of labour militancy, excellent supplies of arms and difficult communications with the rest of Spain – allowed the coal miners who constituted the industrial proletariat to establish a soviet republic. In just two weeks, however, it was all over: experienced troops were brought in by sea from Spanish Morocco, and at the cost of 3,000 casualties, the rising was broken. Arriving at military headquarters in Santander en route from Madrid just in time to miss out on the fighting, Captain José Martín Blasquéz was given a briefing on the current situation that was brief and to the point: 'Everything was as good as ever, and there was no more resistance. Exemplary measures had been taken and that had been the end. It had been proved once more that, as soon as our glorious legionaries and Moorish battalions appeared, the revolutionaries ran for their lives.'[3] Much the same point, meanwhile, was made by the British ambassador, George Grahame: 'The crushing of the uprising of the trade unions and of the rebellion of the Catalan Generality [i.e. the Generalitat, or Catalan government] has shown once more how in these times a government disposing of strong forces of police and able to count on the active loyalty of the army can overwhelm irregular levies, set a limit to the effects of a general strike, and finally reduce to impotence a proletarian revolutionary movement.'[4]

This, perhaps, looks more like a real civil war, but in the end what one gets is really no more than a glorified version of the Floridsdorf affair. What, then, constitutes a civil war? First of all, there are issues of extent and duration: the countries involved must be split into rival zones and the fighting last for more than just a few days. And, second, there are issues of participation: the fighting must embrace more elements than just the armed forces and the police on the one hand and the supporters of one particular political movement or tendency on the other. What these conditions in turn presuppose is a situation in which both sides have extensive popular support, plentiful supplies of arms and the time and space to develop a full-scale war effort, the chief pillar of which must necessarily be a mass army. And perhaps the key requirement here is arms: in a conflict where one side has arms and the other does not, as was the case in Floridsdorf, armed resistance is not going to last for very long, whilst arms, too, represent the factor that is going to clear an adequate geographical base of the enemy and open its resources to general mobilization. In this respect, however, something else is necessary, and this can very roughly be defined as military organization, direction and mentality. Thus, the Asturian miners had plenty of arms – in brief, Asturias housed not just coal mines but also the most important complex of arms factories in the whole of Spain – but a lack of leadership and order ensured that they were unable even to clear their own province of the enemy, let alone expand the area under their control, and the result, of course, was that they became so many sitting ducks.[5]

From all this, it follows that the key to civil war does not lie in the level or intensity of popular politicization. In 1934, France and Austria alike were states that were gripped by politics, and yet civil war made no appearance. If one is seeking an explanation for civil war that is based on engagement in politics, however, then surely the prime candidate for such a conflict is Germany, marked as it was by the emergence of powerful mass movements that were equally violent and equally antagonistic. Yet, whilst there were many months of political disorder in the period leading up to January 1933, in the end Hitler came to power without there being any overt split in the German state. Indeed, it is noticeable that he actually had the backing of the German state, and in particular the German army, whose commanders made it clear that they would have nothing to do with any attempt to resist the Nazis by force. 'Reichswehr', proclaimed the army's chief power broker in 1933, General Schleicher, 'does not fire on Reichswehr', but the real fact of the matter was that by 1933 so many officers had become Nazi sympathizers that there was little risk of any such clash. All that was left, then, was an attempt at an armed revolt for which the Left – a force that was in any case hopelessly divided in its analysis of the situation – was neither armed nor prepared, and which it was, in consequence, not prepared to embark upon.

In discussing the origins of the Spanish Civil War, therefore, we are discussing a crisis whose key elements were military rather than civil, and it is very much in this sense that the subject will be looked at in this chapter. That said, the political history of Spain prior to 1936, nor, still, less, the social situation of the country, can scarcely be ignored. Where, then, to begin? Here the key date would seem to be December 1874, with the overthrow of the first republic by a military coup headed by General Martínez Campos. How Spain had reached that unhappy position is a long and complicated story that need not concern us here, but the chief issue to bear in mind is that, ever since the end of the Peninsular War in 1814, Spanish politics had been marked by endless turmoil as the liberal movement that had arisen from the struggle against Napoleon first struggled to overcome the resistance of the old order to political change, and then split into warring factions eager to enjoy the spoils of office while simultaneously having

both to fight off periodic attempts to turn the clock back by the hard-line supporters of absolute monarchy known as the Carlists and to face down a radical
movement that was growing ever stronger both in numbers and frustration. As
one of the few possible agents of political change, the army could not but be
sucked into the maelstrom, but, under generals such as Espartero, Narvaéz and
O'Donnell, it became a prime mover in the situation, making and un-making
régimes more or less at will by means of endless military coups.[6]

All this culminated in the so-called *sexenio revolucionario* of 1868–74. In brief,
corrupt and ineffectual, the régime of Queen Isabel II was overthrown, and the
ruling Bourbon dynasty replaced by Umberto I, a son of the king of newly unified Italy. This experiment, however, proved a disaster, and in 1872 Umberto
fled into exile, leaving Spain to become a republic. Wrecked by personal rivalries
among the Republican leaders and revolts on the part of the Carlists, the radicals
and the Cuban nationalist movement alike, the republic proved no more of a success than its predecessors, and at the end of 1873 the military intervened to put
an end to the chaos, the result, a year later, being the restoration of the Bourbons
in the person of Isabel's son, Alfonso XII. Thus was inaugurated the so-called
Restoration Monarchy, and with it a political system that was to last until it was
itself overthrown by yet another military coup in 1923.[7]

To that military coup we shall return in due course, it being far more important at the current moment to say something about the nature of the system
established in 1874. The architect of the new régime was Antonio Cánovas del
Castillo, the leader of the ... Partido Conservador Liberal, the ... the current
incarnation of the more moderate of the two blocs into which the original progressive movement had split (the other, headed by Práxedes Sagasta, was the
Partido Liberal Fusionista). These two parties, Cánovas saw, were in practice
divided by very little and interested above all in enjoying the fruits of office, it
having been competition for those self-same fruits of office that had produced
much of the turmoil of the preceding thirty or more years. As each fresh outbreak of trouble ended with the radicals taking to the streets and pressing for
moves in the direction of democratization, what was needed was a mechanism
whereby the two main parties could alternate in power and thereby, so to speak,
take turns at the trough. Also important, meanwhile, was a means of restricting
the influence of the military and the monarch, a further source of destabilization
being the tendency of both ambitious generals and the utterly irresponsible Isabel
II to intervene in the political game with a view to furthering their own interests.
From all this there emerged a unique system of political management whereby
the Conservatives and the Liberals in effect agreed to share power in perpetu
ity by a system of rigged elections. In brief, starting with the Conservatives,
each party took power in turn and ruled for a certain number of years, usually
until such a time that the highly personalized and fissiparous nature of Spanish
politics had rendered continuation in office impossible. At this point the prime
minister would go to the monarch and resign, and the latter, whose ability to
take independent action of any sort was carefully circumscribed, would duly call

on the leader of the other party to form a new administration. Administrations, however, needed a majority in the chamber, and so the next request was invariably for a dissolution of parliament and fresh general elections. These, in turn, would then, be 'made' by the new government (a process the key foundation of which consisted of the immediate replacement of large numbers of civil governors, mayors and town councils so as to pack local and provincial government with personnel who were only too happy to deliver the requisite results). For almost fifty years, then, Spain was a country in which it was not elections that decided the government, but governments that decided the elections, the pattern that resulted being quite extraordinary: in the period 1875–1923, there were sixteen general elections, of which eight were won by the Conservatives and eight by the Liberals, and that by turn, with the two parties literally alternating in power with one another. Nor was this the only symmetry: when the final lists of seats were revealed, the government was invariably revealed to have three-quarters of the deputies and the opposition just one quarter.[8]

Known as the *turno pacífico* ('peaceful alternation'), this system was not without its advantages, on the one hand largely succeeding in keeping the army out of politics and, on the other, putting an end to the endless intrigue and confusion that had marked the period prior to 1868. That said, however, it needs must be recognized that the stability for which it strove represented nothing short of a determination to preserve a social and economic situation characterized by the utmost poverty and inequality, it in fact being this self-same poverty and inequality on which it depended for its survival. Beginning with the countryside, except in a very few favoured areas such as the northern districts of the province of Navarre, the rural populace faced a lot that was hard indeed. In the northern half of the country, the predominant figure was the peasant – the small tenant farmer or petty proprietor – a class whose experience was invariably marked by a combination of poor soil, insufficient land, exorbitant rents, short-term leases and lack of credit, while in the south the need to engage in large-scale monoculture ensured that it was rather the landless labourer, a group whose experience was one of chronic under-employment and pitiful wages. Whichever category the inhabitants fell into, they were utterly at the mercy of the landowners, and thus it was that the latter had only to don the role of *cacique* – in this sense, political bosses – for owner–occupiers, tenants and landless labourers alike to flock to the polling booths to vote for whichever candidate had been recommended to them, knowing full well that the consequences of not doing so could be dire in the extreme. In the larger towns and cities, meanwhile, though not entirely absent, the pressure to vote one way or the other was less severe – indeed, could not be as severe – but here the problem was resolved by drawing the boundaries of each city's constituencies in such a way that they extended far out into the countryside, thereby ensuring that they included large numbers of villages and small towns that could be relied on to vote in the manner desired by the local élites.[9]

So reliable was this system deemed that Spain acquired universal manhood suffrage at a comparatively early date – to be precise, 1890. The confidence that this completely meaningless gesture suggests was soon beginning to unravel, however. Over the next thirty years, indeed, problems began to mount up in the most alarming fashion. In the first place, there was the rise of political movements – Catalan nationalism and organized labour – for which there was no place in the system. In the second place, defeat in the Spanish-American War of 1898 precipitated growing demands for reform. In the third place, a steady rise in urbanization and popular literacy alike began to put pressure on the delivery of the vote. In the fourth place, the Liberal and Conservative parties alike became more and more fragmented and therefore ever more prone to splits and factionalism. In the fifth place, Spain became involved in a gruelling colonial war in Morocco that on the one hand tended to draw generals back into politics and on the other sharpened tensions at home, as witnessed by the bloody insurrection (in its origins an anti-conscription riot) known as the 'Tragic Week' that gripped Barcelona in 1909. And, in the sixth place, the pragmatic and malleable figure of Alfonso XII (and, after his premature death, the equally prudent queen-regent, María-Cristina) was succeeded by the very different Alfonso XIII, a far more interventionist ruler who felt constricted by the bonds that the Constitution of 1875 had placed upon him and was exercised by a wide range of concerns, ranging from a morbid fear of revolution to a determination to modernize Spain's creaking and inadequate infrastructure.[10]

Already alarming, in 1914 the situation was greatly worsened by the outbreak of the First World War. Notwithstanding a vigorous debate in which admirers of Germany and Austria-Hungary pressed for a pro-Central-Powers policy, Spain stayed neutral, but the impact of the conflict was nevertheless enormous. Whilst some areas of the economy benefited – the coal mines of Asturias are a good example – many others were badly hit, the markets for such products as oranges and wine contracting dramatically. With economic hardship, meanwhile, came increased labour militancy: in Barcelona, especially, the powerful anarchist movement that had taken root there and found expression in the formation of a union movement known as the Confederación Nacional del Trabajo (or CNT) embarked on a campaign of revolutionary terror that cost the lives of many factory owners and other representatives of the old order. And, finally, the surging force that was Catalan nationalism was greatly excited by the manner in which the Allies increasingly began to highlight the issue of self-determination, and even at the end to endorse it as one of their war aims. With the constitutional régime seemingly unable to find any means of resolving Spain's difficulties and the Bolshevik revolution looming over all, it is small wonder that Alfonso XIII and many other observers on the Right began to look to an authoritarian solution as the only way forward, their views in this respect being much encouraged by the advent of the Fascist régime in Italy.[11]

Long expected by many observers, the storm broke in September 1923. In brief, the central figure was the captain-general of Catalonia, Miguel Primo de Rivera. A much decorated veteran of the war in Morocco, Primo de Rivera was horrified both by the growing Anarchist violence in Barcelona and its environs and the ever more strident demands of Catalan nationalism, whilst he was at the same time much concerned with putting an end to the colonial conflict, which he was convinced had become unwinnable. This last, meanwhile, had of late become the source of even more tension than normal, in that the summer of 1921 had seen the Spanish forces lose almost all the territory they held in the so-called Spanish protectorate after suffering terrible losses at the hands of the resistance army of Abd-el-Krim in the battle of Anual. A committee of enquiry set up to look into what had happened increasingly looking as if it was (quite correctly) going to incriminate Alfonso XIII, Primo decided that the situation could not be allowed to deteriorate any further, and on 23 September 1923, he launched a coup in Barcelona. The armed forces rallying to his side en masse, within hours he was ruler of Spain, in which capacity he proceeded to establish a military government, ban all existing political parties, clamp down very hard on anarchism and Catalan nationalism alike and prorogue parliament indefinitely. However, the régime that evolved from this development was a failure on almost every count. Such were the contradictions in Primo's position that he had within a very few years alienated almost all his supporters and was left with the backing of only the faction in the officer corps that was particularly associated with Spain's colony in Morocco, where the war had indeed been brought to an end, though, as we shall see, not at all in the fashion imagined by Primo de Rivera. Isolated and friendless, and with the economy in tatters, the dictator was forced to resign in January 1930.[12]

The departure of Primo de Rivera left Alfonso XIII in a very difficult position. Whilst a tame 'court' general named Berenguer was willing to pick up the reins from Primo, it was clear that in the long term, military rule was not an option. But nor could the king easily return to civilian rule. The old parties of the pre-1923 period were in ruins, and most of their leaders were not prepared to co-operate with the king anyway. As for the idea of building some sort of corporate state, there was no mass political force on which such a project could be based, whilst the Right's few ideologues were in any case divided between those who wanted the king to go on as the head of affairs in the style, say, of the royal dictatorship currently in operation in Yugoslavia, and those who saw the monarchy as part of the problem rather than part of the solution. If confusion reigned on the Right, meanwhile, in other areas of politics, there was a growing sense of purpose. Thus, ever since the First World War, Spain's small republican movement had been undergoing something of a revival, and, with this tendency accelerated by Alfonso XIII's complicity in the dictatorship, and, before that, Anual, by the late 1920s there were a number of thriving Republican parties operating under the shelter of an umbrella organization called the Alianza Republicana. To this movement, meanwhile, there began to rally a number of somewhat surprising supporters. From the ranks of the old Right came a number of senior politicians who hoped both to preserve their personal importance and curb the revolutionary imperative by turning Republican, and from the ranks of the army came large numbers of officers irritated by the favour that Primo had shown the officers who had served in Morocco (as we shall see, there were also a number of generals who had fallen out with Primo on personal grounds). By 1930, then, a powerful force was building against Alfonso, and this was strengthened still further when, at a conference held at the seaside resort of San Sebastián, both the Socialists and the Catalan nationalists agreed to join the Republican coalition. Eager for glory, a few hotheads in the officer corps attempted to overthrow the king by launching a coup, and, although this was suppressed, Alfonso managed to turn this into a public relations disaster by shooting the ringleaders and organizing a bungled show-trial of the chief Republican leaders. And in April 1931, there came the final straw: as a first step towards a return to civilian rule, General Berenguer organized municipal elections only to see the Republican coalition triumph in all the main towns and cities – in other words, the only places where there was genuinely a free vote. Realizing that the game was up, Alfonso fled into exile, and on 14 April 1931, Spain became a republic once more.[13]

Before going any further, we must first consider the impact of the war in Morocco, for it was in many ways in that conflict that the struggle of 1936–9 had its origins. This is yet another complicated issue, but the starting point is to recognize that at the end of the nineteenth century, thanks in part to the legacy of the turmoil prior to 1874, and, in part, too, the desire of successive Restoration governments to curry favour in the barracks, Spain had an officer corps that was much too big for her requirements, many officers therefore spending most of their careers on half-pay or occupying make-weight administrative posts of the most tedious character. Being based entirely on seniority – an innovation designed to prevent political interference – promotion was very slow, a situation that was not rendered any sweeter by the fact that officers were not well paid and therefore very much exposed to inflation. When war broke out in Morocco in 1909, the effect was to exacerbate these problems enormously. Eager to persuade officers to serve in Morocco, where it soon realized that it could not make too much use of conscript regiments raised in Spain, but needed rather to recruit specialized formations of professional troops (in brief, the new Spanish Foreign Legion, and the Moroccan tribesmen bribed to enlist in auxiliary units known as *regulares*) the government announced that promotion by seniority would be suspended for all those willing to cross the Straits of Gibraltar, the implicit promise being that deeds of courage on the battlefield would be rewarded by promotions granted on the grounds of merit. For many officers at the start of their careers, this came as a massive boon, and large numbers of young men, including a certain Francisco Franco y Bahamonde, therefore rushed to take advantage of the situation. Often staying on in Africa for many years, these men proceeded to forge glittering careers for themselves in either the Legion or the *regulares*, and had soon emerged as a distinctive group known as the *africanistas*.[14]

For the rest of the army, however, the situation was by no means so rosy. Older officers often had family responsibilities that made it harder for them to volunteer for service in Africa, while those who were not in the cavalry and the infantry (the arms of service that were most frequently in harm's way) had far fewer chances of demonstrating the kind of heroism required to win a battlefield promotion (a further issue here was that officers of the artillery, the engineers and the other service and technical arms had always enjoyed promotion by sen- iority and were therefore particularly aggrieved to see the situation revert to a hated past when infantry and cavalry officers could leapfrog up the ranks and leave them struggling in their wake). Large numbers of officers – indeed, the majority of officers – had therefore gained nothing from the war in Morocco, and by 1923 they were therefore angry and resentful, and all the more so as all the swaggering of the *africanistas* had seemingly produced no other result than complete and total humiliation. Hence in large part the reason why the met- ropolitan army swung so solidly behind Primo in 1923: in brief, knowing that he had come out against the war, the so-called 'stay-at-homes' or *peninsulares*, anticipated that he would put an end to the pretensions of their hated rivals. Yet things did not work out like this. Initially, certainly, to the fury of the *africanistas*, Primo favoured a policy of disengagement that he hoped would lead to a negoti- ated peace, and in the process almost caused a second Anual-style disaster when troops pulling back from the isolated city of Xauen found themselves caught up in a difficult winter retreat. By the middle of 1924, the Spanish forces were holding no more than a series of enclaves along the coast, but, with victory in his grasp, just at this point, Abd-el-Krim turned his armies south and struck across the frontier into the French territory that encompassed the Spanish protectorate. Perhaps the worst move that the Moroccans could have made, this decision led directly to their defeat. A France hitherto happy to let the Spaniards struggle ineffectually in the mountains of the Rif now fell on Abd-el-Krim with the full weight of her colonial war machine, while Primo allowed his African generals to implement a plan they had developed long since for a massive D-Day-style disembarkation in the bay of Alhucemas, this being a spot from which they could easily split the insurgent zone in two. Months of savage fighting later, it was all over, and victory was Primo's.[15]

For the *peninsulares*, all this came as a nasty shock. Far from the *africanistas* being muzzled and demoted, they were rather loaded with honours, appointed to a variety of plum positions and even handed control of the army's whole sys- tem of officer training through the establishment of a new military academy at Zaragoza, command of which was given to Francisco Franco, the latter having a few years earlier become the youngest general in the Spanish army. This was a severe blow, indeed, and in 1926 and 1929 groups of angry *peninsulares* tried to overthrow Primo by force. In the event, these revolts failed, but it was not just the men who had missed out on African glory who hated the regime. On the contrary, so capricious was Primo de Rivera (at best a somewhat volatile and erratic personality) that even some *africanistas* fell out with him, including a number of generals who were ultimately to side with the uprising of 1936, good examples being Gonzalo Queipo de Llano and Miguel Cabanellas.[16] To conclude, then, at the moment that the reign of King Alfonso XIII entered its final agony, the Spanish army was an organization that was shot through with differences and rivalries, and therefore quite unable to take a unified stand on anything. When the king claimed that he was stepping down to avoid civil war, he was in consequence doing no more than speaking the literal truth, for any attempt to use armed force on his behalf by monarchist or *africanista* officers would beyond doubt have produced a violent reaction in many other barracks.[17]

Let us return, however, to the coming of the Republic. In most of Spain's big cities, this development was greeted with genuine excitement. Professor of Spanish at the University of Liverpool, for example, Allison Peers found himself in Barcelona:

> Imagine, if you know Barcelona, the scene as one looks up the plane[tree]-lined Ramblas to the Plaça de Catalunya. As far as the eye can reach, a sea of humanity, a sea with yellow and red sails upon it for the Catalonian Republic [and] red, yellow and purple sails for the Republic of Spain ... Along the tree-lined central avenue, the youth of the Republic, some of them red-capped, others with Republican favours, marching who knows where. Along the outer roadways, no tram-cars for once: on the preceding evening they had all been commandeered by the people, who rode on them without ever paying for a ticket even ... and not only rode on them but filled them to over-flowing, squeezed tightly on top and bottom alike, crowding the platforms, hanging on the back, and swarming up steps and staircase. Black with such shouting loads of humanity, the cars plunged at breakneck speed down the Ramblas, making one shudder both at the thought of their overturning and at the symbolic picture which they offered of a people plunging into the immensity of the unknown.[18]

Amongst the crowds, however, the doubts expressed by Peers were lost amidst the jubilation, if, indeed, they existed at all. Over the years since the late nineteenth century, rates of literacy had been slowly increasing, whilst there had emerged a growing urban middle class that had no contact with the land and felt excluded from a political process that it regarded with the utmost contempt. Meanwhile, the cinema and the radio, not to mention a variety of exciting developments in the intellectual and artistic worlds, had broadened political and cultural perceptions and engendered ever greater expectations, not to mention a strong sense that Spain was backward and ought to be modernized. And beyond the urban elite there was the great mass of the proletariat, both urban and rural, and the peasantry, amongst whom the coming of the Republic naturally aroused hopes of a new age of social justice. Finally, the influence of the Church was clearly on the wane: clung to firmly, though it was, by many elements of the propertied classes as a guarantee of the social order and a symbol of their own respectability, amongst much of the populace it was the subject of indifference and, in many instances, bitter hostility.[19]

Sadly, the story of the next five years is basically the story of how the hopes engendered by the events of 1931 were frustrated. In part, the basic problem here was that the Republic was operating at a moment of world-wide economic catastrophe, the effect of which was to sharpen social and economic tensions and to persuade most governments that the only thing that they could do was to clamp down on government spending, thereby reducing the money available for inward investment.[20] That said, however, it also has to be recognized that the revolutionary coalition that had taken power in April 1931 was a body that was deeply flawed in its views, composition and general behaviour. Let us begin with the simple issue of the various groups that made it up. Starting on the Right, we have the Derecha Republicana (DR), a small group of ex-monarchists headed by an old-style *cacique* from Andalucía named Niceto Alcalá Zamora, who now got to be the Republic's first prime minister. Next there came the Partido Radical Republicano (PRR), an old republican party dating from the late nineteenth century, headed by the extremely disreputable and widely mistrusted Alejandro Lerroux; the Partido Radical Socialista (PRS), a faction that had broken away from the PRR after its leaders had quarrelled with Lerroux; a minor Catalan nationalist party called Acció Catalana (AC); and, lastly, Acciòn Republicana (AR), which was a small group of liberals headed by the well-known intellectual Manuel Azaña.[21] All of these together might roughly be termed the Centre, and to the left of them again there were the Socialists, – more formally, the Partido Socialista Obrero Español (PSOE) – who, not surprisingly, quickly secured the largest share of the deputies when elections were held to a constituent parliament. Fairly obviously, these various parties represented a pretty disparate group with views that ranged from 'let's do nothing' to 'let's do everything'; indeed, many of the supporters of both the DR and the PRR were scarcely Republicans at all, but rather refugees from the old monarchist parties who had come over to these groups in the hope of preserving the local influence they had enjoyed under the old régime. But matters were complicated still further by the facts, first, that there were deep personal divisions within the coalition – Azaña and Lerroux hated both each other and Alcalá Zamora, for example[22] – and, second, that there were deep divisions both between and within several of the parties: many Socialists were not certain they should form part of a bourgeois government at all, whilst the PRR and the PRS were at daggers drawn. And it is worth pointing out that the coalition government did not include two of the most important political forces in Spain in the shape of the chief Catalan nationalist party, which was called the Esquerra Republicana de Catalunya (ERC), a group which had broken away from and largely supplanted AC, and the Anarchists: of these, though very strong and, apart from the PSOE, the only genuine modern political party in Spain, the former was deliberately kept out in consequence of the almost universal loathing with which the Catalans were regarded by all shades of opinion in the rest of the country (so weak was AC, by contrast, that its inclusion cost nothing whilst yet serving to give the impression of a readiness to listen to Catalan opinion), whilst much of the latter would have no truck with the republic. In the words of Anarchist day-labourer Juan Moreno:

> Under the republic, under any political system, we workers would remain slaves … of our work … Of course, one régime can give a bit more liberty

than another, a little more freedom of expression, but most things it can't change ... What did we want? Not the sort of agrarian reform the republic was trying to make. The state and capitalism are the workers' two worst enemies. What we wanted was the land – for the workers to take it over collectively without the state intervening ... We hated the bourgeoisie: they treated us like animals. They were our worst enemies: when we looked at them, we thought we were looking at the devil himself.[23]

The result was not encouraging. After considerable infighting, at the end of 1931, a slimmed-down coalition consisting of the the the PSOE, the PRS and AR took power under the leadership of Manuel Azaña and attempted, with varying degrees of vigour, to push through the reform programme that had already been embarked upon under the provisional government.[24] Yet the reality of what was achieved was deeply disappointing. Immense energy was spent on attacking the Catholic Church and reducing its power, but in large part this anti-clericalism was irrelevant to the immediate needs of the country and in some respects dangerously counter-productive.[25] Autonomy was granted to Catalonia, but only in the most grudging and limited of forms, whilst this was again something that, beyond the frontiers of Catalonia, was of little relevance to the interests of the bulk of the populace, when, indeed, it was not actively offensive.[26] And although a series of reforms were introduced in respect of the position of the landless labourer, they were often either misconceived or bungled in their introduction, so that the results were at best limited (it might also be pointed out that smallholders got next to nothing from the reforms, and in some cases found that they actually made things worse).[27] Typically, there was also much mismanagement. Very interesting here are the views of the prominent Radical, Diego Martìnez Barrio, on the Radical-Socialist minister who was put in charge of the Agrarian Reform Bill:

> What agrarian reform needed was an iron surgeon ... Did Marcelino Domingo possess the qualities necessary to initiate, implement and complete the revolutionary effort that it represented? Evidently not ... Marcelino Domingo had filled the education post in the provisional government and the first Azaña administration with great success. There was no practical reason to transfer him to the Ministry of Agriculture ... The appointment was imposed by the Cabinet reshuffle occasioned by the decision of the Radicals to absent ourselves and the need to avoid giving the impression that the Socialists were in charge of every area of the national economy ... Somebody other than Domingo could have filled the Ministry of Industry and Agriculture, thereby saving the prestige of the Radical-Socialist leader ... and rescuing ... agrarian reform from all too foreseeable collapse. What was done was dictated by party, and the disastrous consequences were soon felt.[28]

We must remember here that all this was being played out against a situation in which industry and agriculture were in the grip of the Great Depression: in the towns and cities there were many unemployed, whilst in the countryside many smallholders were finding themselves unable to pay the rent and many landowners were taking a lot of land out of production. At the same time, many elements on the Right were clearly trying to sabotage the changes that were being introduced or even to block them altogether.[29] All this produced a growing mood of discontent on the Left and amongst the urban and rural working classes, and gave the anarchist movement, which was dominated by forces dedicated to the idea of overthrowing the state by means of launching a revolutionary general strike, the chance to make hay. In July 1931, January 1932 and January 1933, then, gangs of militants attempted to lead revolts against the Republic in various parts of Spain. As the prominent Barcelona Anarchist and member of the secret society known as the Federación Anarquista Ibérica (FAI) (or FAI), a 'ginger-group' that had been established in 1927 to ensure that the CNT did not slip into the heresy of trade-unionism, Ricardo Sanz remembered, 'After seven years of clandestinity, the members generally didn't know where they were going or what they wanted. In such a situation, what was needed was practice, exercise, revolutionary gymnastics. We were the motor or spark that could get those gymnastics going.'[30] On each occasion, these risings were put down with great ruthlessness, but the net result was only to destabilize the government still further. To quote Martínez Barrio once more:

> If men are capable of recognizing the faults that they commit, I would say that the leaders of the CNT in those first years of the Republican regime must since then have lived under a weight of remorse … No sooner had the echoes of the popular acclamations of 14 April died away than … the syndicalists rose in Seville … The tumult overcome, it was repeated in various places elsewhere, sometimes by means of the revolutionary strike, and sometimes by means of odious attacks on particular individuals. All this was intended as an attempt at … social revolution … but nothing was achieved other than to terrify the nation and serve the interests of the conservative classes.[31]

In the end, indeed, the Socialists could take no more, and in the summer of 1933, they therefore surrendered the various ministries that they had held and resigned from the government. Still worse, for the first time, the resolutely reformist line that had been adopted since 1931 began to be questioned by the leadership, and, in particular, by the Minister of Labour and veteran leader of the Socialist Uniòn General de Trabajadores (or UGT), Francisco Largo Caballero. Very much to the fore in this respect was a speech the latter made to the Madrid branch of the Socialist youth movement in the Pardiñas cinema:

> We collaborated in the proclamation of a republic so as to establish a flexible constitution … that will allow us to achieve our aspirations without great bloodshed or violence. We hope to achieve them legally … but

if these gentleman tell us that, because we are workers, because we are socialists, because we are a class party … they will not permit us to take power in accordance with the constitution, we shall have to conquer it by other means.[32]

With the government in tatters, there was no option but to hold new elections. To quote George Grahame: 'Señor Azaña … explained to the President of the Republic that various events had affected the moral authority of the ministry in the accomplishment of its task and suggested that the political situation should be re-examined.'[33] These, however, were held in very different circumstances from those of 1933. In 1931, there had been no political organization on the Right, but this did not mean that there was wholesale acquiescence. On the contrary, whether the subject was the democratization of the electoral system, the expropriation of the great estates, the restrictions imposed on the rights of the Church or the grant of autonomy to Catalonia and also such other regions as Galicia and the Basque provinces, a large part of the traditional élite was up in arms. Indeed, the very coming of the Republic had been seen as a terrible blow. To quote a dispatch written by the British ambassador, George Grahame, just two days after the departure of the king: 'The Spanish aristocracy is in a state of sorrow, dismay and complete gloom. I have had some affecting interviews with those who have been intimate with the king and queen, and several of them broke down entirely. Most of them declare that Alcalá Zamora is a Spanish Kerensky, and that the country will soon be handed over to bolshevism.'[34] Initially, the only course open to the many outright rejectionists was conspiracy and sabotage (especially the expatriation of large amounts of capital), but in the course of 1932, the tiny group of monarchist deputies in the *cortes* blazed a new trail by working within the structures of parliamentary debate to inflict severe damage on the much vaunted Law of Agrarian Reform. Inspired in part by this success and in part by the knowledge that open opposition would only lead to such measures as the suppression of the right-wing press, a Catholic journalist and lawyer named José María Gil Robles had responded by putting together a loose right-wing coalition known as the Confederación Española de Derechas Autónomas (or CEDA). As Gil Robles wrote, 'Given that there was no material possibility of resolving the problem by force … the Right had no other means of gaining power … than taking advantage of the regime that was in operation to penetrate it and make it their own.'[35]

As to what taking power might mean, few people could be in any doubt. While not overtly monarchist, the CEDA was certainly anti-democratic, and Gil Robles made it very clear that he intended to turn Spain into a corporate state. In the words of Claude Bowers, 'His fervent declamations evoked the fanatic emotions of the days of the Crusades.'[36] For example:

We must reconquer Spain … We must give Spain a true unity, a new spirit, a totalitarian polity … For me there is only one tactic today: to form an anti-Marxist front, and the wider the better. It is necessary now to defeat socialism inexorably ... We must found a new state, purge the fatherland of judaizing freemasons ... We need full power and that is what we demand.[37]

With the Republicans and Socialists at odds with one another, and the CEDA in alliance with the pseudo-monarchist PRR, the elections were won by the Right, and there now followed a period of reactionary government known as the 'black biennium.'[38] Reform was frozen at every level, the Catalan government suppressed on a technicality and the Left harassed at every turn.[39] At first Gil Robles stayed aloof from the government, but in October 1934 he demanded three ministries for his party. For the Left, however, this was anathema: in so far as they were concerned, Gil Robles was a fascist and the CEDA a fascist party. Desperate to stop such a development, the Socialists, in particular, had responded with what amounted to a gigantic bluff: in brief, to threaten revolution in the hope that this would dissuade Alcalá Zamora from sanctioning the grant of any ministries to Gil Robles. Yet at the very least, this gifted the Right with fresh ammunition. As Lerroux wrote:

> At the end of September 1934 the political situation was not very agreeable ... The state of public order had many worrying aspects. Those towns and villages where the labour organizations of the Socialists and others predominated were the scene of disturbances and outrages ... A series of unnecessary or insufficiently-justified lightning strikes were continuing as if part of a premeditated plan. The socialist youth organizations were ... marching through the streets in uniform with flags and drums every Sunday. The Socialist Party's threat that it would declare a ... revolutionary strike if the representatives of [the CEDA] entered the government had been made public. Its leaders would not ... resign themselves to living without power.[40]

That the Socialists should have adopted such a line is entirely understandable. In the first place, there was the issue of their power-base. Traditionally a movement whose popular support was centred on the skilled workers whose unions had formed the backbone of the UGT, since 1931 they had made significant inroads amongst the landless labourers of the south and challenged the Anarchist hold on the area by setting up a new and highly combative Federacòn Nacional de Trabajadores de la Tierra (or FNTT). In the summer of 1934, however, this had been provoked into a general strike that had been easily broken, and Largo Caballero knew all too well that its members could well respond by returning to their old allegiance. Politically, then, there was a clear need for a hard line, but beyond the frontiers of Spain there also loomed the spectre of fascism: having come to power in January 1933, Hitler was currently engaged in a violent assault on the German Left, while barely three months had passed since the siege of Floridsdorf. The stakes, then, were very high, but Largo Caballero had nothing in his hand: only in Asturias was there any partnership with the other left-wing movements; the militia that local branches of the party had supposedly been organizing since earlier in the year was little more than a rambling club; and there were few arms. As for allies, the only support that Largo Caballero could hope for came from the Catalan nationalists who were as outraged at the threat to Catalonia's autonomy as the Socialist leader was exercised by the Right's assault on social reform. When the moment of truth came, then, matters fell out exactly as the CEDA leader had hoped: not only were the Socialists revealed in what he claimed were their true colours, but the way was opened for the suppression of not only the Socialists and the other left-wing movements, but also the Catalans.

In brief, the events that followed can be divided into three parts. In the first place, there was the revolt of the Socialists in Madrid and other parts of central and southern Spain; in the second, there was the revolt in Catalonia, and, in the third, there was the revolt in Asturias. Of these, however, neither the first nor the second achieved anything of any note. The Spanish correspondent of the *Daily Telegraph* since before the coming of the Republic, Henry Buckley was a perceptive and well-informed observer of events in the capital and neighbouring districts:

> In all ... ninety-eight people were killed, of whom I think eleven were police or soldiers ... The plan of the Socialists, as far as they had any, was to continue resistance in Madrid over a length of several weeks in order to weaken the government. They had organised groups of young people whose mission was to keep up constant unrest by firing odd shots either in the streets or from house roofs. The police struck a smart blow at this organization from the start, for on the night of 4 October ... they raided the headquarters where the young men were assembling ... and after some desultory firing took fifty youths prisoner and captured most of the arms ... Down in Extremadura the peasants revolted under the leadership of Margarita Nelken, a woman Socialist deputy, but this business did not get far because no sickle or shotgun invented yet can make any showing against ... Mauser rifles.[41]

In Barcelona, meanwhile, the uprising was even less impressive. Supported by the indigenous police force that Catalonia had acquired in the wake of the passage of her autonomy statute, the Catalan leader, Lluis Companys, seized the building that had housed the Catalan government, but not a shot was fired, whilst the rebels surrendered without resistance after only a single night.[42] All that was left, then, was Asturias, but, as related earlier, the coal miners who took over the central part of the province were crushed after just two weeks. In the words of Santiago Carrillo, then the general secretary of the Socialist youth movement, 'The rising was not well-prepared; things moved very fast; the fascists came into the government sooner than we thought, and we were not able to organise the movement in a sufficiently thorough way.'[43]

Across Spain, Gil Robles now harvested the fruits of his cunning. From Gerona to Huelva and La Coruña to Alicante, the entire country was subjected to a ruthless campaign of repression that led to the imprisonment of many thousands of militants, not to mention the dismissal of large numbers of workers suspected of being *rojos*. Thus encouraged, at the end of 1935 Gil Robles (now Minister of War, in which capacity he had been angling for military support by, amongst other things, providing the army with much better heavy artillery by buying a large number of Schneider M1917 155mm howitzers) made a bid for the CEDA to form a government on its own, but this was blocked by Alcalá Zamora, and the result of the crisis was the convocation of new elections for February 1936, and with it immediate confrontation: 'The Right hoisted the anti-Communist flag and frightened prospective voters with accounts of the great damage which a Left victory ... would do to the country ... The parties of the Left ... focused their propaganda on the atrocities which had been committed against the political prisoners after the Asturias rising and on the demand for a general amnesty.'[44]

These fresh polls were fought out in an atmosphere of great bitterness and polarisation. To quote Constancia de la Mora, a very well-connected member of the upper classes who had become a staunch Republican and achieved much notoriety by being the first woman in Spain to avail herself of the Republic's legalisation of divorce, 'I thought during the days between 8 January and 16 February that I would never again live through such weeks of terrible suspense ... We all knew that this election would decide Spain's fate: fascist or democratic, the Middle Ages or the World of Tomorrow, tyranny or justice; which would it be? The existence of the Republic ... trembled in the balance.'[45] On the one hand stood the CEDA and a number of other right-wing groups, including the small Spanish fascist party the Falange Espanola y de las Juntas de Ofensiva Nacional Sindicalistas and the overtly monarchist Renovación Española and Comunión Tradicionalista or Carlists, and on the other, a renewed Socialist–Republican alliance known as the Frente Popular, this coalition also being supported by the Catalan nationalists, the ... Communists (in full, the Partido Comunista Espanol or PCE), a movement that was very weak in national terms, but quite strong in key cities such as Seville and Bilbao, and ... and two tiny fringe groups, of which one – the Syndicalist Party – was a breakaway from the Anarchists and the other – the Partido Obrero de Unificación Obrera (or POUM) – a newly formed breakaway from the Communists. In the event, it was the Popular Front that triumphed, and there now began the slide towards rebellion and, ultimately, civil war. In civil society, this was seen most clearly in the marginalization of Gil Robles as more and more of his supporters rushed to join either the Falange – a movement rendered extremely attractive by the fact that its leader was the extremely personable José Antonio Primo de Rivera – or the Carlists, the point being that both these groups had always been wedded to the violent overthrow of the Republic.[46] And, in the minds of many on the Right, what possible course was there but violence? As the leading conservative newspaper, *ABC*, trumpeted two days after the elections:

We have here the genuinely revolutionary elements of the Pact of San Sebastián, the men who imposed a revolutionary constitution on the constituent *cortes*, in short, those who in October 1934 attempted to install a revolutionary soviet regime and break Spain up into demagogic republics. We have here the Socialists, the Communists, the Syndicalists, the Anarchists, the separatists, the persecutors of religion ... The parties of the socialist revolution are those which dominate the alliance [i.e. the Popular Front] that by force of violence has gained power. Everything is theirs ... and, if they win power, they will pawn it to the rod of Marxism.[47]

Far more dangerous, however, were the developments taking place at the same time in the army (though some officers would beyond doubt have refused to fight the Falange and the Carlists, it can be surmised that enough would have remained loyal to ensure that any rebellion on their part would have failed). To quote Raymond Carr once more, 'The counter-revolution of the extreme Right and the grumbling of the conservative classes would have come to nothing without the generals.'[48] Convinced that Spain was about to be genuinely revolutionized, an impression that was greatly strengthened by the irresponsible rhetoric being engaged in by the left wing of the Socialist party, a group of senior commanders began to hatch a plot for a military uprising under the titular leadership of General José Sanjurjo (Sanjurjo currently being in exile in Portugal, responsibility for the actual conspiracy was rather in the hands of Emilio Mola Vidal, who was in February 1936 commander-in-chief of the Spanish forces in Morocco).[49] Supporting them, meanwhile, was the Unión Militar Española (or UME), a secret society dedicated to winning the army over to the cause of overthrowing the Republic, which had been established by a group of officers of monarchist sympathies in 1933 and had since grown steadily in strength, though its membership had remained almost entirely restricted to men of the rank of captain or below.[50] And, always, beyond the gates of the barracks, there were plenty of voices crying out for the military to save the country and doing all that they could to poison the minds of the officer corps: in 1934, for example, a hysterically anti-Communist and anti-semitic police inspector named Eduardo Carlavilla deluged the army's messes with thousands of copies of an anti-Marxist diatribe entitled *Asesinos de España*.[51]

However, such activists had a much harder task than is often assumed. The army is often assumed to have been solidly anti-Republican, but this was simply not so: many officers had, as we have seen, welcomed the coming of the Republic in 1931. With many *peninsulares* delighted by such measures as the purge of such figures as Mola, the monarchy's last Director-General of Security (in effect, chief of police), the closure of the Zaragoza academy and the reduction in rank of large numbers of *africanistas*, such feelings may even have been strengthened, albeit at the cost of infuriating the Moroccan garrisons, who also had to endure the appointment of a civilian high commissioner and were already much alarmed by the clamour in the Republican and Socialist ranks to abandon

Morocco altogether.[52] At first the balance was positive: in August 1932, a military coup by the *africanista* General Sanjurjo had collapsed for want of support (hence the absence of that general in Portugal).[53] Since then, however, the refusal of the Anarchists to refrain from further uprisings, the frequent strikes and the rebellion of October 1934 had undermined this support, whist it did not help that the Republic's military policy had backfired. Thus, the army was to be reduced in size but given modern weapons, but such were the budgetary constraints on the Republic, that, whilst the first part of the programme was carried out, the second was left unfulfilled: it took until 1934, for example, just to equip the army with steel helmets.[54] Full of rage at the overthrow of the *africanistas* though he may have been, Mola cannot be denied to have had a point when he complained in a book published in 1934 that Spain was all but defenceless:

> After two years ... of Azaña's management, the [army's] units have never been ... more short of troops, whilst the number of officers and NCOs has been run down so much that it would be impossible to put the army on a war footing. The infantry and cavalry divisions have not only seen no improvement in their striking power, but have been left without the most elementary support services ... In so far as mechanised transport is concerned, things are actually worse than they were in the days of the monarchy ... Last but not least, the administration has reached such a pitch of confusion that even clothing has begun to run short ... On top of all this, as a result of the campaign of defamation to which it has been subjected, the officer corps has as little morale as it has prestige. All of this stems from a premeditated plan ... that has been put into execution with all the tenacity and cold bloodedness of a man who has had no other guiding light in his life than the pleasure of destruction.[55]

There is, of course, much here that is wildly tendentious, but the appeal of such arguments cannot be gainsaid, and all the more so as an unfortunate side effect of Azaña's attempts as War Minister in 1931 to reduce the size of the swollen officer corps by offering an extremely generous early-retirement package had been to strip it of many men who were pro-Republican: as the Marqués de Michelina exulted, 'Great numbers of Republican army officers took advantage of the reform to leave the army! They felt that they would have greater possibilities in civilian life now their regime was in power.'[56] Amongst those who stayed, then, were many men whom Azaña must surely have wished to be rid of. To quote an infantry officer named Carlos Bravo, who had been seconded to the Civil Guard, 'The republic wanted to crush the army ... For most of us Azaña was a pervert, a moral disaster. If we hadn't been Christians, we officers would have hanged him by a rope.'[57] With political violence – some of it, at least, inspired by the Right[58] – and labour unrest increasing by the day; the new administration pushing through a far more rigorous programme of land reform than it had attempted in the period 1931–3; regionalism rampant (suppressed in the wake of the revolt of October 1934, the Catalan government was reinstated, and an autonomy statute brought in for the Basque provinces into the bargain); and rumours afoot that the armed forces were to be abolished and replaced by a Bolshevik-style 'Red Guard', plenty of officers therefore rallied to the conspiracy.[59] Yet for all the effort that had been made to subvert the armed forces, only the navy was fully won over, perhaps a third of the army's officers remaining loyal, together with about half those of the police and four fifths of those of the airfiorce.[60] Thanks in part to the efforts of Juan Guilloto León, or to use the alias that he habitually went under, Juan Modesto, a Communist functionary who had been given the task of reaching out in their direction, a considerable number had even been organized into a pro-government secret society known as the Unión Militar Republicana Anti-Fascista (or UMRA).[61] Other officers, meanwhile, had only finally agreed to get involved at the very last minute, and might, in fact, have stayed loyal but for a particularly foolish act on the part of the Left. Thus, on the evening of 12 July, angered by the murder of one of its officers – one Josè Castillo – by a Falangist gunman, a group of the paramilitary police force known as the Assault Guard, which had been specifically formed to protect the republic from subversive activity, went to the flat of the prominent monarchist José Calvo Sotelo and, as the saying went, 'took him for a ride.' In Franco's Spain it was always claimed that the assassination sparked off the uprising, but this is completely false: as we have seen, the conspiracy long predated it. However, what is true is that the discovery of Calvo Sotelo's body at the gates of Madrid's main cemetery came as a profound shock to many waverers and persuaded a number, including, not least, Francisco Franco, to side with the cause of insurrection (ever given to prudence, not to say calculation, consumed though he was by notions of a judeo-bolshevik conspiracy that aimed at the destruction of Christian Europe, the latter had hitherto held back in the hope of acquiring a position similar to that of Francisco Serrano, the general who had in early 1874 been installed as the president of the First Republic in a last-ditch attempt to save it from complete collapse).[62] To quote David Jato, a leader of the Falange's student organization, 'The fact that it was Calvo Sotelo and that he had been assassinated by the government's police forces made people finally take a stand against the government. Many garrisons, many people who a week before had been doubtful or even opposed, now saw the need for a violent solution. Without the assassination, the military rising, I'm convinced, would have failed.'[63]

Of course, not all those on the Left stooped to murder. Yet supporters of the Popular Front were in general aggressive and provocative in their demeanour, thereby increasing the ire of the Right.[64] The hispanist Gerald Brenan, for example, was a prominent member of the English community in Málaga:

> The atmosphere at Churriana was not as easy and pleasant as it was before the election ... The class struggle was very much in evidence. The people felt they were on top, and they meant to take every possible advantage of it. Even quiet workmen, indifferent to all ideologies, put on boastful airs,

while, not only had wages gone up by one third, but farmers and landlords were compelled to take on extra hands whom they did not need.[65]

Afterwards, even observers on the Left were prepared to agree that there was a sense amongst their fellows that power was there for the taking, that they were, indeed, prepared to stop at nothing. In the words of Luis Portela, a militant of the dissident-Communist POUM, a movement that would assume disproportionate importance in the Civil War but in 1936 was all but insignificant: 'They wanted to go forward: they weren't satisfied simply with the release of political prisoners and the return to their jobs of all those who had been sacked as a result of the revolutionary insurrection of October 1934.'[66]

One criticism that has frequently been made of the government of the Popular Front is that it failed to do anything to break up the conspiracy. Very much at the centre of events in Madrid was Constancia de la Mora (her second husband, Ignacio Hidalgo de Cisneros, was a pro-Republican air-force pilot who had supported the failed coup of 1930, gone into exile following the revolt of October 1934 and was currently serving in the office of the prime minister, Santiago Casares Quiroga):

> Madrid was on tenterhooks. Twice a week we got word that the revolt was scheduled for that night or the next. We sat up many a night beside the telephone, waiting for the terrible news that the Madrid garrison, or some other garrison, had risen against the Republic. And every morning after such a sleepless night, Ignacio would go to the War Ministry and beg his immediate superior, the War Minister and, since Azaña's election to the presidency, Premier, Casares Quiroga, to act ... Azaña had lost touch with the people. Remote, uninterested, he had already sunk into the lethargy that was later to overcome him completely.[67]

In the wake of what occurred, such feelings are entirely understandable. Yet, for all that Azaña does indeed appear to have sunk into a mood of ever deeper depression, and for all, too, that Casares Quiroga was a sick man who was inclined to take refuge in delusion, it is difficult to see what more could have been done. On the surface, the measures undertaken against the conspiracy do appear remarkably feeble: if the decision to ban the Falange and arrest many of its chief leaders, including José Antonio Primo de Rivera, was sound enough, the decision simply to transfer the chief conspirators to different postings rather than sack them looks pusillanimous, even downright suspicious, and all the more so as Mola ended up being sent to the Carlist stronghold of Pamplona. As for the repeated interrogations of officers suspected of being involved in what was going on, the men concerned invariably had only to give their word of honour that all was well to be believed. Yet, in truth, what else was the government supposed to do? To purge the army would simply have pushed more officers into the camp of rebellion, as would, for example, arming the people. Nor was attempting to forge links with the non-commissioned officers through improvements in their pay and conditions much better, while the efforts made by the Communist Party in particular to proselytise among the rank and file through the publication of an underground newspaper with the helpful title *Soldado ROJO* can only be described as foolish in the extreme. If these last gained a few hundred recruits, there simply was not enough time for them to achieve anything more than increase the hysteria among those elements of the officer corps who were in favour of rebellion: 'There was a moment in March or April 1936 when *regulares* [i.e. Moorish auxiliaries serving in the ranks of the Army of Africa] had to be brought in to surround certain units of the Foreign Legion', recalled a lieutenant in that force named Julio de la Torre: 'We feared they were going to stage a rising: the sergeants had been promised by the Communists that they would be promoted to officers.'[68]

The conspiracy, then, rolled on unchecked, while the number of its adherents grew by the day, not the least of the recruiting agents acting in its favour being the constant accusations of cowardice and dereliction of duty that resounded in the right-wing press, and, indeed, each and every gathering place of the Right. One such incident was recalled by the monarchist newspaper editor Eugenio Vegas Latapie: 'It was the day after Calvo Sotelo's funeral. I was talking to an artillery major in Segovia when his father, a retired colonel, insulted his son in front of me for not having risen yet. "If I were a young officer I wouldn't tolerate this situation a moment longer."'[69] Yet many difficulties stood in the way of an uprising, not the least of these being that both the Carlists and the Falange were committed to risings of their own. The Carlists, in particular, had been making real efforts to produce a disciplined fighting force: 'It has to be understood', wrote Carmelo Revilla Cebrecos, a young man from Aranda de Duero who had joined the Carlists in Pamplona, 'that, especially in Navarre, the *requetés* were already perfectly organized, being formed into units with their own officers. Amongst these men there were some professionals, but the majority came from their own ranks. That said, however, some of them having travelled abroad to receive military training ... they were well prepared for the tasks which they had to undertake.'[70] Not least because the Carlists were a force with a much longer history, the Falange was much less well advanced in its preparations, a further problem being that the decision of the Popular-Front government to move against it meant that much of the leadership was now in jail.[71]

Given the armed forces' reduced condition, all this might be thought to be very much to the benefit of Mola and his fellow conspirators, in effect presenting them with a reserve army that they could lead to victory. Yet the reality was that nothing could be further from the truth: for the Carlists, the military was the historic enemy, the same force that had imposed the will of Spanish liberalism and executed their grandfathers, great-grandfathers and great-great-grandfathers by the score, whilst for many Falangists, and especially the so-called 'old shirts' who had joined the party prior to February 1936, the generals were part of the problem rather than part of the solution. Neither movement was prepared to accept the lead of the army, and yet neither movement had much hope of success, for the Carlists were above all a regional movement whose mass base was confined to Navarre and the Basque provinces, and the Falange not much more than a gang of enthusiasts with little in the way of arms and ammunition.[72] In short, Mola was faced by the real likelihood that his schemes might be disrupted by what, in the end, was unlikely to amount to anything more than a wild adventure, the consequence being that it took months of negotiation before he could get either the red berets of the one movement or the blue shirts of the other to line up behind his leadership: indeed, as if further proof were needed of the baleful influence of that event, it took the murder of Calvo Sotelo finally to persuade the Carlists to give way.[73]

By the middle of July 1936, then, the battle lines were drawn up. 'The people ... felt the fear of soldiers about to depart for the front' wrote Arturo Barea. 'Nobody knew when and where the attack [would] begin, but everybody knew that the hour had come.'[74] Yet it was anything but a question of the army versus the people. On the contrary, the officer corps was deeply divided on lines that, to a considerable extent, mirrored the long-standing rifts in the Spanish army. Thus, in brief, from Franco down, the vast majority of officers associated with the African campaigns of 1909–23 joined the insurrection, whereas the majority of loyalists were men who had stayed at home and served out their careers in the safety and boredom of some Peninsular garrison. Also clear are certain other distinctions, in that older officers and more senior officers (including, be it said, more than a sprinkling of *africanistas*) and also officers in the artillery, engineers and other technical corps – in other words, those sections of the army that had been most irked by the institution of promotion by merit – were also inclined to stay loyal. To put it another way, the split in the army was not just the fruit of the immediate political situation, let alone of perceptions of what the Popular Front might or might not mean for the future of the military, but rather of deeper jealousies and tensions going back many years. From this in-house quarrel, of course, there followed civil war, but it is vital to note that without the rupture in the armed forces that has just been detailed, there would have been no such development: rather, the suppression of the Asturian rising would simply have been replayed on a nation-wide scale.

Notes

1 M. de Heredia, *Monarquía, república, guerra* (Madrid, 1976), p. 192.

2 R. Carr, *The Spanish Tragedy* (London, 1977), p. 67. As we shall see, the issue was not as clear-cut as this: while some officers were in favour of the Republic and others opposed to it, a number of factors internal to the army were far more important in determining the allegiance of the officer corps.

3 J. Martín Blásquez, *I Helped to Build an Army: Civil-War Memoirs of a Spanish Staff Officer* (London, 1939), p. 14. The 'exemplary measures' mentioned by Martín Blasquéz were exemplary indeed. 'There was a bloody repression, a real massacre', remembered Communist militant David Granda. 'The Tercio [i.e. Foreign Legion] ... killed a lot of people, and 30,000 were taken prisoner and beaten up or tortured. In the prisons the soldiers and the civil guards formed a double line, a *tuba de la risa* [literally, 'tunnel of laughs'], and to make people talk they would be forced to go

down the middle where they would be smashed around. When they came out, they were half dead.' Cit. N. MacMaster (ed.), *Spanish Fighters: an Oral History of Civil War and Exile* (Basingstoke, 1990), p. 50.

4 Cit. A. Elorza et al. (eds.), 'Quo vadis Hispania? 1917–1936: España entre dos rev-oluciones – la visión exterior y sus limites', *Estudios de Historia Social*, Nos. 34–35 (July–December, 1985), p. 451.

5 For a somewhat rose-tinted view of the insurrection in Asturias, see A. Shubert, 'The epic failure: the Asturian revolution of October 1934', in P. Preston, *Revolution and War in Spain, 1931–1939* (London, 1984), pp. 113–36.

6 Though it is now somewhat dated, the standard English-language work on the politi-cal history of the Spanish army is S. G. Payne, *Politics and the Military in Modern Spain* (Stanford, California, 1967).

7 For an introduction to the *sexenio revolucionario*, see M. V. López Cordón, *La revolución de 1868 y la Primera República* (Madrid, 1976). On the restoration, see M. Espadas Burgos, *Alfonso XII y los orígenes de la restauración* (Madrid, 1975). Finally, for a recent biography of Cánovas, see J. L. Comellas, *Cánovas del Castillo* (Barcelona, 1997).

8 For two discussions of the Restoration Monarchy's political system, see G. Brenan, *The Spanish Labyrinth* (Cambridge, 1943), pp. 5–11, and A. Shubert, *A Social History of Modern Spain* (London, 1990), pp. 184–9.

9 For two regional surveys of the operation of *caciquismo*, see J. Tusell Gómez, *Oligarquía y caciquismo en Andalucía, 1890–1923* (Barcelona, 1976), and M.T. Pérez Picazo, *Oligarquía urbana y campesinado en Murcia, 1875–1902* (Murcia, 1979).

10 On the role of Alfonso XIII, see C. Seco Serrano, *Alfonso XIII y la crisis de la restaura-ción* (Madrid, 1979).

11 See J. Tusell Gómez, *Radiografía de un golpe de estado: el ascenso al poder del General Primo de Rivera* (Madrid, 1987), pp. 127–33.

12 In so far as the dictatorship of Primo de Rivera is concerned, helpful works in English include S. Ben-Ami, *Fascism from Above: the Dictatorship of Primo de Rivera in Spain, 1923–1930* (Oxford, 1983), A. Quiroga, *Making Spaniards: Primo de Rivera and the Nationalization of the Masses, 1923–1930* (Houndmills, 2007) and S. Ben-Ami, 'The dictatorship of Primo de Rivera: a political reassessment', *Journal of Contemporary History*, XII, No. 1 (January, 1977), pp. 65–84. For the battle of Anual and its impact, see D. Woolman, *Rebels in the Rif: Abd-el-Krim and the Rif Rebellion* (Stanford, 1969), and M. Leguineche, *Anual: el desastre de España en el Rif, 1921* (Madrid, 1996).

13 On the Right, there was a strong tendency to contest the results of these elections. Here, for example, is José María Albiñana, a Valencian lawyer who founded a minis-cule fascist movement entitled the Partido Nacionalista Español: 'The Republicans won in the majority of provincial capitals and a number of other large towns. But in Spain as a whole the immense majority of the town councillors who got elected were strongly monarchist. ... On 14 April the results of the elections that had thus far come in ... gave a total of 22,150 monarchists and 5,875 anti-monarchists ... In short, the elections of 12 April 1931 were won not by the Republic, but by the mon-archy.' J.M. Albiñana, *España bajo la dictadura republicana: crónica de un periodo putrefacto* (Madrid, 1933), pp. 21–3. Strictly speaking, these claims are true enough, but from Alfonso XIII down, everyone knew that the figures were meaningless. Thus, in the countryside, old-style *caciquismo* was still the norm, the result being that the munici-pal elections delivered town councils recruited entirely from the traditional élites, whereas in the cities the vote was much fairer and therefore much more inclined to represent the popular mood. And that this last was opposed to the king, there was no doubt. On retiring to Málaga in 1927, for example, the erstwhile secretary of the London Zoological Society, Sir Peter Chalmers-Mitchell, found a city whose mood was extremely bitter. 'The dictatorship of Primo de Rivera, beneficent at first, was drawing uneasily towards its end, having lost the support of the army and the intel-ligentsia. Málaga, that is to say the mass of the population of the town and province,

was in bitter poverty, badly housed and badly clothed. Beggars swarmed in the streets and to enter the cathedral you had to push your way through a clamorous mass of deformities ... I should guess that the mass of the population was neither 'black' nor 'red' ... But in one respect they had a political opinion. They were definitely hostile to the king. ... Through the port of Málaga had passed much of the wreckage from the Moorish war and ... the king, rightly or wrongly, was blamed for the huge disaster of Anual.' P. Chalmers-Mitchell, *My House in Málaga* (London, 1938), pp. 21–2. For a good general account of the downfall of the monarchy, see S. Ben-Ami, *The Origins of the Second Republic in* Spain (Oxford, 1978).

14 For the rise of the *africanistas*, see S. Balfour, *Deadly Embrace: Morocco and the Road to the Spanish Civil War* (Oxford, 2002), pp. 82–120, and G. Cardona, *El poder militar en España contemporánea hasta la Guerra Civil* (Madrid, 1983), pp. 27–36. Also of interest is J. A. Alvarez, *The Betrothed of Death: the Spanish Foreign Legion during the Rif Rebellion, 1920–1927* (Westport, Connecticut, 2003). An important point to note here is that, to the extent that Spanish progressives of all sorts tended to oppose the war in Morocco, the *africanistas* acquired a pronounced veneer of reaction.

15 For a recent study of the latter years of the conflict, see W. B. Harris, *France, Spain and the Rif* (London, 2014).

16 Destined to become a major figure in the Nationalist camp in the Civil War, Queipo de Llano was a singularly unpleasant character notorious for his drunkenness, womanizing and penchant for violence, who loathed the very notion of democracy and had nothing but contempt for civilian politicians. If he turned Republican, then, it was for no better reason than his resentment of the favour shown to Franco, of whom he was always deeply jealous, and the fact that his numerous indiscretions led to him being denied promotion to the rank of major-general and transferred to the reserve list. In this particular instance, meanwhile, Primo cannot be blamed for what happened in that he went to considerable lengths to protect Queipo de Llano from the consequences of his actions and sought to sweeten the pill of his enforced retirement by the offer of various posts in the civilian administration. For a detailed analysis, see P. Preston, 'The psychopathology of an assassin: General Gonzalo Queipo de Llano', in P. Anderson and M. A. del Arco Blanco (eds.), *Mass Killings and Violence in Spain, 1936–1952* (London, 2014), pp. 23–58.

17 By far the most detailed study of the army's experience of the Primo de Rivera dictatorship is constituted by C. Navajas Zubeldia, *Ejército, estado y sociedad en España, 1923–1930* (Logroño, 1991). For the situation in April 1931, see Cardona, *El poder militar en España*, pp. 103–15.

18 E. A. Peers, *The Spanish Tragedy, 1930–1936: Dictatorship, Republic, Chaos* (London, 1936), pp. 42–3.

19 The extent of popular hostility to the Church has sometimes been contested, it having been argued that the real source of the Republic's anti-clericalism was, first, the need of the more progressive elements of the Republican movement to find an issue that would retain the support of the Socialists, and, second, the conviction of Manuel Azaña and some other Republican politicians that Catholicism was irreconcilable with democracy. See J. R. O'Connell, 'The Spanish Republic: further reflections on its anti-clerical policies', *Catholic Historical Review*, LVII, No. 2 (July 1971), pp. 275–89. There is more than a measure of truth here – one might even go so far to say that Azaña was not just anti-clerical but also violently hostile to the very principle of organized religion – but to deny that the Catholic Church was facing a bleak future would be short-sighted indeed. As Azaña's brother-in-law, the playwright and stage director Cipriano Rivas-Cherif later wrote, 'Spain had, indeed, ceased to be Catholic, and, in repeating what he had heard long before from his professors at the Escorial and what leaders of the ... Church continued to say, [Azaña] had hardly pointed out something new. Didn't bishops complain about a lack of vocations observable in our seminaries? Didn't they write pastoral letters and thunder from the pulpits about the decline of the faith of our ancestors?' C. Rivas-Cherif, *Portrait*

of an Unknown Man: Manuel Azaña and Modern Spain (Madison, Wisconsin, 1995), p. 174. Meanwhile, if the Church was beleaguered, it was also hostile. In all this it did not help that the clergy had a guilty conscience. To quote a dispatch written by the British ambassador in the summer of 1930: 'The Church in Spain ... is for obvious reasons a bulwark of the throne. The Cardinal-Archbishop of Toledo, Primate of Spain, soon after the present agitation began, issued a manifesto declaring it to be the duty of all Catholics to play their part in the political life of the country ... Catholics understood that he meant them to attend meetings and actively to support the throne. Various bishops have also issued injunctions that the monarchy is to be supported.' Cit. Elorza et al., 'Quo vadis Hispania?' p. 405. For an excellent discussion of the position adopted by the Church, see F. Lannon, 'The Church's crusade against the Republic', in Preston, *Revolution and War in Spain*, pp. 46–78.

20 The implications of this situation were all too clear. To quote the British ambassador: 'One of the Socialist ministers pointed out to a delegation that waited upon him ... that the Republic had had poor luck in one way, namely that, just when favourable economic conditions were needed, Spain began to suffer more and more from the world depression ... On all sides there is an urgent need and an increasing tendency on the part of Spanish and foreign ... enterprises to cut down the number of their employees with the result that there is an ever-growing mass of workmen out of work.' Cit. Elorza, *Quo vadis Hispania?* p. 419.

21 By far the ablest figure in the ranks of Spain's republicans, Azaña was genuinely committed to the cause of reform and modernization. However, in many respects a very shy figure, he was ill-suited to the back-slapping and bonhomie of cafe society, and had a habit of scattering his lengthy speeches with biting remarks that were scarcely calculated to propitiate the undecided. In consequence, his relations with other politicians were at best problematic, the leader of the Derecha Republicana, Miguel Maura, for example, describing him as 'contemptuous, proud, pitilessly and gracelessly incisive, reserved with all those who were not his habitual companions, unkind in his judgements of other people and their actions, in a word insupportable.' M. Maura, *Asi cayó Alfonso XIII* (Madrid, 1962), p. 222.

22 Opportunistic and corrupt, Lerroux was deeply mistrusted and was appointed to the Foreign Ministry for no better reason than that it would pander to his vanity whilst at the same time reducing his ability to engage in political intrigue on the home front. To quote the opinion of Azaña as expressed in his private diary, 'Faced by Lerroux, the only thing one can do is to acquire more authority ... in the eyes of public opinion. He cannot be checked by petty manoeuvres.' Cit. J. Marichal (ed.), *Manuel Azaña: obras completas* (México, 1966), IV, p. 11. Lerroux, meanwhile, was still more abusive: 'There was never any real understanding or cordiality between Azaña and myself ... He is a man whose soul is ... unfathomable, full of early ... that keep him perpetually on guard against his neighbour. And, sheltered behind heavy glasses, eyes like an artillery battery ... and a machine-gun of a ... gaze, this permanent mistrust was like a wall from whose battlements the castellan scanned the horizon, feeling no mercy for the serfs ... who worked his land, scorning the rest of humanity, and ... rejoicing in the contemplation and admiration of himself, knowing – believing – that he was a great man.' A. Lerroux, *La pequeña historia: apuntes para la historia grande vividos y redactados por el autor* (Buenos Aires, 1945), p. 140. Finally, here is Azaña on Alcalá Zamora, for example: '[The President] is capricious, mistrustful and quick to acquire grudges, which he retains forever ... He proceeds in a stealthy and roundabout fashion, adopts the position of a petty lawyer, twists ... words round to make them say what his apprehensions dictate – Can this possibly be endured?' Marichal, *Manuel Azaña*, IV, p. 555.

23 Cit. R. Fraser, *Blood of Spain: the Experience of Civil War* (London, 1979), pp. 94–7.

24 Manuel Azaña quickly became a hate figure for the Spanish Right. As Cipriano Rivas-Cherif complained, 'Caricatures of the Premier's face ... became a new element in the annals of Madrid's satirical journalism. Strokes and flourishes created

a more-or-less ugly ... image, multiplying warts on a fleshy face. A missing tooth became his trademark. In the first months of his ministry, bothered by a minor pain, he had sought relief in a dentists' chair and had allowed ... extraction of an incisor. As a result, from then onwards cartoonists remembered him that way and disfigured him with a gap in his teeth, almost always to suit the malevolent purposes of their editors, themselves servants of subscribers and stockholders. Some editorial commentators who wrote about him every day followed suit. Spite had not ceased to be Catholic.' Rivas-Cherif, *Portrait of an Unknown Man*, p. 179. When the Right was not mocking Azaña's physical appearance, they were insisting that he was not up to the job. Here is the later leader of the conspiracy of 1936, General Mola, on his performance as minister of war in 1931: 'I am not ignorant of the fact that amongst the gentlemen who made up the provisional government, it was difficult to find even one who had dedicated his free time to reading up on a subject that is so arid and inaccessible to the uninitiated as the study of the military world, but even so the mission should have been given to someone who ... could have realised a constructive piece of work within the limits imposed by the Republic's military policy. Unfortunately, however, the task fell to the lot of a man who had none of the necessary qualities ... and did not even enjoy the renown that he believed to be his due as an intellectual ... if one is to judge from the mediocre success achieved by his literary publications ... Cold, vain and sectarian, Manuel Azaña is marked far more by hatred than he is good will, and since the first moment that he took possession of the Ministry of War, he has dedicated himself to the task of grinding down the army; not just that, indeed, but he has attempted to pulverise it.' E. Mola Vidal, *El pasado, Azaña y el porvenir: las tragedias de nuestras instituciones militares* (Madrid, 1934), p. 158.

25 Famously, Manuel Azaña claimed that Spain had ceased to be Catholic. Amongst large sections of the population, most notably the industrial and rural proletariat, this was true enough, but amongst the middle classes and some elements of the peasantry, it was a view that was definitely open to challenge.

26 Thriving, determined and based in a region that contained about one-sixth of the population of Spain as well as her most advanced pockets of industry and urban development, Catalan nationalism was both a force that had to be appeased and one that had considerable right on its side. That said, even in Catalonia, there was a considerable minority – above all, the Anarchists (a very powerful force in Barcelona and its surrounding townships) – that was at best lukewarm in its views on autonomy, while in the rest of Spain, the Catalans were viewed with considerable hostility, even by substantial areas of the Centre and Left. In 1931, then, the Catalans had been silenced when they attempted to proclaim a Catalan republic within a federal Spain, while in 1932 the debate on the Catalan statute had been one of the few issues capable of bridging the yawning gulf between the forces of progress and reaction, To quote Diego Martínez Barrio, 'The attacks on the aspirations of Catalonia took place inside and outside the assembly alike. In the chamber deputies of the Right and Centre, and even some who belonged to parties of the Left, put up a ferocious opposition to the statute's articles in an attempt ... to denude it of any content.' D. Martínez Barrio, *Memorias de Don Diego Martínez Barrio* (Barcelona, 1983), p. 128.

27 By far the most detailed work on agrarian reform under the Second Republic is constituted by E. Malefakis, *Agrarian Reform and Peasant Revolution in Spain* (New Haven, Connecticut, 1970). The essential problem for peasants – here defined as small tenant farmers or owner occupiers – was that legislation to protect them from rack-renting and short-term leases was introduced too late to get it through the *cortes* before the Republican–Socialist coalition collapsed in 1933, whilst if such cultivators happened to take on a few extra hands at harvest time, they were also hit by such measures as the introduction of an eight-hour day and a minimum wage. Thanks to the sabotage engaged in by the Right, little land was made available for re-distribution, and what there was often hopelessly unproductive. The son of a peasant from the village of Navalmorales de Pusa in the province of Toledo, Timoteo Ruiz remembered that,

get two plots of land though his father did, this was a meaningless gesture: 'The land was so poor that when we calculated how much work we would have to put into it for the small return we would get, we realised we were wasting our time. A lot of the landless and the smallholders came to the same conclusion and left the land idle.' Cit. Fraser, *Blood of Spain*, p. 516.

28 Martínez Barrio, *Memorias*, p. 115.

29 The sort of attitude prevalent in the more élite elements of the Spanish Right is typified by a press officer whom Peter Kemp, a Cambridge undergraduate who had come to Spain to fight Bolshevism and enlisted in the Carlist militia, encountered on the Madrid front in 1936: 'Don Gonzalo Aguilera, Conde de Alba de Yeltes ... was a hard-bitten ex-cavalryman of what I believe is known as "the old school"; that is to say, he was a personal friend of King Alfonso XIII, a keen polo player and a fine sportsman ... He had some original ideas on the fundamental causes of the Civil War. The principal cause, if I remember rightly, was the introduction of modern drainage: prior to this, the riff-raff had been killed off by various useful diseases; now they survived, and were, of course, above themselves. Another entertaining theory was that the Nationalists ought to have shot all the boot-blacks ... "My dear fellow," he explained to me, "it only stands to reason! A chap who squats down on his knees to clean your boots ... is bound to be a Communist, so why not shoot him right away and be done with it. No need for a trial: his guilt is self-evident in his profession."' P. Kemp, *Mine Were of Trouble* (London, 1957), pp. 49–50.

30 Cit. Fraser, *Blood of Spain*, p. 546.

31 Martínez Barrio, *Memorias*, p. 166. That the risings had no chance of success and at the same time played straight into the hands of the Right did not perturb Sanz and his fellow hard-liners. Thus: 'We weren't unduly disappointed at the failure: from the beginning, given the situation, we doubted whether they could have effective results. But as we were convinced that such exercises were needed, we carried them out.' Cit. Fraser, *Blood of Spain*, p. 546. However, these tactics were not even justified by success: wanting only the freedom for the CNT to operate in the open, many of its members were not interested in launching a revolution, whilst there was also much hostility to the bullying behaviour of the FAI, the result being a split in the movement that saw thousands of members driven out and a number of moderate leaders set up the short-lived Partido Sindicalista. Within a short space of time, then, the Anarchist threat was receding: 'We lost at least a quarter of our membership in Badalona in that period', complained textile worker Josep Costa. 'A lot of us, who supported neither side, but adopted a centrist position, "went home to sleep." Our ... union was virtually paralysed by the dispute.' Cit. ibid.

32 Cit. F. Largo Caballero, *Escritos de la república: notas históricas de la guerra en España, 1917–1940*, ed. S. Julia (Madrid, 1985), p. 36. So prominent a role was to be played by Largo Caballero in the Civil War that it is worth allotting a few lines to the pen-portrait of him left us by the American ambassador, Claude Bowers: 'It was impossible to doubt the honesty of this pet aversion of the conservatives. He was a plasterer by trade and he had taken his socialism seriously ... Azaña had made him Minister of Labour, and in cases involving employers and employees, his invariable decision for the latter, even where they were clearly wrong, made an unpleasant impression. I do not believe he was consciously unfair, but, instinctively, he supported the workers with a fanatic zeal ... He lived with spartan simplicity, and, because he was incorruptible, he had become the idol of the working class which had so often been betrayed by false friends.' C. Bowers, *My Mission to Spain: Watching the Rehearsal for World War Two* (London, 1954), p. 184.

33 Cit. Elorza, *Quo vadis Hispania?* p. 439.

34 Cit. ibid., p. 415.

35 J. M. Gil Robles, *No fue posible la paz* (Barcelona, 1968), p. 77.

36 Bowers, *My Mission to Spain*, p. 52.

37 Cit. P. Preston, *The Coming of the Spanish Civil War* (London, 1978), p. 48. Yet whether Gil Robles and his followers were genuinely fascists is another matter altogether.

In the words of an Asturian member of the Socialist youth movement named Alberto Fernández, 'The CEDA for us was Dollfuss' corporate social Christian dictatorship, in other words fascism as we conceived it then.' Cit. Fraser, *Blood of Spain*, p. 556. In the end, of course, the truth scarcely matters: however he might be defined, Gil Robles was bent on overthrowing democracy, putting an end to social reform, reversing the anti-clericalism that had among other things seen the Church banned from education, smashing regional nationalism and breaking the power of the Left. And, of course, the impact on the Left was enormous. 'The electoral campaign ... can be seen as a veritable crusade against sincere republicans and socialists. Led by Gil Robles ... the Rightists were exultant: their conduct was marked by vulgarity, cynicism, a belief that power was in their hands. As for their propaganda, it chief characteristic was defamation: affirming that republicans and socialists were thieves and criminals, they demanded that they should be purged from public life.' F. Largo Caballero, *Mis recuerdos: cartas a un amigo* (Mexico City, 1976), p. 121.

38 Just as the Right had contested the legitimacy of the elections of April 1931, so the Left contested the legitimacy of the elections of November 1933. David Granda, for example, was an impoverished Asturian sharecropper form the village of Paladín who joined the Communist Party: 'In little villages like Paladín ... the politics of the Right were organised by the most important people, those who had plenty of land or money, *los caciques*. There was the priest, the secretary to the mayor, the doctor, the local tax-collector; people like that. During an election, even under the Republic, they would visit everyone and buy votes, and, the more miserable and propertyless the people, so much the better, because they were so much the easier to bribe. They were promised a mattress, things like that. There was one election in Asturias, that of 1933, which was called the 'sausage election' because that's what was on offer – sausage. During the 1933 election at Paladín voting took place in the school and a group of right-wingers were waiting outside to interfere with the old people as they went in ... So the old people had to be closely watched by the young, because they were often senile and easily influenced ... The Right was always up to tricks like that.' Cit. MacMaster, *Spanish Fighters: an Oral History*, p. 48.

39 For a succinct guide to the *bienio negro*, see Preston, *Coming of the Spanish Civil War*, pp. 108–16, 151–76. Even when families were unaffected by the arrest of the chief bread-winner or the latter's dismissal from his job or exclusion from employment on political grounds, the populace was hit very hard. Living as he was in rural Málaga, Gerald Brenan was a privileged eye-witness: 'The fall of wages, the dismissals of workmen, the relaxation of the laws safeguarding tenants ... brought an enormous increase in misery ... Some *pueblos* had almost 1,000 men unemployed through nine tenths of the year.' Brenan, *Spanish Labyrinth*, p. 275.

40 Lerroux, *La pequeña historia*, p. 292. In speaking of a premeditated plan, Lerroux was not exaggerating. Santiago Carrillo was the son of prominent Socialist, Wenceslao Carrillo, and a leading figure in the Socialist youth movement: 'I remember, in particular, the preparations for the movement of October 1934. I was a member of the co-ordinating committee, of which Largo Caballero was chairman and which was entrusted with organising the movement on a national scale. That movement ... resulted from our determination to keep fascism in check. At a meeting of the Socialist Party, the UGT and the Socialist Youth, it was decided that, if fascist ministers should enter the government, then it would be necessary to launch a rising and to fight, united with the Communist Party and other working-class forces. Otherwise, as had been the case in Italy, Germany and Austria, the fascists ... would come to power "legally," and afterwards it would be impossible to dislodge them.' S. Carrillo, *Dialogue on Spain* (London, 1976), p. 30. Yet it was a premeditated plan that to the very end, Largo Caballero prayed that he would not have to implement: concerned above all to safeguard the interests and physical existence of the UGT, the Socialist leader was terrified of having to take action that in his heart he realized could not but lead to a shattering defeat, his real goal being no more than the

convocation of fresh elections. As Bowers says, then, 'The rising was conditional on the admission of the CEDA men into the ministry, and Largo Caballero clung to the belief that Alcalá Zamora would continue to oppose their admission.' Bowers, *My Mission to Spain*, p. 98; see also Preston, *Coming of the Spanish Civil War*, pp. 117–20.

41 H. Buckley, *The Life and Death of the Spanish Republic: a Witness to the Spanish Civil War*, ed. P. Preston (London, 2013), pp. 148–9. There was also some trouble in the area round Bilbao, where the UGT declared a general strike, but here, too, it was all over in a matter of days.

42 For a detailed account of these events, see G. Jackson, *The Spanish Republic and Civil War* (Princeton, New Jersey, 1965), pp. 150–3.

43 Carrillo, *Dialogue on Spain*, p. 33.

44 A. Barea, *The Forging of a Rebel* (London, 2001), p. 480.

45 C. de la Mora, *In Place of Splendour: the Autobiography of a Spanish Woman* (New York, 1939), p. 204.

46 The son of the dictator of 1923–30, José Antonio Primo de Rivera had initially gone into politics to redeem the good name of his father, and for this reason was always inclined to be critical of the traditional Spanish élites, whether military or civil, the consequence being that his Falange Española y de las Juntas de Ofensiva Nacional-Sindicalistas made little impact on the political scene till 1936, and all the more so as the CEDA seemed to offer a safer route to the destruction of the cause of reform. See H. Thomas, 'The hero in the empty room: José Antonio and Spanish fascism', *Journal of Contemporary History*, I, No. 1 (January 1966), pp. 174–82. For the Carlists, a movement that traced its origins back to the struggle against the coming of liberalism in the 1930s, see M. Blinkhorn, 'Carlism and the Spanish crisis of the 1930s', *Journal of Contemporary History*, VIII, No. 3 (July 1972), pp. 65–88.

47 Cit. F. Díaz Plaja, *La historia de España en sus documentos: el siglo XX – dictadura y república* (Madrid, 1964), pp. 838–9. Still more hysterical was the view of the then London correspondent of *ABC*, Luís Bolín: 'There was no justification for the exultant excesses of the Left; even after a good deal of cooking, the elections of 16 February [1936] had not shown conclusive results ... But these returns ... were enough for the Left to seize power ... and draw up a programme which included the ousting of Alcalá Zamora ... constraint of army officers, expropriation of property and nationalisation of banks and private industries, destruction of all churches and convents, establishment of a soviet in Morocco, extermination of the bourgeoisie and of bourgeois newspapers, and creation of armed militias as a first step towards a Red Army and the dictatorship of the proletariat ... Loyalty to Russia, and free love, were advocated on the side.' L. Bolín, *Spain: the Vital Years* (London, 1967), p. 150. In such rhetoric, of course, is to be found the heart of the Right's responsibility for the disaster that beset Spain in 1936. Determined to block even the most moderate challenge to the traditional structure of society, they whipped up support for their position by scare tactics and at the same time did all that they could to stir up disorder, whether by provoking the Left into acts of violence, of which the rising in Asturias was but the greatest example, or by engaging in violence themselves. To quote the conservative (but nonetheless staunchly democratic) Republican politician, Diego Martínez Barrio, 'The monarchists ... systematically addressed themselves to exaggerating the difficulties inherent in any political upheaval and instigated numerous incidents whose aim was to weaken the authority of the government. Apart from the damage that it caused the nation, their obstinate stupidity produced a white demagoguery ... that was as prejudicial to the permanent goals of society as the delirium of the extreme Left.' Martínez Barrio, *Memorias*, p. 38.

48 R. Carr, *Spain, 1808–1975* (Oxford, 1982), p. 649.

49 The situation on the Left at this time can only be described as chaotic in the extreme. As noted above, both the Anarchists and the Communists had suffered schisms that had seen breakaway groups set up rival political movements. This, however, was

as nothing in comparison to what was going on in the ranks of the Socialists. In brief, throughout the Republican period, the Socialist party – officially the Partido Socialista Obrero Español (or PSOE) – and its attendant trade-union movement, the UGT had been divided between a right wing that believed in working for social change within the parameters of parliamentary democracy and a left wing that dreamed of much more rapid progress or even violent revolution. In the wake of the elections of February 1936, this dispute erupted in confrontation over the question of whether or not the Socialists should participate in the new government. In the event, it was the Left that won, and Largo Caballero now definitively emerged as the most important figure in the whole movement. If there is one thing that is certain, it is that Largo Caballero was terrified of the idea of revolution, believing that it could only lead to the destruction of Spanish socialism, but he was more than happy to use very violent language as a means of, first, ensuring that the all-Republican Popular-Front government did not renege on all the various reforms it was forcing through, and, second, undercutting the Anarchists and persuading their followers to come over to the Socialists. Nor was this an end to it. Intensely vain, Largo Caballero harboured dreams of absorbing the Communists as well, and he therefore not only contin-ued openly to call for revolution but also to encourage sections of his party to sign unification pacts with their Communist counterparts: hence the emergence at this time of, first, the so-called Partido Socialista Unificada de Cataluña (or PSUC) and, second, the Juventud Socialista Unificada (or JSU). From the point of view of Largo Caballero, what all this represented was a move to tame the revolutionary Left and bring it under his control, but for the Right it looked far more like the preparation of a united revolutionary movement that would take control of the country as soon as the Frente Popular lost headway. In short, Largo Caballero must bear at least some of the blame for what now transpired, while he also failed to see that the formation of the PSUC and JSU did not so much represent the Socialists taking control of major sections of the Communist party as the other way about. At all events, what cannot be denied is that, wherever one looks on the Left, there was a mood that can only be described as breath-taking in its irresponsibility and want of realism. Thus: 'The revolutionaries … were getting ready for battle, and in their minds there was not the slightest doubt that the liquidation of the "squares" was cut and dried. The workers would take to the streets; the militias would storm the barracks; the soldiers, united, as in Russia, with the peasants … would join the people, and in less than a cock's crow all the right-wingers, all the bourgeois republicans, all the democrats, in fact the whole panoply of legalist reaction, would be consigned to the scrap heap.' Heredia, *Monarquía, república, guerra*, p. 194.

50 H. Thomas, *The Spanish Civil War* (London, 1977), pp. 165–6. An insight into the tone that typified the meetings of the Spanish Military Union is provided by the memoirs of the monarchist journalist, Juan Ignacio Escobar: 'About fifteen or twenty officers were present, amongst them my cousin, Carlos Kirkpatrick. I was astonished by the degree of verbal violence which they all expressed themselves, not just against the Republic, but also against the senior commanders of the army … That the gener-als could not be counted on was the refrain of every intervention: they were a bunch of bourgeois old duffers incapable of the slightest daring who would hand us over to Communism for sheer want of decision … That being the case, it was necessary to start afresh on the sole basis of young men below the rank of major.' J. I. Escobar, *Así empezó* (Madrid, 1974), p. 15.

51 P. Preston, *The Spanish Holocaust: Inquisition and Extermination in Twentieth-Century Spain* (London, 2012), p. 51.

52 For all this, see P. La Porte, 'Civil–military relations in the Spanish Protectorate in Morocco: the road to the Spanish Civil War, 1912–1936', *Armed Forces and Society*, XXX, No. 2 (Winter, 2004), pp. 220–1.

53 Amongst those approached in respect of his plans by Sanjurjo was Lerroux, whom the general appears to have regarded as a potential collaborator. 'Very discreetly and

carefully, the general … described the psychological climate that was being created in the army, which was resigned to Azaña's … hasty reforms in the hope that destruction would be followed by renovation … but profoundly alarmed by the extent which social indiscipline had reached, and the weakness … shown by the government. Very gently, he added that this state of affairs was being attributed in military circles to the excessive intervention … of the Socialists, and that … various generals were in agreement with his opinion, and certain garrisons becoming very excited.' Lerroux, *La pequeña historia*, p. 143.

54 The equipment possessed by the Spanish army was an issue that was of genuine concern. In 1931, the army had just twenty obsolescent French Schneider and Renault tanks, no more than 1,000 motor vehicles, all of sixteen anti-aircraft guns and no heavy guns other than a consignment of 150mm Krupp M1913s, a model long since deemed obsolescent by the German army, whilst even its rifles and machine-guns were in many instances worn out and incapable of accurate fire. See Cardona, *El poder militar en España*, pp. 10–13.

55 Mola, *El pasado, Azaña y el porvenir*, pp. 164–5. Equally hostile were the views of a retired infantry lieutenant-colonel named Nazario Cebreiros, who heaped scorn on Azaña's reforms, not only on the political grounds favoured by Mola but also on ones that were purely military, there being, or so he said, too few infantry and cavalry in the new order of battle and too many artillery and engineers. See N. Cebreiros, *Las reformas militares: estudio crítico* (Santander, 1931), pp. 37–54.

56 Cit. Fraser, *Blood of Spain*, p. 565. An artillery officer, Michelina himself took advantage of Azaña's retirement package, going on to rally to the cause of Carlism.

57 Cit. ibid., p. 566. The attitude of Spanish officers to the Republic was analyzed at some length by Antonio Ruiz Vilaplana, a notary from Burgos who became increasingly horrified at what was happening in Nationalist Spain and eventually fled into exile in France. In his eyes, the hatred that many of them clearly felt for the new régime was the product of a mixture of disgust at their miserable pay and frustration at the stagnation of their careers under a régime that was committed to both a peaceful foreign policy and a reduction in the size of the army. See A. Ruiz Vilaplana, *Burgos Justice: a Year's Experience of Nationalist Spain* (London, 1937), pp. 203–12.

58 Typical enough of the sort of tit-for-tat killing that went on was an incident that took place in the small Andalusian village where the poet, Laurie Lee, had ended up in the wake of, as he put it, walking out one midsummer morning: 'June came in in full blast, with the heat bouncing off the sea as from a buckled sheet of tin. All day in the bars the radios spat and crackled – violence in Madrid, demonstrations in Valencia, strikes and riots in Barcelona … [One] morning a group of Falangists in the neighbouring village walked into a bar and shot five fishermen. The murderers, wearing arm-bands, escaped in a car to Granada … In the afternoon I walked out into the country with Jacobo … An hour or so later we returned by another path and found … the figure of a man … sprawled on the river bank. We recognised him as a local Falangist, a boy of about twenty, whose father had once been mayor. He had been shot through the head. L. Lee, *As I Walked Out One Midsummer Morning* (London, 1969), pp. 219–20.

59 See M. Alpert, 'The Spanish army and the Popular Front' in M. Alexander and H. Graham (eds.), *The French and Spanish Popular Fronts: Comparative Perspectives* (Cambridge, 1989), pp. 50–61. That there was a real atmosphere of social and political crisis in the Spain of 1936, it is difficult to deny. Andrés Bernarbé, for example, was the son of peasant proprietor from Villanueva de Huerva: 'I have never heard it said anywhere that Zaragoza was a city that had to all intents and purposes been taken over by the gunmen of the FAI [N.B. Federación Anarquista Ibérica, the political wing of the Anarchist movement] but that really was what it was like immediately prior to the outbreak of war … Bombs were going off every day, and in the streets one saw nothing but machine-guns, tanks [*sic*: there being very few tanks in Spain at this time, Bernabé is presumably referring to the armoured cars employed by the

Assault Guard] and artillery pieces ... The climate was one of the most absolute violence', cit. C. Vidal (ed.), *Recuerdo 1936: una historia oral de la Guerra Civil Española* (Barcelona, 2008), p. 60. Lest it be thought that these remarks are simply the ramblings of an unreconstructed Franquist, compare the very similar remarks about the situation in Catalonia that are to be found in R. Miralles Bravo, *Memorias de un comandante rojo* (Madrid, 1975), pp. 11–14. As so often, however, perceptions were more important than the reality: as Preston has shown, much of Spain was not affected by the wave of violence, whilst something over two-fifths of the 351 people who died between the February elections and the outbreak of the Civil War were killed by the security forces. As for the civilian killings, meanwhile, it is all but certain that the majority were the work of Carlist or Falangist gunmen. For all this, see Preston, *Spanish Holocaust*, pp. 108–23 *passim*.

60 That the army was split was something that was well understood. In the words of Manuel de Heredia, 'One of my brothers-in-law was an officer in the First Infantry, and he told me which generals were on the side of the Republic and which ones were not: Goded, Fanjul, Sanjurjo, Miaja and Mola were all regarded as 'givens' in so far as the cause of rebellion were concerned, whilst it was hoped that Franco would also join the movement. On the other hand, Aranda – at that point still only a colonel – Batet, Pozas, Riquelme and quite a few others were all disposed to defend the regime.' Heredia, *Monarquía, republica, guerra*, pp. 192–3. A keen advocate of rebellion, however, Heredia's brother-in-law was convinced that such reservations had little weight. According to him, indeed, the battle for the soul of the officer corps had long since been won: 'In the end, [he said,] with the exception of one or two figures such as the governors of Valencia and Valladolid, one and all were sick of what was going on and entirely in favour of a coup that would put an end to the current chaos.' Ibid., p. 194.

61 See C. Navajas Zubeldía, *Leales y rebeldes: la tragedia de los militares republicanos* (Madrid, 2011), pp. 119–25; J. Modesto, *Soy del Quinto Regimiento* (Barcelona, 1978), pp. 45–7. According to Modesto, a number of the officers concerned joined the Communist Party, which was thereby presented with a toe-hold in the Republican forces before the war had even started.

62 For a detailed account of the impact of the death of Calvo Sotelo that conveys much of the real drama of the moment, see S. Alcocer, *Y Madrid dejó de reir: andanzas de una periodista por la zona roja* (Madrid, 1974), pp. 5–28. A right-wing journalist, Alcocer was by chance the first person to identify Calvo Sotelo's body. As we have seen, as far as the conspirators were concerned, the murder was but a fortunate accident, but it yet remained a key moment in what now transpired: 'As I crossed the Paseo del Prado my thoughts were given over to the pleasant pastime of dreaming while wide-awake. Intuitively, I divined that the hour of the great decision was about to strike, and that from one minute to the next. The uprising was upon us! There really was no other solution. This chaos that was so affecting the populace with its crop-burnings and land occupations, its attacks on creatures as harmless as humble priests, its murders even; this wave of anarchy that was overwhelming every inch of the country: only the army could stop it. But it would have to be quick, for the Communists were already on the march, already perfectly organised for an assault on power, an assault whose most barefaced steps yet had been taken the night before via the assassination of Calvo Sotelo, and that by agents of authority already won over to the Marxist cause.' Ibid., pp. 28–9. For a less hysterical view, we might cite that of Diego Martínez Barrio: 'All hope of concord had been dissipated. Unreconciled and irreconcilable, the two Spains were facing one another pistol in hand. Any attempt at mediation would now be futile. The historic struggle between black and white – now blue and red – having been revived, the bloody dialogue was about to be renewed.' Martínez Barrio, *Memorias*, pp. 341–3. Finally, for Franco's on-and-off relationship with the conspirators, see P. Preston, *Franco: a Biography* (London, 1995), pp. 120–37.

63 Cit. Fraser, *Blood of Spain*, p. 103.

64 That the Right were just as provocative goes without saying. Sent to Madrid to cover the predictably enthusiastic celebrations of 1 May, John Langdon-Davies witnessed a typical skirmish: 'On the second of May ... I went to the spot in the Paseo del Prado where they commemorate the heroes of the people who died 128 years ago in the rising of the Dos del Mayo. As we stood there, some trouble-seeking students cried out 'Viva la Falange Española!', and at once a thousand people were on their tracks. We chased them round the commemorative column and ... across the Paseo until we reached the *cortes* building, and there the police both rescued and arrested them. They were searched for arms and those that had them were taken off ... while the crowd clapped hands.' J. Langdon-Davies, *Behind the Spanish Barricades* (London, 1936), pp. 55–6.

65 G. Brenan, *Personal Record, 1920–1972* (London, 1974), p. 278.

66 Cit. Fraser, *Blood of Spain*, p. 44.

67 Mora, *In Place of Splendour*, p. 216.

68 Cit. Fraser, *Blood of Spain*, p. 571. In fairness, it ought here to be pointed out that there have been persistent claims that a number of units of the Barcelona garrison, at least, did not rise because of the efforts of Communist agitators to win over the rank and file. See Miralles Bravo, *Memorias*, p. 17.

69 Cit. Fraser, *Blood of Spain*, p. 574.

70 C. Revilla Cebrecos, *Tercio de Lacar* (Madrid, 1975), p. 32. Somewhat less sanguine in his assessment, however, was Emilio Herrera Alonso, a *requeté* from Pamplona who served in the Tercio de Navarra: 'The column was formed of eight companies of *requetés*. Only some of them had proper uniforms and many nothing on their feet but rope-soled sandals, but they all had a red beret, a set of cartridge belts and a good rifle. That said, good rifles or not, the number of men who knew how to use them with any degree of accuracy was not that great.' E. Herrero Alonso, *Los mil días del tercio 'Navarra': biografía de un tercio de requetés* (Madrid, 1974), p. 25.

71 S.G. Payne, *Falange: a History of Spanish Fascism* (Stanford, California, 1961), pp. 110–11. As Antonio Ruiz Vilaplana points out, in much of Spain, the Falange was in any case little more than a paper force: 'In my brief account of what happened in Burgos at the outbreak of the military rebellion, the reader will notice something that seems surprising – that I make no mention whatever of Falangists or fascists. This omission ... is easily explained if one bears in mind that, at Burgos, as at most of the cities where there was a rising, there *were* no fascists to speak of. In each city, there was, it is true, a small nucleus ... composed of young men who had joined the movement without really knowing anything about its aims or ideals [but] their chief reason for enrolling was a desire to be in fashion or to escape from the inevitable tedium of life in the provinces ... It was only in Seville, Valladolid and Saragossa, where the class struggle had brought the Falangists into conflict with the workers' trade-union organizations, that fascism ... had developed to any appreciable extent ... In Burgos, Pamplona and other important centres of the revolt, however, the Falangists were scarcely known and took no part in the coup.' Ruiz Vilaplana, *Burgos Justice*, pp. 26–7.

72 The well-connected monarchist conspirator José Ignacio Escobar was brutal in his assessment: 'The Marxist and Anarchist organizations were the only forces ready for battle other than the army. Neither the Falange – still a mere embryo – nor the more traditional Carlists were in any condition to make head against them.' Escobar, *Así fue*, pp. 40–1.

73 See Payne, *Falange*, pp. 111–14; M. Blinkhorn, *Carlism and Crisis in Spain, 1931–1939* (Cambridge, 1975), pp. 242–50.

74 Barea, *Forging of a Rebel*, p. 510.

2

SPAIN IS DIVIDED

The shots fired on the night of 12 July 1936 were the equivalent of the fusillade heard on the streets of Sarajevo on 28 June 1914. Realizing that it was now or never, Mola responded by ordering his forces to go into action on 18 July. In the meantime, much of Spain was in uproar: not only were the funerals of Castillo and Calvo Sotelo accompanied by massive demonstrations and yet more violence, but also Gil Robles made an inflammatory speech in which he laid the blame for all Spain's ills on the government, asserted that democracy had completely broken down and announced that Spain could expect her liberation forthwith.[1] Warned that trouble was afoot in Morocco in particular, on 17 July, Casares Quiroga ordered several warships to take post in the Straits of Gibraltar and instructed the commander of the Spanish forces at Melilla to arrest a number of his subordinates. The latter, however, were too quick for him: mobilizing a number of troops, they arrested the general concerned – Manuel Romerales Quinto – proclaimed Franco commander of the Army of Africa, declared martial law, instigated a general round-up of all known liberals and leftists and occupied all the key public buildings and military installations. Confronted by a group of Assault Guards who had come to pick up the leaders of the conspiracy in the garrison of Melilla, Lieutenant Julio de la Torre was amongst the very first of the Army of Africa to take up arms: 'My heart was beating wildly, my body trembling. "Have faith in me! Load! Aim!" I shouted, looking at my men … The legionaries aimed their rifles at the policemen … "Surrender! Drop your weapons!" They did … After that it didn't take long to capture the town.'[2] Within a few hours, moreover, the example of Melilla had been followed by all the other garrisons in the protectorate. In an alliance that was to be typical of the next few days, the local representatives of the air force, the Assault Guards and the trade unions fought back bravely, but by dawn on 18 July it was all over. Though nobody realized it as yet, the first battle of the Spanish Civil War had been fought and won.[3]

As the last few shots sputtered in Melilla in the small hours of 18 July 1936, Spain hovered on the very brink of catastrophe, there being three possible outcomes of the situation that had now emerged. The first, of course, was that the rising might achieve the rapid, total and uncompromising effect that had been achieved in Melilla (within a matter of hours, Romerales, the mayor, the acting high commissioner of Morocco and a variety of officers, officials, policemen, trade unionists and political militants of one sort or another had all been shot). The second, meanwhile, was that the rising would go off at half-cock and quickly fall apart. As for the third, and by far the most terrible, Spain might end up divided into two armed camps that would have no option but to fight it out in a prolonged civil war. To the surprise of almost all concerned, it was this last option that prevailed: far from being settled in a few days, the conflict was to drag on for the thick end of 1,000. As Juventud-Socialista-Unificada (JSU) militant Rafael Miralles Bravo wrote, for example, 'What very few – very, very few – people would have dared to predict ... is that those skirmishes ... were nothing other than the first moments of the cruellest civil war recorded in the whole of history.'[4]

Given the efforts that had been made to subvert the armed forces and the police since February 1936, the advantages that the Right had enjoyed in organizing its civilian volunteers and the utter inadequacy of the various left-wing militias, even the very best of whom – possibly the Communist-led Milicia Anti-Fascista Obrera y Campesina (or MAOC)[5] – were untrained, few in number and armed with nothing other than a handful of pistols, shotguns and sticks of dynamite, this might at first sight seem somewhat surprising. However, a number of factors rendered complete success extremely unlikely. Setting aside the fact that the Falangist and Carlist militias were themselves less than spectacular as a fighting force – having gone in mainly for street fighting, for example, the former had never really sought much in the way of military training – not even the fate of Calvo Sotelo was enough to render rebellion universal. Committed Communists, Socialists or even *azañistas* might have been relatively few and far between in the armed forces as a whole, but the air force was imbued with a strongly progressive tradition; the navy possessed of a lower deck radicalized enough to challenge the lead of a largely rebellious officer corps; and the army deeply divided, the preponderance of *africanismo* amongst the conspirators being inclined to ensure the loyalty of many gunners and engineers at the very least.[6]

As some of the conspirators knew all too well, in fact, the strategy that they had been pursuing since February 1936 had been as much of a failure as anything propounded by Gil Robles. However, if too few officers had been won over to the rebellion to guarantee victory, enough had joined it to stave off defeat. If this was the case, it was largely the fault of the Spanish Left, the latter having done everything it could to play into the hands of the conspirators. By advocating – or in many cases pretending to advocate – revolution, they had done nothing to curb the understandable excitement that had swept the working classes in the wake of the Frente Popular's victory, whilst in effect fighting the battles of the Right.[7] In defence of their actions, it is certainly possible to argue that they greatly strengthened popular resistance to the coup, but such arguments ignore not only the greater impetus that was given to the conspirators by the revolutionary threat, but also the absolute inability of the people to prevail except when they fought in the company of elements of the armed forces. In short, Spain was about to be plunged into a holocaust for which the responsibility lies first with the Right's refusal to accept even a modicum of reform; second, the posturing, rivalry and hegemonism that characterized the Spanish labour movement; and only third, the failings of the unfortunate Republican politicians who have been so excoriated by apologists of the Left and Right alike.[8]

Premature though it may have been, the Moroccan revolt was soon seconded elsewhere. At dawn on Saturday 18 July, Franco declared martial law in the Canary Islands and set off by air for Morocco. In Córdoba, Cádiz, Algeciras and Jérez, too, the army, Civil Guard, Carlists and Falange joined the rising and quickly took control. Resistance was often fierce, however – the Assault Guards on the whole stayed loyal – and in Málaga, a rising by some junior officers was defeated altogether, whilst Seville was only secured due to the fact that Queipo de Llano, a sometime Republican who had conspired against the monarchy prior to 1931 but had since been alienated by what he saw as Spain's slide into anarchy, succeeded in deposing the captain general and persuading the garrison and the police to follow his lead, the gallant fight put up by some of the city's workers making no difference whatsoever, and particularly not when two Fokker VII bomber-transports that had fallen into the hands of the Army of Africa began ferrying in squads of Moors and Foreign Legionaries: 'After a couple of cannon rounds from a field piece emplaced by the famous ... arch, we advanced', remembered Rafael Medina, a Falangist volunteer later to become Duque de Medinaceli, of the assault on the Macarena district. 'The revolutionaries started firing. We suffered casualties. A legionary was killed. The man behind him jumped over his body shouting "Long live death!" and advanced down the street ... The legionaries ... were magnificent. The next day the red *barrio* fell.'[9]

What, meanwhile, was the response of the government? Deciding, quite rightly, first, that arming the workers would provoke insurrection throughout the country; second, that such a decision would lead to revolution; and, third, that it would not even guarantee the defeat of the rebels, Casares Quiroga refused to do anything of the sort. Instead, no sooner had news of the Melilla revolt broken than frantic efforts were made to confine the rebellion to Morocco, maintain order amongst the populace and overawe the Army of Africa through aerial and naval bombardment. An important tool here was the radio, the transmitters of every possible station being fed a diet designed, on the one hand, to keep the populace off the streets, and, on the other, to keep potential waverers in barracks. In the words of Arturo Barea: 'Officially nothing had happened. The army had not revolted in Morocco.'[10] Only on the morning of 18 July was it finally admitted that a coup was taking place, but even then, the message was as reassuring as before: 'A new plot against the Republic has been thwarted ...

In the cities of the protectorate loyal elements are continuing to resist the rebellion and thereby to defend the authority of the Republic. With the exception of the units that have already been announced, the army, navy and air force remain loyal to the execution of their duty and are at this moment moving against the insurgents.'[11] Meanwhile, the navy's battle squadron was sent from El Ferrol to join the destroyers stationed at Cartagena. As the rising spread, moreover, the commanders involved were declared to have been dismissed and their soldiers ordered not to obey them, the army as a whole placed on alert and a number of known malcontents rounded up.[12]

By midnight on 18 July, however, it had become all too clear that this strategy had failed, Casares Quiroga therefore quickly resigned in favour of the moderate Martínez Barrio, the aim now being an accommodation with the rebels through the formation of a centrist government of some sort. However, in the early morning of Sunday 19 July, the garrisons of Barcelona, Gijón, Oviedo, Albacete, Toledo, Guadalajara, Cáceres, Salamanca, Segovia, Avila, Zamora, Palencia, Valladolid, Burgos, Vitoria, San Sebastián, Pamplona, Zaragoza, Huesca, Jaca, Teruel, Valencia, Ibiza and Mallorca all rebelled, this example being followed by some forces in Madrid, the Civil Guard of the province of Badajoz and the officers of most of the ships in the navy. As before, however, the rebels found that victory was not going to be easy. It being high summer, many soldiers were on leave, the result being that everything hung on the Assault Guards, the Civil Guards and, in frontier areas, the Carabineers (or border guards). Wherever these joined the uprising, all was well, but elsewhere the rebels faced a difficult task that was not made any easier by the fact that Martínez Barrio had now been left with no option but to arm the people (to the extent that he could: in those places where the military and police were solidly in favour of the rebellion, of course, no arms were forthcoming). How great a difference putting arms in the hands of untrained workers actually made is a moot point, but in Barcelona, the columns of troops who tried to take over the city were shot to pieces and eventually forced to surrender, the numerous prisoners including General Goded, who had flown to Barcelona from his headquarters in Majorca to take command.[13] Also a complete failure was the revolt in Badajoz: here the only elements to rise in the revolt were the Civil Guard, and the forces that defeated them primarily the Carabineers.[14] In San Sebastián, Gijón, Madrid, Valencia and Mahón, meanwhile, the rebels were so intimidated that they hastily barricaded themselves into a variety of strongholds to await relief. However, only in Andalucía was there much prospect of help, and even there, matters were complicated by the fact that the crews of most of the warships in and around the Straits had overthrown their officers and declared for the government. A handful of troops had been got across to Algeciras and Cádiz before the revolt of the lower decks, whilst such few aircraft as were available – three Fokker FVII transport aircraft and two Dornier Wal floatplanes – were used to fly more reinforcements to Seville, but even so matters were clearly hanging in the balance.[15]

Hopes of compromise having failed, on the evening of 19 July, Martínez Barrio therefore resigned in favour of a new cabinet dedicated to military victory headed by the *azañista* José Giral. The new Prime Minister immediately requested help from the Popular-Front government that had recently been established in France under Léon Blum, even if the modest amount of aid that was actually requested – twenty Potez Po540 bombers, 1,000 rifles, fifty machine guns and eight 75mm guns, together with appropriate consignments of spares and ammunition – is redolent of a certain degree of over-confidence. Meanwhile, with their cause in serious trouble, entirely independently of one another, both Franco and Mola had also decided to seek help from abroad, the obvious figures to turn to, in their case, being Hitler and Mussolini. Yet the results of these approaches were very different. Within a matter of days, a variety of factors – hostility to all forms of socialism; the strategic and economic value of a friendly Spain; the desire to try out new weapons of war; and, last but not least, Mussolini's perennial lust for glory – had ensured that help was on the way from Germany and Italy alike: whilst a number of bomber-transports flew direct to Morocco, a variety of fighters and maintenance supplies were dispatched by sea, along with the requisite mechanics. Yet, for all that a 'fascist' Spain was an obvious military danger as well as a negation of everything that the Blum régime stood for, no such help arrived from across the Pyrenees. Terrified of provoking Germany and unwilling to aid what it saw as a Bolshevik régime, the British government effectively told Blum that in the event of trouble, he could not expect any support from Britain, while the French premier himself became increasingly concerned at the possible impact of intervention on French politics. Instead of arms, then, Madrid was offered the assistance of a non-intervention pact that would keep all foreign arms out of the conflict. Had this been implemented fairly, it would have ensured parity between the two sides and possibly even might have brought the conflict to a halt, and by the end of August 1936, Britain, France, Germany, Italy and Russia had all adhered to it. However, while Britain and France honoured their obligations under the pact, the Germans and the Italians simply ignored it and followed up their initial dispatches of aircraft with many shiploads of weaponry of all sorts.[16]

In response to this blatant cynicism, the Soviet Union soon resolved to send aid of its own to the Republic, while at various times shipments of arms, some of them quite considerable, were also obtained from Mexico, Czechoslovakia and even fiercely Catholic Poland (very much a case, this last, of foreign exchange speaking louder than ideology).[17] In Spain, meanwhile, events continued to unfold. Thus, 20 July saw León and Granada fall in the face of ineffectual popular resistance, as well as a series of risings in Galicia in defiance of the military authorities, who in this instance had remained firm in their allegiance. Loyal police and workers did what they could, but they quickly succumbed, along with the crews of various ships that had stayed at El Ferrol, all of which had managed to overwhelm their officers. However, risings at Almería and Cartagena were crushed, as were the ones that had taken place the previous day in Mahón and Madrid, whilst the rebels' titular leader, General Sanjurjo, was killed when the plane that had been sent to pick him up from Portugal crashed on take-off. Waiting for Sanjurjo at Burgos with other insurgent officers was José Ignacio Escobar: 'That night we heard Madrid radio announce the death of General Sanjurjo in an accident. We were stunned. The idea that our movement, though triumphant, was now going to develop along lines other than those which we expected, struck fear into our hearts.'[18]

Before going any further, it is essential to tackle the issue of the role played by the workers in the defeat of the rising in such places where the conspirators were overcome. On the Left, of course, from 1936 onwards it has been axiomatic that victory was the work of the people. Indeed, such claims have continued to be made even by historians whose work is solidly revisionist. In the words of Michael Seidman, for example, 'Hundreds of leftist militants formed ... militias. Without these ... fighters of the CNT, UGT, FAI, PSOE, PCE [Partido Comunista Espanol] and POUM, the military rebellion would easily have succeeded. Milicianos' guerrilla warfare stopped it with enthusiasm and bravery.'[19] As witness descriptions of the fighting in Madrid, however, careful reading of the accounts of at least some of those present those suggests a rather different story.[20] Let us here begin with the memoirs of Arturo Barea:

> Rifle shots were cracking from the direction of the [Montaña] barracks. At the corner of the Plaza de España and the Calle Ferraz a group of Shock Police [i.e. Assault Guards] were loading their rifles in the shelter of a wall. A multitude of people were crouching and lying between the trees and benches of the gardens ... Shouting and screaming, a tight mass of people appeared on the other side of the Plaza de España ... I saw that it had in its midst a lorry with a 7.5cm gun. An officer ... was trying to give orders on how to unload the cannon ... Machine-gun bullets were spraying the street very close to us. I ... threw myself down behind a stout tree trunk, just behind two workers lying on the lawn ... One of the two men in front of me ... gripped a revolver with both hands and pulled the trigger laboriously ... People burgeoned from the ground ... A huge solid mass of bodies moved forwards like a ram against the barracks ... The machine-guns rattled ceaselessly. And then we knew in an instant, though no-one told us, that the barracks was stormed.[21]

Also worth perusing is the account given by the Communists José Sandoval and Manuel Azcárate, both of whom were present in Madrid in July 1936, of the assault on the Montaña barracks:

> Groups of workers, Communist and Socialist party members and members of the CNT ... young lads of the Socialist Youth and the Workers and Peasants' Anti-Fascist Militia, were posted at corners, in trees and behind low walls. The barracks was besieged ... At dawn the next day

the attack ... began. The triumphant arrival of two field guns, with their attendant crowd of eager youngsters and sightseers, redoubled the enthusiasm of the attacking forces, which reached new heights when two loyalist aircraft appeared. Heartened by their presence, the besiegers went into the attack. By noon the gates of the Fascist stronghold were broken down. Madrid had stormed her Bastille.[22]

These passages, of course, give off an impression of overwhelming revolutionary fervour, but deconstruct them and they tell a very different story. If the people are armed, it is only because a handful of officers had broken ranks, while it is clear that what breaks the resistance is the arrival of the cannon dispatched by the artillery and the pair of bombers sent by the air force. Then, too, there is the issue of the bolts belonging to all but 5,000 of the 60,000 rifles that had been distributed to the MAOC at the orders of the Giral government the night before. According to many accounts, these were stored in the Montaña barracks, and, if so, it is hard to see how the men who had received rifles could have done much to assist the assault.[23] As for those rifles that were in working order, they only had a single clip of five rounds of ammunition.[24] Meanwhile, whether by accident or design, the Anarchists had received no arms: at the offices of the CNT in the suburb of Carabanchel Alto, for example, on the evening of 19 July, there were just six pistols and three rifles, of which none of the latter had any bullets.[25] Let no-one deceive themselves, then: exactly ... exactly as had been the case in Barcelona, where the rising was defeated, it was not defeated by the people. At best, all that can be said is that the crowds stiffened the will of the authorities to resist, persuaded at least some officers to take no part in the rising and undermined the morale of the defenders of the various installations in which insurrections took place. In so far as all this is concerned, then, the last word should probably go to the Anarchist militant Gregorio Gallego:

> My personal opinion is that, militarily speaking, the crowd only played a secondary role in the assault on the barracks: they were a chorus, an accompaniment. However, in psychological terms their contribution was decisive. I have always imagined the hours of anguish that must have been undergone by the defenders on seeing themselves surrounded by that mass of ardent humanity, not to mention the gradual collapse of military discipline as the more irresolute elements of the garrison recovered their nerve. Clear to me, too, is the impact which the decisive manner in which soldiers loyal to the Republic directed the siege ... Yet would those officers have acted in the same way had they not felt themselves prisoners of the clamour of voices demanding an immediate assault?[26]

Clearly, we are faced here by questions that cannot possibly be answered. However, like it or not, except, perhaps, in a few insignificant towns and villages, where the only rebel forces were a handful of Civil Guards and Falangists, the fact is there is not a single case of the crowd achieving success against the insurgency on its own.[27] Meanwhile, to return to the general run of events, after three days of fighting, the honours remained about even. The situation was as yet very confused, but the rising may be said to have triumphed in Morocco, western Andalucía, Galicia, northern Extremadura, Old Castile, Navarre and Aragón together with the Canary islands and Mallorca. A number of isolated strongholds aside, meanwhile, the Cantabrian littoral, Catalonia, the Levante, New Castile, southern Extremadura, eastern Andalucía and Menorca were all in the hands of the government, along with the cities of Madrid, Barcelona, Bilbao and Valencia. So much for the geographical division of Spain, but what did all this mean in terms of resources? In brief, the government had the majority of the population, the enormous gold reserves of the Bank of Spain and the bulk of Spain's manufacturing industry, mineral resources and export crops, the only real advantage that had fallen to the rebels, or, to use their own name, the Nationalists, was a rather greater share of the food supply. Many Nationalist supporters, then, later confessed to being deeply alarmed. 'We were by no means out of the woods', wrote José Larios, the scion of an Andalusian magnate family whom the war had caught on holiday in London, 'for the government held most of the tricks ... The news in the papers was terribly depressing ... I boarded the first available ship for Gibraltar ... I shall always remember that four-day voyage as a nightmare. I knew nothing, and there was nothing I could do.'[28]

All things being equal, then, it appeared that the Republic ought to come out on top if it should come to a long war, though the division of its territory into two separate zones was rather unhelpful. In so far as the short term was concerned, meanwhile, it could boast control of a large preponderance of Spain's 260,000 motor vehicles, 275,000 of her 500,000 rifles and carbines, 1,500 of her 4,500 machine guns, 400 of her 1,000 pieces of artillery, fifty of her sixty-five armoured vehicles, 300 of her 400 naval, military and civil aircraft, and twenty-seven of her thirty-one principal naval units (i.e. battleships, cruisers, destroyers and submarines). That said, however, not counting the large numbers of conscripts on summer leave, the rebels had ended up with a notional 91,000 men out of the 159,000 soldiers and policemen who were actually under arms, whilst many of the government's share either could not be counted on – the Civil Guard concerned often went over to the Nationalists at the first opportunity – or had been shattered in unsuccessful attempts at rebellion. Still worse, the Republicans had relatively few of the army's combat units, the Nationalist advantage being augmented still further by the support of the veteran Army of Africa. As for officers, the Republic could rely on no more than 2,000 of the 15,400 officers on active service in the army, the air force and the security forces, the majority even of these being older men employed on the staff or in second-line units. In the navy, meanwhile, the situation was still worse: out of 243 officers of the rank of captain and above, no more than twenty-four were still loyal.[29]

To conclude, then, though seriously disadvantaged, the Republic was not defenceless, whilst the Nationalists appeared to be in real trouble. Thus, in northern Spain, Mola was desperately short of ammunition and open to attack from several different directions at once, whilst many of the Nationalist enclaves dotted around Republican Spain were undoubtedly open to being overwhelmed. Thanks to the combination of, on the one hand, the continued inertia of the government and, on the other, the onset of revolution, within a very few days the opportunity had gone beyond recall, the Republic thereafter being committed to a defensive struggle in which it could at best hope to avoid defeat.[30]

The division of Spain prefigured by the events of the rising had soon more-or-less been formalized. From Burgos, Pamplona and Seville on the one hand and Madrid, Barcelona and Bilbao on the other, hastily organized 'columns' of troops, police and militia drove off in the direction of the nearest enemy. At the same time, 'mopping up' operations continued on both sides, the Republicans putting paid to Nationalist outposts in Alcalá de Henares, Guadalajara, Sigüenza, Gijón, Albacete, Valencia, and San Sebastián, and the Nationalists to Republican ones in a host of *pueblos* in Galicia and western Andalucía. Nationalist garrisons still held out in Granada, Oviedo and the *alcázar* of Toledo, but by the end of July, the country had been divided into two different zones. What this meant, however, was as yet nothing like the situation that pertained on any of the main fighting fronts in the First World War. In the words of Franz Borkenau, an Austrian sociologist involved with the German anti-Nazi resistance who made the first of two visits to Spain in August and September 1936:

> We nearly missed the front, it was so tiny. Driving north on the road to Huesca, we were stopped at the last moment by a guard on the road: otherwise we should have driven into rebel country without noticing it ... Up to a mile behind the lines, there was nothing to suggest its existence ...The 'front' consisted of a concentration of perhaps 300 men in the village of Alcalá [de Obispo] with a few advance guards half a mile ahead. There was no contact with the next militia column, which was stationed in a neighbouring village some miles away. Seeing this I remembered with some amusement the foreign-newspaper reports of sanguinary battles ... fought between tens of thousands of men.[31]

If the front lines remained distinctly permeable, this was just as well given the events that now unfolded. 'One does not need to spend many weeks in Nationalist Spain to marvel, not that there have been reprisals, but that Franco has been so successful in keeping these reprisals within limits, and in substituting courts martial for lynch law.'[32] Thus spake Arnold Lunn, leading skier − amongst other things, he was the inventor of the downhill-slalom Olympic event − and Catholic apologist. If Lunn truly believed this, one cannot but be astonished at his naivety. In fact, no sooner had the rebels taken power than, in accordance with the express order of Mola they set about the physical extermination of all the forces of progress. Having first summarily executed anyone who tried to fight them, they immediately proceeded to arrest anyone who was in any way associated with left-republicanism, socialism, anarchism, or communism, and very often their families as well, the victims also including many people whose only crime was to fail to meet the social norm. Torture was frequent, conditions intolerable, legal process minimal and punishment exemplary: lengthy prison sentences were commonplace and execution routine, the number of those who had been shot by the end of the war probably amounting to at least 75,000.[33] To a degree, terror was the fruit of necessity: the Nationalist forces, after all, were stretched very thin. However, the *limpieza* (literally, 'clean-up') was not the product of circumstances, but rather an inherent plank of insurgent policy that was pursued for its own sake, and that with the utmost relish. At the same time, for those on the Left and in the Centre, it was an experience that was all pervasive, not to mention merciless. Alvaro Millán, for example, was a petty businessman in Córdoba: 'The same terror existed everywhere ... It wasn't only the working class which suffered. Before the war I was a member of a *tertulía*, which had some forty ... members, schoolmasters, lawyers, politicians, sales representatives, etc. Only four or five, including myself, survived the repression ... I never believed it possible to kill people the way they did here.'[34] Meanwhile, in Granada, things were just as bad. 'You've got to realise what it was like', one eyewitness told the writer, Ian Gibson. 'Day and night: there were no rules. Eight people, nine people, fifteen, fourteen, in the first months fifty every day, day and night, a flood.'[35]

Horrific as these events were, they were undoubtedly of great importance in the growing unity that was the second chief characteristic of Nationalist Spain, imbuing it, as they did, with a strong vested interest in victory at all costs. Even had this not been the case, however, there was little chance of the rebel cause being seriously disrupted by internal disputes. Support for the Falange and the Carlists alike had soared – by the end of the first month of the war, the latter may have had as many as 50,000 men under arms[36] – whilst the military situation had given them much power, but neither force was in any condition to press its views upon the generals, and all the more so as their militias were rapidly losing their autonomy (see below). Even if this had not been the case, the Carlists were deeply divided and the Falange headed by figures of the second rank: under arrest since March, José Antonio Primo de Rivera had had the misfortune to be in a prison that ended up in the republican zone, whilst other leaders had been killed in skirmishes in the first days of the fighting. With both the Falange and the Carlists also becoming more and more diluted by large numbers of erstwhile *cedistas* and Alfonsists, not to mention desperate refugees from forces as disparate as the PRR, the Basque nationalists and the Anarchists, the army was in consequence able to do as it liked.[37] As Antonio Ruiz Vilaplana, a Burgos notary who became increasingly horrified at the situation in Nationalist Spain and eventually fled into exile, put it in 1937: 'The army is the master, the ruling element, in Nationalist Spain to the exclusion of all others. All along, neither the Falangists, nor the *requetés*, nor the monarchist group of Renovación Española have exerted any real authority: soldiers alone have enjoyed the substance of power.'[38]

With the rebel zone in the hands of the generals, 24 August saw the organization of a six-man military junta under the presidency of the erstwhile republican
Miguel Cabanellas.[39] Meanwhile, the third characteristic of Nationalist Spain was
being established by the forthright support that the Catholic Church had almost
everywhere lent to the uprising (the only exception was to be found in the Basque
provinces). Driven both by a desire to secure the Church's interests in the new
Spain and to put an end to its persecution under the Republic, the clergy eulogized
the rebellion, invoked divine intervention on its behalf, served with the Nationalist
forces as chaplains and, in some cases, played an active part in the repression. As for
the military authorities, meanwhile, they rushed to welcome the Church's advances.
Thus, the local commanders treated the clergy with great respect, attended mass on
a regular basis, distributed religious insignia among their men, declared war on blas-
phemy, imposed a strict moral censorship and allowed the Republic's anti-religious
legislation to fall by the wayside. With the Carlists and even the Falange happy to
fall into line, the Nationalist cause therefore became a veritable crusade. In the bitter words of Ruiz Vilaplana:

> Clericalism, imperious and supreme ... has seen its might, majesty and
> power challenged ... Reacting, therefore, with characteristic arrogance,
> exploiting its ascendancy ... over the will of those committed to its charge,
> the Church ... has committed the unpardonable crime of transforming a
> fratricidal clash into a holy war ... The function of the priesthood, surely,
> should be to preach peace and charity, yet, actually, day by day, priests have
> been fomenting and whipping up ... hatred and violence.[40]

At the same time, of course, an effective army was quick to appear. Though
arms, uniforms and equipment were initially in short supply, the Nationalists'
human resources were mobilized with some effect. Thus, those conscripts who
had been on leave were compelled to return to their regiments; large numbers
of reservists were called up in accordance with the existing laws of military
service; and the thousands of Falangist and Carlist volunteers were placed under
the command of regular officers.[41] Typical enough was the situation in Carmelo
Revilla Cebrecos' Tercio de Lacar: sent to help take San Sebastián, by the time
the battalion reached the front, all four companies were headed by captains in
the regular army, of whom only one was even Navarrese. Of these men, meanwhile, one was a reservist who happened to be living in Pamplona, one a serving
officer whom the uprising had caught while on leave in Navarre, one a captain
in the Sicilia regiment and one an officer living in retirement in Pamplona.[42]
All too often, however, such complicated nuances were lost to outside observers. Harold Cardozo had been sent to cover the Nationalists' operations by the
Franco-favouring *Daily Mail*:

> It was in this month of August that Spain's national army was being formed.
> Young men were ... standing at the rifle butts or were kneeling round a

machine-gun, all over Nationalist Spain. Some of them were in khaki with a khaki forage cap with a green or scarlet tassel hanging over the forehead: these were the men belonging to the classes of conscripts being called up ... Their discipline was severe, their training hard and they ... had no peers in close hand-to-hand fighting, when it is a case of each man for himself. Despite this my favourites were always the volunteer battalions – the young men of the *requetés* or the Falangists ... The ready supply of volunteers, 300,000 in all, within the first few months of the war, was the best proof that the army movement was really a national one.[43]

Finally, the greatest efforts were made to ensure that the best possible use was made of the Nationalists' scanty resources (rather than hoarding the copious stocks of ammunition that had been amassed in Morocco, for example, at the earliest possible opportunity, Franco sent large quantities of it to Mola, whose reserves were at one point down to less than ten rounds per man). With the labour force subjected to the strictest discipline and the first steps taken in the mobilization of the economy for total war, Nationalist Spain was truly on the march. Yet it should be noted that militarization was far from immediate. A monarchist student, Juan Crespo, for example, had enlisted in Salamanca and soon found himself fighting at the important pass in the Sierra de Guadarrama known as the Alto de León: 'We took the pass and held it. But after three or four days I got fed up. Most of us militiamen ... felt the same ... We had fleas. We were cold. We missed our evening beer. A supply lorry arrived from Salamanca. We got on it and rode home.'[44]

In the Republican zone, by contrast, the very opposite was the case: by rising to save the Republic from revolution – a revolution that could never have succeeded had it been launched prior to the uprising and which almost none of the movements and parties of the Left genuinely favoured at the current moment, if, indeed, they did so at all – Mola and his fellow generals had unleashed the very tiger that they had been intent on chaining up. Thus, no sooner had the decision been taken to arm the people – in practice, the various labour movements – than the revolution finally became a reality, the state – and, for that matter, the autonomous Catalan administration set up in the wake of the statute of 1932 – immediately being supplanted by that of a complex network of local committees whose composition generally reflected the balance of political forces in the towns in which they were established. Foreign visitors to Barcelona were gripped by what they saw, entranced even. Here, for example, is Franz Borkenau:

As we turned round the corner of the Ramblas ... came a tremendous surprise: before our eyes, in a flash, unfolded itself the revolution. It was overwhelming. It was as if we had been landed on a continent different from anything I had seen before. The first impression, armed workers ... They sat on the benches or walked the pavements, their rifles over their right shoulder, and often their girls on their left arm ... They stood, as guards, before the entrances of hotels, administrative buildings and the larger stores. They crouched behind the few standing barricades ... They drove at top speed fashionable cars, which they had expropriated, and covered ... with the initials of their respective organizations ... The fact that all these armed men walked about, marched and drove in their ordinary clothes made the thing only more impressive as a display of the power of the factory workers ... And no bourgeoisie whatsoever![45]

Another foreign arrival was Richard Kisch, a young Londoner of left-wing sympathies who had got on a train at Victoria with three friends to head for Spain almost as soon as the war had begun:

[Barcelona] had become the storm-centre of resistance to the Junta. Thousands of trade-unionists ... were flocking to recruiting depots for the militia ... There was no sex-discrimination. Girls were as welcome as boys. Everyone was in a high state of elation and euphoria after the victory in the streets. They were being packed into trucks and wagons and rushed off to the fronts already being formed outside ... Zaragoza and Huesca. Some had guns. Others went empty-handed to forage for weapons from the dead and wounded ... Barcelona's famous Ramblas thronged with folk in fiesta ... Groups of young men and girls caterpillared their way through the crowd. Mainly they carried anti-fascist banners and Republican flags. They shouted slogans of universal brotherhood and defiance of fascism. Many wore blue denim overalls. The conventional working clothes of labour and industry seemed to epitomize the dignity of work and the spirit of unity ... The walls were vibrant with posters exhorting people to defeat fascism. Public address systems were installed on every street corner and public square ... Popular songs and revolutionary marches blared out day and night.[46]

However, dramatic as all this was, it was killing the Republic. 'The history of those days', wrote Gregorio Gallego, 'belongs to the kingdom of madness. Everything that I saw ... convinced me more and more that our greatest enemy was chaos, and that, if we did not put an end to the abuse and pillage that from the first days took hold of our capital, the enemy would not need much in the way of resources to win the match.'[47] Absolutely chimerical in the *preguerra*, for example, the Left's militias now became a reality. Armed with weapons distributed by the government, captured from the insurgents, or simply commandeered from the army and police, thousands of young men had soon been enrolled in one or other of the various 'red' militias, and all the more so as the new *milicianos* were offered the generous wage of ten *pesetas* a day. Hastily organized into *ad hoc* 'columns', many of them – the bravest and most committed – had soon left for the front, but some were kept back by their own leaders, whilst many more were having much too much fun roaring up and down the streets in commandeered

cars and trucks, swaggering about draped in bandannas and bandoliers and flirting with the thousands of young women for whom the war had come as a liberating experience. One eyewitness was the British newspaper correspondent
John Langdon-Davies:

> Barcelona had done away for the time being with traffic lights and traf-
> fic policemen, and as far as one could see every human being had com-
> mandeered a motor-car from somewhere and was learning to drive and
> break records at one and the same time … Every young man in Barcelona
> had procured a car, a uniform of overalls, and some sort of gun, and so
> long as there was petrol available everyone was going to make use of the
> rare opportunity.[48]

Still more damning was Richard Kisch:

> New recruits brandished weapons like banners and continually shouted
> brazen defiance of the generals and fascism. They all seemed a bit gun-
> crazy … behaved like stereotypes from cowboy and Indian movies or the
> cover pictures of the western pulp magazines they admired on news stands.
> Haphazard casualties were mounting seriously, especially among the kids
> … Any wound seemed good enough to be taken as a token of Republican
> commitment. It was a badge of courage to be flaunted in public. One
> boy who accidentally shot himself through the penis insisted on having it
> splinted and bandaged so it stuck out through the flies of his dungarees like
> a truncheon. He paraded it up and down the Ramblas leering at the girls
> and pointing to his emblem with a grin as wide as Punch.[49]

Whatever else they were doing, such young men were not fighting fascism or
anything else: 'Out of almost every window', wrote Langdon-Davies of the
PSUC's headquarters in the Hotel Colón, 'poked rifles … each manned by a
grim youth in a scarlet shirt. One felt that they were taking life too seriously
by half.'[50] Here too is Franz Borkenau: 'Perhaps thirty per cent of the males on
the Ramblas were carrying rifles … Arms, arms and again arms.'[51] Thousands
of weapons, then, were wasted, whilst the forces who were sent to the front
were often armed with a hotch-potch of arms for which it was impossible to
find adequate munitions.[52] Artillery pieces, too, were dragged off to the front in
ones and twos rather than being massed in larger batteries, whilst the Republic's
pool of motor vehicles was squandered by the conversion of hundreds of trucks
into improvised armoured vehicles that were both militarily useless and desperately vulnerable.[53] Wasteful of weapons and *matériel* as they were, meanwhile,
the militias were also damaging in another sense. Aware that they could get far
higher pay in the militia, many soldiers deserted to their ranks. In the same way,
when the government tried to start persuading reservists to join a new 'volunteer army', many men opted for the easier option offered by the militia. Born in

1915, for example, Elías Biescas Palacio was the son of Andalusian migrants who had settled in Barcelona. When the rising broke out, he had taken no part in the fighting and really wanted no part of it now, but like many others he reckoned that, if he had to take up arms, it would be better to do so close to home:

> When the government began to mobilise the reserves, my friend Eduardo and I decided to join the militia on the Zaragoza front before we were sent our papers and packed off to some unknown destination. We didn't know a whole lot about politics, nor very much about what was happening even … Meanwhile, the fact that it was high summer convinced us that it would be rather like taking a holiday with nothing to do but swim and go fishing … Had I known what it would really be like, perhaps I would have thought better of enlisting.[54]

The seeming reluctance of so many of the militia actually to leave for the front was not helped by a general conviction that the Nationalists were powerless, but the trouble went far deeper than that. Thus, many workers stayed away from work for days or even weeks on end, whilst those who did appear were loud in their demands for higher wages and shorter hours and unregenerate in their absenteeism and pilfering, i.e. Equally, recruitment to the militia quickly fell off, whilst fewer and fewer men actually left for the front.[55] Union membership soared, certainly, but attendance at meetings was very low, there was often a marked reluctance to volunteer even for auxiliary service, and all that mattered for most of those concerned was to obtain an identity card that might serve as a passport to a job, better food, favourable treatment or even, on occasion, life itself.[56] As for the revolutionary committees, if some were scrupulously honest, others became mired in incompetence and even corruption. 'The war', recounted David Granda, 'had only been going on for perhaps six weeks, and I could see that things were deteriorating: there were those who had been unimpeachable and honest before the war, but the moment they were in a position of responsibility and controlled food supplies they began to be corrupted.'[57] Amongst a hardcore of militants, doubtless, there was enthusiasm aplenty, but otherwise the picture was profoundly depressing. For a good example, we have only to turn to Franz Borkenau's account of a speech given by the prominent CNT leader Juan García Oliver to an Anarchist mass-meeting in Barcelona on 9 August. The Aragonese front, the latter admitted, had become a stalemate. One of the reasons being that the militias were short of ammunition, it followed that factory workers should put aside all thought of reduced working hours and work as many as were necessary to win the war. Was the response a standing ovation, a forest of clenched fists? Absolutely not. To quote Borkenau, 'There was a dead silence when these words were uttered.'[58]

Fiesta was accompanied by terror. With arms distributed wholesale, a savage onslaught against all those who were associated with the *status quo* was inevitable. Nothing like as terrible as was generally claimed by the insurgents, there is no doubt that the situation was still quite terrible enough. Setting aside those who were executed at the hands of the state authorities after formal trials – most notably, José Antonio Primo de Rivera (though not till November), but also the leaders of the rebellions in Madrid and Barcelona, Generals Goded and Fanjul – first to suffer were some of those captured in the aftermath of the fighting, a number of prisoners being massacred in cold blood: in Madrid, for example, the crowds who stormed the Montaña barracks shot many men on the spot whilst a number of the defenders were either beaten to death or thrown from the upper storeys of the building, one of the most graphic photographs of the so-called 'three days in July' showing the complex's patio literally strewn with bodies.[59] However, the killing was not just restricted to those directly involved in the uprising. In most of Republican Spain, bands of armed men were soon engaging in a reign of terror, whether on a freelance basis or as the private *chekas* of various parties and trade unions. The Republican Miguel de Heredia was amongst many who were disturbed by what they saw:

> Every day more people were being killed; every day the level of terror increased; and every day the favoured children of the revolution, the so-called 'hyenas', got better at organizing their schemes of assassination and generally running the show. The streets, indeed, were a real spectacle. In the 'Chicote' bar in the Gran Vía, turned into militiawomen by no more than the addition of a set of overalls, a cartridge belt and a showy looking pistol, ladies of the night appeared arm-in-arm with pavement warriors out to restore themselves by drinking cocktails and fondling girls after the orgies of blood of the small hours. Amongst these 'revolutionaries', meanwhile were to be seen the pioneers of the Fifth Column, Civil Guards now renamed National Guards (the name given them by the Republic-in-arms), not to mention Falangists who had gone to ground by donning overalls … The atmosphere was one neither of tragedy nor of fear, but rather one of high-jinks.'[60]

Even on the Left, then, many observers were genuinely frightened. 'This was not the mass which had stormed the Cuartel de la Montaña, mere human bodies against machine-guns', wrote the Socialist Arturo Barea of a pair of militants of the FAI whom he had seen gunning down someone on the street. 'This was the scum of the city. They would not fight. They would not carry through a revolution. But they would rob, destroy and kill for pleasure.'[61] The scenes that resulted were deeply shocking. An eyewitness was the American journalist H. E. Knoblaugh:

> Many mornings after breakfast, Pedro Rosales, the Anarchist chauffeur the government had assigned to us with the requisitioned car we had at our service, and I used to make the rounds of the outskirts of Madrid to check up on the … victims of the night before. Singly and in clusters, they lay along the roadway, riddled with bullets. The wooded Casa de Campo,

former playground of the king, was a favourite execution spot ... [while]
University City, called the finest university campus in Europe, never failed
to produce at least ten or twelve ... each day. Some of the bodies were
horribly mutilated.[62]

Portrayed as a monster by the Right though he still was, a President Azaña helpless
to stop the nightly killings could only wring his hands in horror:

Anxiety about assassination behind the lines greatly burdened my brother-
in-law ... The president felt that our people had some justification for taking justice into their own hands in those first moments of military treason
... He could not, however, excuse ... bands of delinquents who used the
rising ... as an excuse for killing and robbery ... One August morning ...
officials on duty at the palace greeted me ... [with news of] a massacre
at the Model Prison. The previous afternoon some inmates had started a
fire to create a distraction so they could escape. After the fire's extinction
Madrid's populace had responded to this trick by attacking the prison and
killing many persons held there ... I found the president in his audience
chamber ... sitting at a marbled table in the middle of the room, his head
pressed between his hands. He looked up at me, his face contorted as I had
never seen it ... 'Not this! Not this!', he repeated in anguish, raising his
hands violently to his throat. 'I'm sick of the blood. I have had it up to here.
We will all drown in it!'[63]

Needless to say, many Catholic schools, convents and places of worship were
soon in flames, whilst thousands of priests and religious were seized by the revolutionaries.[64] Any representative of the Right was also fair game, however, as,
indeed, was any member of the propertied classes in general. Nor did the humble
escape, victims including Catholic trade-unionists and *caciquista* 'trusties.' As in
Nationalist Spain, meanwhile, arrest all too often meant death, the numbers of
those murdered without trial, executed after the briefest of hearings or killed
in prison massacres provoked by enemy air raids probably amounting to around
50,000, including nearly 7,000 priests and religious.[65] Nor was it just a matter of killing and imprisonment. On the contrary, the property of the rich was
frequently looted, and, on occasion, destroyed, one of the worst such episodes
taking place in Málaga:

Great columns of smoke rose over the hill, and as the brief twilight faded
[they] showed the flickering glow of flames ... After dinner I sat out of
doors until long after midnight and watched the smoke ... slowly creeping along the seafront ... From time to time there were crashes and clouds
of sparks as roofs fell in ... All Sunday morning the flames came closer
and closer to me ... All the afternoon and in the evening until it was
too dark to see, old men, women and children hurried ... up and down

the little lane in front of my house, laden with ... anything they could carry ... On Monday morning the stream of plunderers continued, and houses were still smouldering or sending up columns of sparks as walls and roofs crashed.[66]

If the Terror was greatly exaggerated by the Nationalists – the vast majority of the Republican leadership was dismayed by what was taking place and did its best to restrain the *chekas*, as they became known – Republican Spain was nevertheless soon in the grip of a genuine social transformation. That said, conditions varied enormously from one region to another. The newspapers, clubs and party offices of the Right were universally requisitioned, along with most large hotels, many ecclesiastical buildings and the property of those who had supported the insurrection, whilst the churches were closed, but otherwise the situation was at its most extreme in those areas that were dominated by the CNT and the POUM. Thus, in Barcelona, almost every economic activity was collectivized, whilst the city famously acquired an aspect that was uniquely proletarian. Typical enough was the scene described by the *News Chronicle* correspondent John Langdon-Davies:

> I looked over the road at the Ritz. Across its door was a huge new red-lettered sign: 'HOTEL GASTRONOMIC NO. 1: UGT-CNT' ... In May its waiters and cooks had refused to serve anyone at all; now they were serving thousands of poor men and women daily, for they had taken over the hotel and turned it into a 'Popular Kitchen.' All ... the windows ... were flung open. Within, the huge chandeliers were a blaze of light. Outside was a queue hundreds long of men and women ... waiting their turn to sit at the table of [the rich man] who had gone abroad for his health.[67]

In much of Aragón and Andalucía, meanwhile, *latifundios* and small-holdings alike were pooled in large-scale collectives and farmed according to the principles of libertarian communism. In such areas, money was often either abolished altogether or replaced by a system of coupons; wages paid in accordance with family size; the population fed in communal soup-kitchens; craftsmen, mechanics and agricultural specialists forced to work for the collective in exchange for their food; animals, vehicles, implements and machines held in common; and intensive efforts made to politicize the populace. Last but not least, efforts were soon being made to establish the sort of federal organization that the Anarchists had always envisaged: in Catalonia, for example, there emerged an 'economic council' whose task was to co-ordinate the work of Catalan industry, whilst Aragón acquired a *de facto* regional government known as the Council of Aragón. Impressive as this activity was, however, it was by no means replicated throughout Republican Spain. Indeed, even in those areas where the Anarchists were strongest, the picture was distinctly patchy. Barcelona, for example, was collectivized, whereas the Catalan countryside was not. Similarly, in the liberated areas of Aragón, collectivization was often limited to the estates of those who had joined the uprising, or to those peasants who were willing to join such schemes voluntarily, though there were also places where it was pushed through for one and all willy-nilly whether the locals were in favour of it or not. Meanwhile, such qualifications are still more apparent elsewhere. In many areas – New Castile, for example – the land was for the most part either divided amongst the peasantry and farmed on a co-operative basis or directly cultivated by the revolutionary authorities with the aid of hired labour. There were other pockets of extreme revolution like Gijón and Málaga, but these were countered by places that were positively reactionary, a good example being Vizcaya, where the Basque nationalists did everything that they could to keep social change to a minimum.[68]

If economic change was partial, for many Spanish women, the uprising represented a moment of exciting opportunity. With fathers, husbands and brothers out on the streets or fighting in the militias, they often enjoyed far more personal freedom than had been usual and therefore began to emerge from their customary subservience. All the more was this the case, meanwhile, as the vibrant poster art of Republican Spain frequently made use images of female combatants. This was not so much a call for women to join the militias as an attempt to encourage more men to do so through either simple shame or the hope that life at the front would be fun in more senses than one, but some women, most of them in all probability already political activists, did enlist and in some cases died at the front. Present in both cases in Barcelona for the Communist-sponsored 'people's olympiad' that had been organized in the city in opposition to the Berlin Olympics of 1936, two of the Republic's first foreign volunteers were the British artist Felicia Browne and the Dutch journalist Fanny Schoonheyt, while a much-publicized Spanish example was Lina Odena García, the pre-war head of the Catalan branch of the Communist youth, who, finding herself by chance in Almería when the war started, enlisted in a column raised in that city.[69] Far more common, however, were the many women who flung themselves into a variety of ancillary work, in which last respect a Franz Borkenau who had travelled from Barcelona to Madrid was an interested observer:

> Young working girls in hundreds and perhaps thousands are walking up and down the streets, and are especially to be seen in the elegant cafés of the [Calle de] Alcalá and the Gran Vía. They collect for 'International Red Help'... The couples of girls (they never go alone: walking through the streets completely unchaperoned would still be unthinkable for any decent Spanish girl), well dressed in working-class fashion, who ask everybody for a contribution, are almost a nuisance in Madrid, or at least would be were they not so pleasant to look at.[70]

A wealthy Australian girl of twenty-four who had rejected her privileged upbringing and eloped with a Cuban artist named Juan Brea, Mary Low was yet another of the foreigners who gravitated to Barcelona in the summer of 1936:

The Anarchist trade unions had begun a group, Free Women, which ... decided to ... form a women's regiment ... [it] received more than 500 adherents within the first week ... but dozens of full-blown matrons and young girls confided to me 'Of course I wasn't able to tell my husband (or my father) that I was coming here: he would have had a fit. I just had to say I was joining a sewing circle.' The regiment was in large part composed of these runaways ... I have seldom seen such spirits: they were so glad and gay and seemed like children ... We used to go to the barracks, which were a long way out from the centre of town. On the way, in the tram or metro, the militia boys used to chaff us. We sang *The Internationale* very loudly and tried to convince ourselves that our uniform was as serious as their own. Sometimes they ended by being impressed.[71]

This militia, however, never saw action, and appears to have had but the most ephemeral of existences. Indeed, from the earliest days, it was made clear that women were firstly to be 'home-front' heroines. Such stereotyping was allowed to go largely unchallenged even by the handful of women who were prominent in Republican politics, the increasingly famous Communist leader, Dolores Ibarruri, going so far as to decry the very concept of feminism. Very few women actually went to the front, meanwhile – visiting the Aragón front in August 1936, Borkenau encountered one only, whilst a veteran of the Durruti column named Antonio Navarro Velásquez claimed long afterwards that there were no more than thirty women with it when it left Barcelona[72] – and those that did soon found that the treatment that they received in the trenches differed little from that which they received in their home towns. Highly instructive here is a scene witnessed by Langdon-Davies:

> I stared at the recruiting poster with the young, idealised militia-woman pointing her scornful finger at the slackers in the Paseo [de Gracia]. She was a likeable girl, this recruiting poster girl, with little round breasts, well-painted lips and plucked eyebrows ... Just then a detachment of militia marched by. They happened to belong to a Communist column and carried the hammer-and-sickle. In the middle of the column marched thirty or forty girls, not in the least like the poster-lady, dressed identically with the men in the blue overalls, a few with rifles, but most with cooking utensils strapped to them.[73]

As time passed, moreover, traditional roles reasserted themselves still further, the few women who had reached the trenches eventually being sent home on the pretext that they were infecting many soldiers with venereal disease.[74]

That said, however, the image of the *miliciana* nonetheless remained a liberating one, just as the struggle could not but continue to enhance the position of women in the Republican camp. Thus, women became involved in a wide variety of war work. Most typically, this involved such stereotypical tasks as nursing and the care of soldiers, orphans and refugees, but a minority also became involved in the military administration, the trade unions, the bureaucracy, the civil defence forces and the machinery of propaganda, the progressive nature of Republican Spain creating openings that were generally absent elsewhere. As a good example, one might cite the Milicias de la Cultura, the latter being a force of volunteers whose task it was to combat illiteracy amongst the common soldiers whilst at the same time boosting their political and cultural awareness. To some extent, there were also fresh opportunities for paid employment, whilst even the domestic round acquired wider horizons given the tough conditions faced by most housewives, feminist historians having argued that the war encouraged a new sense of sisterhood. If women were becoming more self-conscious, they were also becoming more organized. In some cases, this was the product of little more than an attempt to mobilize women as cannon-fodder, the Communist-dominated Asociaciòn de Mujeres Anti-Fascistas being a good example of a woman's organization that remained completely uninterested in the advancement of women *per se* (though it did provide an enduring platform for Dolores Ibarruri, the newly elected Communist deputy whom we shall see emerging as *the* voice of Madrid and the beleaguered Second Republic alike). Rather more interesting is the Anarchist group known as the Mujeres Libres, as this not only stemmed from growing resentment amongst female Anarchists of the condescension, harassment and derision that they met at the hands of their male colleagues, but was also disowned by the leadership of the CNT, and that despite – or because of – the fact that by 1938 it had acquired a membership of some 30,000. Meanwhile, not only were women becoming more organized, but they were also making genuine conquests. In Catalonia, though aged just seventeen in 1936, Teresa Pamies i Bertrán acquired a prominent role in the leadership of the Catalan branch of the JSU, whilst in November 1936, Spain gained her first woman minister in the person of the leading Anarchist Federica Montseny. Appointed to the health portfolio, the new arrival was quick to legalize abortion, though in reality few women seem to have been willing or able to avail themselves of the measure. Rather more important, then, are the real efforts that were made to further female education and training, there being no doubt that the war witnessed a significant fall in female illiteracy.[75]

The excitement that gripped the Left produced a political situation that was chaotic in the extreme. On 18 July, the government in Spain had been a wholly Republican affair with Azaña as president and Santiago Casares Quiroga as prime minister, whilst in Barcelona, the autonomous administration had been headed by Luis Companys of the Esquerra, or Catalan Left. Other than the fact that Casares Quiroga had now been replaced by José Giral, on 20 July the situation was unchanged, just as the flags flying over official buildings were still the red, yellow and purple tricolour of the Second Republic or the narrow red and yellow stripes of Catalonia. However, the moderate reformists who had found themselves facing the guns of Mola and his fellow conspirators were now irrelevant: with very few exceptions, such military units as had remained loyal were falling apart, their men deserting in droves; the loyal elements of Civil Guard (now renamed the National Republican Guard), the Assault Guard and the Carabineers were either at the front or desperately trying not to provoke a crowd that often had good reason to hate them; municipal and provincial government alike had been pushed aside by the revolutionary committees; and such militias as the bourgeois Republicans had been able to raise were, at best, exiguous, if indeed they existed at all, an attempt to raise a new 'volunteer army' on the grounds of men in the reserves meanwhile being very slow to get off the ground. As for the question of the high command, the Minister of War in the Giral government, Juan Hernández Saravia, had no means of exercising any authority over the war effort, whilst his attempt to bring a degree of order via the creation of the so-called General Inspectorate of Militias had little effect. Power, then, lay in the hands of the parties and movements of the Left, but these were neither agreed on the path that should be taken nor prepared to step back from their original objectives.

Let us begin with the Communists. Here the pre-eminent force was, of course, the Comintern and in 1936 that meant the principle of 'popular front': in short, the alliance of all good men and true against fascism. A response to a situation in which the Soviet Union feared that Nazi Germany might become the cat's paw of Western capitalism and strike it down, Stalin had decided that the chief object of Russian foreign policy could not be anything other than obtaining the friendship of Britain and France, to which end the Communist parties of Europe and, indeed, the world, were ordered to drop all reference to revolution and pose as the loyal defenders of democracy. This policy being intended to operate on a domestic as well as an international level, further orders were issued to the effect that the Communist movement should also join hands with other progressive forces, including, no less, the hated Socialists (or 'social fascists' as the Communists had been deeming them just months before). In France and Spain alike, the result had been the formation of Popular-Front governments, whilst, somewhat earlier, 2 May 1935 had seen the signature of a Franco–Soviet mutual assistance pact. For Stalin, then, the outbreak of revolution in Spain was nothing short of an unmitigated disaster as the hysterical Nationalist use of the term 'communist' as a label for all their opponents, not to mention the actual facts of the revolution itself, made it seem as if the Soviet Union was the very threat that the European Right was everywhere claiming it to be. However, should Stalin denounce the Spanish revolution outright, the Communist movement's prestige would be hit very heavily. Still another problem, meanwhile, was that, even had the Communists still been in full revolutionary mode, they could not possibly have hoped to take control of the situation: although the PCE had made some headway in the elections of 1936 thanks to its association with the rising of October 1934 and, more particularly, the support it had given the families of the thousands of men who had been imprisoned or thrown out of work in its wake, it was still pitifully small. In short, for the Communists, there was only one policy that made sense, and that was not only to abjure the cause of revolution but also to actively seek the latter's downfall, while making a powerful play for the adhesion of the substantial middle-class elements who now found themselves trapped and isolated in Republican Spain without anyone to protect them or champion their cause.[76] That said, however, just as Stalin could scarcely stand aside while fascism, or something that very much resembled it, rampaged through Spain, the Communists could not – indeed would not – turn their back on their proletarian roots. On an international level, the way forward, as we shall see, was found in a policy of limited aid to the Republic, but on the domestic level, pursuit of the centre continued to be matched by pursuit of the Left: hence the acceptance of the proposals of various parts of the Socialist movement (the Federación de Juventudes Socialistas de Espana and the Unión Socialista de Cataluña) for union with the Communists, and, with them, the birth of the JSU and the PSUC; and hence, too, the frenetic insistence from November 1936 onwards that Madrid had been saved by dint of the heroism of the people. However, it was not just a question of not betraying the proletariat: with Joseph Stalin in power in Moscow, Communism was everywhere in hegemonic mode, and this was as much the case in Spain as it was anywhere else. Himself an ex-Communist who had broken with the party on account of the brutalities of the so-called 'Great Change', Franz Borkenau was only too aware of the realities of the situation: 'Spanish needs are broken, transformed by passing through the prism of Russian interests … Moscow, it is true, proclaims a metaphysical preordained identity of the interests of every proletariat with the interests of the Moscow government, but this is a proposition that can no longer be taken seriously.'[77]

So much for the Communists, the policy of which movement came down to killing the revolution, absorbing the Centre and taking over, if not the whole of the Left, then at least the Socialists. What, though, of this last force? Here the situation was still more confusing. At least the Communists were united, but the Socialists were anything but. Setting aside the tiny handful of dogmatists centred on the speaker of the *cortes*, Julián Besteiro, who wanted nothing to do with either a bourgeois republic or a workers' revolution, as we have already seen, there were two main tendencies. On the Left, the faction headed by Largo Caballero wanted to 'bolshevize' the party in the hope that this would finally persuade the masses to turn away from Anarchism (which Largo continued to hate unreservedly) and, for that matter, Communism, and unite behind the banner of the Socialists, a policy that at the current moment meant driving the revolution forward as fast as possible and staying out of government until such time as it fell into its lap.[78] However, on the Right, the faction headed by the Bilbao leader and sometime Minister of Finance, Indalecio Prieto believed rather that revolution should be shunned and an alliance forged with the bourgeoisie. A leading militant of the UGT in Barcelona named José del Barrio, who was in the Largo-Caballero camp, afterwards remembered an atmosphere of fear and suspicion: 'Something I would like to underline here is the strength of the discomfort that we felt in those great days of struggle on account of the reserve with which we were treated by the leadership of the [local] party. I would so much like to be able to convey how much it cost a militant accustomed to give his all ... to be received with hostility, indeed, almost as an enemy, in the headquarters of his own party ... If anyone thinks that these things can be forgotten, I say that I will never do so.'[79] Yet if the right wing of the movement loathed the latter's left wing, the reverse was equally true. Here, for example, is Largo Caballero on Prieto: 'As far as I am concerned, whether he is judged by his ideas or his actions, Indalecio Prieto was never a socialist, properly speaking ... Jealous, proud and overbearing, he believed himself to be superior to all others and would not tolerate anybody who cast the slightest shadow over him ... At all times all he cared about was to be in the foreground, flattered, praised and admired by all and sundry. To be unable to hog the limelight or make a show of his outstanding gifts had disastrous effects upon him.'[80]

Last but not least, there was the revolutionary Left. Here, as ever, the largest force was the Anarchists. Catalonia, Madrid and parts of Andalucía having stayed in the hands of the government, the CNT had emerged from the rising as a powerful force, and it had enhanced its position by spearheading the drive of the Barcelona militias westwards to do battle with the Nationalists and by taking the leading part in setting up the Council of Aragón (which, in consequence, was very much under its thumb). As to what the CNT, and, hidden in its ranks, the FAI, wanted, the situation was confused. As Gregorio Gallego noted, at the heart of the problem was the fact that the movement was deeply split:

> To understand the attitude of the CNT ... it is necessary to engage in a brief analysis of its internal currents: these could be divided into those who fundamentally considered themselves to be "purists" and those who rather defined themselves as 'alliancists.' Of these the former ... rejected any kind of ... collaboration with forces who did not accept their criteria, and naturally enough were ferocious partisans of direct action ... As for the latter, that is the 'alliancists', recruited above all from anarcho-syndicalists, and, still more so, pure syndicalists, they were much more pragmatic in respect of their positions and in favour of an alliance with the UGT.[81]

In the circumstances of July 1936, what these two positions represented was a choice between implementing revolution and setting this aside in favour of defending the Republic. Confronted with the fact that power was theirs for the taking, that Spanish society was theirs for the re-making, in what amounted to a confession of the bankruptcy of their whole movement, the Anarchist leadership in Barcelona (which effectively meant that in the country as a whole) chose the latter course. A few ultras of the FAI, including most notably the great hero of the Anarchist movement, Buenaventura Durruti, and his close associates, Juan García Oliver and Ricardo Sanz, had initially wanted to press onwards, overthrowing the Catalan government altogether and imposing the full Anarchist programme willy-nilly, but even they were forced to recognize that this would mean subjecting the rest of the Left by force and, in effect, setting up an Anarchist state, all of which would have represented the betrayal of every principle Spanish Anarchism had ever stood for, whilst wiser heads had argued from the start that the current circumstances above all required unity in the defence of the Republic, that in the end it did matter to the Anarchist movement that what was in power was a democracy rather than a dictatorship.[82] In Barcelona, then, the Companys government was allowed to survive, the Anarchists confining themselves to the exercise of a considerable degree of influence through the establishment of the so-called Comité Central de Milicias Anti-Fascistas de Cataluña (CCMAC). Moreover, at least some leaders, such as the erstwhile propaganda secretary of the Zaragoza branch of the CNT, Saturnino Carod Lerín, tried to prevent such acts as church burning and put an end to the Red Terror. Yet the leadership was not the base: acting partly out of conviction and partly out of personal ambition, even some of the leaders – Durruti for one – continued to engage in a forward policy, while many of the rank and file did not possess the same scruples and were in effect uninterested in anything other than posturing, partying and pillaging. As Jaume Miravatlles, a sometime left-winger who had abandoned his original views in favour of Catalan nationalism, said, '[The revolution] bred a lumpen proletariat which now suddenly appeared and overwhelmed the CNT and even the FAI. The latter couldn't disavow these people because they represented the Anarchists' very philosophy: the spontaneity of the masses.'[83] Whichever side of the lines they were in terms of the split in the Anarchist movement, meanwhile, both leaders and led despised everyone else on the Left and were determined to defend such gains as they had made against all comers. Commenting on an incident in Valencia on 30 October 1936, in which unknown gunmen opened up on a CNT funeral, for example, having blamed the attack on 'lowlife, cowardly Communists', Elías Manzanera, an Anarchist militant who had joined the so-called 'Iron Column', wrote,

> Wheresoever the hand of Stalin was felt, the counter-revolution prospered, and the workers' gains ... were whittled away ... Such communism, kowtowing to Moscow, ran up against an impregnable barrier in the battle-hardened Iron Column, made up of manual and intellectual workers, selfless, undemanding women and ... the very flower ... of the Valencian people.[84]

Ranked alongside the Anarchists, yet also apart from them, was the POUM. A completely insignificant force in Spain as a whole, this had nevertheless taken hold in Catalonia where it managed to overshadow both the Communists and the Socialists. Why this should have been the case is by no means clear, but it was nonetheless enough to fill it with confidence, to make it, indeed, the one force on the Left that was truly behind the idea of revolution. With its self-importance further bolstered by the award of a ministerial post in the Catalan government, it was therefore full of swagger and self-confidence, on the one hand attempting to exercise a disproportionate influence in the CCMAC in Barcelona, and on the other openly calling for a dictatorship of the proletariat: just as the Anarchists had believed that the masses would rally to their cause prior to 1936, so now the POUM seemingly believed that they had only to raise the red flag for the same masses to turn to them. That, of course, is not what happened in the slightest – the POUM gained some fresh support but no more than did the other left-wing movements – all that its aggression therefore achieved being to heighten the tension in the Republican camp: in Barcelona, for example, 7 August saw a battalion of POUM militia who had gathered in a cinema or theatre for a political meeting set upon by several lorry-loads of CNT militia and forcibly disarmed.[85] Within the ranks of the POUM, meanwhile, all was frustration and suspicion. As a French sympathizer who had come across the frontier to revel in the revolution wrote:

> The Anarchists are to all intents and purposes the owners of Catalonia, and the POUM the only force strong enough to take them on. They outnumber us by three to one, but that is not so very much, while in the current circumstances the figures could easily change. We have 15,000 armed men as opposed to 40,000–50,000 of theirs. The Communists have united with three or four small parties but they are still a pretty ridiculous affair. On Friday [25 July 1936] they announced in their newspaper that what is afoot is not workers' revolution but rather the defence of the Republic and that anyone who tried to make the revolution would find themselves facing their militias. Their intention, then, is to sabotage the revolution, but I don't believe that they have the strength to do this.[86]

To pretend that there were no political differences in the Nationalist camp would be naïve: on the contrary, the issue of whether or not the monarchy should be restored was one that was deeply divisive (all through the summer of 1936, there were Nationalist supporters who insisted that they were fighting to save the Republic rather than to overthrow it, even Nationalist commanders who continued to fly the Republican flag), whilst at the level of the leadership, the Falange and the Carlists were at best rivals and, at worst, deadly enemies.[87] Also at issue was the position of Catholicism: if Franco was noted for his religiosity, many of his fellow generals were profoundly secular, while some militants were insistent that they wanted nothing to do with the Church. Despite believing in the need to restore the monarchy, one such was Juan Crespo, the student from Salamanca who had briefly fought at the Alto de León: 'The one thing I wasn't fighting for was the Church ... I was fighting to create a better Spain.'[88] Also on view was deep-seated personal rivalry between Franco, Mola and Queipo de Llano.[89] However, such differences were palliated by a number of factors that were not present in the Republican zone. In the first place, if fear of the enemy and hatred of what they were doing was just as universal in Valladolid and Burgos as it was in Madrid and Barcelona, in the Nationalist zone there was no illusion about the task ahead, no heady dreams of victory being obtained by nothing more than revolutionary heroism. In the second, the spiralling numbers

of executions were not only fast outstripping those taking place in the disorganized Republican zone but were also doing so in a form that made it impossible to
claim that they were the work of a minority that was as unrepresentative as it was
uncontrollable, thereby in effect sealing the insurgents in a pact of blood.[90] And,
in the third, thanks to the huge influx of new members since February 1936,
there was little ideological purity in the ranks of the Falange and the Carlists
any more, little sense that the different political movements of Nationalist Spain
represented ideological incompatibilities. Conflict, then, was usually muted,
whilst, with the army in full control, there was far less that the Falange, the
Carlists and the Alfonsists could do to impose their preferences, let alone exert
their independence.[91]

With every day that passed, then, the Nationalist zone slid ever deeper into
social, political and religious conformity. Francis McCullagh was a journalist of
Irish origins from the United States who had travelled to Spain as a correspondent for the Catholic press:

> Before the war every foreign pedestrian who entered a Spanish town
> was pestered by gangs of demoralized boys and youths, corrupted by the
> Soviet schools which with the tireless persistence of bubonic bacilli the
> Communists established all over the country, and by the flood of porno-
> graphic propaganda which the Republic unleashed. Now those boys are
> Catholic scouts who march to school every weekday and to Mass every
> Sunday ... Their fathers and mothers have gained, too, by the great revival
> that has come over Spain. Formerly it was a trial to me to walk down a
> Spanish street in the evening owing to the long vista of lazy women hang-
> ing out of their windows, staring, staring. All the women are now busy
> working for the Red Cross. The young men are under arms. The old men
> are in the civic guard. Everybody is happy because everyone has something
> to do ... Many respectable people have expressed doubts about this reli-
> gious movement in Spain, and ... make no secret of their suspicions that
> religion is being used in Spain for political purposes by generals who have
> very little religion themselves ... But I see clearly that no general however
> brave, no priest however holy, no statesman however popular, no propa-
> ganda however perfect, could ever stir up ... the most tremendous wave of
> enthusiasm I ever witnessed in my life.[92]

In contrast to the horrors that the Right insisted raged on all sides in Republican
Spain, meanwhile, in the Nationalist zone all was quiet. In the words of
Arnold Lunn:

> Franco today has some half a million men on four disconnected fronts.
> Thousands of miles of roads leading to different parts of the front are virtu-
> ally unprotected, and village after village is policed only by middle-aged
> volunteers wearing the scarlet beret of the Carlists or the blue forage cap

of the Spanish Phalanx [i.e. Falange Española]. On lonely mountain roads I have passed isolated and unescorted lorries. In Ireland during the Civil War no unprotected Black-and-Tan lorry would have reached a destination accessible only along deserted roads. If the peasantry in Nationalist Spain were hostile as the Irish peasantry were hostile, roads would be blocked by fallen trees and lorries would be ambushed. But whereas the Black and Tans were fighting for a foreign power, Franco's army is not only national but democratic: national because it represents the reaction against Russian dominance; democratic because within its ranks conservatives and republicans, liberals and socialists, fight shoulder-to-shoulder for the reign of law and order against anarchy and chaos.[93]

If this was peace, then truly it was the peace of the graveyard, but that is not the point. Hardly had the dust settled in the wake of the famous 'three days in July', than Nationalist Spain had in part rushed to embrace, in part been dragooned into accepting, an order in which everything was subordinated to the demands of the war effort and the rational exploitation of the insurgents' somewhat scanty resources. In the Republican zone, by contrast, there was no order whatsoever, but rather the very opposite: central authorities with no power; political movements violently at odds with one another; a logistical system that had no means of functioning effectively; armed forces that had for the most part been replaced by political militias; a commitment to the cause that, if not completely lacking, was frequently as blind to reality as it was bedecked with levity; a want even of geographical unity. What it did have in plenty was revolution, but the extent to which this boosted the Republican cause by encouraging popular support for the struggle

MAP 2.1   Division of Spain at the end of July 1936.

was more than countered by the numerous problems to which it gave rise, including the impact, as yet uncertain, of economic experimentation of every sort, and the alienation of foreign powers – above all, Britain and France – whose support was essential if the aid that was already beginning to arrive from Germany and Italy was to find an answer. Militarily, meanwhile, revolution offered the Republic absolutely nothing: in Madrid, Barcelona and other cities, armed civilians – invariably militants of one or other of the left-wing movements – had been highly visible in the fighting that had led to the overthrow of the uprising, but not once had they triumphed on their own. Far from it, indeed, wherever they had stood alone against the onslaught, they had gone down, gone down fighting, perhaps, but gone down nonetheless. With a long war beckoning – a war in which the government should have had all the advantages – the outlook for the Republic was not good, and it was very soon to darken still further.

Notes

1 'That week', wrote Socialist militant Arturo Barea, 'was one of incredible tension. Calvo Sotelo's funeral was turned into a demonstration by the Right and ended in shooting between them and the [Assault Guards]. In the *cortes* Gil Robles made a speech in Calvo Sotelo's memory which was officially described as a declaration of war. Prieto asked Casares Quiroga to arm the workers, and the Minister refused. Demonstrations and assaults were on the increase in all districts of Madrid ... Expensive cars ... left the town in considerable numbers on the roads to the north.' Barea, *Forging of a Rebel*, p. 512.

2 Cit. Fraser, *Blood of Spain*, p. 48.

3 There are few accounts of the uprising in Spanish Morocco. However, one such is by Carlota O'Neill, the Mexican wife of the temporary commander of the seaplane base at Melilla, Virgilio Leret. Supported by his fellow officers and a number of airmen, the latter fought the rebels for some hours, but was forced to surrender when his ammunition ran out and was immediately court-martialled and shot. Meanwhile, his wife was separated from her two young daughters and imprisoned for two years before finally being released and allowed to settle in Venezuela. See C. O'Neill, *Una mujer en la guerra de España* (Madrid, 2003), pp. 24–244 *passim*. According to Paul Preston, meanwhile, 225 men were executed in Morocco on the night of 17–18 July alone. Preston, *Spanish Holocaust*, pp. 133–4.

4 Miralles Bravo, *Memorias*, p. 26.

5 In existence since late 1933, even the MAOC was of dubious value as a fighting force: by the account of its very leader, the same Juan Modesto who had organized the UMRA, its experience was limited to such tasks as providing armed guards at Communist rallies; of formal military training, indeed, he makes no mention whatsoever. See Modesto, *Soy del Quinto Regimiento*, pp. 47–50.

6 The split in the military estate defies facile analysis. Deeply elitist as it was, it was highly predictable that the naval officer corps would plump for the cause of rebellion, just as it was highly predictable that air-force officers would for the most part back that of the Republic (if Azaña had not been able to re-equip the air force, he was extremely 'air-minded', while the Popular-Front government had just put in orders for a considerable number of new aircraft). In the army, however, matters were more complex. Most *africanistas* backed the rebellion, whilst the latter also tended to have the support of the infantry and cavalry (by the same token, the government got the *peninsulares*, the gunners and the engineers). Yet this seemingly neat division was muddied by the issue of age and rank, in that the older and more senior officers were, the more likely they

were to stay loyal. As has been pointed out on more than one occasion, then, to speak of 'the generals' rising' is highly misleading. Indeed, all too often, it is completely forgotten that, all round Spain, many captains general and military governors refused to join the uprising even at the point of a gun and ended up paying for their loyalty with their lives. For a detailed discussion of the purge of loyalist officers in those areas where the rising triumphed, See Navajas Zubeldía, *Leales y rebeldes*, pp. 163–84.

7 Given the heavy emphasis that was placed by the insurgents and their sympathizers on claims that the Left were committed to revolution, one point that cannot be stressed too strongly is that, with the exception of the miniscule POUM, no party or movement of the Left favoured revolution in 1936, while the Communists opposed it altogether. That said, of course, the leadership were not the same as the militants, and the excitement amongst the latter had become so great that a point might have come when the streets might have swept away the smoke-filled rooms.

8 For a good example of the vituperation hurled at the Republicans, we have only to turn to Largo Caballero. Thus: 'On various occasions I have been asked whether the Civil War could have been avoided. To this question I have always responded in the affirmative: yes, it could indeed have been avoided. Had Azaña and Casares Quiroga treated the warnings they were given with less disdain, the military conspiracy would have been aborted, and we would have been saved from the catastrophe which today has placed Spain in the grip of moral and material misery alike ... Through their pride and *amour propre*, they are responsible for what happened, the one just as much as the other. The two of them knew what was happening and did not lift a finger to prevent or avoid civil war: believing themselves custodians of the truth, they disdained any advice that did not reach them from people who weren't their co-religionists. How much damage was occasioned by the torpor and stupidity of these two individuals!' Largo Caballero, *Mis recuerdos*, pp. 151–4. To repeat a point made in Chapter 1, however, the government was in an impossible position: to have engaged in wholesale arrests or dismissals, let alone armed the people, would have been virtually to guarantee a coup. In effect, then, all that could be done was to constantly reiterate its faith in the armed forces, and, when the storm finally broke, seek to keep the size of the rebellion to a minimum.

9 Cit. Fraser, *Blood of Spain*, p. 108. The seizure of Seville by Queipo de Llano became a central part of Nationalist mythology, but recent research has suggested that the story was much exaggerated. See R. E. L Prazeres Serém, 'Conspiracy, *coup d'état* and civil war in Seville, 1936–1939: history and myth in Francoist Spain', London School of Economics Ph.D. thesis, 2012, pp. 42–128. For general accounts of the fighting on 18 July, see Thomas, *Spanish Civil War*, pp. 222–4; A. Beevor, *The Battle for Spain: the Spanish Civil War, 1936–1939* (London, 2006), pp. 65–78.

10 Barea, *Forging of a Rebel*, p. 512.

11 Cit. Modesto, *Soy del Quinto Regimiento*, p. 53. It was not just the government that engaged in disinformation. In Madrid, for example, on the night of 17 July, the Anarchist militant, Gregorio Gallego, was approached by a retired officer of his acquaintance with a message from an officer involved in the conspiracy to the effect that the Anarchists had nothing to fear from a rising, the only object of which was to rid Spain of 'the Marxist madness and the dictatorial dreams of Largo Caballero.' Gallego, *Madrid, corazón que se desangra*, pp. 46–7.

12 Whilst Azaña gave his consent to the orders releasing troops in rebel units from their oaths of loyalty, he had little faith that they would prove efficacious. To quote Cipriano Rivas Cherif, 'This measure proved largely ineffective. My brother-in-law knew well enough, and he continually repeated it to his Socialist colleagues, most of whom believed otherwise, that the common soldier obeys his sergeant, the sergeant obeys his lieutenant, the lieutenant obeys his captain, the captain obeys his major and the major obeys his colonel. Thus the colonel exercises effective command of our troops. Colonels bring troops into the streets or keep them in their barracks.' Rivas Cherif, *Portrait of an Unknown Man*, p. 278.

13 In Barcelona, it is clear that, having managed to seize some arms just before the storm broke, the CNT, in particular, were somewhat better armed than the crowds we shall later encounter in Madrid, and that the Atarazanas barracks and artillery depot was in the end taken by an assault headed by the Anarchist militants Buenaventura Durruti and Francisco Ascaso (of whom the latter was shot dead in the final moments of the attack), the final blow coming when a group of workers brought up a field gun and, more by luck than by judgement, sent the very first round they fired straight through one of the windows. See Vidal, *Recuerdo 1936*, pp. 77–9. Meanwhile, it was the opinion of Eduardo Pons Prades, a teenage boy who took part in the fighting as a messenger, that without the determined attitude of the people, the Civil Guards and the Assault Guards would have been far less ready to stand firm. See E. Pons Prades, *Un soldado de la República: itinerario ibérico de un joven revolucionario* (Madrid, 1974), p. 56. This last, perhaps, is true enough, while it is almost certainly the case that here and there, workers were by one means or another to get close enough to the insurgent soldiers, many of whom were frightened and confused (they had marched to war under the Republican flag and been told that they were being sent to suppress yet another Anarchist rising) to urge them to surrender. See F. Borkenau, *The Spanish Cockpit* (London, 1937), pp. 845. Yet, for the Socialist Rafael Miralles Bravo, the key moment appears to have been the arrival of a number of aircraft that launched an accurate bombing raid on a key rebel position. See Miralles Bravo, *Memorias*, p. 23. In the end, then, all that we will ever know for certain is that loyal police units played a prominent role in the fighting, and that we do not know what would have happened had they not done so.

14 A. Candelas, *Adventures of an Innocent in the Spanish Civil War* (Penzance, 1989), pp. 18–20.

15 The Fokkers could carry no more than twelve men apiece, while the Dorniers could carry perhaps half that number, of whom several had to make the journey clinging to the wings!

16 Thomas, *Spanish Civil War*, pp. 334–59 *passim*. R. H. Whealey, *Hitler and Spain: the Nazi Role in the Spanish Civil War* (Lexington, Kentucky, 1989), pp. 1–25; J. Coverdale, *Italian Intervention in the Spanish Civil War* (Princeton, New Jersey, 1975), pp. 66–82. Initially, the German and Italian aid was dispatched to Morocco. The reason for this decision was quite simple – in brief, Ceuta and Melilla were far more secure than, say, Zaragoza or Valladolid – and there does not seem to have been any particular desire to favour Franco over Mola. However, as we shall see, favour Franco the decision did, and that in the most decisive of fashions.

17 For a detailed discussion of the Republic's efforts to acquire arms in the wake of the Non-Intervention Pact, see G. Howson, *Arms for Spain: The Untold Story of the Spanish Civil War* (London, 1998).

18 Escobar, *Así empezó*, p. 48.

19 M. Seidman, *Republic of Egos: a Social History of the Spanish Civil War* (Madison, Wisconsin, 2002), p. 34.

20 There are some accounts that not only give all the credit to the people, but also make no mention whatsoever of the presence of troops and police. Later to become a general in the Republican army, the Anarchist militant Cipriano Mera had just been released from Madrid's Model Prison: 'Recalling the page written by the people of Madrid in the assault on the Montaña barracks is a deeply emotional experience. Women and children shouted, "There is the enemy! There are the fascists!" Armed only with sticks and other such weapons, they took the building by assault and overwhelmed the rebels. To attempt to restrain the women from taking part in the assault would have been to risk a jab in the kidneys.' C. Mera, *Guerra, exilio y carcel de un anarquista* (Chatillon-sur-Bagneux, 1977), p. 19.

21 Barea, *Forging of a Rebel*, pp. 529–31.

22 J. Sandoval and M. Azcarate, *Spain, 1936–1939* (London, 1963), pp. 28–9.

23 See Beevor, *Battle for Spain*, p. 70.

24 See M. Tagueña Lacorte, *Testimonio de dos guerras* (Madrid, 2005), p. 104. By all accounts, many of the weapons in store turned out to be in very poor condition. Though he did not arrive in Spain till January 1937, by which time the proverbial bottom of the barrel may have been reached, George Orwell was scathing. Thus: 'There were [two] types of rifle ... The first was the long Mauser. These were seldom less than twenty years old; their sights were about as much use as a broken speedometer; and in most of them the rifling was hopelessly corroded ... Then there was the short Mauser ... really a cavalry weapon. These were more popular ... because they were lighter to carry and less nuisance in a trench ... Actually they were almost useless: they were made out of reassembled parts, no bolt belonged to its rifle, and three-quarters of them could be counted on to jam after five shots.' G. Orwell, *Homage to Catalonia* (new edition; London, 1951), pp. 33–4.

25 Gallego, *Madrid, corazón que se desangra*, p. 52.

26 Ibid., p. 77.

27 Even in such local victories as the ones alluded to here, success did not come easy, if, indeed, it came at all. In the Andalusian town of Baena, for example, the commander of the Civil Guard proclaimed martial law in the wake of the rising in the provincial capital, but, even including such civilian supporters as he could gather to his standard, he had fewer than 100 men. Baena being a town whose population largely consisted of desperate day labourers, he soon found himself under attack from an angry multitude. However, the latter's overwhelming superiority in numbers availed them nothing: when a relief force arrived from Seville nine days later, the insurgents were still holding out in a number of buildings crowning the hill on which the town was built. See Fraser, *Blood of Spain*, pp. 129–31. Rather more lucky were the workers of the mining town of Pozoblanco. Here, too, the Civil Guards rose in revolt but the people managed to surround them and keep them pinned down until they ran out of food and had to surrender, only to face immediate execution. Borkenau, *Spanish Cockpit*, p. 158.

28 J. Larios, *Combat over Spain: Memoirs of a Nationalist Fighter Pilot, 1936–1939* (London, 1974), pp. 22–4.

29 See Howson, *Arms for Spain*, pp. 28–32; Thomas, *Spanish Civil War*, pp. 328–33.

30 Such at least is the contention of the military historian George Hills. See G. Hills, *The Battle for Madrid* (London, 1976), pp. 50–1. As Hills phrases the argument, it is easy to rebut: not only was the government's share of the army riven by desertion and indiscipline and in many instances politically unreliable – many units were commanded by men who were, as the saying went, merely geographically loyal – but its soldiers often belonged to service units of one sort or another: infantry and cavalry units, by contrast, were in comparatively short supply. As for the Civil Guards, the Assault Guards and the Carabineers, even if the detachments concerned were wholly loyal, they were neither trained nor equipped for field operations. That left the left-wing militia, but they were even less capable of taking the offensive and, as we shall see, had the net effect of sapping the ability of the government to wage war. Would it, then, have been better not to have armed the Left? Had the rising still failed to the extent that it did, conceivably not – the government might then have had a better chance of mobilizing its half of the army for battle and going over to the attack – but it would have been a desperate gamble and one that few people who genuinely wished to crush the insurrection could have taken with any equanimity. Arming the people, then, was unavoidable, but the fact remains that, for all the excited talk in Barcelona, say, of marching on Zaragoza, in practice from that moment onwards the initiative lay entirely with the Nationalists. See M. Alpert, *The Republican Army in the Spanish Civil War, 1936–1939* (Cambridge, 2013), pp. 17–28.

31 Borkenau, *Spanish Cockpit*, pp. 99–100.

32 A. Lunn, *Spanish Rehearsal* (London, 1937), p. 36.

33 It is the contention of Paul Preston that, counting the many thousands of victims who were executed in the period 1939–41, the Nationalists executed or put to death

a minimum of 130,000 people; Preston, *Spanish Holocaust*, xviii. For a general discussion of the *limpieza*, See E. de Blaye, *Franco and the Politics of Spain* (London, 1974), pp. 87–96. A good local account, meanwhile, is that of Burgos provided by Antonio Ruiz Vilaplana. See Ruiz Vilaplana, *Burgos Justice*, pp. 32–44.

34 Cit. Fraser, *Blood of Spain*, p. 163.

35 Cit. I. Gibson, *The Assassination of Fedérico García Lorca* (London, 1979), p. 108. According to the figures consulted by Gibson, a minimum of 2,102 people were shot in Granada in the course of the Civil War. Setting aside Lorca, perhaps the greatest writer produced by twentieth-century Spain, the dead included the rector of the university, at least three of his professors and several prominent doctors and lawyers.

36 Blinkhorn, *Carlism and Crisis*, p. 256.

37 For the impact of the influx of new recruits on the Carlists in particular, See Blinkhorn, *Carlism and Crisis*, p. 257–8.

38 Ruiz Vilaplana, *Burgos Justice*, p. 198.

39 For an interesting account of the discussions that produced this development, see ibid., pp. 53–7. Conscious that the failure of the army to retain its unity meant that it could not ignore the Carlists, the Falange and the Alfonsine monarchists, Mola initially wanted to include some civilian politicians, but no names could be found on which everyone present could agree.

40 Ibid., pp. 188–9.

41 Following the uprising, both the Falange and the Carlists grew enormously in size and also raised large numbers of volunteers. However, it should not be inferred from this that the Nationalist cause was universally popular. To quote Antonio Ruiz Vilaplana, 'The ... Falange Española y de las JONS supplied from the very beginning of the rebellion a substantial quota of men for the fighting line ... The growth of this organization, I should perhaps explain, was due to the fact that it opened its doors widely to the masses: workman and peasant saw in it ... a haven from the terrorist regime of the local political boss ... No questions were asked of persons who wanted to join, so that in its ranks will be found thousands of persons of Left sympathies forced to choose between donning the blue shirt or death.' Ruiz Vilaplana, *Burgos Justice*, pp. 219–20.

42 Revilla Cebrecos, *Tercio de Lacar*, p. 35. At least Revilla Cebrecos was allowed to serve in an overtly Carlist battalion. Thus, an alternative solution was to co-opt the political militias into the regular army: when Colonel Francisco García Escámez set off from Pamplona for Madrid on 19 July 1936, his two regular battalions were each brought up to strength by giving them two companies of Carlists and one of Falangists. See J. Martínez Bande, *La marcha sobre Madrid* (Madrid, 1982), p. 68.

43 H. Cardozo, *March of a Nation: My Year of Spain's Civil War* (London, 1937), pp. 57–8. Cardozo is here allowing his enthusiasm to carry him away: whilst the Carlist forces won an excellent reputation that appears to have been well deserved, the Falange were far less impressive. Many of their units were of such poor quality that the rank and file ended up being drafted into the regular army, whilst a considerable number of those that survived never served at the front but were rather employed on internal security duties. See Payne, *Falange*, pp. 142–7.

44 Cit. Fraser, *Blood of Spain*, pp. 116–17.

45 Borkenau, *Spanish Cockpit*, p. 70.

46 R. Kisch, *They Shall Not Pass: the Spanish People at War, 1936–39* (London, 1974), pp. 5, 20, 54.

47 Gallego, *Madrid: corazón que se desangra*, p. 87.

48 Langdon-Davies, *Behind the Spanish Barricades*, p. 137. Describing how he requisitioned a car with a cousin and happily drove round the streets for two days, the CNT militant Antonio Navarro Velásquez, in 1936 a boy of just sixteen, was disarmingly honest, 'I believed that we were living the revolution.' Cit. J. Camps and E. Olcina (eds.), *Les milícies catalanes al front d'Aragó, 1936–1937* (Barcelona, 2006), pp. 275–6. In the Nationalist zone, be it said, the situation was not dissimilar: in the Burgos

area, for example, no sooner had the rising broken out than the followers of a local right-winger named José María Albiñana, who had founded a tiny anti-republican movement called the Partido Nacionalista Espanol, engaged in a reign of terror of which the first victim was a workman who refused to shout 'Long live Spain!' See Ruiz Vilaplana, *Burgos Justice*, pp. 28–30. However, the imposition of military control meant that there was much less space for autonomy and, after the first few days, no room whatsoever for mere death squads. But plenty of small-town bullies who had no intention of getting shot at, not to mention men who had personal connections with the new masters, found safe billets in local detachments of the Falange and the Carlists, or special auxiliary units such as the Mounted Police of Seville, a squadron-sized detachment of horsemen led by a retired *africanista* named Alfredo Erquicia Aranda that in the summer and autumn of 1936 imposed a veritable reign of terror amidst the agricultural labourers of the Guadalquivir valley (a process that the killers sardonically referred to as 'agrarian reform'). As Luis Mérida, a conservative Republican who had rallied to the rising in Córdoba later reflected, 'There were two sorts of people here ... those who went to the front to fight, and the criminals who stayed in the rear.' Cit. Fraser, *Blood of Spain*, p. 162.

49 Kisch, *They Shall Not Pass*, p. 55. Alvaro Cortes Roa, a seventeen-year-old student who enlisted in the Fifth Regiment in August 1936, actually witnessed one such death. See A. Cortes Roa, *Tanquista desde mi tronera* (Madrid, 1989), p. 8.

50 Langdon-Davies, *Behind the Spanish Barricades*, p. 140. For an atmospheric account of the unpleasant effects of 'taking life too seriously by half', see Miralles Bravo, *Memorias*, pp. 34–6. A particular problem was the persistent rumours of cars full of Nationalist sympathizers roaring around the streets at high speed and engaging in what would later be called 'drive-by shootings.' At the very least, accidents could not but be frequent, as when a nervous CNT militiaman shot dead at a checkpoint a JSU militant named Antonio López Raimundo, who was travelling to Barbastro to set up an advanced headquarters for the PSUC militia, for no better reason than he was too well dressed to be anything other than a fascist. Ibid., p. 40.

51 Borkenau, *Spanish Cockpit*, p. 70.

52 Typical enough was the situation that transpired in the Madrid suburb of Carabanchel Bajo. Almost unarmed prior to the assault on the Montaña barracks, local activists now found themselves possessed of a veritable arsenal. To quote Gregorio Gallego, for example, 'In our district there ended up more than a hundred rifles and carbines, a machine-gun, a mortar and almost fifty pistols.' Gallego, *Madrid, corazón que se desangra*, p. 82. How many of these weapons, one wonders, ever saw action against the enemy?

53 For a representative selection of these vehicles, See F. C. Albert, *Carros de combate y vehículos blindados de la guerra, 1936–1939* (Barcelona, 1980), pp. 62–91. Seeing three such vehicles in the Ramblas in Barcelona, Langdon-Davies described them as 'pathetic things with iron sheets a quarter of an inch thick hopefully fastened round their vitals, death-traps for brave amateurs ... bravely flaunting their magic letters CNT-FAI.' Langdon-Davies, *Behind the Spanish Barricades*, p. 145. Interestingly, whereas some 245 such vehicles appear to have been produced in the Republican zone, in the Nationalist one, the figure was possibly as few as twenty-eight. L. Molina Franco and J. M. Manrique García, *Atlas ilustrado de armas y uniformes de la Guerra Civil Española* (Madrid, 2009), pp. 154–63.

54 E. Biescas Palacio, *Memorias de la Guerra Civil Española* (Montevideo, 2005), pp. 7–11. Other men, meanwhile, joined up because they felt threatened. Typical enough here was Carlos Tomás Alvarez, a twenty-eight-year-old textile worker from Madrid with a long history of involvement in the Catholic workers' movement known as the Sindicatos Obreros, who joined up because he believed he was being spied on. Cit. J. M. Garate Córdoba, *Tenientes en campaña: la improvisación de oficiales en la guerra del 36* (Madrid, 1976), p. 93. Another such case, meanwhile, is the Republican playwright and journalist Miguel de Heredia, who volunteered to join the militia as a stretcher

bearer – note the non-combatant role – on account of the fact that he had a brother who had been an early member of the Falange and a brother-in-law who was an army officer. Heredia, *Monarquía, república y guerra*, pp. 200–1.Finally, Joaquín Masjuán, a seventeen-year-old student from Barcelona who chose to write his memoirs under the pseudonym Jack Max and who had so little interest in current affairs that he spent the whole of 18 July sitting at home reading, enlisted because his four best friends were doing so, and he had no wish to be thought a coward. J. Max, *Memorias de un revolucionario* (Barcelona, 1975), pp. 27–8.

55 According to the most recent work, there may have been even fewer militia than there were arms, Madrid probably sending as few as 10,000 men to join the fighting and Barcelona possibly not even half that number. See J. Matthews, *Reluctant Warriors: Republican Popular-Army and Nationalist-Army Conscripts in the Spanish Civil War, 1936–1939* (Oxford, 2012), pp. 22–3.

56 Here, too, we can cite the case of Carlos Tomás Alvarez, the latter admitting that he joined the UGT because 'the rule for any worker who wanted to eat, let alone stay alive, was to become a member of some anti-fascist trade union.' Cit. ibid.

57 Cit. MacMaster, *Spanish Fighters*, p. 64.

58 Borkenau, *Spanish Cockpit*, p. 92. For an interesting discussion of the problems operative here, see M. Seidman, 'The unorwellian Barcelona', *European History Quarterly*, XX, No. 2 (April, 1990), pp. 163–80; M. Seidman, 'Work and revolution: workers' control in Barcelona in the Spanish Civil War, 1936–1938', *Journal of Contemporary History*, XVII, No.3 (July, 1982), pp. 409–34.

59 Preston, *Spanish Holocaust*, p. 260.

60 Heredia, *Monarquía, república, guerra*, pp. 204–5.

61 Barea, *Forging of a Rebel*, p. 544.

62 H. E. Knoblaugh, *Correspondent in Spain* (London, 1937), p. 72. For a general analysis of the killings in Madrid, see Preston, *Spanish Holocaust*, pp. 259–98. In Madrid, at least, the ravages of the *cheka* were accompanied by much racketeering involving various forms of blackmail and extortion, a particularly notorious culprit in this respect being one Agapito García Atadell, a petty criminal who set up a control patrol that was little more than a bandit gang and amassed a considerable fortune before fleeing to France when the Nationalist army arrived before Madrid in November 1936. Taking ship for South America, he fell into Nationalist hands anyway when the ship he was on put in to a port in the Canary Isles, and he ended up before a firing squad. J. Ruiz, 'Defending the Republic: the García Atadell brigade in Madrid, 1936', *Journal of Contemporary History*, XLII, No. 1 (January, 2007), pp. 97–115. Another such case was that of Luis Bonilla Echevarría, a Republican officer put on trial and executed in 1938 on account that he had murdered ten Rightists in Navalmorales in September 1936 out of a desire for personal gain. See J. Ruiz, '"Incontrolados" en la España republicana durante la Guerra Civil Española: el caso de Luis Bonilla Echevarría', *Historia y política*, No. 21 (January, 2009), pp. 191–218. For a grim account of the atmosphere that reigned in the Barcelona area in the course of the Terror, it is worth consulting the diary of Lluis Puig Casas, a devout Catholic and travelling salesman whose elder brother, Josep, was abducted and executed by the FAI. See I. Puig (ed.), *Personal Memories of the Spanish Civil War in Catalan and English* (Lampeter, 1999), pp. 27–31.

63 Rivas Cherif, *Portrait of an Unknown Man*, pp. 284–5.

64 The attack on the Church was ever afterwards to be one of the chief themes of the propaganda of Nationalist Spain, and, later, that of General Franco. In defence of their actions, anarchists and others claimed that the violence was the inevitable response to a situation in which the Church was guilty of 'maintaining and, indeed, reinforcing unjust social structures of a sort that promoted discrimination of every type, not to mention humiliation without end, and denied the lower classes access to the most minimal levels of culture.' Pons Prades, *Soldado de la República*, p. 79. Afterwards there were also frequent claims that priests fired at the crowds from their

belfries and even that coffins were found containing the remains of women who had been done away with after being made pregnant by some ecclesiastic or other, whilst Madrid in particular was gripped by wild rumours to the effect that nuns were poisoning the city's water supply and distributing poisoned sweets to children. See Vidal, *Recuerdo 1936*, pp. 74–7; Gallego, *Madrid, corazón que se desangra*, pp. 66–7.

65 The latest research in Spain places the total figure of those killed in the course of the Red Terror as 49,272, the vast majority of whom perished in the period July–September 1936. Preston, *Spanish Holocaust*, xvi.

66 Chalmers-Mitchell, *My House in Málaga*, pp. 95–102.

67 Langdon-Davies, *Behind the Spanish Barricades*, pp. 136–7.

68 For a general survey of the revolution of July 1936, See Thomas, *Spanish Civil War*, pp. 290–312.As to the ability of all the revolutionary experimentation to meet the needs of the embattled Republic, this is not a topic that can be handled in the space of the few pages available to the author. However, industrial production collapsed whilst the food supply was, at best, patchy. A progressive journalist, José-Antonio Cabezas, was an eye-witness of the situation in Gijón, whence he had decided to evacuate his family in the hope of avoiding the fighting that was raging round Oviedo: 'Given the ... insecurity that reigned in the streets, we parked in a garage near the station .... and spent the night in the cars ... The next day we discovered that there was nowhere where we could get any food for the children. The city was ... subject to the crazy orders emitted by ... the CNT ... They had abolished money and all the comestibles in the place had been requisitioned and stored away ... Crowds of inhabitants, principally women, were therefore setting out on foot or in rudimentary vehicles in the hope of obtaining food from the local peasants in exchange for medicines or silver ... The public dining rooms opened by the CNT were reserved for combatants. If one wanted to obtain so much as a bowl of lentils, it was necessary to have a rifle on one's shoulder.' J. A. Cabezas, *Asturias: catorce meses de guerra civil* (Madrid, 1975), pp. 39–47.

69 Both Browne and Odena García were killed in action, the former in fact being the first Briton to die in the war. For a very enthusiastic account of the participation of women in the fighting, see L. Lines, *Women in Combat in the Spanish Civil War* (Lanham, Maryland, 2014), pp. 71–88. However, it is difficult not to feel that Lines takes her argument too far: whilst no-one would question the courage and determination of some few individuals, to claim that militiawomen made anything more than a symbolic contribution to the fighting is to stretch credulity to its limits. On Fanny Schoonheyt, in particular, meanwhile, see Y. Scholten, 'Fanny, queen of the machine-gun', *The Volunteer*, 4 December 2011, accessed at < http://www.albavolunteer.org/2011/12/queen-of-the-machine-gun-fanny-schoonheyt-dutch-miliciana/ >, 28 December 2017.

70 Borkenau, *Spanish Cockpit*, p. 126. In Nationalist Spain, of course, although both the Carlists and the Falange had female sections, social conventions were much more respected. However, even here, perhaps, there were women who found the war an exciting time. 'The Spanish girls find war exciting, thrilling, entertaining', wrote one American correspondent working in the Nationalist zone. 'Never have they had so much attention. All very polite, all very Spanish. They parade up and down, up and down, pretending to be oblivious to the thousands of eyes which follow them, actually conscious of every youth who looks admiringly upon them.' H. R. Knickerbocker, *The Siege of the Alcázar: a Warlog of the Spanish Revolution* (Philadelphia, 1936), p. 51.

71 M. Low and J. Brea, *Red Spanish Notebook* (London, 1937), pp. 184–7.

72 Borkenau, *Spanish Cockpit*, p. 106; Camps and Olcina, *Les milícies catalanes al front d'Aragó*, p. 276. In unconscious testimony both to the shortage of women at the front and the role that they actually performed, Orwell notes that a neighbouring position was 'an object of fascination to every man in the line because there were three militiawomen there who did the cooking.' Orwell, *Homage to Catalonia*, p. 38.

73 Langdon-Davies, *Behind the Spanish Barricades*, p. 180.

74 For a useful discussion of a fairly balanced nature of the participation of women in the fighting, see M. Nash, 'Women in war: *milicianas* and armed combat in revolutionary Spain, 1936–1939', *International History Review*, XV, No. 2 (May, 1993), pp. 269–82. For a particularly hostile eyewitness account, meanwhile, see Miralles Bravo, *Memorias*, pp. 53–4. According to Miralles, on the Aragón front, all the women concerned were prostitutes from the slums of Barcelona, but, whilst it is probable that some prostitutes did indeed accompany the militias, many of the militiawomen were very far from being deserving of such stigmatization. To take just one example, María de la Luz Mejías Correa, a young JSU militant from Badajoz, fled the city with her fiancé, Juan, and took refuge in the village of Higuera de Vargas, where the couple enlisted in a militia column being organized by the Socialist deputies Ricardo Zabalza and José Sosa. Progressive in her views though she might be, however, Mejías Correa was no believer in free love, Juan's advances in consequence being firmly rebuffed until they had managed to arrange a proper wedding, albeit one of a civil nature. See M. Pulido Mendoza (ed.), *Así fue pasando el tiempo: memorias de una miliciana extremeña* (Seville, 2006), pp. 65–75. Formally expelled from her unit in the midst of the battle of Madrid along with the only other woman serving in it, Mejías Correa spent the rest of the war attached to its headquarters as an orderly, though in order to draw pay she had to list herself under a false identity. Ibid., p. 91. Another woman who remained at the front for much longer than was normal was Mika Feldman de Etchebéhère, an Argentinian dentist of Jewish origin who had been living in Paris with her French husband and moved with him to Madrid following the triumph of the Popular Front. Dissident Communists, both she and her husband (who was almost immediately killed) enlisted in a small POUM column in which she eventually attained the rank of captain and continued to serve in that capacity well into 1937. Yet at the beginning even she found herself forced into a wholly feminine role based on keeping the column's quarters clean, attending to the supply of food, writing letters for militiamen and serving as an impromptu medical orderly. See M. de Etchebéhère, *Mi Guerra de España* (Barcelona, 1977), p. 17.

75 There is a growing literature on the experiences of women in Republican Spain. E.g. L. Willis, *Women in the Spanish Revolution* (London, 1975); M. Ackelsberg, *Free Women of Spain: Anarchism and the Struggle for Women's Liberation* (Bloomington, Indiana, 1991); S. Mangini, *Memories of Resistance: Women's Views of the Spanish Civil War* (New Haven, Connecticut, 1995); G. Herrmann, 'Voices of the vanquished: leftist women and the Spanish Civil War', *Journal of Spanish Cultural Studies*, IV, No. 1 (March, 2003), pp. 11–29; M. Nash, 'Milicianas and home-front heroines: images of women in revolutionary Spain, 1936–1939', *History of European Ideas*, XI, Nos. 1–6 (n.d.), 1989, pp. 235–44; M. Ackelsberg, 'Models of revolution: Rural women and anarchist collectivisation in Civil-War Spain', *Journal of Peasant Studies*, XX, No. 3 (April, 1993), pp. 367–88; M. Nash, *Defying Male Civilisation: Women in the Spanish Civil War* (Denver, Colorado, 1995); F. Lannon, 'Women and images of women in the Spanish Civil War', *Transactions of the Royal Historical Society*, Sixth Series, I (1991), pp. 213–28; T. Kaplan, 'Spanish anarchism and women's liberation', *Journal of Contemporary History*, VI, No. 2 (April, 1971), pp. 101–11. For an account of the perspective of one woman in particular, see T. Pamies i Bertran, *Cuam erem capitans* (Barcelona, 1974).

76 In pursuing this particular objective, the Communists were extremely successful: membership of the party soared dramatically, the new recruits being almost entirely middle class. As José Martín Blásquez wrote in 1937, for example, 'The ranks of the Communist Party have been swelled by thousands of Spaniards who are no more Communist than I am, but have been impressed by its model discipline and its loyalty to the Republic. To talk to these people of the social revolution is like mentioning rope in the house of a man who has been hanged.' Marín Blásquez, *I Helped to Build an Army*, p. 350.

77 Borkenau, *Spanish Cockpit,* p. 290. It should be noted that fighting for democracy was not an end in itself as far as the Communists were concerned. On the contrary, once the war was won, the goal would once more be revolution. As Pere Treball, the editor of the PSUC newspaper, *Treball,* admitted after the war: 'An important element of power is the military. Having an army of proletarians formed in the war, with proletarian officers in command and a proletarian police force ... hegemony would be assured ... With the military and the police in proletarian hands, the government would be able to start on the road to socialism.' Cit. Fraser, *Blood of Spain,* p. 331.

78 If Largo Caballero was still a proponent of 'bolshevizing' the Socialist movement, the growing sensation that the formation of the PSUC and the JSU had played into their hands meant that he was now much more leery of the Communists. To quote Franz Borkenau, 'Comment on the Communists is especially bitter in the Caballero circle ... The Soviet Union does not help us at all, they say, no more than France and England: all they do is to intrigue in our politics, strengthening every tendency towards the right wing of the movement.' Ibid., p. 132.

79 J. del Barrio, *Memorias políticas y militares* (Barcelona, 2013), p. 69.

80 Largo Caballero, *Mis recuerdos,* pp. 135–42.

81 Gallego, *Madrid, corazón que se desangra,* pp. 13–14.

82 For an excellent account of the debate in the Anarchist leadership, see Fraser, *Blood of Spain,* pp. 110–13.

83 Cit. ibid., p. 142.

84 E. Manzanera, *The Iron Column: Testament of a Revolutionary* (London, 2006), pp. 6–7.

85 Borkenau, *Spanish Cockpit,* pp. 91–2. One need not feel too much sympathy for the POUM here: sent to Barcelona with a consignment of valuables following the fall of Tardienta, several carloads of PSUC militia were detained *en route* at a POUM road-block and summarily executed on trumped-up accusations of pillage. Ibid., p. 108,

86 Cit. J. Cervera Gil, *Ya sabes mi paradero: la guerra civil a través de las cartas de los que la vivieron* (Barcelona, 2005), p. 54. Equally combative, meanwhile, was Lois Orr, a nineteen-year-old American woman of Socialist inclinations who had been honeymooning in France with her equally leftist husband, Charles, and joined him in working for the POUM's propaganda bureau. 'The PSUC ... tries never to mention the word "revolution" for fear of scaring their bourgeois allies. The POUM is continually embarrassing them by flinging back at them the slogans of Lenin and Marx, whose prestige with the workers here the PSUC is careful to monopolise, but whose ideas and theories they entirely neglect. Our pet slogan is "War on the Front and Revolution behind the Lines". Cit. G. R. Horn (ed.), *Letters from Barcelona: an American Woman in the Spanish Civil War* (Basingstoke, 2009), p. 81.

87 To quote José Ignacio Escobar, 'The installation of Marxism in power had provoked an extensive ... reaction, but one that was at the same purely negative in that what held it together was the simple idea of overthrowing the regime that had murdered Calvo Sotelo. However, what should be put in its place was another matter. In Navarre ... the state of war had been proclaimed ... amidst the strains of the "Royal March," the loudest possible cheers for the king and a profusion of bicolour flags, but in other places, especially in the south, for a considerable time the movement was celebrated on the basis of the "Hymn of Riego," the tricolour flag and cheers for the Republic ... For their part, meanwhile, the Falangists were trying to impose their red and black flag and the "Cara al Sol." This battle for symbols and emblems was the first sign of discord with regard to the possible direction of the movement.' Escobar, *Así fue,* pp. 44–5. Such was the tension that it appears that on more than one occasion, rival gangs of militia came to blows with one another. E.g. Vidal, *Recuerdo 1936,* p. 135.

88 Cit. Fraser, *Blood of Spain,* p. 174. The general indifference to the Church is confirmed by Enrique Miret Magdalena, a devoutly Catholic student who had joined hundreds of other refugees who had taken shelter in foreign embassies in Madrid. Thus: 'The majority didn't give a hang about the Church or Catholicism. They were

Catholics, but their Catholicism was a sort of social security for the other life. I began to feel like a fish out of water.' Cit. ibid., p. 299.

89 See Ruiz Vilaplana, *Burgos Justice*, pp. 137–40.

90 For an interesting discussion of this point, see M. Richards, 'Civil-war violence and the construction of Francoism', in P. Preston and A. Mackenzie (eds.), *The Republic Besieged: Civil War in Spain, 1936–1939* (Edinburgh, 1996), pp. 197–240.

91 Long after the war, the prominent Falangist Dionisio Ridruejo gave a succinct summary of the situation that would have transpired had he or anyone else attempted resistance; 'Naturally the Foreign Legion would have moved in the next day and captured us, but, much more important, such a move on our part would have brought the war to a halt. I didn't dare take the step: who would have?' Cit. Fraser, *Blood of Spain*, p. 318. In the eyes of many Falangists, however, the struggle was not given up, but merely postponed. Alberto Pastor, for example, was a local leader from Valladolid, 'We were there to fight a common enemy. When the war was won there would be time enough to settle our differences.' Cit. ibid., p. 320.

92 F. McCullagh, *In Franco's Spain: being the Experiences of an Irish War Correspondent in the Great Civil War which began in 1936* (London, 1937).

93 Lunn, *Spanish Rehearsal*, pp. 80–1.

3

FIRST CAMPAIGNS

By the beginning of the last week of July, then, Spain was at war. As yet, however, the situation remained extremely confused. Along the north coast, beleaguered Nationalist garrisons were holding the city of Oviedo together with increasingly battered enclaves in Gijón and San Sebastián, but otherwise the whole of the Cantabrian littoral was in the hands of the government from the frontiers of Nationalist-held Galicia on the one hand to those of France on the other. South of the Cantabrian mountains, it was a different story: Navarre, Old Castile, most of Aragón and the northern half of Extremadura were all held by the Nationalists. Travel further south or further east, however, and one encounters government territory once again: the Nationalists having been confined to the single strongpoint represented by the city of Toledo, Catalonia, Valencia, Murcia and New Castile and the southern half of Extremadura were all bastions of the Popular Front. Finally, Andalucía was divided: the Republicans held the cities of Málaga, Jaén and Huelva and large parts of the countryside, but Seville, Algeciras, San Roque, Córdoba and Granada had all been seized by the rebels. From the very beginning, then, setting aside the long-term aim of winning the war, both sides were presented with short-term objectives that drew them into regular military operations.

Although the circumstances to which the uprising had given rise had very much handed the strategic initiative to the Nationalists, let us here begin with the Republicans. Here, the most obvious need was to suppress the various foci of revolt that had managed to survive the initial fighting as islands of rebellion in a sea of Republican territory. The insurgent forces at San Sebastián being overcome within a few days, the most important of these were Toledo, Oviedo and Gijón. In the first of these places, the military governor, José Moscardó, had secured the city with the aid of the Civil Guard of the entire province on 18 July, but for several days, he had maintained an ambiguous attitude in the hope of gaining time for the arrival of relief forces from elsewhere. However, under increasing pressure from the government to make his position clear, on 21 July he formally declared his support for the rebellion and withdrew all his forces – 800 Civil Guards, six military cadets, 100 officers who had either been stationed at Toledo or taken refuge with Moscardó and 200 assorted civilian volunteers – into the palace-cum-fortress known as the *alcázar* that dominated the centre of the city, taking with him the large amount of rifle ammunition that had been awaiting delivery at a munitions factory on the outskirts as well as something over 100 hostages. Also present, meanwhile, were 670 civilians, most of whom were the wives and children of the Civil Guards. Having served in the period 1931–6 as the Republic's infantry academy, the *alcázar* contained a small arsenal, including a pair of 70mm mountain howitzers and a number of machine guns, but, despite the requisitioning of every comestible in reach, food was in short supply: even with the most careful system of rationing, then, resistance could not be prolonged beyond a certain length of time.[1]

A force of some 8,000 troops, Assault Guards and militia having been dispatched to Toledo, fighting began on 21 July as Nationalist rearguards fought to protect the evacuation of the last consignments of food and ammunition to the *alcázar*. By the next day, the city was completely in the hands of the Republicans, apart from a handful of buildings clustered around the walls of the fortress, and there now began a protracted siege. Stationing their limited number of field guns and howitzers on the hills across the Tagus from the city, the Republicans began by seeking on the one hand to pound the defenders into surrender, and on the other to persuade them to give themselves up (famously, in an exchange later much embellished by Nationalist propaganda, a local representative of the party headed by Manuel Azaña rang Moscardó and told him that his son had been captured and would be shot unless the *alcázar* surrendered forthwith).[2] However, the defenders remained defiant, and progress ranged from slow to non-existent. Lacking proper training and leadership alike, the militia squandered considerable stocks of ammunition by firing at the thick walls with their rifles, and their men came and went at will, in some instances even treating the siege as a tourist attraction to be visited in the course of a day trip. As Arturo Barea complained, for example, 'Milicianos and shock police … crouched in ridiculous positions, vociferating and gesticulating, letting off shots, shouting orders, blowing shrill whistles … Militiamen and militia girls were making merry: they were laughing and singing, the men [drinking] from leather bottles, and their girls [tickling] them in the armpits so that the wine spattered.'[3] According to the highly critical Mikhail Koltsov, an extremely gifted *Pravda* correspondent who had reached Spain as early as 8 August, some even of this activity was entirely artificial, in that the hordes of photographers and cameramen present were forever encouraging the militiamen, whom he described as being got up like Mexican bandits, to strike heroic poses at the barricades and blaze away at the fortress whether or not there was anything to blaze away at.[4] One observer was Cipriano Rivas Cherif:

One afternoon I took advantage of an opportunity to visit Toledo. After my quick trip I gave the president my impressions … It seemed to me that firing from the *alcazár* had turned its besiegers into the besieged. Even our driver entered the city roundabout so as to avoid gunfire from … the fortress, and our troops had adopted a similar defensive attitude … The President commented, 'We can only take the *alcazár* by assault, but we don't seem to be doing that. Our men got as far as the very entry to the castle's central patio and then retreated. That's not the way to do it.[5]

With the passage of time, things became a little more serious. Heavier guns were brought up – by the beginning of September, the Republicans could draw on the services of seven 75mm guns, eight 105mm guns and nine 155mm howitzers – and both the two northern towers soon succumbed to the sustained pounding to which they were immediately subjected, whilst a serious but ultimately unsuccessful attempt was made to occupy some of the buildings that the garrison were holding as outworks, including, most notably, the city's pre-1936 military headquarters. Meanwhile, since the middle of August, the besieging forces had been excavating two mines under the western walls. Detonated on 18 September, these brought down the south-western tower and opened a large breach in the defences. An eyewitness was John Langdon-Davies:

> At a quarter-past six someone pulled a switch, and the distant crowds saw the … tower rise into the air and fall in fragments … Within the city huge blocks of masonry scattered themselves in every direction, crushing roofs and falling shattered in the empty streets … In the Plaza de Zocodover the armoured car used as a barricade was cut in two by the explosion and half of it landed on the fire-station nearby.[6]

Impressive as the explosion was, casualties were minimal and yet another assault was driven off without difficulty: when the attackers got to the foot of the rubble, they found that it was extremely difficult to scale, with the result that they only entered the building in handfuls and were quickly overwhelmed; meanwhile, columns attacking from the north and the south-east also made little progress, and that despite the fact that they were supported by one of the Republic's five First-World-War vintage Schneider CA1 heavy tanks and several other armoured vehicles. Also beaten off, meanwhile, was a second assault that was launched two days later. With the Nationalist forces now rapidly approaching the city from the west, the Republicans were becoming increasingly desperate, and 23 September saw two more attempts to rush the ruins, only for these, too, to be repelled with heavy losses:

> One day some high-ranking army officers led us to some buildings well below the *álcazar*, which lay at a distance of about 200 metres across open ground rising steeply towards the fortress. These professional army officers

had planned an assault … From any direction this was dangerous, and from this particular direction it was suicidal. We clambered out of the buildings, climbed an embankment and advanced upwards on our hands and knees for about thirty metres … Suddenly the enemy opened fire with machine-guns and rifles, and of about 200 men, nearly half fell dead or wounded, and the rest of us had to drag ourselves as fast as we could downhill … and into the buildings where we were safe … After this incident many of the militiamen, including myself, had no doubt that the … officers had planned this attack … so as to inflict as many casualties on the Republican forces as possible.[7]

The defeat of the assault of 23 September was not quite the end. Four days later, yet another mine was exploded under the fortress's only surviving tower, and the defenders subjected to yet another desperate charge. One participant was Antonio Gómez de Zamora, a junior officer in the so-called 'Fifth Regiment' (see below). All through the battle, he had been keeping a diary, and, as the fighting died down, he scribbled a disconsolate summary of events: 'At five o'clock in the morning, our artillery opened fire, not that it achieved very much. Then at dawn our dynamiters exploded a mine. As soon as the smoke cleared, we advanced to the … assault with all the forces that Lister [i.e. Enrique Lister Forján, a prominent commander in the Fifth Regiment] had been able to get together. We kept attacking all morning, but were not favoured by success.'[8]

Toledo being only a couple of hours' drive from Madrid and the *alcázar* being so situated that events there were particularly easy to observe, it occupied a disproportionate share of the attention given to the war (and thereby in a sense tied

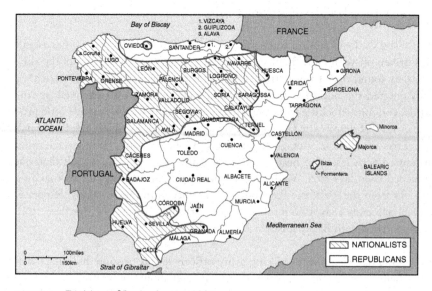

MAP 3.1   Division of Spain, August 1936.

the hands of both sides: for neither the Nationalist nor the Republicans was it possible to ignore Moscardó in favour of more important objectives). Less well reported but just as gripping were the events currently taking place at Oviedo and Gijón. After reducing the odds against them by tricking the authorities into believing that he intended to remain loyal (the effect of this ploy was, as hoped, that large numbers of the battle-hardened militants who had captained the revolt of October 1934 were gulled into heading off to invade León), on 19 July the commander of the garrison, Colonel Antonio Aranda, declared for the rebels, his example being quickly followed by his counterpart in Gijón, Colonel Antonio Pinilla. Immediately, however, the two rebels found themselves facing the wrath of the combined Asturian Left, and they could therefore do no more than take up defensive positions and seek to hold out until help reached them from elsewhere. Scared that the port of Gijón might once again be used to bring in troops from Africa, the revolutionaries at first concentrated on launching assault after assault on the two barracks in which the rebels there had barricaded themselves. Realizing that there was little chance of victory, many of the common soldiers surrendered as the fighting went on, but even so it took until 21 August for the final positions to be overrun.[9]

With Gijón out of the way, the Asturian militias could now turn their attention to Oviedo. Subject only to a loose blockade, Aranda and his 3,000 men had been able to occupy the whole of the city, but his position was extremely difficult as Oviedo was overlooked on all sides by steep hills. Some of these had been seized and fortified, but the perimeter was far too extensive to be held for any length of time. For a little while, life continued more or less as normal, but from early September things began to change with day after day of shelling and bombing raids in which the civilian population suffered more than 1,000 casualties. When the Republican offensive finally began on 4 October, then, one by one the outlying positions were conquered and the defenders driven ever closer to the city centre. Amongst those wartching was progressive journalist, José-Antonio Cabezas:

> The San-Esteban sector was suddenly lit up by a series of flashes that were not dissimilar to lightning. Immediately, the same effect was observed in the direction of Sograndio and La Tenderina and finally, closest to us, San Claudio. A moment later the flashes were joined by the thunder of the guns ... To either side, meanwhile, we heard the rattle of rifles and machine-guns. The noise was deafening.[10]

Despite heavy casualties, by 12 October the Republicans had penetrated the very heart of the city, Aranda and his men being left with little more than a cluster of fortified enclaves. However, even these were soon under attack. Once again Cabezas was on the scene: 'On the morning of the thirteenth ... an attack was launched against ... the convent of the Adoratrices and its adjoining garden ... Very soon, the various buildings grouped around its periphery were on fire and shells bursting in the interior of the convent itself.'[11] Inside the city, meanwhile, the remnants of the defending forces were fighting almost back-to-back. 'We were like wild animals at bay', recalled a Carlist student named Jesús-Evaristo Casariego. 'We were prepared to burn the city, to create barricades of fire between us and the enemy ... Win or die, there was no other choice.'[12]

Like the defenders of the *alcázar* of Toledo, then, the defenders of Oviedo were at length reduced to what seemed to be their last gasp. However, before we conclude their story, we must first examine events on the other side of Spain, and, in particular, Aragón, Catalonia and the Balearic Islands. Only here do we see a sustained attempt to launch what amounts to a strategic offensive on the part of the Republican forces, the targets of this being two-fold. Let us begin with what may be deemed Barcelona's western front. For the Anarchists in particular, the loss of Zaragoza had come as a terrible blow, the city having not only been a very strong bastion of the CNT but also its traditional headquarters. In consequence, within days of the defeat of the rebellion in Barcelona, large numbers of CNT militia in particular were loading themselves into lorries and setting off for Aragón. Amongst the groups concerned was a column – a term from the Moroccan wars made much use of in the early days of the fighting – associated with the famous Buenaventura Durruti:

> In theory, the column was made up of forces of the Alcántara infantry regiment, two machine-gun companies, a section of mortars and infantry guns [i.e. small field pieces designed to be attached to infantry units and used for the purposes of direct support]. and two companies of "militia riflemen" ... However, rather than a military unit, they looked more like a carnival parade, composed, as they were, of a motley crew whose principal characteristic was their complete want of uniformity. Some of them were in full uniform, others in shirt-sleeves and rope-soled sandals; some had civilian hats, others forage caps and a handful steel helmets.[13]

Enthusiasm, however, did not equate to military prowess.[14] Flooding westwards from Barcelona, the militias were able to over-run various towns and villages that had fallen into rebel hands in the course of the uprising, whilst their arrival was generally followed by the imposition of a greater or lesser extent of collectivisation and, very often, dozens of executions: indeed, of all the regions of Spain affected by the Red Terror, the limited area of Aragón (about one third of the whole) occupied by the militias was the hardest hit, the death toll reaching 8.7 per cent of the population.[15] However, not long after they crossed the frontier into Aragón, they began to encounter more substantial opposition in the form of small parties of troops who had been dispatched from rebel Zaragoza, Huesca and Jaca to hold such territory as they could against the oncoming 'Marxist hordes.' Wherever they ran into such groups, the untrained militiamen simply went to ground, whilst in other cases they lost their nerve and halted their advance before they saw even a single enemy.[16] In his memoirs, Elías Manzanera, a CNT militant who had enlisted in the so-called 'Iron Column' in Valencia, claims more than somewhat hyperbolically that 'with four old rifles and little ammunition, the young fighters of the Iron Column helped halt international fascism 150 kilometres outside Valencia.'[17] Yet his description of what happened when he and his comrades ran into the enemy is revealing indeed. Thus, we hear that, after a brief skirmish at the village of Sarrión, the column pressed on to La Puebla de Valverde, and, beyond it, the Puerto de Escandón. At this last place, however, a major battle developed:

> Heavy artillery fire greeted our arrival. Our young men started to dig in and our professional soldiers ordered that the battery they had brought should be set up ... An indescribable racket erupted: the boom of cannons was joined by the crack of rifle fire. The enemy was entrenched a few metres away from us ... The clash that ensued was outstanding, terrifying. And we had to hold out with courage, giving not an inch, but carrying on with the fight. Bullets were raining down everywhere, [but] we were forced to be sparing with our ammunition, wasting absolutely nothing ... Night having fallen, we set to digging our trenches, to await the time to mount our attack on Teruel.[18]

What, however, did this affair really amount to? Reading between the lines, one sees a very different picture, a picture of the advancing militants being pinned down by an enemy force dug in at an obvious defensive position, and then displaying not the slightest degree of initiative. Rather than trying, say, to outflank the enemy, Manzanera and his fellows are rather seen to have taken cover and peppered the enemy with a fire that was doubtless all but useless. By the end of September, the line had therefore stabilized a few miles short of Huesca, Zaragoza and Teruel alike, whilst the defects of the militias as a means of waging war had been cruelly revealed. Training was non-existent; the men were armed with a hodge-podge of different weapons for which the supply of ammunition could not be guaranteed; and there was little willingness to accept the counsel of the few regular officers who had been allowed to accompany the columns as advisers. Meanwhile, not least because no proper arrangements had been made with respect to the establishment of a supply system, food was at best scanty, and many of the militiamen therefore began to drift away on foraging expeditions or even simply to desert altogether.[19] Large parts of the front therefore settled down into a tranquillity broken only by sporadic sniping and shelling. 'Life was a mixture of boredom and discomfort', complained Anarchist militiaman, Joaquín Masjuan. 'The only things that broke the monotony were digging more trenches, mounting guard and going out on patrol, while we were filthy dirty and dressed in rags ... On all sides one saw human excrement and empty cans.'[20] When attacks were made, meanwhile, they came to nothing:

> One day they said to us that an assault company of dynamiters was going to be formed. None of us knew anything about dynamite ... but that did

not stop lots of the lads ... from volunteering ... In return, they were given a special cap with a skull and crossbones badge and excused all fatigue duties, and this led some of them to starting throwing their weight about ... and boasting that they were going to win the war. They were wrong. After some time had passed, they got us of bed in the middle of the night, and whisked us off by lorry to some place or other. None of us small fry ... knew anything about what was going on ... but we nevertheless began to ascend a gully that led towards the crest of a ridge. We had just halted near the top to wait for dawn ... when all of a sudden the silence was broken by a hail of machine-gun fire ... Daylight revealed ... nearly half the dynamiters ... lying dead in front of the enemy positions ... This being our baptism of fire, the sight came as a terrible blow.[21]

Both at the time and since, it was the Anarchist contention that if no progress was made on the Aragón front, it is because it was starved of arms by the Communists. 'Had we had abundant arms and munitions', claimed Elías Manzanera, 'it is a certainty that we would have taken Teruel.'[22] In the summer of 1936, however, if the militia fighting in Aragón were getting little support, it was nothing to do with the Communists. Rather, if the Anarchists were fixated with Zaragoza, the Catalan government was equally fixated with the Catalan-speaking Balearic Islands of which just one – Menorca – had remained in friendly hands. Given the strategic importance of the islands, the Catalan Prime Minister, Lluis Companys, was able to win the support of both the local militias and the Madrid government for an operation for their reconquest, and on 16 August a substantial flotilla of ships started putting ashore a mixed force of militiamen and regular soldiers on the east coast of Mallorca under the command of Captain Alberto Bayo, an air-force officer who had, ironically enough, served for several years in the Foreign Legion. Opposition being minimal, within a matter of hours, a substantial bridgehead had been established, but very soon progress slowed to a crawl, while a dozen Italian aircraft, most of them bombers of various types, were rushed to the island to help bolster the defenders. After two weeks of stalemate, the Nationalists launched a counteroffensive, in the face of which the invaders broke and ran, evacuating the island in a panic-stricken flight that resulted in the loss of many prisoners and much *matériel*. In short, the whole operation was little short of a farce, its only effect being to deprive the Aragón front of resources that might possibly have been sufficient to tip the balance against the desperately overstretched Nationalists (it should be remembered that at the start of the war, Mola had no more than 10,000 men with which to defend the whole line from the Pyrenees to Teruel).[23]

Before we move on the much more impressive picture presented by Nationalist military operations, there is one more aspect of the Republican war effort that we must discuss. As we have seen, the government had ended up in control of most of Spain's military aircraft, whilst their share included a good proportion of the military and naval aviation's bombing strength. Even supplemented with a number of hastily converted civilian planes, the aircraft concerned – a motley collection of De Havilland DH89s, Breguet BrXIXs, Vickers Vildebeests, Savoia-Marchetti SM62bis and Macchi M18s – were hardly an impressive force, but they might yet have given effective support to the militia columns. Alternatively, a concentrated effort in the skies above the Straits of Gibraltar might at the very least have slowed down the flood of troops from Morocco to Andalucía. On occasion, true, planes were used tactically – they appeared both at Toledo and Oviedo, not to mention in the battles for the Sierra de Guadarrama (see below) – but for the most part what dominated in these first weeks of the war were vague notions of strategic bombing that led to handfuls of Republican aircraft being sent off to attack rebel-held towns such as Seville and Salamanca. Militarily, nothing could have been more pointless – such pitiful displays could neither inflict much damage nor, still less, terrify the enemy into submission – whilst, in terms of politics, they were a disaster. The number of casualties was far from great, but most of them were civilians, each and every one of whom immediately became bullets in the Nationalists' propaganda arsenal. Where targets were bombed more regularly – the best example is Córdoba – the impact was rather greater (accounts from the city describe both serious disruption to its economic life and growing demoralization among Nationalist supporters), but the episode cannot be counted a success.[24]

Sadly for the Republic, the picture on the other side of the lines could not have been more different. From the beginning, the Nationalist leadership had accepted that the coup might not be entirely successful, and that it might, indeed, face serious resistance. This, however, was factored into their plans, and the rebels knew exactly what do in the event that this proved the case. In brief, in those cities where it was assumed that popular resistance would be strong – above all, Madrid and Barcelona and possibly Bilbao and Oviedo as well – the rebel forces were expected to dig in and wait for relief (something that was generally assumed would be a matter of a few days only). Meanwhile, with what was hoped would be the unanimous help of the navy, the Army of Africa would be rushed in from Morocco, whilst troops from areas of the country where it was assumed that resistance would be non-existent advanced on Madrid and Barcelona. This was a sound enough plan, but the evening of 20 July saw the conspirators in a far worse position than they had ever imagined: not only had a surprising proportion of the army and police backed the government, but they had only a fraction of the navy and air force and were faced with active opposition not just in the places that they had anticipated but also in a whole swathe of territory across eastern, southern and central Spain. In the face of these difficulties, however, the Nationalists did not panic. Instead, such men as they had in mainland Spain mobilized as quickly as possible and got into the field to ward off the main Republican threats. Given their abundant resources, the obvious dangers here were Madrid and Barcelona, and in the first instance, the chief responsibility for fighting the war therefore fell to General Mola as commander of the forces in northern Spain. Whilst the forces that we have already encountered fighting the militias in Aragón moved to take up strategic positions covering the three provincial capitals of Huesca, Zaragoza and Teruel, other troops headed for Sierra de Guadarrama so as to take the capital. Having gone to say goodbye to her fiancé, a Carlist captain named Mario Ozcoidi, Carmen García-Falcés met with a cheerful scene full of optimism and excitement: '[Mario] said they were all off to Madrid, said it as though they were going on an outing. One of his friends was dressed in his ordinary clothes and white shoes. None of us gave it a second thought: they'd all be back soon.'[25]

Given that a number of columns had set out from the capital in the wake of the defeat of General Fanjul and his fellow rebels to frustrate just such an advance, the Sierra de Guadarrama quickly became the scene of the earliest field battles of the Civil War, the focal point for these being the three main passes across the mountains, namely the Alto de León, the Puerto de Navacerrada and the Puerto de Somosierra. All three of these positions had initially been occupied by columns of militia and loyal troops and Assault Guards that had been hastily dispatched from Madrid (albeit not without a struggle in the case of the Puerto de Somosierra, a small column of civilian volunteers of various sorts, led by a young monarchist named Carlos Miralles, having beaten the Republicans to it). However, only at Navacerrada did the situation remain unchanged: at both the Alto de León and the Puerto de Somosierra, improvised columns of regular troops were able to overcome the defenders and even advance a little way the other side. An eyewitness to the fighting at Somosierra was Harold Cardozo: 'There were two batteries of four-inch guns in position: every minute or so they would fire ... It was a slight affair. Fifty ... shells, a few machine-gun [belts], and the whole of the Nationalist advance guard was pouring forward.'[26] On the other side of the lines, this time at the Alto de León, was the Republican writer and journalist Miguel de Heredia, who had offered his services as a stretcher-bearer:

> The rebels had already crowned their conquest of the *sierra* with success, and ... the Republicans were falling back. As they retired, many of the militiamen were fighting in the open ... without making the slightest attempt to make use of the accidents of the terrain ... It was true enough that the insurgents' attacks were as ferocious as they were daring, but the Republicans had no idea how to stop them, no idea of how to dig in.'[27]

In the Sierra de Guadarrama as much as in Aragón and Mallorca, then, the militia were utterly unprepared for the realities of war. Describing her feelings on setting off to the front in a tiny POUM column commanded by her husband, consisting of just 100 men armed with precisely thirty rifles and a machine-gun without a tripod, Mika Feldman de Etchebéhère wrote, 'We were all dreaming of a brilliant career as guerrillas ... The train that had been assigned to us took hours to get connected up: to endure the robbery of so much time from our hope was hard to endure.'[28] Meanwhile, the student Alvaro Cortes Roa admitted that, for him, until he reached the front line, the war was rather like an excursion, albeit a slightly tiring one.[29] In consequence, the results were all but identical to those seen in Aragón. Heavily outnumbered though they were, the Nationalists were able to beat off the clumsy Republican attacks with the greatest ease, while the militia showed all the same faults as they did elsewhere. Typical enough were the scenes witnessed by the novelist Ramón Sender in the town of Guadarrama at the foot of the Alto de León on 23 July:

> There was a company of the Civil Guard and two of the Assault Guard, all in uniforms ... a strong contingent of workers ... [and] three batteries of light artillery ... But an hour passed without anything being done ... The militiamen ... did not seem to bother about anything ... Rifles in their hands, they felt masters of the world ... Two hours later an aeroplane appeared ... [and] we all saluted it, raising our rifles ... When I saw that it was circling over us, I thought that it might be indicating the position of our column to the hostile ... batteries. I kept silence, as it would have been useless to say so ... When it had fulfilled its purpose, it threw out two bombs ... In less than a minute, more than 3,000 rifles were fired. Some of them were aimed at the quickly vanishing aeroplane. Others were directed blindly at open windows ... as many of the militia thought that the attack had come from the centre of town.[30]

The town soon coming under heavy artillery fire, Sender and a few other men made their way up to the top of the pass in some soft transport, only to find themselves facing an impossible task. 'The lorry in front of ours was overturned by a shell: its occupants fell in a heap ... We heard all round us the gusts of machine-guns and got down hastily and scattered in disorder ... The enemy was stationed on the heights in hidden trenches ... and presently their fire came on us from in front and from the flanks ... Other lorries came up the road, but ... could go no further because rifle shots were shattering the windscreens. The men got out and followed us in open waves ... But it was impossible to advance a single step ... We tried to go higher up, but two of us fell and the rest of us threw ourselves on the ground ... Our guns were silent ... And the command? Where was the command? Why were we there without leaders?'[31]

Given the proximity of the capital, a particular problem was the tendency of many columns to motor up to the Alto de León for the day and then return home in the evening.[32] Success, then, was minimal. Particularly in the area west of El Escorial, a column led by a regular-army colonel named Julio Mangada scored some minor successes in the way of over-running country towns that had been taken over by Civil Guards and Falangists, but an attempt to outflank the troops defending the Alto de León by reaching Avila along the line of the main railway line from Madrid to northern Spain soon petered out.[33] Eventually, then, the whole campaign ended in stalemate, with the Nationalists unable to move down into the plains and the Republicans equally unable to conquer the passes. Casualties were not particularly high on either side – it is unlikely, indeed, that they numbered more than a few thousand – but one notable Nationalist loss was the co-founder of Spanish fascism, Onésimo Redondo, in the absence of José Antonio Primo de Rivera perhaps the only member of the Falange with the political weight to have some chance of pressing the claims of the movement in the construction of Nationalist Spain.[34]

So flaccid was the Republican war effort in respect of Mola's troops that 'the Director', as he was still at this point known, was able to launch two offensives of his own. Of these, the first, an attempt to cut the Republican zone on the Cantabrian coast off from France by securing the city of San Sebastián, is more conveniently dealt with elsewhere, and for that reason we shall here restrict ourselves to dealing with the second, namely the effort that was now made to relieve Oviedo. Having got together a small field force consisting of four companies of infantry, one of Assault Guards, a battery of field artillery and some detachments of civilian volunteers under a Lieutenant-Colonel Ceano, the Nationalists had captured the frontier town of Castropol as early as 30 July. With most of the province's combatants bogged down in the battle for Gijón, there was little to oppose them, and within a few days, Ceano had taken Luarca as well. Even when a column of militia finally appeared, the men concerned were immediately put to flight by a few rounds from the cruiser *Almirante Cervera* and the Nationalists' four field guns. Among the crews of the latter was Faustino Vázquez Carril, a young man from Monforte de Lemos who was performing his military service at the time of the uprising: 'For three hours we vomited fire. Abandoning their positions, the Reds took shelter in some houses, but our shrapnel sought them out anyway and forced them to flee once more. Encouraged by the support of our guns, ... the infantrymen and Assault Guards pursued them without mercy ... So decisive an advance could not lead to anything over than a triumph, but it was a poor triumph, for a wolf was fighting a lamb, a lamb with neither teeth nor even wool to cover itself.'[35]

Now commanded by a long-term associate of General Sanjurjo named Pablo Martín Alonso, and given further impetus by the welcome arrival of a detachment of Moorish troops, the *mariscos* ('shell-fish'), as the relief force called themselves, were soon on the advance once more, in the process engaging in extravagant reprisals so as to dissuade the local populace from any thought of guerrilla warfare. On 28 August, troops coming from the south seized the important Puerto de Espina, but thereafter progress slowed dramatically: on the one hand, the fall of Gijón had allowed the defenders to send more men to the western front, men, moreover, who were much better armed than those encountered in the early stages of the advance, and on the other, the Nationalist forces were becoming increasingly exhausted. Nor did it help, meanwhile, that the Republicans had more planes than the Nationalists and frequently bombed Martín Alonso's columns to some effect (on the other hand, lacking anything other than Breguets, they were unable to prevent a re-supply mission that saw 30,000 rounds of ammunition dropped to Aranda by parachute). For several weeks, then, the Nationalists were held up in front of the town of Trubia, whilst they were further harassed by a series of enemy counterattacks that occasioned some disorder. As Vázquez Carril wrote in his diary:

> Today we were being shot at from every side, and yet the enemy could not be seen. Where was he? Pretty close to us, that's for sure. All we know is that we are completely surrounded by the Reds, that bullets are flying thick and fast and that we cannot move a step. How are we going to get out of this? Our campaign looks as if it is going to end right here ... Night is falling, and we have had no supper as our supplies have run out ... They are ordering us to turn in now. What will happen tomorrow?[36]

To the end, the relief force continued to encounter bitter resistance, but the militia were increasingly exhausted. Amongst the defenders was David Granda:

> After a while everyone began to get a bit demoralised. We had been in the trenches for too long and the food was very bad, and there wasn't enough ... so there were always groups of us going off at night without permission to get hold of eggs, a cow or a pig. And we were filthy and tired ... We were fed up with it.[37]

Sooner or later, then, something had to give, and on the night of 17 October, a number of troops slipped through a gap in the Republican lines and reached Aranda's battered positions. The relief of Oviedo was but a side issue, however. Thus, from the very beginning, it was clear that the force on which everything depended was Franco's Army of Africa. Setting aside various service units and the like who were all composed of conscript troops of the regular army, at the heart of this force were the six battalions of the Spanish Foreign Legion and several different forces of Moorish auxiliaries, including, most importantly, the regular infantry and cavalry known as the *regulares* and the *mehal-la jalifiana* (the household troops of the sultan).[38]

Beginning with the Spanish Foreign Legion, some 4,000 strong in 1936, this force had been formed in 1921 specifically for service in the campaign in Morocco, whilst, unlike its French counterpart, it was 'foreign' only to the extent that it served abroad: until the Civil War, almost all its officers and men were Spanish citizens. In part because of the circumstances of its creation, from the beginning, the *tercio*, as it became known, was instilled with a mystique all of its own. Boiled down to its essentials, this consisted of nothing more or less than the glorification of violence for its own sake. Inevitably drawn from the poorest and most desperate sectors of the labouring poor, the rank and file were subjected to a savage code of discipline whose chief purpose was to brutalize the recruit and ready him for atrocity: not for nothing was the war-cry of the Legion 'Long live death!' In the course of the colonial campaigns, then, brutality was tolerated and, indeed, positively encouraged, the chances of the Legion being able to engage in such behaviour being increased by the fact that, particularly towards the end of the fighting, so many of the Spanish army's operations consisted of punitive expeditions. In battle, meanwhile, legionaries were expected to show the utmost heroism – they were referred to as 'the bridegrooms of death' – this expectation being accompanied by a level of military training that far outclassed anything on offer in the rest of the army.[39] Now, of course, this evil mix was going to be directed against Spain's own people rather than a colonial 'other', but in this, the leadership of the Legion were entirely unrepentant: by succumbing to Marxism, the populace – already little better than Moors in the eyes of many of the élite – had effectively excluded itself from the nation and civilized Europe alike. To paraphrase an old saying, then, Africa now ended at the Pyrenees.[40]

Moving on to the Moorish troops, the 15,000 men that these amounted to were motivated by an ethos that was even cruder than that of the Foreign Legion. For the 'gentlemen legionaries', service was a way out of poverty, even, or so it was portrayed, a redemptive experience (one of the issues that admirers of the Legion often stressed was the claim that many of the recruits had criminal backgrounds). However, for the Moors, whilst poverty was an issue, certainly, the one concrete incentive the men were offered was plunder and with this an outlet for traditions that could no longer be indulged in their homeland.

Nor was Morocco's contribution limited to the men in the ranks in July 1936. On the contrary, the next few months saw a rapid expansion of the Moorish forces, the obvious question to ask here being why the colonial power was able to get so many men to fight for it barely ten years after its forces had triumphed in the devastating war of 1909–27. Though the waters have been much muddied by Nationalist attempts to claim that, as devout Muslims, the Moors were horrified by what they perceived as the Frente Popular's attack on religion, the answer was quite simple. In brief, whilst the colonial authorities certainly did everything that they could to persuade the population that the Republicans were the enemies of Allah as much as they were the enemies of God, and, more than that, affected respect for Islam through such gestures as providing a ship to take a large group of pilgrims to Saudi Arabia, Morocco was desperately poor at the best of times, whilst in 1936 in particular, it was experiencing a prolonged drought. First and foremost, then, the reason why so many men came forward was economic: not only did recruits receive a considerable bounty on enlistment, but also the Franco régime took care to increase the wages of its Moorish troops, thereby rendering service still more attractive, many stories also circulating of the booty that was on offer in Spain. Underlying the obvious economic pressures, meanwhile, were other factors that were also of some importance, whether it was a desire for excitement, nostalgia for a lost past of raids and skirmishes or even the hope of killing Spaniards (given that the Spaniards had now been recruiting Moorish troops for over twenty years, it is also possible that in some tribes or family groups, enlisting in the colonial forces had become a matter of tradition).[41]

Whatever the precise reason, recruits were at first forthcoming in large numbers – by October 1936 alone, 15,000 extra troops had been enlisted, whilst the total eventually reached some 62,000. Yet there were limits to what could be achieved. As the months passed, so stories began to reach Morocco of heavy casualties – in all, as many as 11,000 of the recruits may have died by the end of the war – and of continued bullying and racial discrimination, not to mention absence of opportunity, whilst many areas began to suffer from a serious shortage of labour. Nor did it help that more and more men who had lost arms or legs in the struggle were appearing on the streets, many of whom were quickly reduced to begging. By 1938, then, recruitment had slumped considerably, whilst cities such as Larache and Xauen even experienced serious protests at the constant pressure, something that caused particular anger being the false promises that were frequently made by recruitment officers.[42] As the war continued, then, one suspects that the morale and fighting value of the Moorish units fell off considerably, but in the summer of 1936, they were a valuable addition to the Nationalist forces, and not just because of the numbers that they initially represented. In brief, for most Spaniards, the Moor was a demonic 'other' who inspired widespread terror. The widely reported atrocities that had followed the Moorish victory of Anual had not been forgotten, and there were plenty of tales of Moors running amok in Asturias in 1934. Lingering even deeper in the Spanish psyche, meanwhile, were folk memories of the justly dreaded Barbary pirates. As a result, the mere appearance of Moorish troops in Spain was enough to spark panic, whilst the fact that the *regulares* and the rest were actively encouraged to engage in atrocities of various sorts, including, not least, the mutilation of the dead, could not but increase the terror that the idea produced, this last becoming so great that time and again forces of militia broke and ran at the mere idea that they were facing Moorish troops.[43]

Having secured Morocco for the uprising, then, General Franco had a powerful force at his disposal. Before it could be used in action, however, it had first to be got to Spain. In traditional accounts of the Civil War, much weight has been placed here on the help of Hitler and Mussolini, but the truth is that the importance of this factor has been somewhat exaggerated. As we have seen, both Franco and Mola had sent urgent messages to the two dictators begging them for aid, and the result was the arrival in Morocco from 26 July onwards of no fewer than twenty-nine German and Italian bomber transports.[44] Fully operational by the end of the first week of August, these immediately set to work flying ever-increasing numbers of Moors and Foreign Legionaries across the Straits of Gibraltar. Yet in fact, the problem had already been resolved. The vast majority of the navy's ships having remained in the hands of the government thanks to the loyalty of the lower decks, in the wake of the uprising the Republicans enjoyed overwhelming superiority in the waters off southern Spain. Available to them, then, was the battleship *Jaime Primero*, the light cruisers *Libertad* and *Miguel de Cervantes* (all three of which had been sent down from El Ferrol) and the entire contents of the important naval base of Cartagena, namely fifteen destroyers, eight torpedo boats, five gunboats and twelve submarines, whereas, even counting the ships that had been taken over at Cádiz, Franco had no more than five gunboats and one torpedo boat (the light cruiser,

República, was also in Cádiz, but it was laid up and in such a state of disrepair that it was not got back into service till 1938). If their control of the power-ful coastal batteries that protected Cádiz, Ceuta and Melilla alike was of some help, the Nationalists therefore seemingly had a very serious problem on their hands. As in Aragón, however, what saved them was the revolution. All the ships controlled by the Republicans were now in the hands of committees of their crews, but these proved utterly incapable of running them in an effective fashion. Thus, many of the vessels concerned never put to sea at all (admittedly, not all of them were in a state to do so in the first place), whilst those that did proved extremely timid. Setting aside the five Fokkers and Dorniers that were being used to ferry troops to the mainland by air, Franco had just six Breguet BrXIX light bombers and two Nieuport NiD52 fighters, but a series of attacks on the part of these planes proved enough to send the ships blockading Ceuta and Melilla into a hasty retreat: on 5 August 1936, then, the so-called 'convoy of victory' shipped 1,600 men, six 105mm guns and 100 tons of munitions across the water. Stung into a response, the Republicans responded by a brief foray against Cádiz that led to several of the Nationalist vessels in port there being heavily damaged, but thereafter the Straits belonged in large part to the Nationalists, all that the German and Italian aircraft really did being to speed up the process of getting the Army of Africa into action.[45]

To return to the campaign on land, before very long, Franco had amassed a powerful fighting force in south-western Andalucía. Before anything else could be done, however, the Nationalist hold on the area had to be consolidated: while Seville, Córdoba, Granada and Cádiz were all in rebel hands, much of the terri-tory surrounding them was in the hands of the government, or, more precisely, an assortment of revolutionary committees that were usually dominated by the Socialists and the Anarchists. Some early successes had already been scored – on 19 July, for example, a column of miners from the … the Rio-Tinto mining district … who had set out to fight Queipo de Llano in Seville were put to flight in an ambush, the city of Huelva itself being taken ten days later – but even so, the first priority was to put an end to this situation, the result being that a considerable number of the available troops had to be dispatched into the Andalusian countryside in veritable punitive expeditions that achieved their goal amidst the most lurid scenes of looting, rape and mass murder: in Nerva, 288 men and women were executed; in Moguer, 146; in Aroche, 133; in Alcalá de Gudaira, 137; in Arahal, 146; in Puente Genil, 501; in Constantina, 300; and in Lucena, 118.[46] All that was left for active operations was therefore two bat-talions of the Foreign Legion, two battalions of *regulares*, two batteries of light artillery and assorted detachments of signallers and engineers, together with a pair of Bilbao armoured cars.[47] Organized into two columns of roughly equal size under Lieutenant Colonel Carlos Asensio Cabanillas and Major Antonio Castejón Espinosa, on 2 August, these forces headed north from Seville under the overall command of Juan Yagüe Blanco, an erstwhile battalion commander in the Spanish Foreign Legion and admirer of José Antonio Primo de Rivera who had become an ardent adherent of the Falange. At any other moment to have set out to conquer a country with so few troops would have seemed absurdly quixotic, but the overriding emotion in Seville seems to have been one of complete contempt for the enemy. As Queipo de Llano remarked to American journalist Hubert Knickerbocker in respect of the Republican militia: 'They aren't capable of anything but murder, rape, arson and atrocity. They know how to burn priests alive, but they don't know how to fight trained soldiers.'[48]

Entirely motorized as these forces were (albeit solely on the basis of an extraordinary variety of requisitioned civilian cars, lorries and motor-busses), progress was extremely rapid, and all the more as, periodic bombing raids of a fairly ineffectual nature aside, for the most part the only resistance that was encountered came from pathetic bands of labourers armed with the usual array of shotguns.[49] Other than a short-lived counterattack at Los Santos de Maimona by some troops sent out from Badajoz, not until the city of Merida was reached was any sort of regular defence encountered, and even then the defenders did not last long, being easily outflanked and put to flight with the loss of numerous casualties, four machine-guns, two field guns, two armoured lorries and a considerable number of rifles.[50] Pushing on northwards as far as the frontiers of the province of Cáceres, meanwhile, the leading Nationalist elements encountered the southernmost detachments of Mola's nascent Army of the North, thereby securing one of the Nationalists' principal military objectives. Meanwhile, as in the case of Queipo de Llano's efforts to subject the Andalusian countryside, every advance of Yagüe's troops was accompanied by the most savage wave of killing: at Los Santos de Maimona, the number of deaths in the immediate aftermath of the town's capture was 100; in Zafra, forty; and in Villafranca de los Barros, fifty-six.[51]

As yet, however, the union of the two Nationalist zones was far from secure. To the west of Mérida, the fortress city of Badajoz remained firmly in the hands of the government. In the circumstances, then, there was only one thing to do. Three columns of troops were now available, and on 12 August, two of these set out for the city, whilst the small number of aircraft available to the Nationalists – no more, it seems, than four – launched repeated raids against the unfortunate population. Awaiting the onslaught were perhaps 2,500 defenders ensconced behind the parapets of the very same seventeenth-century Vauban-style fortifications that had been bitterly fought over several times in the Peninsular War (though such value as these still possessed was much reduced by the fact that a great breach had been driven through the wall in order to give more convenient access to motor traffic entering the city from the direction of Seville, and the glacis, ravelin and ditch that had once protected the sector levelled in favour of a public park). The usual mixture of regular soldiers, militiamen, Assault Guards and Carabineers, the Republican forces fought bravely when the assault went in at dawn on 14 August, but they were hit not just by a heavy artillery barrage but also repeated bombing raids, and they lacked both the firepower and the training needed to hold back the attackers.[52] At 182 men, or around 10 per cent of Yagüe's forces, Nationalist casualties were comparatively heavy, whilst it took until mid-afternoon for the attackers to get inside the walls, but, as much as anywhere else, the result was a foregone conclusion. For a good account of what happened next, albeit one that comes to us at second hand only, we may turn to the memoirs of María de la Luz Mejías Correa, a young supporter of the JSU who had taken refuge at the village of Higuera de Vargas:

> The rebel troops rounded up and searched all the men that they could find. Anyone who had compromising documents or political insignia, or even simply a shoulder displaying the bruise of a rifle butt, was led off for execution. Meanwhile, the Moors in particular sacked every house and shop they came to, and in addition raped many women. Franco had told them that they were free to engage in such barbarities … Many people had taken refuge … in the cellars beneath the town hall. Amongst them was my brother-in-law, Manolo, who had hidden there with all his family. When the soldiers finally came … they sent the women and children away, but the men were tied up and lined up outside the town hall … and right there … they were all shot … I've no idea how many they killed, but, taking the city as a whole, it was a great many.[53]

A correspondent for the *Diario de Lisboa*, Mario Neves reached the city a day after the battle:

> Stunned by several successive days of air raids, the population have come out on the streets. White flags can be seen in almost every window, and many women are wandering around dressed in mourning. As for the streets, they are a desolate sight, littered as they are with the debris left by the bombing … The damage caused by the raids is very extensive … Amidst the ruins women of the humbler sort are attempting to remove positive himilayas of rubble in a useless search for their possessions, all the while lamenting their misfortune. At the Puerta de Trinidad … the walls are all topped by sandbag barricades and pockmarked with hundreds of bullet holes … The cathedral, on whose tower we have been told that a number of machine-guns were stationed, is badly damaged, while two corpses are still lying in the nave.[54]

Told that the Nationalists had shot at least 2,000 people since the city had fallen, Neves checked the story out and found several places where it was evident that considerable numbers of executions had taken place, most notably in the infantry barracks and certain parts of the ditch that still lined many stretches of the city walls. In both places, many corpses were still on view, but the worst sights by far were to be found in the city's cemetery, where he discovered a pile of some 300 bodies that had been doused in gasoline and set alight, whilst another 30 or more were lying to one side, awaiting the same fate (curiously, he does not mention the city's bullring, this being the site that is most often mentioned in connection with the mass executions). Shocked to the core, Neves pulled no punches in his reporting of the situation:

> I am going home. Cost what it may, I want to get out of Badajoz as quickly as possible, and make a solemn promise to myself that I will never come back. For all the many years that I remain a journalist, I do not believe that I will ever see a sight as affecting as the one that I have encountered in this burning land ... This is no ridiculous extravagance, no excess sentiment. Even the most modest moral formation ... is enough to make it impossible to remain calm in the face of these horrible scenes.[55]

With Badajoz gone, there was little to stop the Nationalists from marching on Madrid, the only troops in their way being half-a-dozen columns of varying sizes scattered broadcast across the seventy-odd miles separating the northern fringes of the plains of eastern Extremadura and the southern fringes of the Sierra de Gredos. Across the southern marches of this space sprawled the rugged Sierra de Guadalupe, but beyond it there was nothing but the undulating plains of the Tagus valley, this leading straight as a dagger deep into the heart of Spain. Nor were there even any Republican troops to clear away before this inviting axis of advance was reached, almost all the towns and villages along the two routes that could be made use of – Miajadas, Trujillo, Almaraz, Navalmoral de la Mata and Guadalupe – being defended by Nationalist garrisons (furthest of all these to the east, Guadalupe, it is true, was currently being hard pressed by a force of militia that had laid siege to it, but, even were it to fall, the more westerly and, indeed, direct of the two roads would still be at the insurgents' disposal). Within a matter of days, then, the Army of Africa was on the move again, 22 August finding the three columns of which its field forces were now composed – those of Asensio Torrado and Castejón Espinosa, along with a fresh one headed by Francisco Delgado Serrano – all together once more at Navalmoral.[56]

After a brief pause, on 28 August, the advance began once again, the militias that had been facing the Nationalists on the frontiers of Extremadura disintegrating almost immediately and leaving considerable quantities of war material behind them as they fled: after just three days, the haul amounted to nineteen 75mm guns, twelve machine-guns, 500 rifles and carbines, three mortars and large amounts of small-arms and artillery ammunition. Taken, too, were the towns of Oropesa and Puente del Arzobispo.[57] There was little attempt at resistance. 'Talavera is blocked up with cars, carts ... mules and asses. At the bridges across the Tagus and the Alberche, there are long queues of soldiers and civilians who are trying to get away. General Riquelme had ordered a number of *dinamiteros* to get the crossings ready for demolition, but three of the men concerned have been seized as saboteurs and executed and their bodies thrown in the water.'[58] Finally, 3 September saw the capture of the area's largest settlement, Talavera de la Reina, by means of a sweeping envelopment that saw the Moors and Foreign

Legionaries advance triumphantly across the battlefield of 1809 in a rapid move that took them as far as the River Alberche. Captured in and around the town were at least another nine guns and howitzers together with yet more rifles and machine-guns, along with an armoured train. Amongst the men who entered the town was a young Carlist whom we know only as Federico: 'At ten o'clock the *regulares* and the Legion advanced to the attack ... The whole thing was a complete rout: very soon 2,000 Reds were leaving their trenches and running towards the town in the hope of storming one of the lorries and busses that were driving off at high speed.'[59]

One important point that is worth making here is that, despite what has often been claimed, the Nationalists did not enjoy any particular superiority in the air over the Tagus valley. Whilst it is true enough that the Junkers and Savoias that had been ferrying troops across the Straits of Gibraltar had now done all that was needed in this respect and could therefore be employed to harass the Republicans, and, further, that they were in theory supported by twelve Fiat Cr32s and six Heinkel He51s, there were other calls on the Nationalist aviation than the march on Madrid: a number of the Fiats were stationed at Córdoba, for example, while José Larios, now a volunteer bombardier and air-gunner, on several occasions found himself attacking targets in Asturias.[60] Also maintenance appears to have been a major problem: by the end of August, no fewer than five of the twelve Fiats that had been dispatched to Morocco were temporarily out of service on account of mechanical problems.[61] At the same time, such as it was, the Republican air force did surprisingly well, 31 August seeing two Fiats being shot down in a dogfight with Republican Nieuport NiD52s and Hawker Furies somewhere in the vicinity of Oropesa.[62]

As can be imagined, in those sectors of the Republican body politic that were not completely blinded by propaganda, alarm was spreading by the day. In fact, however, the situation was slightly less bleak than it at first appeared. Setting aside the fact that Franco's troops had now been continuously on the move for over a month and were now operating a long way from their base, in the first place the Republicans were falling back on their line of communications and could now count on the services of a main railway line to keep their men supplied. On top of this, meanwhile, two important sources of aid had arrived, the first of these being the so-called 'Escadrille d'Espagne' of the wealthy French writer and adventurer André Malraux. A ferocious opponent of fascism and man of broadly leftist principles, but also an ardent self-publicist, no sooner had the war broken out than Malraux approached the Spanish and French governments with an offer to fund what, to all intents and purposes, amounted to a private air force. Seeing the offer as a means of doing at least something for its fellow Popular-Front régime, the government of Léon Blum fell in with this scheme, as, naturally enough, did the beleaguered Giral government, and the result was that September saw the arrival in Spain of twenty Potez Po540 bombers and a somewhat lesser number of Dewoitine D371 fighters. This was scarcely an impressive force – all the planes involved were, at best, obsolescent, whilst they were also delivered with neither machine-guns nor gun-sights – and any idea that it was crewed by dedicated foreign anti-fascists can be discarded (the pilots and observers were nothing more than mercenaries, pure and simple). Yet in the situation that pertained in the Republican zone in the late summer of 1936, almost anything was better than nothing (not that Malraux achieved very much: even had he known more about air fighting – something that was hardly difficult – he simply did not have the means to do much more than make a show, and in the end, he made himself so unpopular by his general bombast that his return to France in 1937 was greeted with great relief).[63]

Rather more effective than the Escadrille d'Espagne was the so-called 'Quinto Regimiento' or Fifth Regiment. Possessed of its curious name on account of the fact that it was born of a short-lived plan to double the four infantry regiments contained in the garrison of Madrid and originally intended to be the first of these units, this was a brain-child of the Communist Party. As we have already seen, this organization was bitterly opposed to the Spanish revolution, in part because it had little purchase with the Spanish masses, and, in part too, because a left-wing upheaval in Spain ran clean counter to the foreign policy of the Comintern. At the same time, however, it did not want to lose the war and was genuinely anxious to fight the insurgents, and the result was the emergence of a commitment to what was really the only possible way forward, namely the formation of a militia that would be run on military lines, thereby simultaneously undermining the credibility of the other left-wing movements, reassuring the working classes that the Communist Party was committed to fighting fascism, demonstrating to the middle classes that they had a place in the new Spain, establishing a model for the new army that was so obviously needed and, last but not least, giving the Communists a fighting force that they could, if necessary, turn on the Anarchists and the POUM.[64]

In embarking on this policy, the Communists could draw upon the ardent militants of the JSU, not to mention the help and advice of both the increasing number of Comintern agents who had been appearing in Spain from well before the uprising and several trusted militants who had been sent to Moscow some years before to receive a degree of military training (the most important were Juan Modesto and the same Enrique Lister we met in the Sierra de Guadarrama).[65] Also helpful, beyond doubt, was the growing Soviet diplomatic and military presence, the Russian ambassador appointed in consequence of the formal establishment of diplomatic relations between the Soviet Union and the Spanish Republic on 21 August, Marcel Rosenberg, bringing with him an enormous staff.[66] Hardly surprisingly, then, the Fifth Regiment proved a great success. In the course of the next few months, at least 20,000 men passed through its training courses before being channelled into special shock units called the 'Companies of Steel', whilst many of the better qualified recruits were trained as junior officers in the organization's own military academy.[67] Among the units formed was also a women's battalion, but there is no firm evidence that this ever saw combat, and it seems likely that it was never intended to do so, the aim being rather to create some sort of auxiliary force.[68] Needless to say, the Communist propaganda machine made all it could of the results – for example: 'It is very agreeable to be with the Fifth Regiment. Its ranks are a refuge from confusion and disorder, and one is comforted to see the outline of the people's army of tomorrow: although its members look much the same as everyone else around them, they act, think and speak in a different manner – with a certain internal eye, with a certain sense of responsibility'[69] – but it is clear that in many ways the new force was not much better than its predecessors.[70] That said, the Fifth Regiment was not just a crowd of individuals, however enthusiastic: there was no debating of orders and no election of officers, and it is no coincidence that it was from the time of its first appearance that the Nationalists began to have to wage pitched battles on a regular basis.[71]

Meanwhile, it was not just at the front that things were changing. Back in Madrid, the all-Republican Giral government had rapidly been losing all such prestige as it had ever had, and 5 September therefore saw it replaced by a new administration headed by the Socialist leader Francisco Largo Caballero. Composed of representatives of all the main forces in the Republican camp other than the Anarchists and the POUM, the new régime, it was hoped, would be better able to galvanize the working classes and, at the same time, impose the degree of order that was so badly needed.[72] In so far as these objectives were concerned, Largo Caballero certainly did his best. Thus, already in the habit of paying frequent visits to the front dressed in the one-piece overall common among the militia, he was appointed Minister of National Defence and Commander-in-Chief as well as Prime Minister, and now took personal charge of every aspect of the war effort and embarked on the task of subjecting the forces of the Left to the authority of the government and giving a more military form to their motley ranks. As he told the Soviet correspondent Mikhail Koltsov on 8 September, 'My first objective is assuring the complete unity of command and authority ... A complete review of the militia units is being organised ... We are continually receiving exorbitant demands ... for money with which to pay their wages. The sums are enormous: the treasury is not a tunnel with no end: we must have a budget, a plan, accountability.'[73]

In the circumstances of the revolution that gripped the Republican zone, militarizing the war effort was far from easy. Nevertheless, little by little, a degree of order began to be imposed on the situation. In an important move that spelt the beginning of the end for the Red Terror, most of the self-proclaimed heroes of 18 July who had for weeks continued to throng the streets were gradually either disarmed or forced to leave for the front. In recognition of the fact that voluntary enlistment had at best proved insufficient – a fact implicit in the ever more strident efforts of the Communists, Socialists and Anarchists to galvanize the population of Madrid into mass resistance – the first steps were taken towards the use of conscription. And, finally, each of the four geographical zones into which the Republican war effort could be divided was given a single commander, in the case of central Spain one José Asensio Torrado, an *africanista* major who had played an important part in the defeat of the rising in Madrid and had since made something of a name for himself in the Ministry of Defence.[74]

Hastily promoted to the rank of general, Asensio Torrado made an immediate difference on the crucial Tagus-valley sector. Putting the fresh troops who were already being rushed to the front from all directions to good use, within a day of his appointment, he had managed to organize a major counterattack on the line of the River Alberche that was only defeated after three days of heavy fighting.[75] Yet his efforts gained the Republican forces little respite. For a few days, the area fell quiet due to the need to make contact with elements of Mola's forces who had been pushing southwards through the Sierra de Gredos, but on 11 September, the Nationalists renewed their operations. In the meantime, however, a crucial decision had been taken that is often argued to have weighed heavily on the course of the war. In brief, at the town of Santa Olalla, some thirty miles to the east, Franco's forces would have a choice in that they could either march directly on Madrid by way of the main Extremadura highway or strike due eastwards along the River Tagus so as to relieve the *alcázar* of Toledo. After much debate, Franco plumped for the latter, and it has frequently been argued, most notably by Paul Preston, that this cost the Nationalists their best chance of a rapid victory – indeed, that at the very least, Franco sacrificed the military objective of winning the war as quickly as possible in favour of his personal ambitions, the relief of the *alcázar* being the key to realizing his desire to become leader of the uprising.[76] This is going too far, however. That the commander of the Army of Africa was deeply ambitious, no-one would deny, but rushing headlong on Madrid was highly questionable, not least because it came with the danger that the Republican forces besieging the *alcázar* might seize the opportunity to attack him in the rear. In the circumstances, then, saving the *alcázar* was everything: to allow it to fall when the Nationalist forces were within a day's march of its walls would have been both to hand the Republic a massive propaganda victory and to open the way to military disaster. That said, it cannot be denied that sacrificing Moscardó would also have ruined Franco's chances of rising to the top in Nationalist Spain, and there were plenty of officers who were genuinely appalled at the decision. So critical, indeed, was the committed Falangist Yagüe that on 24 September, he was replaced by José Varela Iglesia, an *africanista* of extremely humble origins who was one of only four men ever to win the Cruz Laureada de San Fernando (Spain's equivalent of the Victoria Cross) twice over, and was to emerge as easily the most talented of Franco's generals.[77]

Whatever the thinking behind the decision, on 11 September, the fighting resumed, the three columns of Nationalist troops striking due east across the Alberche. In doing so, however, they encountered more obstacles than had ever been the case previously: with the direction of the Nationalist thrust all too obvious, the way was blocked with successive lines of trenches, some of them reinforced by barbed-wire entanglements and pillboxes, while the Republicans were constantly reinforced by men sent forward from the rear (even allowing for casualties, Republican records show that between 9 and 23 September, the

number of men in the Tagus valley rose from 10,200 to 22,800).[78] Resistance
was still patchy, with many units continuing to succumb to panic – according
to Lister, for example, his unit of the Fifth Regiment beat off several attacks at
Cazalegas but had to withdraw when enemy units managed to get across the
river further north[79] – but even so, it took the Nationalists over a week to fight
their way two-thirds of the distance to Toledo, and that despite the fact that they
were reinforced by a fourth column under the command of Fernando Barrón,
many comments agreeing that the Republican artillery, in particular, was served
much better than had been the case in the past. One Republican participant
in the fighting at the River Alberche was the Communist commander Juan
Modesto: 'Running into well trained forces of a type they had not expected,
the enemy suffered heavy losses ... Our armoured train got into the very midst
of them, and, catching them in the most open terrain possible, made a regular
fight of it.'[80] Thereafter, however, progress was more rapid. As the same Carlist
volunteer we met at Talavera wrote in a letter to his wife, 'On this front not a
day passes on which the Reds escape without a tremendous beating: they throw
away their equipment and their weapons ... in a manner fit to die for.'[81] Fleeing
their defensive positions, the desperate militias invariably made for the nearest
roads in the hope of finding transport, only to find that they then became easy
targets for Nationalist aircraft and machine-guns. As for such prisoners as were
taken, these were wiped out by mass executions such as the one that cost the lives
of seven truckloads of men in the main street of Santa Olalla on 21 September.[82]
For an excellent account of the scenes that resulted, we have only to turn to
Harold Cardozo:

> The road all the way to Maqueda was strewn with bodies ... The stench ...
> was sickening, and the ghastly spectacle lasted for some twenty miles ... At
> one road crossing there was a Red armoured car, a rough-and-ready thing,
> made in some iron factory in Madrid ... There were five dead men around
> it. They were all black in the face and their bodies were twisted and set in
> their agony.[83]

Despite a series of desperate Republican attacks along the axis of the Madrid
highway in the area of Maqueda, on 25 September, the Nationalists got across
the River Guadarrama, the last obstacle between them and Toledo. Here at least
the Escadrille d'Espagne was not without effect. Cecil Gerahty, for example,
was a right-wing newspaperman who was caught in a raid at the broken bridge
over the River Guadarrama that had, before the war, carried the main road from
Maqueda to Toledo:

> The conversation at this point was interrupted by loud cries of 'Enemy
> aviation in sight!' And there certainly were: fourteen big Russian planes
> [sic: there were no Russian planes operational at this point, what Gerahty
> saw rather being Potez Po540s] heading straight for us. Nobody was under

the least delusion as to our being the target, for we presented an ideal objective: with the bridge as centre ... within a half-circle of a quarter-of-a-mile radius, [we] had engineers working on the temporary bridge, troops digging a temporary roadway to and from the river, and some hundreds of lorries, ambulances, guns and staff-cars all parked closely together ... It was impossible to see the effect as dense clouds of smoke and yellow fumes hid everything on the ground ... Several bombs fell within thirty yards and the concussion was terrific.[84]

In the end, however, Malraux's flyers could only delay the inevitable, and then not by very much. By nightfall the following day, the Nationalists had all but cut the Toledo's communications with Madrid and were now literally in sight of the *alcázar*. In the meantime, this was the moment when the Spanish Civil War made its most famous addition to the English language: as Mola observed, there were four columns operating against the capital of Spain and a fifth one waiting to receive them within its walls.[85]

As could hardly be avoided, 27 September was therefore a day of the utmost drama. At five in the morning, Lister launched the attack described by Antonio Gómez de Zamora, but at the very same time, the forces of Barrón, Castejón and Asensio Cabanillas were attacking the outskirts of the city barely a mile away. Progress was slow: in the bullring especially, the defenders held out for a considerable time, and Nationalist casualties were very heavy. Caught between two fires, Gómez de Zamora snatched a moment to write another note in his diary: 'The struggle is desperate. Every moment the combats at the gates are more intense. Various places – bullring, the school of gymnastics, the cemetery – are changing hands without cease. House by house, courtyard by courtyard, flight-of-stairs by flight-of-stairs, hand-to-hand, we are fighting it out with hand grenades ... A real hell!'[86] Wandering the streets after he entered the city, Cardozo bore witness to the ferocity of the struggle: 'I saw one house which had been used as a Red redoubt. Its doors and windows were breached by hand-grenades and a dozen ragged, bloody corpses lay ... clenched as death had met them ... In that first rush no surrenders were accepted, and the Reds were shot down, bombed or bayoneted without mercy.'[87] As the day wore on, however, so it became painfully obvious that the Nationalists were steadily gaining the upper hand. Faced by this situation, most of the militia fled in all directions:

No sooner had we left the trench ... than we found ourselves under fire from Franco's reinforcements ... Bullets were ricocheting past us from front and rear alike, and people were dropping dead on all sides ... In the course of our retreat we had to get across the bridge that lies at the very foot of the *alcázar*. As it was being bombed, quite a few men threw themselves into the river with their rifles and tried to swim for it: many drowned, but others made it to the other side.[88]

Those who got away were lucky. Several substantial parties of militiamen were trapped inside such buildings as the Archbishop's palace, the hospital of Santa Cruz and the diocesan seminary and were wiped out to the last man in the course of mopping-up operations the next day.[89] Meanwhile, any militiamen whose surrender was accepted faced short shrift: October alone saw the execution of no fewer than 835 supporters, supposed or otherwise, of the Popular Front.[90] As for the *alcázar*, it was finally relieved at nine o'clock in the evening (an event that was reconstructed two days later for a propaganda film in which a beaming Franco was shown being welcomed into the fortress by Moscardó and his fellow defenders).[91]

With Toledo in the hands of the Nationalists, an attack on Madrid could not be long delayed, but before we consider this subject, we must first review developments in the Republican war effort, for it was precisely at this moment that the new army that was to postpone Nationalist victory until 1939 came into being. At the heart of this process lay not so much the call-up of fresh conscripts (this process was not begun until December) as the incorporation, forcible or otherwise, of the militias into new structures, the fact that this would be the case being symbolized by the renaming of the General Inspectorate of Militias as the Military Command of Militias, and the announcement as early as 11 September that all men enrolled in the militia were henceforth part of the regular army and therefore subject to military discipline. As to the form the new army should take, this was more complex, but there was general agreement that a return to the terminology of the old army was inappropriate, the way forward eventually being found in the concept of the mixed brigade (for much the same reason, unchanged as they were since days of the monarchy, the rank badges worn by the officers were swept away and replaced by a new system whose centre-piece was the red star). Whilst various theories have been put forward as to why this decision was adopted, the most plausible is that it was a conscious attempt to copy the practice typical of the Moroccan Wars, these having being waged by mobile columns of all arms that in the event of trouble could at least for a time sustain themselves on their own until such time as a relief force arrived.[92] However, in the current circumstances, to follow such a model was utterly irrelevant. In August and September, true, the forces of Yagüe and Varela had been organized in just this fashion and had done very well with it, but all the signs were that a time was approaching when the fighting was going to be taking place on a much greater scale, and, by extension, one that would need to be organized in some other way. A cross between a reinforced regiment and a very small division, however, the mixed brigade was not fit for the purpose for which it was adopted, and the decision to select it may in fact be rated as one of the worst decisions of the entire war. In the first place, there was the issue of the proliferation of staff appointments: consisting, as it was supposed to, of four rifle battalions, an artillery battalion, an engineer company, a signals company, a supply company and a medical company, the mixed brigade needed a very well-staffed headquarters, and this in turn meant that the new force – the People's Army – would require approximately three times as many staff officers and headquarters personnel than one based on the more conventional model of brigades made up solely of battalions of infantry or squadrons of cavalry. Nor was this the end of it: by splitting up the artillery, in particular, the striking power of this last was gravely reduced, it having been a basic principle of military thought ever since the time of Napoleon that artillery should be concentrated in large masses that could not just kill but also terrify.[93]

Thanks to the decision to adopt the mixed brigade as its basic unit, the People's Army was crippled as a fighting force almost from its very inception. As if all this was not bad enough, meanwhile, the decree of 16 October 1936 that formally initiated its history introduced yet another level of complication in the form of the Political Commissariat. Conscious of the pressing need to employ many officers of the old army including some whose loyalty could not be trusted, under pressure from not just the Communists but also the growing number of Soviet advisors, eager to protect his revolutionary credentials, and, last but not least, well aware that the militarization of the militias was unlikely to be popular with many of their members, Largo Caballero agreed that at every level of command, from company upwards, there should be a political commissar. In theory, these men, who were organized in a special corps headed by the Socialist Foreign Minister, Julio Alvarez del Vayo, did not have any military role, being intended rather to look after the welfare and other interests of the rank and file, to help in the upholding of military discipline and to foment enthusiasm for the struggle by means of a wide range of propaganda activities, but in practice the situation was otherwise, especially as part of their duties was to keep watch on the loyalty of any professional officers with whom they might be serving. In some cases, the commissars (in theory, a body of men who were selected on an extremely rigorous basis that laid great stress on a proven record of political militancy) may have done a good job in keeping up morale and ensuring harmony and political commitment in their units, whilst the sheer number of trench newspapers that survive in the Spanish archives suggests that many of them worked extremely hard, but in the end it is hard to see how the same job could not have been done by other means, the chief result of the decision to form the Political Commissariat therefore in the end being to burden the People's Army with yet another layer of bureaucracy.[94]

Nor was it just the question of the Political Commissariat's ability to function without hampering the military command. Also a key issue was the provenance of the commissars. Though a Socialist, Alvarez del Vayo was very much on the left wing of the party and a supporter of Largo Caballero's push to unify the PSOE and the PCE, and this led him to pack the new body, if not with out right Communists, then certainly with Socialist militants who had taken the same position as he had and now thronged the ranks of the PSUC and the JSU. As time went on, then, the increasingly poisonous atmosphere that reigned in Republican Spain was reflected in the People's Army, and the latter opened up to ever greater degrees of Stalinist terror. To quote an observer whose bitter anti-communism does not mean that his views are necessarily devoid of truth:

> There were plenty of commissars of good faith who gave their lives in the holocaust of patriotism and liberty, dying at the head of their units, and there were others who worked honourably for the highest motives. For these, my greatest respect. But, undoubtedly, the mistaken activities of the Commissariat contributed notably to the adverse course of the war. Such things naturally aroused hatred and suspicion among men who were fighting for the same cause. Political differences were increased and passions rose high ... The plan consistently followed by the Communists to get command of the People's Army was stifling.[95]

For the moment, however, all this lay in the future, and all the more as in the first instance there were simply no units to which any commissars could be appointed. Here, however, help was at hand. In the first place, in Madrid, in particular, there remained a few fragments of the old army that had remained more-or-less intact. When Miguel de Heredia reported to his old unit, the First Tank Regiment, for example, he found it remarkably unchanged 'There were three officers there from my time, a captain and two lieutenants ... At a time when the Republic's armed forces were in a state of complete chaos, my regiment had conserved its integrity and even its discipline. Except for a committee of soldiers ... everything went on in the same way as before as if nothing was happening ... There were 130 soldiers ... But why weren't those soldiers at the front? And, incomplete or not, what on earth did the regiment think it was doing carrying on the life of a peacetime garrison?'[96] In the second place, there were a cluster of battalions that had been formed as a result of the Giral government's attempt to set up a new army on the basis of volunteers. And in the third place, the leaders of the Fifth Regiment cheerfully put the whole of their followers at Largo Caballero's disposal, thereby ensuring that men such as Lister and Modesto were immediately promoted to senior commands.[97]

Much more pressing than the need for men was therefore the need for officers. Whilst many officers had continued to serve the Republic – a figure often quoted is 3,500 out of the total of 15,000[98] – captains and lieutenants were thin on the ground, and many of the men were considered too old for service in the field. As early as 11 August, then, the Giral government had decreed the establishment of a new military academy, and other authorities, including, most notably, the governments of Euzkadi (see Chapter 6) and Catalonia, soon followed suit.[99] Thanks to the opposition of elements of the CNT, which, rightly perhaps, argued that such moves could not but lead to the commissioning of numerous representatives of the bourgeoisie, no progress was made in respect of the Giral initiative, whilst an attempt to resuscitate it on the part of Largo Caballero by means of a decree of 15 September was delayed in its implementation by the fact that the military installations chosen as the homes of three new academies that were then envisaged all happened to be in the southern suburbs of Madrid, with the result that they were overrun before they open their doors. In the course of the winter, six fresh sites were found, four of them in the Levante, one in Bilbao and one in Gijón, and by January 1937, they were turning out the first of what proved to be almost 7,000 graduates.[100] For the time being, however, all that could be done was to confirm the leaders of the militia in their existing roles, and that despite the fact that many of them owed their position to nothing other than their posts in some party or trade-union hierarchy.[101]

These efforts to build a new army were in the meantime being boosted by one other source of strength. For the Left in Europe and, indeed, throughout the world, the outbreak of the Spanish Civil War had sounded a clarion call to which it could not but respond with alacrity: from the point of view of Communists and the more reformist elements of the Socialists, democracy was in danger from fascism and had to be defended, while from the point of view of the revolutionary Left, the Spanish people were throwing off their shackles and building a new world. A large number of foreigners of a Socialist or Communist persuasion had happened to be present in Barcelona on 18 July on account of the fact that the city was on the verge of playing host to the People's Olympiad, and, like Felicia Browne, the British artist killed on the Aragón front in late July, many of these had immediately joined the militias, either as individuals or in small national groups. Across the border, there soon came many others, for the most part political exiles from Germany, Italy and eastern Europe who had taken refuge in France, but also numbers of French and English who had simply felt the need to come to Spain to see what they could do (an example is the Richard Kisch we met describing the situation in Barcelona).[102]

Spontaneity, however, was soon replaced by organization. In brief, in Russia, the uprising had been regarded with great concern, not least because a France threatened by a 'fascist' Spain would hardly be likely to be able to do much to honour the provisions of the 1935 Franco–Soviet Pact. As defeat followed defeat, so this concern deepened, whilst there was also a growing desire to stifle the revolution. At a special meeting of the Comintern on 26 August, it was therefore proposed that a force of international volunteers should be organized to fight in Spain, it being envisaged that this would essentially be a Communist venture, albeit one whose gates would be thrown open to all men of a progressive or democratic persuasion.[103] Very soon, then, the initial trickle of volunteers had become a flood: perhaps three-quarters of them Communists or even more, by the end of September 1936, some 5,000 men had arrived at the base that was set up to receive the recruits at Albacete, and it is probable that this number had doubled by the end of the year. The vast majority of the recruits were French, Italian, German, Polish or Yugoslav, but amongst the scattering of other nationalities were to be found two small groups of Britons, of which one ended up in the French Commune-de-Paris battalion and the other in the German Thaelmann battalion, whilst perhaps one-half had some form of military training. Also in attendance were the survivors of the early battles in Aragón, the only foreigners to remain with the militia being a tiny number of dissidents who had elected to enlist with the Anarchists or the POUM, such as Clara Thalmann, a left-wing Swiss journalist who fought in the Durruti column, and Georges Kopp, the naturalized Belgian engineer of Russian origin who was to become George Orwell's commanding officer.[104] As for officers and administrative personnel, these were provided by the party hierarchy or the Red Army (in the form of German and Austro-Hungarian deserters and prisoners of war who had rallied to Communism in the wake of the February Revolution and gone on to forge successful military careers under Lenin and Stalin).[105]

As yet, none of these forces, whether Spanish or international, were ready for action, whilst they were still for the most part very poorly armed. However, the situation in the Republican zone was clearly changing and the balance beginning slowly to tilt against the exhausted Nationalists. To call a halt, however, was not an option – indeed, it was clearly more necessary to press on than ever. For a few days, however, the Nationalist war effort was set aside in favour of politics. In brief, a pressing need had arisen for both the appointment of a commander-in-chief and a concentration of political authority, the various regional commanders having been to a very large extent acting independently of one another, even if it was the case that most of them had been trying to follow the provisions of the plan laid down by Mola prior to the outbreak of hostilities. With the benefit of hindsight, it is easy to assume that Franco, a figure, after all, who had amassed great prestige in right-wing and, more especially, *africanista* circles prior to 1936, was the obvious man to take command of the insurrection: not only had the Army of Africa rallied to him virtually to the last man, but it represented by far the most important fighting force in the whole of Spain and her overseas dominions. In the past, incautious writers have frequently fallen into the trap of implying that he was the leader of the insurrection right from the beginning. This, however, was not the case: Franco's refusal to commit himself to the military coup till the last minute did nothing to endear him to his fellow generals, whilst the two weeks that passed without him being able to take any active role in the fighting meant that the role of hero of the hour, to his great disgust, passed to Mola. To drive home the point, indeed, he was not at first made a member of the military directorate that the latter established to head the uprising under the presidency of the white-bearded Miguel Cabanellas. Needless to say, Franco was not prepared to accept such a snub, and all the more so as his control of the Army of Africa had combined with the widespread failure of Mola's arrangements on the mainland to fill him with the idea, probably for the first time, that he could aspire to something other than being just one general among many others, and he therefore began to strain every muscle to attract support among the Nationalists' civilian backers (in this respect, his use of the radio was especially intelligent) and secure a monopoly of the supply of arms from Germany and Italy, this last being something in which he was quickly successful. Gradually, then, his position improved – somewhat grudgingly, Cabanellas and his colleagues had both to put him in command not just of Morocco, but the whole of southern Spain, and give him a seat on the military junta – and by the time that he was approaching Toledo there was little option but to recognize him as commander-in-chief and head of the government as was agreed at a conference held at Salamanca on 21 September. Yet Franco was not finished, a proclamation issued at his capital of Burgos on 1 October unilaterally proclaiming him to be head of state as well.[106]

Whilst there were many commanders, Alfonsine monarchists, Falangists and Carlists who were outraged by Franco's behaviour, there was little that they could do about it short of declaring themselves in a state of open revolt, and no guarantee of success even if they did. If Franco would doubtless not be easily pardoned were his plans to come to grief on the battlefield, the Nationalist camp was simply not in a position to challenge him whilst he was winning battles. Within a matter of days, then, his war machine was in action again: now organised in five columns – those of Asensio Cabanillas, Castejón, Barrón and Delgado plus a cavalry column that had been brought in from Avila under the command of José Monasterio Ituarte – on 6 October, the troops who had been operating in the Tagus valley struck northwards on a broad front stretching from Maqueda to Toledo, while other forces in the western part of the Sierra de Guadarrama occupied the territory west and south of El Escorial that had been seized by Mangada immediately after the uprising. In a gesture to Mola, meanwhile, on 1 October, the troops fighting under Varela had all been made part of a new Army of the North that was placed under his command, all the Nationalist forces south of the River Tagus being at the same time given to Queipo de Llano as the Army of the South.[107]

At the time that the offensive began, the fifty-mile front between the foothills of the Guadarrama mountains and the River Tagus was protected by no more 10,000 men and twenty guns. Initially, then, progress was extremely rapid, and all the more so as the theatre of operations consisted of rolling plains that were almost completely devoid of natural obstacles. Around the main towns, true, the Republicans had built impressive networks of trenches and pillboxes, but these were easily outflanked and, in any case, often proved defective in their construction. Amongst the men in the area nearest to Toledo was Ramón Sender: 'Our advanced troops were under machine-gun fire from the church tower of Bargas, on which the enemy had a post of observation ... We had no batteries with which to reply to his guns ... The militia had no weapons other than rifles ... The fronts ... were badly disorganised, especially ours. The government wished to arrange fixed lines, but it was facing an enemy of great mobility who always avoided frontal attacks.'[108] Within a matter of days, then, the front had been pushed forward to the towns of San Martín de Valdeiglesias and Santa Cruz de Retamar, and the unfortunate Republican columns caught in the way of the offensive put to flight, leaving behind the usual array of booty of all sorts: at the former town, indeed, the fight was over so quickly that an entire battalion of militia were taken prisoner as they were being served a meal, the latter immediately being fallen upon with great avidity by their delighted captors.[109]

After a brief pause, now supported by the first Nationalist tank unit – a company of Italian L3 tankettes[110] – the attack was renewed once again, and by 18 October, the front ran from Illescas to Chapinería. With Madrid scarcely thirty miles away, Harold Cardozo was as close to the scene of the action as he could possibly get:

> October 17th was the day when the real march on Madrid began ... The troops leap-frogged each other, gaining five kilometres in an hour ... With such open country it was possible to follow closely every incident of the fight. Machine-gun posts could be seen pushing out to a flank, taking advantage of every bit of cover ... Then there would come the moment ... when the rot would set in, and one could see ... lines of men making for the rear.[111]

For the first time, meanwhile, an important part in the Nationalist success was played by the concentrated use of airpower:

> Two squadrons of bombers appeared over Bargas. They were trimotors. They had hardly come over our lines when we saw three other squadrons arriving from the same quarter ... The aeroplanes made a wide sweep round the area of battle ... Bombs of 100 and 200 pounds came one after another. Soon a thick grey cloud rose over Olias ... The concussion ... shook the whole area.[112]

Nor was it just bombers that the Republicans had to deal with. Here, for example, is the acting commander of the Republican air force, Ignacio Hidalgo de Cisneros:

> I was flying over the *sierra* in a Nieuport when I saw a patrol of three aircraft coming from the direction of the enemy's territory. Thinking that the planes were three Breguets ... I gained height in order to attack them. However, as they came closer and I could see them better, I immediately identified them as Italian Fiat fighters. I knew these planes well as I had seen them many times and even flown them when I was at the embassy in Rome. Needless to say, I spun on my axis and returned to Getafe in a state of considerable alarm ... for the Italian fighters were greatly superior ... to our Nieuports.[113]

As Hidalgo de Cisneros predicted, the Republican aviators therefore suddenly found themselves under much greater pressure. Oloff de Wet was amongst the variety of mercenaries piloting Malraux's machines: 'Enemy fighters come over the aerodrome nearly every day. By the time we have our machines up, they are away. None of us is sorry: how can we with our handful of aircraft – only eighteen – now compete with the regular Italian and German units of the rebels? Heinkels, Heinkels and, if it is not the Germans that swarm on top of us, then it is the Italians in their Fiats.'[114] By mid- October, indeed, so many aircraft had been lost or damaged that at one point the only fighter that the Republicans had in action on the Madrid front was a solitary Hawker Fury.[115]

Yet the Republicans were far from beaten. Behind the lines, there were plenty of militiamen who had not yet been involved in the fighting, while, with every step that they fell back, the line that they had to defend contracted. At the same time, though by no means a great commander, Asensio Torrado was at least an energetic personality convinced of the need to take the war to the enemy. Re-organizing the columns that had been beaten and improvising fresh ones from the forces still in Madrid, on 20 October he was therefore able to mount a serious counterattack at Illescas with a force of some 7,000 men that was only driven back after several days of heavy fighting, the troops of Barrón in particular suffering more than 300 casualties.[116] Back in Madrid, meanwhile, an ever more frenetic campaign of propaganda sought to encourage men to volunteer for the front and in general stiffen resistance, whilst Largo Caballero also re-organized the high command, giving the command of the garrison of Madrid to José Miaja and promoting the latter's predecessor, Sebastián Pozas, to the command of the Army of the Centre, Asensio Torrado in his turn becoming Largo Caballero's chief adviser in the Ministry of War. The aim of all this was to respond to the ever-growing criticism, much of it politically motivated, of Asensio's handling of the fighting, whilst at the same time allowing the premier to retain the latter's counsel and support.[117] Last but not least, immense efforts were made to protect Madrid with a triple line of fortifications blocking every access to the capital from the south and west, though it would obviously be a considerable time before these works could be completed.[118]

However, much more important than all this was a new twist in the international situation. As we have seen, the prospect of a Nationalist triumph in Spain had been becoming a matter of ever greater concern in Moscow, and in mid-September, a point was reached when Stalin felt that he could be no longer bound by the provisions of the Non-Intervention Pact: alienate the French though he might by breaking it, a 'fascist' Spain looked certain to cost him far more, while even Stalin could not afford to ignore the ever-increasing chorus of complaint from senior figures in the Comintern that he was doing nothing to help the Spanish working classes. At the same time, too, he also sensed an opportunity: the cause of the Spanish Republic being an ideal medium by which Russian public opinion could be mobilized in support of a régime that had inflicted untold misery upon the populace, hence the dispatch to Madrid of some of the leading lights of Soviet journalism, including Ilya Ehrenburg and Alexander Koltsov, and a team of photographers and film makers. From the beginning of September, then, preparations got under way to send arms to Spain whilst the international committee set up to administer non-intervention was presented with an ultimatum to the effect that, if Italy and Germany did not desist from their repeated breach of their obligations under the original pact, Russia would feel free to act entirely as she thought fit. No satisfactory response being received in this respect, the last days of September saw no fewer than sixteen ships depart from Odessa for the Republic's Mediterranean ports.[119]

As can be imagined, the arrival of the first of these ships – the *Komsomol* – in Cartagena was a cause for much celebration. Yet close consideration of the arms that the Republic received suggests that the response ought to have been more wary. To pay for the shipments, Largo Caballero had agreed to transfer the Bank of Spain's immense gold reserves to Moscow, and the fortune that these represented should have ensured that the Republic got the very best of everything. In reality, however, this was very far from being the case. Some of the 'headline' material, certainly, was very good, indeed absolutely excellent: amongst the cargo retrieved from the ten ships that had docked by the end of October were thirty Tupolev SB2 bombers, seventy-one Polikarpov I15 and I16 fighters, fifty T26 tanks, sixty FA1, BA3 and BA5 armoured cars and 150 DP light machine-guns, all of which were in front-line service with the Russians and the equal, or, indeed, more than the equal, of anything that was in service elsewhere (with its 45mm gun, the T26, in particular, was justly regarded as the best tank in the world, whilst the Polikarpovs far outclassed the He51 and were at least the equal of the Cr32, just as the Tupolevs were superior to the Nationalist Junkers and Savoias).[120] Much of the other material, however, was another matter. Some of it, if old, was solid enough – one thinks here of the 200 Maxim M1910 heavy machine-guns (introduced just before the First World War, these were to remain in service with the Russian army until the end of the Second World War and were frequently encountered in Korea and Vietnam) and the eight Schneider 76.2mm M09 mountain guns, another weapon that had been standard issue in the Russian army – but there was also plenty of material the value of which was questionable, if not non-existent. Assuming that they were in reasonable working order, most of the 1,153 additional machine-guns that appeared were, with some exceptions (the worst offender here was the Saint Etienne), models that were in and of themselves good weapons that had done sterling work in the First World War (they included German Maxim M08s, French Hotchkiss M1914s and Saint Etienne M1907s, British Vickers Mark 1s, Austrian Schwarzlose M07s and American Colt M1895s and Lewis M1914s), whilst much the same was the case with the thirty 37mm McClean infantry guns that were delivered in lieu of proper anti-tank guns, the eight 4.5" Mark 1 Vickers howitzers and the twelve Armstrong Sixty-Pounder Mark 1s. Yet there was a very considerable issue with all this material, for it was mostly all sorts of bits and pieces that had been delivered to Russia in the course of the First World War or captured from the Germans, Austro-Hungarians or the Civil-War Whites, and it has to be asked how much was in proper working order or provided with adequate stocks of ammunition. Meanwhile, if questions could be asked of the artillery and machine-guns, this was even more the case with the rifles. These were provided in plenty, true, but around one-third were outmoded Gras and Vetterlis single-shot weapons dating from the 1870s and, in the former case, possibly even the 1860s, whilst even the more modern weapons were a mixture of Russian Moisin-Nagants, French Lebels, Japanese Arisakas, Austrian Mannlichers and American Winchesters. And even if every single weapon had been properly maintained and was in full working order and supplied with plenty of ammunition, there were four different calibres of artillery pieces, six different calibres of machine guns and seven different calibres of rifles. In short, rather than being simplified, the Republicans' already complicated supply situation was actually being confused still further.[121]

Along with the weapons, meanwhile, there arrived a considerable number of Russian generals, tankmen and air-force pilots (in all some 2,000 Russian military personnel were to serve in Spain, but it is probable that the first batch numbered no more than 300). The generals and other senior officers, of course, were there at the direct behest of Stalin and tasked with defending Russian interests, gaining valuable military experience and, in a few instances – the best examples are the first commander of the tank forces, Semyon Krivoshein, and his successor, Dmitri Pavlov – exercising direct military command, their names including many that were to become famous in the Second World War, including Kirill Meretskov, Nicolai Voronov, Pavel Batov, Konstantin Rokossovski, Yakov Smuskevich, Grigory Kulik, Ivan Konev and Rodion Malinovsky. As for the more junior ranks, it is not entirely clear how they were recruited, but it is probable that at least some were genuine volunteers, or at least, men who had no objection if they were asked to go: thanks to Stalin's considerable efforts to mobilize Russian public opinion, the Spanish Civil War awoke genuine enthusiasm amongst some elements of the population, whilst it cannot be doubted that many young army officers and air-force pilots were eager for combat experience and, one suspects, promotion, nor still less that in many eyes, fighting fascism wherever it raised its head was a patriotic duty.[122]

To return to the battlefields, the Republican counterattack at Illescas having been beaten off, on 24 October, the Nationalists rolled forward yet again, this time advancing to a line connecting the villages of Griñón and Torrejón del Velasco, overrunning, as they did so, the village of Seseña. 'We fought down to the very telephonists and dispatch riders, but it was all in vain', wrote Juan Modesto.[123] With the Nationalists now less than twenty miles away, the government could not but debate the question of whether the capital could (or, indeed, should) be defended. Broadly speaking, the professional officers surrounding Largo Caballero were of the opinion that it was indefensible and should be abandoned forthwith.[124] In this moment of crisis, however, the Communists and the left-wing of the Socialists, supported off-stage by the Anarchists, not to mention the Soviet embassy, insisted that the city should be defended house by house if necessary, and a somewhat unwilling Largo Caballero therefore undertook to make one last effort to halt the Nationalist offensive. In brief, then, it was agreed that a large strike force would drive westwards from the valley of the River Jarama so as to cut the enemy's communications with Toledo by seizing the villages of Seseña and Illescas. Available for the attack were at least 15,000 men, among them the very first mixed brigade to be ready for action, this having been given to Enrique Lister, a company of T26 tanks and two armoured trains mounting 75mm guns, while it was decided to make use of this moment to unveil the Republic's Russian airpower in the form of its Tupolev bombers.

With the only Nationalist troops guarding the line of the Jarama being the cavalry column of José Monasterio, hopes of victory were very high, and Largo Caballero therefore took to the airwaves on the evening of 28 October to make a fulsome speech in which he announced that the Republic was going to launch a great attack the very next day, and, not just that, but it was going to make use of modern tanks and aircraft.[125]

Yet victory came there none. When the attack went in at dawn on 29 October, the Republican armour quickly reached Seseña, but behind them the infantry made almost no progress. 'Our forty [*sic*] tanks', one of their crewmen told the Spanish staff officer, José Martín Blásquez, 'found themselves isolated almost immediately. A few machine-gun nests which we had been utterly unable to destroy were sufficient to hold up the infantry behind us.'[126] On their own, however, the tanks were helpless and all the more so once they had entered the narrow streets of Seseña. As the same man continued, 'When you get inside a tank before an attack, you feel you are in a battle cruiser about to demolish a wooden frigate. But when the enemy opens fire at you ... you feel like a hare ... trying to hit a hidden hunter who is equally or better armed than you. It is obviously easier for a hunter standing still to hit a bounding hare than it is for the bounding hare to ... hit the hunter. And in this case the hunter can always fall back on throwing hand grenades.'[127] The results of this situation were not hard to predict. After one of the tanks was destroyed by a Molotov cocktail, the commander of the little force, a Russian officer named Pavel Arman, retired in the direction of the safety of the Jarama valley, only to lose two more tanks as he did so. Some compensation was obtained when a chance encounter with three Italian L3s led to one being destroyed and another badly damaged, but on the whole, the foray had been a complete failure. As for the aircraft that Largo Caballero had boasted of, these had failed to make their mark: rather than being used to hit the Nationalist front lines, the Tupolevs were wasted in a raid on the Nationalist airbase at Talavera.[128]

There were many lessons here for the European military establishment, but for the time being, the Republicans could only retire to lick their wounds. On 2 November, a half-hearted attempt was made to launch another assault in the same area, but this was driven back in much the same fashion as before, leaving the Republicans no option but to retire to the very suburbs of the capital. At this point, however, they did at last obtain some real succour in that 4 November saw the first appearance over the front of the I15s (the I16s it seems did not enter the battle for another ten days). Organised in three squadrons and crewed entirely by Russians, these instantly out-classed the Nationalist planes, a Ro37 reconnaissance plane and two Cr32s being brought down that same day.[129] Yet, even if they were aware of the new arrivals, for the men on the ground, it must have seemed a question of 'too little, too late.' To quote Antonio Candelas once more:

We were sent to occupy some trenches ... outside the small town of Getafe ... The enemy forces kept on coming in apparently ever-increasing numbers. Again and again we had to withdraw ... From then on, it became an almost continuous battle, day and night.[130]

With the Nationalist forces literally battering at the gates of the capital, the sense of crisis in the Republican camp could hardly have been more dramatic. In this situation, the priority was clearly the creation of the new army, and this in turn meant that none of the Republic's various political parties and social movements could be allowed to remain aloof from the process of militarization: more than that, indeed, they had to be denied any possibility of resistance and forced to take a share in the responsibility. We come here to the problem posed by the Anarchists, a force that was bitterly opposed to the very principle of the regular army and ever since 1931 had been contemptuous of the Republic as a bourgeois sham. To deal with this situation, however, there was an obvious way forward, and Largo Caballero now seized the moment offered by the Nationalist arrival in the suburbs of Madrid to remedy the situation. In brief, then, on 4 November, the Anarchist leadership were offered two ministries – those of Health and Justice – and thereby placed in an impossible position: in brief, to refuse to join the government would have looked like a betrayal of the struggle against Franco, and yet accepting the offer implied abandoning some of the most sacred parts of the Anarchist canon. In the circumstances, however, there could be but one winner, and two leading Anarchists – a well-known libertarian journalist named Federica Montseny and a prominent militant named Juan García Oliver – duly entered the Cabinet. At best, the decision was a controversial one, however – nominated as one of the two ministers by the national committee of the CNT, García Oliver only obeyed the order to go to Madrid under protest – while there were plenty of militiamen in the field to whom it made no difference whatsoever, many militia columns continuing to hold out against militarization until well into 1937.[131]

To conclude, then, what we see in the three months of fighting that we have just reviewed is the utter failure of the Spanish revolution as a weapon of war, and with it the vindication of the Communist argument that the only way to resist the Nationalists was the construction of a new regular army, an army that might be motivated by a different spirit than its predecessor and bedecked with red stars, an army that might even salute with the clenched fist symbolic of the labour movement, but a new regular army nonetheless. In saying this, one does not have to be an admirer of the Communists: on the contrary, Communism was a singularly ruthless and unpleasant force dedicated above all to its own ends that, in Spain in as everywhere else, was determined to achieve a position of complete control. But that is not the point: however ardent they were, men such as Durruti simply had no practical answer to the Communist arguments. All too clearly, militia columns could neither take territory from the enemy nor defend it against attack, whilst arguments to the effect that the Republicans should have turned guerrilla are worth voicing only to subject them to the derision that they deserve: whilst guerrillas can prove of great service if used in conjunction with regular armies, they cannot fight wars on their own. As for the concept of a revolutionary war, to the extent that it has any validity at all, it had little or none in Spain: whilst the militants of the various labour movement may indeed have been committed, even heroic, they were very much in the minority and operated in a sea of apathy, ignorance and indifference. For good or ill, then, the new People's Army was a necessity, and, if the Nationalists were not yet in Madrid, it was because of the progress that had been made in its formation. Yet terrible errors had been made in the conceptualization of that force, whilst the loss of so many rifles, machine-guns and artillery pieces in the fighting (rifles, machine-guns and artillery pieces that could immediately be pressed into service by the Nationalists) had rendered it dependent on the distinctly unpredictable source of weapons and munitions represented by Joseph Stalin, and all the more so as a mixture of *real politik* and revulsion at the Spanish Revolution had led both Britain and France to refuse to send aid to the Republic. By the time the Nationalist forces reached the outskirts of Madrid, then, they had not yet won the war, but their opponents had almost certainly lost it.

Notes

1 In view of the food situation alone, Moscardó's decision to withdraw into the *alcázar* is open to the sharpest criticism. Though the subsequent siege did succeed in tying down many enemy resources, a much better move would have been to use requisitioned transport to reach friendly forces holding nearby Avila.

2 The telephone conversation in which Moscardó was threatened with the execution of his son appears in large part to have been a fabrication on the part of the Nationalist authorities. Moscardó's son – Luis Moscardó Guzmán – was indeed shot by the Republicans, but at a somewhat later date and in circumstances that had nothing to do with the siege as such. Ironically, meanwhile, the young man had progressive views and was on extremely bad terms with his father. See I. Herreros, *Mitología de la cruzada de Franco: el alcázar de Toledo* (Madrid, 1995), pp. 25–41.

3 It should be noted that not all the militia were so lacking in dedication. María de la Luz Mejías Correa, for example, was fighting with the militia column in which she and her husband had enlisted in Extremadura: 'There were many casualties in the trench where I was: indeed, one man was killed by a bullet in the mouth when he was standing at a loophole right beside me. However, we were full of the hope that we were going to win, and things did not seem so very bad.' Pulido Mendoza, *Así fue pasando el tiempo*, pp. 75–6.

4 M. Koltsov, *Diario de la guerra de España* (Geneva, 1963), p. 74.

5 Rivas Cherif, *Portrait of an Unknown Man*, p. 287. One should not imagine, however, that the experience of the defenders was anything other than grim in the extreme. As an un-named Civil Guard wrote in the aftermath of the siege, 'From the day that we shut ourselves up ... we heard nothing but horrible explosions; shells, bombs ... hand-grenades, the lot. Along with this affliction came many others: the worst was our complete lack of contact with the outside world; not only could we not talk to anybody (not that we wanted to), but, still worse, we could not get any news of our brothers, the saviours of Spain and her religion. Such was the moral suffering that tormented us that some of us, at least, began to think that we were the only survivors of the forces who had risen to save Spain.' Cit. Cervera Gil, *Ya sabes mi paradero*, pp. 71–2.

6 Langdon-Davies, *Behind the Spanish Barricades*, pp. 281–2. Like the many other pressmen present, Langdon-Davies had been specifically invited to Toledo to watch what

was billed as the complete destruction of the fortress. As a result, to military failure was added political fiasco, Nationalist morale being given a great fillip.

7 Candelas, *Adventures of an Innocent*, p. 50.

8 Cit. Herreros, *Mitología de la cruzada de Franco*, p. 67. The most detailed account of the siege in English, albeit one of a rather uncritical description, is C. Eby, *The Siege of the Alcázar: Toledo, July to September 1936* (London, 1965). In his memoirs, Lister is utterly scathing: 'There was never a proper plan, nor were any of the measures necessary for the conquest of the *alcázar* even taken. For more than two months, forces of from four to five thousand men – the majority of them Anarchists – accompanied by several hundred "ladies" brought down from the brothels of Madrid bedecked in red and black bandannas, had a wonderful time "fighting" stone walls behind which crouched a bunch of folk who may not have been having such a good time as the Anarchists outside, but were still a lot better off than their friends fighting in the front line.' E. Lister, *Memorias de un luchador* (Madrid, 1977), p. 115.

9 Thomas, *Spanish Civil War*, p. 384.

10 Cabezas, *Asturias*, p. 68.

11 Ibid., pp. 77–8. For a detailed account of the siege by one of its defenders, see A. Cores Fernández de Cañete, *El sitio de Oviedo* (Madrid, 1975).

12 Cit. Fraser, *Blood of Spain*, p. 252.

13 Miralles Bravo, *Memorias*, pp. 39–40. Thus is a fascinating passage, suggesting as it does that the Durruti column was in large part composed of regular troops rather than militia. What is certainly true is that the column was not commanded by the Anarchist leader but rather by a captain of the Catalan police called Pérez Farrás.

14 It was not just that many of the men scarcely knew how to load or fire their weapons. Also on show was an ignorance that defies belief, Joaquín Masjuan describing how he was almost killed when one of his comrades tossed a hand-grenade into a cooking fire for a joke. Max, *Memorias de un revolucionario*, p. 36.

15 For the killings engaged in by the militias, see Preston, *Spanish Holocaust*, pp. 249–50. Meanwhile, the extent to which collectivization was imposed is open to much debate. However, what appears absolutely certain is that the advance was accompanied by considerable disorder. Having decided that he did not want the war to end without him, Rafael Miralles Bravo had abandoned the task to which he had been assigned in favour of pursuing the militia in a requisitioned car with two friends: 'We stopped for the night in Bujaraloz, at this moment the headquarters of Durruti ... The town was full of troops of every type, and offered the most depressing picture ... Complete disorder reigned on all sides, groups of drunken militia filled every tavern, and the air was filled with ... wild shouting.' Miralles Bravo, *Memorias*, p. 45. Another eyewitness, meanwhile, was Manuel Cruz, a barber affiliated with the CNT who had been one of the first to volunteer for the Durruti column: 'I was in Bujaraloz for fifteen days ... What a picture! Nobody wanted to do any work; nobody wanted to dig trenches. All that anybody was interested in was stealing lambs and hens or getting off with some woman ... None of this went down well with me: I thought that, if we were going to have a revolution, then we should set about it properly. As soon as a lorry set off for Barcelona, then, the five of us who had joined up together therefore jumped it: we simply could not stomach the idea of having set out on what turned out to be a mere hen hunt.' Cit. Camps and Olcina, *Les milícies catalanes al front d'Aragó, 1936–1937*, p. 169.

16 Nor did things go very much better when they did finally make contact with the enemy. For the young recruits who had rallied to Durruti, indeed, it was a shattering experience. Within moments of coming under fire for the first time, Joaquín Masjuán saw five men torn apart by the same shell, and both a man who had been standing behind him and his best friend shot dead. See Max, *Memorias de un revolucionario*, pp. 30–1.

17 Manzanera, *The Iron Column*, p. 25.

18 Ibid., pp. 14–15.
19 According to Miralles Bravo, such supply dumps as were established were frequently pillaged more or less at will, with the result that huge amounts of food were wasted. See ibid., pp. 60–2.
20 Max, *Memorias de un revolucionario*, pp. 34–5.
21 Biescas Palacio, *Memorias*, p. 20.
22 Manzanera, *The Iron Column*, p. 23. Here, too, is Joaquín Masjuan: 'Amongst our comrades the rumour spread that the Republican government didn't want the Durruti column to achieve any more success and that it had in consequence sabotaged our operations.' Max, *Memorias de un revolucionario*, p. 36.
23 Exactly why the expedition to Mallorca was undertaken is unclear, but the initiative clearly emanated from the Catalan government, and there is a strong hint that it was above all the product of panic: 'At the sight of the innumerable successes that were apparently being obtained by the Anarchists and Communists, the Esquerra Republicana de Catalunya [or ERC, in 1936 the leading representative of Catalan nationalism] ... was frantically trying to get its own militia together for fear that the war would come to an end before it could take part in the fighting, with all the political consequences – above all, accusations of neutrality – that this would bring with it.' Miralles Bravo, *Memorias*, p. 43. In principle, of course, seizing Mallorca was sensible enough, representing, as it did, an important base that was ideally placed to impede shipping carrying armaments and supplies to Barcelona, and Alpert has argued forcefully that the failure to press the operation represented a major strategic error; see M. Alpert, 'The clash of Spanish armies: contrasting ways of war in Spain, 1936–1939', *War in History*, VI, No. 3 (July, 1999), pp. 346. Yet, even assuming that the island could have been taken, this view begs the question of how it could have been held thereafter. For a detailed account, see J. Massot i Muntaner, *El desembarcament de Bayo a Mallorca, agost–septembre, 1937* (Montserrat, 1987).
24 A concrete example of the damage done by these raids comes from Morocco, where 18 July 1936 saw a single Republican bomber attack Tetuán. As the plane only carried two bombs, what this was supposed to achieve is unclear, but the raid still cost thirteen lives, of which seven belonged to completely innocent Moroccan civilians. See A. Benjelloum, 'Las causas de la participación de marroquíes en la Guerra Civil Española, 1936–1939' in J. A. González Alcantud (ed.), *Marroquíes en la Guerra Civil Española: campos equívocos* (Granada, 2003), p. 45. Meanwhile, the tone of the propaganda diatribes unleashed by such events speaks for themselves: 'Against all reason, against every human right and against all humanity, the Red aircraft have bombarded open cities. Nobody can fail to be aware of this reiterated act of monstrosity, but it is nevertheless important to ensure that it is recorded ... What we see, in effect, is that the Red aviation prefers to avoid military objectives whose bombardment requires skill and sacrifice, not to mention the need to risk death, in favour of sadistically giving itself over to the pleasure of causing casualties amongst the civilian population.' Anon., *Ataques aereos a poblaciones civiles* (Salamanca, 1938), n.p. For a first-hand account of a Republican raid on Soria, see Cardozo, *March of a Nation*, pp. 33–4. Meanwhile, the situation in Córdoba is discussed in Moreno Gómez, *Guerra Civil en Córdoba*, p. 370.
25 Cit. Fraser, *Blood of Spain*, p. 70.
26 Cardozo, *March of a Nation*, pp. 40–1.
27 Heredia, *Monarquía, república, guerra*, pp. 201–2.
28 Etchebéhère, *Mi guerra en España*, p. 14. Typically enough, Etchebéhère and her comrades set off from Madrid in the belief that they were off to Zaragoza, but they got no further than the hills beyond Sigüenza and were immediately routed with the loss of Etchebéhère's husband. Ibid., pp. 23–4. Her account, meanwhile, highlights another problem in the militia, in that her column contained both a man in his sixties, who had fought in the Cuban War, and a boy of fourteen. Ibid., p. 26.

Still another issue that is revealed is the boredom and frustration engendered by the static nature of the war in the *sierra*: forced to camp out for weeks in a drafty and uncomfortable billet in the railway station at Sigüenza, the column became restive, two of its members eventually taking themselves off (or so they said) to fight the enemy elsewhere. Ibid., p. 35.

29 Cortes Roa, *Tanquista*, p. 10.

30 R. Sender, *The War in Spain: a Personal Narrative* (London, 1937), pp. 40–8.

31 Ibid., pp. 55–7.

32 Arturo Barea, for example, describes encountering a lorry-load of militiamen coming back from the *sierra* after a day at the front. Challenged by a woman who loudly demanded to know what they were doing, they responded that they had given the enemy a good beating, that they had met plenty of other men heading for the front line on their way back, that their wives would be frightened without them, and that, in any case, nobody had the right to stop them. Barea, *Forging of a Rebel*, p. 539.

33 Mangada was one of a number of demagogic figures who plagued the Republican war effort at this time (another, be it said, was the far more famous André Malraux). As the Republican staff officer José Martín Blásquez complained: 'Mangada had ... become an idol of the masses. His column was the particular pride of the people of Madrid ... The result was that, whenever Mangada rang up and told us of his desperate plight in the face of some attack, for the rest of the morning we would be overwhelmed at ten-minute intervals by desperate appeals from all quarters relating to the same attack ... On an average, this would be repeated every third or fourth day.' Martín Blásquez, *I Helped to Build an Army*, pp. 172–3.

34 For the battles in the Sierra de Guadarrama, see Martínez Bande, *La marcha sobre Madrid*, pp. 55–121. As a footnote to the main campaign, which was over by the end of August, it ought to be mentioned that the first half of October saw a renewed. flare-up in operations in the form of a Nationalist drive on the town of Sigüenza See ibid., pp. 254–6. Amongst the defenders was Mika Feldman de Etchebéhère: 'Our house creaked and groaned like a ship struck by a tempest. Together, the planes overhead and the artillery in the front line tore great holes in every floor. The men fired back furiously, not because they had a chance of hitting anything, but because it helped them ... endure the unbearable tension. We had two dead [and] ... ten wounded: the girls were trying to treat the latter's injuries or at least protect them from the explosions.' Etchebéhère, *Mi guerra de España*, pp. 67–8.

35 E. Grandío Seoane (ed.), *Las columnas gallegas hasta Oviedo: diario bélico de la Guerra Civil Española, 1936-37: Faustino Vázquez Carril* (Pontevedra, 2011), pp. 123–4. One of the men opposing Vázquez Carril and his fellows was probably the Asturian peasant David Granda, who had set off with a group of volunteers to help halt the Nationalist advance: 'To our right was positioned a company of Assault Guards ... and one morning at about ten or eleven o'clock ... bullets began to fly, pinging all around us. Then we saw that the Assault Guards were telling us to retreat, but there were some who said, "Those bastards up there: perhaps they are not really on our side; we'll stay put." The Assault Guards were retreating because they were in a much better position to see than us, and the enemy was in the process of outflanking us on the other side of the hill. By the time we realised what was going on, the Assault Guards had .... disappeared from sight and we were getting trapped ... One of those in command said, "OK, let's go: we're pulling out," and we began to move back ... Bullets were flying everywhere.' Cit. MacMaster, *Spanish Fighters*, pp. 60–1.

36 Ibid., p. 143. Vázquez Carril is an interesting individual. Caught up in the rising as a conscript, he made no attempt to resist his fate and set off for the front without demur. Privately, however, his sympathies were with the Republic, whilst he regarded the coup as a ridiculous endeavour that was bound to fail. To quote the entry in his diary for 19 July, 'Even if this rebellion really does have support in every part of Spain ... the government will operate in such a way as to ensure that the

workers block the path of these parade-ground louts … It might come as a surprise to find me using such expressions, but the commanders of our dreadful army do not deserve anything better. They have never behaved like men, never won a war except the one in Morocco, and even that victory was only gained thanks to the help of the French and at the cost of thousands and thousands of men … And now they take to the streets to deal with the poor workers. They had better watch out! They think that everything is going to be fine, easy even, but they may well find that they have bitten off more than they can chew.' Ibid., p. 106. As time went on, meanwhile, Vázquez became ever more critical of the 'military scum', not to mention the 'cowardly criminal, Franco', whilst he was deeply shocked at the constant executions, denouncing the death-squads of the Falange, in particular, as 'a bunch of women.' Unfortunately for him, however, he was betrayed to the authorities and sentenced to death for his remarks, being executed by firing squad on 10 May 1937.

37 Cit. MacMaster, *Spanish Fighters*, p. 69.

38 For a brief introduction to the forces that came to make up the Nationalist army, see A. Quesada and S. Walsh, *The Spanish Civil War, 1936–1939 (1): Nationalist Forces* (Oxford, 2014). Also helpful is R. de la Cierva, 'The Nationalist army in the Civil War', in R. Carr (ed.), *The Republic and Civil War in Spain* (London, 1971), pp. 188–212.

39 For all this, see J. Galey, 'Bridegrooms of death: a profile study of the Spanish Foreign Legion', *Journal of Contemporary History*, IV, No. 2 (April, 1969), pp. 47–64.

40 A key figure in all of this was the much-mutilated founder of the Spanish Foreign Legion, General Millán Astray. See R. Jensen, 'Jose Millán Astray and the Nationalist "crusade" in Spain', *Journal of Contemporary History*, XXVII, No. 3 (July, 1992), pp. 425–48.

41 For a discussion of the motives for Moorish recruitment, see Benjelloum, 'Las causas de la participación de marroquíes en la Guerra Civil Española', in González Alcantud, *Marroquis en la Guerra Civil Española*, pp. 42–57. See also S. Fleming, 'Spanish Morocco and the *alzamiento nacional*, 1936-1939: the military, economic and political mobilisation of a protectorate', *Journal of Contemporary History*, XVIII, No. 1 (January 1983), pp. 27–42; A. al Tuma, 'Tangier, Spanish Morocco and Spain's civil war in Dutch diplomatic documents', *The Journal of North African Studies*, XVII, No. 3 (June, 2012), pp. 443–5.The impression that the Moors saw the war in terms of a *jihad* was strengthened by the fact that a number of them were clearly intelligent enough to realize that in Franco's Spain, it was no bad thing to pay lip-service to the notion of a crusade and behaved accordingly. For a good example, see Cardozo, *March of a Nation*, p. 114.

42 See R. M. de Madariaga, 'La guerra colonial llevada a España: las tropas marroquíes en el ejército franquista', in González Alcantud, *Marroquis en la Guerra Civil Española*, pp. 74–84.

43 Hence, perhaps, the stress that both Mola and Queipo de Llano placed on the need for Franco to send them not just reinforcements, but Moorish reinforcements. See N. Cerdá, 'Political ascent and military command: General Franco in the early months of the Spanish Civil War, July–October 1936', *Journal of Military History*, LXXV, No. 4 (October, 2011), p. 1145. See also S. Balfour, 'El otro moro en la guerra colonial y la guerra civil', in ibid., pp. 108–9. Also helpful is R. M. de Madariaga, 'The intervention of Moroccan troops in the Spanish Civil War: a reconsideration', *European History Quarterly*, XXII, No. 1 (January, 1992), pp. 67–98. For a first-hand account of Moorish troops, see Knickerbocker, *Siege of the Alcázar*, pp. 60–2.

44 The planes concerned consisted of twenty Junkers Ju52s and nine Savoia-Marchetti SM81s. Also in attendance were a smaller number of Heinkel He51 and Fiat Cr32 fighters, both of which far outclassed the handful of Dewoitine NiD52 fighters that were all that could be opposed to them by the Republicans, the net result being that the Nationalists were assured of complete air superiority. By far the most detailed

guide to the aircraft employed in the Spanish Civil War is R. A. Permuy López, *Atlas ilustrado de la aviación en la Guerra Civil Española* (Madrid, 2012).

45 There was a brief postscript to these operations. Anxious to do something to prop up resistance in Asturias, in mid-September, the government decided to send the bulk of its fleet to the Cantabrian coast. Exactly what this move was supposed to achieve is uncertain – even the biggest of the ships' guns only had the range to fire a few miles inland – but the impact in the Straits of Gibraltar was catastrophic. Left to watch the Nationalists were just five destroyers and a handful of smaller vessels. Properly handled, this flotilla should have been enough to blockade Ceuta and Melilla, but the Nationalists proceeded completely to out-manoeuvre the Republicans. Thus, no sooner had the Republican battle fleet steamed past El Ferrol than the light cruiser *Almirante Cervera* and the brand-new heavy cruiser *Canarias* (a vessel that was in the final stages of completion when the rising broke out) slipped out of port in its wake and headed south. On 29 September, the two ships came across the Republican destroyers *Gravina* and *Almirante Ferrándiz*, and there followed a completely one-sided action in which the former was badly damaged and the latter sunk. After this, there was not even the slightest attempt at enforcing the blockade, the Republican fleet finally being scared into near total passivity by the dispatch of two German submarines, which in November and December 1936 attacked a number of Republican warships in the vicinity of Málaga and sank an unlucky submarine (also sent to the area were the battleship *Graf Spee*, the heavy cruisers *Deutschland* and *Admiral Hipper* and the light cruisers *Köln* and *Nurnberg*). In fairness to the Republican navy, however, it must needs also be pointed out that its hands were also tied by diplomatic factors, as trying to enforce a blockade of the Moroccan coast, or, for that matter, Cádiz and Algeciras, would have alienated Britain and France. See M. Alpert, 'The Spanish Civil War and the Mediterranean', *Mediterranean Historical Review*, XIII, Nos. 1/2 (June, 1998), p. 154. On the naval war in general, see W. C. Frank, 'Naval Operations in the Spanish Civil War, 1936–1939', *Naval War College Review*, XXXVII, No. 1 (January 1984), pp. 24–55.

46 Preston, *Spanish Holocaust*, pp. 138–70 *passim*. In every case, these figures represent only the summary justice of the first day or two of occupation: over the months that followed, more systematic repression produced hundreds more executions.

47 A typical armoured car of the inter-war period consisting of a turret and an armoured body grafted on to the chassis of a commercial truck, the Bilbao M1932 was armed with no more than a single machine-gun but could also carry a squad of riflemen; prior to the Civil War, meanwhile, it had been a preserve of the Assault Guard. In July 1936, the Nationalists had just seven at their disposal, the other forty having remained in the hands of the government. Albert, *Carros de combate*, p. 59.

48 Cit. Knickerbocker, *Siege of the Alcázar*, p. 32.

49 In fairness, these impromptu militias on occasion showed much courage – in Almendralejo, for example, 100 militants barricaded themselves in the parish church and held out for eight days, only surrendering when they ran out of water – but against the Moors and Legionaries they had no hope whatsoever. For the defence of the parish church of Almendralejo, see ibid., pp. 49–50.

50 According to local legend, the fall of Mérida was accompanied by a spectacular massacre of hundreds of civilian refugees in the city's famous Roman theatre; it is sometimes said, indeed, that every single one of them was decapitated. This seems a little unlikely, but it is all too probable, alas, that many of the women were raped.

51 Preston, *Spanish Holocaust*, pp. 308–9.

52 Amongst the bombers were three Junkers Ju52s that had been handed over to the Spaniards to crew. One of the crew members was José Larios: 'We skimmed over our infantry ... to cheer them on, swooping low over the battlements and firing our machine-guns at the defenders on the high parapets. As we banked steeply, I could

clearly hear the sharp crackling of rifles and machine-guns over the roar of our three engines.' Larios, *Combat over Spain*, p. 45.

53 Pulido Mendoza, *Así fue pasando el tiempo*, pp. 61–63. At the last minute, Mejía Correa's brother-in-law, a man who had never been involved in politics, was saved by the intercession of a Falangist acquaintance, but the next few weeks saw the execution of her mother-in-law and two aunts, of whom the first was shot for no better reason than that her son was in the militia. Ibid., pp. 64–5, 68.

54 Cit. C. García Santa Cecilia (ed.), *La matanza de Badajoz: crónica de un testigo de uno de los episodios más trágicos de la guerra civil de España* (Mérida 2007), pp. 66–7.

55 Cit. ibid., p. 81. In all, the death toll was probably 3,800. Preston, *Spanish Holocaust*, p. 321.Shaken by the coverage that the executions at Badajoz received in the international press, supporters of Franco later tried to deny that anything of the sort occurred, or to put down any killing in cold blood to the confused fighting that took place as desperate militiamen fell back through the narrow streets of the city. Such farragoes of lies and half truths, however, should be treated with the contempt which they deserve, the fact that appalling scenes took place being absolutely incontrovertible.

56 Martínez Bande, *Marcha sobre Madrid*, pp. 153–7.

57 Shortly after its fall, Oropesa was visited by the American correspondent Knickerbocker: 'We parked in the town square beside an armoured car and ... went on up ... to the castle gate ... Every door with a door left had some sort of sign upon it reading "Requisitioned for the [Falange]," or "This is a Patriot's home" ... But many houses had no doors left, and you could look in and see the interior wrecked as though hand-grenades had been set off in each room ... Into the castle we entered ... Two *banderas* of the Legion were quartered here now. They were very tired Legionaries: they had marched and fought all night long and now they ... slept in heaps ... in every corner of shade the castle court afforded ... I went upstairs ... to the quarters of Lieutenant-Colonel [Rolando de] Tella ... He stood at the window ... and showed me how he took the town just a few hours before. "We lost only one dead and eight wounded; the Reds lost I don't know how many.' Knickerbocker, *Siege of the Alcázar*, pp. 67–70.

58 Koltsov, *Diario de la guerra de España*, p. 57.

59 Cit. Cervera Gil, *Ya sabes mi paradero*, p. 64. A poverty-stricken town of Leftist sympathies, Talavera suffered terribly in the wake of occupation, at least 310 of its inhabitants being executed or otherwise put to death, including a nineteen-year-old girl named Luisa Bravo Luna. See J. Pérez Conde et al., *La guerra civil en Talavera de la Reina: conflicto bélico, represión y vida cotidiana* (Talavera, 2008), pp. 240–8.

60 Larios, *Combat over Spain*, pp. 47–50. As Larios recounts, meanwhile, the three Junkers that had been turned over to the Spanish air force rather than being piloted by Germans were not even equipped for bombing missions, their crews rather having to throw their missiles out by hand. One point to note here is that as yet it is wrong to speak of such forces as the Condor Legion: rather, at this point, the German and Italian planes officially composed a new air wing of the Foreign Legion. Meanwhile, the fall of Talavera was not the only defeat that the Republic suffered at this time. Setting aside events in Guipúzcoa (which we will look at in a further chapter), in the province of Córdoba, a force of Republican troops and militia that had been massed at an isolated spot named Cerro Muriano twenty miles north of the capital under General José Miaja in preparation for an offensive was put to flight with heavy losses by a Nationalist surprise attack. Among the large number of journalists who had been summoned to watch what was billed as a great Republican victory was the American photographer Robert Capa, and it was in the course of this fighting that he managed to snap the shot of the Republican soldier falling dead that is perhaps the most famous piece of photojournalism of the entire Civil War. Moreno Gómez, *Guerra Civil en Córdoba*, pp. 351–68.

61 J. Salas Larrázabal, *Air War over Spain* (Shepperton, 1974), p. 75.

62 Ibid., p. 76.The Nationalists were so alarmed at the threat of Republican air attacks at this time that Yagüe actually ordered his men to move only at night. Martínez Bande, *Marcha sobre Madrid*, p. 159.

63 For an assessment of Malraux's role in Spain, see G. Harris, 'Malraux, myth, political commitment and the Spanish Civil War', *Modern and Contemporary France*, V, No. 3 (August, 1997), pp. 319–28.

64 For the Fifth Regiment, see E. Comín Colomer, *El quinto regimiento de milicias populares* (Madrid, 1973). In fairness to the other political movements, they themselves had gradually realized that something needed to be done, the result being that Anarchists and the POUM had already set up improvised military academies in which a handful of serving and retired officers were co-opted or coerced into instilling some of the more promising militiamen with the basic rudiments of officer education. See J. M. Garate Córdoba, *Tenientes en campaña: la improvisación de oficiales en la guerra del 36* (Madrid, 1976), pp. 23–33.

65 Already Party militants for some years, Modesto and Lister both owed their selection for training in Moscow to the fact that they possessed a certain amount of military experience, the former having served for some years in the *regulares* as a white non-commissioned officer, and the latter having taken part in an unsuccessful rising against the régime of General Machado in Cuba in 1931. Comintern agents in Spain prior to July 1936 included the Argentinian Vittorio Codovilla and the Bulgarian 'Stepanov' (actually Stoian Mineff). Thomas, *Spanish Civil War*, p. 123.

66 Along with Rosenberg, there came a consul-general for Barcelona, Vladimir Antonov-Ovseenko; a military *attaché*, Vladimir Gorev; a naval *attaché*, Nikolai Kuznetsov; an air *attaché*, Boris Svieshnikov; an economic *attaché*, Arthur Stashevsky, and a host of GRU and NKVD functionaries, including the senior general Jan Berzin. Also included was the future Marshal Rodimtsev, whose role seems to have been that of special adviser to the Fifth Regiment. Thomas, *Spanish Civil War*, p. 393.

67 According to Lister, by the end of November, no fewer than 69,700 men had passed through the Fifth Regiment training camps, 22,000 of whom had reached the front by the end of September. See Lister, *Memorias de un luchador*, p. 121. It is generally agreed, however, that, even if they are stretched to include such auxiliary organizations as the so-called 'Culture Militia', an educational and propaganda organization that sought to combat illiteracy, whether political or cultural, these figures are greatly exaggerated. Alpert, *Republican Army in the Spanish Civil War*, p. 45.

68 Lines, *Women in Combat in the Spanish Civil War*, p. 80.

69 Koltsov, *Diario de la guerra de España*, p. 88.

70 Training, for example, was frequently rudimentary. On joining the Fifth Regiment in September 1936, for example, Antonio Candelas received no more than two or three days of the most elementary 'square-bashing' before being sent to take part in the siege of the *alcázar*. Candelas, *Adventures of an Innocent*, p. 42.

71 Better though much of the Fifth Regiment was than the other militia, it was not exempt from the latter's problems. In the midst of the Nationalist offensive that took Franco from Toledo to the gates of Madrid, for example, the novelist Ramón Sender found himself having to deal with fifteen men who were demanding to be allowed to leave the front line on the grounds that they were volunteers: 'Like most of my company, the ... men were peasants from ... Córdoba, many of them illiterate ... We had been able to collect and enrol them only because of two facts, the regular supply of food ... and a distribution of overcoats and blankets.' Sender, *The War in Spain*, p. 175.

72 In the Republican parties properly speaking, there also lurked hopes that Largo Caballero would fail in his turn and thereby suffer a serious loss of credibility, though how anyone could think that this could imply anything other than victory for the Nationalists is unclear. See Rivas Cherif, *Diary of an Unknown Man*, p. 288.

73 Cit. Koltsov, *Diario de la guerra de España*, p. 79.

74 José Asensio Torrado is a controversial figure and one who has been much criticized. However, a pro-Communist staff officer who eventually came to welcome his replacement is nevertheless warm in his praise for the contribution that he made in the autumn of 1936. Thus, 'It was [General Asensio] that got the commissariat and supply service, the petrol and oil service, the production of uniforms, etc., etc., going properly. In order to achieve this he had to be a strict disciplinarian and do away with the tradition of camaraderie which had hitherto prevailed. He knew that under the prevalent demagogy the strict fulfilment of his duties would only make him hated, yet he fulfilled them.' Martín Blásquez, *I Helped to Build an Army*, p. 291. Also generous in his assessment is the Communist, Juan Modesto: 'My opinion of him is that he was a brave commander, and, with it, someone who was more than capable of handling the demands of combat.' Modesto, *Soy del Quinto Regimiento*, p. 96.

75 Despite the courage shown by some of the attacking forces, it is impossible not to question the sense of this move. Given that the Nationalists were holding the line of a major river, hopes of success were, at best, limited, whilst the only result was to destroy all hope of stabilizing the front. At all events, driving back to the front from Madrid on 5 September, Mikhail Koltsov came across an Enrique Lister who had been trying desperately to stem the rout beside himself with rage: 'They don't want to fight! The road to Madrid is completely open … Right now the Nationalist could take the city with a single tank!' Cit. Koltsov, *Diario de la guerra de España*, p. 72.

76 Preston actually goes still further here, insisting over and over again that Franco was deliberately seeking a long war that would allow him to teach the Spaniards a lasting lesson on the folly of flirting with revolution. Other historians have not agreed, however. Here, for example, is Nestor Cerdá: 'Franco had no intention of prolonging the war. Had he been given the chance to destroy the Republican forces in a single great battle or series of battles, as the German *Wehrmacht* did in France in 1940, he would doubtless have taken it.' N. Cerdá, 'Political ascent and military command', p. 1157.

77 For a good account of the debates that took place at Franco's headquarters, see A. Kindelán, *Mis cuadernos de guerra* (Madrid, 1982), p. 23. Speaking retrospectively to the British journalist Cardozo, Franco claimed that he had believed the Republican forces were in such disorder that delaying the attack on Madrid for a day or two would make little odds. Cardozo, *March of a Nation*, p. 100. Franco's military leadership has been much debated, with historians favourable to the cause of the Republic (for example, Paul Preston) generally being highly critical and those favourable to that of the uprising (for example, Brian Crozier and George Hills) expansive in their praise. The truth, of course, lies somewhere between the two extremes, but, in line with the most recent scholarship on the subject, it is very much the view of the author that, whilst Franco was no genius and mentally but little equipped to fight battles in the style of those that were to erupt after 1939, his decisions were wholly defensible and his strategy wholly in tune with the resources he actually possessed. For a recent discussion that is inclined to take this view, see L. Lines, 'Francisco Franco as warrior: Is it time for a reassessment of his military leadership?' *Journal of Military History*, LXXXI, No. 2, pp. 513–34. By contrast, a particularly ferocious attack on Franco as military commander can be found in the pages of C. Blanco Escolá, *La incompetencia militar de Franco* (Madrid, 2000). Finally, those wishing for general discussions of the conduct of the Civil War would be well advised to consult J. M. Reverte, *El arte de matar: cómo se hizo la Guerra Civil Española* (Barcelona, 2009) and C. Engel, *Estrategia y táctica en la Guerra de España, 1936–1939* (Madrid, 2008).

78 No sooner had Talavera fallen, for example, than substantial elements of the Fifth Regiment were dispatched to the River Alberche. See Modesto, *Soy del Quinto Regimiento*, p. 92.

79 Lister, *Memorias de un luchador*, pp. 108–9.

80 Modesto, *Soy del Quinto Regimiento*, p. 94.

81 Cit. Cervera Gil, *Ya sabes mi paradero*, pp. 65–6. The constant capture of so many weapons was extremely important: given that, in so far as arms and munitions were concerned, all the material recovered at this time consisted of rifles, machine-guns and artillery pieces in use in the Spanish army in 1936, they could immediately be pressed into service by their insurgents. E.g. C. Iniesta Cano, *Memorias y recuerdos: los años que he vivido en el proceso histórico de España* (Barcelona, 1984), p. 86.

82 Preston, *Spanish Holocaust*, p. 332.

83 Cardozo, *March of a Nation*, pp. 109–10. According to Modesto, by 19 September, his unit of the Fifth Regiment had lost 80 per cent of its strength. Modesto, *Soy del Quinto Regimiento*, p. 97. Many Republican troops, meanwhile, were fleeing for Madrid or scattered across the countryside in a state of complete disorder, Modesto claiming that he came across an entire battalion of Anarchists who had abandoned the front line on the grounds that, as they put it, 'Largo Caballero has betrayed us: the enemy has got aviation.' Ibid., p. 101.

84 C. Gerahty, *The Road to Madrid* (London, 1937), pp. 78–9. Knickerbocker was an eyewitness to the same raid: 'The actual damage inflicted by the bombers was unimportant. The important thing is that when enemy bombers are over the lines all activity ceases. The bateries pull their camouflage of green branches over them and the men sit still beneath them; the infantry lies low in ditches careful not to move … Nobody does a thing until the bombers go away, either chased off by fighting planes or just going home for more bombs.' Knickerbocker, *Siege of the Alcazar*, p. 150. According to Cardozo, who was also present, Nationalist casualties amounted to only ten dead and twenty-five wounded. Cardozo, *March of a Nation*, p. 118.

85 This quote first appeared in a report filed for the *Daily Express* by the reporter Noel Monks. Confusingly, by the time that it was published, there were in fact six columns heading for the capital. See Hills, *Battle for Madrid*, p. 85

86 Cit. Herreros, *Mitología de la cruzada de Franco*, pp. 67–8.

87 Cardozo, *March of a Nation*, p. 127.

88 Pulido Mendoza, *Así fue pasando el tiempo*, p. 77. Another participant in the rout was Antonio Candelas: 'The militiamen … started running towards the bridge … I followed them … On my way across … I saw many men dead. One young fellow was wounded in the right shoulder and I was able to give him a hand … At the other end … there were a few more dead militiamen and some civilians. At that point we were in full view of the enemy in the *alcázar*: bullets were smashing into the masonry walls of the bridge and all around us.' Candelas, *Adventures of an Innocent*, pp. 52–3.

89 Many of those cut off undoubtedly died fighting bravely, but during the night there were unedifying scenes as men frantic to escape the city clashed with elements of the Fifth Regiment led by Lister, who were trying to rally the fleeing defenders at the bridge leading across the river to the south. See Lister, *Memorias de un luchador*, p. 114.

90 Herreros, *Mitología de la cruzada de Franco*, p. 95.

91 For a detailed account of the battle, see Martínez Bande, *Marcha sobre Madrid*, pp. 186–90. Some time later, the journalist Cecil Gerahty visited what was left of the fortress: 'It is almost impossible to describe the destruction that had taken place. The four famous towers at the corners of the building had all fallen. There were masses of masonry, some of which I calculated weighed from forty to fifty tons, lying at the base of the walls, while the heaps of rubble were so big that it was impossible to judge where ground level had originally been. This answered one question which had always intrigued me, viz. how the garrison had survived the shell-fire and the mines. Actually this rubble had provided an entirely shell-proof barrier round the whole building, being twenty to thirty feet higher than the level of the dungeon in which the besieged finally took refuge.' Gerahty, *Road to Madrid*, pp. 162–3.

92 Such, at least, is what is claimed by one staff officer who was directly involved in the process. See Martín Blásquez, *I Helped to Build an Army*, pp. 293–7. One thing that is very clear is that, despite what is often said, it had absolutely nothing to do with the Soviet military advisers who appeared in the Republican zone from the beginning of November onwards.

93 For a hostile view of the mixed brigade as a form of organization, one can turn to Segismundo Casado López, in July 1936 commander of the Presidential Guard. As he later wrote, 'The ... celebrated mixed brigades absorbed an enormous number of men who had no means of fighting, robbing them of their tactical mobility without increasing their firing power. This waste of men meant mobilising a great number of reinforcements which meant in turn an alarming reduction of hands of all work behind the lines. It was [therefore] not possible to practice the fundamental principle of the economy of forces.' S. Casado López, *The Last Days of Madrid: the End of the Second Spanish Republic* (Madrid, 1939), p. 60. In his memoirs, the Communist commander Manuel Tagüeña attempted to defend the mixed brigades by claiming that the fault was not their composition but rather the fact that the Republican high command stuck to the supposedly outmoded concept of a continuous front and refused to fight battles of manoeuvre, but this argument is at best disingenuous. Tagüeña, *Testimonio de dos guerras*, p. 145.

94 For an important recent study of the Political Commissariat, see J. Matthews, 'The vanguard of sacrifice? Political commissars in the Republic Popular Army during the Spanish Civil War, 1936–1939', *War in History*, XXI, No. 1 (January, 2014), pp. 82–101. At least in the International Brigades, the memoir material is inclined to be quite positive. Here, for example, is J. R. Jump, a twenty-one-year-old newspaper reporter who enlisted in the British battalion in 1938: 'The commissar's work, looking after the welfare of the men, was not confined to seeing that the meals were good. They were responsible for education as well. Whenever circumstances permitted, the afternoons were devoted to cultural or political activities. This was not mere indoctrination, though Communist-Party policy was often propounded. Many activities were purely educational ... When we were in action there was no time for education, and the commissar devoted most of his time to looking after the welfare of the men.' Cit. P. Toynbee (ed.), *The Distant Drum: Reflections on the Spanish Civil War* (London, 1976), pp. 118–19. Appointed political commissar of the machine-gun company of the Lincoln battalion, Hank Rubin provides a useful summary: 'My job was to see that the needs of the men in the company were taken care of as well as was possible, that they were as safe as could be in combat, that they were enthusiastic about their work, that they were in good physical condition, that they were learning to be good soldiers, and that they had the correct political attitude.' H. Rubin, *Spain's Cause was Mine: a Memoir of an American Medic in the Spanish Civil War* (Carbondale, Illinois, 1997), pp. 83–4.

95 Casado, *Last Days of Madrid*, p. 58.

96 Heredía, *Monarquía, dictadura, república*, p. 226.

97 As Lister points out, four of the commanders of the first six mixed brigades were drawn from the Fifth Regiment. Lister, *Memorias de un luchador*, p. 140.

98 E.g. R. Salas, 'The growth and role of the Republican Popular Army' in Carr, *Republic and Civil War in Spain*, pp. 191–2.

99 Garate Córdoba, *Tenientes en campaña*, pp. 33–41.

100 Ibid., pp. 49–64.

101 See Alpert, *Republican Army in the Spanish Civil War*, pp. 126–8. Writing in southern Spain early in 1937, Franz Borkenau paints an interesting picture of one such officer: 'The commander of the reinforcements going to Málaga ... was, I believe, a characteristic specimen of the new officer corps. He had been for five years a sergeant in Morocco ... Then he retired, learned locomotive engineering and got a job at the Madrid northern station, one of the strongholds of the UGT. There he became

a trade-unionist and a Socialist. He enlisted again in the Republican forces when the war broke out ... and soon advanced to the rank of captain ... His men obviously liked him, but not in the deferential manner one is used to ... They absolutely treated him as their equal.' Borkenau, *Spanish Cockpit*, p. 214.

102 For a good account of the early volunteers, see J. L. Alcofar Nassaes, *Spansky: los extranjeros que lucharon en la Guerra Civil Española* (Barcelona, 1973), pp. 13–72.

103 From the beginning, the Spanish Civil War was a matter of great concern to the Comintern. For details, see T. Rees, 'The highpoint of Comintern Influence? The Communist Party and the Civil War in Spain', in T. Rees and A. Thorpe (eds.), *International Communism and the Communist International, 1919–1943* (Manchester, 1998), pp. 143–67.

104 A curious exception here is the Dutch journalist Fanny Schoonheyt. Having joined the PSUC militia in July 1936 and fought on the Aragón front until gravely injured in a road accident, she remained in its ranks even after militarization and appears to have ended up as an instructor in a training camp. Scholten, 'Fanny, queen of the machine gun.'

105 Accounts of the formation of the International Brigades are numerous. See, for example, C. Vidal, *Las brigadas internacionales* (Madrid, 1998), pp. 48–70; J. Delperrie de Bayas, *Las brigadas internacionales* (Madrid, 1980), pp. 68–83; R. D. Richardson, *Comintern Army: the International Brigades in the Spanish Civil War* (Lexington, Kentucky, 1982), pp. 31–46; D. Kowalsky, 'The Soviet Union and the International Brigades, 1936–1939', *Journal of Slavic Military Studies*, XIX, No. 4 (December, 2006), pp. 681–704.

106 For all this, see Cerdá, 'Political ascent and military command.' See also Preston, *Franco*, pp. 175–87.

107 Martínez Bande, *Marcha sobre Madrid*, pp. 205–6.

108 Sender, *War in Spain*, pp. 169–70.

109 Iniesta Cano, *Memorias y recuerdos*, pp. 88–9. Behind the collapsing Republican front, meanwhile, there reigned the utmost chaos, as witnessed, for example, in Cipriano Mera's account of his disputes with the regular officers attached to the column of which his men formed a part, a plan to mount a counterattack on San Martín de Valdeiglesias having to be abandoned when Mera insisted on putting it to a vote amongst his subordinate commanders. See Mera, *Guerra, exilio y cárcel*, pp. 50–3.

110 The tankettes were not the only foreign weapons involved in the ground fighting, a newly arrived consignment of twenty-six Italian 65mm M13 infantry guns having also been sent to the front. It should be noted that, poorly protected and armed only with machine-guns, the L3 was all but useless on the battlefield, and that the German Panzer I was only marginally better.

111 Cardozo, *March of a Nation*, pp. 159–62.

112 Sender, *War in Spain*, pp. 202–3.

113 I. Hidalgo de Cisneros, *Cambio de Rumbo: Memorias* (Bucharest, 1964), II, p. 160.

114 O. de Wet, *Cardboard Crucifix: the Story of a Pilot in Spain* (London, 1938), pp. 30–1. Yet the number of planes supporting the Nationalist advance was not so very great: three Savoia SM81s, fifteen Junkers Ju52s, sixteen Heinkel He46 light bombers (twenty of these aircraft had been handed over to the Nationalists in mid-September), twelve Heinkel He51s and nine Fiat Cr32s. See Hills, *Battle for Madrid*, p. 78; Salas Larrázabal, *Air War over Spain*, p. 79.

115 Permuy López, *Aviación en la Guerra Civil Española*, p. 68.

116 For a good description of the counterattack at Illescas, see Modesto, *Soy del Quinto Regimiento*, pp. 110–11.

117 The situation underlying these changes was more complex than it seems. Asensio Torrado, certainly, had presided over a series of defeats, but it is doubtful whether either Miaja or Pozas would have done any better. Far more important was the fact

that Asensio was an independent figure who was not prepared to go along with the Communists. Certainly Koltsov is highly critical: as early as 10 September, he was writing in his diary that Asensio was 'a rather shadowy figure lacking in political and moral formation alike.' Koltsov, *Diario de la Guerra de España*, p. 80.

118 Following the fall of Navalcarnero, Cardozo took the trouble to inspect the defences that had been constructed there: 'I found the barbed-wire belt thin and ill-placed. The trenches themselves, however, were properly dug, had both parapet and parados, and, though not deep enough to need a fire-step, were capable of providing adequate shelter.' Cardozo, *March of a Nation*, p. 176.

119 Thomas, *Spanish Civil War*, pp. 441–3; D. Kowalski, 'Operation X: Soviet Russia and the Spanish Civil War', *Bulletin of Spanish Studies*, No. 1 (January, 2014), pp. 159–78; J. McCannon, 'Soviet military intervention in the Spanish Civil War, 1936–1939: A re-examination', *Russian History*, XXII, No. 2 (Summer, 1995), pp. 154–80.

120 For details of the T26, see Albert, *Carros de combate*, pp. 23–8.

121 For the arms deliveries received in October 1936, see Howson, *Arms for Spain*, pp. 278–82. One weapon that featured in these shipments about which there has been much confusion is the so-called 'Remington rifle.' In reality, this was not a Remington at all, but rather an exact copy of the Russian Moisin-Nagant M1891 7.62mm rifle (the standard Russian infantry weapon of the time), manufactured in the United States by the Remington arms company in the First World War for the Tsarist government. One other source of arms was Mexico whose progressive government sent the Republic 20,000 Mauser 7mm M1936 rifles. These, however, should not be confused with the so-called 'Mexicanski' rifles supplied to some units of the International Brigades. These were more of the same 'Remingtons' we have just described, the difference being that, with Russia in the hands of the Bolsehviks, they ended up being exported to Mexico. No longer needed by the Mexicans on account of the adoption of the M1936, they were then acquired by private arms dealers and sold on to Spain. For Mexican aid to Spain, see M. Ojeda Revah, *Mexico and the Spanish Civil War: Domestic Politics and the Republican Cause* (Eastbourne, 2014).

122 The subject of Russian public opinion is discussed in some detail in G. J. Albert, '"To help the Republicans not just by donations and rallies but with the rifle": militant solidarity with the Spanish Republic in the Soviet Union, 1936–1937', *European Review of History*, XXI, No. 4 (September, 2014), pp. 501–18.

123 Modesto, *Soy del Quinto Regimiento*, p. 111.

124 As George Hills as pointed out, strategically speaking, those in favour of abandoning Madrid were entirely in the right: the capital was not a centre of industry and did not mean that much to a country where there were not only several strong regional nationalisms but also a long tradition of localism and, within older generations of republicanism, federalism as well. Meanwhile, pulling out would save thousands of men, not least because it would mean abandoning the dangerously exposed salient stretching westwards along the foot of the Sierra de Guadarrama and eliminating the looming problem of how to feed the city: already, there was no rail connection between Madrid and the rest of the country and only one major road. Far better, then, to surrender it to the Nationalists, who would thereby be handed a massive administrative problem, and all the more so as the rivers east of Madrid, most importantly the Jarama, provided an excellent defensive position. The kindest thing that can be said about the opposing position, therefore, is that for the time being it saved the population of Madrid from the retribution that the city all too clearly faced at the hands of Franco, though what it was in fact based on, as far as its leading proponents were concerned, was the calculation that a climactic battle for the capital was the policy best served to advance the interests of the Communist Party. Hills, *Battle for Madrid*, pp. 86–7.

125 For an English-language transcript, see Ibid., p. 83.

126 Cit. Martín Blásquez, *I Helped to Build an Army*, p. 286. The failure of the infantry is scarcely surprising: according to Koltsov, some of the troops involved only received their weapons the night before the action. Koltsov, *Diario de la Guerra de España*, p. 159.

127 Martín Blásquez, *I Helped to Build an Army*, p. 287. Far too thinly armoured to be able to fulfil its role as an infantry-support vehicle, the T26 also had too few periscopes and episcopes to be able to operate effectively when closed up for combat. See S. J. Zaloga, 'Soviet tank operations in the Spanish Civil War', *Journal of Slavic Military Studies*, XII, No. 3 (December, 2007), p. 156. Needless to say, the infantry's point of view was very different: according to them, indeed, the disaster was not their fault at all. Thus: 'The tank crews ... should have concentrated on the task of providing fire support, and, especially, knocking out the enemy machine-guns, this being what their commander and I had agreed. Meanwhile, our artillery preparation was too short-lived and undertaken with pieces of small calibre only, the net result being that the enemy's strong points remained undamaged; as for his guns, they were never reached by our shells at all.' Lister, *Memorias de un luchador*, p. 165. A more balanced view is that of Juan Modesto: 'It was the first time our combatants had attacked the enemy with the support of tanks. As for the tank crews, they were fighting alongside an infantry force that was practically unknown to them. The net result was that the necessary co-ordination was never achieved.' Modesto, *Soy del Quinto Regimiento*, p. 114.

128 See S. J. Zaloga, *Spanish-Civil-War Tanks: the Proving Ground for Blitzkrieg* (Oxford, 2010), p. 16.

129 Armed with four machine-guns, the I15 outgunned the Fiats, while, if less well-armed (it only had two machine-guns), the I16 was faster, constructed entirely from metal and possessed of a higher ceiling. C. Shores, *Spanish-Civil-War Airforces* (London, 1977), pp. 10–14 *passim*.

130 Candelas, *Adventures of an Innocent*, p. 57.

131 For García Oliver's account of his appointment to the government, see J. García Oliver, *My Revolutionary Life* (London, 2008), pp. 55–8. Meanwhile, Federica Montseny was Spain's first female minister.

4

THE BATTLE OF MADRID

The battle of Madrid has been described as the central epic of the Spanish Civil War. Presented as a dramatic clash between fascism and democracy or between Christianity and Bolshevism, according to taste, it seized the imagination of the whole of Europe. Perhaps because of this, more nonsense has been written about it than almost any other episode of said conflict. In book after book and article after article, the relics of over-excited inter-war journalism, not to mention outright Communist propaganda, are recycled, and so we read of the first battalions of the International Brigades parading into battle down the Gran Vía led by officers with drawn swords to the acclaim of a cheering multitude; of militiamen commuting to and from the front line on the Metro; of groups of militiamen waiting to rush forward to pick up the rifles of the fallen; of an utterly fictitious women's battalion doing battle with the Nationalists at the Puente de Segovia, and that despite the fact that no Nationalist soldier came within rifle shot of the place.[1] Oral history, meanwhile, has fuelled the flame. In his well-known *Blood of Spain*, Ronald Fraser interviewed dozens of Republican veterans of the siege and faithfully recorded their tales of a city gripped by popular fervour, of women boiling oil ready to throw it on the first Moor who darkened their doors, of union officials spontaneously organizing infantry battalions, of simple workers spurred on to acts of heroism by the endlessly repeated mantra of 'No pasarán!', of old men and women coming forward to offer their services at recruiting offices, of bitter political rivals sinking their differences and lending their weight to a single great endeavour, of taxi-drivers turning themselves overnight into tank-drivers.[2] However, whilst all this is very noble and uplifting, the truth, alas, is more prosaic, if by no means devoid of either courage or excitement.

The logical place to begin an account of the battle of Madrid is the arrival of the weary Nationalist forces on the southernmost outskirts of the city on

6 November 1936. Behind them, as we have seen, lay the famous 'March on Madrid' and, more particularly, over a month of fierce fighting. If progress up until the capture of Toledo had been rapid enough, since then resistance had intensified, not least because the Republicans were falling back ever more closely on their sources of supply. Thus, the famous action at Seseña had been but the latest in a series of battles that had cost the Nationalists hundreds of casualties. Nevertheless, the mood in the Nationalist camp was upbeat, supremely confident even. Determined to be in at the death, Mola was travelling from Avila to join the Army of Africa in the outskirts of the capital, whilst behind the lines lurked a number of battalions of Falangist and Carlist militiamen, not to mention eight mobile courts-martial, the task of these elements being to move into the city

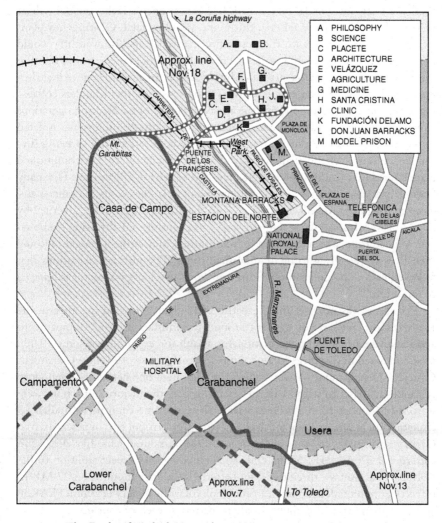

MAP 4.1   The Battle of Madrid, November 1936.

behind the combat troops and embark on *la limpieza* forthwith (fearing that their training was insufficient for the rigours of battle, the Nationalist high command as yet preferred not to make use of such forces in the front line).[3] Meanwhile, the night of 6 November saw the Junkers and Savoias drop thousands of leaflets proclaiming that liberation was nigh, and advising the civilian populace (which had, it was assured, nothing to fear) to remain calm and endeavour to avoid areas of combat.[4]

According to some sources, the arrival of the Nationalists before Madrid provoked a lively debate in Nationalist headquarters, with some elements urging Franco not to launch a direct attack, one of his most trusted staff officers, Antonio Barroso, even going so far as to argue vociferously that a frontal attack could not be pulled off with the troops that were available.[5] The *caudillo*, however, was adamant: Varela, he claimed, had always been a lucky general, whilst he further implied that to falter at this point would be fatal. Contingency plans were drawn up to deal with the possibility that the Republican militia would not simply cave in, but, based as they were on the idea of Franco's troops fighting their way to the heart of the city block by block, it is difficult to believe that they were anything other than a fig leaf: everything rested on the defenders collapsing at the outset.[6] Yet to postpone the attack in favour of outflanking operations aimed at cutting the capital's communications was utterly impossible: isolated in the heart of Spain, Franco's troops were already at serious risk of being surrounded and overwhelmed and could risk neither further delay nor complicated manoeuvres that would stretch their own line of retreat still further. For many Nationalists, there was also a potent human factor. In the words of Franco's airforce commander, Alfredo Kindelán: 'Our operations ceased to be governed by the art of war. Instead what counted was … the sentimental attraction exercised by a Madrid from which thousands of our brothers in imminent danger of losing their lives were calling to us in anguished tones. The military operations that followed cannot be understood if this important psychological factor is ignored or forgotten.'[7]

The scene was now set for the battle of Madrid. Grouped together in the southernmost outskirts of the city around the military base of Campamento and the airfield of Getafe, the Nationalist assault forces numbered some 10,000 men organized in five brigades or columns, namely those of Asensio Cabanillas, Castejón, Delgado and Barrón, together with a new one headed by Heliodoro Rolando de Tella. In support of the assault troops, the majority of whom were seasoned Moors and Foreign Legionaries, there was one company of Italian L3 tankettes, including a section of the flame-thrower version, two of newly arrived German Panzer Is, and one of Spanish 'Bilbao' armoured cars, five three-gun batteries of 37mm PAK36 anti-tank guns (another very recent addition to the Nationalist armoury), three two-gun batteries of Italian 65mm C.65/17 M1913 infantry guns intended for use in an anti-tank role, one battery of 20mm FLAK30 anti-aircraft guns, and eighteen artillery batteries, each of four guns (viz. five batteries 65mm M13, five batteries 75mm Schneider M06, four batteries 105mm

Vickers M22, four batteries 155mm Schneider M1917). Meanwhile, of the 100 aircraft available to the Nationalists, around fifty were being employed on the Madrid front, including eighteen Junkers Ju52s, six Savoia-Machetti SM81s, eighteen Fiat Cr32s and ten Romeo Ro37 light bombers (the latest addition to the aviation available to Franco).[8] Facing them in the front line were about 13,000 Republican militia organized into five different columns – those of Barceló, Escobar, Bueno, Alvarez and Carrasco – supported by something over fifty aircraft, the majority of them now modern Russian Polikarpov I15 and I16 fighters and Tupolev SB2 light bombers, two Renault FT17s of the pre-war army, a variety of improvised armoured lorries, approximately eighty Russian T26 tanks and BA3 armoured cars, all of them armed with either 45 or 37mm guns, forty-five artillery pieces, several armoured trains, and, for whatever they were worth – a point on which there is much debate – a certain number of Russian military advisers, including such future luminaries of the Red Army as Nikolai Voronov and Alexei Rodimtsev.[9] Finally, there were at least 10,000 fresh troops in immediate reserve, including two more columns of militia (those of José María Enciso and Pelayo Clairac, both of whom had been officers in the regular army) and the first three mixed brigades, of which one – the XI – was composed of foreign volunteers.[10]

On the whole, then, the balance was remarkably even: if the Republicans had better tanks and aircraft and superior numbers, the Nationalists were blessed with better morale, organization, leadership and training. However, battles are not just matters of men and machines but also of terrain, and here the Republicans were possessed of a number of major advantages, particularly in respect of any attack coming from the south. Thus, advancing, as the Nationalists were, along the axis of the main road to Andalucía, they would first hit a belt of old villages, impoverished suburbs and shanty towns in which their superior firepower and manoeuvrability would count for very little. Having cleared that, they would then come to the River Manzanares, which at this point was canalized (and therefore impossible to ford) as well as being possessed of only two bridges. And, finally, there was the long climb to the city proper, this being situated on a bluff that rose very steeply from the river and was in many places devoid of any cover, matters being still further complicated by the fact that to reach the city centre, the attackers would have to fight their way through the maze of narrow streets and alleys known as the *barrios bajos*. This formidable succession of obstacles, true, could be outflanked by pushing northwards round the western fringes of the city via the woods and thickets of the old royal hunting park known as the Casa de Campo and taking advantage of the easier terrain that lay beyond, but such a move was possessed of major dangers for so small a force as the one available to the Nationalists. If some of Franco's advisers quailed at the prospect of a direct assault on the city, it was therefore perfectly understandable.

Needless to say, such detachment is easy eighty years after the event. In the Madrid of November 1936, it would have been impossible. For all the boasts of the various left-wing political movements – the Socialists, the Communists and the Anarchists – that Madrid would prove the grave of fascism, it seemed that the Nationalist offensive was invincible, matters not being helped by the fact that the government, now swelled by four Anarchist ministers, abandoned the capital for Valencia on 6 November, leaving the city in the hands of the newly appointed commander of the forces on the Madrid front, General José Miaja Menant. The city, and with it the few roads that still connected it with the outside world, was clogged with refugees, many of the defenders were demoralized and exhausted, and the authorities were in a state of complete confusion. Amongst those who witnessed the panic that gripped the city was the Russian correspondent Mikhail Koltsov: 'All the streets became blocked with traffic ... A compact ... mass of humanity surged to and fro, jostling one another and wearing itself out with its wailing and lamentation. Amidst the crowd could be seen cars, lorries ... carts full of bits of furniture. Particularly noteworthy was an armoured car slung about in the most shameful manner with mattresses, pillows, baskets and bundles of clothing.'[11] It is often claimed, particularly on the Left, that Madrid was saved by the heroism and commitment of its own population, but such a claim is hard to sustain. Certainly, figures such as Dolores Ibarruri, a Communist of Basque origin who had been one of the few Communist deputies elected to the *cortes* in February 1936 and had emerged as a speaker of immense power, made speech after speech proclaiming that it was better to die on one's feet than to die on one's knees; certainly, Communists, Anarchists and Socialists alike vied with one another in a massive propaganda campaign designed to mobilize the popula- tion; certainly, again, many *madrileños*, albeit mostly party militants, volunteered for the front, helped dig trenches and build barricades, or were otherwise actively involved in the struggle; certainly, yet again, the poorer districts of the capital, at least, were solidly pro-Republican.[12] However, the effect of all this is, at best, intangible, and one cannot but wonder what really would have happened had the Nationalists ever broken through. For example, even the committed Anarchist Gregorio Gallego admits that 6 November saw the inhabitants of the southern suburbs flee their homes *en masse* in a desperate rush to reach the safety of the city proper. 'At nine in the morning shells started falling around the Puente de Toledo ... Up until that moment the evacuation of the zone had been proceed- ing relatively smoothly, but there now emerged a tidal wave of people trying to save what they could from their homes. Controlling it was neither possible nor wise.'[13] Present in Madrid throughout the battle, the United States military atta- ché, Stephen Fuqua, was stark in his analysis of the situation:

> It seemed a certainty that ... the capital was doomed. The sight of the demoralised retreating militia, the departure of the government from Madrid, the hurried escape of noted leftists, all combined to make the occasion opportune for the capture of the city by the advancing Nationalist columns, the morale and spirit of which were very high as a result of the uninterrupted series of crushing blows they had inflicted upon the enemy.[14]

The disorder that reigned in the city is epitomized by the circumstances surrounding the establishment of the Junta of Defence. Miaja was only notified that he had been given command of the city on the evening of 6 November, and even then he appears only to have received it on the grounds that he happened to be the commander of the city's pre-war garrison, the now non-existent First Division: such was his conduct during the ill-fated Córdoba offensive that it is impossible to believe that he was selected on the grounds of either competence or tenacity.[15] Sealed in an envelope marked not to be opened until six in the morning of the following day, his orders, which turned out to have been accidentally substituted with those intended for the equally lack-lustre Pozas, were to defend the city at all costs, whilst at the same time putting together a junta of defence, but at that moment Miaja had neither a proper headquarters nor any clear idea of how many men and other resources were at his disposal. In the words of the man he selected as his chief of staff, Vicente Rojo:

> The means available for the defence could only be evaluated approximately on account of the confusion that reigned in a front that ... was constantly being broken and over-run ... Whether because of the difficulties thrown up by the fighting ... or the interference of the ... parties and unions that had organised the militias, the columns ... were constantly being remade or reinforced in a most precipitate fashion without ... the sanction of the high command ... To make matters worse, the defenders' proximity to the capital had greatly increased the confusion on account of the greater ease with which the political movements ... could manipulate those forces which they regarded as their own.[16]

Miaja was no hero. According to Largo Caballero, indeed, his reaction to the news that he would be taking charge of the defence of the city was one of horror. Thus, 'The effect produced on Miaja by my words cannot be conceived of without actually having seen it. He went pale and started muttering something to the effect that, whilst he was at the disposition of the government, his family were in the enemy zone, and not just his family, but much of his property. Cutting him short, I said that I had not come to hear such stuff, but rather to talk of matters that were far more important.'[17] Cometh the man, however, cometh the hour. Utterly lacking in charisma Miaja may have been, but at this moment he somehow found the qualities that the defence needed. Stiffened, perhaps, by the unwavering support of the deputy chief of the Russian military mission, Vladimir Gorev, a thirty-six-year-old Red-Army general who had been much employed in a variety of more-or-less covert missions in destinations as far removed as the United States and China, within a matter of hours he had put together the requisite junta of defence, this body being composed of two representatives each of the Socialists, the Communists, the Syndicalists, the Unión Republicana and the Izquierda Republicana (i.e. all the parties represented in the Popular Front other than the supposedly Trotskyite POUM, which was excluded at the demand of the Communists), together with two representatives each from the JSU, the Federación Ibérica de Juventudes Libertarias (or FIJL), the CNT and the Madrid branch of the Socialist cultural institute known as the Casa del Pueblo. All the members were young, some of them, indeed, very young: Santiago Carrillo, for example, was barely twenty. Each of the nine separate elements thus represented was given a separate area of responsibility, but it was beyond doubt Gorev's doing that the most important – defence, public order and the general secretariat – fell to either the Communists or left-wing Socialists of the sort who had been behind the formation of the JSU.[18] From the beginning, then, the defence was in political terms to be above all a Communist affair, and it is in large part to this fact that many of the myths that it generated can be attributed. As for why Miaja fell for the Communists' scheming, the answer is unclear, but one suspects that it was partly because in this hour of crisis, the Communists were the force best placed to help the defence (apart from backing a policy that made perfect sense militarily speaking, the Communists controlled both the tanks and planes that were so desperately needed and the much-vaunted Fifth Regiment), and partly, too, because they were clearly as opposed to the revolution as he was.[19]

Nor was the Junta of Defence Miaja's only creation. Within hours, too, he had organized a general staff based on such officers as happened to be available in the Ministry of War. That these included conceivably the brightest officer in the entire Spanish army, Vicente Rojo Lluch, an erstwhile professor of the academy of Toledo who had seemingly been so disgusted by the corruption and incompetence that he had witnessed during the four years he had spent fighting in Morocco between 1915 and 1919 that he had become a staunch Republican, was sheer luck.[20] However, it is much to Miaja's credit that he appointed Rojo as his chief of staff, whilst he also showed great energy in establishing proper communications with his miscellaneous collection of defenders and stiffening their resolve: within hours of his having taken command, Carrasco and Alvarez were replaced by Arturo Mena and Adolfo Prada Vaquera, both of whom were officers who had been living in retirement in July 1936. Indeed, having assembled the commanders of his various columns at a meeting held in the small hours of 7 November, he even (or so it is said) managed an appropriately heroic speech. Thus, 'The government has gone. The moment has arrived for us to be men … If there is anyone here who is not ready to die, he had better say so now!'[21]

Yet in the event, thanks to a healthy dose of luck combined with the aggressive posture from the start adopted by the commander of the central front, Sebastián Pozas, things were never quite so serious. Thus, when the Nationalists launched their assault on the early morning of 7 November 1936, their plan called for two of their five columns – those of Barrón and Rolando de Tella – to drive directly northwards through the cluster of villages, slums and shanty towns scattered between the Campamento-Getafe area and the Manzanares. However, this advance was essentially to be a holding attack that would distract the attention of the defenders from the main thrust. This would rather come from the columns of Castejón, Asensio and Delgado, all of which would strike northwards through the Casa de Campo to the vicinity of the Puente de los Franceses railway bridge, where they would cross the river and advance through the open ground afforded by the Parque del Oeste and the brand-new campus of the university of Madrid – the so-called University City – thereby completely outflanking the defenders. Reaching the district known as La Moncloa, they would then be able to advance down the major arteries that lead from that point into the heart of the city.[22] Clever though this plan was, however, things immediately went badly wrong. Rolando de Tella and Barrón made some progress, albeit in the face of desperate opposition, but, just as Castejón's men were getting moving, they were thrown into complete confusion by a sudden Republican counterattack from the north-west. We come here to the role played in the battle by Pozas. Whereas Miaja only commanded the Republican forces actually in the city, Pozas headed all the government troops in central Spain, and, as such, was able to channel a stream of reinforcements to the defenders, one of the first formations to be put on the move in this manner being the newly formed XI International Brigade. Yet Pozas did not solely think in terms of shoring up the defenders by direct means. In advancing on Madrid, the Nationalists had driven a long finger of territory deep into the Republican zone whilst the rolling steppes through which they had advanced offered little protection against counterattacks, all that they had to protect their communications being Monasterio's cavalry and a heterogeneous collection of militia. From the beginning, then, the solution was obvious: by all means man the barricades in Madrid, but fight the real battle outside the city in an endeavour to force the attackers to dissipate their strength or even cut them off altogether. While Miaja struggled to get the situation under control in Madrid, then, Pozas was sending the first of the new mixed brigades to positions on either side of the city: to the south-east, the I Brigade of Enrique Líster occupied Vacíamadrid and Arganda, while to the south-west, the III Brigade of José-María Galán Rodríguez, in July 1936 a lieutenant in the Carabineers, whose brother, Fermín, had been one of the two officers shot following the abortive Republican coup of December 1930, was moved to the vicinity of Aravaca and Húmera.[23]

As dawn broke on 7 November, then, just as the first shells to fall on the city of Madrid itself were exploding in the vicinity of the Paseo de Rosales, the Nationalists were suddenly hit by attacks on both flanks.[24] On the right, Líster was seen off with few problems, but on the left, Galán was supported by numerous T-26 tanks and therefore made some progress. Beaten off though the III Mixed Brigade eventually was, Castejón was badly wounded, whilst the Nationalists were in consequence so much delayed that by dusk they had advanced no further than the southern edge of the Casa de Campo. A captain in the Foreign Legion, Carlos Iniesta Cano was one of those caught up in the fight:

> After a number of combats of singular ferocity in which we had to engage in Retamares in support of Castejón's column, we pressed on towards ... the Puerta de Batán. As we advanced we were attacked by the fire of a Red column that had occupied some dominating heights that overlooked the

road we were following ... Further progress ... being almost impossible, we were forced to launch a strong ... counterattack in order to neutralise this act of resistance. Moving on, we found that the Puerta de Batán had been blocked up, and we therefore had no option but to use picks to open a breach in the wall of the Casa de Campo ... By now night had fallen, and, there being no moon, it ... was decided that we should dig in ... rather than risk a night battle in an area totally unknown to us.[25]

Only in the area of Carabanchel and Usera did the Nationalists make much progress. A medical orderly who we know only as Ramón was advancing with the column of Rolando de Tella on the latter settlement: 'We took one of the hills on which the *barrio* was built without difficulty, but the second one cost us a great deal of effort, and only fell on account of the spirit and daring of our good legionaries ... Obviously enough, we suffered our share of losses, but of course they were much fewer than those suffered by the other side.'[26] True enough, perhaps, but the Republicans had more men to lose. Worse was to come: in the warren-like southern suburbs, the tanks supporting Rolando de Tella and Barrón were at a serious disadvantage, and a number were knocked out by dynamite, petrol bombs or grenades.[27] One such casualty was the command-tank of the L3 company. Manned by a Captain Vidal-Cuadras, this was captured after it bogged down in a drainage ditch and was found to contain a large packet of official papers.[28] Inspected by the Republican high command, these proved to be nothing less than the Nationalists' complete plan of operations, the night of 7 November in consequence witnessing frantic efforts to reinforce the Casa de Campo. Amongst the men sent in was the column of José María Enciso, whose forces included the crack presidential guard, one of the few formations of loyal troops that was still intact.[29] Yet the mood in the city remained febrile. The Socialist press-censor Arturo Barea, for example, was at his post in the great telephone building:

> Towards two in the morning somebody brought me the news that the fascists had crossed ... the Manzanares ... We expected from one moment to the next to hear under our window shots, machine-gun bursts, hand grenades and the caterpillar chains of tanks clanking and screeching on paving stones.[30]

If there were plenty of Republicans who thought the battle had been lost, there were plenty of Nationalists who thought it had been won. Present with the attackers was the ardently pro-Franco Harold Cardozo:

> Rumours ... were flying about everywhere ... Reports came that Nationalist tanks had seized two bridges ... that they had entered the actual streets of Madrid and were being followed by picked assault battalions ... that the Gran Vía and the great Telephone skyscraper were in the hands of Varela's troops ... I must confess that I was confident of rapid victory.[31]

With matters in this state, one issue loomed particularly large in the minds of the defenders. Locked up in the prison mentioned by Barea – a massive structure close to the botanical garden represented by the Parque del Oeste – and other centres of detention were some 5,000 prisoners, including retired politicians, generals and admirals, many of whom had not been active for many years; representatives and sympathizers of the various right-wing movements that had opposed the Republicans and Socialists; Falangists; Carlists; members of the clergy; and, finally, many of the officers taken prisoner at Campamento and the Montaña barracks. To leave these individuals where they were was clearly impossible, as their recapture would have simultaneously both handed a massive propaganda victory to Franco and given him several hundred more-or-less useful army officers. That being the case, the Junta of Defence decided to move them to alternative accommodation at Alcalá de Henares, the night of 7–8 November therefore seeing five convoys of prisoners dispatched from the prison in fleets of busses and trucks. However, only two of them reached their destination safely, the other three being seized by gangs of militiamen and wiped out in mass executions at the villages of Torrejón de Ardoz and Paracuellos de Jarama. For this, the Junta of Defence bore no direct responsibility: indeed, to do the authorities justice, they were at this very time disarming the *chekas* that had been responsible for the purge that had cost so many lives over the past three months.[32] Yet, even so, the Junta's hands were not entirely clean: over the next month, no fewer than twenty-eight further convoys were evacuated from the city with so little protection that several more were waylaid and put to death in the same manner as before. Nor, meanwhile, can the possibility be ignored that some of the more hard-line members of the Junta of Defence were guilty of collusion with the killers. To this day, the death toll is a matter of dispute, but at least 1,000 of the prisoners perished, while the total was probably somewhere between two and three times that number. Whatever the truth, however, it was a singularly unpleasant episode and one that does the cause of the Republic no credit whatsoever.[33]   *Killed prisoners*

Reprehensible though the massacres at Paracuellos undoubtedly were, the Nationalists were scarcely without blame for the situation: not only had they proved still more merciless, but also Mola's boasts of a 'fifth column' were at the very least unwise. Meanwhile, they were losing the battle. Given the superior resources of the Republicans, the rebels' only hope had been to seize the city immediately. Denied a quick victory by the events of 7 November, they were now locked into a struggle of attrition from which they were unlikely to emerge victorious. This, however, is not to say that the defence did not have some alarming moments in the days that followed, of which by no means the least difficult came the very next day. Thus, on 8 November, whilst Rolando de Tella and Barrón fought their way forward house by house through Carabanchel, Castejón's men – now commanded by a Colonel Bartomeu – broke into the Casa de Campo and had by the end of the day reached the line of the main railway to the north and captured the dominant height of Garabitas. Amongst Bartomeu's troops – just 1,100 strong – was Frank Thomas, a young Welshman who had managed to enlist in the Foreign Legion:

> On the second day of our stay in Madrid, Sunday 8 November – notable also for the last wash I was to have for three weeks – we advanced ... into the ... famous Casa de Campo, entering through breaches blown in the twelve-foot-high walls. In this vast hunting park ... we were ... surrounded with huge trees and tangled undergrowth ... Bursting from a thicket, we nearly dropped upon a huge Russian tank ... on the road below us. Before the surprised occupants even realised our presence, its inside was on fire, the result of bottles of petrol ... flung at the loopholes of the tank.[34]

A more distant observer was the American journalist H. E. Knoblaugh. Comfortably ensconced high up in the landmark *telefónica*, he had a view of the battle that was privileged indeed. Thus: 'Loyalist and enemy infantry could be seen as small dots on the landscape, now moving forward under cover of an artillery barrage, now being forced back ... Shellbursts made small puffs on the slopes of the gentle rises to the south of the Casa de Campo.'[35]

The continued advance of the enemy meant that the night of 7 November was anything but one of tranquillity. On the one hand, terrible stories were going round of the savagery of the Moors and Foreign Legionaries, savagery, alas, that was all too real: reconnoitring an abandoned village near the Cerro de los Angeles on 13 November, for example, the International Brigader Keith Watson came across the raped and mutilated body of a woman.[36] If the greatest enemy advances had come in the Casa de Campo, in the southern suburbs the enemy had only been held with the greatest difficulty. Among the defenders was Antonio Candela:

> The enemy attacked with many men, machine-guns and mortars ... We were then forced to retreat to another trench further back ... As we tumbled head first into the new trenches ... we were half-crazy with the dust, the smoke and the terrible noise. We began firing again at the advancing enemy, who were now no more than twenty metres from us, until they had been so decimated that they had to withdraw ... Out of about 100 men in my company, seven men were left. The rest I never saw again.[37]

For a further example of the chaos, we can turn to Lister's I Mixed Brigade. Stationed at the eastern extremity of the front, it found itself completely out of touch. Salvador Múñoz was the commissar of one of its three infantry battalions:

> We had no connection whatsoever, neither by telephone, nor by any other means with the high command. Realising that to hold our position no longer had any object given that the Nationalists had outflanked us by taking Villaverde, and that we could participate in the defence of Madrid

in some other position in which we could be of more help, we resolved to retire in the course of the night and see if we could find somebody who could tell us what to do. Setting off in total darkness, we skirted the Cerro de los Angeles, and made our way with some difficulty towards Vaciamadrid by way of Perales del Río. By dawn we had reached the ... Valencia highway. The whole way we had not seen a single soul, neither friend nor enemy.[38]

Thanks to this completely unauthorized retreat, the Cerro de los Angeles, an isolated hill that dominated the country for miles around, fell into the hands of the Nationalists without a shot being fired. Yet, despite the arrival of a new column under Siro Alonso, which was deployed on the southern edge of the Casa de Campo, thereafter progress slowed once again. Alonso, Rolando de Tella and Barrón became completely bogged down a mile or so south of the Manzanares; every attempt by Delgado to clear the eastern fringes of the Casa de Campo was beaten back; and the repeated efforts of Asensio Cabanillas and Castejón's replacement, Maximino Bartomeu, to seize the Puente de los Franceses and the adjacent Puente Nuevo and get across the river in the Parque del Oeste sector – where, unlike further south, the river did not run in a steep-sided canal but was rather broad and shallow – were mown down with heavy losses. Key here was Republican control of the lofty railway bridge. To quote Rojo, 'Apparently insignificant, but of extraordinary technical importance, one factor that contributed to checking the attack and obliging the troops of Column No. 1 [i.e. Asensio Cabanillas] to go to ground ... was the handful of machine guns that had been skilfully dug in in protected positions on the Puente de los Franceses.'[39]

Virtually surrounded, the Nationalists in the Casa de Campo were constantly shelled and bombed while fresh heart was given to the defenders by the sight of Russian aircraft in the skies above the city and, more particularly, the timely arrival of the first reinforcements dispatched to the city by Pozas. We come here to perhaps the most famous moment of the entire battle. Thus, on the morning of 8 November, a column of troops began to defile through the city from the Atocha railway station in the direction of the Parque del Oeste. This was none other than the newly formed XI International Brigade, and the traditional version of the story tells of a triumphant march through the city in which the volunteers were mobbed by cheering crowds shouting excitedly that the Russians had come, and impressed all and sundry with their disciplined bearing and modern armament. Here, for example, is the oft-quoted account of Geoffrey Cox of the *News Chronicle*:

The next morning I was drinking coffee in [a] bar of the Gran Vía when I heard shouting and clapping outside. I walked out to the pavement edge ... Up the street from the direction of the Ministry of War came a long column of marching men. They wore a kind of khaki uniform and loose brown Glengarry caps [i.e. berets] like those of the British tank corps.

> They were marching in excellent formation. The tramp, tramp of their boots sounded in perfect unison. Over their shoulders were slung rifles of obviously modern design ... Each section had its officers, some carrying swords and revolvers ... The few people who were about lined the roadway, shouting almost hysterically, 'Salud! Salud!'[40]

Both at the time and since, much was made of the arrival of these troops, and it has often been claimed that they saved the city. This is not the case, however. Although undoubtedly mostly brave and well-motivated, the brigade had fewer than 2,000 men and was neither well-armed, nor well-equipped, nor well-uniformed nor well-trained, having, as we have seen, been flung together only days before. John Sommerfield, who was a machine-gunner in the largely Franco-Belgian Commune-de-Paris battalion, describes how he and his fellows were issued with clothing and equipment in such a manner that 'everybody got something and no-one everything', how his battalion was only issued with rifles – 7.62mm Moisin-Nagant M1891s manufactured in the United States for the Tsarist army in the First World War – on the very day they left for the front, and how the machine-gun company only got its guns – the heavy, complicated and hopelessly unreliable St. Etienne M1907[41] – when it actually arrived in Madrid.[42] At the same time, there was no triumphal march across the city – Sommerfield rather describes a plodding, dispirited progress through empty streets[43] – whilst the brigade did not fire a shot on 8 November and was never involved in the crucial fighting round the Puente de los Franceses at all.[44] On the contrary, having spent the night in the comparative safety of the Faculty of Philosophy and Letters on the western fringes of the University City, the brigade advanced across the river in an area well clear of the fighting, and, now armed not just with the dismal St. Etienne but also with a consignment of much more reliable Lewis guns issued on the evening of its arrival, went into the line in the Pozuelo-Húmera sector north of the Casa de Campo.[45] That night saw the death of the first British volunteer to fall under the standard of the International Brigades in the person of a sometime Cambridge student called Maclaurin (another man named Yates went missing and is also assumed to have been killed), but it is clear that it saw no serious action until the counterattack of 13 November (see below).[46] Yet, when all is said and done, the arrival of the XI Brigade, in particular, at least gave the defenders something to cheer themselves up with. 'After the nights of the sixth and the seventh', writes Barea, 'when Madrid had been utterly alone in its resistance, the arrival of those anti-fascists from abroad was an incredible relief. Before the Sunday was over, stories went round of the incredible bravery of the international battalions in the Casa de Campo, of how "our" Germans had stood up to the iron and steel of the machines of the "other" Germans at the spearhead of Franco's troops, of how our German comrades had let themselves be crushed by those tanks rather than retreat.'[47]

Already under serious strain, on 13 November, the Nationalists found themselves having to deal with yet another problem. Thus, attacking from the northern fringes of the Casa de Campo, the III Mixed Brigade, the XI International Brigade, the Palacios militia column and two companies of Russian tanks headed for the dominant Mount Garabitas, only to grind to a halt in the face of heavy fire that appears to have stripped away the infantry supporting the armour and left the latter isolated and exposed.[48] Far from being driven back, then, the Moors and Legionaries actually made some progress and at long last managed to reach the river.[49] On the Nationalist right flank, meanwhile, the fighting centred on the Cerro de los Angeles. Topped by a monastery and the shattered remains of a large statue of Christ that had been dynamited by the militia (a famous photograph shows it being 'executed' prior to the explosion by a *miliciano* firing squad), the hill was well defended, and in consequence the Republicans made little progress. A company of T26 tanks sent to encircle the hill came under heavy artillery fire and beat a hasty retreat, leaving two of their number in flames, whilst the infantry, all of whom were drawn from the newly formed XII International Brigade, became ever more scattered and disoriented. Nor was this surprising. Only 1,500 strong, the brigade had been organized with even more haste than its predecessor and went to the front in a state of complete disorder.[50] One participant was the English volunteer Esmond Romilly (a nephew, no less, of Winston Churchill):

> On both sides west and south-west of the fort [sic] came the flashes and explosions of rifle and machine-gun fire. My dominant feeling was of excitement: then the smack of a bullet in the earth nearby modified this feeling. Jeans ... told us ... that the present orders were for the machine-gun to be prepared for action in a position for continual firing; the rest of us were to take up positions a few hundred yards ahead ... I dug with my bayonet to make a position near the machine-gun. After a lot of clinking and arguing and cursing, I heard the rat-tat-tat of our light-machine-gun ... The effect of this fire was startling and disagreeable. We were suddenly in a hurricane of bullets ... I remembered I was supposed to be doing some protection. Unfortunately I could discern no figures at whom to direct my fire: I discharged five rounds, putting the sights at 1000 metres. It was the first time I had discharged a rifle in my life.[51]

Another man in the same unit (the Thaelmann battalion) was Keith Watson. Temporarily separated from his company, he found himself fighting a one-man war:

> For half the way I was under the cover of a long ridge, [and] I passed an emergency dressing station, stretchers and bandages laid out in readiness. The ridge ended, [and] I came under fire for the first time in my life. Zwiss, zwiss: leaves flew from the bush I sheltered behind ... I felt a deadly cold fear inside my stomach ... The whining noises became more frequent. I was convinced each bullet had a personal venom ... The spoil spurted up

in little clouds all round me. Zwiss, zwiss, zwiss: the machine-gun bullets screamed just above my head. Sobbing with relief, I flung myself under a tree. Sweat soaked me ... The cover was good ... There I lay firing from behind my tree until darkness fell.[52]

Mere long-distance sniping was not going to shift the Nationalists, however, while matters now went from bad to worse. Exhausted and hungry, an entire company of the Thaelmann battalion broke and ran. By nightfall, indeed, the entire brigade was in a state of complete disarray. A White exile who was hoping to work his way back to Russia via service in the International Brigades, Alexei Eisner was an aide-de-camp of the brigade's commander, Mate Zalka (known in Spain as Lukacz):

When night fell, the offensive was abandoned. As the combat had unfolded so the defects of our improvised organization had begun to reveal themselves, but the coming of darkness multiplied them many times over. The commander of the brigade and his general staff had no idea where the first-aid posts, the field kitchens and the other second-line units had got to, while the difficulties were redoubled by the fact that we had no regular contact with the individual battalions just as these in turn had no contact with their constituent companies.[53]

In short, the counterattack of 13 November had been a complete failure. Yet in one sense, this mattered not, the mere fact that the Republicans were capable of such attacks ensuring that the few reserves available to the Nationalists had for the most part to be deployed to protect the flanks of the assault troops rather than being used to reinforce the latter's efforts. The fact was that the balance was now tipping firmly against the Nationalists. Always limited in strength, their forces were depleted by heavy casualties and increasingly exhausted. Even in the air, they were in trouble. Thus, the new Russian fighters that had arrived at Cartagena at the end of the previous month had made their appearance for the first time on 4 November and quickly proved that they had the edge over their Nationalist opponents: the I15 or Chato was better than the He51 and the equal of the Fiat Cr32, whilst the I16 or Mosca more than had the measure of both. Very soon, then, Nationalist planes were falling in appreciable numbers, insult being added to injury by the fact that damaging raids were mounted on the airfields at Avila and Talavera by the fast SB2 light bombers.[54] Flying the desperately slow and under-armed He51, even the most well-trained German pilots were at a hopeless disadvantage, two of them being lost in quick succession over the Casa de Campo.[55] On 6 November, indeed, the commander of the Nationalist air force on the Madrid front had to order his fighter squadrons not to engage the enemy unless they had a clear superiority in numbers.[56] Nationalist accounts such as that of José Larios talk excitedly of pitched battles in which the Fiats and Heinkels inflicted up to twice as many losses as the Polikarpovs – for example:

'November 13 was a … red-letter day: the biggest air-battle to date took place … Ground reports counted twelve fighters and two bombers shot down. During the day our own losses were six fighters and one bomber … There must have been over fifty planes roaring over the battle area at one time.'[57] – but it is noticeable that it was at this time that the aerial assault on Madrid switched increasingly to night-time bombing of the densely populated working-class areas of the capital known as the *barrios bajos*. Designed both to demoralize the population and to impede access to the front line, these raids were scarcely lacking in effect – 'Your house shakes', wrote Knoblaugh. 'The windows rattle like drums. Some of them shatter and the glass falls inside … The planes have passed. Or have they? You go to bed, but you don't sleep … Each time … you remember the … raids you have seen: torn bodies of men, women and children, some inert … some writhing and moaning pitifully; cadavers of donkeys which a moment before … were placidly pulling their little carts; bodies of mothers with babies in their arms … legless, armless torsos flung into the gutter and streaming blood.'[58] – yet the military situation was altered not a whit. In much battered Legazpi or Cuatro Caminos, the population may have cowered beneath the bombs, but, if so, the impact on the morale of the fighting forces was minimal, if only for the simple reason that, with the arrival of ever growing numbers of reinforcements from elsewhere in the Republican zone, *madrileños* were no longer the predominant element on the barricades.[59]

If the defenders of the city were for the most part not *madrileños*, its attackers were not German or Italian. As has already been mentioned, by the time of the assault on Madrid, the Nationalists had received a considerable number of German and Italian aircraft, but neither the Germans nor the Italians yet had a separate air force of their own in Spain of the sort that they were soon to deploy (officially, both flew as part of a hastily formed aviation section of the Spanish Foreign Legion). Angered by Nationalist incompetence, however, in October the Germans had determined to form an independent air corps of their own that would be entirely under their control, the result being the formation of the famous Condor Legion early in November 1936.[60] Consisting initially of three squadrons of Ju52s, four squadrons of He51s, one squadron of He70 reconnaissance aircraft, one squadron of He45 ground co-operation aircraft and one squadron of He59 and He60 floatplanes, the vast majority of them freshly sent from Germany, this constituted a major reinforcement, but it does not seem to have been deployed on the Madrid front until the very end of the battle.[61] Meanwhile, its Italian counterpart, the Legionary Aviation, was not formed until the following month.[62] As for ground troops, at this stage hardly any Germans or Italians were involved. All the Panzer Is and L3s were at least partly manned by Spaniards, as were the thirty-eight 65mm C.65/17 M1913 guns dispatched from Italy, whilst the thirty-odd 20mm anti-aircraft guns and 37mm anti-tank guns and four 88mm FLAK18s received from Germany were wholly crewed by them. Plenty of munitions and small-arms had been sent to the Nationalists, meanwhile, but, as for heavier weapons, the mentions that one comes across of

German and Italian heavy artillery are pure fantasy: at this stage, neither power had dispatched anything of the sort.[63]

To return to the reinforcements being received by the Republicans, if the XI and XII International Brigades were rather less impressive than their press suggests, they were undoubtedly of rather more use than the force of Catalan militia who appeared in the city on 14 November. Some − 1,500 Anarchists commanded by the veteran Anarchist hero Buenaventura Durruti − came direct from the Aragón front, whilst others − a contingent of the PSUC − had rather been raised in Barcelona, but neither were used to the conditions of combat that reigned in Madrid. Meanwhile, although the former in particular radiated revolutionary bravado, their record was, at best, questionable, whilst they were armed with Winchester M1895 rifles, a weapon that was both notoriously flimsy and lacking in hitting power.[64] Of far more value than either Internationals or Anarchists, in fact, was the arrival of much fresh artillery, the number of guns assigned to the defence soon rising to at least eighty; much better organized than before and to a large part concentrated in a single mass in the Retiro Park, this force also had an ideal observation post in the form of the Telephone Building (Madrid's only skyscraper).[65]

The battle, then, was not going favourably for the Nationalists. However, this did not lead to any slackening of their efforts. On 15 November, notwithstanding desperate resistance, a renewed offensive spearheaded by all the Nationalists' Panzer Is finally secured a bridgehead across the Manzanares just north of the Puente de los Franceses railway bridge, the assault troops then pushing up the slopes overlooking the river to occupy the first buildings of the University City. Amongst the artillery supporting the attack, meanwhile, was the Nationalists' solitary battery of four 88mm FK18s: for the past few weeks stationed at the airfield at Talavera, this had now been rushed to the front, and it was therefore in this action that these weapons were first used in the direct-fire role for which they became so famous in the Second World War.[66] Rendered easier though the crossing was by the fact that, as we have seen, the banks were not canalized in this sector, the whole area was still swept by heavy fire by a number of machine-guns mounted on the Puente de los Franceses. Amongst the men crossing the river was Frank Thomas:

> To the screams of artillery and trench-mortar shells and the heavy concussions of the bombs dropped by the twenty-three German three-engined Junkers overhead − the first time we had ever seen them − Madrid awoke from a dreamy dawn ... Incidentally, these bombers were protected by fourteen scouts [i.e. fighters] also of German origin ... The enemy's guns opened up in answer to ours, but company after company ... began to run across the bare plain leading to the river ... We were glad when it came to our company's turn to get off the mark, although ... it meant going through a zone now swept by the bullets of a thoroughly awakened enemy. Between us and the river was the high wall which surrounds ... the royal

park, in which breaches, days previously, had been blown. Halfway to the wall was a royal stables – our first resting place … A hurried dash under crossfire from the heights … in front … got us into precarious safety inside the building … The rest of the … *bandera*, under continuous fire, had already crossed the exposed river and established themselves above us, well within the University City.[67]

This attack took the defenders completely by surprise, the Nationalists being deemed to have been so hard hit that they had lost the initiative. To quote an evidently rueful Vicente Rojo, 'We believed that we were stronger than our adversary.'[68] Nor did it help that the men in the epicentre of the storm were the PSUC militia noted above, these men having been sent to reinforce the Tierra y Libertad column. As the same source continues, 'Having concentrated maximum firepower on a very narrow front, the attackers had the good fortune to provoke panic in an improvised unit which had only just arrived from another front, and in consequence not lived through the moral crisis of 7 November, thereby failing to imbibe the atmosphere generated by the struggle for the capital.'[69]

During the night, fresh troops, including the XI International Brigade and the Durruti column, were immediately rushed in to seal the breach in the Republican front. Amongst the latter's men was Joaquín Masjuán:

I was ordered to occupy a bunker with five other men … We had a Maxim machine gun which we set up in the main loophole … About four o'clock in the afternoon … an extraordinary number of projectiles of every size began to fall around us. After about half an hour … the enemy planes came over and plastered us with a veritable carpet of bombs … Finally, along came the enemy tanks, and with them the Moors, and now the dance really began … The machine-gun vomited fire … Ten, twenty, thirty Moors went down … My rifle was so hot, it was burning my hands.[70]

For the time being, then, the attackers were checked, but throwing them back was another matter. Here, the main role was given to Durruti. To give his men credit, they fought bravely – according to a Nationalist volunteer in one of the units they faced, they came to within thirty yards of the enemy positions – but, as even Durruti's adjutant, Ricardo Sanz, was later forced to admit, they were eventually driven back in disorder.[71] With the Republican counterattack at an end, the tiny handful of Nationalist troops who had got across the river thus far began again to move forward, supported by a thunderous artillery bombardment and heavy bombing raids.[72] Behind them, meanwhile, came a trickle of reinforcements, these having got across the river under cover of a thick mist that had come down in the course of the night.[73] While the Polish Dabrowski battalion manned the defences around the French cultural institute known as the Casa de Velásquez, the Commune-de-Paris battalion was sent to occupy the Faculty of Medicine. Amongst the men taking position in the latter was John Sommerfield:

> We came to a high-up room with big windows ... A few hundred yards away was the Casa [de] Velasquez whose riddled baroque turrets were still pointed at the raining sky ... We were shelled, but not much and not very accurately. Some [projectiles] hit the building, but it was so huge and so strongly built that little damage was done ... They tried to attack with tanks, but they were driven back: the little figures ran and tumbled and lay still.[74]

Desperate resistance by the XI International Brigade and other troops notwithstanding, by the end of the day, several university buildings had been lost, including the Casa de Velazquez – where a company of Poles lost all but seven men – and the faculties of architecture and agronomy.[75] In the midst of the battle, the editor of the newspaper *El Socialista* received a call from a friend on the front line: 'We are still here and are ready to die. Can you hear the explosions? This is terrible. However, don't worry: they won't get by us; rather than let that happen we shall all be killed.'[76] A little later came a second call: 'They are telling us to fall back. The enemy are only twelve meters from us and are firing at us very heavily. If you don't see us again, long live the Republic!'[77]

Curiously enough, a few yards away, many Nationalist soldiers were going through experiences that were not dissimilar. Having crossed the river that morning with his battalion, Juan Urra Lusarreta spent the day pinned down among the pine trees that lined the slopes beneath the university buildings:

> Everybody was flat on the ground ... Nobody dared move, the bullets flew so close amongst us ... To defend the terrain we had occupied, we had formed a front line ... defended by machine-guns placed in such a way as to subject the no-man's land beyond to the heaviest crossfire. Even to enter the open space which made it up was suicide. Nevertheless, at nightfall ... a most tremendous attack was launched against the whole position ... The whole thing was a deluge of rifle, machine-gun and mortar fire. In its way it was imposing enough, but, for all that, it was not enough to unman us. For example, many mortar bombs ... were wasted on account of the fact that they were touched off by the thick roof of branches above our heads. My company ... had orders to hold back until the Reds got to within twenty metres, but things never reached such a pitch, the fire of our machine-guns ... being enough to persuade the militiamen ... to fall back while they were still some way away.[78]

Badly outnumbered and subjected to heavy fire from all sides, the Nationalists nevertheless succeeded in extending their positions the following day as well, occupying yet more schools and faculties, including, most importantly, the ground floors of the as-yet-unfinished shell of the Clinical Hospital (situated on a commanding height, this enormous complex of buildings dominated the whole area).[79] Ever since the crossing of the river, the fighting in the University City had been extremely desperate, with room-to-room and floor-to-floor fighting in the university buildings and repeated charges and counter-charges across the empty *paramos* that surrounded them, but fighting now mounted to a crescendo. Amongst the dead was Buenaventura Durruti, who was shot down in the Calle Isaac Peral whilst frantically trying to rally his fleeing men.[80] Trapped in its upper storeys, the remaining defenders of the Clinical Hospital died to the last man, whilst the Republicans sought frantically to win back the lost ground, with fighting even spreading to the sewers.[81] On 20 November, in particular, the XII International Brigade, which, after a few days' rest and recuperation at the little town of Chinchón, had been brought into line in the area of the Palacete de la Moncloa, attacked from the north-west along the axis of the new highway that had been driven across the heights on which the University City was built in the course of the Republic. Amongst the men moving up with the Thaelmann battalion to attack a building called the White House was Esmond Romilly:

> Four tanks moved up the road. Rebel artillery was active all the time and occasionally the shells sent up great clouds of smoke near the road, but the tanks chugged slowly on. We watched them out of sight round the bend. Then the poum-poum-poum of their guns showed the attack was in full swing. The suspense was maddening. I remembered reading books about the war and for the first time the expression 'going over the top' had some meaning. Jeans shouted, 'Fix bayonets! Everyone ready!' The Italians were lying ready on the ridge. They would cover us with rifle fire. Behind the road four machine-guns started up. 'Forward! Rush ten yards, drop, wait for the next advance, everyone to fire at the windows', shouted Jeans. We reached the wall of the White House. It was a mad scramble ... A few of the Germans dropped on the way: it was like seeing people killed in an American film.[82]

Once again, however, the 'Comintern army' failed, the Nationalists even being able to extend their positions to include the Palacete de la Moncloa (today the official residence of the Spanish prime minister), which was adjacent to the University City on its northern flank. Further counterattacks followed over the next three days, but each time they were beaten off with heavy casualties.[83] As usual, there were serious problems of co-ordination. Watching the Garibaldi battalion – the Italian soldiers mentioned by Romilly – was Alexei Eisner:

> At first all went well for the Italians, and they made rapid progress towards the spot from which they had been driven back the previous day. However, the Thaelmann battalion did not move, and the result was that their left flank was left uncovered. Immediately the enemy opened fire on them with machine guns. Unable to silence them, the *garibaldinos* called up a couple of field pieces, but both of them were destroyed by enemy artillery before they could fire a shot. Taking such shelter as they could, for an hour

more the volunteers tried to withstand the enemy fire, but in the end they had no option but to fall back to their original line.[84]

Exhausted though the Nationalists were, then, they were more than capable of holding their positions. Yet the fighting still wore them down inexorably. 'In effect', wrote Carlos Iniesta Cano, 'the days from 19 November to 30 November were one continuous battle. The tension was constant; when it was least expected, groups of Reds would suddenly erupt out of nowhere and have to be dealt with … The confusion was tremendous, and we went unshaven and dressed in a style that was ever less uniform … It was the most curious episode I remember in the whole war.'[85] Eventually the point came, then, when all they could do was to hold their positions: on 22 November, a last-ditch attempt was made to break through into the city proper across the Parque del Oeste, but this proved a failure. Stationed in some ruined buildings just on the northern side of the main road to La Coruña, Frank Thomas was sent with his unit to attack the imposing Model Prison. Very soon, then, he was in the thick of the fighting:

> The only possible approach for us lay through the open Parque del Oeste so that we were certain of a warm reception … To the sound and sight of the exploding shells fired … by our artillery in the Casa de Campo, the Twenty-Second [Company] left their position to our left … Immediately they had passed us, our company started to follow, *pelotón* by *pelotón*, the machine-gun company being left in position to cover our advance … At this point, the same aerial fleet that had helped us to cross the Manzanares appeared … Bombs then commenced raining down on the barracks to the west of the prison, then on to the prison itself, and, finally, on us! A tragic and unfortunate blunder had been made … I hope someone was shot.[86]

Hit by a hurricane bombardment and saturation bombing, the defenders disintegrated in panic, and for a moment, the Nationalists seemed to have broken through (to this day, indeed, one can read claims that a number of Moors reached the Plaza de España). However, as the attackers emerged from the trees of the park into the open Plaza de la Moncloa, they were cut down by withering fire from Republican troops hidden in the ruins of the Model Prison, and this, together with a dramatic personal appearance by General Miaja, sufficed to turn the tide.[87] Recognizing the inevitable, the very next day Franco ordered the attempt to take Madrid by storm to be brought to an end. Exact casualties are unknown but have been estimated as being some 3,000 for the Nationalists and as many as 8,500 for the Republicans.[88]

What, then, saved the city? The standard – i.e. Communist – narrative stresses a mixture of the heroism of the people of Madrid and the gallantry and skill of the International Brigades. As for the Nationalists, they, too, were keen to stress the importance of foreign aid (that and cowardice): 'The first battle of Madrid had come to an end. The attempt to rush its defences had failed because the Reds, instead of falling back from the "open city" of Madrid when they had been defeated in battle before it, had taken refuge in its maze of streets, and in the fact that there was a great civilian population ...... who would be slaughtered were an assault to be pushed to the bitter end. They had lined the barricades .... with foreign volunteers and with foreign arms, and therefore another way had to be found to capture the capital of Spain.'[89] However, the reality was more complex. For a much more thoughtful view, we may once again turn to Stephen Fuqua:

> While no accurate information is available as to the numerical strength of the Nationalist columns ... it appears ... that these forces numbered ... about one third of the militia and other troops available for the defence ... This may explain the failure of Franco in following up his drive to the Manzanares ... He gave a respite to his troops of a few days for the con-solidation of their positions near the river, preparatory for further advance ... The *junta de defensa* left in charge of the capital by the government took immediate and effective advantage of the halt by Franco's troops and began the re-organization of the Madrid defences, utilizing the contingents which had arrived from Barcelona, Valencia and other places ... while discipline was enforced on the militia for the first time ... as those disobeying orders to hold fast faced death at the point of the pistols of their officers. The marked improvement in discipline, together with the numerical superiority of the government forces ... soon resulted in several attacks on the Nationalists, which, although not attaining their objectives completely, nevertheless served to check further progress of the enemy.[90]

This report is clearly marked by a certain degree of muddle: it is none too clear that either Franco or Varela called a halt to the battle in the manner suggested, while too much weight is given to the role of the Junta of Defence. However, the basic point is clear enough, the substantial German and Italian aid he had already received notwithstanding, Franco had neither the numbers nor the resources that he needed to take the city, and so his attack simply ran into the sand, this process being greatly accelerated by the strategy of envelopment set-tled on by Pozas and his subordinates.[91] At the same time, too, it has to be said that winter had now come, and that the attackers were simply too tired to carry on. For all the men in the front line, indeed, it was the bleakest of times. To quote the Republican militiaman Antonio Candela: 'In Madrid in the sum-mertime one can fry in the heat, but in winter one can die of cold ... There was too much rain ... In most parts of the front line the men had to sleep sitting on one empty munition case with their feet on another ... During the day, if there was no fighting going on, we would pass the time throwing the water and mud out of the trench with empty tins. Through the peep-holes we could see that the enemy faced the same problem. Everywhere we could see little spurts of water flying over the trench parapets.'[92]

Notes

1 For some examples of these myths being regurgitated for a new audience, See Beevor, *Battle for Spain*, pp. 199-219 *passim*; Preston, *Franco*, p. 204; Preston, *Spanish Civil War*, pp. 176-7. As is hinted at here, a particular problem has been constituted by the prominence of the Communist party and, more distantly, the Soviet Union, in the defence of the city. Modern Russian tanks and planes played an important part in the repulse of the enemy; Russian political and military advisers were near ubiquitous; prominent Communists such as Dolores Ibarruri stayed on in the city to encourage the defence when most other Republican politicians had fled for the safety of Valencia; the Junta of Defence that took over the administration was very largely a Communist creature, if not actually a Communist creation; and the International Brigades originated in the deliberations of the Comintern and were organized by the Communist parties of Europe and America, commanded by Soviet-army officers (albeit not Russians, but rather Germans, Hungarians and Poles who had been taken prisoner fighting the Russians in the First World War and been converted to Bolshevism). For a helpful analysis, see R. D. Richardson, 'The defence of Madrid: mysterious generals, Red-Front fighters and the International Brigades', *Military Affairs*, XLIII, No. 4 (January, 1979), pp. 178–85.

2 See Fraser, *Blood of Spain*, pp. 259–70.

3 J. M. Reverte, *La Batalla de Madrid* (Barcelona, 2007), pp. 260–1, 271.

4 Ibid., p. 266. Despite the chaos that reigned in the city, the response of at least some of the defenders was quick enough: 'Militiamen with rifles stood at the street intersections. Anyone making the slightest motion towards one of the leaflets was shot on the spot. At the end of the paper "bombardments," the militia would sweep up the copies and burn them.' Knoblaugh, *Correspondent in Spain*, p. 101.

5 Preston, *Franco*, p. 201.

6 Martínez Bande, *Marcha sobre Madrid*, p. 287.

7 Kindelán, *Cuadernos de Guerra*, p. 90.

8 In all, the five columns destined for the attack on the city consisted of five battalions of the Foreign Legion, nine *tabores* of *regulares* and one battalion of regular infantry. At the end of the first week of November, the aircraft were reinforced by nine more Fiat CR32s and twelve Heinkel He51s. See Martínez Bande, *Marcha sobre Madrid*, pp. 236, 288; Hills, *Battle for Madrid*, pp. 89–91, 100.

9 See Martínez Bande, *Marcha sobre Madrid*, p. 280. Put like this, the defenders sound like a reasonably orderly assembly. In reality, however, the situation was chaotic in the extreme. 'To give an idea of the organic pulverization that reigned amongst our forces, it is enough for me to point out that ... the column of Lieutenant-Colonel Barceló ... contained the remains of [fifteen] small units with effectives that ranged from 600 men to a mere forty ... All the other columns ... were much the same while there were also a number of "autonomous" units whose effectives numbered less than fifty ... All across the front, the armament of the troops was extremely varied whilst weapons were mixed up even within individual units. We had 6.5, 7.0, 7.62, and 7.92mm rifles ... five different calibres of machine gun, three different calibres of mortars, eight different calibres of artillery.' V. Rojo, *Así fue la defensa de Madrid* (Mexico City, 1967), p. 27. At the same time, some classes of arms were notable by their absence: there were, for example, no anti-tank guns and very little in the way of anti-aircraft artillery. Finally, one force that Miaja did not have at his disposal was a women's militia, the nearest equivalent to any such organization being the single *batallón feminina* of the Fifth Regiment already mentioned. That said, a tiny handful of militiawomen who had enlisted as individuals did see frontline service during the battle.

10 Martínez Bande, *Marcha sobre Madrid*, pp. 282–3.

11 Koltsov, *Diario de la guerra de España*, p. 194.

12 If the Communist party took the chief credit for the defence of Madrid, it was in no small part due to Ibarruri. Known universally as La Pasionaria, a term that

stressed her political fervour whilst at the same time recalling her femininity, she not only made frequent speeches to rallies, such as that held at the Monumental Cinema on 9 November, but also spent much time touring the rear areas of the front line, encouraging the exhausted defenders and doing what she could to secure them tobacco, alcohol and hot food. See R. Low, *The Spanish Firebrand* (London, 1992), pp.74–7. One militiaman who remembered her intervention ever afterwards was Antonio Candela. 'We passed ... the whole morning expecting the arrival of the ... enemy Junkers ... The planes came at the very same time that La Pasionaria, accompanied by a group of high-ranking officers and civilians, appeared on the top of our trench. We were busy hiding as low as we could but she and her companions remained standing on the top of the trenches while the bombs were falling all around us. She was calling for courage and determination to face the oncoming enemy, and she went on and on talking to us in a loud voice so as to be heard by as many solders as possible ... Her presence and her encouragement had a good effect on our morale.' Candelas, *Adventures of an Innocent*, p. 57.

13 Cit. Gallego, *Madrid: corazón que se desangra*, p. 199.

14 Cit. J. W. Cortada (ed.), *Modern Warfare in Spain: American Military Observations on the Spanish Civil War* (Washington, 2012), p. 50.

15 The only biography of Miaja is A. López Fernández, *General Miaja, defensor de Madrid* (Madrid, 1975). Born in Oviedo in 1878, Miaja had joined the army in 1896 and served for long periods in Morocco. Unlike many of his fellow *africanistas*, he had not objected to the coming of the Republic and had chosen to back the government when the rising began in July 1936. Given the command of the forces in southern Spain, however, he had, as have seen, failed very badly. Ibid., pp. 17–48.

16 Rojo, *Así fue la defensa de Madrid*, pp. 23–4. Even the exact state of the city's fortifications was unknown to Miaja. As the Nationalists had approached, various organisms – the Ministry of War, assorted political parties and trade-union movements, local committees – had thrown themselves into the work of defending the city, and some areas such as the suburbs south of the Manzanares were now protected by trench systems, barbed wire and even a few concrete bunkers and pillboxes. Yet the works concerned had been constructed in the patchiest of fashions and were often ill-sited and poorly constructed, while no plans existed of their layout, the consequence being that many of the positions concerned were never occupied, some troops falling back past them without even realizing that they were there. Ibid., p. 27.

17 Largo Caballero, *Mis recuerdos*, p. 177.

18 The best study of the Junta de Defensa is J. Arosteguí Sánchez and J. A. Martínez Martín, *La Junta de Defensa de Madrid, noviembre 1936–abril 1937* (Madrid, 1994).

19 It is sometimes said that Miaja was himself a Communist, but, whilst he later joined the party, this was certainly not the case at this stage: what little is known of his political views prior to July 1936 suggests that he was rather a conservative Republican of the same stamp as such Nationalist generals as Cabanellas and Queipo de Llano. Within regard to the Communists, meanwhile, it may simply be that he did not realize just how far he had been manoeuvred into giving them the whip-hand: that representatives of the Socialist Party, the Casas del Pueblo and the JSU were to all intents and purposes Communist agents may have been lost on him. For an excellent discussion, see H. Graham, *The Spanish Republic at War, 1936–1939* (Cambridge, 2002), pp. 171–4.

20 Curiously enough, if Rojo was converted to Republicanism, he remained a devout Catholic and, prior to 1936, appears to have been a member of the Unión Militar Española. For a detailed biography, see C. Blanco Escola, *Vicente Rojo, el general que humilló a Franco* (Barcelona, 2003). Meanwhile, that Rojo was the real motor of the defence there can be no doubt. Here, for example, is Koltsov: 'It is difficult not to take account of Rojo. Without any exaggeration it can be affirmed that he was at his post ... for twenty-four hours a day ... hunched over the map tables ... making notes with coloured pencils, writing memoranda, talking with hundreds of people ... As

chief of the general staff, he held in his hands the complicated web of units ... batteries, isolated barricades, engineer detachments and aviation squadrons, and, without sleep, without a moment's rest even, attentively followed the least movement of the enemy.' Koltsov, *Diario de la guerra de España*, pp. 275–6.

21 Reverte, *Batalla de Madrid.*, pp. 226–7, 234–5. See also Martínez Bande, *Marcha sobre Madrid*, pp. 273–4.

22 Martínez Bande, *Marcha sobre Madrid*, pp. 289–93.

23 Originally Pozas' plan seems to have been to mass the mixed brigadas behind the River Jarama and strike westwards across the Nationalist rear in the direction of Talavera. See Rojo, *Así fue la batalla de Madrid*, p. 49. However, with resistance in the capital all but on the point of disintegration, there was nothing for it but to send them to the Madrid front. Using them in the fashion that Pozas actually did was sensible enough, but for all that, a vital chance was missed that might just possibly have forced the Nationalists to the negotiating table.

24 For the civilian population, the bombardment was a terrifying experience. 'The day dawned with an enormous cannonade', remembered a Nationalist sympathizer named Antonio. 'The projectiles which had previously given us such delight screamed overhead, and we heard them explode nearby. We were all together in the bedroom ... Around ten there was a thunderous explosion and we were enveloped in smoke. A shell had fallen just a few metres away.' Cit. Cervera Gil, *Ya sabes mi paradero*, p. 100.

25 Iniesta Cano, *Memorias y recuerdos*, p. 96.

26 Cit. Cervera Gil, *Ya sabes mi paradero*, pp. 101–2.

27 See Fraser, *Blood of Spain*, pp. 267–8. In the course of these events, a militiaman of Catalan origins named Antonio Col made a name for himself by knocking out two tanks with petrol bombs and hand-grenades, only immediately to be gunned down by a third, his story subsequently being made use of as the centre-piece of a Communist-inspired propaganda campaign designed to stiffen popular resistance, secure volunteers for special anti-tank squads and persuade the troops that there was nothing to fear from the Nationalist tanks, see J. Cabeza San Deogracias, 'Buscando héroes: la historia de Antonio Col como ejemplo del uso de la narrativa como propaganda durante la Guerra Civil Española', *Revista de Historia y Comunicación Social*, X (2005), pp. 37–50.

28 According to Koltsov, after it had been searched, the tank was retrieved, loaded onto a lorry and paraded through the streets of Madrid. See Koltsov, *Diario de la guerra de España*, pp. 199–200.

29 Reverte, *Batalla de Madrid*, p. 267.

30 Barea, *Forging of a Rebel*, p. 586–7.

31 Cardozo, *March of a Nation*, p. 179.

32 López Fernández, *General Miaja*, pp. 108–9. See also Rojo, *Así fue la defensa de Madrid*, pp. 35–6.

33 The most well researched account of the killings is probably I. Gibson, *Paracuellos: la verdad objétiva sobre la matanza de presos en Madrid en 1936* (Madrid, 2005), but see also Graham, *Spanish Republic at War*, pp. 190–1; Preston, *Spanish Civil War*, pp. 181–86. The *sacas* in Madrid were not the only massacres at this time. Koltsov, for example, notes that on 9 December, a heavy air-raid on Guadalajara that cost the lives of 140 of its citizens led to the lynching of 100 Nationalist sympathizers who had been incarcerated in the city's jail. Koltsov, *Diario de la guerra de España*, p. 270.

34 F. Thomas, 'Spanish *voluntario*' in R. Stradling (ed.), *Brother against Brother: Experiences of a British Volunteer in the Spanish Civil War* (Stroud, 1998), p. 66.

35 Knoblaugh, *Correspondent in Spain*, p. 107.

36 Watson, *Single to Spain*, p. 120.

37 Candela, *Adventures of an Innocent*, p. 58.

38 Cit. S. Alvarez (ed.), *Historia política y militar de las brigadas internacionales: testimonios y documentos* (Madrid, 1996), pp. 274–5.

39 Rojo, *Así fue la defensa de Madrid*, p. 88.

40 G. Cox, *The Defence of Madrid* (London, 1937), p. 66; see also D. Ibarruri, *El único camino* (Paris, 1965), pp. 466–7. Though its composition was later altered, at the time of its arrival in Madrid, the brigade consisted of just three infantry battalions – the German 'Edgar André' (510 men), the French 'Commune-de-Paris' (435 men) and the Polish 'Dombrowski' (511 men). In addition, there was a small cavalry squadron of just forty-six men and a detachment of twenty-seven artillerymen, though the latter had not yet been equipped with any guns. In command, meanwhile, was a Hungarian Jew named Manfred Stern: known in Spain as Kléber, he had been captured by the Russians in the First World War and then enlisted in the Red Army. Alcofar Nassaes, *Spansky*, pp. 197–99.

41 The St. Etienne had already been encountered by Manuel Tagüeña Lacorte, a militant in the Communist youth movement, who had spent most of the war thus far manning the lines in the Sierra de Guadarrama. 'We received a consignment of French St. Etienne machine-guns dating from the First World War. Unfortunately, the ammunition proved defective in that the cartridges were leaky and shed powder all over the complicated repeating mechanism, thereby causing it to jam. Having set one up under heavy enemy fire one day, I only managed to get it to fire a handful of rounds before it malfunctioned completely.' M. Tagueña Lacorte, *Testimonio de dos guerras* (Barcelona, 2005), p.140.

42 J. Sommerfield, *Volunteer in Spain* (London, 1997), pp. 48–50.

43 'Soon after the drizzle stopped we formed up and marched off … It was still early, not many people were about. They cheered us and others leaned from windows and shouted. But there was a sense of unhappy apathy everywhere, a feeling of almost hopeless exhaustion … Ours was no triumphant entry: we were a last desperate hope, and, as tired out, ill equipped and hungry, we marched through the windswept streets, past the shuttered shops and the food queues, I thought the hurrying people on the pavements looked at us as if we were too late and had come only in time to die … But soon my own unfortunate circumstances banished these melancholy reflections: I was carrying the St. Etienne and, heavy as it was, the burden of the weight was rendered worse by the pressure of its ridges on my shoulder … After twenty minutes … all of us who were carrying the guns … were drenched with sweat and trembling with exhaustion … I didn't care about the war or Madrid; there was only one thought and desire in my mind – to be able to lie down.' Ibid., pp. 90–1.

44 An account that has the XI Brigade clearing the Parque del Oeste of some Moors who had crossed the Manzanares, recapturing the Puente de los Franceses and then driving deep into the Casa de Campo that is sometimes quoted is wholly imaginary – aside from anything else, the Nationalists not only never captured the Puente de los Franceses, but they did not get across the river for another week – and appears to have stemmed wholly from the brigades' headquarters at Albacete: at all events, slightly different versions of it may be found in the writings of both André Marty and Luigi Longo. See Alvarez, *Historia politica y militar de las brigadas internacionales*, pp. 81, 91–2. None of the first-hand accounts mention anything of the sort, the only excitement being some long-distance shelling that, as a volunteer called Knight remembered, caused a general panic. 'We heard a sound which most of us knew only from the movies as the sound of approaching shell fire. The aim was good and the explosions took place among our ranks. The ground did not offer any cover and most of us simply scrambled forward over the edge of a bank which took us down into a sort of valley which at least got us out of sight … Down on the lower ground we sorted ourselves out and most of us realised ruefully that we had left our weapons behind.' Cit. P. Stansky and W. Abrahams, *Journey to the Frontier: Julian Bell and John Cornford: Their Lives and the 1930s* (London, 1966), p. 376. So much for the disciplined veterans described by Marty and Longo. For a detailed deconstruction of the generally accepted version of the participation of the XI Brigade in the fighting of 8–9 November, see Alcofar Nassaes, *Spansky*, pp. 202–12.

45 See Sommerfield, *Volunteer in Spain,* pp. 92–101.

46 Stansky and Abrahams, *Journey to the Frontier*, p. 376.
47 Barea, *Forging of a Rebel*, p. 595. For another account of the excitement supposedly generated by the arrival of the XI International Brigade, we may turn to Julio San Isidro, an officer (or possibly political commissar) who was stationed with a column of the Fifth Regiment deployed on the steep bluff overlooking the southern fringes of the Parque del Oeste. 'The presence, and decided action, of the Internationals stiffened the entire front and injected it with a consistency and spirit that grew ever greater. With men and women alike electrified by so much heroism, the people of Madrid felt as if they were veritable giants, the comradely action and military activity of the new arrivals crystallizing in a new situation that grew rapidly in depth and greatly helped the defence of the city.' Cit. Alvarez, *Historia política y militar de las brigadas internacionales*, p. 281.
48 For a wildly exaggerated version of this attack, which has the XI Brigade single-handedly clearing 'ridge after ridge of the great park', see R. Colodny, *The Battle for Madrid: the Central Epic of the Spanish Conflict* (New York, 1978), p. 72. That said, it is but fair to point out that Rojo specifically says that it performed 'brilliantly' in this action. Rojo, *Así fue la defensa de Madrid*, p. 87.
49 Martínez Bande, *Marcha sobre Madrid*, pp. 315–16.
50 The XII Brigade was commanded by Mate Zalka, who was, like his XI International Brigade counterpart Manfred Stern, a Hungarian who had been taken prisoner by the Russians in the First World War and enlisted in the Red Army. The brigade consisted of the Italian 'Garibaldi' battalion, the German 'Thaelmann' battalion and the French 'André Marty' battalion, a company of engineers; and a battery of three 75mm guns. Alcofar Nassaes, *Spansky*, pp. 214–16.
51 E. Romilly, *Boadilla* (London, 1937), pp. 103–4.
52 Watson, *Single to Spain*, pp. 121–2.
53 Cit. Alcofar Nassaes, *Spansky*, p. 224.
54 Attacking Franco's airfields made some sense, but there was also a continued fetish for strategic bombing. Thus, it should not be forgotten that, while Nationalist Junkers and Savoias were dropping bombs on civilians in Madrid, Republican Potez Po540s of the Escadrille d'Espagne were winging their way to Seville on missions that were exactly similar, if much smaller in scale and effect. See De Wet, *Cardboard Crucifix*, pp. 47–55.
55 R. Proctor, *Hitler's Luftwaffe in the Spanish Civil War* (Westport, Connecticutt, 1983), p. 64.
56 Salas Larrazábal, *Air War over Spain*, p. 99.
57 Larios, *Combat over Spain*, pp. 81–2.
58 Knoblaugh, *Correspondent in Spain*, pp. 103–4.
59 Martínez Bande, *Marcha sobre Madrid*, pp. 280–1; the reinforcements included III, IV, V and VI Mixed Brigades, all of which were raised in Valencia, Murcia or New Castile and a mixed detachment of Catalan militia sent round from the Aragón front (see below). At the same time, there were strict limits to what the Nationalists could achieve: even the heaviest raid – that of the night of 18 November – was launched by no more than fifty bombers, whilst the combined pay-load of these planes was a mere forty tons. Casualties, meanwhile, were grievous, but scarcely over-whelming: between 14 and 23 November, there were 1,119 civilian air-raid casualties, including 133 deaths. Salas Larrazábal, *Air War over Spain*, p. 105.
60 Proctor, *Hitler's Luftwaffe in the Spanish Civil War*, pp. 51–2.
61 Whealey, *Hitler and Spain*, p. 49. In addition to the planes, the brown-uniformed Condor Legion had a complete staff of mechanics and other service personnel, as well as a searchlight detachment and seven batteries of anti-aircraft artillery, four of which were equipped with the deadly 88mm FLAK18. Though the 88mm batteries, in particular, were sometimes used for ground support in a direct-fire role, it is important to note that these ground troops were primarily intended for airfield defence. Meanwhile, given the matter's constant repetition, it should be emphasized that the

Legion never had an armoured element. Whilst such tank instructors as were sent to Spain appear to have been brigaded with it, the machines they served were always supplied directly to the Spanish army. See Proctor, *Hitler's Luftwaffe in the Spanish Civil War*, pp. 59–61.

62 A. Emiliani et al., *Spagna, 1936–39: l'aviazione legionaria* (Milan, 1976), p. 5. The name 'Legionary Aviation' was a survival from the first days of the war, these having seen the German and Italian pilots fight, officially at least, as part of the Spanish Foreign Legion.

63 For the initial dispatches of Italian weapons and their employment in the battle of Madrid, see J. L. de Mesa, *El regreso de las legiones: voluntarios italianos en la Guerra Civil Española* (Madrid, 1994), pp. 19–22. Aside from the anti-aircraft and anti-tank guns mentioned in the text, the only German artillery pieces to have been received in Spain by the time of the battle were fifty Ehrhardt 76mm mine throwers dating from the First World War. A species of trench mortar of a particularly cumbersome nature with a very limited range, these do not appear to have been sent to the Madrid front. See A. Mortera Pérez and J. L. Iniesta Pérez, *La artillería en la Guerra Civil: material de origen alemán importado por el bando nacional* (Valladolid, 1996), pp. 27–8.

64 The arrival of these forces is described at some length by the Anarchist Gallego. Far from being eager to rush to Madrid's defence, Durruti rather initially demanded that he be given the arms he needed to launch an attack on the Aragón front that, or so he claimed, would immediately cause Franco to abandon the assault on the capital, and he then was enraged to discover that he was not going to be allowed to command the entire contingent but rather only his own CNT militants. At the same time, Gallego all but openly acknowledges that the veteran Anarchist was entirely lacking in military talent. Gallego, *Madrid, corazón que se desangra*, pp. 213–15, 225–6. See also Max, *Memorias de un revolucionario*, p. 38.

65 That this was the case, the Nationalists were perfectly well aware, and in the latter part of the battle in particular, the building suffered very heavily. Thus: 'Correspondents finally had to give up their choice observation point in the telephone building when the insurgent artillerymen, discovering that the loyalists had placed an artillery observation post in the tower of the building, began to aim directly at it … They placed shells in nearly every floor of the building, making its steel-reinforced frame shake under the impact. Built along American lines, with huge I-beams welded into a strong skeleton … faced with brick and stone, the … building was in no danger of being razed, but the shells went through the outside walls and left great holes in the south and west façades.' Knoblaugh, *Correspondent in Spain*, pp. 106–9.

66 Mortera Pérez and Infiesta Pérez, *Artillería en la Guerra Civil: material de origen alemán*, p. 50.

67 Thomas, 'Spanish *legionario*', pp. 68–9. The reference to close air support (and, still more so, Thomas' claim that he had not witnessed so heavy an aerial attack before the crossing of the Manzanares) is interesting: clearly the Nationalists were still prepared to mount major daylight operations, but only in connection with major attacks of the sort launched on 16 November.

68 Rojo, *Así fue la defensa de Madrid*, p. 88.

69 Ibid., p. 89. It is often claimed that the troops who broke were rather Durruti's Anarchists, but there is no direct evidence that they were in the front line when the fighting began, whilst the Communists and their allies had very strong motives for wanting to denigrate them, as well as equally strong motives for wanting to protect the reputation of the PSUC (the PSUC, or United Socialist Party of Catalonia, was, as we have seen, like the JSU, or United Socialist Youth, the result of a merger between the Communists and elements of the Socialist movement). See Alcofar Nassaes, *Spansky*, pp. 228–35. This theory is backed by Gregorio Gallego, the latter also openly accusing the Communists of deliberately seeking to blacken the reputation of Durruti. Gallego, *Madrid: corazón que se desnagra*, pp. 229–31. However, whether Durruti's men would have done any better had it been them in the front line is a moot point.

70 Max, *Memorias de un revolucionario*, pp. 40–1.

71 R. Sanz, *Los que fuimos a Madrid: Columna Durruti , 26 División* (Paris, 1969), p. 116. Many other Republican counterattacks also came to grief. A good account of one such is afforded by the memoirs of the Fifth-Regiment volunteer Alvaro Cortes Roa. In brief, ordered to go over the top, he and his comrades were immediately assailed by heavy fire against which they found it impossible to proceed. Pinned down, Cortes Roa considered trying to hurl his grenades at the Nationalists, but decided, first, that it would be impossible to light their fuses, and, second, that, even if he could manage this, he would not be able to throw them far enough to do any damage. Eventually, then, he gave up the fight, inching his way back to the trench from which he had joined the attack. Cortes Roa, *Tanquista*, pp. 110–12.

72 For the contribution of the Nationalist air force to the new advance, see Salas Larrazábal, *Air War over Spain*, p. 104.

73 See J. Urra Lusarreta, *En las trincheras del frente de Madrid: memorias de un capellán de requetés herido de guerra* (Madrid, 1967), pp. 119–20.

74 Sommerfield, *Volunteer in Spain*, pp. 141–53.

75 The defence of the Casa de Velasquez by a group of Poles – apparently Company No. 3 of the Dabrowski battalion – is well attested to. However, stories of a desperate battle in the Faculty of Philosophy and Letters appear to be completely fabricated. For a good example of the genre, here is Delperrie de Bayac: 'On the night of the 14th [*sic*] the XI International Brigade was brought up ... to counter-attack in the University City. The commander of the Commune-de-Paris [battalion] said to his men, "The Arabs are afraid of cold steel, so let's go after them with the bayonet." Immediately the Frenchmen threw themselves into the attack. Commanded by Marcel Sagnier, No. 1 Company got into the Faculty of Philosophy and Letters. The battle raged in the classrooms, in the lecture theatres, in the corridors. When the ground floor had been taken, the Internationals moved on to the floors above. Neither one side nor the other faltered. Insults and jeers flew to and fro. Legionaries and Moors rolled grenades down the stairwells, whilst the Internationals responded by loading bombs into the lifts and pressing the button.' Delperrie de Bayac, *Brigadas internacionales*, p. 107. All very exciting, were it not for the fact that very few Nationalists ever reached the Faculty of Philosophy and Letters, Sommerfield making it clear that the building was reoccupied very quickly and without any real difficulty. See Sommerfield, *Volunteer in Spain*, p. 140.

76 J. Zugazagoitia, *Guerra y vicistitudes de los españoles* (Barcelona, 1977), p. 209.

77 Ibid.

78 Urra Lusarreta, *En las trincheras del frente de Madrid*, pp. 123–5.

79 It was only at this point that the panic that is so often said to have sent the Durruti column into a disorderly retreat occurred. Having been forced to evacuate his position near the Casa de Velásquez, Joaquín Masjuan was an eyewitness: 'In the afternoon ... the enemy broke into the Clinical Hospital. One of its wings fell into their power immediately, but in the other a furious fight broke out ... I was in the wing where the defence collapsed, alternately firing my submachine-gun and throwing hand grenades. Suddenly I heard men shouting that we had been betrayed and, looking round, saw a crowd of militia in full flight, abandoning the ruins as if pushed along by a hurricane.' Max, *Memorias de un revolucionario*, pp. 45–6.

80 Ibid., p. 46. The death of Durruti has always been the subject of much debate, but stories that he was shot by one of his own men appear to be completely unfounded.

81 The climax of the battle for the Clinical Hospital is vividly described by Urra Lusarreta: 'Very soon the upper floors resounded with the explosions of hand grenades, and through the holes in the walls we saw two or three of the enemy ... fall to their deaths on the ground below.' Urra Lusurreta, *En las trincheras del frente de Madrid*, p. 145. Meanwhile, by all accounts, the fight for the building was claustrophobic in the extreme. From the other side of the front line, we have Jesús Izcaray, a left-wing journalist who provided copy for a number of different newspapers during the

battle. In one article, he described an interview he had with some defenders who had been evacuated when they were wounded. 'The company ... to which the wounded belonged had occupied two wards of the hospital ... The ward next door, by contrast, was held by the other side. In the few moments of quiet, they said that they could hear them talking to one another. They were legionaries, and most of the time they talked about nothing but girls ... However, one of them was constantly on about a legacy that someone or other was going to leave him, and boasted that as soon as he got it, the Legion could go and screw itself.' J. Izcaray, *La guerra que yo viví: crónicas de los frentes españoles, 1936–1939* (Madrid, 1978), pp. 104–5.

82 Romilly, *Boadilla*, pp. 145–6.

83 Delperrie de Bayac, *Brigades internationaux*, pp. 109–10.

84 Cit. Alcofar Nassaes, *Spansky*, pp. 242–3.

85 Iniesta Cano, *Memorias y recuerdos*, pp. 97–8.

86 Thomas, 'Spanish *legionario*', pp. 76–7.

87 Miaja's personal intervention in the fighting is retailed in some detail by his biographer, López Fernández. Having driven to the Carcel Módelo to observe the fighting from close quarters, the general and his staff narrowly escaped with their lives when it was struck by the self-same air-raid mentioned by Thomas. Running out into the courtyard, they found their cars in flames and the whole area littered with dismembered bodies. Still worse, from outside came screams of panic: 'The Moors are coming! The tanks are breaking in!' If the story is to be believed, however, Miaja responded to the situation with the utmost *sang froid*: 'Without considering the temerity of his deed in the slightest, the general rushed out pistol in hand into the very centre of the Plaza de la Moncloa, and, with the enemy less than fifty metres away, began to shout in the angriest of tones. "You lot running away, where do you think you're going? Are you the soldiers who have been defending Madrid? I'll kill anyone who takes a step back. Get back in your trenches you cowards. Once and for all, get on with it!"' López Fernández, *General Miaja*, p. 123. Much the same story is retailed by Rojo. See Rojo, *Así fue la defensa de Madrid*, pp. 96–8.

88 Martínez Bande, *Marcha sobre Madrid*, pp. 341–2. Save Madrid the XI and XII International Brigades most certainly did not, but, for all that, they paid a heavy price: in what was to be a recurring pattern, by the end of the battle, around half their men had been killed or wounded. Alcofar Nassaes, *Spansky*, p. 244.

89 Cardozo, *March of a Nation*, p. 181.

90 *Cit.* Cortada, *Modern Warfare in Spain*, pp. 50–1.

91 Giving up the battle when the Nationalists were seemingly only metres from success was a difficult pill to swallow for many of Franco's supporters, and there was a certain amount of angry muttering. However, even the air-force commander Kindelán, an officer who at the end of the war fell out with Franco very seriously over the question of the monarchy, could not but agree that the decision was justified: 'Nothing is easier to justify than Franco's prudent decision not to risk the loss of his miniscule army ... in a hazardous bout of street fighting. With the enemy receiving daily reinforcements, to do so would have been to put at risk all the territory that had been captured and, with it, his lines of communication ... Defended though these were by the moral influence of our glorious advance, there was nothing to protect them in a physical sense.' Kindelán, *Cuadernos de guerra*, p. 91.

92 Candelas, *Adventures of an Innocent*, pp. 64–5.

5

WINTER BATTLES

The decision to abandon the direct assault on Madrid did not put an end to the fight for the capital. On the contrary, local fighting continued to rage around the periphery of the Nationalist pocket in the University City as one side or the other sought to gain some local advantage over their opponents, whilst on 11 December, a mine dug under the Clinical Hospital produced a spectacular explosion that killed thirty-nine soldiers of the Foreign Legion. In the slums of Carabanchel and Usera, too, there was constant sniping and periodic attempts to take houses held by the enemy. Amongst the men enduring the stress and fatigue of such fighting was Peter Kemp, a young Cambridge undergraduate who had interrupted his studies to travel to Spain and join the Nationalists and was now serving in a Carlist battalion:

> We were subject to frequent night attacks. The first came on the night of January 2nd ... Suddenly there came a burst of fire from one of our machine-guns upstairs, followed by a series of sharp detonations ... In a moment the whole house was shaking with the blast of mortars and grenades [while] the night became a chattering cacophony of rifle and machine-gun fire. I snatched my rifle and ... blazed away until it occurred to me I must be wasting a good deal of ammunition ... The same thought seemed to occur to [Lieutenant] Urmeneta, for, coming up behind me, he shouted into my ear, 'Don't shoot unless you've got a good target: we must conserve our ammunition. The same goes for grenades.' I had lobbed a few grenades, more for practice, and to give myself the impression that I was doing something, than for their effect ... The standard hand-grenade used by both sides was the percussion 'Lafitte' ... As the case was very thin, there was little danger of fragmentation, and the blast effect was limited to a few feet.[1]

Such clashes, however, were small beer compared with what was happening elsewhere. Thus, baulked in his attempt to rush the defences head-on, Franco now switched to the strategy of envelopment put forward by some of his commanders at the beginning of November. Before that task could be embarked upon, however, a more immediate problem had to be dealt with. In brief, in driving deep into the defences of Madrid, the Nationalist forces had left themselves with a tactical problem that was extremely delicate. For the troops holding the University City, their situation was very difficult, certainly: confined to an area that was not just surrounded and frequently overlooked by the enemy, but also so narrow that there were places in which it could be crossed from one side to the other in less than five minutes, they were dependent for all their supplies on a single narrow footbridge that was overlooked from close range by the Republican machine-guns on the Puente de los Franceses. Yet it was not just the Nationalist positions in the University City that were under threat. To the east, the fact that the insurgents had captured the Cerro de los Angeles helped a little, but from there to the River Tagus at Aranjuez there was nothing but a few squadrons of cavalry, whilst to the west the situation was little short of catastrophic. Thus, ensconced in such villages as Pozuelo, Húmera and Aravaca, the Republicans were ideally placed to threaten communications with the University City, whilst there was almost nothing to stop them: the column of Bartomeu was dug in around Mount Garábitas and a few more troops stationed a little further to the south-west at Retamares, but beyond that there was only empty countryside. To think, meanwhile, of the trench lines of the First World War would be entirely unrealistic. 'The tangle ... of the lines all round Madrid ... was such', wrote the English journalist Harold Cardozo, 'that it became very dangerous to motor up to any part of the front line ... for fear of driving into the Red forces.'[2]

No sooner had the direct assault on Madrid ceased, meanwhile, than the Nationalists had a serious scare. Many miles to the southwest, their chief line of communications continued to run through the town of Talavera. Situated on the north bank of the River Tagus, this was literally no more than the width of the river from government territory and, what is more, a river crossed by a bridge that had yet to be blown up. As for garrison, there were just 300 militiamen supported by two First-World-War German mine-throwers, and it was therefore with the utmost alarm that, at dawn on 24 November, these forces suddenly found themselves under attack. In the event, the attack could barely even be called a damp squib: the Republican artillery made no attempt to concentrate on the handful of machine-gun posts dominating the bridge, while few of the infantry involved in the fighting even so much as approached it, preferring instead to go to ground in the scrub that cloaked the southern bank (not that this provided any safety): with the Nationalists over their initial panic, for much of the rest of the day the attackers were heavily bombed by relays of Junkers and Savoias. Nevertheless, if Talavera was successfully defended, the incident was still a worry. Scarcely had the Nationalist troops scrambled back into their trenches after the fighting on 23 November, then, than Franco and his commanders were planning another attack, though this one was aimed not at taking Madrid but rather securing the thin corridor of territory that was all that linked them to the city against any further counterattacks. Thus was born the battle that has gone down in history as Boadilla or, alternatively, the Corunna Road. In brief, fighting began on 29 November with a violent attack on Pozuelo and Húmera that got the Nationalists a little more territory in the vicinity of the Casa de Campo but was checked by a combination of the weakness of the Nationalist forces involved in the action (the weary columns of Bartomeu and Alonso, plus a handful of cavalry), the extensive fortifications that the Republicans had constructed in the area over the course of the previous month and, finally, the series of counterattacks launched by the defenders, who were also supported by much more artillery than that available to their opponents. Amongst the troops rushed to the area, meanwhile, were the XII International Brigade and the newly organized X Mixed Brigade, a composite unit made up of various Anarchist formations including the remnants of the forces brought to Madrid by Durruti. One eyewitness to the fighting was Harold Cardozo:

> Two columns of legionaries and Moors, without much backing in artillery and tanks, captured … Humera and … even the villas around Pozuelo. The heads of the columns had been deflected from Aravaca … the approaches to which were beaten by the Reds from three different directions. This side-slipping was a fatal error, as it left the whole Nationalist line … in the air. It was so evident that orders were speedily given for the advance guards to fall back along the railway line … and to concentrate in a semi-circle north and west of Humera.[3]

After dying down overnight, the fighting broke out again the following day, the Republicans making furious efforts to break through. Prominent amongst their forces were the X Mixed Brigade and the battalion of T-26 tanks commanded by the Russian Semyon Krivoshein. As the latter later wrote:

> The tanks deployed in combat formation and soon passed the Anarchists units that were attacking with us. Arriving in front of the Casa Quemada, they were received by a hail of artillery fire and musketry. One tank received a direct hit and went up in flames, but, enveloping the Casa Quemada by its left and right alike, the others kept going and obliged the fascists to abandon it. However, the infantry advanced very slowly … Only five men entered the Casa Quemada, and even they rejoined their fellows after firing on the enemy for a while.[4]

As at Seseña, then, so at the Casa Quemada. On occasion, the Republicans could attack bravely enough, but they had little idea of how to co-ordinate the movements of tanks and infantry. It was a besetting sin that, as we shall see, was to cost them very dear. On the other hand, the Russian tanks did establish their superiority over their enemy counterparts once and for all: in what was probably the biggest tank battle of the civil war to date, a company of Italian L3s lost one-third of its tanks. In the hit-and-run fighting that raged in the Casa de Campo, meanwhile, the Russian BA10 armoured cars proved particularly useful. To quote Koltsov, 'Hidden behind small rises in the ground, clumps of trees or isolated buildings, they stalk enemy tanks, rush out at them from one flank or the other, fire a single shot ... and then drive off at high speed.'[5]

With both sides utterly exhausted, on 1 December, the fighting petered out, but the respite was only temporary. In brief, conscious of their lack of numbers, the Nationalist commanders were now hoping to force the elimination of the Republican pocket west of Madrid centred on the historic town of El Escorial, and to this end, planning was soon in hand for a new attack, hopes being boosted in this respect by the arrival at the front both of substantial forces of the old army and of the first combat-ready elements of the Falangist and Carlist militia. Meanwhile, a change in the Nationalist command structure had paved the way for a more centralized direction of the fighting, whilst at the same time symbolizing the Nationalists' tacit recognition that they were facing a long war. Thus, it was at this point that the 'columns' of the operations up to and including the battle of Madrid disappeared from the scene. In brief, all the forces holding the front line that snaked its sinuous way from the frontiers of Soria in the north-east to Talavera in the south were united in a single army corps – the Cuerpo de Ejército de Madrid – under the command of Andrés Saliquet, and the troops organised into the divisions of Soria, Avila and Madrid and an independent brigade charged with the defence of the Tagus valley. As yet, the order of battle of these forces was not entirely regular: placed under the command of Luis Orgaz, the Madrid division numbered three brigades, each of which numbered not the conventional four battalions, but rather as many as twenty (to render such oversized assemblies manageable, they were divided into 'groups of battalions', i.e. in practice, the old columns by a different name). In command of the First Brigade – the main strike force – was the same General Varela who had headed the attack on Madrid, and he had 10,000 men, two companies of tanks and around fifty guns – an imposing array, but certainly not the fascist horde spoken of by some writers.[6] As for aerial support, this was relatively copious, but hampered both by poor weather conditions – the last weeks of 1936 happened to be ones of constant rain – and vigorous Republican opposition: on 4 December, for example, a surprise air-raid on the airfield of Navalmoral knocked out an entire squadron of Spanish-crewed Ju52s.[7]

On the other side of the lines, things had also been changing. As the battle of Madrid had died down, so the defenders also began to look to their own organization. With more and more mixed brigades ready for action, a more regular means had to be found of articulating the Republican forces, and thus it was that 27 November 1936 saw the first appearance of conventional divisions in the Republican zone, the first part of the front that was chosen for this experiment being the sector north and west of Madrid (in brief, each of the new divisions contained three or four mixed brigades, the latter formations thereby losing the independent nature that was their one real rationale).[8] As yet, however, the change was by no means complete. Thus, the forces defending Madrid itself continued to be organised into *ad hoc* 'sectors' rather than divisions, whilst the conversion of the old columns into mixed brigades was proceeding more slowly than Miaja and his staff would have liked: if the Fifth-Regiment column of Antonio Ortega had become a force that was temporarily designated 'Y Brigade', that of Barceló had survived untouched.[9]

In fairness to the Republicans, however, the time available for re-organization was short indeed. On 14 December, then, Varela advanced to the attack once more under the convenient cover of a dense fog, the target this time being the Republican salient west and south-west of Pozuelo, and, more particularly, the isolated village of Boadilla de Monte. In brief, whilst two columns commanded by Monasterio and Barrón pushed northwards from Villaviciosa de Odón into the empty spaces west of Pozuelo with the aim of enveloping Boadilla, those of Eduardo Sáenz de Buruaga (another new face who had taken the place of Rolando de Tella, the latter having been badly wounded towards the end of the direct assault on the capital) and Alonso launched a direct attack from the south and east. Defending the area were some 13,000 Republican troops supported by two armoured trains and up to forty-seven guns of calibres ranging from 75mm up to 155mm. Commanding them was the erstwhile commander of the XI International Brigade, Manfred Stern, whose exploits, whether real or imaginary, in the assault on the capital had brought him what was in effect command of a division. The day was marked by thick fog, but by nightfall, the Nationalists had pushed through Pozuelo and occupied the first houses of Boadilla. Here, however, a desperate stand by the XI and XII International Brigades, in particular, checked the attackers, and continued fog held them in place for the whole of the next day. That said, success was short-lived: thanks in part to a brief reappearance of conditions favourable for enemy air attack, 16 December saw the Republicans driven from the whole of the village. Amongst the last to leave was the Thaelmann battalion, and, with it, its single section of British volunteers. 'We were firing all the time', wrote Esmond Romilly of the desperate flight that followed. 'I copied the others and fired in the same direction till the barrel was red-hot. And always, starting every few minutes, there was the deadly cross-fire … There were bombing planes over us and shrapnel bursting behind.'[10]

By nightfall, only two of Romilly's original ten-man squad were still alive. With the fall of Boadilla, however, the battle soon ended, the Nationalists having now secured all their objectives: though Republican apologists have always tried to claim that Varela had somehow been defeated, there had never been any intention of pushing any further north at this stage.[11] If there is any doubt about the result of the battle, meanwhile, one has only to look at the fate of Manfred Stern. A Jew from Bukovina who had joined the Red Army in 1917 and was known in Spain as Lazar Kléber, Stern had arrived in Madrid as the commander of the XI International Brigade. In this capacity, he seems to have performed well enough, but he had otherwise played no role in the defence of the city. Yet the Communist propaganda machine had built him up to be something much more – to this day, it is possible to find him billed as the commander of the entire Madrid front – and as such he had been given charge of the crucial Boadilla sector. That said, Stern was extremely vulnerable, having for understandable reasons incurred the hatred of both Miaja and Rojo (in this respect, it did not help that he was boastful and vain-glorious). Having been revealed as an idol with feet of clay, he now paid the price: coming to the conclusion that they needed the general and his chief of staff much more than they needed an over-promoted brigade commander of no special competence, the Communist leadership dropped Stern overnight, the result being that Miaja was permitted to replace him with the Spanish regular officer Cuevas de la Peña.[12]

Victory at Boadilla had not come cheap for the Nationalists: one Carlist battalion alone had lost 300 of its 500 men.[13] That said, the situation in the Republican camp was very dark. The XI International Brigade had been practically destroyed and many other units subjected to a severe beating, while the Madrid front's reserves of munitions had been almost completely drained and many weapons of various sorts captured by the Nationalists. Conscious of the need to do something to relieve the pressure on the capital, the Republican high command reverted to the diversionary strategy that it had first had recourse to in September. In brief, then, three different attacks were mounted on the Nationalist front lines in areas well away from Madrid, the targets selected being Sigüenza, Teruel and Córdoba (in this last region, the Nationalist forces in southern Spain had on 15 December launched an offensive of their own, which had succeeded in taking such towns as Bujalance). Each of the operations received the support of an International Brigade – the XII in the case of Sigüenza, the XIII in the case of Teruel and the XIV in the case of Córdoba, the two last named both having just been organized – but it is not the case, as is sometimes implied, that the attacks were wholly the work of foreign volunteers. Also committed to the offensives were limited numbers of tanks, guns and aircraft. Had all the resources involved been committed to a single front, something might have been achieved, but, as it was, the Republicans contrived to be weak everywhere and strong nowhere. Though few in numbers and often deployed in widely separated strong points, the Nationalists held out grimly, and within a matter of hours, the Republicans had for the most part been brought to a dead halt. In many instances, particularly in the south, the advance was conducted in the utmost disorder, whilst on the Sigüenza front, Republican aircraft repeatedly strafed their own men. Here and there, a few insignificant villages fell into the attackers, but even these had to be given up after no more than a few days. Casualties, meanwhile, were frequently very heavy: the XIII International Brigade lost half its strength, whilst the XIV International Brigade, a unit that appears to have been composed of recruits of very poor quality and had a reputation for drunkenness and indiscipline, was also badly hit: one battalion was wiped out when it advanced into Nationalist territory entirely on its own and without the slightest knowledge of the enemy's positions, whilst the rest of the brigade was decimated while trying to attack the villages of Porcuna and Lopera and ended up all but disintegrating, insult being added to injury by the fact that the Nationalist forces in the area had never numbered more than 2,000 men, most of whom were neither Moors or Legionaries but rather conscripts and militia.[14]

In the face of these failures, the Republican leadership sought desperately for some crumb of comfort. To quote Tom Wintringham, the Grimsby-born Communist who commanded the British battalion of the XV Brigade in the battle of the River Jarama (see below), 'The appearance of one of our brigades down there on the straight road to Seville, Franco's base, must have made him detach troops from his Madrid army to cover his own "goal."'[15] Setting aside everything else, however, in all three of the offensives, the much vaunted International Brigaders had shown not just want of training but also want of spirit, many men having gone absent without leave or even deserted altogether. Still worse, these operations did nothing to reduce the pressure on the capital. On the contrary, on 3 January, the Nationalists attacked yet again, their object this time being to bring relief to the beleaguered garrison of the University City by advancing from Boadilla to the highway to La Coruña in the vicinity of the towns of Majadahonda and Las Rozas. Amongst the attackers was the Welsh foreign legionary Frank Thomas:

> 1 January [*sic*] saw us advancing out of the village … under cover of our artillery and tanks … The next day another advance took us across barren plains to an unfinished highway … Here we took up positions, digging small holes … for sleeping and defence purposes. It was well that we did so, for the following midday an attack burst forth from the woods a quarter of a mile from us. We were not caught napping, and well-directed fire drove the enemy infantry back into the woods after they had only gone a few yards. However, four or five Russian heavy-cannon tanks in front of them continued to come on. Two anti-tank gun units we had with us fought a duel with them, though we had to kick the gunners' backsides to make them do it … Halting half-way … the tanks began to methodically pelt us with steel, but, their ammunition seeming to run out, they eventually retreated.[16]

Once again there was heavy fog, but the Nationalist pressure was unremitting, and by 9 January, substantial insurgent forces had occupied Las Rozas and the village of Aravaca, thereby forcing the Republicans dug in along the western flanks of the Casa de Campo and the University City to withdraw in disorder. Once again, the International Brigades were in the thick of the fighting: already in the area at the start of the battle, the XI International Brigade had to be withdrawn after suffering heavy casualties, but, with the fighting elsewhere now at an end, the XII, XIII and XIV International Brigades were all thrown into the battle, along with a variety of Spanish formations including the I, III and XXI Mixed Brigades.[17] However, progress was all but non-existent and losses very heavy. To quote an evidently rueful Koltsov, 'We have been attacking for two days. We have got a wealth of means, but for the time being the results are very disappointing.'[18]

As the Nationalists had no intention of advancing any further, on 16 January, the fighting once again ground to a halt with the troops in positions that were to remain unchanged to the end of the war. Both along the highway to La Coruña and around the University City and in the Casa de Campo, Nationalists and Republicans alike began to construct elaborate trench lines that were eventually to turn the whole zone into a miniature version of the Western Front, complete with bunkers, pillboxes and dense wire entanglements. Inside the city, meanwhile, the primitive barricades of November were supplemented by the conversion of entire city blocks into fortresses by knocking holes in the walls separating each apartment from the next and blocking doors and windows alike with massive sandbag barricades. That said, Madrid was still very much in danger. Now that their flank and rear was secure, the Nationalist troops massed before the capital could turn their attention to cutting the vital Valencia highway, this having long since become the beleaguered city's only practicable source of food, munitions, arms and reinforcements. On 6 February, then, 19,000 Nationalist troops, the vast majority of them either Moors or Foreign Legionaries, left their positions south of the city and struck due east towards the River Jarama. Supporting them were around sixty Panzer I tanks, almost all of them crewed by Spaniards, and no fewer than 101 guns, including six batteries of 155mm howitzers, together with much of the newly organized Condor Legion, the Italian Legionary Aviation and the rather more exiguous resources of the Nationalist air force (as well as planes, the Condor Legion appears also to have contributed the services of its four batteries of 88mm FLAK18's).[19]

At first, progress was rapid. No more than 3,000 Republicans were deployed in the area hit by the Nationalists, while the terrain consisted of little more than rolling uplands, which offered no obstacle to the attacking forces. In just five days, then, the Nationalists were approaching the River Jarama, leaving the defenders in shreds. At this point, however, the situation got more difficult, not least because the eastern bank of the river was dominated by a line of low hills covered with a mixture of scrub and olive groves. Behind the river, meanwhile, were substantial reserves, the Republicans having themselves been massing for an attack on the insurgent positions south of Madrid. All of them dependent not on Miaja but rather on Pozas as overall commander of the Army of the Centre, these consisted of XI, XII and XIV International Brigades; I Shock Brigade; and I, XVII, XVIII, XIX, XXI, XXIII, XXIV, LXV, LXVII, LXIX and LXX Mixed Brigades.[20]

Saying a great deal, as it does, about the state of decision making in the Republican camp, the aborted offensive to which these troops had been committed is worth considering at some length. To attack on the Jarama front was by no means a foolish plan, for success there could very soon endanger Orgaz's communications with the Tagus valley. However, the scheme was deeply entangled with a series of political tensions centred on the fact that Largo Caballero had become increasingly uncomfortable with the prestige that the Communists had derived from the defence of Madrid, and all the more so as his pride had been deeply wounded by his flight from the city as Franco's troops had closed in at the beginning of November (it did not help here that Largo Caballero was simultaneously finally beginning to wake up to both the extent of Communist influence in the People's Army and the extent to which his ambitions to take over the Communist party immediately prior to the war had backfired). Also a source of much trouble was the constant friction between the Communist-dominated Junta of Defence and the central government; a key issue here being the determination of the Communists to get rid of, Asensio Torrado, the latter having made the mistake of refusing point-blank to join the party. To quote Largo himself:

> Ignoring every order that it was sent, the Junta of Defence of Madrid set itself up in open opposition to the government. It was not at the orders of Miaja: rather, things were the other way about. Whenever I called something to his attention in my capacity as Minister of War, he took refuge in the argument that it had been done at the behest of the Junta ... Some of the members took to insulting the authority of the government and, especially ... General Asensio ... but General Miaja took no action against them despite the fact that he was in the chair ... The campaign ... against General Asensio was quite unspeakable ... Already I had had to relieve him from the command of the Army of the Centre and appoint him Undersecretary in the Ministry of War, but now they wanted to exclude him from the government altogether.[21]

With his irritation increased still further by the pretensions of the Russian advisers that swarmed around him, Largo therefore attempted to push an offensive in Extremadura in the hope that by doing so, the Republican forces could reach the Portuguese frontier and thereby cut the Nationalist zone in two. This plan, however, was vetoed by the Communists and, indeed, Pozas: the Republicans would attack, yes, but only in an area that would redound to their credit.[22]

To return to the course of the battle, on 12 February, the first Nationalist troops got across the Jarama near the village of San Martín de la Vega, having captured a railway bridge that the Republicans had failed to blow up. Ascending the hills beyond the river, the Moors and Legionaries then ran into fresh opponents in the form of the XV International Brigade. A new formation, composed of the British battalion (a unit that had just been put together from the remnants of the various British detachments that had fought at Madrid, Boadilla and Lopera and some 400 men who had come out from Britain in the course of the winter), the Slavic Dimitrov battalion, the largely French Sixth-of-February battalion and the American Abraham Lincoln battalion, the XV International

Brigade had been in training – a very sketchy activity that left many men barely able to fire a gun – in a number of villages round the Internationals' main base at Albacete, but the Nationalist breakthrough south of Madrid soon had the first three of these units being rushed to the front.[23] Sent forward into the line with little or no knowledge of the enemy positions and the most inadequate of armament – the rifle companies of the British battalion, for example, were armed with a mixture of Colt M1895 and Chauchat M1915 machine-guns, but the canvas ammunition belts supplied with the former (survivors of some of the very large consignments supplied to Russia in the First World War) proved to have perished, whilst such was its propensity to jam that the latter is for good reason regarded as one of the worst machine-guns ever to have seen the light of day – they were cut to pieces.[24] Deprived of adequate fire support by the fact that the lorry carrying the machine-gun company's eight Russian Maxim M1910s had not turned up, the three rifle companies attempted to hold a line of isolated knolls, only to be shot to pieces by enemy troops who had occupied some high ground immediately to the north. Walter Gregory was a young brewery worker from Nottingham who was attached to the commander of No. 3 Company, Bill Briskey: 'Shells were dropping all around me and I weaved about in the hope of gaining added protection … The carnage was horrendous. There were not only dead and dreadfully wounded men lying all over the ground, but there were bits of bodies thrown all over the hillside.'[25]

Badly armed as they were – even the Moisin-Nagant rifles with which the men were armed could not be fired with any degree of accuracy due to the fact that the volunteers had stripped them of the spike bayonets with which they had arrived, without realizing that the sights were calibrated to take account of the extra weight which the former exerted[26] – the British battalion had no chance, whilst it did not help that two of the company commanders were amongst those cut down. After several hours, the troops on the hillocks were therefore overrun and forced to flee. One of the small minority of middle-class recruits in the battalion was Jason Gurney, a South African sculptor who had been living in London in 1936:

> At this particular moment we were a broken battalion … Seventy per cent of those who had been holding the forward positions were either killed or wounded … Gradually, a few members of the three companies came drifting back. All their automatic weapons had been lost or abandoned, and many of them had no weapons at all … They were all in a state of greater or lesser shock, hungry and suffering from a tremendous thirst.[27]

Eager to exploit their success, the Nationalists moved forward onto the plateau that overlooked the positions that had been defended by the broken rifle companies from the rear. Ahead of them lay nothing more than the hitherto helpless machine-gun company. Commanded by Harry Fry, an Edinburgh cobbler who had seen service as a sergeant in the First World War, this was dug in a few hundred yards to the rear. Fortunately, just at this very point, its eight Maxim guns had finally been readied for action, the triumphant Moors therefore receiving an unexpected bloody nose. 'For the first time ... we opened fire in earnest, the strategically placed Maxims giving devastating cross-fire', recalled David Hooper, an unemployed Londoner who had volunteered to serve in Spain in the wake of the failure of his marriage. 'I could see dead men all over the place ... To be honest, I was bloody scared, but I kept on firing. Then we stopped ... and we could hear the wounded enemy's moans and groans [but] no-one came to help them.'[28] If Fry had managed to buy the shaken battalion a little time, the night that followed was but the most short-lived of respites: no sooner had the day dawned, indeed, than the Nationalists not only attacked again but scored an early success by overrunning Fry's badly isolated men and taking many of them prisoner, together with all of their guns. Though in theory attached to battalion headquarters as a cartographer, Jason Gurney found himself not only in the front line, but also participating in a desperate counterattack:

> The sheer weight of noise was tremendous ... Wintringham stood up to lead the charge [but] was almost immediately shot through the thigh and collapsed ... Aitken [the battalion commissar] and about ten others jumped to their feet ... and charged. Very, very reluctantly I followed them ... By the time that I had run about sixty yards I realised that there was no longer anyone in front or alongside me, and I dived for cover under one of the small hills built up around the foot of every olive tree.[29]

For the whole of the next day and well into the next, the survivors of the battalion held out in a sunken lane that crossed the plateau in the rear of the positions that had been held by the machine-gun company, but on 15 February, the appearance of some enemy tanks put paid to what little remained of their resolution. 'All that was now left of the battalion was a handful of men rushing up and down ... in a state of utter confusion', wrote the same observer. 'This was only increased when two Russian tanks appeared from the main road and started to bombard the Moors in the machine-gun trench. Their fire was erratic and there was a moment of panic when we thought that they were shooting at us ... One unfortunate individual ... was rushing round in a cocoon of insulated wire and crying, "I have captured the fascist communications! I have captured the fascist communications!" Eventually he leapt up on to the parapet and was shot dead by a burst of machine-gun fire.'[30]

According to the usual version of events, a gallant counterattack late in the day reversed the tide of battle and drove the Nationalists from their positions, but this is almost certainly a myth, for the front line occupied by the British volunteers at the close of the battle was well short of the edge of the plateau.[31] Nor, meanwhile, did the Moors and Legionaries have very much interest in advancing too far. Thus, what the myriad accounts of the British battalion's gallant stand ignore is the fact that, positioned where it was, the battalion was not in the Nationalists' direct line of march, but rather on its flank. Heroic though the British battalion may have been, it had clearly not stopped the enemy advance. On the contrary, the real fight was taking place some miles to the north. One participant in the defence was Joaquín Masjuán, who, in a change of allegiance that says a lot for his level of politicization, had just transferred from the Durruti Column to Enrique Lister's I Mixed Brigade:

> On we trudged and by-and-by we reached the battlefield ... Huge col-
> umns of black smoke were rising into the air, and gouts of earth were being
> flung into the air by the shells ... Pretty soon ... we suffered our first losses
> ... In front of us was a great mass of smoke that was coming from scrub
> fires produced by the shelling, and this made it very hard to see ... Finally,
> the enemy attacked us: it was four o'clock in the afternoon. They were
> protected by tanks, but they got an unpleasant surprise in the form of our
> Russian anti-tank guns, which quickly put paid to four of the latter. One
> of them went up like a roman candle, and at this the others backed off,
> leaving us free to mow down the infantry with our cross fire.[32]

Such bravery, however, was not enough. On the contrary, the Nationalists con-tinued to push north-eastwards. Amongst the troops in the front line of the advance was Carlos Iniesta Cano:

> As we moved forward ... the enemy attacked our right flank with tank
> support ... However, the impetus and daring of my legionaries, the deter-
> mination with which they sought to engage in hand-to-hand fighting and
> the manner in which they set fire to the tanks with bottles of inflammable
> liquid, soon persuaded [the Reds] to desist in their endeavour.[33]

Yet for all the efforts of officers like Iniesta Cano, the Nationalist attack was appreciably slowing down. Setting aside the fact that two weeks' fighting had cost Franco's forces heavy casualties, the Republicans continued to show consid-erable aggression, even if this was not accompanied by much in the way of skill. On the morning of 17 February, for example, Peter Kemp found himself facing a counterattack against the left flank of the original Nationalist breakthrough near La Marañosa:

> At dawn on the morning of the 17th we awoke to the sound of heavy firing
> away to our left. We ran to our trenches and took up firing positions. At first
> we could see nothing, but, as the haze rolled back in the rising sun, we saw
> groups of little dark figures moving towards us ... We held our fire, letting
> them reach the olive trees undisturbed. Surely, I thought, they can't mean to
> attack across those open fields in front with no artillery preparation? It's sheer
> suicide ... But in a moment they emerged from cover and began to advance
> at a trot towards us. We waited until they were well in the open, [and] then, at

a sharp word from the platoon commander, our machine guns opened up ...
The little trotting figures halted and toppled down in heaps ... Some of the
enemy ... tried to cover the advance of their comrades with light automatic
weapons, but ... they stood no chance against our fire.[34]

As usual, meanwhile, dogged by the perpetual problem of how to co-ordinate its
operations with those of the infantry, the Republican armour was able to achieve
far less than might have been expected. Only after the infantry had been routed,
then, did any enemy tanks appear on this occasion, and even then it did not take
much to neutralize them. To quote Kemp again:

Suddenly we heard the sound of heavy engines, and from our right front
appeared six Russian tanks, each carrying a [45mm] gun in its turret. One
after another they crossed in front of the olives, then turned towards us and
began to approach in line. This looked awkward for us, and would have
been if any infantry had followed them, but the latter had no fight left in
them ... At that moment our artillery, silent before, came into action ...
and soon we saw black puffs of smoke bursting all round the tanks. They
wavered, then came to a halt. A moment later one of them was enveloped
in thick black smoke as a shell struck it squarely; it began to burn. Then
another was hit at the base of the turret. The remaining four turned, spread
out and made off.[35]

Whilst every Republican attack was beaten off, more and more men had to
be left behind to guard the flanks of the breakthrough. At the same time, the
Nationalists were frequently hard pressed. Yet the fighting on this sector of
the front has received little attention. Instead, the presence of the International
Brigades has ensured that most of the coverage has been focused on events on
the other side of the Jarama, a good example being the attack mounted by the
American Abraham Lincoln battalion on 27 February. The fourth battalion
in the XV Brigade, this had been late reaching the line and had only turned
up on 16 February. Fed into the line to the right of the British battalion, on
22 February the Americans had already lost sixty casualties in an attempt to rush
the Nationalist positions on the Morata de Tajuna road, and it was therefore
with some consternation that they were ordered by the Brigade's commander,
a Croatian Communist called Vladimir Copic, to move forward once again.
Spanish troops would be advancing on his right, the battalion commander,
Robert Merriman, was told, and the rest of the XV Brigade on his left, and
there would be plentiful tanks, artillery and air cover in support. Rightly sus-
pecting that such support was likely to prove illusory, Merriman begged Copic
to call off the attack, only to be ordered to go ahead anyway. The result was a
slaughter. No sooner had they left their trenches, than the Americans were falling in swathes. One survivor of the charge was a trade-union activist from New
Jersey named John Tisa:

At the outset, one of our tanks ... was hit and burst into flames ... belching an awful bonfire; my thoughts for a moment were of the crew trapped inside ... Rodolfo de Armas, leader of the Cuban section, was the first man killed ... Cries of 'First aid! First aid!' came from everywhere. Men fell in front, to the right and to the left of us, dead or wounded. Enemy machine guns kept hammering away steadily, ploughing up the ground around us ... Stalled in our advance by the enemy's wall of fire, many of us laboured desperately, chopping up the damp earth with bayonet and helmet to make some sort of trench ... A few, close enough to enemy positions, hurled grenades, but then they too were silenced, either killed or wounded.[36]

By the end of the day, 127 of the American volunteers were dead. That said, 27 February was the last day of the battle: their losses having mounted alarmingly, the Nationalists simply did not have the strength to push on any further, whilst their troops were utterly exhausted. Nevertheless, if Franco's triumph was incomplete, he had scarcely suffered a defeat: Republican casualties numbered as many as 10,000 men; Pozas' plans for a counter-offensive had been ruined; and the Nationalists had advanced close enough to the Valencia highway to bring it under shell-fire. Might more have been achieved, however? Given the fact that Franco's troops occupied the whole line of the Sierra de Guadarrama, they had the potential to strike deep into the Republican rear as well as to advance across the River Jarama. Had the two fronts been attacked simultaneously, the result could easily have been a crushing victory, for, even as it was, the Republicans had only come through with the greatest difficulty. Such an idea, it seems was certainly discussed, but for logistical reasons – above all the fact that the Nationalists did not have the resources to fight two battles at once – it was eventually agreed that the troops holding the frontiers of Soria would only advance once Orgaz's forces cut off the Valencia highway.[37] Given that the result was failure, there has been a tendency to invest this decision and others like it with political significance. We return here, of course, to Preston's claims that Franco wanted a long war, but, once again, it is very difficult to accept such arguments: as before, such a plan conflicted with the need to avoid the conflict in Spain becoming conflated with a wider European struggle, whilst Franco's political position was not so secure that he could afford to risk defeat. Militarily perfectly sensible, what the decision reflected was not Machiavellianism but rather the caution that remained a feature of Franco's generalship throughout the rest of the war, the bloody nose he had received in the direct assault on Madrid very much inclining him to favour set-piece battles in which the odds were loaded heavily in his favour over more daring attacks that were accompanied by greater risk.[38]

The fighting around Madrid, then, was not yet over. Before examining the struggle that resulted, however, we must first turn to an episode in southern Spain, and all the more so as it made an important contribution to the erosion of Largo Caballero's prestige and authority. Ever since the start of the war, the province of Málaga had been holding out for the Republic (not that it had ever been hard pressed, the Nationalist forces in southern Spain having far too few troops to push through the ring of rugged mountains that protected it on three sides). All but totally isolated from the rest of the Republican zone – the only route into and out of the zone was the coastal road running east from Málaga city to Motril – and defended solely by left-wing militias that had not been touched in the slightest by the moves that led to the establishment of the People's Army, it was clearly ripe for the picking, all that was wanted being the force needed to march in and crush such feeble resistance as could be expected. Unfortunately for the defenders of Málaga, in December 1936, just such a *masse de manoeuvre* emerged. Eager for more military glory than had been on offer in the assault on Madrid and contemptuous of commanders whom he regarded as old-fashioned and over-cautious, Mussolini had decided to send not just arms or even an air force to Spain, but an entire army corps, this being christened the Corpo di Truppe Voluntarie (or CTV).[39] This move was not at all to the taste of the Nationalist high command, but such was the importance of Italian aid that there was little that they could do about it, and so from the middle of December 1936, ever larger contingents of Italian troops began to disembark at Cádiz. With the forces concerned landing, as they were, in Andalucía, the obvious place to make use of them was Málaga, and all the more so as this was a target that was far too valuable to ignore: the capital, after all, was a major port, while the province's capture would considerably shorten the Nationalist front line. Nor were such considerations the only ones pushing the Nationalists in the direction of an attack: Málaga being a bastion of the CNT and, to a lesser extent, the Communists, taking it would deal a heavy blow to Republican morale and give Franco the chance to appease the blood-lust of his more radical supporters, amongst whom were many figures of whose loyalty he could not be entirely certain.

By the middle of January, then, substantial forces were massing against Málaga. From the Nationalist Army of the South came 15,000 Foreign Legionaries, Moors, Spanish regulars and Carlist and Falangist militia, while the CTV contributed another 10,000 men, together with some artillery batteries and a battalion of tanks and armoured cars, these forces being poised to invade the beleaguered province from no fewer than four different directions. Ready to fly overhead, meanwhile, were strong elements of the Legionary Aviation together with a motley assembly of planes from the pre-war Spanish air force, albeit mostly antiquated Breguet BrXIXs, whilst at sea lurked a small flotilla of Nationalist warships headed by the modern cruisers *Baleares*, *Canarias* and *Almirante Cervera*. Also a feature of the build-up was an ever increasing number of air-raids. As the retired zoologist Sir Peter Chalmers-Mitchell later wrote, 'From 4 January to 23 January … only four days passed without warning signal; actually bombs fell on the town eleven times.'[40] Against such an array the defenders had no chance whatsoever, and all the more so as they had almost no combat experience: there were barely 12,000 men under arms, of whom only 8,000 had modern rifles; there was little in the way of ammunition; there were very few machine-guns and only sixteen pieces of artillery; there were hardly any aircraft of any sort; and such few defence works as existed were both poorly built and poorly sited.[41] Yet the atmosphere in the province was anything but despondent: even if the Nationalists managed to get through the mountains, revolutionary zeal, it was confidently believed, would triumph. As Chalmers-Mitchell remarked of one acquaintance, he 'was so sure of the bravery and spirits of the defenders, and of their wise choice of points of vantage, that he was full of confidence.'[42] Indeed, so infectious was the atmosphere that, visiting the city just a few days before the Nationalist attack began, the chief correspondent of *The Daily Worker*, Claude Cockburn, predicted that an enemy offensive would 'be faced with a very different and much more exhausting resistance than anything seen on the Málaga front before.'[43]

As in many other parts of Republican Spain, meanwhile, as even many of its supporters recognized, the revolution had produced complete chaos in Málaga. 'I was in agreement with it', remembered Jaime Alarcón, a marble cutter from a small village near Fuengirola named Tajos, 'but things weren't done as they should have been ... One flag, another flag, flags all over: UGT, FAI-CNT, Communists – all those parties! What could come of all that? There wasn't union enough ... I didn't have any position in the union or the revolutionary committee: I didn't have the education for that. Not that those on the committee understood very much: there were some on it who were there for their personal advantage. One man in particular, a real reactionary, the committee trusted, I don't know why ... There were a few like him: they thought that the revolution was eating and drinking without working.'[44] Still more damning, meanwhile, is the account of the chairman of the committee concerned:

> A revolution isn't made by shooting off revolvers, by violence and nothing else. And yet that was what a lot of people thought ... There was too much freedom: everyone had his own idea of what could be done, of what should be done ... The militia took things into their own hands. They'd go into a shop or a house and requisition goods, saying the order came from me ... We on the committee couldn't throw them out ... In some places it was necessary to shoot militiamen and the like who assassinated people and looted, but they were too strong here: they had all the arms.[45]

With strong leadership, a degree of order might have been restored, but higher up, the issues were in some ways even worse. De facto authority in the province was in the hands of a revolutionary committee, but this had little power in the face of the unruly militias.[46] As for the military commander, an obscure colonel named José Villalba Rubio, he was at one and the same utterly at odds with the revolutionary committee, the militias and the commander of the Republican Army of the South, General Martínez Monje.[47] Finally, as if all this was not enough, no help could be expected from outside: with the fighting round Madrid in full swing, there was in any case little enough to send, but, even had this not been the case, Largo Caballero and Asensio Torrado regarded Málaga as a bastion of the Communists and were therefore little interested in rushing to the province's defence.[48]

In short, the situation could not have been more calamitous. Angry Anarchists later argued that all was not lost – that had the ever more depressed and disaffected Villalba been prepared to fight a revolutionary war, the city might yet have been saved – but rhetoric was no substitute for a well-armed and well-disciplined defence force, even were there not plenty of reason to suspect that the enthusiasm of the masses was in reality little more in evidence than in any other region of Republican Spain. Out in the countryside, gangs of peasants and landless labourers dug defences in return for a few *pesetas*, but no new recruits were forthcoming to man their efforts. 'The most surprising aspect of the situation', wrote Franz Borkenau, who, like Cockburn, happened to visit the province just before the Nationalist offensive, 'was the relation between the population of the [city] and the front. There was very little contact at all ... The enemy was approaching and large posters asked for new ... recruits, but very few seemed to come in.'[49]

What followed, then, was a foregone conclusion. On 3 February, the four Nationalist columns crashed into the defenders. Resistance being all but nonexistent, in just five days, the attackers were in the capital. Fleeing along the coast road, meanwhile, were a mass of terrified refugees desperate to escape the trap. A witness to the *grande battue* that the campaign became was Chalmers-Mitchell, who, tiring of the suspense, climbed one of the hills behind the city to watch the approach of the Nationalists: 'Slowly drawing near ... field-guns barked, machine-guns clattered and rifles spluttered. Now and again [there came] a duller, heavier sound as of a large shell bursting ... Armies were advancing from every point of the compass except due south where the Mediterranean glittered.'[50] Málaga having been the scene of scenes of particular violence during the revolution of the previous summer – taking the province as a whole, 2,600 Nationalist sympathizers are believed to have been murdered, including some 270 prisoners who were put to death in reprisal for enemy air raids [51] – the victors were in no mood to show mercy. On the contrary, as commander of the rebel forces, Queipo de Llano had over the course of the autumn and winter been repeatedly threatening the Republicans with the most terrible vengeance (a vengeance that he had already been exacting across those areas of southern Spain controlled by the Nationalists), and Málaga now felt the full weight of his fury. As they struggled along the narrow coast road, a journey made all the harder by flooding resulting from months of heavy rain, the fugitives were repeatedly both bombed and strafed from the air and shelled from the sea. In its last action of the war, Malraux's squadron tried bravely to cover the retreat, but it was outclassed by the Italian Fiat CR32s and driven from the skies, though it is very much to its credit that it tried to do anything at all: by contrast, gripped by indiscipline and lethargy, the Republican fleet remained in port at in its base at Cartagena and did not make a single attempt to challenge the Nationalist ships.[52] The flight from the city was witnessed at close quarters by Chalmers-Mitchell:

We went to the front of the house … The narrow lane … was packed close with a miserable stream. Donkeys laden with children and bundles, old women, young women, here and there a dejected soldier still dragging his rifle, but helping along some hobbling old woman, or with a child under his arm and a bigger child holding on to the end of his jacket. Hurrying, pushing, groaning, screaming, faces mottled with grey and green and dull red, fear and misery turning them into one of Goya's dreadful pictures … Down the Camino Nuevo, along the *arroyo* at the foot of the garden, were similar streams. The streams converged as they approached the Motril road, and … we could see … that its wide breadth was filled. The streams went on all night, rustling and sighing like the wind in trees. And during the night rebel warships came along, patrolling backwards and forwards, playing searchlights on the curves of the road and following the stream with shells. At dawn, aeroplanes swooped down, spraying with machine-guns.[53]

How many died on the road, no-one will ever know, but a conservative estimate might be 3,000, whilst another 1,884 people were executed in the ten months following the Nationalist victory.[54] As was in part the intention, of course, such ruthlessness spread great alarm in the Republican zone. More seriously, perhaps, the fall of Málaga badly undermined the position of Largo Caballero. As Prime Minister and Minister of National Defence, he could scarcely avoid the responsibility for the defeat, and the Communists exploited this situation by organizing massive street demonstration in Valencia and elsewhere calling for greater energy in the conduct of the war. The message underpinning these demonstrations was all too clear, namely the need for Largo Caballero to step down in favour of an administration dominated by the Communists, but for the time being, the premier was allowed to remain in office. Not so the trusted figure of Asensio Torrado, however. Labelled 'the general of the defeats', he was openly vilified by the Communists, whilst the men who might have been thought to be his natural allies – namely, the officers of the old army still serving the Republic – for the most part turned their back on him, the fact being that, according to his admirer Martín Blásquez, at least, he had frequently shown them up as incompetent. Had Largo Caballero been in a stronger position, the general might yet have brazened things out, but, as matters stood, his situation was impossible, and at the beginning of March, he duly tendered his resignation. It was a tragic loss: Asensio Torrado was scarcely a great military commander, but, if the Republic now had an army, it was in large part due to his efforts, whilst it was as much the manner in which he slowed down the final advance on Madrid in October 1936 as anything else that saved the capital from falling.[55]

With the conquest of Málaga behind him, the commander of the CTV, General Roatta, cast about for fresh operations with which to satisfy Mussolini's dreams of martial glory. In so far as these were concerned, there were two possibilities, the first being a drive from Teruel to the Mediterranean Sea that would cut the Republic in two, and the second an offensive in the province of Guadalajara that would finish off the encirclement of Madrid.[56] It being the latter plan that was agreed upon, in late February, the 47,000 men of the CTV were duly transferred to the Soria front. On paper, it seemed that a great victory was certain, but in practice all was far from well. In the first place, an enthusiastic follower of Mussolini, Roatta was, as Sullivan has put it, 'an officer more a politician than a general, with no command experience above the battalion level and no combat duty since World War I.'[57] In the second place, there was the weapons and equipment with which his men were provided. The defects of the L3 tankette we have already noted, but there were also serious issues with the weapons supplied to the infantry: with a calibre of only 6.5mm, the Italian M91 rifle lacked hitting power and in addition suffered from persistent problems with the quality of its ammunition due to the shoddy standards of Italian industry, whilst both the Fiat-Revelli M1914 heavy machine-gun and the Breda M30 light machine-gun were dogged by comparatively low rates of fire and complex feed systems that made them both difficult to operate and prone to jamming; as for the artillery, this was dominated by First-World-War weapons, including some that had already been obsolete in 1914.[58] In the third place, while the role of the CTV was supposed to be rapid blitzkrieg-style operations, it had just eighty-one even of the near-useless L3, sufficient motorized transport for only one of its four divisions and nothing at all in the way of such necessary accessories as half-tracks and self-propelled guns. In the fourth place, training and discipline were poor, and many officers in the blackshirt divisions retired 'dug-outs' glad to eke out meagre pensions with what they essentially saw as a paid holiday in the sun.[59] In the fifth place, the organization of the troops was defective: with only two infantry regiments, the model of division currently favoured by the Italian army was too weak to function in an effective manner, whilst the organization of the infantry platoon was equally odd in that, for want of sufficient light machine-guns, it was divided into not three squads but two.[60] And, in the sixth place, Roatta's men were hardly ardent crusaders bent on fighting Bolshevism wherever it raised its ugly head: one division – the Littorio – was a regular unit of the Italian army recruited entirely from conscripts that had simply been posted to Spain lock, stock and barrel, whilst the other three had been recruited from the blackshirt militia and were for the most part poverty-stricken landless labourers or industrial workers who had only signed up for the relatively generous pay rates that were on offer.[61] Add to this such problems as the facts that knowledge of both the terrain and the enemy was limited, that there had been insufficient time for proper planning and that even proper maps were lacking, and it can be seen that Mussolini's forces were heading for disaster. As Preston has observed, then, 'The mood in the Nationalist headquarters was notably more pessimistic than that of Roatta and his staff.'[62]

With the situation already bad enough, it was promptly compounded by two further factors that were quite beyond Roatta's control. In the first place, scarcely had the attack crossed its start line on 8 March than the weather closed in and made it very difficult for the Nationalist air squadrons, all of which were operating from airfields north of the Sierra de Guadarrama, to reach the battlefield (by contrast, whilst the Republican fighters also had to cope with the endless rain and low cloud, they were operating from Madrid's airport at Barajas and were therefore both close by and unimpeded by any high ground). And, in the second place, despite previous promises that they would do so, the troops on the Jarama front did not make the slightest effort to advance, their inactivity having led to speculation that a Franco increasingly angry with the pretensions of his Italian allies was at the very least seeking to teach them a lesson, if not actually to engineer their defeat (just as suspicious here is that fact that when Roatta came to him after things had started to go wrong and begged him to relieve the Italian forces, he insisted that the CTV should rather rely on its own resources and persevere come what may).[63]

From the very beginning, then, the attack was doomed. Thanks in part to the assistance of the Nationalist forces posted on the Soria front, not to mention the fact that the Republican defenders were desperately thinly stretched, at first, progress was reasonable.[64] Indeed, sufficient alarm was caused in Madrid for the Communists to demand the removal of the chief of the general staff, Toribio Martínez Cabrera.[65] However, tied to the only two good roads that crossed the empty region at which the attack was directed, the advance soon slowed to a crawl, whilst many units showed little in the way of initiative or offensive spirit. Still worse, despite everything, the Italians remained absurdly over-confident, making no attempt even to throw out flank-guards to protect the ever-lengthening columns that jammed the roads.[66] After two days of rain and cold, the leading Italians of the left-hand column had advanced some thirty miles to the town of Brihuega, but attempts to push on the next day towards Torija were checked by a massive Republican airstrike delivered by virtually every plane in the region. To quote a French analyst writing after the event:

> It was a catastrophe. General Bergonzoli's troops were immediately stopped dead … It was impossible to thin out the formations, for the cars and trucks could not be deployed in the fields. It was impossible to turn around. It was impossible for the column even to defend itself. Flaming lorries barred the road. Those crushed by the bombs formed a barricade against the others. There was no help from their own aircraft, which could not be warned in time. The soldiers scattered over the plateau in disorder: anything was better than to remain on a road which had become a target.[67]

The air assault coincided with the arrival of increasing numbers of Republican troops who had been brought up from the Jarama. Amongst them were the XI and XII International Brigades, and the result was that on several occasions, rival groups of Italians found themselves fighting one another. In the first clashes, the CTV did not disgrace itself, but it was clear that further progress was unlikely, the point being reinforced still further by a serious counterattack that shook the leading troops so badly that they had to be relieved by Roatta's two remaining divisions, this being a process that took up several days and in the process completely handed the initiative over to the Republicans.[68] On 18 March, then, came the final blow: supported by large numbers of bombers and fighters and T-26 tanks, brigade after brigade of Republican infantry was launched against the shivering Italians holding the area round Brihuega. Here and there, resistance was creditable enough, indeed, even quite stiff, but very soon the CTV was in full retreat. Amongst the foremost Republican commanders was the Anarchist Cipriano Mera:

> About four o'clock in the afternoon, we received the order to attack ... Hardly had the firing begun ... when we observed that the enemy were beginning to abandon their front-line positions ... That being the case, I immediately ordered our men to speed up their advance and bypass Brihuega so as to get control of the side-road to Torija, the troops ... stationed in the most advanced positions in the meantime being ordered to enfilade the road to Sigüenza so as to ensure that no enemy reserves could reach the town. To tell the truth, however, there was little chance that anything of the sort was likely to happen. On the contrary, hardly had the battle begun than the Italians fell into a state of complete disorder: on all the roads leading from Brihuega to the enemy zone, we could see crowds of soldiers in flight, some of them on foot and others attempting to jump on lorries.[69]

Also very much in the front line was Alvaro Cortes Roa, the latter having now transferred to the armoured corps in order to escape the misery of life in the trenches:

> Using my right foot I worked the pedals that controlled the firing mechanism ... The target being at point-blank range, my viewing slit was immediately obscured by the explosion of the shell: there was a great deal of smoke and dust whilst I could hear debris raining down on the tank's armour ... Not without caution, I opened my ... hatch and raised my head above the turret. Before my eyes was a scene of absolute chaos. Soldiers running in all directions without order or concert ... their equipment thrown off, their jackets unbuttoned ... Dead bodies too ... Right in front of us was a group of men: some of them threw themselves to the ground and froze, whilst the others threw away their weapons and held their hands high in the air so that there could be no doubt that they were surrendering.[70]

Not least because the line was stabilized well-short of the Italians' starting positions, to talk of a great victory (as the Republican press and many pro-Republican journalists and other foreigners did) was ridiculous, but, even so, the battle still ranked as a defeat for Franco. Some 400 Italians were dead and another 1,800 wounded, while, along with perhaps 500 prisoners, a considerable amount of weaponry had fallen into Republican hands, including twenty-five artillery pieces.[71] 'I entered Brihuega at about six o'clock accompanied by my three friends', wrote Joaquín Masjuán. 'We found the town full of smoke from all the fires. Many of the houses were in ruins ... Pressing on beyond the town, we encountered no resistance: on all sides there was nothing but abandoned tanks and the bodies of Italians who had died in the battle ... Dirty, demoralized, hungry, terrified and utterly humiliated as they were, the sight of the prisoners could not but fill one with pity.'[72] Yet victory had not come cheap. On 29 March, Masjuán and his men were relieved and fell back to the village of Cogollor; 'It was ten o'clock at night ... The only light came from some candles, and it was in their pallid gleam that Major Cacho called the roll. Of our company of 109 men, only twenty-eight were left.'[73] Meanwhile, for the time being, the struggle for Madrid was at an end. Direct assault had failed and now, too, strangulation, whilst the conviction was beginning to grow in Franco's headquarters that, even were the city to fall, it would not mean the end of the war. That being the case, it followed that the struggle could not but be a long one, a battle of attrition even. To win such a conflict would require more foreign aid, indeed more resources of every sort, and this in turn focused attention on one theatre and one theatre only, namely the long strip of territory that the Republic still held on the north coast of Spain. Consisting of most of the province of Asturias together with those of Santander and Vizcaya, this contained important mineral resources that could be used to keep German support, much of Spain's heavy industry and, finally, a large population of which substantial elements could be relied upon to support the Nationalist war effort. Capturing it, meanwhile, would also release large numbers of troops who could be better employed elsewhere. For weeks, senior officers at Franco's headquarters had been urging him to exploit the opportunity that the northern zone so clearly represented – it was not, after all, as if

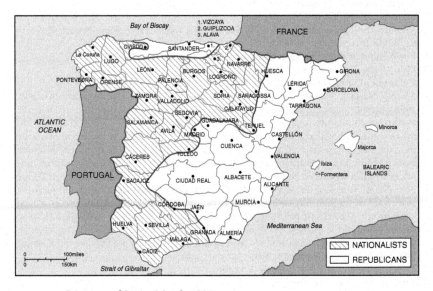

MAP 5.1   Division of Spain, March 1937.

the Republican forces there seemed likely to put up much of a fight – but the Nationalist commander had refused to listen, clinging instead to the idea that one more effort would bring him Madrid. However, after Guadalajara, even Franco could not argue the point any longer, the result being that fresh battles now threatened, and that in a very different part of Spain.[74]

Notes

1 Kemp, *Mine were of Trouble*, pp. 60–2.
2 Cardozo, *March of a Nation*, pp. 197–99. For the general situation of the Nationalist forces in and around Madrid in the wake of Franco's suspension of the assault, see J. M. Martínez Bande, *La lucha en torno a Madrid en el invierno de 1936–1937* (Madrid, 1984), pp. 46–7.
3 Cardozo, *March of a Nation*, pp. 224–5.
4 Cit. Alcofar Nassaes, *Spansky*, p. 301. Krivoshein's complaints of being let down by Anarchist militia should not be taken too seriously: it is probable that the troops involved were, indeed, Anarchists, but the behaviour of virtually any Republican infantry at this stage in the war was likely to have been much the same. According to the Anarchist Cipriano Mera, whose column was among the troops incorporated into the X Mixed Brigade, the failure of he and his men to keep up with the tanks was due to misdirected Republican artillery fire that hit them just as they were crossing the start line and cost them 150 casualties. Mera, *Guerra, exilio y carcel*, p. 105.
5 Koltsov, *Diario de la guerra de España*, p. 257. By contrast, the Nationalist armour made little impact on the fighting, the chief-of-staff of the Condor Legion, Wolfram von Richthofen, complaining bitterly that the behaviour of their almost wholly Spanish crews was, or so it is implied, completely lacking in aggression. See Beevor, *Battle for Spain*, p. 212.
6 Martínez Bande, *La lucha en torno de Madrid*, pp. 52–5.
7 Larios, *Combat over Spain*, pp. 91–2.
8 Alpert, *Republican Army*, p. 76.
9 Martínez Bande, *Lucha en torno a Madrid*, pp. 45–6; 56.
10 Romilly, *Boadilla*, pp. 279–282. Confusingly, originally in the XII International Brigade, the Thaelmann battalion had in the first week of December been transferred to the XI International Brigade.
11 For the end of the battle, see Alcofar Nassaes, *Spansky*, pp. 313–14.
12 Hills, *Battle for Madrid*, p. 114.
13 Cervera Gil, *Ya sabes mi paradero*, p. 107.
14 Alcofar Nassaes, *Spansky*, pp. 247–92; C. Vidal, *Las brigadas internacionales* (Madrid, 1998), pp. 94–9. According to legend, the only troops of the XIV International Brigade to distinguish themselves was a company of British recruits who had been attached to the so-called Marseillaise battalion. Made up both of new recruits who had managed to make the long journey from England and the survivors of the two British squads who had fought in Madrid, this lost eighty-three of its 150 men, the dead including both John Cornford and the prominent Communist writer and journalist Ralph Fox. Needless to say, however, the Republican propaganda machine made such use as it could of the fighting. 'For the first time,' wrote Mikhail Koltsov, 'we have seen large numbers of fascist prisoners, They were captured on the Guadalajara front in the conquest of the villages of Algora and Mirabueno. Four hundred strong, they … were paraded through the streets … amidst the … enthusiasm of the crowd.' Koltsov, *Diario de la guerra de España*, p. 301.
15 T. Wintringham, *English Captain* (London, 1939), p. 139.
16 Thomas, 'Spanish *legionario*', pp. 84–5.
17 Modesto, *Soy del Quinto Regimiento*, pp. 124–5.

18 Koltsov, *Diario de la Guerra de España*, p. 303.
19 Persistent claims that the attackers also numbered two battalions of German machine-gunners should be dismissed as fantasy: for the ground troops with which the Nationalists actually opened the battle of the River Jarama, see Martínez Bande, *Lucha en torno a Madrid*, pp. 102–3. With regard to the aerial component, the Condor Legion deployed twenty-seven Ju-52 bombers, fifteen He51 fighters and eighteen reconnaissance aircraft, half of them high-speed He70s and half of them obsolescent He45 biplanes; the Legionary Aviation sixty CR-32s and an unknown number of Savoia SM81 bombers and Ro37 reconnaissance aircraft; and the Nationalists contributed nine Ju52s and three Ro37s.
20 Martínez Bande, *Lucha en torno a Madrid*, p. 100.
21 Largo Caballero, *Mis recuerdos*, pp. 179–80.
22 For a detailed discussion of the growing tension between Largo Caballero and the Communists, see Graham, *Spanish Republic at War*, pp. 199–212. In fairness, the Communists did have some reason to complain of Largo Caballero, the latter being possessed of a manner that was blustering and uncouth. Also unfortunate, meanwhile, was the fact that he insisted on having cognizance of every last jot and tittle of the business of government, the result being that many important decisions went untaken for weeks at a time. E.g. Koltsov, *Diario de la Guerra*, p. 330.
23 Even worse off in terms of its state of preparation than the other three units, the Abraham Lincoln Battalion did not reach the front until 16 February.
24 For the rifle companies' machine-guns, see J. Gurney, *Crusade in Spain* (Newton Abbott, 1976), pp. 78–9.
25 W. Gregory, *The Shallow Grave: A Memoir of the Spanish Civil War* (London, 1986), pp. 45–7. The highest of the knolls was crowned by a small white house. In consequence, Gregory refers to it as Casa-Blanca Hill, but in other accounts it is rather called 'Suicide Hill.'
26 See B. Clark, *No Boots to my Feet* (Shelton, 1984), p. 28.
27 Gurney, *Crusade in Spain*, p. 110.
28 D. Hooper, *No Pasarán! A Memoir of the Spanish Civil War* (London, 1997), p. 20. The saga of the British battalion's machine-guns is all too typical of the chaos that dogged the Republican war effort. Eventually, the guns and their attendant ammunition were located by a squad of men sent to the rear and dragged up to the front line under heavy fire. Thomas Hyndman was a sometime British soldier who volunteered for the job because he did not trust his rifle to be serviceable: 'The enemy fire was increasing. Dive-gunning planes swooped on us. The dead and wounded were everywhere ... I lost my partner: bullets got him in an almost straight line down his back. I pushed him off the gun, moved forward a few feet with it and went back for the cases.' Cit. Toynbee, *The Distant Drum*, p. 125. However, this was not the end to the story. When the guns were finally got into position, it transpired that the wrong ammunition had been supplied for them, so that a second expedition had to be dispatched to get fresh supplies. Even then, the travails of the machine-gun company were not at an end, for it now transpired that the new bullets were not loaded into belts but rather loose, the net result being that, with enemy shells bursting all around them, the gunners were forced to strip all the ammunition out of the old belts and replace it with the supply that had just been brought up. For a recent account of the battle of 12 February, see R. Baxell, *British Volunteers in the Spanish Civil War: The British Battalion in the International Brigades, 1936–1939* (London, 2004), pp. 69–73.
29 Gurney, *Crusade in Spain*, p. 121.
30 Ibid., p. 123.
31 Koltsov is particularly exaggerated here, speaking of a constant battle for the control of the Pingarrón plateau in which the Nationalists ruthlessly threw in unit after unit in an attempt to wrest it from the defenders. Koltsov, *Diario de la guerra de España*, p. 340.
32 Max, *Memorias de guerra*, pp. 59–61. What is particularly interesting about this passage is the very strong suggestion that Nationalist tanks did not like getting shot up any

more than Republican ones did. The anti-tank guns, meanwhile, were brand new Russian 45mm M1932s.

33 Iniesta Cano, *Memorias y recuerdos*, p. 104.

34 Kemp, *Mine were of Trouble*, p. 73.

35 Ibid., pp. 75–6.

36 J. Tisa, *Recalling the Good Fight: An Autobiography of the Spanish Civil War* (South Hadley, Massachusetts, 1985), pp. 42–3. Accounts of the attack of 27 February are numerous. See, for example, A. H. Landis, *Death in the Olive Groves: American Volunteers in the Spanish Civil War* (New York, 1989), pp. 20–4; and M. Merriman and W. Lerude, *American Commander in Spain: Robert Hale Merriman and the Abraham Lincoln Brigade* (Reno, Nevada, 1986), pp. 106–13.

37 For a recent analysis of the battle of the Jarama, see L. Díez, *La Batalla del Jarama* (Madrid, 2005).

38 For a summary of Preston's position, P. Preston, 'Franco as military leader', *Transactions of the Royal Historical Society*, Sixth Series, IV, pp. 21–42. Much more balanced are the views contained in G. Jensen, *Franco: Soldier, Commander, Dictator* (Washington, District of Columbia, 2005).

39 For an interesting discussion of this development, which was at least as much inspired by the manoeuvrings of competing factions in the Italian general staff as it was by Mussolini, see B. Sullivan, 'Fascist Italy's military involvement in the Spanish Civil War', *Journal of Military History*, LIX, No. 4 (October, 1995), pp. 704–5.

40 Chalmers-Mitchell, *My House in Málaga*, p. 239. On 11 January ,the city was also subjected to a two-hour naval bombardment 'directed to no military object except terrorism and wanton destruction, two of the favourite "military objects" of the rebels.' Ibid., p. 240.

41 Borkenau, *Spanish Cockpit*, p. 220.

42 Chalmers-Mitchell, *My House in Málaga*, p. 254.

43 Cit. J. Pettifer (ed.), *Cockburn in Spain: Dispatches from the Spanish Civil War* (London, 1986), pp. 147.

44 Cit. R. Fraser, *The Pueblo: A Mountain village on the Puerta del Sol* (London, 1974), pp. 63–4. In fairness, Alarcón goes on to stress that the opportunists were in a minority, but, even so, his story is a depressing tale of petty abuses of power.

45 Cit. ibid., pp. 67–9.

46 E.g. Borkenau, *Spanish Cockpit*, p. 218.

47 Borkenau is scathing: '[Villalba] was ... very formal in his manner ... obviously not caring for any contact with the popular movement, uneasy and even nervous in the ... situation he was sent to master ... Such a man was certainly the type least suited to the task of holding Málaga.' Ibid., p. 219.

48 Largo Caballero's views on the subject were most trenchant; 'The departure from Málaga of the then Colonel Asensio left the direction of the defence of that city in the hands of the Communists. Those soldiers who were not partisans of the latter were a nullity as far as the Left was concerned, whilst the other political groupings – the Socialists, the Republicans, the Anarchists, etc., – were all excluded. The de facto commander of the resistance was the Communist deputy for Málaga, Señor Bolivar.' Largo Caballero, *Mis recuerdos*, pp. 188–9.

49 Ibid., p. 219. For a very negative view of the state of revolutionary spirit in Málaga, see Seidman, *Republic of Egos*, pp. 76–7. Writing of Churriana, Gamel Woolsey paints a picture of the most limited levels of politicization: 'In our village they were all Anarcho-Syndicalists. That is, everyone belonged to a Syndicalist trade union ... Most of them weren't politically minded at all.' G. Woolsey, *Death's Other Kingdom* (London, 1988), p. 70. Part of the problem, Woolsey continued, was the survival of old modes of thought that had little bearing on the current struggle. Thus: 'Everyone thought in provinces, a Spanish habit at the best of times. "Granada is attacking us," people said ... The capture of a town in the province of Granada was regarded us as putting one up on Granada ... This extreme federalism was more important to most

of the country people than the class-war aspects of the struggle which some of their leaders were emphasising.' Ibid., p. 78.

50 Chalmers-Mitchell, *My House in Málaga*, p. 264.

51 A. Nadal, *Guerra Civil en Málaga* (Málaga, 1984), pp. 172–3. It goes without saying, however, that there were limits to the savagery. According to Gerald Brenan's wife, Gamel Woolsey, for example, 'Our village, which was a large one by English standards – it contained over 2,000 people – was perfectly safe, quiet and orderly during the entire Civil War except when invaded on several occasions by gangs from Málaga … It was managed by a syndicalist committee … chosen by a meeting of the entire village and serving without salary … There was perfect order and respect for private property. There were, for instance, three or four large houses in the village belonging to rich landowners who did not live there, but came occasionally for short visits. These houses, though they belonged to individuals who were popularly suspected of fascist sympathies, stood vacant during the entire period up to the taking of Málaga, even at a time when refugees from the interior were sleeping under trees in the rain. There was a suggestion at one time that some of the poorest people might be put in them, but it was decided by the authorities in Málaga … that, as the big houses were furnished, it would not be right to occupy them: the furniture might get hurt!' Woolsey, *Death's Other Kingdom*, pp. 69–73.

52 The most shameful aspect of the fall of Málaga was the failure of the Republican fleet to come out from its refuge at nearby Cartagena and do battle with the Nationalist squadron; had this been attempted, the death toll amongst the refugees would, beyond doubt, have been much reduced.

53 Chalmers-Mitchell, *My House in Málaga*, pp. 266–7.

54 Nadal, *Guerra Civil en Málaga*, p. 190.

55 Martín Blásquez, *I Helped to Build an Army*, pp. 316–19.

56 Some Italians, notably the Foreign Minister, Ciano, also suggested that the CTV should thrust up the Mediterranean coast through Almería, Cartagena and Alicante to take Valencia, but this scheme was so ridiculous that even Roatta seems to have shrunk from putting it forward. See Coverdale, *Italian Intervention*, pp. 209–10.

57 Sullivan, 'Fascist Italy's military involvement in the Spanish Civil War', p. 707.

58 For an interesting discussion of the Italian army's small-arms and artillery in the early part of the Second World War (and, by extension, the Spanish Civil War), see R. Carrier, 'Some reflections on the fighting power of the Italian army in North Africa', *War in History*, XXII, No. 4 (November, 2015), pp. 510–12. A particular problem for the CTV, meanwhile, was that it was provided with very few anti-aircraft guns: in the whole corps, there were just twelve Breda 20mm M1935s and twelve 75mm M1915s, this last being a particularly antiquated weapon that had been hastily improvised to meet the Italian army's requirements in the First World War and was now utterly out-dated. See A. Mortera Pérez and J. L. Infiesta Pérez, *La artillería en la Guerra Civil: material de origen italiano importado por el ejército nacional* (Valladolid, 1997), pp. 88–94 *passim*.

59 In the words of one commentator, 'The [Littorio] division and other units of the army enjoyed the advantages of being staffed by fairly competent regular officers and partially manned by reasonably trained conscripts. But the quality of the officers and men of the blackshirt units generally varied from mediocre to truly miserable.' Sullivan, 'Fascist Italy's military involvement in the Spanish Civil War', p. 706. So bad was the situation, indeed, that even Roatta could not ignore the problem. As he afterwards wrote, 'During the recent operations it has become far clearer than in the previous ones that the officers are quite deficient especially at the company and platoon level. A certain percentage is made up of men who will get themselves killed, but who do not know how to give orders, [and] do not make their authority felt. They are not demanding, are unfamiliar with the rules of warfare, and often do not even know how to provide for the logistic needs of their men.' Cit. J. Coverdale, 'The battle of Guadalajara, 8–22 March, 1937', *Journal of Contemporary History*, IX, No. 1 (January, 1974), p. 74.

60 Sullivan, 'Fascist Italy's military involvement in the Spanish Civil War', p. 709.

61 For an interesting discussion, see Coverdale, *Italian Intervention*, pp. 181–6. Persistent stories that the blackshirt recruits joined up thinking that they were signing on to take part as extras in the filming of 'Scipio Africanus' in Libya do not seem to have any basis in fact, though it is possible that the story was put about for public consumption in the hope that it might disguise the reality of what was going on. A more plausible version of events is that the recruits included a number of men whose contracts as 'extras' had just come to an end and were in consequence desperate for employment. See D. Poulain, 'Aircraft and mechanised land warfare, 1937: the battle of Guadalajara', Journal of the Royal United Service Institution, LXXXIII, No. 530 (May, 1938), p. 366. According to Borkenau, meanwhile, many of the prisoners taken in the battle claimed that they had thought they were signing up for voluntary labour in newly conquered Ethiopia rather than combat duties in Spain. Borkenau, *Spanish Cockpit*, p. 270.

62 Preston, *Franco*, p. 230.

63 See Coverdale, 'Battle of Guadalajara', pp. 70–2. Given the importance Franco placed on prestige, the idea that he hoped to see the Italians defeated seems a little far-fetched. More likely, he envisaged nothing more than a mild check that would see them grind to a halt after just a few miles.

64 In many ways, the Guadalajara front was a much more promising sector for an offensive than that of the River Jarama. Not only was the terrain more favourable, but, organized though they now were in the five-brigade-strong Twelfth Division, the defenders had been little touched by militarization. As for the defences, these were little short of token. As one Russian military adviser noted, 'The trenches' lack of concealment struck one at the merest glance: beside them could clearly be seen little piles of the earth excavated from them. At the same time they were full of water from the recent rains, the soldiers manning them giving us the very strong impression that they had only got in when they saw us coming. In front of each section, at a distance of between 100 and 200 metres, there was a barbed wire fence, but this consisted of but two strands and was so low that it could easily be jumped ... With respect to the defenders, meanwhile, they were strung out in a single line without any reserves.' Cit. Martínez Bande, *La lucha en torno a Madrid*, p. 176.

65 Thomas, *Spanish Civil War*, p. 598. Martínez Cabrera's replacement being the hero of the defence of Madrid, Vicente Rojo, not the least of the results of the battle of Guadalajara was the fact that the Republican war effort was henceforward in the hands of the best strategist in the whole of Spain. Indeed, if the Republican response to the Nationalist offensive was so vigorous, it was in large part due to Rojo's appointment.

66 Borkenau, *Spanish Cockpit*, p. 267.

67 Poulain, 'Aircraft and mechanised land warfare, 1937', p. 365; note, however, that the troops involved were not those of Bergonzoli, who commanded the Littorio division, but rather the 'Black Plumes' division of General Luigi Nuvoloni. For a good account of the air operations over Guadalajara, see Salas Larrázabal, *Air War over Spain*, pp. 126–9.

68 For the role of the International Brigades in this fighting, see Delperrie de Bayac, *Brigades Internationales en Espagne*, pp. 216–20. According to Rojo, one factor that heavily favoured the Republicans was the open woods that cloaked the countryside around Brihuega, as these masked the Italians' field of fire and made it harder for them to defend themselves. See Rojo, *Así fue la defensa de Madrid*, p. 181.

69 Mera, *Guerra, exilio y carcel*, pp. 125–6.

70 Cortes Roa, *Tanquista*, pp. 122–3. The passage from which this quote is taken is not just interesting for its account of the climax of the battle of Guadalajara. Also of note is its description of what it was like to man a T26 in action. 'Everything inside a tank is noise when it is shut down for combat: the roar of the engine, creaking, banging. And movement, too: despite the cramped nature of my position, jammed between the wall of the turret and the recoil mechanism of the gun, at every moment I was

being flung from one side to the other and getting all sots of knocks in the process, some of them very painful.' Ibid. p. 121.

71 For general accounts of the battle, see Coverdale, 'Battle of Guadalajara', pp. 59–67; Martínez Bande, *La lucha en torno a Madrid*, pp. 186–247; Hills, *Battle for Madrid*, pp. 125–34.

72 Max, *Memorias de un revolucionario*, p. 71.

73 Ibid., p. 74.

74 For the arguments that raged at Franco's headquarters with regard to the northern zone, see Preston, *Franco*, pp. 235–7.

6

THE WAR IN EUZKADI

For the reasons that we have seen, then, following Guadalajara Franco turned north. In doing so, he was presented with three targets in the form of the provinces of Asturias, Santander and Vizcaya, but of these there was little doubt which he would hit first. Thus, much more accessible than Asturias and Santander, both of which were protected by rugged mountains, Vizcaya was also the only one of the three that had shown any propensity for offensive action. What really marked out Vizcaya as a target, however, was its political situation: in the first place, a considerable proportion of the population was lukewarm in its support for the Republic (if the dominant force in the area was currently Basque nationalism, historically Vizcaya had strong links with Carlism, whilst it had become clear that, as Catholics, many Basque nationalists were less than comfortable with their left-wing allies); in the second place, the Basque nationalists were hated by the Socialists and Communists; in the third place, the *rojo-separatismo* of the Basque nationalists was a particular bug-bear of the Spanish Right; in the fourth place, relations between the Basque nationalists and the Republican government were extremely poor; and, in the fifth place, the fact that the Catholic Church in the Basque provinces had on the whole stuck with the Basque nationalists, and, by extension, the Republic, was a constant source of embarrassment to Franco. To conclude, then, attacking Vizcaya offered, or so it seemed, an easy victory and one that would bring many benefits, and it can therefore have been no surprise to anyone when 21 March 1937 saw Franco issue an order for his armies to march on Bilbao.[1]

Although the long northern front had for the most part been relatively quiet since the start of the war, it was not the first time that the Basque provinces had been involved in the fighting. On the contrary, conflict had erupted there as early as the last week of July 1936.[2] Thus, desperately alarmed that foreign arms might flood across the border from France and, in the beginning, possessed of some hope that he could relieve the garrison of San Sebastián, which at this point was still holding out in its barracks, Mola had organized several columns consisting of Carlist militia and regular troops and ordered them to push into the province of Guipúzcoa from the south, whilst at the same time having some of the Nationalists' few available warships bombard the defenceless capital.[3] Commander of the land operations was Alfonso Beorleguí, a hardened *africanista* who had been living in retirement in Pamplona when the uprising broke out on 18 July. What followed was a precursor of the later campaign in Vizcaya: hopelessly outclassed, the militia and their police allies (as elsewhere, an important part of the defence fell to loyal Civil Guards, Assault Guards and Carabineers) fell back on strong defensive positions around Irun, whereupon, having distracted the defenders by seizing Oyarzún, a hill village a mile or two short of the main road from San Sebastián to the frontier, the Nationalists concentrated all their firepower on a single access of attack – the narrow road from Pamplona to Irun – and proceeded to drive the defenders from one position after another by a mixture of concentrated artillery bombardments and infantry assaults. Though the Nationalists were soon reinforced by a handful of troops from the Army of Africa, they were still in very small numbers – at most Beorleguí had some 4,000 men – and for several days, militiamen who were dug in on the Puntza-Zubelzu ridge around the isolated chapel that marked the 1813 battlefield of San Marcial therefore managed to hold them off. At the same time, the defenders were supported by heavy artillery firing from three massive forts constructed at the end of the nineteenth century to stave off a hypothetical invasion from France. For an eyewitness account, we can turn to the memoirs of a correspondent of *The Times*, George Steer: 'Infantry moved up through the maize in stealthy groups … The young man in a beret who carried the red-yellow-red flag fell flat by the first house, grasping his stomach. He tried to rise, then fell again … Their officer … shouted orders: we could hear every syllable above the gun fire; his men, crouched waiting behind walls, cried 'Viva España!' and 'Mañana a San Sebastián!' The whole Frente-Popular line [then] began serious shooting: every machine-gun sprang to quarrelsome life.'[4] Around Oyarzún, too, the defenders managed to beat off several attacks, notwithstanding the capture of the initial commander of the Republican forces in Guipúzcoa, Major Augusto Pérez Garmendia, when his car strayed into Nationalist territory.[5] Some of the desperate urgency of the moment is captured by Marcelo Usabiaga, a young Communist militant who had enlisted in the militia and joined the defence of the border village of Behobie:

> At length the situation became so bad that Margarida [i.e. Manuel Margarida Valdés, an Assault-Guard lieutenant who was in command of the defence] called for a representative of each of the political parties to come to the town hall … 'Gentlemen', he said, 'each party has got to take responsibility for the defence of one key position in particular … And I don't want to hear the word "retreat": either you die at the front or … you're not coming back anyway.' Lots were chosen to see where we should

go, and when it came to my turn I got ... a [hill] ... near the Carabineer barracks. Having grabbed a lift in a car, when I got there I found that the defenders were dug in ... with a couple of machine guns. There were quite a few of them and I told them that I had come from the Popular Front and that its military committee had given orders that there could be no retreat. At this, they began to argue, saying that if the enemy came in any force they would have to pull back. 'No you won't!' I said. 'If anybody runs away, they will shoot me, so we're not going anywhere!'[6]

The courage of the defenders in this area is verified by George Steer: 'At the Carabineros' house ... the defenders stood their ground with the coolest courage. The armoured cars poured hail into their sandbags and ripped the massive plaster front of the house to pieces. Soon the top sand-bags were all shorn away.'[7] However, gallantry was not enough. Supported though the defenders were by an improvised armoured train and some equally improvised armoured lorries, not to mention a handful of foreign volunteers, most of them French or Belgian, the battle was hopelessly one-sided.[8] Not the least of the problems was ammunition. According to Miguel de Amilibia, the head of the revolutionary committee that had been established in San Sebastián, the only help received in this respect was the daily dispatch from Madrid of a single transport aircraft loaded with forty boxes of rifle cartridges, of which only half were allocated to the defence of Guipúzcoa.[9]

As if the situation was not bad enough already, it was compounded by disunion amongst the defenders. At this point, although some individual militants did take part in the fighting, the main Basque nationalist movement had not openly declared for one side or the other in the conflict and was sitting on the sidelines. Many militants genuinely had no idea how to respond to a situation in which their bitterest enemies had overnight become their *de facto* allies (it should be remembered that the nationalist party was a deeply conservative force with strong links with both the Catholic Church and Carlism), whilst the Basque nationalists had no tradition even of street violence, let alone a party militia.[10] In consequence, the campaign was soon over. In part torched by Anarchist militiamen, Irún fell on 5 September, whilst San Sebastián followed it a week later and, with it, almost all the rest of the province.[11] As the Nationalists closed in, desperate scenes were witnessed at the so-called 'International Bridge' that connected France and Spain. Caught on holiday in San Sebastián when the uprising broke out, Claude Bowers was an agonised observer: 'I saw pitiful scenes. Hundreds, thousands, of women and children and old men poured across the frontier from their ruined homes ... Penniless, friendless, they staggered into an alien land, bringing as much of their pathetically meagre belongings with them as they could carry on their backs. Many of the old women, with fear and misery stamped on their faces, carried chickens under their arms – their sole defence against starvation ... Some carried a few kitchen utensils. And all their faces were marked by tragedy and horror.'[12]

All this makes for a depressing story, but, as elsewhere, it cannot be told simply in terms of well-armed 'fascists' crushing the unarmed Spanish people. Certainly, arms were short among the defenders, but Beorlegui's troops were few in number and had only a limited amount of heavy armament and air support. Also crucial was what can best be described as the rotten heart of the militia system. In much the same way as in other parts of Spain, the militiamen considered themselves to have taken up arms of their own free will and shied away from any idea that they were soldiers. Nor, meanwhile, were they necessarily hard-line militants enthused by a vision of nirvana: if some were, indeed, devoted to Communism, to Socialism, to Anarchism or Basque Nationalism, others had signed on to take advantage of the generous pay, to escape the drudgery of day-to-day life, to impress some girl or to act out some teenage fantasy. As more committed combatants later admitted, little of this, ideology included, was proof against the rigours of campaigning, let alone the horrors of war, and the consequence was that, long before San Sebastián had fallen, hundreds of men had slipped away to homes that were often but a few miles away.[13]

In one sense, however, the fall of Guipúzcoa simplified the political situation in the Basque country. In the first place, if the Partido Nacionalista Vasco had ever hoped, as has sometimes been alleged, to come to some sort of arrangement with the rebels, all such aspirations were now dashed. And, in the second place, the cause of workers' revolution had received a fatal blow: Irún and the port of Pasajes being Anarchist strongholds, their loss created something of a power vacuum that the Basque nationalists were able to exploit. When a government of Euzkadi – the name by which the three Basque provinces (Alava, Guipúzcoa and Vizcaya) are known in Basque – was created by virtue of the statute of autonomy accorded to the Basque country that had been under negotiation at the time that the uprising took place and was finally voted through by the *cortes* on 1 October, the chief positions were taken by the Basque nationalists,. The leader of the Partido Nacionalista Vasco, an erstwhile professional footballer named José Aguirre, became both Prime Minister and Minister of War, whilst other Basque nationalists occupied the posts of Minister of the Interior, Minister of Justice and Minister of Finance, leaving the other five parties represented in the ruling coalition to fight among themselves for the remainder.[14] As for the Anarchists, they were excluded from power, the non-revolutionary character of the new state being further emphasized by the creation of a Basque-nationalist-dominated gendarmerie known as the Erzaña.[15] To the dismay of the Left, meanwhile, Aguirre and his supporters immediately moved to protect the Catholic Church and to forestall any attempt at the socialization of industry and property. With exception of the lynching of forty prisoners by sailors from the battleship *Jaime Primero* in October 1936 in reprisal for the sinking of the *Almirante Ferrández* off Gibraltar, and a serious prison massacre provoked by a particularly vicious air-raid on Bilbao in January 1937, then, Euzkadi remained free of the turmoil that gripped the rest of Republican Spain.[16] As for revolution, this was entirely absent: there was no collectivization, no expropriation, no democratization of the work-place, no local committees, nothing. Far from creating a new world, then, the proletariat continued to work under the same conditions as it had done before.[17]

Aguirre's determination to prevent revolution was also expressed in a push to seize control of the armed forces. At the time that he took power, the Republican forces in northern Spain were denominated the Army of the North and divided into three regional commands, one each for Asturias, Santander and the Basque provinces. This, however, was not a situation that the new Prime Minister was prepared to tolerate, and on 26 October he openly challenged it by issuing a decree placing all Euzkadi's military resources under his personal control, thereby cutting out the commander of the Army of the North, General Llano de la Encomienda, and uniting all the forces concerned with the militia that the Partido Nacionalista Vasco had been putting together ever since its decision to throw in its lot with the Republic. Thus was born the so-called Euzko Gudarostea or Basque Army, and on 6 November, Aguirre formalized the break with the rest of the Republican forces by setting up a separate general staff under the leadership of Alberto Montaud Noguerol, an engineer officer who had been professor of fortification at the army's Escuela Superior de Guerra in Madrid in July 1936 but had been dispatched to Bilbao to help organize resistance in the northern zone. Though Aguirre himself was the titular Commander-in-Chief, of course, effective command was wielded by his Chief of Operations, Captain Modesto Arámbarri Galasteguí, a sometime *africanista* whom the uprising had found in charge of Bilbao's municipal police force. Finally, to drive home the point of the Basque forces' independence, a further decree insisted that officers would wear not the red bars of the People's Army but rather the gold stars of the regular army, something that failed to materialize at all, meanwhile, being the political commissariat.[18]

Of what, however, did the Basque Army consist? The regiments of engineers and heavy artillery that had constituted the garrison of San Sebastián having been destroyed in the course of the uprising and that of Bilbao – a single mountain battalion – fallen apart, at its heart could not but lie the political militias, and, as everywhere else, these were transformed into infantry battalions of around 500 men and reinforced by large numbers of conscripts and reservists (by February 1937, the call-up had been extended to all men between the ages of eighteen and forty-five).[19] As many as seventy-eight infantry battalions may have been formed altogether, and some idea of the political composition of this force may be gleaned from the fifty-nine whose origins are known for a certainty: thus, twenty-six were affiliated with the Partido Nacionalista Vasco, twenty-one with the Socialists or Communists, six with the Anarchists, three with Acción Nacionalista Vasca (a dissident nationalist party that rejected the confessionalism of the main nationalist movement) and three with one or other of the two Republican parties.[20] Though there were ever fewer volunteers and much resistance to conscription, manpower was not too serious an issue. Far more problematic was the question of arms and officers. Taking the question of armament first of all, in July 1936 in the whole of the northern zone, there appear to have been about 15,000 rifles, 400 mortars and machine-guns and 100 artillery pieces, together with seven Breguet light bombers. Given that much of this arsenal was held in Asturias and Santander and that a considerable amount of weapons had also been lost in the fighting in Guipúzcoa, the situation was anything but rosy, and it was never really rectified. Fortunately for the defenders the Nationalist navy was never strong enough to amount a completely effective blockade, the only ships available being the battleship *España*, the cruisers *Almirante Cervera* and *Canarias*, the destroyer *Velasco*, one mine-layer, two auxiliary cruisers and seven armed trawlers, a force that was reduced still further when the *España* was lost to a mine on 30 April 1937[21] That being the case, a steady trickle of armaments did get through to the northern zone – some reports, indeed, give a minimum figure of 90,000 rifles, 1,000 sub-machine-guns, 1,300 light and heavy machine-guns, 250 mortars, 280 artillery pieces and 120 tanks and armoured cars[22] – but, even if this total is accurate, it should be remembered that no more than one third ever reached the Bilbao front. Nor could much be done to remedy the want in terms of local production: whilst Vizcaya possessed a number of small armament plants, for the most part they only produced such ancillary weapons as pistols and hand-grenades.[23] Meanwhile, such weapons as did arrive were variegated in the extreme and often sub-standard: there were eight different models of rifle, while the artillery included Japanese mountain guns dating from before the war of 1905 that had neither shields nor modern recoil mechanisms, and the armour a batch of First-World-War Renault FT17 tanks bought from Poland that, even when brand new, had only been able to manoeuvre at walking pace. As for aircraft, the northern zone saw the arrival of just fifteen I15s, ten antiquated Latvian Bristol Bulldog fighters and twenty-five Dutch Koolhoven FK51 light bombers.[24]

If weapons were always short in the Basque forces, the question of officers was even worse. With only a very limited number of even retired regular officers available and some of those who did offer their services distinctly lukewarm in their loyalty (in November 1936, two engineer officers working on the fortifications of Bilbao were shot for trying to pass the plans of the defences to the Nationalists, while, as we shall see, February 1937 saw the notorious *caso Goicoechea*), Aguirre had little option but to confirm the appointments of the many commanders who had emerged in the militias and try to improvise others from militants of one movement or another who were put through emergency training programmes. In all, some 400 officers were produced by this last method, but quality and commitment alike remained very low. In the words of an officer on Llano's staff:

> Incompetent and badly trained, the officers spent their time in Bilbao …
> abandoning the care of their men in a manner that was quite disastrous …
> Puffed up by the attack on Vitoria, which was stopped dead as soon as it
> met any resistance, they relaxed the rigid discipline which is indispensable

(supposing that it ever existed) and didn't live with their men, but spent their days, and, above all their nights, merry-making ... In sum, they lived as if the war was already won.[25]

The weakness of the Basque forces was soon to be demonstrated all too clearly. With Madrid under heavy attack, the government of Largo Caballero requested an attack in the northern zone, and, Aguirre being vain and over-ambitious – his few weeks as Commander-in-Chief had been enough to earn him the scornful nickname *Napoleontxu* ('little Napoleon') – he therefore sat down with Montaud and Arámbarri to plan an offensive against nearby Vitoria. In the wake of the establishment of a Basque state, however truncated, the atmosphere was enthusiastic, not to say wildly optimistic. Speaking of the situation in after years, Anarchist militant Manuel Chiapuso was blunt in his assessment: 'So great was the euphoria produced by obtaining the statute [of autonomy] that it ... was believed that Vitoria could be reached very easily ... that from Vitoria we could march to Aranda de Duero, even that from there we could make contact with the armies defending the centre of the country, and all this as if it was a mere nothing.'[26] On 29 November, then, twenty-nine infantry battalions, twenty-five guns and eight improvised armoured vehicles struck the Alavese town of Villareal from two directions at once. However, the result was, if not a disaster, then at the very least distinctly disappointing. Although the defenders consisted of only two infantry battalions, a single battery of mountain guns and a handful of other troops, they were able to fend off every attack without difficulty, and the offensive therefore quickly stagnated. One observer was Miguel de Amilibia:

> The offensive did not prosper. A few old aircraft and a handful of guns did what they could to prepare for the assault, and then the infantry came down to the plain. They fought bravely and ... bogged down in front of Villarreal. Together, lack of means and coordination slowed down the pace of the attack, and so the enemy was able to bring up his reserves in good time. Very soon he began to counter-attack and ... little by little the ground that had been taken had to be given up.[27]

Fighting continued to flare up on and off for almost a month, but in the end, the battle petered out with little gain for either side. Amongst the attackers, especially, casualties had been heavy – perhaps one-fifth of those engaged – while the troops had suffered terribly from cold and wet (Nationalist dead, by contrast, had numbered just 225 men). To put it mildly, it was not an auspicious beginning, whilst its one concrete result – the dispatch to Bilbao of the Russian military adviser Vladimir Gorev – made not the slightest difference. [28]

After Villareal, there was no further movement on the Basque front until the start of the Nationalist offensive in March.[29] On the contrary, thoroughly chastened, Aguirre set his troops to fortifying their positions in readiness for the attack that he knew must come. Such as they were, his dominions were to be defended by two rings of fortifications. Around the outer perimeter, the Cantabrian mountains were to be sown with field defences – trenches, machine-gun nests, road blocks and barbed-wire entanglements – but the main line of defence was to be constructed much further back in a circle around Bilbao. Known as 'the Iron Ring' and stretching for a total length of some seventy-five miles, this was to feature not just field defences but also numerous con-crete bunkers and pillboxes - as many as 1,400, according to the original plan. Inevitably, however, construction lagged behind schedule, and by the time the defences came to be tested, they were only half-complete: whilst some sectors were comparatively strong, others were much weaker or even all but completely unprotected. Still worse, many positions were poorly constructed or ill-sited, with pillboxes that could not withstand anything bigger than a 105mm shell and trenches that were either too shallow or dug in straight lines so that they were hopelessly vulnerable to enfilade fire, these problems being so marked as after-wards to provoke wholesale accusations of treachery against the engineer officers charged with the planning and execution of the works.[30] One suspects that these allegations were unfounded – the problems for the most part probably stemmed from inexperience or poor supervision – but it did not help that in February, the officer in charge of the construction of the Iron Ring, Alejandro Goicoechea, deserted to the Nationalists with a complete set of plans.[31]

Rumours of espionage, treason and betrayal did nothing to help the morale of the defending forces, and all the more so as the Anarchists, Socialists and Communists hated the Basque nationalists as Church-loving crypto-fascists. By the same token, however, the militants of the Partido Nacionalista Vasco and, indeed, much of the civilian population away from the immigrant slums of Bilbao loathed the representatives of the Left as church-burning Bolsheviks pos-sessed of a violent hatred of traditional Basque culture.[32] The many clashes that had erupted in the course of the flight from San Sebastián as Basque-nationalist militia had confronted Anarchist groups eager to use scorched-earth tactics had created further bitterness, while, in January 1937, an Anarchist show of force designed to secure a place in the government led to a clamp-down that included the detention of the CNT's central committee, the suppression of the *CNT del Norte* newspaper and severe restrictions on the right to hold public meetings and organize demonstrations.[33] If the clash with the Anarchists was particularly acute, squabbles over supplies were constant and desertion widespread, whilst weeks of tedium and guarding water-logged trenches in the endless rain of a Vizcayan winter sapped morale and discipline alike. Nor, meanwhile, was any love lost in respect of the professional officers with whom Aguirre surrounded himself, and all the more so given the comparatively luxurious life which many of them enjoyed at the commandeered Bilbao hotel that housed the headquarters of the Euzko Gudarostea. 'In so far as we were concerned', remembered Miguel de Amilibia, 'we did not trust the regulars, not least because of the character ... of the uprising. ... If there was one thing that Aguirre sinned in in particular, it was the way that he favoured the professional soldiers over the commanders who had emerged from the militias.'[34] And, last but not least, arms remained desperately short: at the time the offensive began, the Vizcayan front could muster just seventy-one pieces of artillery, most of them with comparatively little ammunition, whilst at least twenty battalions had no machine-guns.[35] As Steer wrote, then, 'In every way except in numbers of men, the insurgents were superior ... It was obvious the Basques had no chance.'[36]

The sheer one-sidedness of the campaign that beckoned is reinforced if we examine the military resources that were available to the Nationalists.[37] The offensive, then, was launched by the so-called 'First Group' (Agrupación Primera) of General López Pinto's Sixth Organic Division, a formation that actually was nearer an army corps in size, each of its two 'groups' being larger than a pre-war division.[38] Commanded from Vitoria by General José Solchaga Zala, said 'First Group' consisted of four so-called 'Brigades of Navarre', which could together muster some 28,000 effectives, organized in no fewer than thirty-two battalions, many of them Carlist militia who were in many instances themselves Basques.[39] Also available, meanwhile, was General Piazzoni's 8,000-strong 'Flechas Negras' brigade of the CTV (a formation that was actually almost entirely Spanish, apart from its officers).[40] Supporting this force, meanwhile, was an impressive array of firepower: in addition to the seventy-two guns attached to the five infantry brigades, there were a further 128 guns organized in twenty-five Spanish batteries and seven Italian batteries under the direct control of Solchaga, the latter also having the Nationalist army's single tank battalion and the 'Agrupazione Celere', or mobile group, of the CTV (a total of over 100 tanks and armoured cars). Finally, ready to fly in overhead were something over 100 planes: sixty-six bombers and fighters of the Condor Legion (which also sent up its sixteen 88mm FLAK18s to the front line); ten Cr32s and eighteen SM81s and SM79s of the Legionary Aviation; and two or three six-plane squadrons of Nationalist Breguet BrXIXs and He45s.[41] Backing up these forces, meanwhile, were considerable reserves: by the middle of May, each of the existing Brigades of Navarre had been built up to a strength of twelve battalions, and two fresh brigades had been created, each of them supported by their own battalions of field artillery, whilst, if necessary, Solchaga could also call on the services of the remainder of the CTV, namely two and one-half divisions of infantry and six batteries of artillery.[42]

Such were the advantages possessed by the Nationalists that, when the offensive began on 31 March, progress could hardly be anything but steady. Whilst some of the defenders were subjected to saturation bombardments that either incapacitated them or forced them to flee – on the first day of the campaign alone, seventy tons of bombs and 150 tons of shells pounded Aguirre's forces[43] – other positions were outflanked by columns that infiltrated the valleys that separated the peaks on which the Euzko Gudarostea invariably tended to range itself. Here and there, the attackers ran into sharper resistance than normal or even found themselves facing fierce local counterattacks, while, trapped by steep slopes and thick forests, their armour was condemned to advancing at a snail's pace along winding mountain roads. Nor, meanwhile, were the Nationalists aided by the constant rain. Yet the pressure was unremitting and the strain upon the defending forces immense. Supply arrangements broke down; unable to change their positions except at night, the troops became more and more exhausted; reserves were used up faster than they could be replenished; political divisions were exacerbated as units from rival movements accused one another of betrayal; repeated promises that fresh planes and tanks were on the way – promises that were, of course, never made good – eroded faith in the leadership; and morale was worn down by the crushing superiority of the enemy's firepower, not to mention the constant retreats. To quote the Basque commissary-general, Luis Ruíz de Aguirre, 'When soldiers labouring under the most tremendous fatigue are forced to retreat day after day to the accompaniment of constant rearguard actions, it is only natural that their morale should suffer.'[44]

Particular problems, meanwhile, were caused by the Nationalists' control of the air. Against the swarms of Nationalist aircraft, the defending pilots did their best, but the lack of suitable airfields meant that such few aircraft as the defenders could muster were desperately vulnerable to destruction on the ground, while in the air they consistently lost more planes than their opponents: in the biggest dogfight of the campaign, for example, five I15s were shot down compared with just two Cr32s.[45] Free from any fear of attack by enemy fighters, then, the Junkers and Savoias ranged the battlefields at will, disrupting the movement of men and supplies, silencing the defenders' artillery, severing communications and devastating defensive positions that might otherwise have held out for much longer, whilst at the same time driving home the message that Euzkadi had been abandoned to its own devices.[46] So great was the problem, indeed, that it began to undermine the whole of the defence: eager to explain away the constant retreats, the Bilbao press emphasized the role of the Nationalist aircraft to such an extent that the troops began to see the mere fact of being bombed as sufficient excuse to abandon their positions without a fight.[47] Demoralization, too, was spread by repeated attacks on targets that might, on the one hand, have been seen as headquarters and centres of communication, but were also densely populated market towns and industrial centres in which every bomb was likely to take the life of innocent civilians: struck very heavily on the first day of the campaign, for example, Durango lost 127 dead and perhaps three times that number seriously wounded in just half an hour, many of the casualties coming from a church hit while a priest was celebrating Mass.[48] Also difficult to avoid, meanwhile, was the pull of the 'Ring of Iron': constantly told that the fortifications were impregnable, many militiamen saw no reason to risk their lives in unnecessary battles. As Mikhail Koltsov wrote in his diary after paying a brief visit to Bilbao at the beginning of June (an enterprise that involved a hair-raising trip by plane via Toulouse that culminated in a landing on the golden sands of a Basque beach):

> The defenders of Bilbao have built what is referred to as 'a belt': a belt of fortifications, a belt of iron, a belt of steel. Indeed, some of the armchair experts who write for sensationalist publications have even taken to calling

it the 'Basque Maginot Line.' This liking for grandiose names will do the defence of the city no good. It has created a mistaken idea of the extent of the fortifications and led people to believe that they absolutely impenetrable, hermetic even ... Faith in the magic properties of the 'belt' has given birth to the idea that the fighting in the area beyond the city is of little consequence, and that the real battle will only begin once the troops have fallen back within the defences. This idea is as false as it is dangerous. There never was a line of fortifications that can provide a guarantee of defence in and of itself. Everything depends on the use that is made of the defending army in the course of the battle, and in what circumstances the struggle begins.[49]

In the circumstances, then it is only surprising that it took the Nationalists some three weeks to force their way through the mountains and enter the heart of the province. An eyewitness to the decisive breakthrough was George Steer:

On the morning of April 20th the great air fleet appeared once more in the skies of Euzkadi. On the clustered ... trenches of Tellamendi, they dropped a few tons of bombs. Where they could, the militia went underground; the rest cowered with fear in shallow trenches, which were now roofed in with ... shrapnel. Meanwhile, the rebel infantry moved tranquilly through the pines on either side of Tellamendi and sent a few machine-guns up the slopes to east and west. When the bombardment was over ... the Basques ... came out to find that they were being shot at from behind ... 'We are cut off!' they shouted, and away they ran down the back of Tellamendi between the flanking machine-guns.[50]

The next ten days were marked by utter chaos. Completely outflanked and out of food and ammunition, many units fled in disorder or disintegrated altogether: according to the Carlist Carmelo Revilla Cebrecos, for example, the advance from Elgoibar to Echeverría and, finally, Marquina, was 'almost a mere stroll.'[51] Between 20 and 30 April, the Nationalists were therefore able to over-run the whole of the eastern part of the province, and it is probable that, had they driven hard for Bilbao, they might have brought the campaign to an end in a matter of days. However, themselves weary and in some disorder, Solchaga's forces checked their pursuit in order to regroup, and the defenders therefore lived to fight another day. Nevertheless, this period of the fighting was marked by one of the most famous events of the war. From the beginning of the campaign, the Nationalists had been unsparing in their employment of bombing against the towns and cities of the Basque country: Bilbao, of course, had been a prime target, but the bombers had also, as we have seen, struck small towns such as Durango, the aim being both to increase the demoralization of the men at the front and to clog the roads with terrified refugees. Most of the time, the amount of damage caused by the raids was not particularly great, but on the afternoon of

26 April, something very different happened. For over three hours, the town of Guernica – the site of the oak tree under which generations of Spanish monarchs had sworn to respect the traditional code of Basque liberties – was devastated by wave after wave of Condor-Legion bombers, whilst numerous flights of fighters dived and wheeled over the narrow roads leading out of the town, machine-gunning terrified fugitives trying desperately to escape to the open country. It being market day, the town was crowded with inhabitants from local villages, whilst it was also full of refugees hoping that they could catch a train on the narrow-gauge railway that led to Bilbao. No-one knows exactly how many were killed or wounded in the general mayhem – estimates of the former range from 1,645 claimed by the Basque government to 250–300 or even as few as 126 – but what is true is that three-quarters of the town was laid waste. The first reporter on the scene was George Steer:

> We drove down the street which led into Gernika ... carefully, for it was a street no longer. Black or burning beams and tattered telephone wires rolled drunkenly ... across it, and the houses either side streamed fire ... In the centre of the town the smaller tongues of fire were turning into a single roar ... We tried to enter, but the streets were a real carpet of live coals; blocks of wreckage slithered and crashed from the houses, and from their sides ... the polished heat struck at our cheeks and eyes.[52]

If questions hang over the physical impact of the bombing of Guernica, the reasons for what happened are even less clear. The operation was initiated by the commander of the Condor Legion, Hugo Sperrle, certainly, but whether it was intended as a deliberate experiment in terror bombing is unknown, what is often forgotten being that at this point a large part of the Basque army was trapped on the heights just east of the town, its only route to safety being Guernica's single narrow bridge across the River Oca. In short, the raid has a tactical significance that cannot be ignored, and it is significant that no other target either in the Basque country or anywhere else in Spain was subjected to anything like the same treatment, a treatment, meanwhile, the physical effects of which were artificially inflated by a series of factors unlikely to be replicated anywhere else, namely, the complete absence of anti-aircraft defences of any sort; the consequent ability of the bombers to fly at rooftop height; the proximity of the Nationalist airfields to the target; and the ease of locating Guernica, positioned, as it was, at the uppermost reach of a very distinctive estuary.[53]

Whatever the truth, the events of 26 April had little impact on the events of the campaign, the battered Basque forces being able to file across the River Oca and regroup on the heights on the western bank. Indeed, they even hit back, a foolhardy crossing of the river in their wake on the part of the Italo-Spanish Flechas Negras being checked by a sudden counterattack at Bermeo.[54] To an extent, then, the destruction of Guernica may even have stiffened the will of the defenders to fight: at all events, the second half of the campaign was much harder going for the Nationalists than the first had been. Also instrumental here, perhaps, was an improvement in the defenders' military organization. Desperate to prevent the fall of his home city – prior to the Civil War, he had been the head of the Socialist Party in Bilbao and the director of one of city's leading newspapers – Indalecio Prieto, the War Minister in the new government that, as we shall see, had been established in Valencia under Juan Negrín, had resolved to restore order to the Basque front by sending a new commander for the Euzko Gudarostea in the person of General Mariano Gámir Ulibarri, a career soldier of Basque origin of no particular political affiliation, whom he hoped might be acceptable to Aguirre (for good measure, Gámir Ulibarri was accompanied by several officers who had played important roles in the International Brigades, including the Hungarian Dezsö Jazz, the Italian Nino Nanetti and the Frenchman Joseph Putz).[55] Exhausted and despondent, the Prime Minister at last gave way and finally accepted that his forces should officially become I Corps of the Army of the North and formed into standard brigades and divisions. With the heartland of Basque nationalism in Vizcaya – the mountain villages and country towns of the east and south-east of the province – now in the hands of Franco's forces, the idea of sending aid to Bilbao was no longer quite as repugnant as it had been at the beginning of the campaign, and the period between late May and early June saw the dispatch of no fewer than fifty aircraft, all of which, of course, had to be flown across Nationalist-held Old Castile from Madrid. At the last minute, too, a shipment of mostly Czech arms arrived at Bilbao, which brought in no fewer than fifty-five light anti-aircraft guns, thirty field guns and two squadrons of I15s, Gámir Ulibarri in the meantime making frantic efforts to mobilize fresh troops for his much-reduced infantry battalions, some help being derived in this respect from the tardy arrival of a number of infantry battalions from Asturias and Santander.[56]

Further fighting continued throughout the month of May, and the Nationalists continued to make steady progress, albeit only at the cost of some ferocious battles that saw the Euzko Gudarostea make desperate efforts to recapture important peaks such as Bizcargui and Pena Lemona with the more-or-less unwilling aid of a number of Asturian battalions that had been sent across from Oviedo.[57] If the Nationalist rate of advance was surprisingly slow, meanwhile, it was in part because there were to be no more Bermeos, impetus and daring being sacrificed in favour of prudence and method.[58] With the Basque forces now for the most part back at the 'Ring of Iron', there was some hope that the position might be stabilized, but, if Aguirre and other Basque politicians took comfort in its concrete pillboxes, the soldiers detailed to man its positions were not deceived. Thus, camouflage was almost non-existent; in many areas, the defences either lacked adequate fields of fire or were over-looked by hills and ridges; there was too little barbed wire; the trenches were laid out in straight lines and in places little more than shallow ditches; and the concrete pillboxes and block-houses that were supposed to be the mainstay of the system were badly designed, poorly sited and desperately vulnerable to enemy fire. As one astonished militiaman observed, then, it was a ring not of iron, but of silk.[59] In the city, meanwhile, morale was low, with food very short and the population demoralized by the constant bombing, there being no sense whatsoever of a desire to defend the city street by street. 'The most terrible confusion is reigning here', wrote Koltsov. 'There is a constant struggle between rival interests and rival influences. Basques are pitted against Spaniards, nationalists against non-nationalists; parties against themselves and one another alike.'[60] Something of the mood that reigned among the civilian population comes over from the memories of the distinguished Basque historian and writer Martín de Ugalde: 'There was much hunger ... We talked of hunger, nothing but hunger. If we got hold of a bit of bread, we ate it that instant, but after that there would be nothing to eat all day. It was horrible.'[61]

The Nationalists having much to do to re-organize and re-equip their forces following the bitter struggle in the mountains, there was now a lull in operations, a further factor that slowed things down being the death of Mola in an air crash near Burgos. At length, however, all was ready, and the full power of Franco's régime descended on the defenders with a vengeance. To quote Cardozo, 'General Franco, always a believer in having the utmost strength at the vital spot, had crowded the valley behind Bizcargui ... with batteries. Never had I seen so many ... in so small an area. There were guns of every calibre up to huge twelve-inch howitzers, and all of them were firing at full speed.'[62] Faced by such ruthlessness, the last Basque troops outside the 'Ring of Iron' were routed and forced to seek its shelter, and on the 12 June, it was at last the turn of the positions on which so much hope had been placed.[63] The sector chosen for the breakthrough – the hill called Gaztelumendi near the village of San Martin de Fica – being the weakest in the entire line of defences, the assault troops burst through within a matter of hours. A journalist who, throughout his time covering the Basque campaign, showed extraordinary courage, George Steer was in the front line at the moment of collapse:

> Suddenly everything was in movement ... Their artillery was shooting faster than ever, before, the planes were back again in monstrous progression, the hillside in front of Gaztelumendi was wrapped in smoke ... One could see nothing ... Tank shells hit our parapet. In front of us there were men ... Our machine-guns opened fire: they dropped, then moved right. The shells were now falling in the trench, and, to my left, one exploded through one of the brushwood canopies. Two good lads had stood there firing. Both their faces were blown off, and there was nothing underneath the hair but red rags of flesh ... At this moment a man came running breathless along the trench from the right. He was the first officer I had seen that day. He whispered to the corporal, 'There is shooting behind us: they say they have got in at Gaztelumendi.'[64]

All that was left now in the way of the victorious Nationalists was the ridge called Archandasarri directly overlooking the city. This being protected by a number of reserve positions, the troops stationed there – elements of the Euzko Gudarostea's First Division under the erstwhile International Brigadier Joseph Putz – held out bravely for eighteen hours. Having narrowly escaped death at the 'Ring of Iron', Steer was watching from the streets below:

> Thursday morning ... we woke to a crack like Doomsday ... The whole ridge from Berriz to the radio station was a ribbon of smoke ... We took out our watches and counted. Over eighty a minute and sometimes a hundred. No intermission ... It continued for two hours ... An infantry attack was driven back between eight and nine. There was a pause for about an hour, and then the artillery hammered the ridge again for two more hours. It was terrible ... At midday another infantry attack, another failure ... We had many dead. Reserves went up. As they moved, the enemy aviation intervened: it made fire spring wildly from the mountain side and choke itself in earth and ashes.[65]

Nearby was another Englishman. Having been on leave in England, Peter Kemp had missed the entire campaign, but, as luck would have it, he managed to catch up with his battalion in the immediate aftermath of the position's capture:

> It was early evening before I found the Tercio de Nuestra Señora de Begoña. They were resting in woods on the heights of Archanda which they had stormed that afternoon. This ridge was the last enemy line of defence, and now there was nothing between us and Bilbao ... They had fought a bloody battle all day, struggling up the almost vertical hillside through the trees under a murderous fire of mortars and machine-guns from the defences on the top ... Already well under strength, [the Tercio] had started the assault with 170 men: there were barely forty left when I joined them.'[66]

In the city below, chaos reigned. 'We were completely penetrated by a spirit of defeat', admitted Anarchist militant Manuel de Chiapuso. 'This is the only truth: everything else is fantasy. Nowadays people want to make themselves feel good, and so they say this that and the other. One has to have actually been there to see what it was like.'[67] Having taken the decision not to defend Bilbao, Aguirre and his government had retired to the village of Trucios, leaving behind a Junta of Defence headed by the Basque-Nationalist Minister of the Interior, Jesus María de Leizaola. Seeing that the game was up, the latter now ordered the complete evacuation of the city, and long columns of troops now joined the thousands of civilians already fleeing along the main road that followed the left bank of the River Nervión to the sea and then turned westwards for Santander. According to orders that had been received from Prieto, the city's industries should have been destroyed rather than see them fall into the hands of General Franco, while, as in San Sebastián, there were plenty of left-wing militiamen eager to turn the whole

city into a wasteland. As before, however, the Basque nationalists were not prepared to tolerate such a course of action, and to this end, Leizaola had retained a
number of Partido Nacionalista Vasco troops in the city, these now being used to
clear the streets and herd all the remaining militiamen across the river. Evidently
feeling that their war was at an end with the fall of their homeland, a considerable number of the men concerned then quietly piled their arms and sat down to
await the arrival of the enemy.[68] At the last minute, the bridges were blown up,
and an hour or two later, the first representatives of Franco's army – a small party
of officers – entered the city. With them was Harold Cardozo, a newsman in his
way just as intrepid as George Steer:

> We were seized upon and pulled this way and that … the centre of a crowd
> of enthusiastic patriots simply mad with joy. Processions were formed and
> marched up and down … with the national flag at their head. We were
> assembled in the midst of one which escorted us in triumph to the place of
> the provincial assembly … There the old separatist guards … six-footers
> every one of them, presented arms and flung open the great iron gates.[69]

How far this joy was genuine, it is hard to say. Amongst the crowds there must
have been many who reasoned that turning out to cheer and give the fascist
salute was a wise move in the circumstances. Yet the Bilbao bourgeoisie had far
less reason to love Basque nationalism – a cause whose links with the Basque language ensured that it was above all associated with primitive country villagers[70]
– than their Barcelona counterparts had reason to love the equivalent movement
in Catalonia, and just as much reason to fear the revolutionary Left. At the same
time, too, of course, rich and poor alike were desperately hungry after months
of a diet of little more than black bread and chick peas, this being a fact that was
quite enough in itself to prompt many to rejoice at the sight of Franco's troops.
As Kemp wrote, 'The condition of the civilian population was tragic. The first
day we were constantly besieged by pathetic, emaciated figures … begging pite-
ously for a little bread. The Nationalists tackled the problem at once, rushing in
supplies of meat, potatoes, rice and bread, and opening restaurants where any
civilian could get a free meal.'[71] If Franco's army hastened to restore the situation to normal, it was not out of concern for the populace but rather because the
factories and shipyards of Bilbao, few of which had even been stripped of their
tools and machinery, not to mention the iron-ore mines of its hinterland, were
a valuable asset to the Nationalist cause that needed to be pressed into service
as quickly as possible. Nor was it just a matter of acquiring an industrial base
and substantial mineral resources. Thus, the population of Vizkaya was itself an
important asset. Once again, the point is made very effectively by Peter Kemp:
'We stayed a fortnight in Bilbao, recruiting officers and men from sympathisers who had remained underground … during the Republican regime: we had
more applications than the shortage of equipment and instructors allowed us to
enlist.'[72] In short, the destruction of Euzkadi, an achievement rendered all the

sweeter by the fact that it eliminated the only pocket of Spanish Catholicism that had not lined up behind the Nationalist crusade, was not some mere side-show: rather, it was the key to victory.

Notes

1 For the decision of 21 March and the background thereto, see M. Martínez Bande, *Vizcaya* (Madrid, 1971), pp. 15–17.

2 Away from the bitter fighting in San Sebastián itself, the first clash seems to have come in the village of Vera de Bidássoa on 20 July. This, however, was a somewhat a comic affair. Entering the sprawling village from opposite directions at exactly the same time as one another, the rival forces – a tiny band of Socialist militia on the one hand and an equally tiny band of Carlist militia on the other – both turned and fled at the mere mention that there were enemies in the vicinity. See M. Usabiaga, 'Asi fue la batalla de Irun', < http://www.asociacionrepublicanairunesa.org/cas/batalla_irun. php >, accessed 20 February 2016.

3 The naval resources available to the Nationalists on the north coast at this stage were minimal. Thanks to their control of the naval base of El Ferrol, they had obtained the services of the battleship *España* and the destroyer *Velasco*, but, of these, the former had not been to sea for two years and had been stripped of some of its secondary armament, while the latter had been experiencing serious mechanical problems and was barely sea-worthy. See J. Cervera Valderrama, *Memorias de guerra: mi labor en el estado mayor de la armada afecto al cuartel general del Generalísimo durante la Guerra de Liberación Nacional, 1936–1939* (Madrid, 1968), pp. 19–20.

4 G. Steer, *The Tree of Gernika: a Field Study of Modern War* (London, 1938), p. 34. The difficulty faced by the Nationalists in this operation should not be underestimated. For example: 'Centred, as it was on the left bank of the River Bidássoa, the terrain through which the battalion was expected to attack was very difficult. Below Enderlaza, the river runs through a deep gorge. On one side of this lay France and on the other the enemy positions, these last being very strongly entrenched. In consequence, there was no chance of manoeuvre.' Revilla Cebrecos, *Tercio de Lacar*, p. 42.

5 The fighting around Oyarzún was very fierce. Despite stubborn resistance, the village fell to the Carlist Tercio de Lacar on 27 July, but the latter then came under sustained artillery bombardment from the guns of the coastal battery of San Marcos, and the attackers therefore had no option but to withdraw. Revilla Cebrecos, *Tercio de Lacar*, p. 47.

6 Usabiaga, 'Asi fue la batalla de Irun.'

7 Steer, *Tree of Gernika*, p. 45. The armoured cars featured in Steer's account were two lorries clad in boiler plate of much the same sort as those used by the Republicans, whilst they were manned by a detachment of the Falange of Navarre, each vehicle being under the command of two erstwhile Civil Guards. See Revilla Cebrecos, *Tercio de Lacar*, p. 57. A noteworthy feature of the fighting was the presence of a handful of women in the ranks of the Anarchist militia, amongst whom was Casilda Mendéz Hernáez. Lines, *Women in Combat*, p. 80.

8 For the presence of foreign volunteers in the defence of Irún, see F. M. Vargas Alonso, 'Voluntarios internacionales y asesores extranjeros en Euzkadi, 1936–1937', *Historia contemporánea*, XXXIV (2007), pp. 325–7.

9 Cit. L. M. Jiménez de Aberásturi and J. C. Jiménez de Aberásturi (eds.), *La guerra en Euzkadi; transcendentales revelaciones de unos testigos de excepción acerca de la Guerra del 36 en el País Vasco* (Barcelona, 1978), p. 29.

10 See Fraser, *Blood of Spain*, pp. 189–91.

11 The burning of Irun was in many ways a particularly lamentable episode. A crude attempt at a scorched-earth policy, it achieved nothing other than to afford the

Nationalists a considerable propaganda coup and, later on, a useful means of covering up the bombing of Guernica. For a dramatic account, see Steer, *Tree of Gernika*, p. 53.

12 Bowers, *My Mission to Spain*, p. 284.

13 For an excellent discussion of these issues, see the recollections of Basque nationalist militant Joseba Elosegui in Jiménez de Abarásturi, *Guerra de Euzkadi*, pp. 167–8.

14 Steer, *Tree of Gernika*, pp. 82–3.

15 Ibid., pp. 100–1. Among the Left, the Erzaña had an evil reputation as both a bourgeois militia and a soft option for the sons of the élite. E.g. M. de Amilibia, *Los batallones de Euzkadi* (San Sebastián, 1978), p. 108. An early victim of the Basque nationalists' hostility appears to have been Santiago Carrillo. Away in France at a meeting in the week before the uprising, he arrived on the night train from Paris on the morning of 18 July to find himself in the middle of a war. Unable to carry on to Madrid, he attempted to make his way to Bilbao, but on the way was arrested by nationalist militia and, or so he later claimed, threatened with execution. Saved by a lucky chance, he then briefly fought on the Santander front and eventually got back to Madrid by taking a boat from Bilbao to Bayonne and then travelling on by train via Barcelona. Carrillo, *Dialogue on Spain*, p. 45.

16 For these massacres, see Steer, *Tree of Gernika*, pp. 79–80, 116–18. In taking the stance that they did, the Basque nationalists had the support of the two Republican parties, the small secular nationalist party known Basque Nationalist Action and, above all, the Communists, this last seeing Aguirre and his followers as prime examples of the sort of non-revolutionary allies they needed to cultivate if they were ever to achieve their goals in the highly complicated situation that had developed since the uprising.

17 See Jiménez de Abarásturi, *Guerra de Euzkadi*, pp. 232–3.

18 Ibid., pp. 93–5; See also Martínez Bande, *Vizcaya*, pp. 29–33. For the uniform regulations of the Euzko Gudarostea, see J. M. Bueno, *Uniformes militares de la Guerra Civil Española* (Málaga, 1974), p. 189. Not satisfied with setting up his own army, Aguirre also established a small navy consisting of a number of armed trawlers (not that he could really be blamed for this: although the battleship *Jaime Primero*, two cruisers, six destroyers, a torpedo boat and four submarines had been sent to Bilbao as a gesture of solidarity in September, most of the ships were quickly withdrawn, while the crews of the few vessels left behind – a destroyer, two submarines and a torpedo boat – did absolutely nothing to challenge the Nationalist blockade). See Alcofar Nassaes, *Fuerzas navales*, pp. 119–23; Jiménez de Abarásturi, *Guerra de Euzkadi*, p. 260. Other acts of defiance, meanwhile, included ignoring the Largo Caballero government's decree of 25 October making all troops subject to the code of military justice, substituting numbers for the distinctive names with which the old militia columns had gone to war and excluding militia chiefs who had not been confirmed in some military rank from command, and disregarding Llano de la Encomienda's later order ordering the formation of brigades and divisions throughout the Army of the North.

19 In Euzkadi, as everywhere else, the overwhelming majority of the combatants were Spaniards. However, perhaps as many as 100 foreign volunteers enlisted in the Euzko Gudarostea, the vast majority in Socialist or Communist battalions. See Vargas Alonso, 'Voluntarios internacionales y asesores extranjeros en Euzkadi', pp. 330–33.

20 There were also a variety of artillery, engineer and tank or armoured-car units, all of which appear to have been preserves of the Partido Nacionalista Vasco. See Amilibia, *Los batallones de Euzkadi*, pp. 106–7. One issue that caused serious problems was Aguirre's point-blank refusal to permit the establishment of brigades and divisions, the trouble with this being that it greatly complicated the command and control of the Basque forces. See Jiménez de Abarásturi, *Guerra de Euzkadi*, p. 43. Also problematic was the fact that the Partido Nacionalista Vasco units undoubtedly contained many individuals who, at best, were hoping to sit out the war as quietly as possible and, at worst, favoured the cause of Franco. Amilibia, *Batallones de Euzkadi*, p. 106.

21 Cervera Valderrama, *Memorias de guerra*, pp. 86–7, 135–44. If the Nationalist squadron could not be everywhere at once, on the only occasion it was openly challenged, it gave a brutal display of its firepower. Thus, moving in to take a transport heading

for Bilbao, on 5 March 1937, *Canarias* was challenged by the armed trawlers *Vizkaya*, *Nabara*, *Guipúzkoa* and *Donostía*. The four Basque vessels having just seven three-inch and four-inch guns between them, they were badly outranged by the six-inch guns of the Nationalist vessel, the net result being that the *Nabara* was sunk and the *Guipúzkoa* badly damaged. As for the ship the Basque squadron was trying to bring in, it made port safely, only for it to be discovered that a large part of its cargo was militarily useless due to the absence of key parts such as fuses and firing pins. See Steer, *Tree of Gernika*, pp. 294–7.

22 See Martínez Bande, *Vizcaya*, pp. 54–7. It should be noted, however, that only two shipments of Russian arms arrived in Bilbao. Both unloaded in November 1936, these brought in fifteen I15 fighters, thirty armoured cars, six Sixty-Pounder Mark 1s, eight 76.2mm mountain guns, fifteen 37mm McClean M16 infantry guns, 453 machine-guns, fifty mortars and 23,000 rifles. Howson, *Arms for Spain*, p. 282.

23 One Bilbao concern did manufacture 41mm and 81mm mortars, but the sights came from beyond the Basque country, with the result that the finished products left much to be desired. Jiménez de Aberásturi, *Guerra de Euzkadi*, pp. 255-6. When weapons systems were improvised from scratch, meanwhile, the results were even worse. We come here to the story of the so-called Carro Euzkadi. A tiny light tank that was turned out in small numbers in one of Bilbao's many shipyards on the basis of the Landesa agricultural tractor, this was all but useless, being mechanically unreliable, hopelessly under-powered, extremely cramped, poorly ventilated and armed only with light machine-guns. According to legend, indeed, when the first models were paraded before Aguirre, every single one of them broke down before they had travelled more than a few yards. See Albert, *Carros de combate*, pp. 35–7, and M. González, 'M36 Euzkadi', < http://director.io/tanquesyblindados/articulos/gce/republicano/euzkadi/euzkadi.htm >, accessed 21 February 2016.

24 The best weapons that the Basques received from abroad were a consignment of some thirty Russian armoured cars, of which two-thirds were the cannon-armed BA10 and the remainder the much smaller and less impressive machine-gun armed FA1 or BA20. See Steer, *Tree of Gernika*, p. 97.

25 Cit. Martínez Bande, *Vizcaya*, pp. 239–40. Told of these allegations whilst he was being interviewed for Jiménez de Abarásturi's *Guerra en Euzkadi*, the Socialist Miguel de Amilibia dismissed them as 'exaggerated and tendentious.' Cit. Jiménez de Abarásturi, *Guerra en Euzkadi*, p. 42.

26 Cit. Jiménez de Abarásturi, *Guerra en Euzkadi*, p. 150.

27 Amilibia, *Batallones de Euzkadi*, p. 116. A refugee from Guipúzcoa, Amilibia remarks that he was bitterly disappointed that the target for the attack was Vitoria rather than San Sebastián. To political differences, then, we see added a certain provincialism.

28 For a general study of the battle of Villareal, See J. A. Aguirregabiria Parras, *La batalla de Villareal de Alava: ofénsiva sobre Vitoria-Miranda de Ebro* (Bilbao, 2015). The role played by Gorev, if, indeed, he played any at all, remains unclear. Steer, certainly, is sceptical: 'Gurieff [*sic*] … struck none of us as a genius, and the Basques resolutely refused to employ him except in an advisory capacity, where his advice was in nearly every case rejected. I found him a likeable personality, but, as I thought, inexperienced in war.' Steer, *Tree of Gernika*, p. 99. A number of other foreign advisers were also present at various times. See Vargas Alonso, 'Voluntarios internacionales y asesores extranjeros en Euzkadi', pp. 339–42.

29 If there was no fighting on the frontiers of Alava and Guipúzcoa, in February 1937, six battalions of the Euzko Gudarostea were sent to Oviedo to support a fresh offensive against the beleaguered Nationalist garrison. 'A simultaneous attack was launched in every sector chosen for the ambitious operation … However, right from the beginning things went wrong … Many of the objectives were never secured, and as the days went on, whilst always very fierce, the battle degenerated into a confused struggle of a roughly balanced nature that was particularly demanding, cruel and exhausting for the attackers.' Amilibia, *Batallones de Euzkadi*, p. 119. For a detailed account, see Cabezas, *Asturias*, pp. 111–24.

30 E.g. Amilibia, *Batallones de Euzkadi*, p. 145.

31 Steer, *Tree of Gernika*, p. 99. In the post-war era, Goicoechea won fame as the designer of the famous Talgo.

32 For good measure, the more radical elements of the Partido Nacionalista Vasco also hated the secular nationalists of Acción Nacionalista Vasca. E.g. Jiménez de Abarásturi, *Guerra de Euzkadi*, pp. 251–2.

33 See Steer, *Tree of Gernika*, pp. 121–2. In response to these events, a number of Anarchist battalions abandoned their positions at the front and briefly embarked on a march on Bilbao to rescue their leaders before being turned back at the point of machine-guns by Basque-nationalist troops sent to block their way. See Jiménez de Abarásturi, *Guerra de Euzkadi*, pp. 152–3, 156–7.

34 Cit. Jiménez de Abarásturi, *Guerra de Euzkadi*, p. 43. See also Fraser, *Blood of Spain*, p. 397.

35 The artillery pieces were a motley collection indeed, the inventory of those whose presence is known for certain including twelve 155mm Schneider M1917 howitzers, three 150mm Krupp M13 guns, three Vickers Sixty-Pounder Mark Is, two Vickers 105mm M1922 howitzers and forty-one assorted 75mm or 77mm guns of no fewer than six different models and four different countries of origin. Significantly, however, anti-aircraft guns were all but non-existent, the only weapons that had turned up of this sort being six Oerlikon 20mm cannons. See Martínez Bande, *Vizkaya*, p. 35.

36 Steer, *Tree of Gernika*, p. 158.

37 After the event, left-wing observers were keen to criticize the Basque government for failing to mount a revolutionary war, and, still more so, offer the proletariat significant gains on the home front. E.g. Jiménez Abarásturi, *Guerra en Euzkadi*, p. 231. However, setting aside the fact that the Communists were just as much opposed to such a line as Aguirre and his followers, it is difficult to see how such a policy would have done anything than push the more conservative elements of Basque society into the arms of the enemy.

38 A month after the offensive began, the terminology caught up with reality, the Sixth Organic Division being relabelled the VI Army Corps and its two groupings the First and Second Divisions (later Sixty-First and Sixty-Second).

39 The Brigades of Navarre appear to have been conceived as a gesture to the Carlists, the latter being very strong in Navarre. Thus, dominated by the red-bereted Carlist militia, they served as a symbolic reference to the Carlist armies that had battled the march of Spanish liberalism in the course of the nineteenth century. In military terms, meanwhile, the theory was that they would be crack, fast-moving mountain troops who were particularly suited to the demands of war in the rugged *cordillera cantábrica*. In practice, however, it is evident that they were little different from the rest of the Nationalist forces and above all served as a means of subjecting the militias of a region where political differences between rival nationalist factions were likely to be particularly acute to military authority. For an adulatory account by a veteran, see J. Nagore Yárnoz, 'Las brigadas de Navarra: su espíritu', < http://www.requetes. com/brigadas.html >, accessed 21 February 2016.

40 The Flechas Negras and its sister brigade, the Flechas Azules, were somewhat different from the rest of the CTV in that their only Italian elements were the officers and non-commissioned officers, the whole of the rank and file being composed of Spaniards, the general idea being that the expertise Italy had gained in the war in Ethiopia could in this fashion quickly be instilled into a comparatively large number of Spanish troops. Originally, the intention was to ensure the political enthusiasm of the new units by forming them from volunteers from the Falangist militia, but the recruits that came forward were of such poor quality that the attempt had to be abandoned, and the two brigades had to be filled up with conscripts, most of them from Extremadura. In the wake of the battle of Guadalajara, meanwhile, the CTV had been thoroughly reorganized. The regular Littorio Division was kept more or less as it was, but, many of their recruits having been deemed to be useless and sent home, the three blackshirt divisions were amalgamated into just one and those troops that

were left over used to form a new brigade known as the XXIII March. Mesa, *Regreso de las legiones*, pp. 67–8; Coverdale, *Italian Intervention*, pp. 167, 177–9, 275–6.

41 It will be noted that the Nationalist air cover included a number of new planes, including not just SM79, He111 and Dornier Do17 bombers but also the Henschel Hs123 ground-attack aircraft and the Me109 fighter, this being a model that from the first moment of its appearance far outclassed the Republican I15s and I16s. Permuy López, *Aviación en la Guerra Civil Española*, pp. 118–19.

42 Coverdale, *Italian Intervention*, pp. 279–80. The new commander of the CTV, Ettore Bastico, would beyond doubt have loved a more prominent role in the campaign, but in the end, the only other Italians formations to join the fighting, and then only very briefly, were the six batteries of artillery mentioned in the text and the XXIII Marzo brigade: in the wake of Guadalajara, it seems that there was little desire to trust Italian bombast.

43 Salas Larrazábal, *Air War over Spain*, pp. 135–6; Proctor, *Hitler's Luftwaffe*, pp. 118–2; for a detailed first-hand account of the first day of the battle, see Amilibia, *Batallones de Euzkadi*, pp. 123–4.

44 Cit. Jiménez de Aberásturi, *Guerra de Euzkadi*, pp. 261-2.

45 See Salas Larrázabal, *Air War over Spain*, p. 165. To quote Mikhail Koltsov, 'Here on the northern front it is the aviation which is doing all the fighting. The only trouble is that that comment only applies to the Nationalist aviation: the Republican aviation doesn't exist.' Koltsov, *Diario de la guerra de España*, p. 396.

46 E.g. Fraser, *Blood of Spain*, p. 403. Just as significant here was the issue of the Republican navy. Thus, following the start of the offensive, the government dispatched a destroyer and two submarines to reinforce the token naval force that had been left at Bilbao the previous autumn, but, to the fury of Aguirre's government, the vessels concerned did not make the slightest effort to interfere with the Nationalist blockade. Alcofar Nassaes, *Fuerzas navales*, p. 123.

47 In the memorable words of George Steer, 'The mystique of the air was drugging the troops and rearguard, and the rearguard re-injected the troops in double portion.' Steer, *Tree of Gernika*, p. 182. Meanwhile, it is important to note that airpower had its limitations. As the war correspondent Harold Cardozo admitted, 'The whole of this campaign in Vizkaya illustrated the immense difficulties attending the co-operation of bombing and machine-gunning aircraft with infantry advancing actively across enemy positions ... In many attacks fully fifty per cent of the casualties were caused by errors on the part of the squadrons of bombing planes.' Cardozo, *March of a Nation*, p. 273. Even when planes found their targets, the effect was not always that great. On the same day that Gernika was bombed, for example, George Steer and another correspondent were shot up by six He51s when their car was caught in the open near the village of Arbaceguí: 'For between fifteen and twenty minutes they dived over our hole at full throttle, loosing off their double guns at us from anything down to 200 feet ... Of course, it's all noise. The shooting was wild and after a quarter of an hour we could not find a bullet in the bomb-hole.' Steer, *Tree of Gernika*, p. 235.

48 See Steer, *Tree of Gernika*, pp. 164–8.

49 Koltsov, *Diario de la guerra de España*, pp. 394–5.

50 Steer, *Tree of Gernika*, p. 214.

51 Revilla Cebrecos, *Tercio de Lacar*, p. 84.

52 Steer, *Tree of Gernika*, pp. 243–4. For a dramatic full-length account of the raid, see G. Thomas and M. Morgan Witts, *The Day Guernica Died* (London, 1975). One thing that is certain is that the concentrated bombing of civilian targets was not an idea that was limited to the Germans. Thus, at a conference in early April, Mola shocked the chief of staff of the Condor Legion, Wolfram von Richthofen, by suddenly demanding that he abandon the tactical attacks on which the Nationalist planes had been concentrating from the beginning of the campaign in favour of a massive assault on Bilbao, designed not just to destroy the factories and shipyards but to kill large numbers of workers, the only argument put forward in favour of this being that, along

with that of Catalonia, the Basque proletariat had become far too dangerous and in consequence needed to be eliminated. See Proctor, *Hitler's Luftwaffe*, p. 122.

53 For an interesting discussion, see Proctor, *Hitler's Luftwaffe in the Spanish Civil War*, pp. 127–30.

54 For an account of this battle, see ibid., pp. 265–74, whilst the role of the Italian and Italian-led forces in the campaign is discussed in Mesa, *Regreso de las legiones*, pp. 83–91. In the end, however, the lines collapsed once more, Steer alleging, rightly or wrongly, that the fault lay with some of the few Asturian troops who had been taking part in the fighting, these last having abandoned the key position of Monte Sollube without orders.

55 For some details on these International Brigade officers, see Vargas Alonso, 'Voluntarios internacionales y asesores extranjeros en Euzkadi', pp. 335–7.

56 For the shipment of Czech arms, see Steer, *Tree of Gernika*, p. 292. Like the rest of the Republican zone, Bilbao was at the mercy of an international arms trade that frequently mercilessly cheated the buyers sent out to track down useful consignments. Of three shiploads brought in from the Baltic by the *SS Yorkbrook* in March 1937, two were discovered to have been badly sabotaged. See Howson, *Arms for Spain*, p. 195.

57 Revilla Cebrecos, *Tercio de Lacar*, p. 91; Steer, *Tree of Gernika*, pp. 284–9.

58 Cardozo, *March of a Nation*, p. 284.

59 Martínez Bande, *Vizcaya*, pp. 45–6; Jiménez de Abarásturi, *Guerra en Euzkadi*, pp. 154, 187–8.

60 Koltsov, *Diario de la Guerra de España*, p. 397.

61 Cit. Jimenez de Abarásturi, *Guerra en Euzkadi*, pp. 308–9.

62 Ibid., pp. 292–3. The enormous weight of the bombardments to which the defenders were subjected highlights one area in the aid received by the Nationalists that far outstripped that received by the Republicans. Thus, taking the war as a whole, it is generally agreed that, whilst the former got fewer guns than is often supposed, and, what is more, that the guns concerned were not that modern, they received far more ammunition and, still more importantly, a constant supply of ammunition as almost all the guns they received were still in service. For the sake of argument, then, the 65mm mountain guns supplied to Franco in 1936 were still blasting the Republican lines in 1939. In the Republican zone, by contrast, things were very different in that, whilst plenty of guns arrived, they were only rarely standard-issue models and therefore frequently came with limited supplies of ammunition, the result being, of course, that Republican gunners had to hoard every shell, while Nationalist ones were able to deluge their targets with a veritable hail of fire.

63 Passed over here very briefly though it must be, the fighting of 11 June was just as severe as anything that followed. One man who experienced it was the Guipúzcoan Socialist Miguel de Amilibia. 'At that time I was attached to the headquarters of the First Division … We were bombed very heavily … Nine big enemy bombers … turned up with no other intention than that of flattening the command post. They left the whole area a mass of craters, while the house we were based in … was left in a state of semi-ruin. We didn't suffer many dead, losing just a couple of men … That said, we had a dreadful fright: a number of incendiary bombs fell on the shelter in which we were hiding. Given the reduced nature of the space available and the very large number of people who had crammed themselves inside, we could hardly breathe … People were screaming, 'Air! Give us some air!' Every minute seemed an hour.' Cit. Jiménez de Abarásturi, *Guerra en Euzkadi*, pp. 47–8.

64 Steer, *Tree of Gernika*, pp. 313–14.

65 Ibid., pp. 352–3.

66 Kemp, *Mine were of Trouble*, p. 92.

67 Cit. Jiménez de Abarásturi, *Guerra de Euzkadi*, p. 155.

68 According to Miguel de Amilibia, the troops concerned were all members of the Erzaña. See Amilibia, *Los Batallones de Euzkadi*, p. 108. The subject of whether or not

Bilbao could have been defended has ever since been the subject of much controversy, with almost all those on the Left bitterly critical of the Basque nationalists, and the Communists, especially, insistent that had they been in command, they could have rallied the populace and emulated the defence of Madrid. This, however, is just so much grandstanding: such troops as were left were in total disarray; ammunition was extremely limited; most of the Euzko Gudarostea's heavy weapons had been lost in the course of the campaign; the Nationalists had complete control of the air; food and medical supplies were running out; the populace was deeply divided; and, to cap it all, Bilbao's physical situation meant that it was almost impossible to defend, the city being overlooked from all sides. Granted that such men as Leizaola had always been ambivalent about the war, it is difficult to see how he or anybody else could have come to any other conclusion.

69 Cardozo, *March of a Nation*, pp. 299–300.
70 E.g. Fraser, *Blood of Spain*, p. 406.
71 Kemp, *Mine were of Trouble*, pp. 94–5.
72 Ibid., p. 95.

7

DIVERSIONS AND DISASTERS

From 31 March 1937, as we have seen, the chief weight of the Nationalist war effort switched to northern Spain. However, this did not bring peace to the other fronts. Far from it: desperate to relieve the pressure on Vizcaya and Oviedo, and in part, too, driven by a variety of political factors, the Republicans proceeded to launch a series of offensives on various parts of the Nationalist lines that at Brunete and Belchite produced two of the biggest battles of the whole Civil War. In every sense, however, these offensives were unsuccessful: sometimes a little territory was won, but the cost was appalling and the respites that were secured on the northern front were at best temporary, all resistance having been brought to an end there by the middle of October. On top of this, whilst the Nationalist zone had witnessed further political consolidation by means of the unification of all its political parties into the single Falange Española Tradicionalista y de las Juntas de Ofensiva Nacional-Sindicalistas, in the Republican zone, the tensions of 1936 had erupted in a tragic civil war within a civil war followed by a fresh cabinet crisis that produced the overthrow of Francisco Largo Caballero. Truly, then, 1937 was for the Republicans a year of disaster and the Nationalists a year of triumph.

Before we go on to discuss the campaigns, we need first to review the two armed forces that were in contention with one another. Beginning with the Republic, the process of building a new army that had begun in the autumn of 1936 was now complete, at least in organizational terms. The militia columns that had set off to seek the enemy in July 1936 and then proceeded to fail so miserably and at such terrible cost had now all been converted into mixed brigades, of which there were 117 by the end of April 1937: for example, the so-called Iron Column was the LXXXIII Mixed Brigade and the Durruti Column the CXIX, CXX and CXXI Mixed Brigades. That done, the mixed brigades had in turn had been subsumed into a conventional structure of divisions, corps and, finally, field armies (initially those of the North, the South and the Centre): taking the three brigades established on the basis of the Durruti column as an example, they had become the Twenty-Sixth Division and been assigned to what eventually became the Army of the East's XI Army Corps. Most of the military and police units that had remained loyal to the Republic had been swallowed up in the columns, but the Carabineers had survived as a species of private army headed by the Socialist Minister of Finance, Juan Negrín (as the country's customs guard, the Carabineers had always been responsible to the Ministry of Finance) and contributed four brigades to the total (III, V, LXXXV, LXXXVII). Also distinct were the Russian-commanded tank and armoured car battalions and the five International Brigades, these last being controlled by the autonomous directorate that had been established at their base in Albacete. At division, corps and army level, command was overwhelmingly in the hands of officers of the old army (though there were exceptions: the Eleventh Division was headed by Enrique Lister, and the Twenty-Sixth Division by Durruti's erstwhile second-in-command, Ricardo Sanz), but at brigade level, there had been no option but to make use of militia commanders and even erstwhile sergeants and corporals of the pre-war armed forces. Men of little education and no military training beyond the rudiments of parade ground and barrack room, whether they were capable of fulfilling their roles was at best uncertain, but, despite this, measures that might have recruited large numbers of middle-class young men of some education to the officer corps by means of accelerated training courses were never pushed for fear of outraging working-class sensibilities.[1]

As the creation of so many mixed brigades suggests, manpower was not in short supply. Although there were never more than 20,000 International Brigaders in Spain at any given time, foreign volunteers continued to come in in reasonable numbers till the middle of 1937, whilst in 1936, the voluntarism of the first months of the war had been replaced by resort to conscription, no fewer than six year-groups having been called up by May 1937.[2] By March 1937, then, some 360,000 Spaniards were under arms in the People's Army, around 250,000 of them in the four armies holding the central and eastern zone, though it should be remembered that that, thanks to the unpardonable decision to adopt the mixed brigade, as many as one quarter of the whole were to all intents and purposes non-combatants; to quote Hugh Thomas, 'While the republic had organised a modern army if anything sooner than their opponents had done, they also had reproduced the bureaucracy ... which characterised the old army.'[3] On a more positive note, on the whole this was an army that actually looked like an army. On paper, at least, a modern battle-dress-style uniform had been adopted that was very reminiscent of that worn by the British army in the Second World War, and, if this had not yet been issued very widely, the revolutionary panto-mime outfits of the summer of 1936 had mostly disappeared. Though their use was never universal, steel helmets – the vast majority the stylish French 'Adrian' model of the First World War – were also increasingly common. Certainly Franz Borkenau found a noticeable change when he returned to Barcelona after an absence of several months in January 1937: 'The troops were entirely different from the militia I had known in August. There was a clear distinction between officers and men, the former wearing better uniforms ... The uniform of the privates was not yet quite unified, but ... there was a definite attempt towards a uniformity of clothes.'[4]

Arms for these new-style troops were by no means abundant – there were many battalions that had no machine-guns, many mixed brigades that had no artillery batteries – but the situation was not quite so chaotic as it had been in the autumn of 1936 (most units now seem to have been armed with one type of rifle only, for example).[5] Along with the weapons that had been inherited from the pre-1936 armed forces, there were now to be seen the plentiful supplies of arms that had come in from the Soviet Union, although, as we have seen, these included a host of weapons that were not Russian at all, but had rather been imported by the Tsarist government during the First World War or captured from the Whites, and, indeed, some that were frankly awful.[6] Russia, however, was not the only source of supply. Bizarrely, meanwhile, to pro-Republican Mexico, which had, as noted, sent 20,000 rifles in the immediate wake of the uprising, had been added deeply Catholic Poland. In brief, the military régime that had governed Poland since 1926 was no friend of the Republic, and, with this, a particular enemy of Soviet Russia, but it was anxious for hard currency that it could use to fund its own re-armament. In consequence, Republican agents found Warsaw eager to do business. From the spring of 1937 onwards, then, large quantities of rifles, machine-guns and artillery began to reach the Republic from this source, the shipments even including a considerable number of FT17 tanks. However, most of these weapons were no more Polish than the Russian weapons were Russian: once again, what we see is a wide range of arms that had been supplied to the Polish legions serving in the French, German and Austro-Hungarian armies in the First World War, together with large numbers of weapons that had been captured from Russia in the war of 1920–1 (in fairness, however, included in the whole were several consignments of more modern weapons such as Polish variants of the Browning light machine-gun and Mauser rifle dating from 1928 and 1929 respectively). At the same time, given that the Poles were not disposed to regard the Second Republic with any degree of friendship, the quality was in all probability even worse than was the case with the material shipped from Russia (what is certainly true is that the prices were outrageous: though the Poles had deemed the FT17 to be completely useless for military purposes, they had no hesitation in charging the unfortunate Republicans $35,000 dollars for each vehicle whereas the Russians – themselves by no means generous – were only asking for $21,500 for a T26).[7] And, above all, for the Polish and Russian arms alike, there was the issue of ammunition: let us say that delivery was taken of a battery of Vickers 4.5" howitzers, and that said howitzers were in excellent condition; so far, so good, but without copious supplies of shells, the new arrivals would be of no use whatsoever, and, indeed, just one more drain on the Republic's scanty resources. With the stocks of ammunition reaching the Republic always much more limited than those that reached their opponents – according to

Hugh Thomas, whilst Italy alone provided Franco with 7.000,000 shells, Russia only sent the Republic some 4,000,000[8] – the sort of artillery support available to Republican commanders was never going to equal that of their opponents. Only in the air were things any brighter, the miscellany of aircraft that took part in the battles of the summer and autumn of 1936 having now almost entirely given way to squadrons of Polikarpov I15 and I16 fighters, Polikarpov R5 and R7 ground-attack aircraft and Tupolev SB2 bombers.[9]

Before moving on to other issues, it is worth pausing here to discuss the enormous problems involved in arming and supplying the Republican army. Given the fact that the industrial base available to the Republicans in the central and eastern zone was lacking in organization, short of raw materials, limited in its capacity and largely unsuitable, the vast majority of the arms and munitions that were needed had to come from outside.[10] With the French frontier firmly shut, however, that in turn meant that supplies could only arrive by ship and thereby run the gamut of the Nationalist blockade. In the northern zone, this was at best patchy, but along the far more important Mediterranean coast, it was a very different story. Here, there were even fewer Nationalist vessels (though Mussolini did his best to make good the want by making over four destroyers and two submarines to the insurgents, the latter also receiving no fewer than five motor torpedo boats from Germany), but their absence was more than made up for by the Italian navy, which attacked many ships bound for Republican ports, for a period over the winter of 1937 engaging in what amounted to a policy of unrestricted submarine warfare so brutal that even Britain could not stomach it and sent destroyers to patrol the sea lanes. Some attempt was made by a Republican navy increasingly beset by shortages of every kind to provide cover in the western reaches of the Mediterranean, but the Russians, whose ships might conceivably have made a real difference, made no attempt to help whatsoever, whilst the growing Nationalist air superiority meant that even those ships that got through the blockade were often bombed in port or the last stages of their journey (particularly important here were not just Italian aircraft operating from Mallorca, but also the often neglected floatplane component of the Condor Legion, this being equipped with the highly effective He59 torpedo bomber).[11]

By the spring of 1937, then, the People's Army had organic existence, large numbers of men and a level of armament that represented a considerable improvement on what had gone before. What, though, about the key question of morale? Implicit in the destruction of the militias was the destruction of the revolution, and many observers on the Left have been insistent that this was a death-blow in so far as the chances of the Republic were concerned: in brief, left with nothing to fight for, the people lost all enthusiasm for the struggle and retreated into cynicism, even apathy. To quote the Anarchist apologist Vernon Richards, 'By removing the initiative from the workers, the responsibility for the conduct of the struggle and its objectives were also transferred to a governing hierarchy, and this could not have other than an adverse effect on the morale of the revolutionary fighters.'[12] Nor was this just so much theory. In the words of Lois Orr, a young American girl working as a volunteer in POUM headquarters in Barcelona, 'The revolutionary fervour ... has disappeared ... and now what goes on is political manipulation by the heads of the labour organizations.'[13]

Although the question is highly debatable, it is at least arguable that the new atmosphere hit voluntary enlistment. Coming back to Barcelona after an absence of several months in January 1937, Borkenau was astonished: 'Very little recruit-ment is now going on in Barcelona ... During the week of my stay I did not see a single convoy leave for the Aragón front.'[14] What is certainly true is that, amongst such groups as the Anarchists and the POUM, there was no liking for the idea of the People's Army.[15] Militarization therefore did not go through without resistance, many Anarchists, in particular, remaining utterly opposed to it. As one Valencian militant wrote, 'We do not wish to be under military command of any sort, and are ready to fight anyone who tries to impose such a measure, or, for that matter, does anything that will impose limits on liberty: Anarchists as we are, we don't want discipline.'[16] Many columns in consequence did all they could to drag their feet, the Iron Column managing to hold out against being refashioned as the LXXXIII Mixed Brigade until March 1937, and only giving way even then in a spirit of anger and resentment. To quote the manifesto that it issued in its dying moments:

> The people's militias are no more. In short, the social revolution has had the life strangled out of it ... We know the drawbacks to militarization: the system does not fit in ... with any of us who have ever had a proper understanding of freedom. But we also know the drawbacks to remaining beyond the purview of the Ministry of War. It pains us to concede the fact, but we have but two options open to us: dissolution of the column or militarization.[17]

To protest, meanwhile, was sometimes added non-compliance – for example, the refusal to wear uniform or to adhere to basic military forms – or, in the most extreme cases, desertion. Though he only turned sixteen on 20 November 1936, Antonio Navarro Velásquez had been at the Aragón front with the Durruti col-umn from the very beginning:

> Militarization arrived. Some of us, the minority, were in favour of it, but the majority were not. Personally, I was against it. Even if we were to win the war, creating an army was to risk everything staying the same as before. Winning the war without making the revolution would be of no benefit to anyone. To see the truth of this one had only to look at Russia: they had kept an army and kept a state alike, and look where that had got her ... There being some discussion of turning guerrillas, several units in the column began to make moves in this direction, and one, the so-called 'Black Band' actually set off for enemy territory to engage in a sabotage

mission. However, those who wanted an army won out, and so, in January or February 1937, I left the front.[18]

To a degree, then, some material can be found that seems to substantiate the arguments of the critics of militarization. However, it is important to note that all the evidence that can be put forward in this respect comes from the ranks of the militants, the latter being implicitly assumed to stand proxy for the whole of the Spanish people. To accept this last, however, is to fall into the trap of believing that in city and countryside alike, the lower classes were united in a passion for revolution. This is certainly the picture that emerges from George Orwell's famous depiction of the Barcelona that he found when he arrived in the city in January 1937, but, in fact, nothing could be further from the truth.[19] As the thoughtful and reflective José Martín Blásquez argued, the population of the Republican zone could be divided into a minority of militants who were in favour of one form or other of the socialization of society, and the rest, an enormous mass of people who knew little about politics, and, indeed, were but little engaged with politics. The majority of the first group having rushed to do battle with the enemy in 1936 and in many cases paid the price, what was left was a lumpen mass who were Republican only because they happened to find themselves in the Republican zone and had little interest in the result of the struggle either way. If called upon to fight, they would turn out if there was no way to escape such a fate, but neither valour nor vigour were to be sought amongst them.[20] That this was the case, meanwhile, is suggested all too clearly by the fact that even soldiers who might have been expected to be enthusiastic about the fight soon proved to have a strong streak of cynicism. In the Fifth-Regiment unit of Alvaro Cortes Roa, for example, by the end of the battle of Madrid, one of the men's favourite songs was a ditty that went as follows: 'What happens to those who go off to Madrid? They shoot them! And what do we want? That they shoot us too!'[21] Equally, in the British battalion of the International Brigades, by the spring of 1937, the men were singing (to the tune of 'Red River Valley'), 'There's a valley in Spain called Jarama; it's a place that we all know too well. 'Twas there that we spent our young manhood, and most of our old age as well.'[22]

In short, most Republican soldiers did not rush to embrace the war, but rather hoped that it would not embrace them, and, when it did finally catch up with them, they remained aloof from the politics of the moment, whilst doing as little as they could. In consequence, political commissars who engaged in long harangues and staged long political meetings had an effect that was entirely counterproductive. And this was just the soldiers who were politically neutral or in some way vaguely left-wing: with the introduction of conscription, the ranks could not but include men who remained at least culturally Catholic or who disliked the social implications of the revolution (it should be remembered that, for many peasants as opposed to landless labourers, even the reforms of the period 1931–6 had proved problematic, whilst they were now frequently threatened by collectivization to boot, on top of which it has to be recognized that, from the beginning, plenty of men with a questionable political background had joined militias as the best way of ensuring their survival). As in the northern zone, buried in the ranks were not just plenty of soldiers whose dearest wish was for the war to end as quickly as possible and cared little for who actually won, but also more than a few who actually wanted the Nationalists to triumph. To complicate matters, in this 'new' army, there was as yet much reluctance to enforce military discipline in a proper fashion, soldiers who infringed regulations in one way or another being encouraged in their actions by the fact that they knew full well that very little would happen to them, the same thinking also sapping aggression on the battlefield: in the People's Army, the soldiers were most certainly not more afraid of their own officers than they were of the enemy (as they most certainly were: believing, as many did, that falling into the hands of the enemy meant a firing squad if they were lucky, and the knives of the Moors if they were not, to say that the soldiers were inclined to err on the side of caution is an understatement).[23] At all events, foreign observers were often exasperated in the extreme. In May 1937, for example, a Polish agent of the Comintern named Wlodzimierz Poplawski sent a damning report to Moscow with regard to the People's Army:

> The Spanish soldier is usually a bad soldier, and one who participates in the war in a most unwilling manner. Does he march to the attack? Not a bit of it. Instead, by necessity of course, he limits himself to manning trenches. As a result almost all the attacks which have supposedly covered the Republican army with glory have been the work of the International Brigades ... For all practical purposes, it is these units that are waging the war.[24]

Here, too, is Jason Gurney on a Spanish unit he encountered during the battle of Jarama:

> Every Spanish unit I had [anything] to do with appeared to be devoid of any military sense These were men of the Lister Brigade [i.e. I Mixed Brigade] which was built up from the old Fifth Regiment which fought with such fantastic courage ... in Madrid ... In spite of ... this, they looked and acted less like soldiers than any other bunch of fighting men I had ever seen. They lay around the olive grove in a haphazard way with their rifles discarded beside them on the ground. Nobody seemed to be in charge of anything or to care very much what happened.[25]

For many soldiers, then, life in the army was about nothing more than doing the absolute minimum and staying alive, but there were plenty who went well beyond this and actively sought a way out, and all the more so as life at the front was at best dreary and at worst marked by extreme privation: soldiers might spend months living in rat-infested trenches and dug-outs without proper food and clothing or even systems of regular reliefs. As Gurney wrote of his experiences in the wake of the battle of the Jarama, 'For the majority of the battalion, life was becoming very hard indeed, as month after month dragged by with no prospect of leave or any break in the dreariness, the dirt and the scarcity of food ... It began to seem that we would sit up there in the dirt and stink of the Jarama trenches until we were gradually whittled away without having achieved anything at all.'[26] At the same time, every soldier was all too well aware that in the rear, there were plenty of men who had used political connections to secure cushy billets or were otherwise having an easy war; as Joan de Milany, a young Catalan aviator who had volunteered to train as a pilot as a means of escaping Anarchist-dominated Catalonia and Aragón, wrote of the air force, for example:

> In the course of the war the air arm attained a strength of some 20,000 men, but very few of these were aircrew, and only a minority even of these men actually served at the front. If we say that there were around 200 pilots employed in combat positions at any given time, it was therefore the case that for every authentic combatant, there were 100 men who wore the wings of a flyer whilst yet experiencing far less danger. So many of these last were there, and so ostentatiously did they strut about the place, that the friction between the pilots who did the fighting and those who did no more than fly a desk reached the gravest of levels.[27]

Pay, too, was often wildly in arrears, while, deeply aware of the rising cost of living, soldiers worried about their loved ones.[28] For obvious reasons, then, getting away was very important, a favourite trick being to 'get lost' while undertaking some errand to the rear.[29] Self-inflicted wounds, too, were not uncommon, whilst a rather less unpleasant way of getting to hospital was seeking to become infected with venereal disease, an easy enough task given the number of prostitutes clustering in villages behind the front lines and working the bars and streets of all the major towns and cities.[30] More drastic a remedy, of course, was desertion, sometimes to the enemy, though much more usually to the home front.[31]

Perhaps all this can be taken too far. Even amongst the most miserable conscripts, there were men who were dimly aware that an enemy victory could not but be disadvantageous to ordinary people, just as men who had felt the full weight of the Nationalist war-machine in the fighting in the autumn for the most part regarded the formation of the People's Army as a cause for celebration. Amongst such men, perhaps, was the veteran of the Durruti column, Joaquín Masjuán, who was clearly converted to the idea of a regular army by his traumatic experiences in the University City, for in December 1936, he applied for a place on a sergeants' training course at the Fifth Regiment's 'People's School of War', and, having graduated, secured a transfer to Enrique Lister's I Mixed Brigade.[32] Equally, it took no more than a day or two of fighting at the Alto de León to persuade an earlier recruit to the Fifth Regiment that learning the rudiments of soldiering was a necessity: 'We had not taken San Rafael. We had not cut the road to the Alto de León, the object of our operation. We had wasted an opportunity to force the enemy to retreat from the proximity of Madrid. The only thing we had done was to learn a lesson, and I, for one, had learned it very well.'[33]

Yet herein lies the rub. If the experiences of the International Brigades – supposedly the very cream of the Republican army – are anything to go by, the level of training was abysmal. Having escaped Málaga on a British ship, in the autumn of 1937, Laurie Lee returned to Spain to fight, only to discover that the army he was joining was amateurish in the extreme:

> An official ... asked me my name and my next of kin and wrote down my answers in a child's exercise book ... Next he gave me ... a forage cap with a tassel and said, 'You are now in the Republican army' ... The next morning ... scattered committees ... began to gather in the courtyard ... By majority votes it was agreed we should have some exercise and drill. Somebody blew on a bugle. Men sauntered out on to the parade ground and ... then marched up and down, shouting orders at each other, forming threes and fours, falling over, falling out, standing still, arguing, and finally parading past the commandant from several different directions, while he stood on a chair saluting ... We finished the day's training with an elaborate anti-tank exercise. A man covered a pram with an oil cloth and pushed it round and round the square while we stood in doorways and threw bottles and bricks at it. The man pushing the pram ... was cross when a bottle hit him.[34]

One could continue in this vein *ad infinitum*: miracle though it was that it had been got together at all, the People's Army was deeply flawed. More to the point, on most levels it remained deeply inferior to its Nationalist opponents. Turning our attention to them, we discover that, counting the 50,000 Moors and the 35,000 Italians of the CTV, by the spring of 1937, Franco had perhaps 200,000 men at his disposal.[35] As in the Republican zone, there had been an initial burst of volunteering that probably produced some 50,000 men all told, but conscription had come into operation at a much earlier date, and regular battalions of the old army were therefore coming to fill a larger and larger proportion of the Nationalist order of battle. In the rebel zone as much as the government one, then, there were large numbers of men who did not want to be fighting or, still worse, found themselves fighting for a cause that they despised. Nor was this last situation just the fruit of conscription: as repression took hold in the insurgent zone, so thousands of men took refuge from a suspect past by volunteering to fight for Franco, favoured destinations in this respect being a Falange keen to embrace the workers and a Foreign Legion that had always prided itself on providing a means for criminals, however defined, to redeem themselves.[36] In the Nationalist army, however, the impact of this situation was far less severe. There were 'reluctant warriors' aplenty, and, like their Republican counterparts, they used every trick in the book to improve their lot and avoid excessive danger, yet the very different ethos of Franco's Spain meant that such activity could not be pushed nearly as far: in extreme cases, to have done so would have literally been a death sentence. At the same time, there was less to complain about – life at the front was no more pleasant for Nationalist troops than it was for Republican ones, but pay, if lower, was more regular, whilst there was much more in the way of clothing, food and other comforts[37] – and less to desert to: the more it became apparent that the Nationalists were winning the war, the less sense it made to cross the lines.[38] And, finally, Nationalist troops were much better commanded: large numbers of officers had to be improvised, certainly, but it was necessary to have a certain level of education to obtain access to the training programmes, whilst the fact that the insurrection had gained the support of the majority of officers of junior and middling rank meant that the new arrivals were not thrust into higher posts overnight. Particularly important here was the Condor Legion. Whilst its combat personnel were limited to its aircrew and the crews of its seven anti-aircraft batteries, it also featured a training element divided into Gruppe Dröhne and Gruppe Imker, of which the first handled tanks and armoured vehicles and the second such matters as engineering, signals and infantry and artillery tactics. Under the supervision of General Wilhelm von Thoma, officer training schools were established at Avila, Granada and Pamplona, as well as centres specializing in tanks and anti-tank guns, artillery, mortars, infantry tactics and chemical warfare, the number of Spaniards who eventually passed through the training courses on offer being some 56,000.[39] Finally, as well as staffing the three training schools mentioned here, German instructors appear to have been seconded to individual battalions deemed to be in need of some assistance. To quote one Irish volunteer, 'We went into intensive training: from dawn to dusk we were legging around like mad. Many of us had had some kind of military training at home … but this made it all the worse, since we had to unlearn all we knew and knuckle under to everything the German instructors said … To complain was useless because these Nazis were out to show us who was boss.'[40]

As we have seen in the case of the Republican soldier, an important means of retaining the confidence of the fighting man was providing him with decent weaponry, and here, the insurgents again did much better. For the most part, the weapons supplied to the Nationalist army were little different from those supplied to its Republican counterpart in that they came from exactly the same generation of armaments. If not armed with the 7mm Mauser M1893 of the pre-war army, then, the Nationalist infantryman was armed with either the German 7.92mm Mauser M98 or M98K or the Italian Mannlicher-Carcano 6.5mm M1891. Equally, setting aside the Hotchkiss and Trapote machine-guns in use in the Spanish army in 1936, fire support came from the German Maxim MG08, MG08/15 and MG13 or the Italian Fiat-Revelli 6.5mm M14, Fiat-Revelli 8mm M1935, Breda 6.5mm M1930 or Breda 8mm M1937, the Italians also sending a little over 1,000 French Saint Etiennes and Austrian Schwarzloses. That said, there were some key differences. Not all of these weapons were especially good

– as we have seen, both the Saint Etiennes and the Italian machine-guns suffered from some appalling design faults – but they were in general in a much better state than their counterparts in the Republican army and also came with plentiful supplies of ammunition, the result being that, when a Nationalist soldier pointed his weapon at the enemy, he could generally count on it to work and not have to worry about where the next box of cartridges was going to come from. At the same time, he might well be encouraged by the immense quantity of booty taken from the enemy, one list of captures taken by May 1937 alone speaking of 110 tanks and armoured cars, 119 artillery pieces, 1,831 heavy machine-guns, 1,658 light machine-guns, twenty-four mortars and 17,043 rifles.[41] On such details does the confidence of an army rest more than almost anything else, and here there is no doubt that the Nationalists always had the edge.[42]

Also very heartening to the Nationalist army was the quality of its artillery and aerial support. As 1937 wore on, so the arrival of both more aircraft and better aircraft – one thinks here, especially, of the Messerschmitt Me109 fighter and the Heinkel He111 bomber, but the Italians sent some Fiat BR20 and Savoia-Marchetti SM79 bombers and Breda BA65 ground-attack aircraft – meant that the sky began more and more to belong to the Nationalists.[43] At the same time, the simple fact that they got more guns (though not that many more guns: according to the figures usually quoted, the balance in favour of the Nationalists was only about 500 – in other words, perhaps 25 per cent) and, above all, more ammunition, also tipped the artillery battle in their favour.[44] Here again, however, the issue was not the quality of the individual pieces. With the exception of the extraordinary 88mm FLAK18 and such modern anti-tank weapons as the 37mm PAK36, the artillery that appeared was that of the First World War, but, again, standards of maintenance were higher, whilst the pieces were for the most part taken from standard stock and fully supplied with ammunition and spare parts. Held back at divisional level and above, the Nationalist artillery could also be used more effectively in that its fire was more concentrated and easier to direct. Tanks, too, were better used, and, for the most part, more aggressively used, than was the case on the other side – here, at least, the opinion of the German instructors dispatched with the Condor Legion appears to have been decisive[45] – while one also sees the improved co-ordination between ground forces and air support that was one of the chief hall-marks of the *blitzkrieg* tactics that served the German army so well at the start of the Second World War.[46] Given the fact that scarce resources – above all, the tiny handful of guns heavier than 150mm – were regularly shifted from front to front in accordance with strategic need rather than being held back to protect one politically privileged area or another, Nationalist troops could generally feel that orders to take a given objective did not constitute a suicide mission.[47]

As the above comment with respect to the Nationalist artillery has already implied, the Nationalist army was also aided by its superior organization. Although it took some time for Franco's forces to develop a full pyramid of brigades, divisions, corps and field armies, this can be seen in embryonic form as early as the battle of Madrid and was in full operation by the end of 1937. Setting aside the obvious point of difference – the fact that in the Nationalist army, brigades consisted of infantry battalions and cavalry squadrons only, assisted on occasion by an attached anti-tank battery – the most interesting issue here is the very different form that was given to the Nationalist order of battle in political terms. In the Republican army, the needs of the moment at the time of their formation had led to many mixed brigades, and, in some cases, divisions, acquiring an identity that was very distinct: the Twenty-Ninth Division, for example, was a POUM formation, just as the Forty-Fifth Division was a Communist one. The result of this, of course, was bitter rivalries and jealousies of all sorts as well as much fear and distrust when it came to the execution of operational plans. Under Franco, however, the situation was very different, in that brigades tended to be of very mixed composition, with, for example, one battalion of regular infantry, one of Falangists, one of Carlists and one of Moors. Partly the product of political considerations – the need, first, to ensure that the Falangists and Carlists were never able to field substantial masses of troops that could take the credit for particular battles or even stage a coup, and, second, to watch over battalions of potentially unreliable volunteers and conscripts – this also served a solid military purpose, in that it was hoped that it would foster a sense of unity and encourage a spirit of co-operation, qualities that were at least in theory institutionalized when the Falange and the Carlists were unified as the Falange Española Tradicionalista y de las Juntas de Ofensiva Nacional-Sindicalistas in April 1937.[48]

At the mention of this development, we must needs pause and consider the political situation that had developed in Nationalist Spain. Ever since the collapse of the CEDA in the wake of the elections of February 1936, the politics of the Spanish Right had revolved around two movements, namely the Falange Española y de las Juntas de Ofensiva Nacional-Sindicalistas of José Antonio Primo de Rivera and the Carlist Comunión Tradicionalista. In theory, the two were separated by a massive ideological divide – in principle, the Falange was a fascist movement bent on the destruction of the old order and the modernization of the Spanish state, and the Comunión Tradicionalista a conservative one devoted to preserving the values and society of the past – and at the level of the leadership, there was bitter rivalry, with each side professing to despise the other and aspiring to a position of hegemony. Yet even by the time that the Civil War had broken out, the ideological differences between the two had been massively eroded, and this process had since progressed still further. In brief, then, the failure of Gil Robles' parliamentarian strategy had led the Right to embrace the cause of revolt, but in doing so it had acted more or less indiscriminately, flooding the ranks of the Falange and the Carlists alike without much in the way of consideration for their political principles or the sort of Spain that they theoretically stood for, what mattered being (in the case of Carlism especially) family traditions, local political allegiances and perceptions of both the local and national leadership. In consequence, July 1936 found the two movements much grown in size but also much diluted in ideological commitment, and in the wake of the uprising, this situation was enhanced still further by the rush of all and sundry in Nationalist Spain to demonstrate their political conformity and secure the patronage and protection of the only political organizations that had survived the coup. To quote a founder member of the women's branch of the Falange, for example, 'In the weeks between the eighteenth of July and the end of August, the Falange opened wide its arms and gates, in a gesture poorly understood and worse utilized. The absence of the best leaders and the lack of political sense of others permitted the party of José Antonio to be infiltrated by all sorts of people look-ing for shelter: those who had never joined anything, those who had never risked their skin, throwing the rock but hiding their hand, those who had much to hide, the saboteurs, even those of opposing ideas. This mass corrupted the essence of the Falange, and the few remaining idealists were overwhelmed.'[49] At base could be discerned certain echoes of the past – middle-class families that had remained devout Catholics were likely to be Carlist, for example, just as those that had moved in a more secular direction were likely to be Falangist – but that was about all. Meanwhile, if its rank and file had been transformed, the Falange in particular had suffered grievous losses at the level of the leadership. Rounded up en masse in the spring of 1936 and, to their misfortune, confined in loyalist Alicante rather than, say, Seville or Burgos, Primo de Rivera and most of his closest collaborators were out of action, while many other 'old shirts', as they were known, were either quickly arrested (for example, Ramiro Ledesma Ramos) or killed in the fighting (for example, Onésimo Redondo).[50] Somewhat more fortunate in respect of their own militants though they were, the Carlists, meanwhile, suffered an additional blow in that their chief ally amongst the generals was the now-dead José Sanjurjo.[51]

From the beginning, then, the Carlists and Falangists were operating at a grave disadvantage and all the more so as many of the new leaders who came to the fore were mediocre figures of limited grasp or talent, the prime example here being the new leader of the Falange, Manuel Hedilla, a man who is often somewhat unkindly described as a mechanic (in fact, he was a trained engi-neer, albeit one whom personal misfortune and the economic difficulties of the inter-war years had denied the professional opportunities to which he might have aspired). Also a problem was bitter personal rivalry: as someone who was convinced that the movement should reach out to the proletariat in the manner that had been espoused by Primo de Rivera, Hedilla was opposed by a variety of powerful provincial satraps who conceived of fascism in much more conservative terms, whilst the Secretary General of the Comunión Tradicionalista, Manuel Fal Conde, Fal Conde, an Andalusian, was regarded as an upstart by the leader-ship of the traditional Carlist heartland of Navarre. The net result, of course, was that neither the Falangists nor the Carlists could do anything to check the man-ner in which their militias were incorporated into the ranks of the Nationalist army, let alone resist the *de facto* coup that made Franco not just commander in chief but also head of state, the realities of the situation being driven home still further when Fal Conde, was exiled to Lisbon in December 1936 following an abortive attempt to establish an independent Carlist military academy.[52]

By the end of 1936, then, the potential for political disunity in Nationalist Spain had already been much reduced, a further factor here, as we have seen, being the collective responsibility imposed by the *limpieza*. For Franco, however, this was not enough. Profoundly suspicious of any threat to his authority whatsoever, he was therefore soon moving in the direction of the imposition of an even tighter measure of political control, and all the more so as, neutered though they were, both the Falange and the Comunión Tradicionalista had thrown themselves into the task of melding their masses of new recruits into vibrant party organizations with branches in every town and city in Nationalist Spain. In doing so, however, Franco realized that he could not simply proceed by main force, what we rather see being a process of 'divide and rule.' Thus, if the Carlists found themselves held at arm's length and even subjected to bullying and harassment, in a number of speeches, the *generalísimo* appeared to align himself very closely with the twenty-seven points of the fundamental charter of the Falange Española y de las Juntas de Ofensiva Nacional-Sindicalistas whilst at the same time elevating the conveniently deceased José Antonio Primo de Rivera to the status of a secular saint. Behind the scenes, meanwhile, intensive negotiations were undertaken with the leadership of the two movements, which secured the acquiescence of such figures as Fal Conde's replacement, the Conde de Rodezno, for the formation of a single political movement. The *dénouement*, then, was not long in coming, and on 19 April 1937, Franco was able to announce the unification of all the political forces in Nationalist Spain into the single Falange Española Tradicionalista y de las Juntas de Ofensiva Nacional-Sindicalistas. Needless to say, this was not at all to the taste of either Fal Conde or Hedilla, but the former was still in exile while the latter's efforts to mobilize his followers in opposition to the decree led to his immediate arrest and, not just that, but the passage of a death sentence, commuted though this was to life imprisonment, Franco having belatedly recognized that to shoot Hedilla was to risk uproar.[53]

The decree of unification never quite produced the monolithic political unity at which it aimed: allowed to return from exile in October 1937, for example, Fal Conde fought a long and unsuccessful battle to protect the property of the Comunión Tradicionalista from being appropriated by the new party and to maintain some degree of autonomous political organization, but open disputes were kept to a minimum and serious challenges to Franco's leadership avoided. In the long term, this was, of course, a huge advantage, but for the time being, the situation in the Nationalist camp remained anything but perfect: indeed, an offensive that was launched in the Sierra Morena by Queipo de Llano in the midst of the battle of Guadalajara in an attempt to relieve a force of Civil Guards that had declared for the rising and barricaded itself in a remote mountain-top monastery deep inside Republican territory called Santa María de la Cabeza was repelled with heavy losses (the force that Queipo de Llano had been trying to rescue was overwhelmed at the beginning of May).[54] Yet, all in all, one is forced to the conclusion that the Nationalists had in general coped much better with the task of improvising a war effort than their Republican opponents. Circumstances were against the latter, certainly, but, even so, grievous errors were made that were now to be put to the test in the most brutal fashion.

Thus, in strategic terms, by the spring of 1937, it had long since become quite clear that the war could not be won by the efforts of the Spanish Republic alone, not least because the international situation was such that it could not possibly build up the three-fold superiority in men and *matériel* that the First World War had suggested was the minimum needed to secure an offensive victory. In this situation, there was but one way forward, namely to pursue a strategic defensive until such time as Europe was once again gripped by a general war that would at one and the same time deprive Franco of his chief supply of arms and rescue the Republic from its pariah status. However, tailored though such a strategy was to the Republic's needs – it was both cheap in terms of the resources it required and accommodating in respect of the enormous deficiencies in the Republican war-machine – it was a political impossibility. At bottom, it rested on trading territory for time, but that was simply out of the question when the territory involved included the Socialist stronghold of Bilbao and the iconic mining district of Asturias. Mouthpiece of a Communist Party increasingly opposed to Largo Caballero though she was, Dolores Ibarruri was not just being *parti pris* when she claimed that, when she and the rest of the Communist leadership finally broke with the Prime Minister in May 1937, it was because 'we hoped to turn the steering wheel in the right direction and head north with all the means at the government's disposal to aid the Basque combatants and those in Asturias and Santander.'[55]

Such as they were, then, the Republic could not rest on its laurels. Nor was this just a matter of trying to do something for the Basque country, Santander and Asturias, for the month of May 1937 had been marked by a fresh convulsion in the Republican zone. The story of this affair has been told many times, and so no attempt will be made to do so here other than in outline. In brief, over the winter, the fault lines already apparent in the Republican camp had intensified dramatically, and there were now two camps who were bitterly opposed to one another, although both of these were shot through with differences of their own. By the end of 1936, the revolution was much curbed, New Castile and the Levant having in large part been forced to accept the authority of the government and allow their militias to be incorporated in the Popular Army. Meanwhile, in Catalonia, too, the Generalitat had to a large part ended the situation of dual power that it had been forced to tolerate since the uprising. In Aragón, especially, however, Anarchism continued to reign unchecked, whilst the Catalan industrial belt remained very much dominated by collectivization. Whilst the Nationalists concentrated on Madrid, this situation could be ignored, but Franco's attack on Vizkaya called forth a response not just from the forces of the capital, but also from those of Catalonia and Aragón. War in the north, in short, meant the final death-knell of the Spanish revolution. To quote Dolores Ibarruri, 'The news arriving from the Basque country and Asturias was alarming. Unless the government radically changed its policies, its localistic military and political approach, a swift defeat was inevitable.'[56] If this comment is rather opaque, the rising star of the Communist war effort, Juan Modesto, makes things quite clear. Complaining that the struggle against Franco was being undermined by 'political problems that should never have been permitted', he continued, 'I am here referring to the tolerance shown by Largo Caballero with respect to the extremists of the FAI and, especially, the manner in which their extra-legal socio-political activities were tolerated and their control-patrols allowed to exercise power in the shadows ... the result of this being that a small group of men who could be counted on the fingers of one hand ... were allowed to impose a reign of terror in the towns and villages of Catalonia and Aragón.'[57] And, if proof of the pudding was needed, there was always the fact that the Aragón front remained completely static. 'Only on the Aragón front did [the Anarchists'] red and black banner wave above some of the combatants ... combatants who never went into battle.'[58] Of course, the revolutionary Left's answer to this was that everything was the fault of the Communists. In the words of the American POUM-ista Lois Orr, 'There have been no ammunition and no guns on this front because the Stalinists are afraid that, if they give them to the Anarchists, they will return to Barcelona when they are through with the fascists and finish making the revolution.'[59]

Yet, whatever the reason, the fact remained that no-one was marching on Zaragoza. As Orr was forced to admit, 'There has been absolutely no action on this front during all the long months since the start of the war.'[60] Nor was Aragón the only chink in the revolution's armour. Also very damaging to them was the fact that the Republic was facing economic disaster. It is but fair to point out that this was not necessarily the fault of collectivisation *per se*, transport difficulties, lack of capital, shortages of fuel and raw materials and lack of skilled management all combining to ensure that the difficulties faced by the revolutionaries were immense. In the case of agriculture, in particular, meanwhile, the weather had been unfavourable and labour badly hit by the imposition of conscription. Yet certain facts cannot be gainsaid. While some collectives flourished, many others did not. To quote POUM volunteer Richard Kisch, 'The real snag about collectivisation in the countryside was that the benefits in terms of conditions of work, freedom of behaviour, communal living and share-outs were not matched by serious economic gains. At no stage did collectives get anywhere near an effective take-off point capable of making them economically viable or establishing a genuinely prosperous agriculture. What was being established, in fact, was the collectivisation of poverty.'[61] By the autumn of 1936, food prices had already risen dramatically, whilst many commodities were in short supply, the inflationary spiral having been worsened still further by the wholesale emission of tokens, vouchers, coupons and paper money of all sorts. Food supplies from Russia helped enormously, but as the months passed, so the situation continued to deteriorate. To quote Franz Borkenau, 'It was a problem to get bread. So it was to get sugar, meat and many other foodstuffs.'[62] Also very difficult was the matter of tobacco. 'I was never so glad I don't smoke as now', mused a virtuous

Lois Orr. 'There is a shortage, and all the people we know spend their time ...
worrying about where [and] how to buy cigarettes.'[63]

Whatever the responsibility of the revolutionary movement may have been,
then, growing economic difficulties were pretext enough for the government
to intensify its offensive. As we have seen, even before the battle of Madrid,
an important goal had been secured in this respect in that the unremitting
Nationalist advance had persuaded the Anarchists to accept two posts in the government, a number that had since been increased to four. Meanwhile, supported
by the Communists and the Republicans, Largo Caballero was able to proceed
with the next step of the counter-revolution. Thus, December saw a general
move to sweep away the revolutionary committees, re-establish the traditional
machinery of government, end the power of the *chekas* and tighten the control of
the Ministry of War over the remaining militias. Whilst the writ of the central
government still did not reach as far as Catalonia, there, too, the revolution was
in full retreat, the PSUC forcing a cabinet reshuffle that led to the exclusion of
the POUM, the abolition of the committees of supply that had hitherto controlled the distribution of food to the populace and an increase in the power of
the Generalitat with regard to both taxation and industry. In Catalonia and the
rest of Republican Spain alike, meanwhile, all attempts at further collectivization
were firmly blocked.[64]

The situation in the Republican zone did not, of course, change overnight.
Many of the revolutionary committees refused to dissolve themselves, just as
many militia columns tried to ignore militarization. Yet the power of the revolutionary left was as clearly on the wane as that of the Communist Party was on the
increase. In this respect, the advantages that the latter had derived from a vigor-
ously counter-revolutionary domestic policy and the arrival of Russian arms had
been swelled by its appropriation of most of the credit for the defence of Madrid.
Needless to say, this brought a flood of fresh recruits, including still more leading
army officers, whilst at the same time exposing the forces of the revolution to
further denigration (it was, for example, claimed that the militias who held the
Aragón front had not lifted a finger to help the capital). Whilst the ground was
being cut from under the feet of the revolution in this fashion, a complex sub-
plot was also beginning to emerge. Thus far, Largo's interests had largely coincided with those of the Communists, but it was not long before a gap had begun
to emerge between the two. Jealous of the Communists' appropriation of the
defence of Madrid, Largo came increasingly to resent the patronizing behaviour
of the Russian military advisers, whilst he was full of resentment at the overthrow
of Asensio Torrado, something else that added fuel to the fire being the constant
complaints that were reaching him to the effect that Communist units were
getting the best of everything when it came to food, clothing and equipment.
Even more alarming, perhaps, was the fact that the Communists were beginning
to attract many converts from the PSOE and its sister organizations and were
pressing for it to merge with the PCE, and still worse that it was clear that many
of his sometime allies within the Socialist party, such as the Foreign Minister,

Julio Alvarez del Vayo, were effectively acting as Communist agents. Eager to do what he could to stem the onward march of the Communists, on 14 April, the Prime Minister therefore published an executive decree that placed control of the whole edifice of the political commissariat under his direct control.[65]

To act in such a fashion was clearly to provoke open warfare in the government, it being precisely through their preponderance among the political commissars that the Communists exercised their growing hegemony in the army. So complex is the situation that now prevailed, however, that it almost defies description. Largo, the Communists, the Esquerra Republican de Catalunya, the right wing of the PSOE and the remnants of left-republicanism were all agreed on the necessity of crushing the revolution, but the first two were bitterly at odds with one another, the third the object of the united dislike of the other four and the fourth at war with the first. In the revolutionary camp, meanwhile, the Anarchists, left-wing Socialists and the POUM were all opposed to the policies of the government and the Generalitat, whilst in many instances loathing each other's blueprint for the new Spain.[66] The *dénouement* is well known. Amidst a climate of increasing tension, the government, the Generalitat and the Communists continued with their efforts to destroy the revolution, and on 3 May 1937, a relatively minor dispute over control of the telephone exchange in Barcelona sparked off the inevitable explosion. Flinging up barricades, large numbers of the CNT and the POUM sprang to arms, there following a confused struggle that eventually cost some 500 lives. Within five days, the rising had been put down, however.[67] With it died the revolution, the last remnants of trade-union power and the militia system now being firmly swept away. Thus, a strict deadline was set for the surrender of all weapons, the control patrols and revolutionary committees were finally dissolved, the revolutionary tribunals were purged and placed under the control of regular judges, the industrial collectives were subjected to tighter control than ever and the last of the militias were turned into regular troops. As Orwell put it, 'The Spanish Republican flag was flying all over Barcelona – the first time I had seen it, I think, except over a fascist trench.'[68]

By the end of May 1937, then, the revolution was dead. Also broken, however, were Largo, the POUM and the Generalitat. Taking Largo first of all, the premier was at loggerheads with his former allies. Determined to break the Communists' control of the army, the Socialist leader had dissolved the Junta of Defence of Madrid and was now again proposing to switch the main Republican military effort to Extremadura, where he hoped to strike west in the direction of Badajoz and Cáceres and cut the Nationalist zone in two, the sub-text here being that such an attack could not but weaken the influence of the pro-Communist Miaja, of whom he was deeply jealous. Hurling the blame for what had happened in Catalonia at Largo, the Communists therefore walked out of the cabinet, though their object in the first instance does not seem to have been to remove the premier from the government altogether but rather to replace him as Minister of National Defence. Their example being followed by virtually all the other ministers apart from the four Anarchists and two loyal Socialists, Largo was placed in an impossible position. For a brief moment, he essayed resistance, but fears of losing Russian aid proved too much, and on 18 May the Socialist leader surrendered, being replaced in the premiership by the erstwhile Minister of Finance, Juan Negrín, and in the Ministry of National Defence by his arch-enemy, Indalecio Prieto.[69]

Turning now to the POUM, the Communists had long since desired its elim-ination, the rising therefore coming as a godsend in that its leaders could be accused of treason. So long as he was Prime Minister, Largo refused to go along with such attacks, but, once he was gone, the POUM's enemies had a free hand. Masterminded by senior representatives of the Comintern and the Soviet secret police, a plot was hatched to prove that the POUM was linked to a Nationalist spy ring that had just been unmasked in Catalonia, whilst the new government was quickly persuaded to make the POUM illegal, order the arrest of its leading militants and place its militias under reliable commanders. Meanwhile, despite efforts on the part of elements of the government, most notably the new Minister of the Interior, Julián Zugazagoitia, to save him, its leading figure, Andrés Nín, was tortured in an effort to get him to admit the ludicrous charges that had been laid against him. Refusing to give way, Nín was eventually killed, the show trial that had been organized to deal with his followers in consequence falling flat (the few men brought to trial were only convicted of rebellion rather than col-laboration with the enemy). Nevertheless, things were quite bad enough, many party militants being either murdered or held in prison for a considerable time.[70]

Last of the casualties of the 'May Days' was the cause of Catalan autonomy. With its territory flooded by police loyal to the Valencia government, the freedom of manoeuvre open to the Generalitat was obviously circumscribed, and all the more so as it was in June remodelled so as to exclude the CNT. Still worse, Companys had been forced to agree that the central government should resume responsibil-ity for defence and public order, the independent army that he had been trying to form henceforth being absorbed into the Popular Army, and, as a new 'Army of the East', placed under the same General Pozas who had previously commanded the Army of the Centre. Meanwhile, of course, the PSUC was also very much in the ascendant. The final seal on the situation was not imposed until the autumn of 1937, when the government moved *en bloc* from Valencia to Barcelona, but the fact was that Catalan autonomy was as dead as the Spanish revolution.[71] Nor is there any reason to be surprised at any of this. Like most Castillian-speakers of whatever shade of opinion, Negrín detested the Catalans. As he told Zugazagoitia in 1938: 'There is only one nation, and that is Spain. Muffled though it now is, the separatist campaign is as persistent as ever, and it is not to be tolerated. If I am to continue … to direct the policy of the government – a policy that is a national one – then it must be torn out at the roots. Nobody is as keen as I am on the distinctive features of their home region – I dearly love those of the Canary Islands, and I not only do not scorn, but actively glory in those of other regions – but Spain must take priority over all these differences.'[72]

So much for a bare outline of the events that took place in the *retaguardia* in the period November 1936–May 1937. What, however, are we to make of them? Whilst the subordination of Carlists, Falangists and Alfonsists alike to the will of General Franco was beneficial to the insurgent cause, the destruction of the revolution is regularly claimed to have sounded the death-knell of the Second Republic in that the people were deprived of the will to resist, and the Popular Army condemned to fight a war that maximized the advantages of its opponents. To say this, however, is to go too far: amongst those Anarchist and POUM supporters who realized what was going on, the Communist moves came as a body blow, but there were plenty of areas in Republican Spain where neither movement had had much support, and plenty of observers, too, with whom they had been very unpopular. However outrageous, then, the stories of a 'fascist plot' were by no means generally dismissed, and it seems entirely probable that the affair quickly receded from the public consciousness. To quote British volunteer James Jump, 'We had heard the word "Trotskyist" many times. It was synonymous with "defeatist" or "fascist." A Trotskyist was one who claimed to be anti-fascist, but, because he did not accept the current political line of the Republican government, was in fact said to be helping Franco by destroying the unity of the Republicans. This logic we accepted, for how were we to know anything different?'[73] As for the idea that enthusiasm for the war was damaged, as there was very little to start with, one may assume that this argument has been overstated.[74] On the other hand, the new régime was clearly faced with a need to restore its credibility, and, coupled with the need to do something about the Northern Front, this persuaded it to take the offensive. Even now, however, Largo Caballero was not to be honoured by acceptance of his very sensible plan for an offensive in Extremadura. On the contrary, the first thought of Negrín and his advisers was rather for an offensive in the direction of Segovia via the only one of the three main passes over the Sierra de Guadarrama to have remained in the hands of the Republic, namely the Puerto de Navacerrada. With Republican troops already holding positions some miles in advance of the summit, this seemed on the surface to be a sensible option, a blow, indeed, at the 'soft under-belly' of Old Castile.[75]

From the very beginning, however, the whole affair proved a grave disappointment. The area that was the immediate target of the attack, the picturesque town of La Granja, with its royal palace and the hills that commanded the place from all sides, were held by no more than a single brigade against which there were deployed two whole divisions and a substantial part of a third, while the attackers could count on fifty pieces of artillery and twenty tanks, not to mention the participation of the XIV International Brigade, and, or so it was supposed, the full support of the Republican squadrons based at Barajas. On top of this, La Granja was not only vulnerable to attack from the south, but also to attack from the east, given that the Republicans held not just the Puerto de Navacerrada but also a more minor crossing of the mountains called the Puerto de Reventón. Yet when the attack began on 30 May, progress was extremely slow and in places absolutely non-existent, whilst matters were not helped by bombs from Russian planes frequently hitting their own troops. One participant was Manuel Tagüeña, a Communist student who had risen to the command of XXX Mixed Brigade: 'I will never forget that dawn. In a single instant the whole outline of Cabeza Lijar was lit up by a gigantic flash and a hail of rifle and machine-gun fire unleashed. The enemy's advanced posts were over-run and fighting reached the very summit, but we were thrown back, only to return to the charge over and over again ... We lost many casualties.'[76] Confined to the main road due to the rocky and heavily forested terrain, the tanks were unable to lend much weight to the attack, whilst the artillery-pieces were too few in number to do much damage to the well-dug-in Nationalists. In consequence, the crucial positions of the Cerro del Puerco, Valsaín and Matabueyes all held firm, while the mountain known as Cabeza Grande was only take after a bitter two-day battle. At length, a handful of Republican troops managed to reach the gardens of the royal palace, but they were quickly expelled, whilst a counterattack delivered by fresh troops rushed up from other sectors of the front also recaptured Cabeza Grande. By 4 June, then, all was quiet, all that the attack had achieved, and then entirely by happenstance, being the death of General Mola, the plane crash in which he was killed on 3 June having occurred in the course of an attempt on his part to fly down from Pamplona to take personal charge of the battle.[77]

If the battle of Segovia showed anything, it was that pin-prick operations launched by small numbers of troops were futile. Within two weeks, however, the government tried again. This time the sector chosen was the Aragón front and, in particular, the northern city of Huesca. The attack being very much a political statement, an augury, indeed, of what the Aragón front would be expected to deliver in the future, troops were brought up from the Madrid front to show the local forces how such things should be done. Involved in the attack, then, were the Forty-Fifth Division of the Hungarian commander, General Lukacz (the Hungarian Communist, Mate Zalka), this consisting at this point of the XII International Brigade, an *ad hoc* Spanish formation and the LXXII Mixed Brigade; and four local divisions, including the wholly POUM Twenty-Ninth Division. Once again, however, the effects were nugatory. This time the air support on offer was more impressive, if not effective, but again there was too little artillery preparation, while the command arrangements were extremely muddled (in this respect, it did not help that Lukacz was killed by a stray shell the night before the battle, nor, still less, that his replacement was the same Manfred Stern – General Kléber – whose achievements in the battle of Madrid had been so much exaggerated). In consequence, when it was launched on 12 June, the attack broke down almost immediately, many units barely leaving their trenches. Fighting continued sporadically till 19 June, when news of the fall of Bilbao led to the battle being called off, but by then, the Republicans had suffered over 1,000 casualties. Indeed, other than temporarily diverting a number of aircraft from the Basque front – the aerial battles over Huesca are generally agreed to have been truly spectacular[78] – the only effect of the battle was to increase the simmering tension in Aragón, a number of clashes having taken place between International Brigaders and erstwhile CNT and POUM militiamen.[79]

This tension was to be worked out in full in the course of the summer, but in the meantime, we must turn our attention to a much bigger operation than either of those that had taken place at La Granja or Huesca. We come here to the battle of Brunete. By far the biggest battle of the conflict thus far, this took place on the rolling plains west of Madrid in the blazing heat of a Castilian summer. Too late to do anything to help Bilbao, the object was now to delay the impending attack on Santander and Asturias. In principle, the idea was simple enough, whilst it was not even new, having already been attempted, albeit with much less in the way of resources, in the failed counterattack of 13 November 1936. Thus, the Nationalist troops holding the trench-lines that snaked from the Cerro de los Angeles through the Casa de Campo and the University City and then lined the highway to La Coruña as far as the village of Las Rozas occupied the leading edge of an immense salient that was perhaps ten miles deep and twenty miles wide. With Madrid no longer the chief target of Franco's attentions, the troops holding the Nationalist lines were stretched thin, and they therefore constituted an obvious target: pinch off the salient, indeed, and Franco would be forced to turn his attentions back to a battleground of the Republicans' choosing (and one, be it said, whose physical proximity to the capital meant that it fitted in very well with the determination of the Communists – always the leading backers of the scheme – to prioritize their political objectives at the expense of virtually every other consideration). In brief, then, what was supposed to happen was that the flanks of the salient would be hit simultaneously by troops driving south from the area of El Escorial and west from the southern reaches of the River Jarama.[80]

In the event, this plan was modified: rather than being launched simultaneously, the two thrusts would rather be delivered sequentially in that the troops mustered for the offensive west of Madrid would strike first, the operation in the southern outskirts of the capital being delayed until such time as the former had reached the important road junction of Navalcarnero (presumably, it was hoped that by the time that Navalcarnero had been taken, the Nationalists would be so preoccupied with the fighting that they would have little left to deal with anything else). Everything, then, depended on the western thrust. Heavily reinforced, this was to be delivered by two entire corps, namely V Corps and XVIII Corps, of which the former was headed by Juan Modesto and the latter by Enrique Jurado Barrio, an artillery officer who had stayed loyal despite strong *africanista* antecedents and played a major role in defeating the uprising in Madrid. Each of these corps, meanwhile, had three divisions, no fewer than four of which – the Eleventh (Lister), Fifteenth (Gal), Thirty-Fifth (Walter) and Forty-Sixth (González) – were billed as shock troops (included in their order of battle was not just Lister's old I Mixed Brigade, but also the XI, XIII and XV International Brigades). Supporting the attack were no fewer than 250 guns and some 170 tanks and armoured cars, by far the largest force of armoured vehicles the Republican had ever assembled, whilst the Madrid area was the base for around 300 aircraft.[81]

Facing these imposing forces, meanwhile, were no more than 3,000 men. Indeed, there was not even a front line properly speaking, but rather simply the loose chain of fortified strong points represented by the villages of Quijorna, Villanueva de la Cañada and Villanueva del Pardillo, each of which was held only by two or three companies of infantry, whilst a few troops were also deployed on the summit of a low rise called Llanos. Still worse, most of the defenders were Falangist militia, the only decent troops in the whole area being a single battalion of Tiradores de Ifni (Moorish infantrymen who, prior to July 1936, had served as the garrison of the tiny Spanish enclave of Ifni in the south-west of present-day Morocco), whilst the whole area was overlooked by the Republican positions, clinging, as these did, to the foothills of the Sierra de Guadarrama. When the attack went in at dawn on 6 July, it should therefore have been overwhelmingly successful, and at first all did, indeed, seem to go smoothly enough. Lacking in firepower, Rojo had eschewed any form of preliminary bombardment – something that was to be a feature of all five of the great Republic offensives launched between July 1937 and January 1939 – and plumped instead for a silent approach that sought to outflank the scattered enemy positions and insert large forces of troops deep inside enemy territory under cover of darkness.[82] Still only eighteen, Joaquín Masjuán was with the leading elements of I Mixed Brigade:

> Surprise was total. The enemy not having realised that his front had been broken, our forces were able to get through it without difficulty. On our right was the village of Quijorna and on our left that of Villanueva de la Cañada, the two of them being separated by a gap of approximately four kilometres. The terrain was dusty, arid and covered in scrub ... In the distance we could see a large farm-house: from it there came the sound of a dog barking, and this caused us to send a patrol to check it out. Coming to a run-down small-holding, I gathered up a large number of tomatoes ... but nobody wanted any, so I ate the whole lot myself ... By-and-by, we began to hear the sound of a tremendous battle that appeared to have broken out around the villages that we had flanked in the course of our march ... By contrast, we kept going in the most perfect tranquillity ... Rather than a military operation, it was more like a pleasant stroll in the country.[83]

Very quickly, however, the battle developed into something much more dramatic than Masjuán's pleasant ramble. By the midday, the leading troops had taken the village of Brunete, which fell without much in the way of resistance, but closer to the old front line, real problems were developing in that the grievous faults in the People's Army's leadership and training were becoming cruelly apparent.[84] Coming under fire from the tiny garrisons of the three front-line villages, many soldiers took cover and refused to advance any further, while their officers showed a woeful lack of initiative and enterprise, the whole plan in consequence starting to stagnate. As cautious as ever, meanwhile, the tanks and armoured cars hung back, restricting themselves to firing at the enemy positions from long range. Watching the scene from the rear was Fred Thomas, a Londoner serving with XV International Brigade's anti-tank battery:

> Seven a.m. On top of the world ... Down in the plain are villages held by the fascists, and these our side has got to take. From just behind us our artillery is blowing hell out of the villages. This is big stuff shaking the ground: villages are on fire. Eight a.m: moved up another half mile; from here we have an almost bird's-eye view. Immediately in front of our sector is a village ... Villanueva de la Cañada, a mile or away, which our troops are attacking ... About twenty-five of our tanks are closing in on the village. Our artillery has stopped. Troops can be seen behind the tanks ... Horrible sight watching one ... go up in flames; I hope the occupants were killed first. Nine a.m: our artillery starting up again; tanks holding back a bit; can see smoke and hear firing from villages to right and left. Twelve noon: village not yet taken apparently ... We are still waiting for orders.[85]

Given that Villanueva de la Cañada was held by nothing more than an incomplete battalion of Falangist militia, two anti-tank guns and two 75mm field guns, this performance was hardly inspiring. Afterwards, Lister was particularly hard on the use made of the tanks. In his words, 'The manner in which the tanks and armoured cars was used could not have been more lamentable. For all its ... strength and capacity for manoeuvre, the force which they represented ... was employed in the most foolish of manners: there is no other word for it. They were just thrown straight at the guns, when beyond them stretched ground which offered the most wonderful opportunities to armoured forces.'[86] On one level, this is true enough, but the fact is that the bulk of the Republican infantry were so poor that without armoured support, they could not be relied on to make head against determined opposition. Walter Gregory was with the British battalion:

> We swung round towards our objective, Villanueva de la Cañada ... First we had to isolate the village by cutting off the road on its southern side to prevent a relief column making an unwelcome arrival on the scene and restrict the possibility of enemy troops escaping ... With the road cut, we began a cautious advance towards the village itself ... As we drew closer we were subjected to a murderous hail of machine-gun fire ... I threw myself into a road-side ditch and began to crawl on all fours towards the village ... It was the very devil fighting in that heat with no protection from the sun's searing rays. Accurate shooting was impossible because everything was shimmering ... All day we stayed in that ditch, ducking down low whenever a machine-gun swung in our direction and sprayed us with bullets, popping up as soon as it had traversed away and firing back with every weapon at our disposal. It was an awfully long day.[87]

Gregory and his comrades were beyond doubt very brave, but this was no way to win a battle: apart from anything else, with the tank crews understandably extremely concerned by the increasing modern number of anti-tank guns with which the Nationalists were equipped, they could hardly be expected to move in to finish the job from close quarters.[88] In addition, the idea that the Republicans were wildly outgunned by the enemy was one that was deeply ingrained. Milt Fersen, for example, was a New York Jew who had come to Spain to fight in the Abraham Lincoln Battalion:

> High, very high, invisible in the shimmering sky, German bombers circled at their leisure and dropped sticks of bombs that made the earth leap and tremble. Each soldier, lying helpless on the ground, could hear the scream of the bomb as it fell and knew that it was aimed at the very centre of the small of his back. When ... the explosion came, it made a sound we had never heard before, ear-splitting and totally terrifying ... 'Where the hell are our fighter planes?' came a wistful complaint. Where indeed? We would discover that for every plane of ours, the fascists had fifty. For the three 75mm guns in the John-Brown battery, the other side had a hundred, and the same for tanks and supplies and manpower.[89]

As a result of such factors, although they were completely surrounded, the three villages were able to hold out for far longer than had been expected – Villanueva de la Cañada was taken on 7 July, but Quijorna continued to resist until 9 July and Villanueva del Pardillo for a day longer still – whilst Republican attempts to expand the breakthrough by capturing positions such as Villafranca del Castillo and Boadilla del Monte were uniformly unsuccessful. Amongst the men deployed against the latter was Joaquín Masjuán:

> The next day, 7 July, we ... were sent towards Boadilla del Monte to help the International Brigades. About twenty of our planes flew past overhead on their way to bomb the place, while we advanced under a blazing sun along rough tracks that led us through scrubby pinewoods ... Under heavy fire all the way, we got as far as the town's cemetery, but, such was the strength of the resistance that we encountered there, that we had to give up ... That being the case, we dug in and spent the night in the open, watched over by our sentries.[90]

Finally, though Lister and his men could literally see Navalcarnero, they did not dare advance any further for fear that they would end up being cut off. Though the Communist commander is very obviously a partisan voice, his general conclusions cannot really be questioned:

> 11 Division occupied Brunete at six o'clock in the morning on 6 July. A single battalion continued on to Sevilla la Nueva and one company even

got as far as the outskirts of Navalcarnero. The enemy front was broken, and our forces more than ten kilometres inside their lines. What would have been the right thing to do in this situation? Surround Villanueva de la Cañada with one brigade and Quijorna with another and send all the rest of the forces of V Corps through the gap opened by 11 Divison … What actually happened? For the whole day of 6 July, 34 Division did nothing but launch frontal attacks on Villanueva de la Cañada, losing many men and ten tanks in the process … Two desperate days passed by … I begged for reinforcements … until I was utterly frantic, but not a word did I get in response, and yet all that time … men and resources were being thrown away in stupid frontal attacks.[91]

Within a matter of days, then, the offensive had broken down. By their heroic resistance, meanwhile, the front-line positions had bought time for the arrival of fresh troops to be rushed up from elsewhere, including the northern front, where Franco was forced to delay his attack on Santander for two weeks. By the time of the first anniversary of the uprising on 18 July, the Nationalist forces, now swelled to five divisions and two independent brigades, were counterattacking in an attempt to win back all the territory that had been won. Included among the new arrivals were many Moors and Foreign Legionaries. In the face of this onslaught, the Republicans resisted with considerable determination, and the fighting was so intense that even on the Nationalist side of the lines, the tension was stretched to breaking point: at one point, indeed, a furious row broke out between a Yagüe desperate for reinforcements and a Franco insistent that he should fight to the end with what he had.[92] Yet such were the forces deployed against them that the Republicans were pushed back until all that was left in their hands to mark their initial success was Quijorna, Villanueva de la Cañada and Villanueva de Pardillo. Though wounded in the arm earlier in the battle, Walter Gregory had returned to the fighting line: 'Although we had support from Soviet-made tanks and, at least for the first few days, the Republican air force … the battalion received a terrible battering. The suffering from the heat and thirst was dreadful … Day after day the sun beat remorselessly down, the dust clutched at our throats, the flies drove us wild, and our losses crept inexorably upwards.'[93] By the time fighting came to an end on 25 July, over 20,000 men had been killed or wounded, whilst losses in terms of aircraft were probably around fifty (in this respect, the fact that the fighter pilots of the Condor Legion were now fully equipped with the Messerschmitt Me109 was decisive, the Nationalists, by contrast, losing just seventeen aircraft).[94]

A triumph for Franco in every respect, the battle of Brunete was followed by further victories in Santander. A deeply conservative province with only a limited amount of heavy industry and a rural populace that was better off than its counterparts in many other areas, Santander had not shown much vigour since the start of the uprising, and its defenders were low in morale – many of the troops who had escaped from Vizcaya no longer wished to fight at all, believing that, with Euzkadi gone, the civil war no longer had anything to do with them – and holding positions whose fortifications were rudimentary in the extreme. As had been the case in the Basque provinces, meanwhile, air and artillery support alike were extremely limited. Facing this pitiful array, meanwhile, were the battle-hardened Brigades of Navarre, together with some additional Spanish troops and the whole of a CTV that had been purged of its more unreliable elements and was now much better trained and organized than it had been at Málaga and Guadalajara. Hardly had the attack begun on 14 August, then, than resistance collapsed. Here and there, there was fierce fighting, but within three days, the Nationalist forces had taken the main passes of the Cantabrian mountains and were heading for the city of Santander itself, leaving thousands of Republican troops trapped in their wake. With the roads clogged with refugees, many other units were over-run as they struggled to escape westwards to Asturias, while the Basque-nationalist elements of the Eusko Gudaraostea abandoned the front and decamped to the town of Santoña, from whence its leaders attempted to make such terms as they could with the Italians in the hope that they could get a better deal from them than they would be able to from the Nationalist army. Meanwhile, there were desperate scenes in Santander as thousands of people attempted to secure places on boats or ships that might take them to France, while the Basque government, the revolutionary authorities in Santander and the chief military commanders all managed to get away by plane or submarine. Finally, on 26 August, the Nationalist forces marched into the capital, where they appear to have received a welcome that was probably more sincere than that which they had got in many other towns and cities. In prisoners alone, the Republican loss came to 45,000 men, while Nationalist casualties were extremely limited: according to the Carlist, Carmelo Revilla Cebrecos, for example, the Tercio de Lacar had only lost nine dead and thirty-six wounded.[95]

Just as one battle was ending, so another was beginning, this time on the Aragón front. Once again, the aim was to buy time for the defenders of the northern zone, but in massing troops to attack Zaragoza, there was also a hidden agenda in that the Negrín government and its Communist backers were determined to break the hold of the Anarchists on the area, what this meant above all being to break up the council that the latter had set up to co-ordinate all the collectives that had been established in the wake of the advance of the militias the previous year, and to get rid of Joaquín Ascaso, the tough and brutal FAI militant who had emerged as the most dominant personality in the region. Also doomed was the whole principle of collectivization: allowed to survive for a little longer so as to ensure that the harvest was brought in, this, too, was to be smashed. With troops designated the Army of Manoeuvre pouring into the region from the Madrid front, including the whole of Modesto's Communist-dominated V Corps, all this was easy enough: the Council of Aragón was dissolved, Ascaso and at least 600 other militants arrested, and many collectives restored to their original owners, the only ones that were allowed to survive being those which could demonstrate that force had played no part in their establishment. With Anarchist power in Barcelona already broken by the May Days, the Spanish revolution was finally at an end.[96]

Before a shot had been fired, then, the Negrín government had secured a major political victory. However, winning a military victory was to prove far more difficult. By the beginning of the third week of August, the whole of the Army of the East and the Army of Manoeuvre – some 80,000 men or about the same number as those employed at Brunete[97] – were ready to go into action, but the attack was spread over a much wider front – attacks went in from Jaca in the north to Caudé in the south – while there were fewer tanks and aircraft. Backed by even less weight of fire than the Nationalists had faced the previous month and struggling to contend with the same intense heat that had marked the battle of Brunete, every single Republican advance had soon broken down, whilst the front-line village of Belchite, a few miles south of Zaragoza, witnessed an epic struggle that was an exact repeat of those seen at Quijorna, Villanueva de la Cañada and Villafranca del Castillo. Except among the more ideologically motivated units, there was once again a great deal of evidence that the troops were lacking in enthusiasm for the struggle: fighting as a runner near Codo, for example, Esteban Biescas Palacio saw large numbers of Republicans flee in panic from a single Nationalist armoured lorry that had been sent from Belchite to reinforce the defenders (just half a battalion of Carlists).[98] Meanwhile, an initial British assault on a hill near Quinto called the Cerro del Purburrell was repelled with heavy losses:

> Expecting little resistance, the British battalion began its ascent of the steep hillside, only to be met by a murderous machine-gun fire ... Our commander, Peter Daly, was wounded in the opening moments of our initial attack and later died of his injuries ... Those of us fortunate enough to have survived the first onslaught sought what protection we could as, throughout a long, hot, bloody day, we waited for the sun to go down and the arrival of darkness to shield our retreat from those bullet-swept slopes. Many died before nightfall gave us the protection we so desperately needed to fall back and regroup.[99]

Gradually, however, the Republicans made progress: the Cerro del Purburrell, for example, was taken the next day after the British battalion took the precaution of using its anti-tank guns to smash many enemy positions before they went into the advance.[100] Yet in Belchite, 'progress' was a question of taking a single room here, a single bunker there, a single cellar somewhere else. Inside the town were some 3,000 men plus another 2,000 civilians, all the males amongst the latter eventually being pressed into service to help with the defence. Ordered to hold on to the end, the defenders put up a desperate fight amidst scenes of the utmost horror. Joaquín Moreno Miranda, for example, was a Falangist volunteer from Zaragoza:

Against a wall, miraculously still on his feet ... was the body of my good friend, Fernando. Hung up like a joint of meat, his face was slack, his eyes starting from their sockets. Recognise him though I did, there was nothing for it but to keep going: there was simply no way I could have stopped to recover his remains ... Meanwhile, the war went on creating fresh victims ... On 3 September, a Galician soldier, another good friend, a pleasant and agreeable chap, ended up like a puppet that had been pinned to a wall when a mortar that he had been crewing blew up and sent a large piece of the barrel straight through his head. Around the base-plate various other corpses were left sprawling, including that of the mayor ... My distress was such that I just didn't have the tears to express it.[101]

Another of the defenders was Angel Artigas, an eleven-year-old boy who was first put to building barricades and carrying messages, but ended up helping to man a field-gun at the Puerta del Pozo:

Every day the enemy came closer ... There were days on which the town was bombarded several times over ... Soon we were fighting house-to-house ... The very buildings were crashing around our ears. You would throw yourself in a doorway and the walls would come down on all sides ... If you weren't on the ball, you would get squashed flat ... Very often one floor of a building would be held by one side while the one above was controlled by the other ... When they reached our barricades, they went down like flies. At night it was even worse. The Nationalist soldiers attacked with white rags tied round their arms. If they came across anyone who didn't have such an armband, the fellow got a bayonet in the guts before he could even open his mouth.[102]

Frantic efforts to re-supply the defenders by air notwithstanding, Belchite fell on 6 September after the last survivors of the garrison had made a desperate attempt at a break-out that saw a handful of them, including Joaquín Moreno Miranda, got back to the Nationalist front line. Also taken were the villages of Codo and Quinto. Lluis Puig Casas was a devoutly Catholic travelling sales-man from Terrassa who had been conscripted in the summer of 1937 and was now serving in the signals section of an infantry battalion in CXLIII Brigade, 44 Division:

Quinto came into view ... We shuddered as we saw innumerable corpses, semi-decomposed and abandoned, which gave off an unbearably putrid stench ... No more than a few dozen houses could still be of any use ... We could hear the pitiful howling of dogs calling their masters ... We went into the houses ... and saw ... trunks, chests of drawers and shelves all turned upside down ... You cannot imagine how terrible a war is until you have seen what I saw with my own eyes.[103]

In the wake of these successes, the darkest side of the civil war yet again raised its head. In the Republican zone, the efforts of the authorities to put an end to the revolution had brought in their train an end to the terror: after December 1936, the vast majority of those executed were not 'fascists' but rather dissident Republicans. Yet the capture of large numbers of prisoners gave rise to scenes that were the equal of anything produced in Nationalist Spain:

> When the Republican soldiers finally took control of the town [i.e. Belchite], they ... flushed us all out and then marched us all over to Codo ... On our arrival ... a crowd of militiamen ... took us into some olive groves. After a while, several men appeared and began to pick out any-body who had been a soldier. Pretty soon they had ... about 400 men ... Falangists, *requetés*, one or two Civil Guards. Seeing what was about to happen, one of the prisoners took to his heels. Immediately the guards opened fire on him, but he managed to cover a clear kilometre before he was finally brought down ... His body was left where it had fallen. And not just his: having set up some machine-guns, the guards then proceeded to shoot all the others. Some while later, a convoy of lorries turned up and took us off in the direction of Alcániz. At one of the villages on the way, another selection was made, and a whole lot more people were shot.[104]

However, if the Republicans had no difficulty shooting prisoners, once again attempts to push on beyond the initial objectives came to naught:

> At five o'clock on the dot our artillery began to fire at the enemy posi-tions. ... The machine-guns began crackling. Our soldiers came out from the trenches and within a few moments enemy mortar bombs were rain-ing down on them. It was impossible to move as the ground was covered with corpses. The company commanders ordered a retreat. The tanks fled because they were under constant fire from the Nationalist anti-tank guns ... The attack had failed. We could hear cries of victory ... The Nationalist air force appeared. Three squadrons of Junkers could be seen. Overcome with panic we all took to the shelters ... Moments later a series of heavy bombs fell around us. The whole shelter shook and with every bomb that fell our hearts jumped ... Next to me was a good companion from Mataró called Coma. He was frail and at every bomb that fell he went into a state of panic, and ... would grab me, saying, 'Puig! I can't breathe. I need air! I am dying!'[105]

By 6 September, the battle was over. In the front line, the men who had bypassed such strong points as Belchite and Codo had managed to beat off the enemy counterattacks that had repeatedly assailed them, but this was at best an empty achievement. Republican casualties were once again very heavy, whilst even less had been achieved than at Brunete, in that 1 September had seen the troops that had just over-run Santander go into action against Oviedo: some planes had temporarily been transferred to the Aragón front, but that was all.[106] To make matters worse, meanwhile, there was much muttering to the effect that the offensive had failed because the Anarchist units involved had failed to pull their weight or had even collaborated with the enemy.[107] With the Nationalists soon making steady progress, it became imperative to renew the battle, and on 10 October, a desperate attempt was made to break through to Zaragoza. For this new attack, the spot chosen was Fuentes de Ebro, a small village on the front line just south of the Ebro, whilst some effort was made to find a solution to the problems that usually beset Republican attacks. In brief, a new battalion of fifty Russian tanks of a new model – the BT5, a 'cruiser' design intended for fast-moving deep-penetration style operations rather than the infantry-support work that was the intended role of the T26[108] – had just arrived in the area. Taking advantage of this piece of luck, Pozas ordered the battalion to load a number of infantrymen on each tank and charge straight at the enemy lines. Supporting the attack, meanwhile, would be elements of the XV International Brigade, including the newly arrived Canadian Mackenzie-Papineau battalion. However, the results were disappointing in the extreme. To quote Lluis Puig Casas once more:

> [The attack] started at twelve noon on the dot. Once the artillery had prepared the ground, all our tanks moved in. They advanced together in groups of five, and headed for the Nationalist trenches; in all, there were forty of them. Later we learned that they were powerful Russian tanks called BT5s ... On each tank there was a group of infantrymen riding it as if it were a bus, but they were an easy target and the enemy weapons picked them off one-by-one ... The enemy batteries were spitting shells non-stop ... Some tanks got stuck, but others kept on going ... They destroyed the barbed-wire entanglements and made their way to ... the trenches. At that moment Franco's troops came out ... throwing powerful hand-grenades. It was such an unequal battle: steel monsters fighting against men! However, our infantry ... did not come out of their trenches and the tanks were left defenceless, and ... had no alternative other than to retreat, leaving about twenty of their number in the hands of the enemy.[109]

Ridiculous almost beyond belief, this attack did not deserve to succeed. Delivered, as it was, in broad daylight, there was no chance of achieving surprise. The unfortunate 'tank-riders' had never been trained in the role they were supposed to undertake – did not, in fact, know anything about it until the tanks turned up – whilst the tank crews were as much in the dark as they were. The tanks offered few places to sit or even hold on, and many men were therefore thrown off, in many cases being crushed under the tracks of vehicles coming on behind. There was almost nothing in the way of artillery support, just two batteries of 75mm guns with a very limited supply of ammunition. The Spanish mixed brigade that was supposed to follow immediately in the rear of the attack was notoriously unreliable. And, finally, no chance having been given them to reconnoitre the approaches to the enemy lines, the tank crews found that they were expected to cross an area criss-crossed with numerous drainage ditches and, still worse, barred by a steep ledge some twelve feet high.[110]

Launched on 13 October as it was, the attack at Fuentes de Ebro also came too late to attain its object. Even had a breakthrough been obtained, Zaragoza could not possibly have fallen for some days, and yet the Asturian front was on the brink of collapse. With the fall of Santander, which incidentally had cost the Asturians fourteen of the twenty-seven infantry battalions that they had sent to the aid of the neighbouring province, the defending forces had sunk into defeatism. As Cabezas put it, 'The [defending] army no longer lacked arms, but it lacked discipline and suffered from a surfeit of politics ... To reach Gijón, true, there were many mountains to climb, many rivers to wade, but the superiority of the enemy forces, supported as they were by a powerful aviation, was all too evident.'[111] Meanwhile, to hold the line, there were but 40,000 men. To make matters worse, when the Nationalists attacked, they chose to do so not along the obvious axis of attack afforded by the coastal plain, but rather through the mountains to the south, the net result being that the defenders were thrown into complete confusion. All the time, meanwhile, the Condor Legion, the Legionary Aviation and the Nationalist air force pounded the beleaguered Republicans' lines of communication: 'All troop movements ... had to be made by night because during the day the roads were bombed and strafed ... At Posadas, at Poo, at Celorio, the author had on many occasions to abandon his car to save himself from the enemy's machine-guns.'[112]

Needless to say, the defenders had little in the way of air cover themselves. One of the few fighter pilots operating in the region was Francisco Tarazona Torán, a young Valencian who had joined the air force and been selected for pilot training in the Soviet Union. Now in the cockpit of an I16, he and a group of other pilots had volunteered to take their planes and attempt to reach Asturias from the airfield at Alcalá de Henares. Hazardous a flight though this was, Tarazona survived, only to find himself plunged into a battle that could not have been more one-sided:

> Every day the enemy gets closer to Gijón ... Our missions are becoming ever more frequent and that despite that fact that our fighting force is becoming ever more feeble: sixteen, fourteen, sometimes ten planes only ... We are on the brink of complete exhaustion ... Every day one of us goes down ... The enemy can put twenty planes in the air for every one of ours, and that is probably putting the figure too low ... Nobody talks about the disaster that is approaching: we have been forbidden to speak of defeat and are optimists perforce.[113]

Despite the Nationalist air superiority, aided by the constant rain of the Cantabrian autumn, for some weeks the defenders put up a good fight. On 14 September, for example, the Tercio de Lacar was ordered to assault a rocky ridge in the Sierra de Mazuco:

> Commanded by Major Luciano, the battalion advanced with its third and fourth companies deployed as a vanguard ... Such was the volume of fire that it had hardly left its positions before it started to suffer casualties. Immediately, the two companies out in front were reinforced by a section of the first company, but Luciano quickly saw that the men in the front line were too few to launch an assault by themselves, and all the more so as they were not only being fired at from in front but also ... from the right flank. That being the case, he ordered the entire battalion to advance as one ... The assault that followed being extremely dashing, very soon the enemy positions were being attacked with bayonets and hand-grenades.[114]

The end came on 15 October, when troops who had fought their way into the province from the east finally made contact with Aranda's forces in the vicinity of Oviedo. To quote Cabezas again, 'All the rest was nothing more than running up and down mountains in an attempt to keep ahead of the enemy.'[115] As had been the case in Santander, there was a desperate rush for the coast, and all who could left by boat, or in the case of a few senior commanders, by plane. At Gijón, of course, the situation was one of complete disintegration: 'Everyone, men, women, children, soldiers were in a panic, pushing and fighting their way to the quayside ... In the port everyone was trying to get onto a little coal ship ... What with the general panic and people screaming that the fascists were coming, things were out of control ... Some people were trying to climb up the sides and ... falling in the water. It was sickening.'[116] Many got away, but many did not, and when the Nationalists marched into Gijón on 21 October, there was the usual round of arrests and executions, whilst the town was badly sacked and many women raped.[117]

Other than a few thousand men who tried to carry on a guerrilla war in the mountains and were gradually whittled away by betrayal, hunger, disease and police action, the war in the north was over, while in the rest of the Republican zone, the People's Army was counting the cost of a succession of offensives that had achieved very little other than to squander precious resources of men and *materiel*.[118] Hardly surprisingly, the fall of Gijón also gave rise to a fresh burst of intrigue and recrimination: obsessed with the idea of Asturias as a bastion of the proletariat and eager to deflect any blame from themselves, the Communists discovered another 'spy-ring', those accused this time being not the POUM but rather Generals Asensio Torrado, Martínez Cabrera and Martínez Monje, all of whom had been prominent under Largo Caballero, only for the case against the three men to have to be abandoned for want of evidence.[119] In Madrid, a Mikhail Koltsov coming to the end of his time in Spain, looked round his hotel bedroom and spouted defiance: 'A year ago the cannons of world fascism were directed against these walls. They killed but they did not conquer. Madrid ... did not surrender, is not surrendering now and will not surrender in the future.'[120] Brave words, perhaps, but many such brave words had been uttered since Koltsov arrived in Madrid, and the truth was that the outlook for the Republic was no better in November 1937 than it had been in November 1936.

Notes

1 Alpert, *Republican Army*, pp. 126–44. In fairness, some of the militia commanders were very good, Alpert singling out Juan Modesto and Manuel Tagüeña for particular praise in this respect, whilst giving only slightly less credit to the Anarchist Ciprano Mera. One figure who was distinctly dubious, by contrast, was the Communist-backed Valentín González: universally known by the nickname El Campesino, he was an avid self-publicist, whose contribution on the battlefield was frequently dogged by accusations of incompetence and cowardice.

2 J. Matthews, *Reluctant Warriors: Republican Popular Army and Nationalist Army Conscripts in the Spanish Civil War, 1936–1939* (Oxford, 2012), p. 26. Conscription had actually been introduced as early as September 1936 with the mobilization of the 1932 and 1933 year-groups, but professed Anarchists were initially allowed to join militia columns. Thomas, *Spanish Civil War*, p. 433.

3 Thomas, *Spanish Civil War*, pp. 542, 781.

4 Borkenau, *Spanish Cockpit*, pp. 173–4. Difficulties of supply of all sorts ensured that the People's Army was never fit for the parade ground. To quote the American volunteer John Tisa, 'You can easily go mad trying to pick two identical Republican uniforms.' Tisa, *Recalling the Good Fight*, p. 112. Meanwhile, Orwell provides an excellent description: 'I have spoken of the militia "uniform" which probably gives a wrong impression. It was not exactly a uniform. Perhaps a 'multi-form' would be a better name for it. Everyone's clothes followed the same general plan, but they were never quite the same in any two cases. Practically everyone in the army wore corduroy knee-breeches but there the uniformity ended. Some wore puttees, others corduroy gaiters, others leather leggings or high boots. Everyone wore a zipper jacket, but some of the jackets were of leather [and] others of wool. The kinds of cap were about as numerous as their wearers. It was usual to adorn the front of your cap with a party badge and in addition every man wore a red or red-and-black handkerchief round his throat. A militia column at that time was an extraordinary-looking rabble.' Orwell, *Homage to Catalonia*, pp. 6–7. By far the best modern guide to the uniforms and equipment of the Republican forces is F. Flores Pazos and R. Recio Cardona, *Ejército Popular Republicano, 1936–1939: uniformes y pertrechos* (Madrid, 1997).

5 On the level of the individual soldier, there were still enormous deficiencies. As George Orwell complained, 'We had no tin hats, no bayonets, hardly any revolvers or pistols, and not more than one bomb between five or ten men. The bomb in use at this time was a frightful object known as the FAI bomb, it having been produced by the Anarchists in the early days of the war. It [worked] on the principle of a Mills bomb, but the lever was held down not by a pin, but a piece of tape. You broke the tape and then got rid of the bomb with the utmost possible speed: it was said ... that they were impartial – they killed the man they were thrown at and the man who threw them.' Orwell, *Homage to Catalonia*, pp. 34–5. That said, according to an estimate made by the French military *attaché*, by March 1937, fully two-thirds of the infantry were armed with Spanish or Mexican Mauser rifles or one variant or another of the Russian Moisin-Nagant. Thomas, *Spanish Civil War*, p. 548.

6 Amongst all the leftovers from 1914–21, a few new types of weapon turned up that had not been seen in the first consignments of armaments. Most important here was the 45mm M1932 anti-tank gun, which we first saw being used in action at the battle of the Jarama: the standard Russian anti-tank gun of the first part of the Second

World War, this was by far the best such gun of its day. One point to take into consideration with regard to the weapons dispatched from Russia was that the capacity of the Communist régime to supply Spain with modern weapons has been greatly over-stated: the new weapons starting to reach the Russian army were certainly better than most of what was sent to the Republic, but Stalin also needed to think of the enormous needs of his own army and air force, whilst by 1937 Soviet industrial production was being badly hit by the impact of, first, the Great Purge, and, second, the ongoing moves to relocate heavy industry in Siberia. Graham, *Spanish Republic at War*, p. 321.

7 With regard to Mexican aid, the initial shipment of 20,000 rifles and 8,000,000 cartridges was followed by two further shipments totalling fifty-one pieces of artillery, 165 machine-guns, forty-four trench mortars, eighty submachineguns and 17,000 rifles, though the first of these was captured in its entirety by the Nationalists when the ship carrying it was seized in the Bay of Biscay. See J. Lezamiz, 'La conección mejicana: armas y alimentos para la República', *Revista electrónica iberoamericana*, IX, No. 1 (January, 2015), pp. 1–18. For Polish arms deliveries to the Republic, see Howson, *Arms for Spain*, pp. 260–75. In terms of quantity, by the time that shipments ceased in September 1937, the figures appear to have been considerable: sixty-four tanks, 294 artillery pieces, 700 heavy machine-guns, 7,500 light machine-guns, 109,000 rifles and carbines, 250 mortars. Just as happy to participate in the bonanza, meanwhile, were dictatorships in Finland and Estonia and a number of South American states, shipments of arms appearing from, amongst others, Bolivia, Paraguay and Argentina.

8 Thomas, *Spanish Civil War*, pp. 979–82. In fairness, very considerable efforts were made to produce arms and ammunition in the Republican zone: by early 1937, a hitherto wholly non-existent Catalan armaments industry was producing 500,000 rifle cartridges per day, whilst Catalan factories also managed to turn out Mauser rifles, a completely new model of submachinegun called the Labora-Fontbernat and even a number of I15 fighters, though it is probable that, of the 300 planes that were ordered, no more than 151 were delivered to the Republican airforce, all the rest remaining incomplete on account of the failure of the engines to arrive from Russia. In Valencia, meanwhile, a modern armoured car known as the UNL 35 was manufactured from January 1937 onwards, albeit at the glacial rate of five vehicles a month, as well as a copy of the Soviet BA6 and another submachinegun – the 9mm Naranjero M1938. Hand-grenades, too, were a major product, the most common being the same Lafitte that had equipped the pre-war army, together with newly developed models known as the Sifón and the Castillo. For all this, see Molina Franco and Manrique García, *Armas y uniformes* pp. 162–201 *passim*. That said, there were often complaints about the quality of the bullets that emerged from the factories and workshops in Barcelona and elsewhere: elaborated on the basis of spent cartridge cases collected up in the trenches by young volunteers, many of them female, they were notorious for their unreliability. See Cortes Roa, *Tanquista*, p. 68.

9 One of the persistent myths of the Spanish Civil War is that the Republicans were constantly outnumbered in the air. Whilst the Nationalists generally achieved local superiority thanks to the continued division of the Republic's territory into two different zones and an on-going tendency to spread those planes that were available out to cover as much of the front as possible, the actual number of planes sent to Spain from abroad was not dissimilar: up until March 1937, then, both sides had received some 450 planes, while from then until July the Republicans got 231 planes and the Nationalists only 144. To some extent, the resultant discrepancy was made up by much higher Republican losses but, even so, at the time of the battle of Brunete, the Republicans could put 377 planes in the air as opposed to only 351 on the part of the Nationalists. Permuy López, *Aviación en la Guerra Civil Española*, pp. 149–50.

10 If the index of Catalan industrial production for January 1936 is taken as 100, by December 1936, it was down to sixty-nine and by December 1937 fifty-eight.

There are no figures later than September 1938, but at that point it had dropped to thirty-three, a rate of decline roughly twice that experienced the previous year. Thomas, *Spanish Civil War*, p. 973.

11 Alpert, 'Spanish Civil War and the Mediterranean', pp. 155–62; J. M. Campo Rizo, 'El Mediterráneo: campo de batalla de la Guerra Civil Española: la intervención naval italiana – una primera aproximación documental', *Cuadernos de Historia Contemporánea*, XIX (1997), pp. 55–87. For the travails of the Republican navy, see Thomas, *Spanish Civil War*, p. 549.

12 V. Richards, *Lessons of the Spanish Revolution* (London, 1972), pp. 42–3.

13 Cit. Horn, *Letters from Barcelona*, p. 127.

14 Borkenau, *Spanish Cockpit*, p. 176. See also Orwell, *Homage to Catalonia*, p. 118.

15 Curiously enough, even some volunteers to the International Brigades were also less than enthused by the process to which they, too, were subjected. As one early English volunteer put it, 'Oswald [his company commander] seems to think this is a capitalist army, trying to make everyone jump up and salute or something ... I came out here to fight bleedin' fascism: I didn't come to have a soldier made out of me.' Romilly, *Boadilla*, pp. 136, 164. Still more explicit was an American: 'Jesus! They told me this was a revolution, but it's nothing but a f★★★★★★ war!' Cit. ibid., p. 137.

16 Cit. Cervera Gil, *Ya sabes mi paradero*, p. 91.

17 Cit. Manzanera, *The Iron Column*, pp. 24–5. According to the admittedly hostile account of Martín Blásquez, some elements of the Iron Column refused to accept the decree and had to be suppressed in a shoot-out with loyal troops at the village of Chantada. Martín Blásquez, *I Helped to Build an Army*, pp. 323–4.

18 Cit. Camps and Olcina, *Les milícies catalanes al front d'Aragó*, p. 277. Whether militarization sapped the fighting spirit of the Republic in the manner that is often claimed is hard to say. However, what is true is that the Republican camp became gripped by a mood of cynicism that became ever more apparent. Here, for example, is Rafael Miralles Bravo: 'In response to the growing indifference ... the PSUC began an unprecedented campaign to obtain recruits ... On every side one saw posters encouraging men to come forward, the slogans that these employed being picturesque in the extreme ... Yet all these appeals were in vain, and the party ... therefore had to order its local branches to oblige the many *emboscados* contained in their ranks to sign up. The number of such men was far greater than expected, but, even so, in order to mount the parade of 10,000 volunteers which the party had decided to hold on 14 April 1937, it had no option but to call large numbers of combatants back from the front and disguise them as civilians who had just come forward in response to its appeals ... When these 'volunteers' were sent back to the front the day after the parade, we were left with only a few hundred men, almost all of whom ... had already seen service on the Aragón front.' Miralles Bravo, *Memorias*, pp. 85–6. Meanwhile, Miralles Bravo was himself no longer much inclined to risk his neck at the front, and in the summer of 1937, he duly obtained a position in one of the Republic's many new military academies. As he wrote, 'Thus it was that I became one more of the thousands of officers of the Popular Army who were holed up on the home front ... In contrast to what had happened in the first months of the war when everybody had been fighting to get a place at the front, most people were now using every scrap of influence they possessed to secure a cushy billet in the rear. As for me – I confess it quite sincerely – I could not bring myself to be an exception to something that was becoming a general rule.' Ibid., p. 122.

19 Plenty of eyewitnesses can be found whose accounts are very different from that of Orwell, but, for a sustained critique of *Homage to Catalonia*, see P. Preston, 'Lights and shadows in George Orwell's *Homage to Catalonia*', *Bulletin of Spanish Studies*, XCV, Nos. 1–2 (October, 2017), pp. 1–29.

20 Martín Blásquez, *I Helped to Build an Army*, pp. 348–9. Corroboration of this point can be found in the diary of Franz Borkenau. Thus, 'The large majority of the Spanish peasants are poor, and they are used to regarding the landowner, the police,

the troops and even the priests as their natural enemies against whom they now seek shelter behind the lines of the Republican army. But at the same time these peasants have given very few volunteers indeed to the government troops ... They know from what to flee, but they hardly know for what to fight. The insurgents would take much from them, but the Republic has given them nothing substantial. Their attitude is in accordance with this situation.' Borkenau, *Spanish Cockpit*, p. 206.

21 Cortes Roa, *Tanquista*, p. 117.

22 Gurney, *Crusade in Spain*, p. 150. By 1938, disillusionment had gone beyond the mocking. Here, for example, is John Bassett on his first encounter with the British battalion: 'They were ... very cynical ... All their idealism had gone ... One afternoon ... a sleek Spanish captain ... summoned us to an *hora política*. Nobody was interested and after an argument he forced us all downstairs at the point of his gun. We sat sullenly in the shade of some olive trees while a Spanish Commissar read an article from *Frente Rojo*, a badly printed paper that was always pretending that the Republic was winning on all fronts, even when retreating. After the interpreter had made translations in four or five languages, questions were invited. The British gave one concerted roar; "When are we going home?"' Cit. P. Toynbee (ed.), *The Distant Drum: Reflections on the Spanish Civil War* (London, 1976), pp. 134–5.

23 For some interesting discussions of these problems, see Thomas, *Spanish Civil War*, p. 543; Matthews, *Reluctant Warriors*, pp. 140–2, 151–2. An added problem that resulted from the general slovenliness and inattention to duty was that weapons and equipment were frequently poorly maintained and therefore much given to malfunctioning or breaking down.

24 M. Requena Gallego and M. Eiroa (eds.), *Al lado del gobierno republicano: los brigadistas de Europa del este en la Guerra Civil Española* (Cuenca, 2009), p. 102.

25 Gurney, *Crusade in Spain*, p. 115. Also worth quoting here is George Orwell on his experiences in the POUM's Lenin barracks in Barcelona: 'The whole barracks was in the state of filth and chaos to which the militia reduced every building they occupied ... In every corner you came upon piles of smashed furniture, broken saddles, brass cavalry helmets, empty sabre-scabbards and decaying food ... The Spaniards are good at many things, but they are not good at making war. All foreigners alike are appalled by their inefficiency, above all their maddening unpunctuality.' Orwell, *Homage to Catalonia*, pp. 6, 11.

26 Gurney, *Crusade in Spain*, pp. 140–2.

27 J. Milany, *Aviador de la República* (Barcelona, 1971), p. 126.

28 For all this, see Matthews, *Reluctant Warriors*, pp. 159–64.

29 E.g. ibid., p. 154.

30 Ibid., p. 157.

31 Ibid., pp. 187–9. Desertion was not just a problem among conscript troops. In XV International Brigade, the long period spent in the cold and dirt of the trenches in the wake of the battle of Jarama without any sort of respite, let alone leave, led to a number of men sneaking off to Madrid for a few nights or even seeking to escape the war altogether. Gurmey, *Crusade in Spain*, p. 141.

32 Max, *Memorias de un revolucionario*, pp. 48–51.

33 Cortes Roa, *Tanquista*, p. 18.

34 L. Lee, *A Moment of War* (London, 1991), pp. 23–43 *passim*. Detailed accounts of the sort of training that was received in Spanish units are fairly infrequent, but it can be presumed that George Orwell's experiences in the POUM in early 1937 are far from unrepresentative: 'We were taught nothing about the use of weapons. The so-called instruction was simply parade-ground drill of the most antiquated, stupid kind: right turn, left turn, about turn ... and all the rest of that useless nonsense which I had learned when I was fifteen years old.' Orwell, *Homage to Catalonia*, p. 8. In fairness, some accounts are less scathing. An International Brigader from Liverpool, for example, Robert Clark writes that by the time he went to the front in the summer of 1937, the draft of recruits he was with was 'fairly proficient' in the

use of machine-gun, rifle and hand-grenade, and that he himself had been through an intensive training course designed to produce competent corporals and sergeants. R. Clark, *No Boots to my Feet* (Shelton, 1982), pp. 28, 32.

35 Providing almost no ground troops as they did, the Germans of the Condor Legion are not included here. However, by this stage, Franco had acquired the services of several thousand miscellaneous foreign volunteers. Of these, the largest group were the 1,000 Portuguese, the majority of them poverty-stricken landless labourers who were recruited to fight in an independent Portuguese unit called the Legion of Viriato but ended up being sent into the ranks of the Foreign Legion. Otherwise, the numbers were relatively small: a grandiose endeavour on the part of the Croix de Feu to form a 'Legion of Joan of Arc' ended up producing precisely sixty-seven recruits who were again sent into the Legion. Nevertheless, foreigners were not uncommon: Russian exiles came in some numbers, while there were individual adventurers, soldiers of fortune and anti-Communists from many different countries, including a handful from Britain, two of whom – Frank Thomas and Peter Kemp – we have already met. Finally, the winter of 1936 had seen the arrival of an Irish battalion that had been organized by the Irish fascist leader Eoin O'Duffy, but this proved so shambolic an outfit that it was withdrawn from the front within weeks of its arrival and sent home. For all this, see J. Keene, *Fighting for Franco: International Volunteers in Nationalist Spain during the Spanish Civil War, 1936–1939* (Leicester, 2001). One Italian volunteer who made his way to Spain independently was Alfredo Roncuzzi, a devout Catholic from Rome who was persuaded to enlist with the Nationalists for religious reasons and ended up in the Carlist militia. See A. Roncuzzi, *La otra frontera: un requeté italiano de la España en lucha* (Madrid, 1982), pp. 18–19.

36 To give credit where credit is due, the Nationalists generally honoured the bargain implicit in these arrangements: men who had joined up voluntarily, conformed to the social and religious norms of Nationalist Spain and showed themselves to be willing to serve the cause were, if carefully monitored, left alone, whilst they appear to have been able to count on the support of their officers if their families ever came under threat on the home front. See Matthews, *Reluctant Warriors*, pp. 146–9. For a wider discussion involving such issues as surveillance, see the same author's '"Our Red soldiers": the Nationalist army's management of its left-wing conscripts in the Spanish Civil War, 1936–1939', *Journal of Contemporary History*, XLV, No. 2 (April, 2010), pp. 344–63.

37 The subject of the uniforms of the Nationalist army has been the victim of a degree of political misrepresentation. In works such as J.M. Bueno, *Uniformes militares de la Guerra Civil Española* (Madrid, 1997), Nationalist soldiers are invariably shown looking extremely spick and span in parade-ground style uniforms (their Republican opponents, by contrast, come over as being at best raffish and, at worst, ruffianly). However, photographic evidence provides us with a very different picture, with officers and men alike wearing a wide range of clothing. Also telling is some of the memoir material. For example, here is Seamus Mackee, a veteran of O'Duffy's Irish battalion: 'Some time after we got to Cáceres we were given uniforms – and our *bandera* was a sight to see! Shoddy blouses, various kinds and shapes of trousers ... A more ill-equipped, slovenly gang it would be hard to imagine!' S. Mackee, *I was a Franco Soldier* (London, 1938), p. 17.

38 That said, there were still occasional revolts, Frank Thomas recounting an incident in the battle of the Jarama in which three conscripts from the Canary Islands overpowered the other two members of their squad and forced them to cross the lines with them at gun-point. Thomas, 'Spanish *legionario*', pp. 100–1.

39 Whealey, *Hitler and Spain*, p. 102; Proctor, *Hitler's Luftwaffe in the Spanish Civil War*, p. 51. It was not just German training that boosted the Nationalist cause behind the scenes. Also important was the excellent communications equipment supplied by the Nazi régime.

40 Mackee, *I was a Franco Soldier*, pp. 16–17.

41 Bolín, *Spain: the Vital Years*, pp. 350–1.

42 As more and more Republican weapons fell into their hands, so the Nationalists pressed a great deal of it into service. For example, eventually posted to a machine-gun company in the Foreign Legion, Peter Kemp found himself commanding eight Russian Maxim M1910s. However, they appear to have been quite selective in this respect, only making use of weapons that were in good condition and could be assimilated into their armoury with relative ease (although there are some surprises here: it seems that the Saint Etienne and Chauchat machine-guns, both of them weapons with a terrible reputation, were taken into service in large numbers). What is also clear, meanwhile, is that many such weapons went to second-line troops or units deployed on the more inactive fronts. Finally, to correct one claim that is often made, one weapon that does not appear to have put in an appearance, except in very small numbers for the purpose of evaluation only, was the famous German MG34.

43 According to Thomas, by May 1937, there were approximately 300 Russian aircraft in Spain and a somewhat larger number of German and Italian ones. Given that the Messerschmitt 109 – the one plane that could consistently outperform the I15 and I16 – never became the mainstay of the Nationalist fighter force, it is probable that the steady decline in the performance of the Republican air force from this time on was the result of the fact that the well-trained Russian pilots who done most of the fighting hitherto were increasingly replaced by hastily trained Spanish flyers (trained in Russia, the consensus is that the men concerned were not selected rigor-ously enough, and, further, that the courses they were sent on were too intensive). Thomas, *Spanish Civil War*, p. 678; Alpert, 'Clash of Spanish armies', p. 350.

44 According to the figures quoted by Hugh Thomas, the Nationalists got approxi-mately 2,000 artillery pieces as opposed to the Republicans' 1,550; Thomas, *Spanish Civil War*, p. 985.However, this data is in other respects clearly completely wrong: it is, for example, difficult to believe that the Republicans received 900 tanks and armoured cars. For more up-to-date figures, please see Appendices 1–3, these sug-gesting that in reality the Republic was only outclassed in numerical terms in the air. However, the whole area is the subject of bitter debate, with broadly pro-Nationalist historians such as Pérez-Mortera posing angry challenges to the minimal figures for aid to the Republic given by Howson's *Arms for Spain*. For the conflict between Pérez-Mortera and Howson, see < http://www.sbhac.net/Republica/Fuerzas/Armas/Polemica/Polemica.htm >.

45 As Michael Alpert has pointed out, in the German army, rapid strides were already being made towards the concept of *blitzkrieg* in 1936, whereas in the Russian army experimentation with such techniques was at an early stage at that point, and was in general characterized by much muddle and confusion. See Alpert, 'Clash of Spanish armies', pp. 349–50. Here it is worth noting that the quality of Nationalist tank units was steadily improved by the impressment of captured Republican vehicles: by the end of the war, each company of fifteen tanks had two sections of Panzer Is and one of T26s or BT5s. At the same time, a small number of the former were given extended turrets mounting Italian Breda 20mm cannon. Zaloga, *Spanish Civil War Tanks*, pp. 30–2.

46 On the Republican side, by contrast, there was little liaison between the army and the air force, whilst it has also been argued that the increasing quality of Nationalist anti-aircraft fire tended more and more to discourage low-level ground-support missions. See Alpert, 'Clash of Spanish armies', pp. 342–3, 350.

47 If this was true enough, the constant use of certain units – initially, the columns of the Army of Africa, but later the Brigades of Navarre – as shock troops came at a certain cost. To quote Frank Thomas, 'I had come to Spain willing to expect fair risk of death or serious injury, but this permanent use of the *bandera* as shock troops converted the risk into certain death which I was not prepared to accept. For national or even strong political motives, yes, but for love of adventure at four *pesetas*

a day? No!' Thomas, 'Spanish *legionario*', p. 121. A further issue that Thomas felt strongly about was that the heavy casualties meant that the quality of the officers he had served under had declined significantly, too many of them now being somewhat inferior products of the metropolitan army. Ibid., p. 120.

48 The Nationalist army was by no means free of tensions. Brawls between rival units were not uncommon, whilst there was a considerable amount of jeering: the Carlist militia, for example, were referred to as 'tomatoes' on account of their red berets, but they turned this around by referring to the green-bereted Alfonsine-monarchist militia (a comparatively small force that is rarely mentioned in accounts of the war) as 'green tomatoes', i.e. fruit that were basically fine, but still needed to mature a little. See Mackee, *I was a Franco Soldier*, pp. 18–19; Roncuzzi, *La otra frontera*, p. 42. Yet brawls between groups of soldiers from different units are a common feature of life in every army, and there were simply not enough committed militants of the various pre-1936 parties and movements for ideological division to be a factor of any significance.

49 Cit. S. G. Payne, *Fascism in Spain, 1923–1977* (Madison, Wisconsin, 1999), p. 207.

50 Ibid.

51 Blinkhorn, *Carlism and Crisis in Spain*, p. 250.

52 For a highly favourable account of Hedilla written by a historian sympathetic to the Falange in general and the 'old shirts' in particular, see M. García Venero, *La Falange en la guerra de España: la unificación y Hedilla* (Paris, 1967). Meanwhile, the position of the Carlists is covered by Blinkhorn, *Carlism and Crisis in Spain*, pp. 271–7.

53 For the decree of unification and the background thereto, see S. G. Payne, *The Franco Régime, 1936–1975* (Madison, Wisconsin, 1987), pp. 167–73. J. M. Thómas, *El gran golpe: el caso Hedilla o cómo Franco se quedó con la Falange* (Barcelona, 2014); S. Ellwood, 'Falange Española and the creation of the Francoist "new state"', *European History Quarterly*, XX, No. 2 (April, 1990), pp. 209–25; Blinkhorn, *Carlism and Crisis*, pp. 285–91.

54 Moreno Gómez, *Guerra Civil en Córdoba*, pp. 558–91.

55 Ibarruri, *They Shall Not Pass*, p. 287.

56 Ibid., p. 287.

57 Modesto, *Soy del Quinto Regimiento*, p. 154.

58 Ibarruri, *They shall not Pass*, p. 282.

59 Cit. Horn, *Letters from Barcelona*, pp. 128–9.

60 Cit. ibid., p. 128. Accounts of the static nature of the Aragon front are legion. José Lacunza Benito, for example, was a village schoolteacher who had enlisted in a socialist column: 'We were sent to a place called Bielsa. When we got there, there were trenches and other defensive positions for us to occupy, but the whole time nothing important happened in the way of combat ... We were totally isolated from the world ... Our life was the trenches and the blockhouses in which we lived ... Between one blockhouse and the next there was nothing but empty space.' Cit. Camps and Olcina, *Les miliciés catalanes al front d'aragó*, p. 212. See also Orwell, pp. 22–3.

61 Kisch, *They Shall Not Pass*, p. 97.

62 Borkenau, *Spanish Cockpit*, p. 231.

63 Cit. Horn, *Letter from Barcelona*, pp. 138–9.

64 For all this, see Graham, *Spanish Republic at War*, pp. 228–38.

65 B. Bolloten, *The Spanish Civil War: Revolution and Counter-Revolution* (London, 1991), pp. 372–3.

66 It should be noted that the issue was not just the issue of Communist power. Largo Caballero was deeply opposed to this, certainly, but he was also absolutely determined not to relinquish his hold on the Ministry of War. This, however, was his Achilles' heel: if the Communists were able to garner as much support as they did, it was because Largo Caballero was patently ineffectual in so far as the tenure of this post was concerned. Here, it was not just military defeat that told against him – given the evident military superiority of the Nationalists, this could well have been

forgiven – what was really hard to stomach being his stubbornness, incompetence as an administrator and preference for surrounding himself with personal advisers of the most dubious quality. Graham, *Spanish Republic at War*, p. 297.

67 The best account of the fighting in the English language is beyond doubt that offered by George Orwell in *Homage to Catalonia*. What is particularly interesting about his account is that the participants showed little more desire to engage in offensive action than they had in the hills of Aragón. Thus: 'The devilish racket of firing went on and on, but, so far as I could see, and from all I heard, the fighting was defensive on both sides. People simply remained in their buildings or behind their barricades and blazed away at the people opposite.' Orwell, *Homage to Catalonia*, p. 142.

68 Ibid., p. 154.

69 Graham, *Spanish Republic at War*, pp. 297–306; Bolloten, *Spanish Civil War*, pp. 462–73.

70 For the destruction of the POUM, see Graham, *Spanish Republic at War*, pp. 284–92; Bolloten, *Spanish Civil War*, pp. 498–509.

71 For the destruction of Catalan autonomy in the wake of the 'May days', see A. Balcells, *Catalan Autonomy Past and Present* (Basingstoke, 1996), pp. 120–3.

72 Cit. Zugazagoitia, *Guerra y vicisitudes de los españoles*, p. 454.

73 Cit. Toynbee, *Distant Drum*, p. 118.

74 The difficulty of generalizing in respect of the triumph of militarization is exemplified by the case of José Zamora. A CNT militant from Barcelona, he deserted from his unit in July on grounds that were ostensibly strongly political. Thus, 'They were militarising us, and in my Anarchist mind this meant that it was no longer our war.' All very telling – until one discovers that Zamora only volunteered for the front in the wake of the May Days on the grounds that these made such a move advisable. Vidal, *Recuerdo 1936*, pp. 244–5. Another man who took shelter with the Anarchist militia on the Aragón front for fear that otherwise he might risk arrest was the French Trotskyite we met before named Benjamín. See Cervera Gil, *Ya sabes mi paradero*, p. 297.

75 J. M. Martínez Bande, *La ofensiva sobre Segovia y la batalla de Brunete* (Madrid, 1972), pp. 63–4.

76 Tagüeña, *Testimonio de dos guerras*, p. 154.

77 For the battle of Segovia, see Martínez Bande, *La ofensiva sobre Segovia y la batalla de Brunete*, pp. 76–100.

78 Salas Larrázabal, *Air War over Spain*, pp. 162–3.

79 For a detailed account of the battle of Huesca, see J. M. Martínez Bande, *La gran ofensiva sobre Zaragoza* (Madrid, 1973), pp. 39–56. The best source on the role of the International Brigades is Delperrie de Bayac, *Brigades internacionales*, pp. 243–5.

80 Hills, *Battle for Madrid*, pp. 143–6.

81 Modesto, *Soy del Quinto Regimiento*, p. 158.

82 Unlike anything seen in the First World War, this tactic was feasible because of the complete absence at Brunete and elsewhere of anything like the continuous lines of trenches of 1914–8. With the front line no more than a chain of widely separated fortified villages, infiltration tactics were comparatively easy, while the battlefield of Brunete, in particular, was cloaked in groves of ilex and pine that did not get in the way of movement but at the same time provided excellent cover.

83 Max, *Memorias de un revolucionario*, pp. 85–6.

84 Brunete housed a small field hospital, and its capture therefore saw a number of Nationalist nurses fall into Republican hands. Amongst the women concerned were two sisters of the pilot José Larios, whilst, in a slightly odd twist of fate, the sergeant who first came across them was none other than Joaquín Masjuán. Ibid., p. 87.

85 F. Thomas, *To Tilt at Windmills: a Memoir of the Spanish Civil War* (East Lansing, Michigan, 1996), pp. 34–5.

86 Lister, *Memorias de un luchador*, pp. 257–8. Manning one of the tanks concerned was Alvaro Cortes Roa. For him, the battle was above all an inferno of heat. 'The tanks

that we had got now had been fitted with a new device for observing the battlefield and aiming the gun in the form of a periscope: in my view, this was much better than the old visor: one could see far more ... and obtain much greater accuracy. Some had a second periscope for the loader as well, whilst others had been fitted with a machine gun on top of the turret for use against aircraft as well as another projecting from its rear ... All of these improvements were important, but nothing had been done to ensure a decent supply of fresh air or a means of extracting all the fumes from the cordite, the oil and the gasoline. Still worse, however, there was no device to keep the temperature in the interior of the tanks at a reasonable level when they were closed down for battle: it was like being in an oven.' Cortes Roa, *Tanquista*, pp. 145–6.

87 Gregory, *Shallow Grave*, pp. 69–70.

88 Cortes Roa provides a dramatic account of the experiences of the Republican tank crews. Thus: 'As soon as a tank appears ... all the furies of hell ... converge upon it ... On all sides, then, there is nothing but fire, smoke, shrapnel and great gouts of earth. ... Meanwhile, sweating feverishly, the drivers are frantically ... zig-zagging from side to side in the hope of impeding the enemy's aim ... With so much movement, however ... the task of their comrades in the turrets above their heads also becomes very difficult as the latter have to constantly struggle ... just to keep their weapons pointing at the enemy ... Occasionally, a hit is obtained, and whenever this happens the successful tank heads straight for the gap in the enemy defences, and does all that it can to increase the increase the damage ... But, all too often, the crew perceives that they are alone, that they have advanced too far, that the infantry ... have not been able to keep up ... either because they have been pinned down by the enemy's fire or because the tank has been too fast for them. If such is, indeed, the case, there is nothing for it but to retire.' Ibid., pp. 149–50.

89 M. Fersen, *The Anti-Warrior: a Memoir* (Iowa City, 1989), p. 63. Setting aside the ludicrous odds in favour of the Republic on the battlefield of Brunete on the morning of which Felsen writes, by the time that the battle began, the Republic had received 678 planes from abroad as opposed to 594 for the Nationalists. Permy López, *Atlas ilustrado de la aviación en la Guerra Civil Española*, pp. 149–50. Moreover, the Republican air force had the better of the air battle at this stage. To quote a letter written by Australian volunteer Lloyd Edmonds to his father on 8 July: 'In the air we have the ascendency. The fascist planes run for their lives and are indiscriminate as to where they drop their "eggs". They have to fly so high that accurate bombardment is impossible.' Cit. A. Inglis (ed.), *Lloyd Edmonds: Letters from Spain* (Sydney, 1985), pp. 122–3.

90 Gregory, *Shallow Grave*, pp. 91–2.

91 Lister, *Memorias de un luchador*, pp. 256–8.

92 The clash did not occur face-to-face but rather over the telephone via an unfortunate staff officer who was faced with toning down 'the most ugly words in our language ... the vilest remarks that anyone could possibly make.' Cit. Cervera Gil, *Ya sabes mi paradero*, p. 211.

93 Gregory, *Shallow Grave*, pp. 73–4.

94 Franco has been much criticized for his decision to counterattack – regaining Brunete and the other villages that had fallen to the enemy was in military terms of little consequence, after all – but in fact the decision rested on the very sound principle that, a substantial Republican army having in effect offered itself up to destruction, it was best to take advantage of the opportunity. Meanwhile, defeat though it was, in one sense the battle of Brunete made an important contribution to the overthrow of fascism. Thus, the military situation that developed at Stalingrad in the autumn of 1943 was all but a carbon copy of the one that had developed before Madrid in the winter of 1936, whilst the Brunete offensive bore a strong resemblance to the one that finally cut off the German VI Army off on the banks of the Volga. Given the fact that so many Soviet commanders of the Second World War rotated

through Republican Spain, it is therefore difficult to believe that precedent and plan alike were forgotten. For detailed accounts of the battle, see Hills, *Battle for Madrid*, pp. 147–66, and Martínez Bande, *La ofensiva sobre Segovia y la batalla de Brunete*, pp. 103–201, whilst the role of the International Brigades is recounted, sometimes at the level of the individual battalion, in Vidal, *Brigadas internacionales*, pp. 179–99; Delperrie de Bayac, *Brigadas internacionales,* pp. 249–59; Landis, *Death in the Olive Groves*, pp. 39–57; Baxell, *British Volunteers*, pp. 82–6. Finally, for the role and experience of the rival air forces, see Salas Larrazabal, *Air War over Spain*, pp. 173–7.

95 Revilla Cebrecos, *Tercio de Lacar*, pp. 104–10. For a detailed account of the campaign, see J. M. Martínez Bande, *El final del frente norte* (Madrid, 1972), pp. 41–105.

96 For all this, see Thomas, *Spanish Civil War*, pp. 723–5; Lister, *Memorias de un luchador*, pp. 263–78. Partial only though it was, the destruction of the collectives has again been held up as having been extremely damaging to the Republican war effort. However, as has been pointed out by the revisionist American historian Michael Seidman, collectivization only affected 18.5 per cent of the land in the Republican zone, whilst even in heavily affected Aragón, the figure only amounted to 40 per cent. M. Seidman, 'Agrarian collectives during the Spanish Revolution and Civil War', *European History Quarterly*, XXX, No. 2 (April, 2010), pp. 210–11. If so, then the argument is at the very least open to challenge.

97 Many of the troops were also the same, just as the troops that had fought at Brunete had in many cases been the same as those that fought the Jarama, and, before that, Boadilla. It is above all this that explains the terrible losses suffered by units such as the International Brigades. In brief, Communist influence having designated certain units as crack troops and ensured that to some extent they got the best of everything, they became natural 'fire brigades' that were rushed from place to place to cope with some crisis here or take part in some offensive there, a tendency that was increased still further by the Communists' desire to maximize on their investment in terms of propaganda. The result, of course, was that the assets concerned rapidly diminished in value: in the International Brigades, for example, the constant pressure to provide replacements meant that the British and American Communist parties, and probably others too, became less and less selective in their screening of recruits, whilst by the end of 1937, at least a third of the rank and file were Spaniards.

98 Biescas Palacio, *Memorias*, p. 26. Still more interesting is Biescas Palacio's devastatingly honest account of what happened when Codo was finally taken: 'That our troops committed many barbarities on entering Codo is something that I cannot deny. Amongst other things I saw sick and wounded enemy soldiers being thrown out of the windows of the hospital ... It is possible, I suppose, that nothing can contain young men who have friends, or even brothers, die by their side ...We lost many men, among them my friend, Eduardo Castillo ... I spent the whole of the next morning looking for him and even scraped the earth clear of a few corpses who had been buried during the night, but I never found any trace of him: in all probability, he took a direct hit from a bomb and was blown to bits.' Ibid., pp. 26–7.

99 Gregory, *Shallow Grave*, p. 79.

100 Ibid., p. 80.

101 Cit. *El Mundo*, 30 March 2014, < http://www.elmundo.es/cronica/2014/03/30/ 5336b1beca47418d308b456d.html >, accessed 8 April 2016. Unbeknown to him, Moreno Miranda's brother, Luis, in 1936 a conscript who had been doing his military service in Barcelona, was amongst the troops attacking the town.

102 Cit. Vidal, *Recuerdo 1936*, p. 211.

103 Puig, *Personal Memories of the Spanish Civil War,* pp. 73–5.

104 Cit. Vidal, *Recuerdo 1936*, p. 214. A number of prisoners were also shot earlier in the battle by the Croat commander of the XV International Brigade, Vladimir Copic, and, possibly, the commander of the Lincoln battalion, Robert Merriman. P. N. Carroll, *The Odyssey of the Abraham Lincoln Brigade: Americans in the Spanish Civil War*

(Stanford, California, 1998), pp. 155–6, 158. It is unfortunate that Paul Preston's seminal *Spanish Holocaust* fails to make any mention of these executions.

105 Puig, *Personal Memories of the Spanish Civil War*, p. 99.

106 For a detailed account of the battle, see Martínez Bande, *Gran ofensiva sobre Zaragoza*, pp. 77–183, whilst the role of the International Brigades is recounted in Vidal, *Brigadas internacionales*, pp. 203–23; Delperrie de Bayac, *Brigadas internacionales*, pp. 260–4; Landis, *Death in the Olive Groves*, pp. 69–87; Baxell, *British Volunteers*, pp. 89–91.

107 Candelas, *Adventures of an Innocent*, pp. 102–3.

108 For details of the BT5, see Albert, *Carros de combate*, pp. 39–42.

109 Puig, *Personal Memories of the Spanish Civil War*, pp. 107–9. See also Koltsov, *Diario de la guerra de España*, p. 477.

110 Zaloga, 'Soviet tank operations in Spain', pp. 145–7; Landis, *Death in the Olive Groves*, pp. 88–91.

111 Cabezas, *Asturias*, pp.144–5.

112 Ibid., p. 145.

113 F. Tarazona Torán, *Yo fui piloto de caza rojo* (Madrid, 1974), pp. 68–84 *passim*.

114 Revilla Cebrecos, *Tercio de Lacar*, p. 113.

115 Cabezas, *Asturias*, p. 147.

116 *Cit.* MacMaster, *Spanish Fighters*, pp. 91–2.

117 The best military history is Martínez Bande, *Final del frente norte*, pp. 111–94. For details of the repression in the Oviedo-Gijón area, see Preston, *Spanish Holocaust*, pp, 444–6. Not counting those who were murdered by Falangist death-squads or simply shot out of hand at the moment of surrender – a total that probably amounts to at least 500 – a minimum death-toll would appear to be 1,339 at Oviedo and 1,245 at Gijón. Meanwhile, the Moorish troops in particular wreaked havoc amongst the defenceless civilian population, though to a certain extent they were kept in check by growing racial sensitivities about African men satisfying their lusts with white women: in a few cases, *regulares* who made the mistake of molesting women too publicly were court-martialled and shot. E.g. Vidal, *Recuerdo 1936*, p. 217.

118 Those units used as shock troops had suffered particularly heavily. In the British battalion of the International Brigades, the 300 men who had gone into line at Brunete had been reduced to just forty-two by the end of the battle, of whom only twenty-four were unwounded. Rebuilt to a strength of about 400 in time for Belchite by dint of the incorporation of 200 Spanish conscripts, it had then proceeded to lose another 150 casualties. With the number of British recruits steadily falling, meanwhile, thereafter the proportion of British combatants was never more than 25 per cent of the whole. Gregory, *Shallow Grave*, p. 88.

119 Thomas, *Spanish Civil War*, p. 781.

120 Koltsov, *Diario de la guerra de España*, pp. 484–5.

8

COLLAPSE IN ARAGÓN

The onset of the second winter of the war brought with it a new mood in the Republican zone that was encapsulated by the slogan 'Resistir es vencer' ('To resist is to conquer'). As the Australian truck driver Lloyd Edmonds put it, 'The nature of the war has changed considerably since the capture of Asturias. Now the slogan here is "Fortification": no more "Pasaremos."'[1] Instrumental in this was not so much the impact of political turmoil but that of military defeat. If the Anarchists and the POUM were embittered by what had happened, plenty of observers who had sided with their opponents also had little faith in victory. Here, for example, are the views of the father of the Republican journalist Miguel de Heredia, himself a minor Republican politician, on the generals of the Republic:

> Of all of them the only one who is any good is Rojo and maybe Saravía, though, for all his loyalty to the Republic, the latter is a weakling with little faith in the cause which he serves. Pozas? A pompous ass who in his inner being is a monarchist, but who switched to republicanism overnight, and only failed to turn Communist because the Communists wouldn't have him? Tell me: what did Pozas achieve at Belchite, or, for that matter, the Jarama or Guadalajara. And Miaja? Do you know what I believe? That he was as much in favour of the coup as Franco ... As for his role as the heroic defender of Madrid, I hear tell that his price for taking charge of the defence was a permit for his family to leave Spain. And these are the fellows that have been put in charge! Far better the commanders who are springing from the ranks of the people: some of them might even turn out to be men of the stamp of the marshals who emerged from the French Revolution.[2]

By the time that Gijón fell, the Republican government had for some five months been in the hands of the Socialist academic and erstwhile Minister of Finance,

Juan Negrín López. Much vilified by anti-Communist writers, the new Prime Minister was a rather more complex figure than many of his detractors have allowed. The scion of a prosperous bourgeois family who was very much on the right of the Socialist party, he was in full agreement with the need to end the revolution – had personally saved many Catholic friends from the Red Terror, even – whilst he was slow to recognize just how far the Communists had been able to dominate the army and security forces, and extremely foolish in the extent of his contempt for Largo, whose personal mediocrity blinded Negrín to the need to give him his backing in May 1937. If the Communists had supported him as the replacement for Largo Caballero, meanwhile, it was precisely because they believed that they could manipulate him with greater ease than they could Indalecio Prieto, the only other potential candidate. That said, however, Negrín was no mere Comintern catspaw. Prepared to sup with the devil for the sake of winning the war, he was a sincere democrat who had as little time for Communist hegemonism as he did for left-wing revolution, whilst he soon became increasingly resentful of the pretensions of the Communist Party and its Russian and Comintern advisers. Whether he could actually have broken away from them is a moot point – the deeply divided PSOE was hardly an effective powerbase – but for the remainder of the war, he did all he could to restrict their influence and secure the British and French support that was the only hope of shattering their grip.[3]

Genuine though he was in his intention to challenge the Communists, Negrín was facing an uphill task. Unwilling and unable to join the Left, he was also estranged from Largo Caballero (not that the latter could have offered him much support: in the summer and autumn of 1937, he was stripped of his remaining positions of influence and eventually silenced altogether). Nor did it help that his

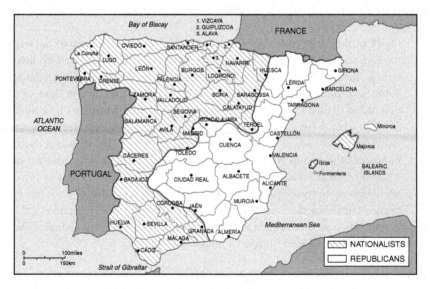

MAP 8.1   Division of Spain, October 1937.

considerable intellect and utter determination to take the war effort in hand made him, as Thomas puts it, 'ten enemies a day'; that he lived in great opulence; that he was a glutton, a drunk and a womanizer alike – something that his opponents claimed did not sit well with a situation in which what was needed was personal rectitude and dedication to the struggle – and that his irregular lifestyle produced a situation in which his unfortunate ministers frequently found themselves summoned to meetings in the dead of night.[4] Meanwhile, Communist influence was greater than ever. Desperate for protection against the Red Terror in particular and the revolution in general, and at the same time attracted to the fact that the Communists seemed to offer a new model of politics that cut across obvious class divisions, enormous numbers of the bourgeoisie, the professional classes and, to a somewhat lesser extent, the peasantry had flocked to the haven that they represented, whilst the Party had a strong appeal to young men and women entering the world of politics for the first time, the result being that by the middle of 1937, party membership stood at around 400,000.[5] Inevitably, all this had had a powerful impact on the armed forces, and all the more so given the role played by the Fifth Regiment in the process of militarization. Nearly half the Popular Army were members either of the PCE, the PSUC or the JSU, whilst Communist representation at the rank of battalion commander and above was even higher: over two-thirds of the mixed brigades had Communist commanders, whilst prominent converts included Pozas, Miaja, and the commander of the air force, Hidalgo de Cisneros. The erstwhile militia leaders Lister and González were divisional commanders, and Modesto the head of a corps; Communists peppered the general staff, the war ministry and, especially, the political commissariat; and the security forces, the International Brigades and the air force were essentially Communist preserves, even if the number of this last's pilots who were actually Russian was in rapid decline as more and more young Spaniards came back from the training courses that had been set up for them in the Ukraine. At the same time, meanwhile, the Communists had also built up an impressive array of nominally independent civilian organizations – the Asociación de Mujeres Anti-Fascistas is just one example – whose aim was to put pressure on the government, whilst, in at least some cases – that of Dolores Ibarruri, for one – they were also clearly still angling for unification with the Socialists, or, to put it another way, the formation of a single left-wing movement in which they themselves would predominate.[6]

Whilst Negrín quickly killed off the pressure for unification, the most prominent figure in the resistance was rather his long-term friend and ally, Prieto, the latter having become more and more concerned at both the general 'Communization' of the Republic and the ruthless manner in which the Communists had dealt with the POUM (in many ways the most attractive figure in the Republican camp, Prieto was a sincere democrat who believed that the only road to social justice was parliamentary politics and respect for all). Thus, appointed Minister of Defence, Prieto lost no time in banning all party propaganda from the armed forces; engineering the removal of many Communists from the upper echelons of the political commissariat; ending the administrative independence of the International Brigades; transferring many Communist staff officers to less sensitive posts; and trying to ensure that the new secret police force known as the Service of Military Investigation (or SIM) that was being forced upon the Republic by the Russians did not immediately fall under Communist control.[7] Realizing that the Communists were in consequence out to get him, in the early winter, Prieto decided to secure his position by means of a major military victory, the obvious target being the Nationalist bastion of Teruel, which was almost surrounded, lightly garrisoned and difficult to defend. Entrusted to a specially created force – the Army of the Levante – under the non-Communist Republican Juan Hernández Saravia, the assault began on 15 December. Aided by the fact that, as Prieto had hoped, the Nationalist air force was grounded by inclement weather, 100,000 Republican troops surrounded the Nationalist garrison and occupied a large expanse of territory to the north and north-west. In the new capital of Barcelona, meanwhile, there was much jubilation: '"I am now Minister of Defence and Attack alike!" This announcement was made to the journalists assembled in the building in the Paseo de Gracia where the cabinet had its meetings, Prieto then going on to give us some details of the military operations … My colleague was beside himself with glee … Not being used to receiving good news, we were utterly astonished.'[8]

There remained, however, the city of Teruel. Trapped inside the Republican ring were 2,000 troops under the governor, Domingo Rey d'Harcourt, and another 2,000 civilians. For a little while, the defending troops made an attempt to hang on to a hill called La Muela that overlooked the city, but very soon it became clear that the only hope was to withdraw inside the built-up area and await relief. Here, however, there was an ideal refuge. Perched on the very edge of the bluff on which the city was built was a close-set cluster of substantial buildings including the diocesan seminary, the Bank of Spain, the convent of Santa Clara and the offices of the civil government, and Rey d'Harcourt and his men duly barricaded themselves inside together with many civilians, including the city's bishop, Ramón Anselmo Polanco. All of a sudden, then, the Republicans' triumphal advance came to an end. Amongst the leading Republican troops was the erstwhile militiaman Esteban Biescas Palacios:

> Our objective was to enter the capital, and this we set about without delay … My battalion happened to pass close by the station. Seeing some goods wagons, our first thought was to go and see what we could requisition from them, but we were not allowed to do so, and kept going until we reached the first buildings of the town … The enemy had no option but to hole up in a large building which turned out to be the seminary, a great, big block of a place with walls a metre thick. I can say this because we dragged up a cannon and opened fire with it at point-blank range, only to discover that the only result was to knock a few chips out of the brick-work … On top of all this, it also had lots of little windows from which the defenders fired continually and cost us many casualties, many of them mortal.[9]

As so often before, the result was that the advance came to a dead halt. Having got into the web of streets surrounding the enemy strong points, the Republican troops found themselves completely pinned down. As the same observer continued, 'The streets around the seminary were very narrow, and, as can well be imagined, we always crossed them at full speed. None of this sufficed to spare us many dead, but then someone had an idea. Some blankets having been fixed to a rope and the rope in turn having been firmly tied up, one of our men dashed across one of the worst of the streets with the resultant bundle and tied the end of the rope to a pole somewhere out of sight of the enemy. In this fashion ... the enemy snipers were deprived of their mark, but even so we still took care to make the crossing at a run just in case!'[10]

However, hopes that such a shock had been administered to the Nationalists that they could be forced to accept a compromise peace – the sub-text of the whole operation – were soon dashed. Though taken by surprise – he had actually been massing his forces for a fresh offensive against Madrid via the old battlefield of Guadalajara – Franco quickly launched a massive counteroffensive, this being something in which he was much assisted by the fact that his forces were now finally organized into proper First World War–style army corps, each of them composed of several divisions.[11] Hampered by a prolonged blizzard, the relief forces did not reach the city in time – after a Stalingrad-like struggle, the garrison surrendered on 8 January[12] – but even so, the Nationalist advance continued, the increasingly exhausted Republicans not only being driven back but also losing large amounts of territory that they had held at the start of the battle. Hitherto kept back for political reasons, the International Brigades were sent into the line in the empty steppes north-east of Teruel. Bob Clark was a casual labourer from Liverpool who had arrived in Spain to fight with the British battalion in the autumn of 1937 and was now undergoing his baptism of fire with the machine-gun company in an entrenchment a little way behind the front line:

> The fascist artillery opened up ... The whole trench trembled and showers of earth poured from the parapet above. This shelling continued for about half an hour. After our first fright we began to feel fairly safe: the shells were continually dropping about fifty to one hundred yards in the rear of our trench and a surprising number of them were duds ... Suddenly what looked like black ants came crawling up the valley evidently intent on occupying the forward positions ... We sprang to life ... and in a few seconds had a perfect bead on the advancing enemy ... We kept on firing for quite a long time. How exhilarating it all was: I felt almost ashamed of myself when I remembered afterwards how full of joy I felt.[13]

At first the Nationalist attacks (as in this instance) were beaten off, but the pressure mounted inexorably. Another British volunteer was the anti-tank gunner Fred Thomas. To quote the entry in his diary for 17 January:

At the moment I am watching ... the biggest artillery barrage and long-est air-raid I have seen so far in this war. It began about seven o'clock this morning when their heavy guns opened up. After shelling more or less indiscriminately for an hour or so, they concentrated everything on a small crest to our right. At the same time, judging by the sound of rifle and machine-gun fire, their troops began a fierce attack in that area which is still going on at 3 p.m. A thick pall of black smoke hangs over the sur-rounding crests. They probably have more artillery here than at Brunete, and that beat all records for this war. Twenty-odd of their bombers and twice as many chasers are giving us some unpleasant moments ... The whole damned ground is shaking: ever since they have first come over, they have been circling round and round, bombing, bombing, bombing.[14]

The pressure was utterly relentless, with day after day of shelling and bombing. Another entry in Thomas' diary scrawled on 22 January reads as follows:

Well, we have just had a very nasty half hour. About 4.30 we sent over twenty shells ... to the hill in front of us and of course enjoyed it. However, then their '75's', a much bigger gun, had us bang in sight, and, oh boy, the bloody things came one-two-three-four, one-two-three-four, for half an hour, hitting everywhere except the actual gun. By a sheer stroke of luck there were no casualties, but you feel like a wet rag after that sort of experi-ence. If we had tried to keep firing we would have had no gun crew left. Everything is covered now by a foot or so of earth and debris (as we were also at times), and has to be dug out.[15]

What Thomas does not say, however, is that over the previous three days, the forces of which the British battalion had been a part had suffered a heavy defeat in that, posted to hold the strategic heights of El Muletón and Alto Celadas, they had eventually been driven from their positions and forced to retreat over the River Alfambra, a tributary of the River Turia that joined it at Teruel. Meanwhile, just keeping the battle going was a bitter battle against the elements. 'The snow was feet thick (one day the temperature was sixteen below zero)', wrote Lloyd Edmonds, 'and we went with tow ropes on the back of each truck so that when a truck slid off the road, we could pull them back again without a waste of time ... Each night we let the water out of the radiator so as not to freeze, but we had so much trouble in the mornings that we took it in turns to stay up all night and run each truck for five or ten minutes each hour to keep them warm.'[16] In the skies above the battlefield, meanwhile, the pilots of both sides suffered terribly. Still convalescing in hospital after injuries he had received when he was shot down in Asturias, Francisco Tarazona was unable to take part in the fighting, but the account that he gives is nonetheless convincing enough. As he noted in his diary, 'Pilots coming from the front talk of the terrible cold that they have encountered at height: fifty degrees below zero. The idea is truly terrifying. Some of them have had to have fingers and toes amputated, whilst others have suffered frostbitten noses or chins.'[17]

The battle unleashed by the Nationalist counterstroke lasted for over six weeks. Checked before Teruel itself (although they still got close enough to it to be able to pound it with their artillery), the Nationalists shifted the axis of attack to the barren mountain region to the north of the city in the hope that they could outflank the troops blocking their way. The new phase of the battle, known as the battle of the River Alfambra, began on 7 February. Initially, the fighting was fierce enough. Iniesta Cano, for example, was sent to attack a line of hills protected by successive lines of Republican trenches: 'Well dug-in and possessed of a very advantageous position, the enemy fiercely opposed our advance ... I overcame the first line of defence, but to take the second I had to make prolonged use of our 81mm mortars, and even then the defenders were only overcome at the cost of hand-to-hand fighting ... that went on till two in the morning. However, the enemy were not finished. Counterattacking with great valour and decision alike, they managed to get into the positions held by my Legionaries and had to be driven off by dint of further hand-to-hand fighting. Such was the confusion that the two sides kept mistaking their own men for the enemy.'[18]

At best patchy – it was at its fiercest in precisely the area in which Iniesta Cano was operating – such fighting was short-lived, however. Once the Nationalists had broken through the Republican defences, they found little to stop them, not least because the heavy snow made it almost impossible to send in reinforcements. Even had this not been the case, morale in many units was at a low ebb: when the LXXXIV Mixed Brigade (a unit that had been heavily involved in the capture of the city) was ordered back into the fray, it refused point-blank to obey and was immediately disarmed and subjected to a series of summary court-martials that cost the lives of forty-four of its men. Virtually unopposed, then, the Nationalists had reached all their objectives in a matter of days, Republican casualties coming to well over 20,000 men, most of them prisoners. As one Carlist veteran of the campaign wrote, 'This operation could not have been more encouraging: in the entire division there were fewer casualties than the battalion had suffered in the conquest of any single ridge in the first days of the battle of Teruel, whereas the enemy had suffered heavy losses including not just those who fell in the fighting, but also large numbers of deserters and prisoners of war.'[19] It was in this battle, meanwhile, that the terrifying dive-bomber known as the Stuka – more properly, the Junkers Ju87 – made its first appearance on the battlefield: equipped with sirens on its fixed landing gear that gave off an ear-splitting howl as it dropped vertically towards the ground to release its load, this was as feared in Spain as it was to be on the early battlefields of the Second World War, though in fact the Condor Legion only ever got three of them.[20]

Having badly shaken the Republicans, Franco's forces now bore down on Teruel itself. Pouring across the River Alfambra immediately to the north of the city, within forty-eight hours they were threatening the defending forces with complete encirclement. Inside the city, the Forty-Sixth Division of Valentín González held out bravely enough, but it was clear that resistance was a lost cause, and the last days of the fighting were chiefly marked by desperate attempts to evacuate the many sick and wounded. Amongst the men trying to get these unfortunates away was a political commissar named Enrique de la Jara:

> I will never forget the sight of the Plaza del Torico full of wounded soldiers ... The Moors were very close ... and we had to evacuate the wounded as best we could ... We did it using mules – good Spanish mules of the sort that no longer exist. A stretcher was hung on each side of each animal and they were led away like that. To understand what it was like ... takes a lot of imagination.[21]

On 21 February, however, the trap snapped shut, and the few men left inside the city were left with no choice but to give themselves up or try to slip away through the Nationalist lines. With Teruel itself reconquered, by 23 February the battle was over, Republican casualties numbering some 54,000 and Nationalist ones perhaps 10,000 less.[22] Privately, many Republicans were very shaken. 'The campaign of Teruel', wrote Francisco Tarazona, 'was a palpable demonstration that we lacked war *matériel*: the impetus of the offensive was undermined; the latent disproportion of our means made itself felt: whenever a single Republican plane appeared, five fascist machines fell upon it and riddled it with bullets; down on the ground, the only thing we had enough of was men.'[23]

In stressing the superiority of the resources available to the Nationalists, Tarazona had a point: with every battle that was fought, the greater strength of Franco's forces was becoming more apparent. Yet, as the appendices at the end of this work demonstrate, the issue was not simply that the rebels were getting more foreign aid than their Republican opponents: on the contrary, the People's Army actually got more of some categories of weapons. To emphasize a point that has been made before, the central issue was that the mixed-brigade system effectively ensured that the Republicans were weak everywhere and strong nowhere, true though it is that they would have been short of artillery support whichever model of organization they had adopted. Whether it was at Brunete or Belchite or Teruel, then, the Republican forces simply did not have the firepower that they needed. At the same time, there is another point that needs to be made. We come here to the question of armament production in the rival zones. Possessed of a substantial industrial base though they were, the Republicans were able to extract little profit from it. Taking the great arms plant of Trubia as an example, between July 1936 and October 1937 – the period when it was in the hands of the Republicans – it managed to produce no more than twenty 105mm and 150mm howitzers, together with a few dozen 40mm infantry guns. Once under Nationalist control, it was a very different story, the same plant turning out no fewer than 117 pieces of field and heavy artillery between October 1937 and the end of the war. Indeed, the figures for armament production in the Nationalist zone are extremely impressive: 185 cannon and howitzers, 3,900 machine-guns, 5,000 light machine-guns and 137,000 rifles. To this, meanwhile, must be added the efforts of the Servicio de Recuperación: charged with the task of sorting, refurbishing and, where necessary, repairing, the enormous quantities of material taken on the battlefield, by March 1939 this had supplied Franco's forces with 100 tanks, 1,897 pieces of artillery, 6,990 mortars, 25,306 machine-guns, 576,301 rifles, 100,000,000 hand-grenades, 3,683,086 shells and 1,136,260,000 cartridges. In large part this was the result of ruthless discipline on the home front – cowed by savage reprisals, the labour force was left with no choice but to accept long hours and low wages – but it is impossible not to draw a stark contrast with the situation in the Republican zone.[24]

Fought in arctic cold and heavy snow, Teruel was perhaps the toughest battle of the whole conflict.[25] Meanwhile, the early months of 1938 found the Republic in a situation that was increasingly desperate. Setting aside the terrible losses in the North, Brunete, Belchite and Teruel had between them stripped it of much its stock of arms and munitions. Supplies of Russian aircraft, in particular, were drying up thanks to the need to send assistance to the Chinese Nationalists in their war against Japan, while Stalin was in general losing interest in the Spanish war. Yet Soviet aid was more essential than ever, the battle of Teruel having shown that even Franco's Spanish fighter pilots were now better trained than their Republican counterparts (in the fighting over Teruel, setting aside the contribution made by the Me109s, formations made up entirely of Fiat Cr32s had regularly driven off superior numbers of I15s and I16s, and that despite the fact that many of the latter were now improved models with more machine-guns).[26] Gone, meanwhile, were many of the militants who had for the past year provided the cutting edge of the Republican war effort. For evidence of this, one only has to look at the British and American battalions of the International Brigades. In both cases, it was not just the fact that losses had been appalling and that many of such few replacements as were still arriving in Spain were, in the words of American volunteer Alvah Bessie, 'a scurvy lot ... weak and unreliable elements.'[27] Amongst those killed, invalided out or transferred to political work at home were most of the party stalwarts who had always been the heart and soul of the two battalions: Tom Wintringham, the British battalion's first commander; George Nathan, the immensely popular Jewish homosexual who had risen to be chief of staff of the XV International Brigade; Oliver Law, the first Black American ever to command an infantry battalion; Steve Nelson, the first commissar of the Lincolns; Harry Fry, the machine-gun officer captured at the Jarama and released in an exchange of prisoners, who had come back to command the British battalion only to die at Fuentes de Ebro; the early company commanders Paul Burns, William Briskey and Christopher Conway. In the International Brigades, perhaps, things were better than they were elsewhere: though ever increasing numbers of the rank and file were Spaniards, the men concerned had all asked to be assigned to the Brigades and may therefore be assumed to have been either dedicated Communist or Socialist militants, or, at the very least, young men bent on seeing real action.[28] But in the army as a whole, all that was left was the unwilling conscripts whom we met in the previous chapter. Typical, perhaps, were the little group of men whom a Laurie Lee who had come back to Spain to fight for the Republic encountered when he became separated from the British battalion in the fighting round Teruel:

> As the gully widened ... we came to a bunker scraped out of rock and snow and half covered by a sheet of tin. There was a dog and a cooking pot, and a few shivering men eating out of rusty cans. Grey-faced and in rags, their heads moved in quick animal jerks as they ate, up and down, left and right, as though they were hunted ... I stayed with the Spaniards for several days in the frozen vault of their bunker. Never had I seen men so drained of hope and spirit. Except when the bucket of food came up each morning they seldom stirred from the foetal position in which they hunched themselves. They had no field telephone, the place seemed to have no purpose, and their leader ... said he had no idea what his men were supposed to be doing.'[29]

As the same observer reflected, 'The gift of Teruel at Christmas had become for the Republicans no more than a poisoned toy. It was meant to be the victory that would change the war; it was instead the seal of defeat.'[30] Behind the lines, meanwhile, living conditions were now downright desperate. The Republican navy having shown itself to be utterly incapable of protecting the beleaguered shipping lanes that led to Valencia and Barcelona, food was very scarce and prices very high (a further problem here was that, following the loss of several vessels to Italian submarines, the Russians were no longer willing to risk their limited supply of merchant shipping on the run to Spain, the full burden of supplying the Republic in consequence having to be borne by the Republic's increasingly threadbare merchant marine, together with foreign skippers willing to take enormous risks for the sake of equally enormous profits). The winter had been bitterly cold throughout, and, with fuel for heating limited, the civilian population in consequence suffered terribly. Shivering and malnourished, they also began to suffer from disease, whilst hunger was a constant companion.[31] Meanwhile, in many instances, they also had to endure the direct attention of the Nationalists. Heavily bombed in the course of the Nationalist assault in November 1936, Madrid had thereafter been constantly shelled, but the steady increase in Nationalist airpower led to ever more bombing raids on towns and cities well behind the lines. In the very midst of the battle of Teruel, indeed, the Italian Legionary Aviation hit Barcelona no fewer than eight times between 1 and 30 January, while other targets that were struck included Valencia, this last also being shelled by the Nationalist cruiser squadron, albeit at heavy cost to the *Almirante Cervera*, which was badly damaged in a Republican air attack; on leave in the city, meanwhile, Francisco Tarazona had a narrow escape when he was caught in the centre of the city by an enemy raid: 'I threw myself to the ground in the doorway of the telephone headquarters, whilst various other people followed my example, some of them even landing on top of me ... A number of bombs fell near us: the report was horrendous, whilst the blast wave hit us in the most violent of fashions: it stank and tasted of burnt stone, whilst fragments of metal ... struck the doors and windows of the great building. Driven by sheer terror, we huddled together as close as we could. Our mouths were filled with a bitter taste and were as dry as a bone: we could not move a muscle.'[32] Despite efforts to maintain popular enthusiasm, morale was therefore clearly in decline. At the front, perhaps, things were better, but even so there was a general air of wrangling and mistrust (it did not help that Valentín González had fled Teruel in dubious circumstances at the end of the battle, thereby giving rise to accusations of cowardice). With the SIM in addition busily turning the Republican zone into a police state, the situation could not have been more dispiriting.[33] On leave in Madrid after his experiences at Teruel, Antonio Candelas voiced what must have been the feelings of many ordinary combatants: 'I had a strong feeling that ... the cause of the Republic would be lost. No matter what we did our efforts would be wasted. That is what was in my mind as was the case with many others, although not many people talked about it at the time ... I began to see that we could not possibly win the war.'[34]

Weary and demoralized, Candelas went absent without leave when the time came for him to return to the front, and for some weeks he lived from hand to mouth before handing himself in for want of any other means of subsisting himself and being drafted into a new battalion and sent to the front in Extremadura. In Aragón, meanwhile, fresh troubles were building for the Republic. In brief, for the first time in the war, Franco resolved to embark on one of the bold strategic strokes that were constantly being urged on him by the representatives of Germany and Italy. Rapidly re-deploying his troops (a task in which he was much aided by the large numbers of trucks that the Nationalist cause had been able to acquire from the decidedly friendly American automobile industry), he arrayed four Spanish army corps and the Italian CTV along the length of the front stretching from Teruel to Huesca, and by the first week of March, he had 150,000 men ready to go into action backed by 700 guns and 200 tanks. In the trenches facing them were just two Corps – XII and XXI – most of whose men were nothing but raw conscripts, many of them not even fully armed. At dawn on 9 March, the offensive began with a thunderous artillery bombardment and numerous air attacks on Republican airfields that destroyed many planes on the ground (so thinly spread were the defenders that it was deemed to be wasteful to use airpower against them until such time as knots of resistance had been identified).[35] Alfred Lunt was a gunner in one of the Condor Legion's batteries of 88mm Flak18s:

> From the meandering front lines on our maps ... pencilled arrows sprout towards the Mediterranean ... The four ... guns are poised to fire at

low-angle from an open position next to an olive grove. They stand in kite-shaped formation with three front pieces in action against ground targets. The fourth is waiting for enemy planes that never seem to come ... I cannot help marvelling at our own vast superiority in numbers and material. Streams of Heinkel 111's protected by Messerschmitt fighters and alternating with Italian Caproni and Savoia bombers, carry out their missions unopposed but for the occasional twin puffs of smoke from the enemy's double-barrelled French anti-aircraft guns. Some four miles away the mountains resemble erupting volcanoes ... Our groups of *flak* shell bursts are clearly discernible. We are known as one of the 'mad' batteries because of our firing speed and precision. We never have to worry about the supply of ammunition.[36]

Almost immediately, the front gave way before the very eyes of horrified onlookers, amongst them the signaller Lluis Puig:

All around, all we could see ... were soldiers who were retreating: there were thousands of them! We arrived at ... a very high hill from where I could observe ... the enemy advancing. You could see Spanish flags ... and large numbers of armoured vehicles ... firing non-stop as they advanced. Also visible was a throng of soldiers ... They were protected by steel helmets which were shining under the rays of the sun. The anti-Marxist artillery didn't stop firing ... The bullets were continually whistling past, and the shells exploding in our rear ... A lieutenant who saw the enemy near his trench ... abandoned it without receiving an order from his superior, and the latter ... shot him three times with his pistol, killing him instantly.[37]

In the face of such an onslaught, there was little that the Republicans could do, and within three days, all the gains that they had made in the battle of Belchite, including not least the much battered town itself, had been lost to the enemy. A week later, the Nationalists were threatening Caspe, an advance that had not been equalled since the days of the march on Madrid. For the first few days, meanwhile, in many sectors resistance was non-existent: according to the diary of one legionary named Luis Hernaiz Gracia who took part in the occupation of Moyuela, Albalate del Arzobispo, Calanda and Alcániz, it was 14 March before he and his comrades encountered any opposition at all, and even then it came not from ground forces but a number of Republican bombers that managed to catch a cavalry regiment out in the open.[38] Not until 18 March did the battalion lose any casualties, and even then these only amounted to a few wounded inflicted by a single Republican shell.[39] Also involved in the advance was an infantryman named Domingo Fernández: 'We began our attack on 9 March. No sooner had we done so than we discovered that our adversaries had abandoned their positions ... for fear that we would cut them off, and dug themselves around Quinto. At around ten o'clock in the morning we came up with them, but once again they retired without putting up a fight.[40] Very soon, then, the biggest problem the Nationalists faced in respect of the Republicans was what to do with all their prisoners.[41]

Behind the Republican lines, meanwhile, all was confusion. When the Nationalist hammer-blow struck, Lister's Eleventh Division was at rest at Sagunto:

> On 9 March ... we got the news that the enemy had begun an offensive in Aragón ... Over the next three days the accounts that we received got more and more alarming, and on 12 March we heard that Rojo had gone to the headquarters of XVIII Corps at Alcañiz to take personal charge of operations. The next day I got an order to get my division on the road and report to Rojo as quickly as possible. At about ten o'clock that night, I reached Alcañiz. The state in which I discovered the commander of XVIII Corps and his staff could not have been more lamentable. To my questions, their only response was that they had no idea where the front was, nor still less what the situation was of either their forces or those of the enemy.[42]

As ever, Lister's troops were ready to fight, but around them there was nothing but panic. Stationed on the southern flanks of the Nationalist onrush, Elias Biescas Palacios' battalion was amongst the many that found any meaningful resistance an impossibility:

> Very soon everything was a case of disintegration and rout ... From this moment on ... we never fired a single shot, but rather just kept retreating, albeit for the most part only at night, being so frightened of the enemy's aviation that we hid up during the day. As was only natural in all this disorder, food was distinguished by its absence, the field kitchens and supply trains having got themselves God knows where, and we were therefore reduced to grabbing whatever we could.[43]

Amongst the forces caught up in the nightmare were the XI, XII, XIII, XIV and XV International Brigades (though initially only the first and the last were near the front line, the XII and XIII Brigades being rushed up from reserve after some days and the XIV Brigade sent round from the Madrid front). Inevitably, it is the travails of the XV Brigade that are best covered in the literature, and such is the wealth of material that it would be perverse not to use it as a case-study in the disasters that now befell the People's Army; with regard to the other four, all that need be said is that their experiences were not dissimilar, and that by the end of the campaign, they had all been reduced to mere shadows of their former selves, if not destroyed altogether.[44] At rest in the area south of Belchite when the attack began, on 10 March, the four battalions of which the XV Brigade consisted – the British, the American Abraham Lincoln, the Canadian Mackenzie-Papineau and the Spanish Fifty-Ninth – were ordered into the line, only to encounter a hail of fire that cut them to pieces in a matter of hours. Crouching in a trench, the Canadian volunteer Harold Smith recorded the events of the day in his note book:

> Things begin to happen. A heavy movement of troops to the left, ours falling back. A sporadic shelling, flat trajectories, German eighty-eights. Heavy bombings to the rear and on both flanks. Brigade anti-air battery (Oerlikons) knocked out. Artillery now zeroing in on Lincoln trenches. Heavy damage, heavy casualties. Flights of fighter-bombers over Lincoln trenches. Strafing runs ... Blain Owen of my squad is wounded, Lincoln ammo dump is blown up ... Twenty fascist tanks spread out ... and advance towards us ... Two of our armoured cars and some heavy machine-guns using armour piercing bullets hold the tanks at bay ... Heavy enemy movement on the right flank and to the rear ... Small groups of enemy advancing in skirmish line.[45]

Another witness to the fighting was the Liverpool volunteer Bob Clark. In hospital with dysentery for the previous week, he returned in the very midst of the Nationalist attack to find the Brigade caught up in a desperate battle in which he could play no part (like most men sent to the rear, he had been stripped of his rifle on departure):

> The military situation was bad: there was no doubt about that ... Runners were dashing along the communication trenches with messages ... It was all very bewildering. The crump of shells was ... very close. The enemy had obviously got the range on brigade headquarters: a large lorry with an anti-tank gun on it had sunk its front wheels into one of the communication trenches, offering a beautiful target ... Shellfire became heavier and continuous and the sharp rat-tat-tat of machine-guns could be heard very close. At that moment a company ... came staggering along the trench. They were Americans ... They had been dive-bombed for hours on end and were nearly all in.[46]

Thanks to the excellent leadership of Robert Merriman, the commander of the Abraham Lincoln Battalion, and a number of other officers, the XV Brigade was kept from breaking and running altogether, but the hours of darkness inevitably found it trudging towards the rear with the rest of the Republican forces. Desperate rearguard actions at Lecerra and Hijar notwithstanding, the dwindling ranks of the Brigade had no option but to keep going. Constantly attacked from the air, after three days, they reached Caspe in a state of considerable disorder. As Walter Gregory remembered:

> As we slumped to the ground ... it was difficult to think of ourselves as a fighting force ... It had been at least three days since any of us ... had slept for even a few minutes. The almost total absence of food and water, the

energy-sapping marches across rough country under a ferocious sun and the constant harassment by the enemy ... meant that we were completely drained, physically and mentally ... Not one of us could have offered even token resistance had we been attacked at that moment.[47]

Behind them, meanwhile, the road was strewn with the detritus of a beaten army:

> The evidence of an army in retreat was everywhere. Here a large lorry loaded with hundreds of picks and spades lay with its back axle in a ditch, the driver's heavy coat lying discarded on the roadside. Further along, another lorry had run into a clump of trees ... A dead Spaniard lying with a bullet hole neatly drilled through his head and a number of bullet holes in the lorry's mudguard testified to enemy aircraft strafing. Everywhere lay empty and full ammunition boxes, odd rifles, bayonets, gas-mask containers, discarded greatcoats. A donkey with a raw bleeding wound hobbled pitifully alongside the road.[48]

Weary and demoralized, the men who reached Caspe nonetheless made a brave effort to defend the town when the Nationalists attacked on 16 March. For a little while, fighting was very fierce and there was afterwards much German muttering along the lines that the problem could have been avoided if only the Spaniards had been prepared to use modern tactics. At one point, indeed, a gallant counterattack supported by eight T26 tanks even succeeded in driving the Nationalists back.[49] Amongst the men fighting in the latter's ranks was Peter Kemp, now the commander of a rifle platoon in the Sixteenth Bandera of the Foreign Legion:

> We were on our feet .... before dawn ... As the sun rose, we heard the first sounds of battle over on our left ... I was relieved to note that the enemy seemed to be very short of artillery: apart from the [45mm] of their tanks, I could hear none ... Taking advantage of the cover afforded by the banks and ditches, I disposed my platoon with a view to giving the maximum depth to my defence ... There was, of course, no time to cut away the olives that blocked our field of fire ... One moment we were waiting ... the next, bullets were hissing through the trees ... All we could see of the enemy was an occasional glimpse of a crouched figure darting from tree to tree. For a while we held them off, but at the end of twenty minutes, when the firing died down, I had lost half a dozen men and we knew the enemy were appreciably closer.[50]

However, in reality, the check was only momentary. With no than 700 men able to fight, the XV Brigade was overwhelmed:

> Events grew very confused and hand-to-hand fighting became the order of the day. I abandoned any attempt to give orders to what remained of

my company: it was simply a case of each man for himself ... Somehow, and I do not know how even to this day, those of us who were still able to stand and fight formed a defensive cordon on the east side of Caspe ... By nightfall the fascists had brought tanks into Caspe itself, and we were forced to retreat.[51]

As if all this was not enough, on 22 March, the Nationalist forces north of the Ebro joined the fray and were soon pushing towards the frontiers of Catalonia, driving all before them in the process. Andrés Bernabé was an infantryman in a Falangist battalion: 'The breakthrough was something else. No war film could possibly depict it adequately: one would have had to witness it in person to understand what it is like to see row upon row of guns firing without cease ... And all this with lots of bombers dropping their loads and lots of fighters doing their usual *cadena*.'[52]

To the south, meanwhile, the whole of the Army Corps of Morocco made an impressive assault crossing of the river Ebro and struck the defenders in the flank. Desperate fighting led by the controversial figure of Valentín González checked the attackers for a week at Lérida (a delay that sufficed to get the vast majority of the population loaded on to trucks and trains and evacuated to Barcelona), and there were briefer stands in other places, but as soon as a few units managed to regroup and make a stand, they were outflanked by further breakthroughs elsewhere. Sent to the front in an attempt to hold the line, a new International Brigade – the CXXIX, a formation made up mostly of Slavs of various nationalities – was decimated by heavy bombing and put to flight. Not until the Nationalists reached the River Segre, then, did their onward march come to an end. Everywhere Franco's forces went, meanwhile, there were the usual executions and massacres, the number of victims running into many hundreds. 'My battalion was very hard on the prisoners', remembered Bernabé. 'Except in the case of those we knew for certain were on our side, the whole lot were shot as a matter of course.'[53]

In all this, the Germans and Italians played a prominent part. On the ground, a CTV that had been re-organized yet again put in a much more impressive performance than before, whilst a major role was played by both the Condor Legion and the Legionary Aviation, whose aircraft strafed the endless columns of troops and refugees in the most unmerciful manner and also pounded such targets as Lérida, where 400 perished in a single raid on 27 March. Also hammered, of course, were the Republican lines of communication. 'Since the ... retaking of Teruel, the fascists have had such an influx of material that they [have] gained supremacy in the air, the first time since May' complained truck driver Lloyd Edmonds. 'And they [have] used it. Every day they have been over, bombing and strafing. They [have] bombed our camp four times. We have become artists in camouflage: if we stop anywhere only for a few minutes, we camouflage our wind shields and lights ... I was ... strafed yesterday morning, but my customary luck still holds ... I was out of the cabin ... in less time than it takes to think

... Some of these towns – Tortosa, for example – are bombed twice or three times a day.'[54] Combined with all this was a new wave of strategic bombing. As Caspe was falling into the hands of the Nationalists, so Italian bombers based in Mallorca were returning to Barcelona. At the direct orders of Mussolini on 16, 17 and 18 March, the city was subjected to heavy bombing raids that caused 924 dead, including 117 children, and more than 1,500 wounded. Damage was heavy. The American volunteer John Tisa was employed at International-Brigade headquarters:

> The first building we got to was the one closest to us. Half the building was out on the street; the other half looked like it was hanging from a tightrope ... Windows in adjoining buildings were partially damaged; a few roofs had caved in ... We left this area and soon approached a bakery shop in flames ... A *tranvía* (street car) fifty feet from an explosion had all its windows knocked out ... Two blocks from the Paseo de Gracia, a house was levelled and its white rock and brick barricaded the street ... Not far from here, a building behind the Catalonian Generalitat propaganda head-quarters was in flames ... Another short walk and we came to the *Treball* building with its iron doors and windows blasted out by concussion. A bomb ... had exploded on the street near it. The same blast smashed in the front of a bookstore and set a parked automobile on fire ... The telephone and electric wires seemed to be everywhere. A dead man, a blanket cover-ing his body, lay in the middle of the *paseo*. Part of his head was visible, and one open eye stared at us as blood trickled along the ground from his body.[55]

And this was only the first raid. Still little more than a teenager, the Barcelona Anarchist Eduardo Pons Prades, who had taken part in the suppression of the uprising of July 1936 as a messenger, had been serving in the army in Madrid, but the bombing caught him on leave in his home city. As he later wrote:

> On 16 and 17 March 1938, Barcelona had to endure a raid every two hours, its attackers displaying the most cold-blooded punctuality ... On the six-teenth, a Thursday, I was in the offices of the Partido Sindicalista ... when all of a sudden there came the sound of the sirens and bombs dropping in unison. It was the second or third raid of the day: I don't remember. The building shook like a house of cards. Every time the planes flew over, what struck me was the paradoxical nature of my reactions: at the front I was always convinced that I would get off scot-free, but in the city I always felt like a defenceless rabbit waiting to be killed. To put it another way, the fear I felt in Barcelona was incomparably greater.[56]

Unable to return to his unit, for the next two days, Pons Prades helped drive some of the many wounded to hospital, along with, at one point, a woman in labour who actually gave birth in the car that he was driving. On the evening of 17 March, however, he became a casualty himself when two lorries full of explosives that were parked nearby were hit by a bomb:

> In a fraction of a second there came through the door ... a great blast of hot air and with it an enormous cloud of dust: it was as if some terrible dragon with seven heads was breathing fire and smoke at me with each one of its seven mouths. Thrown to the ground with great violence, I was next sucked out of the building and tumbled across the ground, ending up semi-conscious and badly battered on the pavement on the opposite side of the street.[57]

As was only to be expected, the collapse in Aragón sparked off a fresh political crisis in the Republican zone. Determined to get rid of Prieto, the Communists had for some time been accusing him of defeatism, in which respect it is but fair to say that the Minister of Defence was by now so demoralized that he had openly begun to advocate surrender (it did not help, meanwhile, that he was in extremely poor health and also suffered from bouts of clinical depression). Organizing angry demonstrations to demand Prieto's resignation, the Communists also put it about that Stalin was only prepared to send more aid to Spain if he went. Negrín himself having decided that Prieto could not remain at his post, he moved in for the kill. At first, there was some attempt to retain his services, but the Minister of Defence proved absolutely unmoveable and rejected every alternative position he was offered, and on 5 April, the Prime Minister therefore took over his position himself and excluded him from the government altogether. Yet he was not the only casualty. Also gone was the Foreign Minister, the same José Giral who had served as Prime Minister in the summer of 1936 and was extremely close to a Manuel Azaña who had to all intents and purposes withdrawn from politics and was known to think the Republic was a lost cause. Replaced by the crypto-Communist Alvarez del Vayo, like Prieto, he was a victim to Negrín's determination to instil the Republican camp with an iron resolve that could admit of not even the slightest hint of demoralization.[58]

Back at the front, meanwhile, the battle was continuing unabated. In particular, the end of the month saw the final destruction of what remained of the XV Brigade. After the fighting at Caspe, the brigade fell back to Gandesa, while its ranks were filled up to a limited extent by a mixture of raw recruits (now almost entirely Spanish) and men who had for one reason or another missed the first part of the campaign. The Abraham Lincoln Battalion, at least, even received a fresh supply of hand-grenades and Moisin-Nagant rifles, the new weapons being part of the first fruits of Negrín's success in opening up the French frontier to the supply of weapons (see below). Dug in around the town (an important road junction that would for that same reason feature prominently in the later battle of the Ebro), the Internationals might have achieved something, but they were instead ordered to advance on the enemy and pushed north and west into open country. There was, however, little knowledge of the exact positions of the enemy, and the result was disaster, 30 March seeing the British battalion suffer terrible casualties when they were taken by surprise by an Italian tank unit near Calaceite, the many dead including both yet another battalion commander, one George Fletcher, and the battalion commissar, Wally Tapsell.[59] Also badly hit was the Mackenzie-Papineau battalion and the Spanish Fifty-Ninth, both of which ran into more Italians north-east of the site of the rout of the British battalion and had to conduct a day-long fighting retreat.[60] Further to the east, the Americans had an easier day and had pushed northwards past the village of Batea, where the XV Brigade's commander, Vladimir Copic, established his headquarters. What Copic was completely unaware of, however, was that a substantial force of Nationalist troops – to be precise, an entire infantry division – was pushing round his right flank through the rugged terrain between Batea and the River Ebro. Still worse, the danger was not discovered till late in the afternoon of 31 March, when a party that had been sent back by truck to pick up extra ammunition reported shelling in the hills beyond the town. Having already been driven southwards the day before, the British and Canadians were in no real danger, but the position of the Abraham Lincoln Battalion was another matter altogether, for the Nationalists had only to take Gandesa to cut them off. Rejecting a ridiculous demand on the part of the brigade commissar to the effect that the battalion should hold its ground and fight to the last man, Copic and his chief of staff, Robert Merriman, the erstwhile commander of the Lincoln Battalion, ordered the Americans to retreat, and dawn on 1 April saw them reach the outskirts of Gandesa. Here, however, they encountered a scene of total panic, for the Nationalists were themselves on the verge of taking the place. Amongst the men of an advance party sent to reconnoitre was seaman and labour activist Harry Fisher:

> The civilian population was frantically loading carts with belongings and food ... People were piling sacks of sugar, rice, bread, coffee, canned goods and tobacco onto their carts. One old woman was trying desperately to drag a tremendous sack of sugar along the road, but she could scarcely budge it. Small children, five or six years old, were running like mad with their hands full of food. Women were screaming at the children to hurry and get more, while they guarded the carts as though they were gold mines ... Everyone kept looking up at the skies with terror in their eyes, always expecting the fascist planes to begin an attack.[61]

Realizing that they were trapped, the Americans now launched a desperate attempt to break through to the River Ebro, only to be driven back with contemptuous ease and forced to take refuge in some olive groves north of the town. When night came, they tried to slip through the enemy forces and make for Tortosa, but it was too late: there were simply too many Nationalists in the area, and the result was that most of the battalion was either killed or taken prisoner, amongst those who disappeared without trace being Robert Merriman and the brigade commissar Dave Doran, both of whom are believed to have been taken prisoner and summarily executed. After many adventures, a few men reached the River Ebro and swam to safety, whilst some others managed to join up with the battered remnants of the British and Canadian battalions, with whom they helped fend off the CTV for a full day near the village of Pinell some miles south-east of Gandesa, but to all intents and purposes the Abraham Lincoln Battalion had ceased to exist.[62]

Traumatic though it was, the destruction of the XV Brigade was but a detail in a much wider picture. While the fighting for Gandesa was still raging, other columns of Nationalists were bypassing the town to the south and pushing ever closer towards the Mediterranean, one notable advance taking the remote town of Morella. Resistance, meanwhile, was ever more sporadic, most units having long since been reduced to little more than bands of fugitives. Indeed, army and civilian population alike were in full flight. Having escaped the disaster at Gandesa, Bob Clark had somehow made it to the bridge across the Ebro at Tortosa with about a dozen other survivors of the British Battalion:

> It began to look as if the entire Republican army was retreating across the Ebro … What a spectacle, literally thousands of almost exhausted khaki-clad troops, many hundreds of civilians, even cripples on crutches and flocks of sheep and goats streamed along the highway. Huge six-wheeled lorries laden with ammunition, even larger lorries laden with four-inch and six-inch howitzers, armoured cars, an odd tank or so, then a company of troops still keeping their formation and trailing their wheeled Russian machine-guns behind them, followed in succession. Many lorries were loaded with civilians with piles of bedding … All were making their way to that solitary girder bridge.[63]

With matters in this state, the culmination of the great offensive could not be long postponed, and on 15 April, the leading Nationalist troops reached the Mediterranean at Vinaroz: the Republican zone was cut in two. However, massive propaganda victory for the Nationalists though this event was, the Republic was not yet lost. Realizing that there was going to be no way of preventing the Nationalist forces from reaching the Mediterranean, the Negrín government had been taking every step it could to make ready for this development, dividing its forces into two army groups – Army Group Centre under Miaja and Army Group East under Hernández Saravia – turning the battered remnants of the forces defeated in southern Aragón into a new army known as the Army of the Ebro commanded by Modesto, and transferring as many troops as it could to a Catalonia that at this point was almost undefended.[64] In response to the terrible losses that had been incurred in the campaign, meanwhile, draconian measures were instituted against desertion and the age range of conscription extended to a crippling 17–45, the many teenagers who were now incorporated into the draft following the new measures being referred to as the 'baby-bottle class.'[65]

Beaten on the battlefield, meanwhile, Negrín also launched a major peace offensive. Less than two weeks after Vinaroz was occupied, then, there appeared a thirteen-point plan that in effect offered surrender on terms (most importantly, the formation of a coalition government, life and liberty for all the Republic's combatants and the renunciation of reprisals of any sort). There was much in the document that the Nationalists could legitimately object to – to expect Franco to accept what amounted to the old Frente-Popular programme in such areas as workers' rights, regional autonomy and agrarian reform was at best wishful thinking, and the demands concerned were therefore doubtless included as a basis for negotiation only – but the offer of a compromise peace was nevertheless entirely serious whilst yet being designed to rekindle support for the war effort.[66]

Whether any of this would have been enough to turn the tide is a moot point. At this point, however, something unexpected happened. The Republican leadership was convinced that Franco would now turn on Catalonia, whilst there was also strong support for such a move in Nationalist circles.[67] Yet in the event, the *caudillo* instead turned south and directed his armies to march on Valencia. Reference has here often been made to worries about provoking French intervention, and there was, in fact, some concern at this point that the government of Léon Blum was seriously considering intervention in the civil war (it had, as we shall see, already opened the frontier to arms shipments to the Republic).[68] However, there were also plenty of other factors in play, not the least of these being that the gains to be made in the Levante seemed to be much greater than those on offer in Catalonia: in brief, take Valencia, and the whole of the central zone might well be forced to surrender on account of the impact this would have on the import of food and munitions. Also very likely to have been of some influence is the fact that, jealous of his fellow generals, General Varela, whose Army Corps of Castile was holding the Teruel area and had therefore taken no part in the battles in Aragón, was eager to secure a share in the glory and therefore lobbied hard for the southern option. By contrast, encouraged by claims from both sides of the battle lines that victory would have come many months earlier than it actually did had Franco turned on Barcelona, Preston advanced the thesis that the *caudillo* 'was motivated ... by a reluctance to move to the definitive victory before further destruction and demoralization of the Republic's human resources.'[69] All that can be said is that this thesis remains unproven, that a long war was replete with danger and, finally, that there is every reason to think that securing the fall of Madrid would bring the war to an end far more quickly than securing the fall of a region whose isolation now rendered it little more than a sideshow. In the event, Franco got things badly wrong – not only did the new offensive prove disappointing in its results, but Catalonia also turned out to be much more of a danger than was ever anticipated – but even a figure as deeply unpleasant as the *caudillo* does not deserve to be judged on the basis of hindsight.[70]

For whatever reason it was undertaken, the new battle began on 23 April. While Aranda's Army Corps of Galicia struck south along the axis of the coastal road that linked Valencia with Tarragona and Barcelona, Varela's troops pushed into the deep Republican salient that had been created in the mountainous region north-east of Teruel in the course of campaign of Aragón. On the coastal plain, progress was smooth enough, but in the mountains to the west, Varela made only a limited amount of progress before several days of heavy rain completely paralyzed the whole offensive. Thereby provided with a handy breathing space, the Republicans rushed in reinforcements whilst at the same time doing all they could to fortify the threatened sector, the result being that when the offensive was renewed, it ran into heavy resistance and made even slower progress than before, and that despite the fact that the attacking troops now received the support of the independent division of García Valiño. Amongst the forces of this last commander was the Tercio de Lacar and, with it, Carmelo Revilla Cebrecos:

> In spite of the time of year, the weather was terrible: it was very cold and there was rain all day every day. On top of the difficult nature of the terrain through which they had to pass, the *requetés* therefore had to cope with being completely soaked, the result being that the operation was subject to repeated delays ... On the fifteenth and sixteenth so torrential was the rain that there was no possibility of making any advance at all.[71]

Particularly notable in the fighting was the recovery of the Republican air force: on 13 May, for example, José Larios' wing of eighteen Fiats encountered a large force of Chatos and Moscas over the village of Allepuz and were forced to engage in a prolonged dog-fight.[72] On this occasion, the Republican flyers were routed with, or so Larios claims, the loss of seven planes and several other possibles, but on many other occasions, they were more fortunate, Revilla Cebrecos complaining that his Tercio de Lacar was repeatedly strafed by enemy aircraft.[73] Even without this added inconvenience, he found that the campaign was becoming ever harder: forced to engage in full-scale frontal assaults at Mosqueruela and Lucena del Cid, in this last action alone the battalion lost ten dead and twenty-four wounded, and all this in a terrain so difficult that it was impossible to bring up the battalion's field kitchens, the troops therefore often going without hot food for many days.[74]

In contrast to the extraordinarily rapid advances made in Aragón, what became known as the campaign in the Maestrazgo – the area of rugged mountains in which most of the fighting took place – was therefore a disappointing affair: by 26 May, indeed, Aranda, Varela and García Valino had advanced no more than thirty miles. Not surprisingly, then, there was fresh muttering at Franco's headquarters, and all the more so as 22 May had seen some sharp fighting flare up on the northern reaches of the Catalan front when the Army of the East mounted a surprise offensive designed both to regain control of the important hydro-electric plants located in the upper reaches of the valley of the River Segre and to rescue a Republican division that had been cut off in the Pyrenees in the fighting in late March and had been holding out ever since. The results of this offensive were distinctly disappointing, however. Herewith Julián Zugazagoitia:

> When the first bulletin came in, it was vague and lacking in sparkle, while the second one was much the same … The reconquest of Tremp began to look not just problematic but impossible. And so it transpired: after three days Negrín … without much conviction assured me that things were going well. "What we intended has in part been achieved. The number of enemy troops on the Levant front has been reduced whilst their aviation has been sent up here. In consequence, we have got a chance to re-organise our troops down there and shore up our defences. But these objectives could not be revealed to the combatants for fear that they would be discouraged." "But weren't we hoping to reconquer Tremp with all that it means for our supply of electricity?" "Only if it had proved possible. Personally, I always thought it unlikely due to the difficult nature of the terrain. How anybody could have thought that the area would be given up so easily is beyond me. The possibilities the area offers for defence are unbeatable."[75]

Indeed, even as a diversion, the operation failed, the forces in the Maestrazgo simply pushing on notwithstanding. In the event, however, progress was disappointing: fierce counterattacks forced some of the Nationalist spearheads to fall back, while it took a full month for Aranda to take the major town of Castellón.[76]

Increasingly frustrated, Franco now threw in still more troops: García Valino's division, already much stronger than such a unit would ordinarily have been, was given enough fresh troops to allow it to become the Army Corps of the Maestrazgo; still more men were brought up and given to General José Solchaga as the Army Corps of the River Turia; and, finally, the three divisions of the CTV were also sent to the front. On 2 July, then, this great mass of troops was hurled at the Republican defences and immediately broke through, only to be blocked by a solid defensive line that had been constructed in the imposing Sierra de Espadán, a range of mountains that ran some way in the rear of the Republican front line (these fortifications, incidentally, were no gim-crack 'ring of iron' but rather an affair that was expertly engineered, with deep bunkers, well-sighted trenches and pillboxes and plenty of artillery support). Manning this 'XYZ Line', as it was known, meanwhile, were large numbers of fresh troops who had not been caught up in the fighting in Aragón. Attack after attack followed, but the ferocious shelling and bombing to which the attackers were subjected had little effect, the Nationalists therefore being able to make no progress whatsoever. Inevitably, meanwhile, their casualties were very heavy.[77]

The battle for the XYZ Line lasted from 13 to 23 July, but in the end, the troops involved were so exhausted that it had to be abandoned. Thus ended eight months of fighting that had been among the fiercest and most sustained of the war so far. The Republic had endured terrible losses in terms of men and *materiél* and seen the Nationalists occupy thousands of square miles of territory, whilst at the same time beginning to experience the full weight of their enemies' superior firepower, a problem that was much exacerbated by the increasingly precarious nature of the supply of arms to the Republic. Living conditions were increasingly terrible, while there was an overwhelming mood of war-weariness. Yet, if down, the government of Juan Negrín was not yet out, and determined to keep fighting as long as possible in the hope that the international situation would change in Europe. With war seemingly looming, to resist was indeed to conquer.

Notes

1 Cit. Inglis, *Letters from Spain*, p. 152.
2 Cit. Heredia, *Monarquía, república y guerra*, p. 284. Implicit in these remarks is a deep-seated anti-militarism, the roots of which can be traced back as far as the Spanish War of Independence of 1808–14 and possibly even earlier. Exacerbated by the military uprising, the resultant distrust of military opinion and expertise alike was to be something that dogged the Republican war effort from start to finish.
3 Thomas, *Spanish Civil War*, pp. 665–6. G. Jackson, *Juan Negrín, Physiologist, Socialist and Spanish Republican War Minister* (Eastbourne, 2010) is a recent biography.
4 Thomas, *Spanish Civil War*, pp. 667–8.
5 Ibid., pp. 521–3; Graham, *Spanish Republic at War*, pp. 181–2.
6 Graham, *Spanish Republic at War*, pp. 328–9. As Graham points out, this hegemonism was increased by pressure from below: large numbers of the party's new membership had been implicated in the clientelism that had characterized Spanish politics even under the Republic and therefore expected the Communist leadership, like any other party leadership, to reward their loyalty with patronage and favour of all sorts.
7 Thomas, *Spanish Civil War*, pp. 774–9.
8 Zugazagoitía, *Guerra y vicisitudes de los españoles*, pp. 35–4.
9 Biescas Palacios, *Memorias*, p. 33.
10 Ibid., p. 34. For an account of the battle up to and including the Republican entry into the city, see J. M. Martínez Bande, *La batalla de Teruel* (Madrid, 1974), pp. 60–90.
11 As with other such instances, Preston is inclined to be critical of the decision to counterattack: 'The sound advice of the senior German and Italian officers in Spain was to abandon Teruel and go ahead with the planned operation to cut off Madrid. His own staff ... also believed that he should not let himself be diverted from his original plans. However, his determination to bring the Republic to total humiliating annihilation did not admit of allowing the enemy such successes. The capture of Madrid would have hastened the end of the war, and, possibly, with Rojo having thrown everything into the Teruel offensive, at little cost. In contrast, to snuff out the move against Teruel had little strategic significance, and might, and indeed did, take a bloody toll. However, to Franco its attraction was that it provided the opportunity to destroy a large body of the Republic's best forces.' Preston, *Franco*, pp. 292–3. The key sentence here is the last one, however. Whilst the case for Franco wanting a long war is, at best, unproven, and that for the capture of Madrid ending the war downright dubious, the destruction of the People's Army was a guaranteed road to victory.
12 For the siege of the Nationalist strongholds, see Martínez Bande, *Batalla de Teruel*, pp. 105–20, 139–61. Rey d'Harcourt, Polanco and the other prisoners were at first spared, but on 7 February 1939, the colonel, the bishop and forty-two other survivors of the battle were summarily executed by their guards as they were being evacuated to France in the wake of the fall of Barcelona.
13 Clark, *No Boots to my Feet*, pp. 51–2.

14 Thomas, *To Tilt at Windmills*, p. 73. Amongst the Nationalist pilots was José Larios: 'On 19 January 1938, one of our biggest and most concentrated raids of the war took place over the Teruel battlefield. Around 400 bombers and fighters swept backwards and forwards during the whole day and 110 tons of high explosives were dropped over vital targets. We were briefed … to escort the Junkers, Savoias, Heinkel 51's and Romeos: this meant that we would be flying in wide circles over the target area, some of us at the same level of the bombers, the rest high above them … The patrols lasted from two to two and a half hours from take-off to landing: we were over the lines between sixty and ninety minutes. It was a strain on the neck muscles to continually swivel one's head around in all directions, especially above and behind, two most vulnerable spots, but it was the best way to keep alive … During this period we were flying two or three patrols daily.' Larios, *Combat over Spain*, pp. 160–1.

15 Ibid., p. 76.

16 Cit. Inglis, *Letters from Spain*, p. 166.

17 Tarazona Torán, *Yo fui piloto de caza rojo*, p. 101.

18 Iniesta Cano, *Memorias y recuerdos*, p. 120.

19 Revilla Cebrecos, *Tercio de Lacar*, p. 141.

20 Permuy López, *Aviación en la Guerra Civil Española*, p. 178.

21 *Cit.* Vidal, *Recuerdo 1936*, p. 236.

22 For the latter part of the battle of Teruel, see Martínez Bande, *Batalla de Teruel*, pp. 165–209.

23 Tarazona, *Yo fui piloto de caza rojo*, p. 102. Again we see here the Republican fixation with the idea of Nationalist air superiority. The Nationalists did a better job of concentrating their planes, but the overall superiority in favour of Franco's forces at the start of the battle of Teruel was only about four to three, while the Republicans were still ahead in the quality of their fighters. Permuy López, *Aviación en la Guerra Civil Española*, pp. 178–80. On the other hand, Tarazona is right to imply that the Republicans had heavy losses at Teruel: so many of their fighters were downed that a number of squadrons had to be amalgamated. Ibid., p. 183.

24 Molina Franco and Manrique García, *Armas y uniformes*, pp. 40–1, 229.

25 Descriptions of the suffering endured by the troops on both sides are legion. E.g. Revilla Cebrecos, *Tercio de Lacar*, p.131; Candelas, *Adventures of an Innocent*, p. 110; Biescas Palacios, *Memorias*, pp. 35–6.

26 For the air battles over Teruel, see Salas, *Air War over Spain*, pp. 209–18.

27 Cit. V. Johnston, *Legions of Babel: the International Brigades in the Spanish Civil War* (Harrisburg, Pennsylvania, 1967), p. 136.

28 One problem that beset shock units such as the International Brigades and the still more élite tank battalions (all of which were recruited entirely from volunteers) was combat fatigue. Several leading members of the British battalion, notably Fred Copeman and Jock Cunningham, had nervous breakdowns in the wake of the battle of Brunete, while the T26 commander Alvaro Cortes Roa is disturbingly frank in his account of the impact of the battle on both himself and other 'tankers': 'We had a hard time of it. I witnessed various psychological crises amongst my comrades and often myself thought that it was impossible to carry on.' Cortes Roa, *Tanquista*, p. 148.

29 Lee, *Moment of War*, pp. 158–9.

30 Ibid., p. 158. Anxious to discredit a critical voice, the Communist-dominated International Brigade Association responded to the publication of *A Moment of War* with claims that Lee was never in Spain. Certainly, he was not in Spain for very long – only some eleven weeks – whilst his experience of the front was limited to its rear echelons, but that he served with the XV Brigade on the Teruel front there is no doubt whatsoever. See < http://blogs.bl.uk/english-and-drama/2014/04/laurie-lees-lost-diary-discovered.html >, accessed 1 October 2016.

31 For some grim memories of life in Madrid and Barcelona, see A. Bullón de Mendoza and A. de Diego (eds.), *Historias orales de la Guerra Civil* (Barcelona, 2000), pp. 115–18.

32 Tarazona, *Yo fuí piloto de caza rojo*, p. 109. The Nationalists did not quite have it all their own way at sea at this point. On the night of 5–6 March was waged the battle of Cape Palos. The biggest naval action of the war, this pitted the three Nationalist cruisers in service at this point – *Canarias*, *Baleares* and *Almirante Cervera* – against the light cruisers *Libertad* and *Méndez Núñez* and no fewer than eleven destroyers. In brief, the Nationalist ships were convoying two merchant ships crammed with much-needed Italian war material to Cádiz when, a little after midnight, they suddenly encountered the much stronger Republican flotilla some fifty miles due east of Alicante. Attacking out of the darkness under the cover of the light cruisers' 152mm guns, the destroyers launched a salvo of torpedoes, several of which hit the *Baleares*, which sank some three hours later with the loss of approximately 740 lives. However, having fired their torpedoes, the triumphant Republicans turned for home, probably because they had no desire to risk being bombed with the coming of dawn. All in all, it was a fairly pointless episode, and all the more so as the loss of the *Baleares* was partially made good by the arrival in service a short while later of the newly modernized light cruiser *República* (now renamed *Navarra*). For a recent account, see J. Peñalva, 'Combate del Cabo de Palos (6 de marzo de 1938): el hundimiento del crucero Baleares', < http://www.revistanaval.com/www-alojados/armada/batallas/palos.htm >, accessed 30 April 2016.

33 The extent of the SIM's activities has been the subject of much debate: that it carried out hundreds of arrests, operated without due legal process and had many secret detention centres and torture chambers is undeniable. Yet it never had quite the free run that is sometimes imagined, even if the estimate of 1,000 executions in 1938 alone is still a damning indictment. See Thomas, *Spanish Civil War*, p. 779.

34 Candelas, *Adventures of an Innocent*, p. 112.

35 For a detailed account of the operations of the Condor Legion in the first days of the battle, see Proctor, *Hitler's Luftwaffe in the Spanish Civil War*, pp. 191–5. On 9 and 10 March, losses amounted to no more than one Heinkel He111 and one Messerschmidt Me109. Amongst the many pilots caught unprepared was Francisco Tarazona, whose squadron was based at Caspe. On the morning of 9 March, he recounts, his squadron was in the process of getting ready to take off for its usual dawn patrol when the airfield was struck by a heavy air-raid. 'My mouth was filled with the taste of death. Somehow I managed to take off though my Mosca was all the way buffeted from side-to-side. Twisting and turning, in an attempt to dodge the enemy bombs, I gained some height, and began to feel a bit better: the enormous fighter escort that was protecting the bombers notwithstanding, at least I was in my element. Yet, such was the vigilance of the carnivorous enemy that every inch of sky seemed a no-go zone: I could hardly move for the hail of fire. Just like it had been in the north, there was nothing for it but to fight like mad men. There were Fiats on all sides: it was their job to attack us whilst, far above us, the Messerschmitts waited to pounce on any prey that escaped the pack of hounds. Two of the former got on my tail, but the lightning speed of my plane saved me from being caught … We had been taken by surprise … but what was no surprise was the enemy's numerical superiority.' Tarazona, *Yo fuí piloto de caza rojo*, p. 112.

36 Cit. Toynbee, *The Distant Drum*, pp. 99–100.

37 Puig, *Personal Memories of the Spanish Civil War*, pp. 163–5.

38 V. Hernaiz Grijalba (ed.), *Memorias de mi padre: Guerra Civil Española, 1937–1938* (Barcelona, 2012), pp. 26–8.

39 Ibid., p. 30.

40 Cit. Vidal, *Recuerdo 1936*, p. 235.

41 For the experiences of one harassed guard, see Revilla Cebrecos, *Tercio de Lacar*, pp. 158–9.

42 Lister, *Memorias de un luchador*, p. 327. Another commander plunged into the maelstrom at Alcáñiz was Manuel Tagüeña, whose crack Third Division had been hastily rushed in from the Madrid front: 'We covered the last few miles with great difficulty,

the road clogged with all kinds of vehicles and artillery pieces, not to mention large number of fugitives travelling on foot, all of whom were heading in the opposite direction. The town, too, was jammed with soldiers whilst its narrow streets were all full of lorries: at headquarters, meanwhile, there reigned the most horrible confusion, while nobody had the slightest idea where General Rojo had his command post.' Tagüeña Lacorte, *Testimonio de dos guerras*, p. 171.

43 Biescas Palacios, *Memorias*, pp. 36–7.

44 In brief, sent up to defend the area of Codo, the XI Brigade was quickly overwhelmed and forced to retreat on Hijar and Alcáñiz, eventually being all but wiped out in the vicinity of Calaceite, and the XII, XIII and XIV overwhelmed in a series of combats that enveloped them as soon as they entered the line. Vidal, *Brigadas internacionales*, pp. 262–73; Delperrie de Bayac. *Brigadas Internacionales*, pp. 282–92. An eye-witness to the fate of the XIII International Brigade was Andrzej Rozborski, a sometime Communist who became disillusioned with what he saw in Spain and managed not just to desert but also to return to Poland, where he made a series of declarations to the Polish secret services: 'At this point [i.e. when the Brigade reached Alcáñiz] a panic broke out that was so severe that it is difficult to describe. The men took off in all directions; there were terrible losses; and the enemy aviation strafed without cease any group that tried to escape. The brigade lost all its transport, tanks, machine-guns and ammunition ... and casualties among the troops were so heavy that the second battalion ended up with just thirty-seven men ... As punishment for the defeat, several battalion commanders and others were executed on suspicion of cowardice. However, no such fate was suffered by any of the political commissars or other party functionaries.' Cit. Requena Gallego and Eiroa, *Al lado del gobierno republicano*, p. 106.

45 Cit. Landis, *Death in the Olive Groves*, pp. 128–9. Mention of the Nationalist tanks is interesting. Now officially a part of the Foreign Legion, Franco's single battalion of German Panzer Is was deployed at Belchite, and it is sometimes claimed that the senior German tank officer in Spain, von Thoma, insisted that they be used en masse to drive through the enemy lines in true *blitzkrieg* fashion. Judging from this account, however, it seems more likely that they were used in their usual role of infantry support. On the other hand, they were not just driven straight at the Republican trenches but were used to envelop them from each flank. As Harry Fisher wrote in a letter to his family, 'There were many breaks in the line. We had to keep low. Too much shrapnel from shells landing nearby. Gosh, but I felt shaky then. Meanwhile, I still saw the planes strafing the hills. While the planes were keeping our comrades low, a bunch of their tanks got around the hill. In this way many of our comrades were killed or captured. They never had a chance.' Cit. C. Nelson and J. Hendricks (eds.), *Madrid, 1937: Letters of the Abraham Lincoln Brigade from the Spanish Civil War* (New York, 1996), p. 374.

46 Clark, *No Boots to my Feet*, pp. 60–1.

47 Gregory, *Shallow Grave*, pp. 105–6.

48 Clark, *No Boots to my Feet*, p. 73.

49 Landis, *Death in the Olive Groves*, p. 135.

50 Kemp, *Mine were of Trouble*, pp. 177–8. In the course of the fighting that followed when the Republican assault was resumed, Kemp was both creased in the neck by a bullet and blown off his feet by a hand-grenade. Meanwhile, according to him, by the time that Caspe fell the next day, his company had barely twenty men left on their feet out of the 110 with which it had commenced the action. Ibid., p. 184.

51 Gregory, *Shallow Grave*, p. 106. The fall of Caspe brought to an end what is generally regarded as the first phase of the Nationalist offensive. For a general account of the fighting of the period 9–17 March, see J. M. Martínez-Bande, *La llegada al mar* (Madrid, 1975), pp. 25–68.

52 Cit. Vidal, *Recuerdo 1936*, p. 247. The *cadena* (literally 'chain') was a manoeuvre whereby aircraft strafing a ground-target dived down upon it one after another in line astern, thereby concentrating their fire on one small area.

53 Cit. ibid., p. 249.The fighting north of the Ebro is chronicled in Martínez Bande, *Llegada al mar*, pp. 71–137. For details of the repression, see Preston, *Spanish Holocaust*, pp. 459–61. As Preston points out, if anything, things were even worse than they had been on other occasions: such was the hatred of the Nationalists of the Catalans that towns such as Lérida and Fraga were treated with even more savagery than normal. With every advance, meanwhile, tales of Red savagery fanned the flames of hatred. 'Every so often we see unpleasant things', wrote a Jesuit novice serving as a medical orderly. 'In Molinos de Sipán, for example, we found thirteen women and five children who had been shot dead. As well as that there was the corpse of a man who had been shot lying in the doorway of a house. Going inside ... we found a woman who had been hacked to pieces lying on the stairs ... Let the Reds talk of humanity now!' Cit. Cabezas Gil, *Ya sabes mi paradero*, p. 311; assuming that this account is true in its basic details, there is, of course, no way of knowing how the victims died. There was some disappointment in the Nationalist ranks that the offensive was not continued deep into Catalonia with a view to taking Barcelona, but fear of provoking France led Franco to decide for the time being to confine his operations to the area south of the Ebro. See Preston, *Franco*, pp. 304–5.

54 Cit. Inglis, *Letters from Spain*, pp. 171–5.

55 Tisa, *Recalling the Good Fight*, pp. 134–5. One result of the bombing was that several fighter squadrons were pulled back from the front to protect Barcelona. Until this point, it seems that the protection of Barcelona and other coastal cities had been left to the handful of Dewoitines and Nieuports left over from the fighting of 1936, these simply being too slow to catch the Italian Savoia-Marchettis that carried out the raids from their bases in Mallorca. See Milany, *Aviador de la República*, pp. 85–6.

56 Pons Prades, *Soldado de la República*, pp. 248–9.

57 Ibid., pp. 253–4.

58 For the crisis that brought the exclusion of Prieto from the government, see Graham, *Spanish Republic at War*, pp. 360–62. Negrín's position here is completely understandable. In reality, he no more believed that the war could be won than Prieto had, and had for some months been working behind the scenes to secure some sort of negotiated settlement. Unlike the erstwhile Minister of Defence, however, he saw that the latter goal precluded any form of defeatism, for Franco could clearly only be brought to the table by the prospect of a long and costly struggle that could well be subsumed into a wider European struggle. In his insistence on 'resisting to conquer', he may have echoed the Communists, but, whereas they in effect advocated war for its own sake, he dreamed not of war to the death, but rather of war to the peace table.

59 Walter Gregory provides an excellent account of this action. Thus: 'As we turned a bend in the road we ran foul of a column of enemy light tanks ... Another group of tanks broke cover from a wood on our flank and Italian infantry in large numbers entered the fray in support of their armour ... We broke into ones and twos and sought cover wherever we could find it. Fortunately our machine-gun company, which had been at the rear of the battalion, was able to secure some high ground and bring its guns quickly into action, thus affording crucial covering fire while those of us on the road sought to ... make good our escape.' Gregory, *Shallow Grave*, p. 108. For a more general account, see Baxell, *British Volunteers*, pp. 98–9.

60 For the experience of the Mackenzie-Papineau battalion of the campaign of March–April 1937, see V. Howard and M. Reynolds, *The Mackenzie-Papineau Battalion: the Canadian Contingent in the Spanish Civil War* (Ottawa, 1986), pp. 174–95.

61 H. Fisher, *Comrades: Tales of a Brigadista in the Spanish Civil War* (Lincoln, Nebraska, 1998), p. 127.

62 The most detailed account of the destruction of the Abraham Lincoln Battalion is C. Eby, *Comrades and Commissars: the Abraham Lincoln Battalion in the Spanish Civil War* (Harrisburg, Pennsylvania, 2007), pp. 313–46, but see also R. Rosenstone, *Crusade of the Left: the Lincoln Battalion in the Spanish Civil War* (new edition, New Brunswick, New Jersey, 2009),pp. 290–6; and Landis, *Death in the Olive Groves*, pp. 144–55.

63 Clark, *No Boots to my Feet*, p. 86.

64 Martínez Bande, *Llegada al mar*, pp. 194–5; Thomas, *Spanish Civil War*, pp. 815–16. Army Group East had two armies, (those of the Ebro and the East) and Army Group Centre five (those of the Centre, Andalucía, Extremadura, the Levant and Manoeuvre).

65 Matthews, *Reluctant Warriors*, p. 198; Alpert, *Spanish Republican* Army, p. 157. In all, the Republic mobilized twenty-seven classes of conscripts or roughly twice as many as did their opponents. In part, this discrepancy was the result of the ever-shrinking nature of their demographic base, but in part, too, it was the result of the adoption of the mixed brigade and the disproportionate demands that this placed on manpower. At all events, the impact on morale is all too easy to imagine. To quote Luis Bolín, 'Out of a total of 19,653 men captured during [the Battle of the Ebro], forty-five per cent were approximately the same age as our soldiers, ten per cent were older, and the remaining forty-five per cent younger.' Bolín, *Spain: the Vital Years*, p. 314.

66 Thomas, *Spanish Civil War*, pp. 820–22.

67 E.g. Kindelán, *Mis cuadernos de guerra*, pp. 157–8.

68 How genuine these concerns were, it is difficult to say. The opening of the frontier to French arms on 17 March clearly was not an encouraging sign, while two days before, Blum had proposed to a cabinet meeting that Franco be sent an ultimatum warning him to cease his use of foreign troops and aircraft or risk French intervention, some careless talk on the part of certain ministers leading to reports in the French press that an expeditionary force was being prepared in readiness for dispatch across the Pyrenees. Yet the danger was at best minimal. Not only was Blum's gambit rejected by a cabinet deeply alarmed that such a move could not but lead to war with Germany and Italy, but many generals were inclined to sympathize with the Nationalists and take the line that, as they looked increasingly likely to win, France's interests would be best served by cultivating friendly relations with them in the hope of persuading them not to 'go Axis' once peace had come. Setting all this aside, meanwhile, France was simply not ready for war in 1938: there were too few tanks and too few planes, while the military budget had been cut so savagely that there was no way of funding even the traditional annual manoeuvres. Still worse, there would be no support from anyone other than the entirely unknown quantity represented by the Soviet Union: the British had made it very clear that they would not fight in a war whose *causus belli* was Spain, while Italy was all too clearly now firmly in Germany's orbit. See P. Jackson, 'French strategy and the Spanish Civil War', in C. Leitz and D. Dunthorne (eds.), *Spain in an International Context, 1936–1959* (Oxford, 1999), pp. 55–79. As Preston says, then, 'Franco's anxiety about the activities of the French cannot entirely account for his cautious turn away from Catalonia.' Preston, *Franco*, p. 305.

69 Preston, *Franco*, p. 305.

70 For a detailed discussion of the debate, see J. M. Martínez Bande, *La ofensiva sobre Valencia* (Madrid, 1977), pp. 13–24.

71 Revilla Cebrecos, *Tercio de Lacar*, pp. 217–18.

72 Larios, *Combat over Spain*, pp. 191–2. An interesting comment on the experience of aerial combat can be found in the memoirs of the Catalan aviator Joan de Milany: 'In the dogfights one had the sensation of pitting oneself more against machines than against persons of flesh and blood, persons with feelings. Shooting an aircraft down produced a sense of triumph that was essentially sporting, something along the lines, perhaps, of scoring a goal against a rival team ... I doubt whether any pilots concerned themselves with the idea that what they had in their gun-sights were human beings. We only felt any sentiment in respect of those who did not threaten us, and sometimes not even then.' Milany, *Aviador de la República*, p. 124.

73 For an interesting personal account of the operations of the Republican air force in the battle of the Maestrazgo, see Milany, *Aviador de la República*, pp. 115–21. Not surprisingly, it is his contention that the Nationalists did not have it all their own way and were defeated just as frequently as the Republicans were.

74 Revilla Cebrecos, *Tercio de Lacar*, pp. 217–32, 238–9. For a general discussion of the campaign, see Martínez Bande, *Ofensiva sobre Valencia*, pp. 45–98.
75 Zugazagoitia, *Guerra y vicisitudes de los* españoles, pp. 437–8.
76 Martínez Bande, *Ofensiva sobre Valencia*, pp. 98–148.
77 For the final drive on Valencia, see ibid., pp. 151–78. Amongst the men wounded in these attacks was the Carlist Revilla Cebrecos. Revilla Cebrecos, *Tercio de Lacar*, pp. 249–50.

9

ENDGAME

Viewed with the benefit of hindsight, the victory of General Franco in the Spanish Civil War appears all but inevitable, the Republic's unfavourable diplomatic situation alone meaning that it was very unlikely that its cause would ever have prevailed. Add to this such issues as political disunion and the technical incompetence that had marred its mobilization for total war, and one has to wonder why anyone ever doubted that the struggle could ever have ended in any other manner than it did. Yet the early summer of 1938 saw Nationalist Spain, or at least its leadership and political circles, plunged into gloom. To quote a dispatch that the German ambassador, Von Stohrer, penned from San Sebastián on 19 May:

> Every time a military reverse or even a stalemate occurs in the military operations of Nationalist Spain, the same phenomenon appears again and again: the optimistic appraisal of the situation and the confidence in victory change to the opposite, giving way to deep disappointment, great mental depression and dissatisfaction, and allowing the internal political differences to come to the fore. This has been experienced once more since the brilliant advance of Franco's troops to the Mediterranean has more or less come to a halt and the collapse of the Reds, which many had been expecting, had not occurred.[1]

The extent of the crisis of confidence to which Von Stohrer is referring is open to question, but that some sort of slump in morale should have occurred was unavoidable. Always questionable in military terms, Franco's decision to advance on Valencia had proved abortive; the fall of Prieto had removed a distinctly defeatist influence from the Republican government; and Negrín's peace plan was sufficiently uncompromising to suggest that the situation in Republican Spain was far less drastic than might have been expected. Still worse, the international situation

MAP 9.1 Division of Spain, July 1938.

suddenly looked much darker than it had done for some time. Thus, much shaken by the *anschluss*, the second Léon Blum administration had adopted a more relaxed attitude with regard to non-intervention. On 17 March, the frontier opened and large quantities of arms began to enter Catalonia (strictly speaking, it had been possible to get arms shipments across the border for the previous few months, but the amount brought in had been much reduced by the fact that the trains were only allowed to make the journey at night).[2] How much came in until the flow was cut off in July by the much more conservative Daladier government cannot be established with any certainty, but the total suggested by Howson is fifty-seven aircraft, most of them a new version of the Polikarpov I16 armed with four machine-guns instead of two; 194 assorted field guns; 274 modern Soviet 37mm and 45mm anti-tank guns; thirty-two Soviet 76.2mm M31 anti-aircraft guns (like the Soviet anti-tank weapons, thoroughly up-to-date models that were used throughout the Second World War); twenty-five T26 tanks; 2,083 heavy machine-guns; 2,500 light machine-guns; and 125,000 rifles.[3]

All this made for an impressive picture, and yet there were still desperate problems. In general, there were too few automatic weapons, too few mortars and too few anti-tank and anti-aircraft guns, whilst the new artillery pieces coming across the frontier were but a drop in the ocean compared to what was needed, and all the more so as such artillery as had survived the battles in Aragón was frequently either hopelessly antiquated or in desperate need of refurbishment. Here, for example, is Manuel Tagüeña's account of the situation in his XV Corps:

> The Third and Thirty-Fifth Divisions … could count on a total of seventy-one guns of different sizes, but … many of the pieces were old and in poor repair … As for the Forty-Second Division, all it had was four batteries of

guns dating from the last years of the nineteenth century that lacked modern recoil mechanisms, real museum pieces which our penury left us with no option but to use … At the same time, we had been informed that, once the immediate reserves of ammunition had been used up, shells were likely to be in short supply as the production of our factories was insufficient to satisfy the likely daily requirement of our guns.[4]

For a more detailed picture, we can turn to V Corps' Thirty-Fifth Division. Composed of the XI, XIII and XV International Brigades, this might have been expected to have got the cream of what was available, and yet the 9,600 men in its front-line infantry units had only some 5,400 rifles, 143 light machine-guns, twenty-three machine-guns, eighteen mortars and four anti-tank guns.[5]

If the situation with respect to armaments remained poor, things were not much better with respect to manpower. Acutely conscious of the danger to Catalonia, the Republican authorities made frantic efforts to galvanize public opinion and increase support for the war effort.[6] Yet for all the fiery speeches and radio broadcasts, for all the meetings and rallies and for all the vibrant poster art, the populace remained as dispirited and apathetic as ever: volunteers for the front were notable by their absence, while the armies were only reconstituted by dint of a variety of forms of compulsion; not only was the civilian population subjected to unprecedented level of conscription but also deserters were hunted down without mercy and every base and barracks ransacked for men who had managed to ensconce themselves in comfortable postings in training units or the military administration. By these means, plenty of fresh blood was forthcoming, but the results were distinctly unprepossessing, even the International Brigades being reduced to mere shadows of their former selves: if there was still a hard core of militants who had either somehow reached the bridge at Tortosa or swam across the river, their Spanish components – two-thirds or even three-quarters of the whole – were no longer volunteers but unwilling conscripts, many of them little more than boys.[7]

In the circumstances, a defensive strategy might have seemed the obvious choice, but Negrín and those around him saw clearly that such a policy equated to doing little more than exposing the Republic's collective neck and waiting for the axe to fall. Boosted by the windfall represented by the opening of the frontier, they therefore decided that the forces in Catalonia should rather seek to capitalize on Franco's difficulties in Valencia and launch a great offensive that, much as Prieto had attempted at Teruel, would bludgeon the Nationalists into coming to terms, and in the process might even re-open communications with the central zone. With this end in mind, then, a new Army of the Ebro was established under the command of the erstwhile sergeant Juan Modesto, this eventually consisting of three corps (the V Corps of Enrique Líster, the XII Corps of Etelvino Vega and the XV Corps of Manuel Tagüeña, each of which had three divisions); four companies of tanks; three companies of armoured cars; two brigades of heavy artillery; two anti-aircraft brigades, each consisting of three batteries of Russian 76.2mm M31s, two batteries of

40mm Bofors guns, eight batteries of 20mm Oerlikon guns and a single company of quadruple Maxim machine-guns; a brigade of cavalry; a heavy machine-gun battalion; a signals battalion; and a specially formed bridging battalion.[8] As for the target of this array, the greatest in the history of the Republican war effort, there was but one possibility, namely the area in which the Ebro forces its way through the chain of mountains that, all round the periphery of Spain, marks the frontier between the *meseta* of the interior and the coastal plain by means of a great bend that in effect traces three sides of a square: not only was the river much narrower here than was usually the case, but the defenders – a single division of the Army Corps of Morocco – were vulnerable to being surrounded and wiped out.

The situation brooking no delay whatsoever, on the night of 24–25 July, 80,000 Republican troops therefore began to cross the River Ebro between Cherta and Mequinenza, the operation showing a degree of sophistication that the People's Army had never yet demonstrated. Simply getting across the river required the construction of several pontoon bridges and the use of large numbers of assault boats, whilst, as at Brunete and Belchite, the Republicans foreswore any form of preliminary bombardment. Instead, ahead of each unit went special squads of commandos whose task it was to cause chaos in the Nationalist rear. Originally from Almería, Francisco Pérez López had spent most of his life either in France or Algeria but had returned to Spain to take his chances in the Republican forces rather than endure conscription to the French army:

> At one in the morning we got the order to cross … Once on the enemy banks we took out the cables we'd prepared and tied them to a tree: they would be used to guide the boats that would be used to transport our troops and weapons … Leaving the troops to take their positions, we set off … marching ten yards apart in single file. After two or three miles we reached the main road to Madrid. There near a little bridge we got in some pits with our machine-guns and light mortars in firing positions. The order was to fire without question on all vehicles that passed … Near the bridge there was a large house. All of a sudden one of the windows lit up. I dispatched a patrol of four men. They came back with seven prisoners, all Civil Guards. So as not to make any noise we killed them with our daggers. We stripped them and threw the corpses into a pit and seven of us changed our Nationalist uniforms for those of [the] Civil Guards … Then we stood guard on the bridge, while the others hid in the pits, ready to fire.[9]

Thus began the most terrible battle of the war. Rapidly overwhelming the thin defending forces, the Republicans had soon occupied a major bridgehead, this news being greeted with delight by the Negrín government. 'On the banks of the Ebro things were going well', wrote Julián Zugazagoitia. 'The first communiqué, that of 25 July, was eminently satisfactory. … The most difficult part of the operation – the crossing of the river itself – had gone off without a hitch. One hundred and fifty metres wide even at its narrowest point, the Ebro had been waded without the enemy even being aware of what was going on.'[10] At first, meanwhile, resistance was minimal. 'We reached the Ebro at dawn', recalled Harry Fisher. 'Scores of small boats were carrying troops to the west side of the river. I realised that thousands of troops were involved in this offensive. On one boat an American was standing, probably because he had just gotten aboard. Someone shouted at him, "Hey! Get down! Who the hell do you think you are? George Washington crossing the Delaware?" As we crossed the river, a small fascist observation plane flew over us. Immediately, hundreds of rifles fired at the plane, and it quickly disappeared. After landing on the fascist side … we began marching inland. It was still very quiet. The morning dragged on. The heat became intense, as did the thirst, reminding me of Brunete, but there was still no fighting and only a smattering of rifle fire up ahead. At about noon, we passed hundreds of fascist prisoners who had … surrendered and were now being taken to the rear. They seemed so young, so frightened, so helpless.'[11] That said, from the very beginning, the outnumbered Nationalists made lavish use of airpower to slow down the Republican advance. Amongst the thousands of men trudging along the narrow mountain roads was Fred Thomas of the XV Brigade's anti-tank battery:

> Christ! That last hour had the worst bit of bombing I have ever experienced. At about five p.m. we got orders to move down … an old dusty track leading to the pontoon bridge our men have put across. About half an hour after we arrived over came fifteen or so bombers, and, blimey, I never want bombs closer. Lousy to be once again at the old game of burying your nose in the ground.[12]

As so often before, however, initial success was followed by stalemate, this time at the town of Gandesa. Faced by determined resistance – typically enough, Franco had rushed reinforcements to the sector from far and wide[13] – the Republicans suffered heavy casualties and were brought to a halt. As ever, Walter Gregory was fighting with the British Battalion, the objective of this unit being a steep-sided knoll officially known as Hill 481 but more commonly termed 'the Pimple':

> We launched our first attack against 'the Pimple' on 27 July … Our first attempt was repelled with heavy casualties … On 30 July it fell to my company to lead another assault … Just before dawn we started our … ascent, crawling from rock to rock, keeping as low as possible and trying to leave the loose shale undisturbed … We had moved but a short distance beyond our own front line when we were greeted by a fusillade of rifle and machine-gun fire and any semblance of an orderly advance disappeared as each man sought cover for himself … It was now simply a matter of returning fire whenever each man thought that it was safe enough for him to expose himself for as long as it took to discharge a few rounds of ammunition at the heights above.[14]

Gregory was wounded that same day. Meanwhile, another account of the fighting comes from Fred Thomas, whose anti-tank gun was supporting the Abraham Lincoln Battalion:

> With the sun just coming up, we opened fire, first making sure our chaps were not there already ... With daylight their planes came over, bombing all round us and, for the first time in this action, their big guns favoured us with some close attention, not without success ... Confusion spread as machine-fire came over from our extreme right. They [i.e. the enemy machine-guns] were quickly sighted and we sent over twenty to thirty shells. Then the Lincolns went over yet again in a brave but costly attempt on the ridge.[15]

Fighting with one of the rifle companies of the British Battalion was the same Bob Clark who had managed to escape the earlier disaster at Gandesa:

> The whole crest of the hill was a death trap ... By some piece of sheer luck, I found that I had reached a position from where I could see the enemy machine-guns ... Peering cautiously around, I noticed a dip in the hillside which would give a measure of protection. Slowly crawling along on my belly ... I suddenly felt as if I had been hit in the face with a sledge-hammer. Jumping about five feet in the air, I felt a terrible emotion of seeing a searing wall of flame followed immediately by a dreadful darkness.[16]

With paralysis spreading all along the line, the Republicans were at length forced to suspend the offensive. 'The purpose of the attack ... had been to take Gandesa', wrote Harry Fisher, 'but it had been a complete failure. The fascists had sent more and stronger forces to the area with artillery, tanks and planes. There was no way we could have succeeded unless we had supporting forces; we just didn't have any. We were fighting with rifles, machine-guns, a few pieces of artillery and very few tanks. If our artillery sent three rounds of shells into enemy territory, the fascists would answer with a barrage of dozens of shells.'[17] In fairness, however, the Republican forces had suffered heavy losses since crossing the river – at least 12,000 men according to Martínez Bande[18] – while such was the shortage of motorised transport, the wretched condition of the roads in a mountainous district almost totally devoid of centres of population and the sheer distance of the new front line from the Ebro that keeping the assault going was never really a serious possibility. For a good account of the problems that dogged the Republicans, we may turn to American medic Hank Rubin:

> As the days of the offensive passed and our troops moved forward, a few trucks were ferried over which were immediately put to double duty. After delivering their supplies to the front, they collected the wounded and brought them back to the river. After a ride in these jolting trucks,

the *heridos* had to be carried by bearers on foot over the pontoon bridges to ambulances waiting on the eastern bank ... Often the wounded had to lie on their litters or on the ground for hours, shaken by bombings, choking on dust, waiting to be taken across the river. Yet nothing could be done for them until the action quieted for a moment or until destroyed pontoons could be replaced ... The terrain ... over which the troops were fighting was so steep and treacherous that often the wounded were brought to aid stations by ... *artolas* [i.e. litters designed to be carried on mules]. And sometimes the ground was so difficult to traverse or so open to enemy fire that the only way to bring out a wounded man was piggyback on a bearer.[19]

Digging in, the Republicans were then subjected to a ferocious counteroffensive designed, first, to restore Franco's faltering prestige, and, second, to wreck the forces defending Catalonia beyond repair. We come here to reaction to the offensive in Franco's headquarters. According to Franco's chief press officer, Luis Bolín, the attack had come as something of a shock. Thus: 'The Red onslaught on the Ebro was launched on 25 July. For some time we had known that our opponents were planning to cross the river, but so stealthily was the operation carried out and so well had it been rehearsed beforehand that part of our troops were taken by surprise.'[20] That said, Bolín continued, the generalissimo reacted with characteristic phlegm. 'The situation was not reassuring, for in a single day our front had been pierced to a depth of almost thirteen miles, but Franco was not too perturbed ... After hearing Mass that day – it was the feast of Saint James, patron saint of Spain and of the Spanish infantry – he moved to a set of maps on which every phase of the situation had been noted ... "I feel tempted," he said, "to allow the enemy to penetrate as far as they wish while we ourselves hold fast to both ends of the gap. In this way our troops will maintain a stranglehold upon the Red salient and in due course destroy their opponents on the very ground chosen by them."'[21] In fairness, this course of action was very much the one that the Nationalists adopted in the course of the battle, but there is more than a hint of hagiography here. Beneath the surface, there was much panic in the air; witness, for example, the repeated requests that were sent to Hitler for more artillery.[22] At the same time, Franco's decision to throw the full weight of the Nationalist war-machine against the Republican bridgehead caused much controversy. With so many Republican troops concentrated on one small sector of the right bank of the Ebro, the rest of Catalonia was wide open to attack, and there is good reason to believe that an attack on the Segre front would have produced the fall of Barcelona in a very short space of time. This opportunity, however, was thrown away in favour of what Preston calls 'a desperate and strategically meaningless battle ... involving a blood bath worse even than those of Brunete, Belchite and Teruel.'[23] To quote the same observer, Franco 'preferred to turn Gandesa into the cemetery of the Republican army rather than secure a swift and imaginative victory.'[24]

There was some logic to Franco's decision: as at Brunete, Belchite and Teruel, the engagement and destruction of the main enemy fighting force could be argued to trump even the most important of geographical objectives. At the Ebro, however, there was a crucial difference in that every inch of the ground occupied by the Republicans was a tangle of jagged limestone *sierras* that offered far better defensive positions than the plains of Brunete or the steppes of Teruel. Joaquín Masjuán's memories of one Nationalist assault are therefore by no means atypical: 'The artillery bombardment having come to an end, the ... enemy infantry began to advance. As they did, however, we saw the majority of them go down. A few of them tried to take shelter in the irregularities of the terrain, but our artillery soon drove them out into the open, whereupon our automatic weapons did the rest. In all, they launched three consecutive attacks, and all three failed with heavy loss of life ... Meanwhile, we destroyed three enemy tanks, each one of which was reduced to a smoking heap of scrap metal.'[25]

Afterwards, then, more than one Nationalist commander felt the need to explain why the battle of the Ebro went on for so long when the somewhat similar Republican offensives at Brunete, Belchite and Teruel were reversed in a matter of weeks. In the eyes of the head of the air force, Alfredo Kindelán, for example, the problem began with the corps and divisional commanders (of Franco, of course, he was careful to speak only in terms of the utmost praise). Thus, men who had prior to July 1936 led nothing more than tiny columns of colonial troops had only progressed to the command of the sort of formations which they now led relatively recently, and, accept though Kindelán did that they faced a very difficult task – as he admitted, in no other battle had the Nationalists faced either quite such difficult terrain or quite such a density of opposing forces – they therefore made frequent mistakes, not the least of these being to restrict their attacks to very narrow fronts, thereby sacrificing manoeuvre in favour of swamping the enemy with sheer weight of fire when in fact they did not have the resources to produce the results that they hoped for. Nor was this an end to it. If the corps and divisional commanders were not up to the task, problems had also emerged lower down the chain of command. Thus, whereas in 1936, the Nationalists had been well favoured in that the vast majority of those officers who had either seen front-line combat or were of an age to be particularly useful in that capacity, by 1938, many of the men concerned had been killed or incapacitated, and others still promoted up the chain of command, sometimes, or so it is implied, to positions beyond their level of competence. That being the case, platoons, companies and battalions alike were in the hands of new men hastily trained up in the course of the war, who, as Kindelán put it, only knew how to die with courage. Add to all this a series of technical deficiencies – an artillery that, however imposing, was still insufficient for the tasks required of it and could not be moved forward quickly enough for want of adequate transport, and a tank force that was relatively small, not well used and mostly composed of light tanks equipped with nothing more than machine-guns – and it was only to be expected that progress on the ground had proved less than dramatic.[26]

That something was amiss even relatively lowly members of the Nationalist war-machine were well aware, and such was the scale of the fighting that the trust that had hitherto sustained the Nationalist army so well began to be eroded. Falangist Andrés Bernabé, as we have seen, was fighting in an infantry battalion:

> Many errors were also seen on our side. For example, there was never any real connection between the men in the front line and the high command. In the whole battle ... I never saw a staff officer except for a single lieuten-ant-colonel. One day Fonseca, who commanded our brigade, got in touch with García Valiño and told him that that there had been many casualties, and that the objectives we were set could not be achieved because units that normally counted 110 men had been reduced to a mere sixteen or twenty. The answer given him by García Valiño was that whilst there was one man still on his feet, it was necessary to keep going. ... At times the lack of co-ordination was astounding. I remember, for example, that there was a little hill close to us which was pounded by artillery fire, only for us to discover that there had been no-one there, no-one at all ... The truth is that the high command was not that good in some respects.[27]

Victory therefore took over three months, the last Republican troops not being withdrawn until 16 November. Typical enough of the experience of the defend-ers was that of Harry Fisher of the Abraham Lincoln Battalion:

> On our second day at Hill 666, the order came for the Lincolns to attack the enemy position on another nearby hill ... The Americans were sched-uled to lead the attack and at mid-afternoon two of our batteries opened fire ... The First and Third Companies ... spearheaded the attack and suf-fered tremendous casualties. Aaron Lopoff, the commander of one of the companies ... lost his eyes and died two days later in a hospital. A Spanish company commander was also killed. A number of men were missing and we had to presume they were dead. Many men were wounded, some very badly ... The next day the fascists answered with a terrible barrage, the worst I have ever seen or heard. It sounded as if thunder were crashing directly overhead. Our men on top of the hill were blown to bits. The most popular man in the battalion, Joe Bianca, commander of the machine-gun company, was hit; he died a few hours later ... The scene was awful: the terrain was covered with a haze of dust; bullets flew over our heads. We wondered if anyone out there was still alive.[28]

Another combatant was Eduardo Pons Prades:

> The orders we had received were stricter than ever: we were not to give up an inch of ground whilst we had a single bullet left to us. Hardly had dawn broken than the enemy aviation paid us a number of visits. However,

given that we had become pretty good at the art of imitating moles, that was all more noise than anything else. For the rest of the day there was a bit of everything – artillery bombardment, mortar fire, the lot – but nothing in the way of proper attacks. These came the next morning. The key point in our position was Hill 424 … In the course of the day, five or six assaults were launched against it, but to no avail. Only on 8 September was the hill given up, and then only to a third wave of attackers. That night, meanwhile, we organised a serious of energetic counter-attacks, and managed to get it back … This business of holding out by day and hitting back at night became our normal routine.[29]

Not only was the fighting grim in the extreme, but it also took place in intense heat, the result being not just that the combatants were even more exhausted than normal, but also that the field of battle was particularly unpleasant. As Milt Fersen remembered, 'It had been one of the hottest summers on record, bad news for gladiators. When soldiers fell, they began to swell almost at once, bloating until they looked like huge over-stuffed dolls, turning black in the sun and stinking horribly.'[30] Nor did it help that much of the battlefield consisted of solid rock in which it was simply impossible to dig proper graves. If the Ebro was therefore remembered as a place of unique horror, it is scarcely surprising. Sent with another man to pick up some replacement communications equipment from brigade headquarters, Harry Fisher was suddenly confronted by a sight that cannot have been atypical: 'We didn't dare go via the road below: the fascists would have spotted us in a minute. We decided to go east, around the hill, and into a valley. What we saw there appeared to be a battalion at rest: soldiers were lying all over the ground. We realised that they were not "at rest": there was an awful stench, and insects were buzzing round the men. They were all dead, as many as two hundred, very possibly soldiers from both sides.'[31]

An important feature of the battle was the manner in which it finally established Nationalist air superiority. Initially, the absence of most of the Republican fighters in the Levante meant that the Nationalists had things very much their own way – a factor that may, indeed, have been decisive in the final result of the battle – but more and more I15s and I16s soon began to join the fight, fighter pilots such as José Larios therefore frequently finding themselves in action against large formations of enemy aircraft.[32] Yet in the end, the Nationalist flyers proved superior, much aided by the superiority to everything else in the air of the Messerschmitt Me109. In the course of the battle, then, the Condor Legion claimed at least fifty-nine enemy fighters and bombers for the loss of just one Messerschmitt shot down and a few others that were forced to make emergency landings after sustaining serious damage.[33] As their losses mounted, meanwhile, so the surviving Republican pilots came under ever greater pressure. As Francisco Tarazona confided to his diary on 25 August: 'We have had an exhausting week. Our sorties over the Ebro front follow one another in one great blur. As soon as we land, we fall asleep wherever we happen to be. Up top all we have no time to do anything but pull the trigger ... The enemy aviation covers the sky.'[34] More and more, then, the morale of Republican fighter squadrons began to crumble, whilst on 1 November, the air-force high command gave up the fight altogether and ordered its squadrons not to engage with the Fiats and Messerschmitts at all. This, however, was easier said than done. Early in November, for example, Joan de Milany found himself flying his first sortie with an I16 unit to which he had recently been posted in a machine that, to his considerable misfortune, was suffering from persistent engine problems:

> It was early in the afternoon ... As my motor kept misfiring, I was keeping up with the formation with some difficulty ... Suddenly, well above us, a group of Fiats shot through a gap in the clouds. No sooner had he seen them, than the commander of our squadron banked and headed off in the direction of our lines with all the other planes in the formation in hot pursuit. With every moment that passed, my dodgy engine meant I was left further and further behind ... In horizontal flight, the Fiats were slower than the Moscas, but in a dive they were like so many arrows ... In a moment ... I was surrounded by ... tracer shells. Something smashed into my back and struck me brutally on the shoulder while the Mosca ... went into a violent spin ... In the end, it was instinct ... that saved me. Pulling violently with my left hand, I ripped open the buckle that fastened the straps that held me in my seat and in that same instant the centrifugal effect of the spin flung me out of the plane whereupon ... I pulled the ripcord of my parachute.[35]

Once again, a set-piece battle had proved catastrophic for the People's Army. Casualties were about 70,000 as opposed to 60,000 for the Nationalists, whilst the Republicans had lost thirty-five tanks, fourteen field guns (a figure that says a great deal in respect of the difficulties the Republicans faced in bringing up artillery support), 181 machine-guns, 214 light machine-guns, forty-five mortars and 24,000 rifles.[36] In terms of aircraft, the situation was even worse, the battle having seen well over 100 bombers and fighters go down for no more than forty of their opponents.[37] At the very least, however, this was a bad bargain, for whereas Franco's losses could easily be replaced, the same could not be said for those of the Republic. In the first place, there was the question of manpower. Once again, the militants on whom the People's Army depended had paid a terrible price for their political convictions. As Lister lamented, 'It is impossible to give the names of all those who fell ... Domiciano Leal, an experienced class-warrior from pre-war days ... [who] had attained the command of the Forty-Sixth Division ... Angel Barcía, the commissar of the Eleventh Division ... Manuel Yagüe, a land-worker ... [who] fell at the head of IX Brigade in the Sierra de Pandols ... Paulino Llorente, a battalion commissar and founder-member of the Fifth Regiment, Tiburcio Minaya, a combatant from the first days of the struggle who fell at the head of his battalion ... Joaquín Moreno, the commissar of the Second Armoured Brigade.'[38] Nor was it just a question of Party *apparatchiks* of varying degrees of military aptitude, if not dedication. Also gone, as we have seen, were many thousands of common soldiers. Returning from the front on leave, at the beginning of October 1938, Eduardo Pons Prades records a picture that is infinitely more moving than that of the list of Communist worthies tendered by Lister: 'No sooner had I got home ... than I began to ask around about my acquaintances from the neighbourhood ... A dozen of my closest friends had been killed, as many others had been wounded, and two had disappeared.'[39] To fill the gaps in the ranks, meanwhile, there were only the resources of Catalonia, and it was only with the greatest difficulty that even 20,000 reinforcements – a mixture of new conscripts and men transferred from the rear echelons – could be found for the front-line units.[40] Still chief of the general staff, Vicente Rojo painted a picture that could hardly be more bleak:

> On the home front morale was fragile. On the one hand, there was an awareness of danger, an awareness that rigorous measures were on the way, measures that everybody considered necessary, indispensable even, to keep the ship of state afloat, and yet, on the other, no sooner had measures been introduced to get the many shirkers out of their comfortable posts in the rear, than, far from being applauded, they met with enormous resistance: senior functionaries, even ministers, had no hesitation in pulling strings so as to get exemptions for friends or relatives, this being something that gave a most lamentable example. Yet it was understandable that fighting spirit should have been at a low ebb, for danger and privation were mounting by the day without anyone lifting a finger to correct the disorder which reigned with regard to the distribution of foodstuffs, and in the administration: this gave rise to general disgust, while the mass of the population displayed the most manifest war-weariness.[41]

At the same time, there was also the question of armaments. Here, too, losses had been terrible, and there was no way that they could be made up, a search of the Republican rearguard turning up just 8,000 rifles.[42] Although Catalonia was still capable of producing large quantities of munitions and aircraft (several factories had been equipped to turn out I15 and I16 fighters under licence), production was increasingly being disrupted by shortages of raw materials and the earlier Nationalist capture of many of the hydroelectric plants on which the region depended, not to mention growing illness, absenteeism and resistance to work among the proletariat. 'At the end of 1938', says Michael Seidman, 'Catalan workers had lost any remaining desire to sacrifice for the Republic ... At the San Adrián de Besos [power] plant ... rampant tardiness among the workers caused periodic blackouts ... Part of the explanation was that food shortages forced workers to spend much time in search of sustenance.'[43] Meanwhile, other than aircraft, Catalonia had never produced much in the way of actual weaponry, most of its efforts having rather gone into the production of munitions. In the vast majority, rifles, machine-guns, artillery pieces and armoured vehicles had all had to come from abroad. Yet the French frontier was firmly shut, whilst the Munich agreement had caused Stalin to put an end to the supply of Russian arms, not that ships – the only hope now that the French frontier was closed once more – had very much chance of getting through to Barcelona anyway. In the Nationalist zone, true, talks with the Italians had led to an agreement that the CTV should be reduced to a single division and the 10,000 troops who were thereby rendered surplus should be withdrawn from Spain, but Franco had so many men of his own that this mattered little, whilst the fact that it was to all intents and purposes balanced by a decision on the part of Negrín to send home the 12,000 foreign volunteers who still remained in the People's Army meant that the Nationalists remained ahead of the game, the Italians who were withdrawn being ordinary infantrymen of no particular value, whereas the International Brigaders were all hardened veterans.[44]

In the wake of their withdrawal from the front, the surviving International Brigaders tried to come to terms with their experiences and, in particular, to find some sense of achievement. Typical enough was the line settled on by the medic Hank Rubin: 'As I waited through the long days for our departure, it seemed time for me to assess ... what the International Brigades had contributed ... The Republic had needed time to create and train a disciplined army and space to recover from its political mistakes. We'd helped give them that time. The presence of the [International Brigades] had also generated a great deal of international support, both politically and financially, and had given courage and hope to many Spaniards.'[45] Others took refuge in Communist propaganda.

> 'It would be hypocrisy to pretend that we British regretted our involuntary withdrawal from the fighting. When, suddenly and unexpectedly, the government ordered us out of the battle ... we excused our immense relief by the bland assertion that the Republican army was now judged strong enough to stand on its own, no longer in need of the International Brigades' aid to achieve that final victory. This was, of course, another illusion to add to the many that we had nurtured throughout the war, based on hope and dedication to our cause, rather than on fact and even probability ... but our explanation helped assuage the unease our new role as bystanders caused us.'[46]

Readers of this work will have to come to their own decisions, but it is difficult to escape the feeling that, militarily, the International Brigades contributed very little – whether at Madrid, the Jarama, Brunete, Belchite, Teruel, the Ebro, they performed no better than the Spanish units around them – and that, politically, the situation was not much better: there is little firm evidence that even in Madrid in November 1936, the presence of the International Brigades inspired a single Republican soldier to fight harder. What one is left with, then, is a rather dark conclusion, but one that seems unassailable. To quote the American historian

R. D. Richardson, 'Despite their relative decline in military significance, the brigades continued to be a highly important component in the Comintern's overall operations regarding the Spanish Civil War and the Popular-Front strategy in general. The brigades were held up as the most concrete and heroic example of the Popular Front and anti-fascism in action ... The Comintern's success in this meant that the International Brigades remained to the end what they had been from the beginning, an interlocking part of the Comintern's directorate in Spain.'[47]

To return to the military situation, the position of Catalonia was desperate: if Negrín issued an order laying down new norms for the regulation and administration of the People's Army on 1 October 1938, it was on the one hand a brave attempt to bluff both Franco and the population of the Republican zone into believing that the situation was not as grim as it actually was – the army, he announced, consisted of seventy infantry divisions, two armoured divisions, four anti-aircraft brigades, two coast-defence brigades and four cavalry brigades, a claim that was true enough in itself but completely ignored the fact that many units existed only on paper – and on the other a real effort to force the thousands of men who had found safe billets behind the lines into combat positions. As Alpert writes, 'Much of the emphasis in this ... order was, understandably, on the full use in fighting units of all men available and the reduction of second-line troops to the minimum possible. From then on rearguard units and service echelons might only use war invalids and others exempt from active duty. Nobody would be permitted to serve for more than three months in any of the main artillery and service depots.'[48] As for weapons, in November, the staunchly Communist commander of the air force, Ignacio Hidalgo de Cisneros, was dispatched to Moscow in a last-ditch effort to secure fresh dispatches of arms, and that despite that fact that the credit constituted by the gold reserves dispatched to the Soviet Union had now been spent, something of the penury to which the Republican forces had been reduced being suggested by the extraordinarily ambitious nature of the requests: 250 aircraft, 250 tanks, 650 guns and 4,000 machine-guns.[49]

Nor were matters made any easier by the politics of the Republican zone. Ever since the government had moved to Catalonia, the Generalitat had been complaining bitterly about the manner in which Catalan autonomy had increasingly become a mere fiction. Determined to put an end to this situation, in the very midst of the battle of the Ebro, Negrín had faced Companys with the choice of complete capitulation or accepting the task of heading the Republican government. His bluff called, Companys duly climbed down, whereupon Negrín imposed still tighter controls.[50] Meanwhile, rumours of treason were rife and personal disputes of all sorts manifold, the population in the meantime having to endure both the onset of another winter and a further series of air attacks. Conditions on the home front, meanwhile, could scarcely have been worse. Due to a combination of the blockade, the Nationalists' control of so much of Spain's agriculture and, especially, wheat, and the disruption attendant upon collectivization, food was short, while the spiralling inflation did not help in the slightest, many peasants being understandably unwilling to sell their produce for money that was so much worthless paper and especially not given the frequent attempts to impose price controls, ineffective though these were. In consequence, even the most basic food-stuffs were beyond the reach of most people: oil was 150 *pesetas* a litre; a dozen eggs 200, a chicken 400–500.[51] And with starvation came degradation. Convalescing in Barcelona, for example, British International Brigader Bob Clark had a sad encounter at a Barcelona café: 'I was approached by a young girl who was sitting at the next table. I was able to enquire why she was doing this. Her age, she told me was seventeen, but she looked even younger. Asking her why she did not work in a government factory, her reply was that the money was not so bad, but … it was almost impossible to buy anything with it. Food, tins of corned beef, sardines, canned milk or cigarettes, these were the real money. A tin of milk was worth almost half a week's wages.'[52] Another volunteer who remembered the general misery was Fred Thomas:

> As in all Republican Spain, hunger was a major weapon on Franco's side. In Marsa swarms of children and even some adults, mostly women, waited patiently outside the church where we were fed hoping for scraps from our meal. One day the BBC announced that fascist planes had bombed Barcelona with loaves of bread together with leaflets exhorting the population to come over to their side for 'Peace, Bread and Work.' If true, the bread would have been acceptable![53]

In these circumstances, Franco was hardly likely to pay any attention to Negrín's ever more pathetic suggestions of a compromise peace. On the contrary, indeed, on 23 December, the full force of the Nationalist armies was flung against Catalonia. Only in numbers of men did the Republicans equal the enemy, the Nationalists' superiority in artillery and aircraft being extremely marked. From the first day, then, it was clear how things were likely to end: supported by a barrage from some 500 guns, for example, the four divisions of the CTV alone, one of them Italian and the other three Spanish with Italian officers, advanced over twenty miles in the first twenty-four hours.[54] To quote Henry Buckley, 'Luck or treachery gave the Franco forces a great send-off. At the point they crossed the river Segre, south of Lérida, were Carabinero forces … Some of [these] units were good, but others were very bad indeed. This one was one of the worst. After the first few shells the officers in command got into their cars and drove away. The bewildered troops broke, and within a few hours General Franco's forces had swept through and outflanked the whole … Segre line.'[55] The campaign was not quite a walk-over – after the first day the Nationalist advance was for some time slowed to a crawl, whilst the élite V Corps made repeated attempts to counterattack – but gradually the superior firepower of Franco's troops began to tell. On the scene, once more, was the same Henry Buckley:

> Out at Castelldans, I and Herbert Matthews and Willie Forrest found Lister with his army-corps headquarters in a cave about a mile from the

front line holding on grimly while the Italian troops in front battered furiously against his positions. The air was full of Nationalist planes. The Franco guns thundered mightily and were only answered faintly by the few Republican guns ... We did not need telling things were bad ... We ran through a barrage of shells, found our car had luckily escaped damage, and raced furiously down a terrible shell-pitted road through the now completely deserted village of Castelldans ... By now we were all specialists in covering retreats, and were not easily impressed by the streams of refugees, the weary soldiers filing back, the chaos and confusion. But this time we soon saw that things were very grave indeed. The officers who knew us spoke freely enough ... It was the same tale everywhere. Nothing like enough machine-guns, scarcely a single anti-tank gun, the artillery few in number of pieces and all worn out.[56]

Even in Aragón, nothing had been seen like this. To quote Lister, 'In the first twenty days of battle, the casualties suffered by the Republican forces surpassed 70,000 dead, wounded and missing, whilst their losses in terms of weapons were also very serious.'[57] At length, then, even the toughest Republican troops could take no more, and on 3 January, the Nationalists finally broke through. It was the end. As Lister admitted, 'From this moment all hope of maintaining a solid line passed beyond the realms of reality. With what forces could we have done this in the face of the enormous superiority of the enemy in men and material, not to mention the deep salients that had been driven in on either flank?'[58] Here and there, a few die-hards still fought on, buying a few hours' time here or mounting some petty counterstroke there, but within a matter of days, the whole of the Republican forces were fleeing in panic or laying down their arms, whilst fast-moving Nationalist columns sliced through their ranks in the direction of Tarragona and Barcelona. Someone who experienced in the rout was Feliciano Gracia, a young officer who had just emerged from cadet school and now could not even find his unit: 'The truth is that that there was no front any more. All we could do was to keep retreating: there just wasn't anything else we could do.'[59] For a Nationalist perspective, we may turn to one Domingo García: 'The Reds did nothing but flee: the truth is that the campaign of Catalonia was nothing but one big rout. I remember that they resorted to scorched-earth tactics and tried to destroy everything as they went so as to leave us with nothing. For example, in Artesa de Segre ... there were some flour mills that still had large stocks, and they burned the lot.'[60] Rumours of all sorts just increased the confusion, while so low was morale amongst the troops that even the sound of shelling was enough to provoke a stampede.[61] As Larios notes, 'The Red command had mustered around 200,000 troops in Catalonia, but their morale was low, for their best shock troops had been sacrificed on the Ebro. They had also mobilised 100,000 men of ages varying from the very young to the very old to fortify ... the approaches to Barcelona. But they had planned the defence too late. The will to fight had been drained out of them.'[62]

Amongst those who found themselves caught up in the disaster was Eduardo Pons Prades:

> In the last days of December and the first days of January ... the topic of conversation that came up most frequently was the defence of Barcelona. Very few people were prepared to admit that the Catalan capital would be allowed to fall without putting up a fight. All sorts of stories were in circulation, then. One rumour that did the rounds was that the Anarchists ... were setting up combat groups that would dispute the city street by street and house by house. In practice, however, such a project was completely lacking in viability, not least because of the all too evident exhaustion, not to say prostration, of the civilian population ... Another rumour that circulated in a particular insistent fashion was that the International Brigades had refused to cross the frontier and had rather turned on their heels in order to march back to Barcelona where they would repeat the prowess that they had displayed in the autumn of 1936 in Madrid ... Thus was established a vicious circle in which more and more people shut themselves up, and from which it was only possible to escape by admitting that Catalonia had been lost for good.[63]

We come here to the Communist claims aired earlier to the effect that the population of Catalonia had rallied behind the Republican war effort to the last man and, indeed, the last woman. From the very moment of the mass mobilization that had taken place in the wake of the loss of Aragón, it was clear that the populace had no desire to fight to the last, even if they had sympathized with the Republican war effort in the first place. Not just in Catalonia, but right across the Republican zone indeed, there was utter indifference. Black-marketeering, embezzlement and pilfering were widespread; officers made little or no effort to care for their troops; nepotism was universal; conscription was defied or evaded; men competed for places in the National Republican Guard (the old Civil Guard), the Assault Guards and the Carabineers in the hope that this would save them from service at the front; officer cadets deliberately failed examinations so as to have to repeat their training courses; desertion was wholesale; trenches were not dug properly but rather skimped: the list of malfeasance or downright crime is almost endless.[64] Meanwhile, so bad was the problem of gangs of runaways who turned to banditry to live that the security forces had to conduct regular sweeps against them that almost reached the intensity of full-scale counterguerrilla operations.[65] There was therefore massive resistance to the Negrín draft, large numbers of conscripts desperately trying to fake illness or alternatively going into hiding, taking to the hills or trekking to the French frontier in an attempt to get across the border, the response of the state being to employ wide range of sanctions against the families of the men concerned, up to and including pressing fathers or brothers.[66]

By one means or another, sufficient men were rounded up for the Army of the Ebro to be brought up to strength, but rounding them up was one thing and keeping them quite another. Hardly had it gone into battle on 25 July, than it began to shed troops right and left: whilst some men tried to make it back across the river, others went over to the Nationalists, typical enough of these last being around twenty Assault Guards who had been sent to Eduardo Pons Prades' battalion as replacements and tried to cross the lines after just two nights, the fact being, as Pons Prades remarked, that the men concerned 'had enlisted in the forces of public order precisely so as not to have to go to the front.'[67] Recaptured shortly afterwards by a Republican patrol, six or seven of the Assault Guards were immediately executed, this being a fate that befell increasing numbers of deserters, stragglers and men who had failed on the battlefield, one of Harry Fisher's darkest memories being of coming across a teenage boy who had been cornered in a small cave pleading for his life in floods of tears.[68] In the course of the battle, it seems that at least sixty-five men were shot out of hand in such circumstances.[69] With demoralization in the rear rampant and the authorities determined to root out deserters, defeatists and Fifth Columnists, meanwhile, the ever more hated SIM and the other forces of public order – men who were generally suspected of having used private influence of one sort or another to secure a safe position in the rear – became ever more heavy handed: Pons Prades, for example, spent weeks in jail when he was arrested for having borrowed a car belonging to the army to take the relatives of a wounded friend of his to visit him in hospital in Granollers.[70]

To return to the campaign in Catalonia, then, desperate attempts on the part of the Communists to rally the defenders had no more effect than the arrival of a few more arms from France, Paris having been panicked into once more opening the frontier, this being something that provoked much clutching at straws: amongst the wilder rumours in circulation was that Companys had declared Catalonia's independence from Spain and secured a promise of French intervention.[71] Such rumours had no effect when it came to galvanizing resistance, however. Tomás Roig Llop, for example, was a Catalan nationalist, but one who had prior to 1936 always voted not for the dominant Republican Left of Catalonia but the older and more conservative Catalan League. Called up in January 1939, he reported for duty, but found the barracks in a state of total confusion and therefore had no hesitation in joining a particularly inventive attempt at a mass break-out:

> After three hours ... one of the men spoke up. 'Do you want to leave here?' 'Of course', we all chorused. 'Well, then: form up in a column of fours. I will act as the commander, and you will keep in step, shouting, "One-two! One-two!" as we march out.' We formed up, and with the man giving the orders and us shouting as he had told us, we marched out of the building. We marched past the guard, still shouting, 'One-two! One-two!' until we had gone a short distance round a corner ... and, with that, we scattered and ran. The army never saw us again.[72]

In the skies overhead, the Nationalists reigned supreme. Here and there, the Republican flyers continued to do their best – on 30 December, for example,

Francisco Tarazona downed a Messerschmitt whilst escorting some Chatos which had been sent to strafe the road from Lérida to Granadella[73] – but their efforts were unavailing. On 28 December, the Condor Legion alone shot down three bombers and a fighter; on 29 December, four fighters; on 30 December, four fighters; on 31 December, one fighter; on 1 January, two fighters. To quote Raymond Proctor, then, the Germans alone 'were taking a devastating toll of the enemy aircraft.'[74] But, of course, it was not just the Germans, the Italians and Spaniards also bringing down a number of Republican planes.[75] With control of the air entirely theirs, meanwhile, the Nationalists were able to rain bombs on the unfortunate Republicans without let-up. José Zamora was an administrator in the prison service:

> The air-raids on Barcelona were terrible and had an effect that was extremely demoralising. Every single one of the bombs could be seen as they fell from the aircraft, and as they came down so their sound became louder and louder until you believed they were heading straight for you even if they were in fact half a kilometre away. Towards the end, in order to terrify the population and paralyse the factories, there were times when they were coming over every half an hour … The whole thing was carefully worked out: no sooner had the factory workers come out of their shelters, than they had to take shelter once again.[76]

Heavily bombed and torn by food riots, meanwhile, Barcelona was in a state of turmoil, whilst there were no proper positions from which it could have been defended even had it been possible to rally the ragged mobs of unarmed men to which the Catalan forces had been reduced.[77] As for the civilian population, none had any thought for anything other than their own safety. Another eye-witness was Constancia de la Mora: 'When we left the country roads and turned onto the main highway to the frontier, we found the people of Barcelona, hungry, wretched, cold, desperate, fleeing from General Franco. The road was absolutely jammed with people in cars, in trucks, on donkeys, on foot. Peasant women holding a child or a goat or a chicken to their breasts; young women trailing their children behind them. We stopped to talk to some of them: a young woman with four children. Her husband was at the front; she had left Tarragona with all her household goods, and now she walked with nothing but the shawl over her head.'[78] In the midst of the general chaos, the only personnel who emerged with any credit were the medical services, whose doctors and nurses worked heroically to get as many of the thousands of sick and wounded in the base hospitals onto northbound trains and ambulances as they could, and, in many men who were too ill to be moved.[79]

With all possibility of resistance at an end, on 23 January, the government fled to Gerona, the Nationalists rolling in to the Catalan capital three days later. No sooner had they done so than they embarked on a *limpieza* of truly apocalyptic proportions. Amongst the first Nationalist soldiers to enter the city was Carlos

Iniesta Cano: 'Our journey through the streets was unforgettable. Mad with joy and full of patriotic emotion, the inhabitants embraced the troops, threw flowers at our feet, joined us in giving cheers so hearty that they strained our throats, and invaded our ranks.'[80] Stationed near the city with his squadron, José Larios took advantage of an early opportunity to visit the city with some of his fellow pilots:

> The great capital of Catalonia looked like 'the morning after the night before.' Filthy and disorganised, [it was] yet full of bustle and activity. The harbour had suffered extensively, for our bombers had caused great devastation: thirty ships were sunk, with their masts sticking out of the water, and many more were damaged ... The shops were already boom-ing, for the shrewd and thrifty Catalans had hoarded their wares awaiting better times.[81]

To the accompaniment of a few brave rearguard actions, one last meeting of what remained of the *cortes* at Figueras and another fruitless offer of peace negotiations, some 460,000 men, women and children flooded across the French frontier into what was to prove a miserable exile. Eventually released from prison, Eduardo Pons Prades had been posted to the administration of the People's Army's medical services: 'Many times over we wished that the earth would swallow us up so as not to have to see that interminable procession of women, children, old men ... soldiers who had lost their units, trudging along in the rain ... without the slightest idea of when they would next eat. Just as bad was the sight of tanks shoving lorries blocking their path out of their way, leaving them either overturned on the verge or crashing down into some ravine. Privileged as we were by the fact that were had a car to take us to and fro, on official business as we were, we could not but feel that in the eyes of those unfortunate people we were one more motive for their demoralization.'[82] The government having also fled to France, the fact was that there was noth-ing but disorder and disintegration. Fairly typical were the scenes described by Tarazona when he landed at the airfield at Figueras after his squadron was evacuated from its normal base further south:

> In the hut that housed the headquarters ... there reigned the most phe-nomenal confusion. The personnel charged with keeping the airfield in operation were just milling about without achieving anything useful; vari-ous aircraft undergoing repair offered an excellent target for the enemy aviation; immense tankers full of gasoline lined the margins of the airfield ... without the drivers or anyone else having given any thought to the dangers of having them out in the open ... All round the place oozed dis-organization like pus from a wound ... When I asked who was in charge, nobody could give me an answer for certain. Indeed, nobody even knew for certain where the senior officers were.[83]

For Tarazona, there was worse to come. Returning to his aircraft, he managed to taxi it to the shelter of some trees, but no sooner had he done this than the airfield was attacked by Nationalist aircraft:

> My attention was attracted by a noise in the sky: several flights of Fiats were approaching from the southwest. At once all the personnel in sight ran for cover in the most bare-faced of fashions ... Just at this point a few Chatos appeared over the airfield. Immediately the Fiats hurled themselves upon the poor devils: out of ammunition and with little fuel, these were easy meat. At once I gave Manolo, who had just got his plane into cover, a shout. Arming ourselves with a couple of machine guns, we rushed to protect the Chatos which were now trying to land ... Taking up a position in the very middle of the runway, we opened fire on the Fiats ... One by one meanwhile, the Chatos got in, though in a couple of cases their pilots were wounded. When the planes were all down, we rushed to get them out of the way, but then along came a gang of Messerchmitts. That put an end to everything. Everything was destroyed by them: petrol tankers, planes undergoing repair, cars, everything became fuel for the flames.[84]

One by one, meanwhile, the border crossings were occupied, and by 10 February, it was all over, the scale of the defeat being worsened still further by a revolt that led to the surrender of Menorca.[85] Enrique Lister provides a dramatic picture of the scene at the frontier as the battered remnants of his V Corps reached the end of its life as a fighting unit:

> I put myself at the head of the column and led it in the direction of the French border post ... An officer having come out to greet us, I asked for the presence of the most senior officer present, whereupon there appeared a lieutenant-colonel. After I had told him who we were, he said that he saluted me, and not just me but my entire command ... That done, how-ever, he told me that, as one soldier to another and with the greatest sadness, he had no option but to communicate to me the orders that he had received which were to disarm any force that crossed the frontier and conduct it to the nearest camp ... Having thanked him for his words of greeting ... I drew my pistol and threw it on the ground, whilst at the same time giving the order to my men that they should do the same. At this they began to file past me, and, before abandoning their rifle, their machine-gun, their hand grenades, their pistol, each man looked into my face, and I saw the sadness ... in their eyes. It was the most bitter moment of my whole life.[86]

With the Republican government soon back in such territory as remained to the loyalists (though not Rojo, Azaña and the president of the *cortes*, the conservative Republican Diego Martínez Barrio, all of whom elected to remain in France and thereby by implication effectively made a public statement against continuing the struggle), the policy of resisting to conquer might yet have continued for a while longer. The international community, true, was now openly coming out in favour of the Nationalists – Britain and France, for example, formally recognized Franco on 27 February – whilst Madrid had been reduced to near starvation. Moreover, the Republicans were not only short of food, but also almost entirely bereft of industry, their manufacturing potential having been almost entirely concentrated in Catalonia. Yet, whilst aircraft, in particular, were in short supply, it seemed that something might yet be done. The four field armies that held the central zone still had 500,000 men under arms. That said, the auguries were not good. The morale of the soldiery could not have been lower, whilst their most recent record of combat was scarcely encouraging. In fairness, in August 1938, a renewal of the Nationalist offensive in Extremadura had been thrown back by a vigorous counterattack, but since then there had ensued many months of hunger and inactivity that had sapped the morale of the Republican forces.[87] Far more telling, then, is the battle of Peñarroya. Often overlooked by histories of the war, not least because the International Brigades played no part in it, this struggle deserves to be treated as something other than a footnote. The fruit of a long-term ambition in some Republican circles to launch an attack in an area of real strategic interest that had generally been left only thinly garrisoned by the Nationalists, the plan called for Antonio Escobar's Army of Extremadura to strike westwards in the direction of Mérida in the hope of cutting the crucial line of communications represented by the railway line from Seville to Salamanca and possibly taking Badajoz. Launched by the XXII Corps of Juan Ibarrola Orueta, in 1936, a captain of the Civil Guard who had fought in the Basque country and Asturias prior to escaping to the central zone; a scratch three-division *agrupación* under an erstwhile militia commander and sometime amateur boxer named Nilamón Toral, who is sometimes spoken of as the best military leader produced by the Spanish revolution other than Juan Modesto, and sundry other units, the attack at first made good progress, smashing a wide breach in the thinly held Nationalist front line and occupying 500 square kilometres in just three days. This was the greatest Republican advance of the entire war, but it was not sufficient to achieve either its primary or its secondary goals: thus, as usual, the Republican forces were checked by the arrival of fresh troops drawn from other parts of Andalucía and Extremadura and thereby prevented from reaching even Mérida (it did not help in this respect that torrential rain turned the country into a quagmire), while no troops were transferred to Extremadura from Catalonia. Still worse, on 17 January, the Nationalists launched a counteroffensive. Ill-clad, ill-fed and badly under-armed, Escobar's soldiers were in an impossible position – the salient they were defending would have been completely untenable even for well-equipped regulars – and they therefore fell back in ever greater disorder. Victory, then, had become yet another defeat, and by 4 February, all the survivors – there had been at least 40,000 casualties, of whom about half were prisoners – were back in their original positions.[88]

In the wake of this affair, the military position was worse than ever. Precious stocks of munitions had been used up; there had been many deserters; and many commanders, including, not least, Escobar, were won over to the growing pressure for peace at all costs. Even away from the fighting in Extremadura, meanwhile, desertion was running at an all-time high: for example, by the end of February, the Madrid-based Eighteenth Division was losing at least fifteen men a day.[89] Nor was this surprising: soldiers on the Madrid front were often going barefoot and suffering from various forms of scurvy.[90] To quote Michael Seidman, 'Troops simply did not wish to fight and hoped that the war would end as soon as possible. Soldiers lost all confidence in their officers who had concluded that certain divisions would be totally useless in the event of an enemy attack.'[91] Typical of the general mood was that in the unit of Elias Biescas Palacios: 'Apart from a few skirmishes, in our sector all was quiet: the enemy, it seemed, had no interest in conquering fresh territory where we were. For our part, meanwhile, we had neither the will nor the means to attempt anything positive, and spent our time wandering aimlessly about without the slightest idea what to do for the best.'[92] Nor was there anything but cynicism with regard to the government, not least because, as Seidman notes, 'Negrín's famous girth did not lend credibility to his calls for sacrifice.'[93] Yet in public, Negrín remained unshaken: not only had secret contacts revealed that Franco would not offer even the slightest concessions to the Republicans, but on 13 February, the generalissimo had issued a decree that made it clear that the repression would be savage indeed. That being the case, Negrín determined to fight on to the bitter end (although in practice, what this meant would probably have been a gradual retreat towards the coast whilst frantic efforts were made to get all those in the central zone in most danger of imprisonment or execution on to such ships as still remained to the Republic).[94]

The commanders in the central zone had other ideas, however. Dominated by officers of the old army, of whom the few who had become Communists – most notably Miaja, who was the overall commander – had only done so out of opportunism, they were jealous of such figures as Modesto, convinced that Franco was only proving obdurate because of the Communist complexion of the régime and sceptical of the chances of their troops putting up much of a fight. To quote the central figure in the events that followed:

> Both from a military and a political point of view, the war was long since lost, and, if we had been governed by a Spaniard [willing to] learn and interpret the will of the people, it would have ended in 1937 ... All that remained of our government was a group of men who ... practically constituted a dictatorship, since for some time past they had suppressed the rights of the head of state, followed a war policy that was fatal as well as un-Spanish, and coerced certain ministers who seemed to be the slaves of their own timidity.[95]

If this was what moved the military, many Socialists and Anarchists rather feared what appeared to be the ever onward march of Stalinism (at the end of February,

Negrín had unleashed a wave of new appointments in the army that seemed – although this has been strongly disputed – to presage a tightening of Communist control of the armed forces). 'If the Communists succeeded in monopolising power', claimed Eduardo de Gúzman, an Anarchist journalist who was living in Madrid, 'it could only be at the expense of all other organizations. It was impossible to know whether the Communists were manipulating Negrín or whether Negrín was manipulating them. Our reaction was designed as a purely defensive movement against a Communist take-over.'[96] Thus emerged one of the most tragic episodes of the war. Under the leadership of Colonel Segismundo Casado, the commander of the Army of the Centre, a plot was hatched to over-throw the government, arrest all those in favour of resistance and deliver the remaining loyalist territory to the Nationalists. Also involved in the plot were a variety of dissident Anarchists and Socialists, the most prominent being Julián Besteiro. Promised by Franco that he would spare all prisoners except those actually with blood on their hands, on 5 March, Casado duly seized control of Madrid, being joined in his revolt by Miaja, the fleet and parts of the garrisons of Valencia, Murcia and Cartagena (the latter also witnessed an uprising on the part of the local 'fifth column'). Deciding that the game was up, Negrín (who may, in fact, have himself been about to offer peace on more or less the same terms as those that Casado thought he had himself secured) and his allies all fled by air. However, elements of the Republican forces were still opposed to surrender, and the result was a confused struggle in the heart of the capital that eventually saw Casado triumph, though not before the fleet had set sail for Bizerta rather than risk surrender. Resuming his negotiations with Franco, the rebel leader discovered that, other than safe passage abroad for himself and a few of his closest collaborators, the only terms on offer remained unconditional surrender.[97]

In short, the game was up. All that was left was for those who could to escape or go into hiding. On 28 March, for example, Mera fled Madrid with twenty of his closest friends and subordinates and headed for Valencia in a convoy of four cars guarded by two motor-cycle outriders along a route whose every town was already bedecked with monarchist flags.[98] However, the Nationalists were not disposed to grant their defeated foes any lee-way, and on 29 March, they finally went into action. With nothing left to give, everywhere the Republican forces collapsed, whilst Cartagena, Alicante and Valencia were besieged with frantic refugees, the last pockets of Republican territory being occupied on 31 March.[99]

Thus ended the Spanish Civil War (at least in the immediate military sense: there are some who would contend, including, not least, the author of this work, that it has in some senses never ended). So far as a retrospect is concerned, let us begin with the conflict's military lessons: after all, one of the many ways in which it has been billed is as a rehearsal for the Second World War. In so far as these were concerned, in many ways there was little new to talk about, the guidance that had been received from the infinitely larger battles of the First World War having simply been confirmed. Thus, on the defensive, the battle of Brunete, in particular, had shown that the best way to hold a position was not to establish a continuous trench line held by large numbers of troops that could easily be broken, but rather a series of interlocking defended localities that could command the ground around them and slow down the forces of an attacker whilst at the same time laying them open to counterattacks by fresh forces held back in the rear (or, in the case of the thinly stretched Nationalist armies, rushed in from other parts of the country altogether).[100] Equally, on the advance, the Nationalists had shown that, except in circumstances where opposition was so weak and disorganized as to be negligible, what worked was the 'bite and hold' techniques developed by the British army in the First World War: confronted by a series of mountain ranges at the Ebro, for example, the Nationalists had concentrated as much firepower as possible against each one in turn and then occupied them with infantry, the same process then being repeated all over again. Perceived by the Germans and Italians, not to mention such latter-day critics as Paul Preston, as slow and unimaginative, these tactics were essentially the only ones that made any sense in a situation where the attacking forces lacked the self-propelled guns, armoured personnel carriers, supply vehicles and, last but not least, fleets of tanks that characterized the armies of the Second World War. Indeed, on the two occasions when the Nationalists tried something more ambitious in the face of opponents whose fighting power had not already been completely worn down – the battles of the Jarama and Guadalajara – they found that their offensives ran into the sand: whilst initial gains were often spectacular, the momentum of the advance could not be maintained. Only when the opposition was so weak that it was unable to respond or even function in an effective fashion was it possible to stage breakthrough-style offensives, and it is but fair to note that when such opportunities arose – for example, in Aragón in the spring of 1938 and Catalonia in the winter of 1938–9 – Franco was quick to seize them. That said, there is no reason to regard Franco as a military genius. As Anthony Beevor remarks, 'Franco did not so much win the war: the Republican commanders, with the odds already stacked heavily against them, squandered the courage and sacrifice of their troops and lost it.'[101]

In one sense, however, this judgement is a little harsh. Whilst the decision to launch the series of offensives – Segovia, Brunete, Belchite, Teruel, the Ebro and Peñarroya – that ended by doing no more than incurring losses that the Republicans simply could not afford, these yet showed a considerable degree of flexibility in the manner in which they were planned. Not for Vicente Rojo, then, the massive bombardments of the First World War. Recognizing that he simply lacked the firepower to achieve decisive results, in every case except the first, the People's Army relied on long approach marches in the cover of darkness as well as infiltration tactics designed to get their forces deep inside the Nationalists' lines before the defenders could rush up fresh troops. At the Ebro, too, we see the use of special commando units dressed in enemy uniforms, this being a tactic that the Germans made good use of in the Ardennes offensive of 1944. Amongst the reliance on the proven, then, there was also a search for the innovative that showed a keen recognition of the weaknesses of the Republican forces.

If the Spanish Civil War harked back in many ways to the First World War, 1938 was not 1918, the intervening twenty years having witnessed many changes in the field of armaments. First of all, of course, we have the tank. A technology the possibilities of which had been amply demonstrated in the final year of the First World War – at Cambrai and, still more so, Amiens, spectacular breakthroughs had been achieved by substantial forces of armour – but the models on offer at the time had been too slow, unreliable and unpleasant to operate to have more than a very limited radius of action and combat life. To a very considerable extent, these problems had now been resolved, but, for all that, the Spanish Civil War did not provide much evidence that a new age of warfare was on its way. In the first place, neither side had access to that many tanks, the most that either of them were ever able to concentrate on a single battlefield being about 200, whilst these were often split up into company-sized units and, particularly on the Republican side, used in the most timid fashion. That this was so was in part the reflection of continued technical deficiencies: all the armoured fighting vehicles used in the conflict were very thinly protected against enemy fire, whilst the German and Italian tanks were equipped only with machine-guns. However, there was also another problem, in that both Nationalist and Republican tankers were well aware that they could not count on the infantry support vital for their survival. Invulnerable to enemy small-arms fire and, in the case of the Nationalists in particular, challenged by only a limited number of anti-tank guns, they could roll forward indefinitely, but behind them it was a very different story: unlike tanks, infantrymen are creatures of flesh and blood and they were all too easily cut down by the fire of the defending forces and forced to go to ground. With the sort of leadership and training available to the Nationalist forces, these problems could to a limited extent be overcome, but even then there was the problem of how men on foot could keep up with vehicles travelling even at comparatively low speeds or communicate with the men inside them to arrange a joint course of action (until late in the war, few tanks were fitted with radio). Desperate to find a way forward, the Republicans had come up with the idea of actually mounting infantry on the back of tanks, but this had proved an unmitigated disaster. Like it or not, then, whatever they might have wanted – and there is considerable evidence that some of the foreign theorists present had dreams of much more exciting things – the tank forces on both sides had little option but to confine themselves to backing up infantry assaults from the rear (the Republican solution) or to screen attacking infantry battalions behind the shelter of First World War–style creeping barrages (the Nationalist one).[102]

All this meant that the Spanish Civil War offered few obvious lessons for the future. In terms of the actual vehicles, things were clear enough: in brief, mere machine-gun carriers were no longer sufficient. Realizing all too well that the Panzer Is and L3s that they had sent to Spain were all but useless, both the Germans and the Italians busied themselves with the development of the new models, namely the excellent Panzer III and the rather less impressive M13/40, that were to serve as the work-horses of their armies in the period 1940–3, whilst the Russians phased out the slow and poorly armoured T26 in favour of the much superior BT7 (a modification of the BT5s that had been thrown away so wastefully at Fuentes de Ebro) and also embarked on the design process that was ultimately to lead to the introduction of the seminal T34.[103] However, could much more ever be expected of tanks than had been seen in Spain? Here, opinion was divided. While the British, French and American general staffs were initially inclined to conclude that dreams of autonomous 'tank fleets' tearing into the enemy rear were visionary, and therefore that armour should be tied to the infantry (much to the horror of such proponents of tank warfare as J. F. C. Fuller), after some debate, the Germans rather decided that what they needed to do was in effect to discount the whole experience as irrelevant and press on with the development of the armoured divisions that their own devotees of tank warfare had been demanding since the beginnings of re-armament. In this, of course, they were quite correct, and so it might be surmised that the correct lesson to be learned from the tank warfare of the Civil War was that that conflict was no lesson at all (except, perhaps, in what the Duke of Wellington once termed 'what one ought not to do').[104]

In contrast to the tank, the other technology that had come on in leaps and bounds since 1918 made a considerable impact on the conflict. In all the major battles of the war, control of the air had played a major role in victory, whilst there was also overwhelming evidence, on the tactical level, first, that poorly trained troops were highly susceptible to air attack; second, that aircraft could deliver a significant weight of fire support to armies that were attacking and defending alike; and third, that the movement of supplies and reserves could be significantly indicted by the application of airpower. Also on view were plenty of examples of strategic bombing and also such ancillary uses of aircraft as the transport of troops and supplies (though given the constant insistence in most air forces that the bomber would always get through, also notable was the vulnerability of even modern bombers to fighters such as the Messerschmitt Me109). Finally, in addition to the usual bombers and fighters, there had appeared the first specialized ground-attack aircraft ever seen in battle – the Henschel Hs123, Junkers Ju87, Romeo Ro37, Breda Ba65 and Polikarpov R5 and R7. What, however, was the impact of all this? In brief, not entirely what might have been expected. In Britain, France and the United States, whilst a handful of enthusiastic young officers wrote detailed analyses of what had taken place in Spain, their superiors were less impressed. Despite the fact that such terrifying examples as the bombing of Guernica were mirrored in very few other places, despite the fact that Madrid, Barcelona and Bilbao had all been battered by the Nationalist bombers but never bombed out of existence, and, finally, despite the fact that the modern anti-aircraft guns available to both sides by the time of the battle of the Ebro had inflicted significant losses on the Heinkels and Savoias of the one side and the Tupolevs of the other, there was a stubborn insistence on the primacy of strategic bombing that was challenged only in France and then only temporarily. Fortunately, in Britain, at least, civilian thinkers were not so blinkered, and thus it was that the Royal Air Force (RAF) acquired the modern fighter force that allowed it to win the battle of Britain, but even then it was a victory that for a considerable while hung in the balance, thanks to the insistence of many squadron commanders in flying in tight wingtip-to-wingtip formations rather than the more open patterns developed by the Germans in Spain.[105]

Unfortunately for Britain and France, in Germany and Italy, the picture was entirely different. Even before the Civil War, thinkers in both countries had been moving in the direction of the tactical deployment of airpower, and they were now confirmed in this by their experiences of the fighting, even if these experiences came about as much by happenstance as anything else: in part, interest in ground-attack operations amongst the Germans snowballed because the Heinkel He51 was so inadequate as a fighter plane, and, in part, too, because most of the Condor Legion's officers had perforce started their military careers in the infantry or cavalry and were therefore highly attuned to the needs of the men on the ground. Henceforward, in both countries, considerable resources would be poured into the development of substantial ground-attack resources and the development of long-range strategic bombing scaled back (it was particularly noted here that the bombing of Madrid and Barcelona had produced no military effect whatsoever). At the same time, it was also perceived that airpower was never to be squandered or dispersed but concentrated in support of the immediate point of attack. Here, however, there was a serious sting in the tail. In the short term, certainly, there were huge benefits, in that in 1939–40, the massed ranks of Ju87s in particular tore first the Poles and then the Dutch, Belgians, British and French to shreds. Yet for this concentration on the tactical, the Allies could be grateful: not only did the Ju87 prove desperately vulnerable in the face of the next generation of fighters, but the fact that so many resources went into intervention on the battlefield also meant that the Germans were never able to mount the sort of strategic bombing campaign that tore the heart out of their cities in 1943 and 1944. At the same time, meanwhile, both the Germans and Italians fell prey to an almost unbelievable misjudgement in the case of their bombers. Given that their fighters had been increasingly available to shoot the Republicans out of the skies, their bombers eventually really had been able always to get through, and so no attention was paid to the bomber–fighter co-operation that might have produced devastating results against the RAF in the Battle of Britain. And nor was this the end of it: almost all the Condor Legion's bomber losses were due to anti-aircraft fire, whilst its 88mm FK18s and various lighter weapons accounted for large numbers of Tupolevs and other aircraft, and from this it was deduced that the defence of the homeland could be left to anti-aircraft guns only, something that was not the case and meant the Luftwaffe did not have an effective air defence system in place when Germany came under sustained aerial attack from 1941 onwards.[106]

One country that must needs be assessed separately here is the Soviet Union, for the simple reason that its response to the Spanish Civil War was affected by a set of unique factors that had nothing to do with what happened on the battlefields in Spain. In brief, the Civil War had not been going on for very long when Stalin unleashed the 'Great Purge', the result being that many men who had taken part, say, in the defence of Madrid, were liquidated, along with such forward thinkers as the father of Soviet armoured warfare, Mikhail Tukhachevsky, and the head of the air force, Alexander Lapchinsky. Both these men having been won over to the cause of deep strategic penetration on the one hand and the tactical use of concentrated airpower on the other, their deaths meant that it was dangerous to push their ideas too hard, and the Russian armed forces therefore found themselves facing Operation Barbarossa clinging to hopelessly outmoded doctrines that did not serve them well in the slightest. In the air force, true, a powerful interest in close-support operations survived and, as in Germany, this meant that strategic bombing was neglected, the difference being that such were the circumstances in which Russia was eventually placed was that this was something that was not damaging at all. Indeed, the Russian air force gained the Ilyushin Il4, or Shturmovik, this being an infinitely better bargain than the Ju87 ever was. A significant problem, however, was the failure to engage with the problem of tank warfare in a satisfactory fashion: whereas the experience of the Spanish Civil War led the Germans to develop the Sd.Kfz. 250 and 251 half-track armoured personnel carriers, the Russians neglected this area and therefore had to wait until they were provided with large numbers of M3 scout cars and M4 halftracks from 1942 onwards under the Lendlease system.[107]

One final issue of a specifically military nature that is particularly relevant to the Soviet Union is that of the employment of cavalry. Thanks in part to the Russians' neglect of the need to equip its army with vehicles equivalent to the Sd.Kfz. 251, Stalin entered the Second World War with a large force of cavalry. As one expert on the subject writes, indeed, 'At the beginning of World War II, the Red Army was the only force using large cavalry formations apart from Poland and Rumania.'[108] Here, too, it is probable that the Spanish Civil War seriously confused matters. Cavalry were not employed in large numbers on either side, and, in one or two actions in which Nationalist cavalry came up against Republican tanks, as at Seseña in 1936, they were duly shot to pieces. That said, there were occasions when mounted units had played a major part in Franco's success. In the advance on Madrid, for example, Monasterio's cavalry column had done a good job in screening Varela's exposed right flank, while in the battle of the Alfambra early in 1938, the same commander's cavalry division was able to launch a rapid strike that took it clean through the centre of the Republican forces and, particularly at Visiedo, even saw it employ traditional cavalry charges to rout such enemy troops as it encountered, though it should be noted that these attacks enjoyed the support of both tanks and airpower and were launched against men who were already beaten. There is, in addition, a serious caveat to be made here, in that the Republican forces lacked the firepower of even third-class armies of the inter-war period. Spain, in short, was once again a poor model for the rest of Europe. Writing of the campaign in Catalonia, Henry Buckley is very interesting here:

> Down by the Ebro [General Franco] threw in his cavalry under General Monasterio, but I do not think this played a great part in breaking through … The Republican forces hardly used cavalry at all during the war. General Franco had more opportunity because the Republican forces did not have the machine-guns or the chaser planes [i.e. fighters] which today make the life of the cavalry a most unpleasant business. Except in guerrilla warfare in broken country with plenty of cover, the horse has little chance of staying alive. The man can take cover, but the horse is less adaptable and remains an excellent target for even a distant machine-gun … Spain, with a battlefront of almost 1,000 miles for a considerable part of the war … most of which was but thinly held … offered more scope to cavalry than most wars.[109]

What, meanwhile, of the cost of the war? Not counting the many thousands who died in the post-war repression or were lost to the ravages of disease and malnutrition, some 340,000 people had been killed: 200,000 on the battlefield, 75,000 in the Nationalist *limpieza*, 55,000 in the Terror and subsequent acts of judicial murder in the Republican zone, and 10,000 in air raids and the like: it is not, then, true, as has often been claimed, that Spain lost a million dead (though it should be noted that that the 500,000 dead were equalled by another 500,000 men, women and children who fled Spain, around half of them for good).[110] As for physical damage, this was, too, more plentiful than overwhelming. Only a few places had suffered real devastation – Irún, Oviedo, Guernica, Teruel and Belchite are the most obvious examples – whilst even Madrid was still more or less intact. By dint of heroic efforts, particularly in the beleaguered Republican zone, much of the country's archival, artistic and architectural heritage had survived untouched. Most factories were undamaged, meanwhile, infrastructural damage only attaining serious proportions on the railways, though many important road bridges had inevitably been bombed or dynamited and some ports, most notably Barcelona, temporarily put out of action. And, finally, unlike in nearby France, the fighting had not left large stretches of valuable farming land irredeemably poisoned from repeated saturation with poison gas (that said, in such places as the Casa de Campo in Madrid, it is still possible to see areas where hasty attempts to cover up the devastation to the natural flora by means of the importation of large numbers of quick-growing evergreens produced damaging long-term changes to the environment). Spain, in short, had escaped comparatively lightly in physical terms, even if the total cost of the war was still calculated as some 30,000,000,000 *pesetas*.[111]

Yet physical terms are scarcely everything. In Franco's Spain, there was neither peace nor reconciliation. Mass executions continued in the country's wildly over-crowded prisons until 1942; long sentences kept many unfortunates incarcerated for as long as thirty years after the conflict; anyone remotely associated with the Republican cause was blocked from teaching and government service, and, unofficially at least, employment at professional levels in the private sector as well; thousands of women who had been pregnant when they fell into the hands of the Nationalists had their babies taken from them as soon as they were born and handed over to 'suitable couples'; monuments to the victors of the most tasteless nature erected by slave labour appeared at every site associated with the fighting; Avenidas del Generalísimo, Plazas del José Antonio and Calles del 18 de Julio became *de rigeur*; new housing developments commemorated a variety of lesser-known Nationalist commanders and *apparatchiks*; Republican memorials were bulldozed out of existence; every 1 April, grandiose military parades reminded the Spanish populace of just who had won the war; in schools and colleges across the nation, Church and state combined to ram home a version of Spain's recent history that demonized the Republican cause; and, finally, the thousands of Republican *mutilados* were left entirely without succour, just as the thousands of families who had lost loved ones in the repression were left with no option but to sign up to versions of their deaths that put them down to such euphemisms as trauma, lead poisoning or sudden effusions of blood (in many families, indeed, such was the fear that later generations would be victimized that the fact of execution was suppressed altogether, even in the very closest circles: there are most assuredly Spaniards who are alive today who are unaware that they lost grandparents or great-grandparents to Franco's firing squads; equally, and still more sadly, there are also many others snatched from imprisoned mothers at the earliest of ages who do not know that those they have known all their lives as their parents have nothing to do with their ancestry whatsoever). All this, meanwhile, was coupled with endless pretty acts of vindictiveness and humiliation, not to mention wholesale sexual violence and extortion: whether arrested or not, women perceived as 'Reds' could expect to be raped, just as the wives, sisters and daughters of prisoners were often forced to engage in sexual intercourse in order to elicit small favours such as permission for brief visits. As for democracy, social justice, the rights of trade unions, women and the national minorities, freedom of speech and freedom of political organization, these were, of course, notable by their absence.[112]

Following the death of Franco in 1975 – an event followed by a compromise peace (the Constitution of 1978) of the sort that Negrín had proposed exactly forty years earlier – there was a hiatus. Hitherto largely in the hands of foreign historians, the academic historiography was increasingly hispanized, while there were some moves at the level of both central and local government towards the dismantling of the memorialization of the Nationalist victory: in many places, street signs were changed back to the original, while 1 April now became simply the 'Day of the Armed Forces'; equally, as any visit to the civil section of the Cementerio de la Almudena in Madrid will testify, families were able to commemorate dead veterans as soldiers or airmen of the Republic (or, in the case of one Communist couple, 'two Marxist-Leninists for ever'). In 1986, too, a large group of International-Brigade veterans were welcomed back to Madrid and Barcelona. Yet on both Left and Right alike, there was a conscious effort not to mention the war, even to suppress its memory altogether, in order not to rock the boat of the transition, and this reticence paid dividends in the form of a process of democratization that was in the end remarkably smooth, even if this featured an amnesty law that essentially meant that the cause of justice was sacrificed to the cause of democracy.

Under the surface, however, all was not well: the looming statues of General Franco, the continued absence of any public recognition of the Republican cause, the want of justice for the victims of the repression and many other issues were festering sores that finally burst forth in the wake of the Madrid bombings of 11 March 2004. Elected to office just two days after this tragedy, the new Socialist government headed by José-Luis Rodríguez Zapatero launched what can only be described as an attempt to gain the total victory that the Left had not obtained in 1978, let alone 1939. Setting aside a variety of legislative changes affecting, most notably, the position of the Catholic Church, in October 2007, the Spanish parliament passed the so-called 'Law of Historic Memory', this being a bill that condemned the Franco régime out of hand, rehabilitated all those who had fought on the side of the Republic, offered Spanish nationality to all surviving members of the International Brigades, denied the legitimacy of all laws and court sentences passed in the period 1939–75, offered state help to all victims of Franquism and all those who wished to discover the whereabouts of the remains of family members executed by the Nationalists and ordered the cleansing of all public spaces of all reference to the Nationalist cause. This is not the place to discuss the explosion of mutual hatred that followed, including, not least, the latter-day 'revolt of the Catalans' that marked the autumn and winter of 2017, but, however understandable, it has been a sad episode that has done Spain little good and, above all, revived the hatreds that led to civil war. In the process, meanwhile, old myths have been revived, including many relating to the battles, and it is partly with this in mind that this book has been written.

Why, though, had the war taken the Nationalists so long to win? Given the conventional picture of a powerful Franco supported by all the resources of two mighty war machines, and a defenceless Republic cheated and betrayed at every turn, it might have been thought that victory ought to have come far more rapidly than it did. In answer, it is usually claimed either that Franco deliberately postponed the defeat of his opponents, or that the Republic was sustained by the fervour and heroism of its inhabitants. However, neither argument is particularly satisfactory. Whilst Franco may have missed certain chances, except just possibly with respect to the battle of the Ebro, there is little real evidence that he deliberately lengthened the war. Equally, the undoubted courage of many of those who fought for the Republic was of limited value in a military context, whilst in any case co-existing with a rather more varied pattern of behaviour than has often been admitted. At the simplest level, the chief factors that delayed the Nationalist victory were, first, the fact that the balance of technology was rather less favourable to Franco than has sometimes been imagined; and second, that the Republic, in the very nick of time, turned its back on the militias and organized a regular army. Constantly sapped though the Republic was by the baneful effects of the revolution, the political rivalries that divided the loyalist forces, the deficiencies of the scheme of military organization that it adopted and the problems that it met in actually building the new armed forces that its situation required, including, not least, a level of political commitment among the masses that was at best low, if not altogether non-existent, the mere existence of the People's Army was enough to ensure that war was long and drawn out. In the event, the British and French relief forces of which Negrín and Prieto dreamed never materialized, but the policy still came close to success: had the Czechoslovak crisis led to the war that was generally expected, for example, the fortunes of the Republic might have been very different (though this is a considerable assumption: unable as they were to go to the aid of Poland, it is difficult to imagine the British and the French doing much better in respect of the Republic, and all the more so if Italy had initially stayed out of the war as was actually to be the case in 1939).[113] None of this is to say, of course, that foreign intervention was unimportant, nor still less to deny that Franco received far more help than did his opponents. Mere quantity is not everything, however: whereas the Nationalists invariably maximized the impact of what they were sent, the Republicans just as invariably squandered it, or at the very least proved unable to make use of it effectively.

This brings us, of course, to the question of why the Republic lost. Given everything that has appeared in this book, it is probably safe to say that nonsense about the armed people winning the revolution and the People's Army losing the war is just that — nonsense: there is simply not a shred of evidence either that an overtly revolutionary policy would have created a more effective fighting force or that it would have done a better job in getting the population of the Republican zone to engage with the war effort. Given the socio-political reality faced by the successive governments of José Giral, Francisco Largo Caballero and Juan Negrín — in brief, a populace whose general level of political education and commitment was not the mass fervour of legend, but rather the very opposite — what counted was bread and tobacco (with Spain a country in which levels of smoking, at least among men, were extraordinarily high, cigarettes were worth almost more than bullets).[114] Provide for the basic needs of the population, and there was some hope of winning its support, and all the more so if those basic necessities were accompanied by a progressive social policy based on shorter hours, higher pay, better health care, better education and access to the land. Partly on account of the war, partly on account of the weakness of the Republican state, partly on account of its own errors and partly on account of the international situation, there was no hope of satisfying this agenda, while the extraordinary stupidity of the policy of the mixed brigade compounded the problem by raising the army's demands for manpower to levels much higher than those in the Nationalist zone. Very soon, then, the Republic was at war not just with Franco but also with its own people. In the Nationalist zone, a similar problem, at least in so far as the forces of the Left were concerned, was resolved by wholesale terror, but that was not a route that even the most ruthless figures in the Republican camp were prepared to go down: though, deserters and political dissidents were shot in some numbers, most of those who died behind the lines were representatives of the enemy. Whether greater use of terror would have done anything to effect the final result is a question to which we will never know the answer, but in the end, for all the unpleasantness of the SIM, the Republic chose to operate on a higher level, thereby ensuring that, to answer the question with which the current author closed his earlier *Spain in the Liberal Age: From Constitution to Civil War*, Franco did not win the peace.

Notes

1 E. von Stohrer to J. von Ribbentrop, 19 May 1938, cit. HMSO. London (ed.), *Documents on German Foreign Policy, 1918–1945, from the Archives of the German Foreign Ministry. Series D, vol. III: Germany and the Spanish Civil War* (London, 1951), p. 657.

2 Thomas, *Spanish Civil War*, p. 805.

3 Howson, *Arms for Spain*, pp. 297–9. Included in the new arrivals were a large consignment of Czech rifles and machine-guns that had been acquired in the winter of 1936–7 but only just now reached Spain. These were particularly appreciated. 'When the first cases of light machine-guns were opened', remembered Manüel Tagüeña, 'we were amazed at their lightness and excellent finish. Having bought the patent, the British army made them famous in the Second World War under the name of the Bren Gun.' Tagüeña, *Testimonio de dos guerras*, p. 194. With the rifles and machine-guns came an equally large number of the distinctive Czech steel helmet, this being a common feature of photographs of Republican troops fighting in the battle of the Ebro. In addition, the Czechoslovak government had also sold the Republicans forty Avia 101 reconnaissance aircraft, but these had all fallen into the hands of the Nationalists when the ship carrying them was stopped in the Bay of Biscay.

4 Ibid., pp. 205–6.

5 J. M. Martínez Bande, *La batalla del Ebro* (Madrid, 1978), pp. 84–5.

6 E.g. Del Barrio, *Memorias*, p. 90.

7 E.g. Gregory, *Shallow Grave*, p. 116; Fisher, *Comrades*, pp. 148–9.

8 For all this, see Martínez Bande, *Batalla del Ebro*, pp. 87–97. Not only was the Army of the Ebro a powerful force in military terms, but it was also overwhelmingly Communist: Modesto, Lister and Tagueña were all, as we have seen, stars of the Party's war effort, while the less well-known Vega was a long-standing Communist stalwart who had been a member of the Party's national executive in 1931; equally, the army, corps and divisional commissars were all Communists, as were all the divisional commanders.

9 F. Pérez López, *A Guerrilla Diary of the Spanish Civil War* (London, 1972), p. 67.

10 Zugazagoitia, *Guerra y vicisitudes de los españoles*, p. 453. In fact, things were not quite as rosy as Zugazagoitia suggests: on the southern edge of the battlefield, an attempt on the part of the XIV International Brigade to get across the river at Campredó was defeated with heavy losses, the Commune-de-Paris and Henri Barbusse battalions being wiped out when they were trapped on the south bank after the footbridge that had been thrown across to allow the passage of reinforcements was destroyed by enemy aviation. Delperrie de Bayac, *Brigadas internacionales*, pp. 304–6.

11 Fisher, *Comrades*, p. 143.

12 Thomas, *To Tilt at Windmills*, p. 117. As usual, one of the Nationalist pilots involved in the fighting was José Larios: 'There was no rest for our air force ... and thousands of tons of bombs were shattering vital targets. On the day of the breakthrough over thirty reconnaissance flights were carried out low over the enemy's bridgeheads, strongly defended by AA guns. During the first twenty-four

hours the situation was fluid and chaotic and nobody knew where anybody else was on the Nationalist side. The complete surprise had caught us napping to say the least, but our troops gradually began to regroup and put up an organized and well directed resistance. A continuous shuttle service going back and forth to the Ebro was kept up by forty Savoia 79's, thirty He111's, eight Dorniers, thirty Junkers 52's, nine Bredas, twenty Savoia 81's, seven *cadena* squadrons and Morato's fighter group ... The sky over the Ebro would become dark with bursting shells, jolting and peppering our machines as we swept back and forth.' Larios, *Combat over Spain*, pp. 223–4.

13 The ease with which the Nationalists were able to move large numbers of troops from one area of the front to another begs an interesting question. In brief, Spain was a country greatly suited to guerrilla warfare, and from the very start, this had played a certain role in the struggle. Thus, in 1936, large numbers of Andalusian and Extremaduran day labourers took shelter in hills rather than risk death at the hands of the Nationalists, and in October 1937, thousands of Asturian soldiers in particular managed to slip through the Nationalist lines and carry on the fight in the Cantabrian mountains. Meanwhile, given that the Communists in general, and the Russian military advisers in particular, greatly favoured the idea of partisans, it was not long before the military authorities were organizing properly armed and equipped companies of guerrillas and sending these out to make a nuisance of themselves in the Nationalist rear. Alpert, *Republican Army*, pp. 70–2. Later in the war, more use was made of irregulars, but it is the contention of one of the few scholars to have looked at the subject in detail that the results were at best limited. Thus: 'The Loyalist government's guerrillas constituted only an ancillary behind-the-lines force. At most they achieved marginal success in disrupting Rebel lines of communication and in tying down some Rebel troops in security duties. Furthermore they played only a nominal part in organizing popular resistance.' B. Whaley, 'Guerrillas in the Spanish Civil War', Massachusetts Institute of Technology research paper, 1969, p. 3. Just as sceptical, meanwhile, is Michael Seidman: 'In June 1938 a regular guerrilla unit's 100 soldiers ... attached to the Army of Extremadura, raided Nationalist territory around Badajoz and blew up a bridge and four cars. This limited success came at a high price ... Only nineteen returned; most of the survivors were either sick or injured. The head of the information section of the Extremadura Army came to question the effectiveness of guerrilla operations: he believed that raids did little damage to the enemy and that raiders falsified their reports.' Seidman, *Republic of Egos*, p. 215.

14 Gregory, *Shallow Grave*, pp. 124–6.

15 Thomas, *To Tilt at Windmills*, pp. 122–3.

16 Clark, *No Boots to my Feet*, pp. 107–9. Clark had fought his last battle. Evacuated from the front, he was still convalescing when the decision was taken to withdraw the International Brigades from Spain (see below), and he was therefore among the handful of British volunteers who eventually made it back to Britain.

17 Fisher, *Comrades*, p. 145. The Republicans did, indeed, employ few tanks in the battle of the Ebro, but this was as much as anything because the terrain weas so unsuitable. That said, the performance of the few that did go into battle was lamentable. Thus, as Kindelán noted, they were used only as 'artillery pieces of great mobility or [moveable] blockhouses that could be used to protect retreating troops.' Kindelán, *Mis cuadernos de guerra*, p. 194.

18 Martínez Bande, *Batalla del Ebro*, p. 162. Eduardo Pons Prades records that in his heavy machine-gun battalion (the one such unit possessed by the Republicans), casualties reached 50 per cent by 30 July, the unit therefore having to be withdrawn to the other bank of the Ebro to be rebuilt with fresh conscripts. Pons Prades, *Soldado de la República*, p. 270.

19 Rubin, *Spain's Cause was Mine*, p. 123.

20 Bolín, *Spain: the Vital Years*, p. 312.

21 Ibid., p. 313. Lister, especially, argues that Nationalist claims that Franco from the first moments conceived of a battle of annihilation are exaggerated, and that what he rather intended was simply to push the Republicans back across the river. See Lister, *Memorias de un luchador*, pp. 349–50. However, this is mere jousting with semantics: after all, ejecting the Republicans from their conquests was scarcely incompatible with inflicting crippling casualties upon them and neutralizing the Army of the Ebro as a fighting force.

22 E.g. Memorandum by the Under-State-Secretary, 22 October 1938, cit. HMSO, *Documents on German Foreign Policy*, 22 October 1938, p. 777. In an interesting comment on the Germans' ability or, perhaps, willingness to support the Nationalist war effort, the only guns that were sent were 100 77mm Krupp M96 N.A. field guns, a weapon that had been the most common field piece of the German army in 1914 but had had to be replaced in the course of the First World War by the much more effective 77mm M16. See Mortera Pérez and Iniesta Pérez, *La artillería en la Guerra Civil: material de origen alemán*, pp. 19–21.

23 Preston, *Franco*, p. 311.

24 Ibid. The cost of victory appears to have shaken even Franco: 'At night when the reputedly cold-blooded general read the list of casualties, he would lean his head on his clenched fists and occasionally break down. Our losses were heavy. One army corps, after five weeks' fighting, reported two field officers, fifty-five officers and 423 men killed, four field officers, 280 officers and 4,411 men wounded; three weeks later another field officer, forty-six officers and 838 men had been killed, and nine field officers, 263 officers and 8,450 men wounded.' Bolín, *Spain: the Vital Years*, p. 314 (N.B. The term 'field officer' is used to describe officers of the rank of colonel and above). However, even if Bolín is telling the truth here, the *caudillo* did not hold himself responsible for the situation, but instead rounded on his field commanders. As Von Stohrer reported to Von Ribbentrop, 'Morale at headquarters is … low. Violent scenes between Franco and his generals, who do not carry out attack orders correctly, are multiplying.' E. von Stohrer to J. von Ribbentrop, 19 September 1812, cit. HMSO, *Documents on German Policy*, 19 September 1938, p. 743.

25 Max, *Memorias de un revolucionario*, p. 270.

26 Kindelán, *Mis cuadernos de guerra*, pp. 182–6. In one sense, Kindelán is not fair here: such was the terrain, not to mention the inadequate nature of the tanks available to the Nationalists and their complete lack of such assets as armoured personnel carriers and self-propelled guns, that it was ridiculous to talk as if blitzkrieg-style operations were a serious possibility.

27 Cit. Vidal, *Recuerdo, 1936*, pp. 279–80. Transferred to the Ebro front from that of Valencia early in September, by the end of the month, the Carlist Tercio de Lacar had lost at least thirty-nine dead and 150 wounded, whilst an attack on Hill 361 on 1 October cost it another thirty-seven dead and 143 wounded.

28 Fisher, *Comrades*, p. 152.

29 Pons Prades, *Soldado de la República*, pp. 273–6.

30 Fersen, *The Anti-Warrior*, p. 105.

31 Fisher, *Comrades*, pp. 151–2.

32 For a detailed account of some of the dogfights in which Larios was involved, see Larios, *Combat over Spain*, pp. 230–45. In the course of the fighting, Larios claimed two kills, his second and third.

33 Proctor, *Hitler's Luftwaffe in the Spanish Civil War*, pp. 223–35.

34 Tarazona, *Yo fui piloto de caza rojo*, p. 210. As early as 13 August, the same author was noting the strain he and his fellow pilots were under. Thus: 'The aviator often feels as if he is waging a war that apart, a war that is completely distinct from that of the soldier on the ground. Perhaps because he has more time to think, his morale is of a different nature with the result that he is more tense, more fragile even. That said, at the moment time is something we haven't got much of as we are flying as many as five sorties in a single day.' Ibid., p. 203.

35 Milany, *Aviador de la República*, pp. 165–6. Badly wounded, Milany was rescued by Republican troops and spent the rest of the war in hospital, eventually having the good fortune to be evacuated to France.

36 Martínez Bande, *Batalla del Ebro*, pp. 300–4. Whilst Martínez Bande's account of the battle is as detailed as it is reliable, for an alternative, see J. Llarch, *La batalla del Ebro* (Barcelona, 1972).

37 These figures are, it is admitted, estimates only: however, a loss rate of between two and three Republican aircraft for every one suffered by the Nationalists does not seem implausible.

38 Lister, *Memorias de un luchador*, p. 356.

39 Pons Prades, *Soldado de la Republica*, p. 277.

40 Lister, *Memorias de un luchador*, p. 388. Amongst the troops, meanwhile, there was not the slightest desire to continue the struggle. At the end of the battle, Joaquín Masjuán found himself on a bluff watching the last remnants of the Army of the Ebro file over the bridge at Flix. Supposedly, he and his comrades were in reserve, but, as he acknowledged, 'We had little desire to fight, supposing, that is, that we had ever had any to start with. Indeed, the spectacular sight of so many men in flight had our morale draining from the very soles of our feet.' Max, *Memorias de un revolucionario*, p.285.

41 V. Rojo, *Alerta los pueblos! Estudio político-militar del periodo final de la Guerra Española* (Barcelona, 1974), p. 33. This gloomy picture might be thought to be contradicted by the cheering crowds that attended the last parade of the International Brigades in Barcelona on 12 October, but such scenes were at best ephemeral, whilst one suspects that said cheering crowds had essentially been got up through the mobilization of Communist and PSUC activists.

42 Lister, *Memorias de un luchador*, p. 388.

43 Seidman, pp. 225–6.

44 In the end, of the 12,673 foreigners found to be present with the Republican forces, only 4,640 were actually repatriated, those who went consisting of almost all the surviving British, French, Dutch, Belgians, Swiss, Scandinavians and Americans – in other words, those national groups with countries that offered them some sort of future – and a limited number of Germans, Italians and Slavs who were given refuge in Russia as men deemed to be valuable for the future (a great many of the Germans, in particular, ended up in senior positions in post-war East Germany). As for the remaining 6,000, they remained behind to endure the collapse of the Republic in 1939, many of them being reassigned to other units. Thomas, *Spanish Civil War*, pp. 851–3. For the withdrawal of the Italians, meanwhile, see Coverdale, *Italian Intervention*, pp. 362–6.

45 Rubin, *Spain's Cause was Mine*, p. 145.

46 Thomas, *To Tilt at Windmills*, p. 165.

47 Richardson, *Comintern Army*, pp. 179–80.

48 Alpert, *Republican Army*, p. 272.

49 Hidalgo de Cisneros, *Cambio de rumbo*, II, pp. 242–7. Extraordinarily enough, Stalin agreed to these terms and in the course of December dispatched several substantial shipments to France in the hope that they could then be got across the frontier, but by the time they arrived, it was far too late. Howson, *Arms for Spain*, pp. 242–3.

50 Thomas, *Spanish Civil War*, pp. 844–5.

51 Seidman, *Republic of Egos*, p. 225.

52 Clark, *No Boots to my Feet*, p. 113.

53 Thomas, *To Tilt at Windmills*,

54 Coverdale, *Italian intervention*, p. 376.

55 Buckley, *Life and Death of the Spanish Republic*, p. 405.

56 Ibid., pp. 406–7.

57 Lister, *Memorias de un luchador*, p. 393.

58 Ibid., p. 392.

59 Cit. Castells, *Recuerdo 1936*, p. 292.

60 Cit. ibid., p. 293. García is probably correct in so far as people with little or no record of political involvement is concerned (though such were the horror stories in circulation that it may be assumed that there were plenty who thought discretion was the better part of valour).

61 Seidman, *Republic of Egos*, p. 223.

62 Larios, *Combat over Spain*, p. 255.

63 Pons Prades, *Soldado de la República*, p. 326.

64 For all this, see Seidman, *Republic of Egos*, pp. 165–75.

65 E.g. ibid., pp. 202–3.

66 Matthews, *Reluctant Warriors*, p. 197. Martínez Bande, *Batalla del Ebro*, p. 86.

67 Pons Prades, *Soldado de la república*, p. 276.

68 Fisher, *Comrades*, p. 153.

69 Matthews, *Reluctant Warriors*, p. 197.

70 Pons Prades, *Soldado de la República*, pp. 277–319. Pons Prades' account of the ever worsening conditions of his captivity is harrowing. Particularly significant is the fact that, whilst his numerous fellow prisoners included a number of Nationalist sympathisers, the vast majority were 'draft evaders, deserters, particularly from the class of 1941 ... functionaries who had been arrested in the Pyrenees trying to get to France with money and valuables.' Ibid., p. 285. So poisonous was the atmosphere, meanwhile, that perhaps the very last British volunteer to cross the frontier with the aim of joining the International Brigades, the extraordinary adventurer Peter Elstob, was immediately thrown in prison as a spy

71 Pons Prades, *Soldado de la República*, p. 323.

72 Cit. Fraser, *Blood of Spain*, p. 481.

73 Tarazona, *Yo fui piloto de caza rojo*, p. 283–4. At least, such is the claim made by Tarazona. In fact, the enemy plane was only damaged, the records of the Condor Legion suggesting that it lost no aircraft on that day.

74 Proctor, *Hitler's Luftwaffe in the Spanish Civil War*, p. 244.

75 Salas Larrázabal, *Air War over Spain*, pp. 287–95.

76 Cit. Vidal, *Recuerdo 1936*, p. 290. Given the impact of the bombing, captured Nationalist pilots, whether Spanish, Italian or German, were in real danger of being lynched. Frantic to avoid anything that might discredit the Republic in the eyes of the international community, a few days before the loss of Barcelona, Negrín ordered the commander of the air force, Hidalgo de Cisneros, to escort all the enemy flyers held in captivity after being shot down over Catalonia to safety in France. Hidalgo de Cisneros, *Cambio de rumbo*, II, p. 248.

77 In a frantic effort to provide some sort of defence, Rojo ordered the formation of static machine-gun battalions whose task it would be to man the fortifications that were hastily being constructed to defend the capital, but, whilst this was sensible enough, the men were the sweepings of the barracks and rear areas, whilst in several cases they had to be armed with machine-guns designed as the armament of fighter planes and therefore lacking such necessities as tripods or bipods. Rojo, *Alerta los pueblos!* pp. 100–1.

78 Mora, *In Place of Splendour*, pp. 387–8. According to Mora, the crowd was neither broken or demoralized but defiant. '"We shall come back," the women said, and the children echoed them, "We shall come back and then let them tremble!"' Ibid., p. 388. Well, perhaps.

79 Pons Prades, *Soldado de la República*, p. 325. Sadly, for all these efforts, the fate even of the wounded who were got away was not a happy one: of the 15,000 men evacuated from Barcelona, the French only admitted one fifth of their number, the rest being captured as their trains and ambulances were over-run by the Nationalists. Lister, *Memorias de un luchador*, p. 396.

80 Iniesta Cano, *Memorias y recuerdos*, p. 135.

81 Larios, *Combat over Spain*, p. 258. For an account of the Nationalist repression in Barcelona (of which Larios, of course, says nothing), see Preston, *Spanish Holocaust*, pp. 464–5.

82 Pons Prades, *Soldado de la República*, p. 343.

83 Tarazona, *Yo fuí piloto de caza rojo*, p. 293–4.

84 Ibid., pp. 295–6.

85 For general histories of the campaign in Catalonia, see L. Romero, *El final de la guerra* (Barcelona, 1976), pp. 53–96; J. M. Martínez Bande, *La campaña de Cataluña* (Madrid, 1979).

86 Lister, *Memorias de un luchador*, p. 398.

87 For the fighting on the Extremadura front in August 1938, see Moreno Gómez, *Guerra Civil en Córdoba*, pp. 63–4.

88 For a detailed account of this all but unknown battle, see ibid., pp. 65–82.

89 Matthews, *Reluctant Warriors*, p. 184.

90 Ibid., p. 189.

91 Seidman, *Republic of Egos*, p. 211.

92 Biescas Palacios, *Memorias*, p. 45.

93 Seidman, *Republic of Egos*, p. 218.

94 Bolloten, *Spanish Civil War*, pp. 687–8.

95 Casado, *Last Days of Madrid*, pp. 100–1.

96 Cit. Fraser, *Blood of Spain*, p. 491.

97 The Casado coup is a complicated affair that has understandably been the subject of bitter controversy. For a highly critical account, see A. Viñas, 'Playing with history and hiding treason: Colonel Casado's untrustworthy memoirs and the end of the Spanish Civil War', *Bulletin of Spanish Studies*, XCI, Nos. 1–2 (January, 2014), pp. 295–323. In brief, Viñas' thesis is that Casado was motivated above all by concern for his own safety, and that, but for him, large numbers those who went on to suffer imprisonment and execution could somehow have been evacuated. However, whilst it is beyond doubt true that Casado's various accounts of his actions are completely untrustworthy and, still more so, that he was deeply self-serving, this line of argument is distinctly problematic. Complete fool to have believed Franco though Casado may have been, there is no guarantee that the demoralized Spanish forces could have held out for more than a few hours against a full-scale Nationalist attack, whilst the thousands at risk from Franco's firing squads have to be balanced against the hundreds of thousands at risk of starvation with every day that the war continued: with average calorie intake down to just 770 per diem in Madrid, civilians were literally dropping dead of hunger in the streets; Seidman, *Republic of Egos*, p. 219. More balanced (and more detailed) than Viñas' contribution, then, is Romero, *El final de la guerra*, pp. 133–402. For a more recent study, see L. Español Bouché, *Madrid, 1939: del golpe de Casado al final de la Guerra Civil* (Madrid, 2004). Finally, a highly pro-Casado account is that contained in Bolloten, *The Spanish Civil War*, pp. 702–42.

98 Mera, *Guerra, exilio y carcel*, p. 226.

99 The 'campaign' of the last days of March 1939 is described in detail in Romero, *El final de la guerra*, pp. 403–54. Typical enough was the experience of Luís Bolín when he entered Madrid in the immediate wake of the first Nationalist soldiers: 'Shabbily dressed people lined the thoroughfares and watched with bewilderment in their faces. Republican soldiers, some of them still carrying hand-grenades and rifles, stared sheepishly at me, unable to believe their eyes. For years they had been assured that we would never break through ... and now we were here.' Bolín, *Spain, the Vital Years*, p. 324. Victory, of course, was everywhere followed by a wave of arrests and summary executions. For events in Madrid, see J. Ruiz, *'They have passed!' The Beginning of Francoist Rule in Madrid, April 1939* (Oxford, 2005), pp. 29–52.

100 This technique may be observed on a small scale on the ground today in the form of the well-preserved remains in the Casa de Campo in Madrid: the terrain in the

park consisting of a series of spurs projecting towards the River Manzanares, the Nationalists can be seen to have established defensive redoubts on each one of these whilst leaving the ravines in between empty of all defence other than the cross-fire to which they could be subjected from the trenches and pillboxes above.

101 Beevor, *Battle for Spain*, p. 476.

102 For a general discussion of armoured warfare in the Spanish Civil War, see. K. Macksey, *Tank Warfare: a History of Tanks in Battle* (London, 1971), pp. 103–6; I. Hogg, *Armour in Conflict: the Design and Tactics of Armoured Fighting Vehicles* (London, 1980), pp. 62–7.

103 For all this, see B. T. White, *Tanks and Other AFVs of the Blitzkrieg Era, 1939–1941* (London, 1972).

104 For all this, see P. Wright, *Tank: the Progress of a Monstrous War-Machine* (London, 2000), pp. 213–17. For an interesting discussion of one particular case-study, see G. Hoffmann, 'The tactical and strategic use of *attaché* intelligence: the Spanish Civil War and the U.S. army's misguided quest for a modern tank doctrine', *Journal of Military History*, LXII, No. 1 (January, 1998), pp. 101–33.

105 J. Corum, 'The Spanish Civil War: lessons learned and not learned by the Great Powers', *Journal of Military History*, LXII, No. 2 (April, 1998), pp. 316–24.

106 Ibid., pp. 324–9; Proctor, *Hitler's Luftwaffe in the Spanish Civil War*, pp. 254–9.

107 Corum, 'The Spanish Civil War: lessons learned and not learned', pp. 329–31; 153–7; Zaloga, 'The inter-war period: Soviet tank operations in the Spanish Civil War', pp. 153–7. To quote Hugh Thomas, 'General Pavlov told Stalin that the Spanish war proved that tank formations could not play an independent operational role. He may have given that advice to escape being branded as an admirer of Marshal Tukhachevsky, who had had faith in such formations. The large Russian army of heavy tanks was, probably in consequence, in 1939 distributed as an infantry support force.' Thomas, *Spanish Civil War*, p. 945.

108 J. Piekalkiewicz, *The Cavalry of World War II* (London, 1979), p. 252.

109 Buckley, *Life and Death of the Spanish Republic*, pp. 408–9.

110 For these figures, see Thomas, *Spanish Civil* War, p. 927; to these figures should be added a considerable number who died of hunger or disease, but calculating figures of this sort is much harder. Preston puts the number of those executed by the Nationalists as at least 130,000 and possibly as many as 180,000, but this figure includes the large numbers who faced the firing squad in the period 1939–42. Preston, *Spanish Civil War*, p. 302. Notwithstanding the terrible losses suffered by the International Brigades, the foreign component of these figures pales into insignificance beside the Spanish totals: Italian dead came to 2,794; German 131; International Brigade 10,000. Coverdale, *Italian Intervention*, p. 418; Proctor, *Hitler's Luftwaffe in the Spanish Civil War*, p. 253; Delperrie de Bayac, *Brigadas internacionales*, p. 324.

111 Thomas, *Spanish Civil War*, pp. 927–9.

112 For a detailed analysis of the form that peace took in Franco's Spain, see S. Holguín, 'How did the Spanish Civil War end? Not so well', *American Historical Review*, CXX, No. 5 (July, 2015), pp. 1767–83. Also excellent is Preston, *Spanish Civil War*, pp. 301–17.

113 A serious issue to consider here is the attitude of the British government. In theory, this was characterized by the principle of non-intervention, but in practice, the politicians who made up the so-called 'National Government', the heads of the army, navy and air force and the 'mandarins' of the Foreign Office were united in their loathing of the 'Reds', this feeling extending even to the staunchly anti-fascist Winston Churchill. For a detailed study, see E. Moradiellos García, *La perfidia de Albión: el gobierno británico y la Guerra Civil Española* (Madrid, 1996). For an interesting study of how even the most moderate Republican leaders had to struggle for acceptance in the eyes of the British establishment, see P. Preston, 'Great statesman

or unscrupulous opportunist? Anglo-Saxon interpretations of Lluis Companys', *Bulletin of Spanish Studies*, XCII, No. 8–10 (December, 2015), pp. 493–509.

114 For an interesting discussion of the role played by tobacco in the Spanish Civil War, see M. Cortes Blanco, 'El tabaquismo en la Guerra Civil Española' at < http://www. bvsde.paho.org/bvsacd/cd37/pt41p37.pdf >, accessed 28 December 2017. Although the literature on the subject is very limited, amongst the soldiers of both sides, smoking was near universal, whilst it was also common amongst the civilian population. Given such levels of addiction, cigarettes could not but figure in the dynamics of the war. Soldiers possessed of tobacco, then, were liable to enjoy higher morale than men who had none; the promise of tobacco featured extensively in leaflets dropped on Madrid and other cities, not to mention the propaganda that was frequently blasted across no-man's-land from loud-speakers; and the hope of obtaining tobacco could often be a strong inducement to enlist. Meanwhile, it is highly probable that the Civil War made a considerable contribution to the spread of smoking among Spanish women, not least because of the prevalence of the habit amongst the foreign women who arrived in Republican Spain: amongst the many smokers in this group were the journalist Martha Gellhorn, the photographer Gerda Taro, the POUM sympathizers Mary Low and Eileen Blair (the wife of George Orwell) and the militiawomen Fanny Schoonheyt and Clara Thalmann.

APPENDIX 1

Organization of the Spanish Home Army, 1936

First Organic Division (Madrid)

First Infantry Brigade:	Infantry Regiment No. 1 (Wad-Ras), Madrid
	Infantry Regiment No. 2 (León), Madrid
Second Infantry Brigade:	Infantry Regiment No. 3 (Castilla), Badajoz
	Infantry Regiment No. 4 (Covadonga), Madrid
First Artillery Brigade:	Light Artillery Regiment No. 1, Getafe
	Light Artillery Regiment No. 2, Vicálvaro
First Engineer Battalion:	Carabanchel
Seventh Engineer Battalion:	Alcalá de Henares

Second Organic Division (Seville)

Third Infantry Brigade:	Infantry Regiment No. 5 (Lepanto), Granada
	Infantry Regiment No. 6 (Granada), Seville
Fourth Infantry Brigade:	Infantry Regiment No. 7 (Pavía), Algeciras
	Infantry Regiment No. 8 (Vitoria), Málaga
Second Artillery Brigade:	Light Artillery Regiment No. 3, Seville
	Light Artillery Regiment No. 4, Granada
Second Engineer Battalion:	Seville

Third Organic Division (Valencia)

Fifth Infantry Brigade:	Infantry Regiment No. 9 (Otumba), Valencia
	Infantry Regiment No. 10 (Guadalajara), Valencia
Sixth Infantry Brigade:	Infantry Regiment No. 11(Tarifa), Alicante
	Infantry Regiment No. 12 (Vizcaya), Alcoy
Third Artillery Brigade:	Light Artillery Regiment No. 5, Valencia
	Light Artillery Regiment No. 6, Murcia
Third Engineer Battalion:	Valencia

Fourth Organic Division (Barcelona)

Seventh Infantry Brigade:	Infantry Regiment No. 13 (Badajoz), Barcelona
	Infantry Regiment No. 14 (Alcántara), Barcelona
Eighth Infantry Brigade:	Infantry Regiment No. 15 (Almansa), Tarragona
	Infantry Regiment No. 16 (Albuera), Lérida
Fourth Artillery Brigade:	Light Artillery Regiment No. 7, Barcelona
	Light Artillery Regiment No. 8, Mataró
Fourth Engineer Battalion:	Barcelona

Fifth Organic Division (Zaragoza)

Ninth Infantry Brigade:	Infantry Regiment No. 17 (Aragón), Zaragoza
	Infantry Regiment No. 18 (Gerona), Zaragoza
Tenth Infantry Brigade:	Infantry Regiment No. 19 (Galicía), Jaca
	Infantry Regiment No. 20 (Valladolid), Huesca
Fifth Artillery Brigade:	Light Artillery Regiment No. 9, Zaragoza
	Light Artillery Regiment No. 10, Calatayud
Fifth Engineer Battalion:	Zaragoza

Sixth Organic Division (Burgos)

Eleventh Infantry Brigade:	Infantry Regiment No. 21 (Valencia), Santander
	Infantry Regiment No. 22 (San Marcial), Burgos
Twelfth Infantry Brigade:	Infantry Regiment No. 23 (América), Pamplona
	Infantry Regiment No. 24 (Bailén), Logroño
Sixth Artillery Brigade:	Light Artillery Regiment No. 11, Burgos
	Light Artillery Regiment No. 12, Logroño
Sixth Engineer Battalion:	San Sebastían

Seventh Organic Division (Valladolid)

Thirteenth Infantry Brigade:	Infantry Regiment No. 25 (San Quintín), Valladolid
	Infantry Regiment No. 26 (Toledo), Zamora
Fourteenth Infantry Brigade:	Infantry Regiment No. 27 (Argel), Cáceres
	Infantry Regiment No. 28 (La Victoria), Salamanca
Seventh Artillery Brigade:	Light Artillery Regiment No. 13, Segovia
	Light Artillery Regiment No. 14, Valladolid

Eighth Organic Division (Seville)

Fifteenth Infantry Brigade:	Infantry Regiment No. 29 (Zamora), La Coruña
	Infantry Regiment No. 30 (Zaragoza), Lugo
Sixteenth Infantry Brigade:	Infantry Regiment No. 31 (Burgos), León
	Infantry Regiment No. 32 (Milán), Oviedo
Eighth Artillery Brigade:	Light Artillery Regiment No. 15, Pontevedra
	Light Artillery Regiment No. 16, La Coruña
Eighth Engineer Battalion:	Gijón

Cavalry Division

First Brigade (Palencia):	Cavalry Regiment No. 2 (Villarobeldo), Palencia
	Cavalry Regiment No. 3 (Calatrava), Salamanca
Second Brigade (Barcelona):	Cavalry Regiment No 9 (Santiago), Barcelona
	Cavalry Regiment No 10 (Montesa), Barcelona
Third Brigade (Vitoria):	Cavalry Regiment No 4 (España), Burgos
	Cavalry Regiment No 6 (Numancia), Vitoria
Horse Artillery Regiment	Campamento
Cyclist Battalion	Alcalá de Henares
Armoured Car Battalion	Aranjuez
Signals Regiment	El Pardo

First Mountain Brigade

First Half-Brigade:	Mountain Battalion No. 1 (Chiclana), Figueras
	Mountain Battalion No. 2 (Asia), Gerona
	Mountain Artillery Regiment No. 1 (Barcelona)
Second Half-Brigade:	Mountain Battalion No. 3 (Madrid), Seo de Urgel
	Mountain Battalion No. 4 (Ciudad Rodrigo), Gerona

Second Mountain Brigade

First Half-Brigade:	Mountain Battalion No. 5 (Flandés), Vitoria
	Mountain Battalion No. 6 (Arellano), Bilbao
	Mountain Artillery Regiment No. 2 (Barcelona)
Second Half-Brigade:	Mountain Battalion No. 7 (Arápiles), Estella
	Mountain Battalion No. 8 (Sicilia), Pamplona

Naval-Base Garrisons

Cádiz:	Infantry Regiment No. 33 (Cádiz),
	Coastal Artillery Regiment No. 1
Ferrol:	Infantry Regiment No. 35 (Mérida)
	Coastal Artillery Regiment No. 2
Cartagena:	Infantry Regiment No. 34 (Sevilla)
	Coastal Artillery Regiment No. 3
Mahón:	Coastal Artillery Regiment No. 4

Asturias Mixed Mountain Brigade

Infantry Regiment No. 32 (Milán), Oviedo
Infantry Regiment No. 40 (Simancas), Gijón
Mountain Artillery Battalion (Oviedo)
Mounted Battalion

Baleares Command

Infantry Regiment No. 36 (Palma), Palma de Mallorca
Infantry Regiment No. 37 (Baleares), Mahón
Mixed Artillery Group, No. 1 (Mallorca)
Mixed Engineer Group, No. 1 (Mallorca)
Mixed Engineer Group, No. 2 (Menorca)

Canarias Command

Infantry Regiment, No. 38 (Tenerife), Santa Cruz
Infantry Regiment No. 39 (Canarias), Las Palmas
Mixed Artillery Group No. 2, Santa Cruz
Mixed Artillery Group No. 3, Las Palmas
Mixed Engineer Group No. 3, Santa Cruz
Mixed Artillery Group No. 4, Las Palmas

Independent Units

Cavalry Regiment No. 1 (Castillejos), Zaragoza[1]
Cavalry Regiment No. 5 (Farnesio), Valladolid
Cavalry Regiment No. 7 (Lusitania), Valencia
Cavalry Regiment No. 8 (Taxdir), Seville
Machine-Gun Battalion No. 1, Castellón
Machine-Gun Battalion No. 2, Plasencia
Machine-Gun Battalion No. 3, Almería
Machine-Gun Battalion No. 4, Manresa
Tank Regiment No. 1, Madrid
Tank Regiment No. 2, Zaragoza
Heavy Artillery Regiment No. 1, Córdoba
Heavy Artillery Regiment No. 2, Gerona
Heavy Artillery Regiment No. 3, San Sebastián
Heavy Artillery Regiment No. 4, Medina del Campo
Artillery Intelligence Group No. 1, Carabanchel
Artillery Intelligence Group No. 2, Barcelona
Artillery Intelligence Group No. 3, Valladolid
Railway Regiment No. 1, Leganés
Railway Regiment No. 2, Leganés
Anti-Aircraft Battalion No. 1, Campamento
Anti-Aircraft Battalion No. 2, Zaragoza
Searchlight Battalion (Madrid)
Regiment of Sappers and Miners, Madrid
Balloon Regiment, Guadalajara
Pontoon-Bridge Battalion, Zaragoza
Presidential Battalion, Madrid
War-Ministry Detachment, Madrid

Commentary

1. Infantry regiments consisted of two battalions, each of four rifle companies, one machine-gun company and one heavy-weapons platoon (this last had two mortars and one infantry gun.) Each regiment had sufficient weapons in store to equip a third battalion in time of war.
2. Cavalry regiments consisted of two squadrons of sabres and one of machine-guns.
3. Artillery regiments consisted of two battalions, each one of three four-gun batteries, together with sufficient material to equip a third battalion in time of war. In the light regiments, odd-numbered units were equipped with 75mm guns and even-numbered ones with 105mm howitzers. In the heavy regiments, the first battalion was equipped with 150mm guns and the second with 155mm howitzers.
4. Tank regiments were supposed to consist of a headquarters echelon of seven tanks plus four companies of fifteen tanks apiece. In reality, each of the two regiments had just five vehicles.
5. Each anti-aircraft battalion consisted of two companies of cannon and one of machine guns.

Note

1   In time of war, it was intended that these four regiments should be split up so as to provide each organic division with a reconnaissance squadron.

APPENDIX 2

Organization of the Army of Africa, 1936[1]

A. MOROCCO

Eastern Division

First Regiment, Spanish Foreign Legion
Indigenous Regular Regiment No. 2 (Melilla)
Indigenous Regular Regiment No. 5 (Alhucemas)
African Light Infantry Brigade: Light-Infantry Battalions Nos. 3 (Melilla) and 7 (Ceuta)
Cavalry Brigade
Artillery Brigade
Machine-Gun Battalion
Melilla and Rif Cyclist Detachments

Eastern Division

Second Regiment, Spanish Foreign Legion
Indigenous Regular Regiment No. 1 (Tetuan)
Indigenous Regular Regiment No. 3 (Ceuta)
Indigenous Regular Regiment No. 4 (Larache)
African Light Infantry Brigade: Light-Infantry Battalions Nos. 1 (San Fernando), 2 (Las Navas), 6 (Ceriñola) and 8 (Serrallo)
Cavalry Brigade
Artillery Brigade
Machine-Gun Battalion
Ceuta, Tetuan and Larache cyclist detachments
Moroccan Engineer Battalion
Moroccan Signals Battalion

Forces of the Caliph

Mehall-la Regiment No. 1 (Tetuan)
Mehall-la Regiment No. 2 (Melilla)
Mehall-la Regiment No. 3 (Larache)
Mehall-la Regiment No. 5 (Rif)
Mehall-la Regiment No. 6 (Gomara)

B. OTHER COLONIES

Ifni: Ifni Sharpshooters.
Spanish Sahara: Forces of the Sahara
Equatorial Guinea: Colonial Guard

C. AIR SUPPORT

Group No. 1 (Tetuan/Melilla/Larache): 2 squadrons Breguet BrXIX (20 planes)
Bomber Squadron: (Villa Cisneros/Ifni): 1 flight Fokker FVII (4 planes)
Group No. 6 (Atalayón): 1 squadron Dornier-Wal (6 planes)

Commentary

1. The Spanish Foreign Legion was divided into two regiments known as Legiones del Tercio. Each regiment was divided into three battalions or *banderas*, each of which had three rifle companies and one company of mortars and machine-guns.
2. The 'indigenous regulars,' otherwise known as *regulares*, consisted of five regiments each of three battalions – *tabores* – of infantry and one of cavalry, these last being brigaded to form the two cavalry brigades listed above. Infantry *tabores* had three companies and cavalry ones three squadrons, but the strength of both was only 225 men.
3. In contrast to the *regulares*, the African Light Infantry, or Cazadores de Africa, were considered not as native auxiliaries but as an integral part of the Spanish army, and as such enjoyed the same organization as normal infantry battalions, i.e. four companies of rifles and one of machine-guns, together with a section of heavy weapons.
4. The artillery brigades had two battalions: one of three batteries of 105mm and one of 155mm howitzers, and one of three batteries of 105mm howitzers. In 1935 six more batteries were dispatched to Morocco, including two of 75mm guns, two of 105mm howitzers, one of 150mm guns and one of 155mm howitzers, but it is not known how they were deployed.
5. The Mehall-la was in effect the bodyguard of the puppet Caliph of Morocco. Setting aside one *tabor* that was retained at the Caliph's palace and two

mounted *tabores*, in 1936, each regiment or *grupo* consisted of three *tabores* and each *tabor* of three *mías*. Why there was no Regiment No. 4 is unclear.

6. Beyond Morocco, the resources of the Army of Africa were at best exiguous; the troops in Spanish Sahara and Equatorial Guinea consisted of no more than one battalion apiece, while Ifni (the only one to send troops to Spain) had just three *tabores* of infantry and one *mía* of cavalry.

Note

1   Salas Larrázabal, *Air War over Spain*, pp. 351–2.

APPENDIX 3

Spanish military and naval aviation, 1936[1]

Military aviation/Aeronautica militar

Wing No. 1

Group No. 11 (Getafe): 3 squadrons Nieuport–Delage NiD 52
Group No. 21 (León): 3 squadrons Breguet BrXIX
Group No. 31 (Getafe): 2 squadrons Breguet BrXIX

Wing No. 2

Group No. 22 (Seville): 2 squadrons Breguet BrXIX

Wing No. 3

Group No. 13 (Prat de Llobregat): 2 squadrons Nieuport Delage NiD52
Group No. 23 (Logroño): 3 squadrons Breguet BrXIX

Independent units

Group No. 1 (Tetuan/Melilla/Larache): 2 squadrons Breguet BrXIX (20 planes)
Group No. 6 (Atalayón): 1 squadron Dornier-Wal (6 planes)
Group No. 31 (Getafe): 1 flight De Havilland DH89 (3 planes)
Cuatro Vientos: 1 squadron BrXIX
Villa Cisneros/Ifni): 1 flight Fokker FVII (4 planes)
Guadalajara: 1 flight Hawker Fury (3 planes)
Granada: 1 flight Nieuport-Delage Nid52 (3 planes), 1 squadron Breguet BrXIX

Naval Aviation/Aeronautica Naval

Bomber group (San Javier): 1 squadron Dornier Wal flying-boats (5 planes)

Torpedo group (San Javier): 3 squadrons Vickers Vildebeest torpedo bombers (27 planes)

Reconnaissance group (San Javier): 2 squadrons Savoia-Marchetti SM62bis flying boats (18 planes)

Reconnaissance patrol (Mahón): 1 flight Savoia-Marchetti SM62bis flying-boats (5 planes)

Reconnaissance patrol (Marín): 1 flight Savoia-Marchetti SM62bis flying-boats (5 planes)

Fighter group (San Javier): 1 squadron Martynside F4 fighters (10 planes)

Training group (Barcelona): 1 squadron Macchi M18 flying boats (10 planes), 1 flight Savoia Marchetti SM62bis

Commentary

Discounting unarmed trainers of various types, total planes in service in 1936 were as follows: 60 Nieuport-Delage NiD52, 125 Breguet BrXIX, 3 Hawker Fury, 3 De Havilland DH89, 4 Fokker FVII, 27 Vickers Vildebeest, 8 Dornier Wal, 21 Savoia-Marchetti SM62bis, 10 Macchi M18, 10 Martynside F4. It has not been possible to list the exact strengths of the military aviation's squadrons in mainland Spain, but at full strength, a squadron should have numbered ten planes. Plans were underway to build a complete bomber wing in Madrid on the basis of military versions of the DH89 and to replace the NiD52 with the Hawker Fury, but these had not advanced very far. As it was, the bulk of the aircraft available to the Spanish forces were obsolescent at best – the top speed of the NiD52 and the BrXIX was in both cases no more than 180 miles an hour – whilst many aircraft were out of service: of the Naval Aviation's ninety combat aircraft, for example, no more than fifty-seven were capable of taking to the air.

Note

1   Salas Larrazábal, *Air War over Spain*, p. 354.

APPENDIX 4

Spanish Navy, 1936[1]

Battleships

España (laid up)
Jaime Primero

Cruisers

Canarias (under construction)
Baleares (under construction)
Miguel de Cervantes (under repair)
Libertad
Almirante Cervera
Mendez Núñez
República (laid up)

Destroyers

Churruca
Almirante Valdés
Sánchez Barcáiztegui
Lepanto
Almirante Antequera
Almirante Ferrándiz
Almirante Valdés
Almirante Miranda
José Luis Díez
Alcalá Galiano

Alsedo
Lazaga
Velasco (under repair)
Gravina (under construction)
Escaño (under construction)
Císcar (under construction)
Jorge Juan (under construction)
Ulloa (under construction)

Submarines

B1–B6
C1–C6
D1–D4 (under construction)

Gunboats

Dato
Canalejas
Laya
Cánovas del Castillo

Torpedo boats

Nos. 2, 3, 7, 9, 14, 16, 17, 19, 20, 21 and 22

Minelayers

Jupiter (under construction)
Velasco (under construction)

Commentary

The warships available to the Spanish navy were at best a mixed bag. Launched in 1909 and armed with eight 305mm and twenty 105mm guns, the two battleships were the smallest dreadnought-type vessels ever launched and represented an absurd prestige gesture designed to salve the feelings of a Spanish navy humiliated by its defeat in the War of 1898; even at their best, they had never been capable of taking on the equivalent vessels possessed by other fleets, while in 1936, the *España* was laid up and to all intents and purposes out of service. Much better were the cruisers. Laid down in 1931 and in an advanced state of completion, the heavy cruisers *Canarias* and *Baleares* were both fast and comparatively heavily armed – they carried eight 203mm guns – but only lightly protected, as witness the loss of the *Baleares* in 1938. In this, however, they were very similar to many cruisers of a similar vintage (the Washington Treaty of 1926 had laid down strict limitations on tonnage that caused many navies to trade protection for speed), while four of the five light cruisers – *Libertad*, *Almirante Cervera*, *Miguel de Cervantes* and the somewhat less well-armed *Méndez Núñez* – were all directly comparable to similar vessels currently in service with the Royal Navy (based on a design dating back to before the First World War and extremely slow, the *República* was a different question, her state in any case being so poor that it took the Nationalists till 1938 to get her armed and ready for sea). Depending on the class, all the light cruisers were armed with a varying number of 152mm guns, but, like all the other vessels in the fleet, they were very weak when it came to anti-aircraft weapons, both sides therefore having to put much time and energy into providing them with extra cannon and machine-guns. In many ways, then, pride of place was occupied by the fleet's destroyers and submarines, all of which are described as having been as good as anything in service in the other fleets of Europe and the wider world (by contrast, the gunboats and torpedo boats were all extremely antiquated and good for little more than patrol work, no fewer than eleven of the original twenty-two representatives of the latter type of vessel having already been taken out of service).

Note

1   Alcofar Nassaes, *Fuerzas navales*, pp. 15–43.

APPENDIX 5

Weapons in service with the Spanish Army, 1936[1]

Rifles/carbines/submachineguns

7mm Mauser M1898 rifle
7mm Mauser M1895 carbine
7mm Mauser M1916 carbine
9mm Star SI-35 submachinegun

Machine-guns

7mm Hotchkiss M1907 heavy machine-gun
7mm Hotchkiss M1922/M1927 light machine-gun
7mm Astra-Unión M1927 light machine-gun
7mm SECN M1924/1925 light machine-gun
7mm Trapote M1932 light machine-gun

Mortars

60mm Valero M1926
50mm Valero M1932
81mm Valero M1933

Artillery

40mm Ramírez-Arellano M33 infantry gun
70mm Schneider M08 infantry gun
75mm Schneider M06 field gun
76.5mm Skoda M1919 anti-aircraft gun

105mm Schneider M06 mountain howitzer
105mm Vickers M1922 field howitzer
150mm Krupp M1913 gun
155mm Schneider M1917 howitzer

Note

1   Molina Franco and Manrique García, *Armas y uniformes,* pp. 183–206. For a detailed survey of the artillery pieces in service in 1936, see A. Mortera Pérez and J. L Infiesta Pérez, *La artillería en la Guerra Civil: material reglamentario en 1936* (Valladolid, 1999).

APPENDIX 6

Obsolete weapons brought back into service, 1936[1]

Rifles/carbines

11mm Winchester M1873 carbine
11mm Tigre M1915 rifle
11mm Remington M1871/79 rifle

Artillery

75mm Saint Chamond M1900 field gun
75mm Krupp M1903 field gun
75mm Krupp M1896 mountain gun
75mm Schneider-Canet M1900 field gun
80mm Krupp M1878 field gun
80mm Sotomayor M1880 field gun
80mm Plasencia M1880 mountain gun
80mm Plasencia M1883 field gun
90mm Krupp M1875 field gun
90mm Krupp M1878 field gun
90mm Mata M1891 mortar
120mm Plasencia M1891 gun
150mm Verdes-Montenegro M1891 gun
150mm Krupp M1892 gun
150mm Mata M1891gun
150mm Mata M1891 mortar
210mm Plasencia M1885/1891 howitzer
210mm Mata M1895 mortar

Commentary

Particularly at the beginning of the war, both sides made extensive use of the large number of obsolete or otherwise superfluous weapons to be found in Spain's bases and arsenals. For example, photographic evidence suggests that, perhaps not least because they brought to mind romantic images of the 'Wild West,' the Winchester M1873 and its derivative, the Tigre M1915, were extremely popular with the Republican militias, while the Nationalists employed several batteries of the Plasencia M1885/1891 and the Mata M1895 during the campaigns of 1936–7. However, the field pieces, especially, were so outmoded that they were soon relegated to training camps or phased out altogether.

Note

1 For small-arms, see Molina Franco and Manrique-García, *Armas y uniformes*, p. 184. Artillery is covered by A. Mortera Pérez and J. L. Infiesta Pérez, *La artillería en la Guerra Civil: material fuera de servicio incorporado en la campaña* (Valladolid, 2000).

APPENDIX 7

Aircraft, tanks and other weapons supplied to Nationalist Spain[1]

Aircraft

(a) Germany	
Arado Ar68E	4
Arado Ar95A	3
Dornier Do17E/F/P	34
Heinkel He45	45
Heinkel He46C	20
Heinkel He50G	1
Heinkel He51B/C	134
Heinkel He59B	27
Heinkel He60E	70
Heinkel He70 E/F	8
Heinkel He111B/E	97
Heinkel He112V/B	17
Heinkel He115A	2
Henschel Hs123A	6
Henschel Hs126A	8
Junkers Ju52 3/m	167
Junkers Ju86D	5
Junkers Ju87V/A/B	13
Messerschmitt Me109V/B/C/D/E	139
(b) Italy	
Breda Ba64	1
Breda Ba65	23
Cant Z501	10
Cant Z506	4
Caproni Ca310	10
Fiat BR20	13
Fiat Cr32	377
Fiat G50	10
Macchi M41	3

Romeo Ro37	68
Romeo Ro41	28
Savoia-Marchetti S55X	3
Savoia-Marchetti SM79	90
Savoia-Marchetti SM81	84

(c) Poland

PWS-10	20
Total:	1544[2]

Tanks and other armoured vehicles

Panzerkampfwagen I A/B	117
Panzerbefehlwagen I	4
Carrovelocce CV3/33 (L3)	155
Lancia-Ansaldo IZII 1917	8
Total:	284

Heavy/field artillery

(a) Germany

150mm sFH18	4
105mm lFH18	4
100mm K18	4
77mm FK16	36
77mm C96na	104

(b) Italy

305mm O.305/17 M1917	8
260mm M.260/9 M1916	8
152mm C.152/37 M1915/16 (Skoda M15)	12
149mm C.149/35 M1910	16
149mm C.149/12 M1914 (Skoda M14)	84
105mm C.105/28 M1913 (Schneider M1913)	84
100mm O.100/17 M1914 (Skoda M14)	260
75mm C.75/27 M1906/M1911	356
75mm O. 75/13 M1932 (Skoda M15)	12
Total:	992[3]

Anti-aircraft artillery

(a) Germany

88mm FLAK18	79
75mm FLAK14	90
37mm FLAK18	12
20mm FLAK30	116

(b) Italy

75mm CAA.75/46 M1934	4
75mm CAA.75/27 M1915	24
20mm CAA.20/65 Breda M1935	60
Total:	385[4]

Anti-tank/infantry-support weapons

(a) Germany	
37mm PAK35/36	302
76mm lMW Ehrhardt M1914	80
(b) Italy	
65mm C.65/17 (Schneider M1906)	220
47mm CCC.47/32 (Bohler M1936)	12
Total:	614

Mortars

(a) Germany	
GWM1916	160
81mm sGW34	?
(b) Italy	
81mm Breda M1935	70
45mm Brixia M1935	1,426
Total:	1,496[5]

Machine-guns

Germany	
7.92mm Dreyse MG13, Maxim MG08, Maxim MG08/15	5,000
Italy	
6.5mm Fiat-Revelli M1914, 8mm Fiat M1935	2,449
6.5mm Schwarzlose M07/12, 8mm Saint Etienne M1907	1,055
6.5mm Breda M1930, 8mm Breda M1937	5,250
Total:	19,004

Submachineguns

(a) Germany	
9mm Bergmann MP18/MP28, 9mm Erma EMP-35	?
(b) Italy	
9mm Beretta M1918/M1918/30	?
Total:	?[6]

Rifles

(a) Germany	
7.92mm Mauser M98/M98K	207,000
(b) Italy	
6.5mm Mannlicher-Carcano M1891	240,000

Grand total

Combat aircraft	1,544
Armoured vehicles	284
Field and heavy artillery pieces	992
Anti-aircraft guns	385
Anti-tank, infantry and mountain guns	614
Mortars	3,000 (?)
Machine-guns	19,004
Submachineguns	10,000 (?)
Rifles	447,000

Notes

1   The best guide to the artillery pieces supplied to the Nationalists is constituted by A. Mortera Pérez, and J. L. Infiesta Pérez, *La artillería en la Guerra Civil: material de origen alemán importado por el bando nacional* (Valladolid, 1996) and A. Mortera Pérez, and J. L. Infiesta Pérez, *La artillería en la Guerra Civil: material de origen italiano importado por el ejército nacional* (Valladolid, 1997). For rifles and machine-guns, by contrast, see Molina Franco and Manrique García, *Armas y uniformes,* pp. 184–5, 206–7. Finally, for aircraft, see C. Shores, *Spanish-Civil-War Air Forces* (London, 1977).

2   This figure does not include trainers and unarmed transport aircraft. These numbered some 188, the most numerous being the Bucker Bu131 trainer.

3   This figure excludes a small number of coastal guns that were acquired for the defence of Cádiz and El Ferrol.

4   Excluded from this figure are 43 Italian 75mm and 76mm guns on fixed mountings designed for naval use that were used to strengthen the armament of a number of Nationalist warships or equip auxiliary cruisers.

5   This is obviously a minimum. No record can be found of the number of mortars supplied by Germany, but the 81mm appeared in some quantity so an educated guess for the overall total might be 3,000.

6   No figures have been found for the number of submachineguns supplied to the Nationalists, but the photographic evidence alone suggests that they arrived in considerable numbers: a minimum of 10,000 does not seem unreasonable.

APPENDIX 8

Aircraft, tanks and other weapons supplied to Republican Spain

Aircraft

(a) Russia	
Polikarpov I15	153
Polikarpov I15-bis	30[1]
Polikarpov I16	276
Polikarpov R5	31
Polikarpov RZ	93
Tupolev SB2	93
(b) France	
Bleriot Spad 51	1
Bleriot Spad 91	1
Dewoitine D371/372	18
Dewoitine D510	2
Loire46	5
Potez Po540/542	14
Marcel Bloch MB210	7
Breguet 460	1
Gourdou-Lesseure GL32	16
Potez Po25	5
(c) Other	
Aero A101 (Czechoslovakia)	6
Letov S231 (Czechoslovakia)	17
Bristol Bulldog (Estonia)	8
Potez Po25 (Estonia)	8
Grumman GE-23 Delfin (Canada)	34
Fokker C.X (Holland)	1
Fokker C.XXI (Holland)	1
Koolhoven FK.51 (Holland)	22
Seversky SEV3 (USA	1
Vultee V.1/V.1A (SA)	8
Northrop 2/5 Gamma	2
Total:	854[2]

Armoured vehicles

BT5	50
T26	281
BA3/6	80
FA1	60
Renault FT17	64
Total:	535

Field guns

75mm Schneider M1912S	4
75mm Schneider-Canet M1898/01	16
75mm Schneider LD	4
75mm Schneider M1922	4
75mm Krupp M06	122
76.2mm Schneider/Saint Chamond M1897	51
76.2mm Obujov-Putilov M1902	8
76.2mm Putilov M02/30	79
76.5mm Krupp M1916	6
76.5mm Skoda M05	56
77mm Krupp C96na	47
77mm Krupp FK16	60
80mm Saint Chamond/Mondragón M1878	8
80mm Schneider	18[3]
87mm Krupp M1877/95	11
100mm Skoda M14/19	4
100mm Krupp M1904	63[4]
105mm Krupp M1904	2
105mm Schneider M1913	14
107mm Putilov M1877	10
107mm Meiji Type 38 M1905	74
Total:	661

Field howitzers

100mm Skoda M14/19	4
105mm Krupp FH1916	23[5]
114.3mm (4.5") Vickers QF Mk 1 M1910	159[6]
Total:	186

Heavy artillery

119.3mm (4.7") Vickers QF Mk 1	8
127mm (5") Armstrong 60-pounder Mk 1 gun	12
127mm Krupp M1902 howitzer	12
150mm Krupp M1875 howitzer	5
150mm Krupp M1892 gun	6
150mm Krupp sFH13 howitzer	4
152mm (6") Vickers BL Mark VII gun	14

152mm Perm M1884 howitzer	28[7]
152mm Metall-Plant M1931 howitzer	86
152mm Putilov M1909 howitzer	24
155mm De Bange M1877 gun	32
155mm Schneider M1917 howitzer	40
155mm Perm M1881 gun	32
170mm Erhardt mMW M1913 bomb-thrower	21
240mm Korotkostvolny Minomet bomb-thrower	8
250mm Erhardt sMW M1910 bomb-thrower	1
Total:	333

Anti-aircraft guns

20mm Oerlikon	210
20mm Solothurn ST5-100	4
20mm Hispano-Suiza HS-404	18
40mm Bofors M32	28
57mm Nordenfeldt M1929	9
76.2mm Lender M1915	18
76.2mm Soviet M1931	64
Total:	351

Anti-tank, infantry-support and mountain guns

20mm Semag M1923 anti-tank gun	8
25mm Hotchkiss M1934 anti-tank gun	16
37mm Puteaux M1916 infantry gun	14
37mm Rosenberg M1915 infantry gun	5
37mm Maclean M1916 infantry gun	30
37mm M1928/1930 anti-tank gun	250[8]
37mm Bofors M1934 anti-tank gun	28
45mm M1932 anti-tank gun	138
60mm Krupp M1898 mountain gun	4
70mm Mondragón M1898 mountain gun	70
75mm Krupp M1907mountain gun	7
75mm Krupp M1913mountain gun	4
75mm Schneider MPC2 mountain gun	4
75mm Arisaka M1898 mountain gun	56
75mm (2.95") Vickers QF mountain gun	4
76.2mm Putilov M1910 mountain gun	8
Total:	646

Mortars

60mm Stokes-Brandt M1935	100
75mm Jouhandau-Delandres M1917	127
75mm Delaunay M1923	?
76mm Erhardt lMW M1914	369
81mm Stokes-Brandt M1930	150
Total:	746[9]

Machine-guns

Soviet Union	20,486
Poland:	8,718
Other countries:	682
Total:	29,886[10]

Rifles

Soviet Union	495,685
Poland:	104,430
Other countries:	28,119
Total:	628,234[11]

Grand Total

Combat aircraft	854
Armoured vehicles	535
Heavy artillery	333
Field howitzers	186
Field guns	661
Anti-aircraft guns	351
Anti-tank, infantry and mountain guns	889
Mortars	3,000 (?)
Machine-guns	29,886
Rifles	628,234

Notes

1　The I15-bis was a variant of the I15 in which the original 'gull-winged' configuration was eliminated in favour of a more conventional biplane design. According to most accounts, it was not a success, but this scarcely matters as the small batch that reached Spain arrived so late in the war that they never saw combat.

2　This total does not include another 238 aircraft that could be used as trainers, transports or improvised bombers. Also excluded, meanwhile, are a considerable number of I15, I15bis and I16 fighters that were built in the Republican zone under licence.

3　No trace has been found of such a weapon, probably the De Bange M1878.

4　Sold to other countries for production under licence, this weapon was invariably rebored to a calibre of 105mm. It is probable that these particular pieces were the version used by Japan.

5　This figure is a minimum. Other sources give a total of 63.

6　Possibly as many as 217.

7　Possibly as many as 40.

8　There is some mystery about this weapon. Sometimes listed as the M1928 and sometimes as the M1930, it appears to have been based on a Hotchkiss design. However, no trace of it has ever been found in the Nationalist records, and the consignment may therefore never have been dispatched.

9　Only a limited number of consignments of mortars have been identified with any certainty, whilst no trace exists of shipments of the Delaunay M1923. However, it is clear that mortars appeared in some quantity, and a reasonable overall total might therefore be 3,000. Thomas cites figures giving a total of 15,000, but this seems rather high. See Thomas, *Spanish Civil War*, p. 982.

10 For details, please see Appendix 9.

11 For details, please see Appendix 9.

APPENDIX 9

Machine-guns and rifles supplied to the Republic[1]

Machine-guns

7mm/7.62mm Colt M1895
7.62mm Maxim M1910
7.7mm (0.303") Vickers Mark 1
7.92mm Maxim MG08
7.92mm Browning M1917
7.92mm Browning wz-30
8mm Schwarzlose M1907
8mm Hotchkiss M1897
8mm Saint Etienne M1907

Light machine-guns

7mm Mendoza C-1934
7.5mm Neuhausen M1922
7.62mm Maxim–Tokarev M1926
7.62mm Degtyarev M1930
7.62mm/7.92mm Madsen M1896
7.65mm Vickers–Berthier M1928
7.7mm (0.303") Lewis Mark 1
7.92mm Maxim MG08/15
7.92mm Bergmann MG15
7.92mm ZB vz-26
7.92mm Browning wz-28
7.92mm Hotchkiss M1922/M1925
8mm Chauchat M1915
8mm Hotchkiss M1909

Single-shot rifles

10.4mm Vetterli M1870
10.6mm Berdan M1868/1870
11mm Chassepot M1866
11mm Gras M1874/80/84
11mm Gras M77/80
11mm Gras-Kropatchek M1874/85

Repeating rifles

6.5mm Arisaka M1897/1905
6.5mm Mauser-Mannlicher M1892/1893/1895
7mm Mauser M1895/1901/1910 (Mexican)
7mm Mauser M1895/1912 (Chilean)
7.62mm Winchester M1895
7.62mm Krag-Jorgensen M1892
7.62mm Moisin-Nagant M1891/M1891/1930
7.65mm Mauser M1889 (Belgian)
7.7mm (0.303") Lee-Metford M1888
7.7mm (0.303") Lee-Enfield M1895/1913
7.7mm (0.303") Ross M1910
7.92mm Mauser-Obendorff M1888
7.92mm Mauser-Moisin wz-25
7.92mm Mauser vz-24 (Czech)
7.92mm Mauser M1898/M1898K (German)
7.92mm Mauser wz-1929/1930 (Polish)
7.92mm Mauser M1890 (Turkish)
7.92mm MauserM1897/1907/1927 (Paraguayan)
7.92mm Mauser M1891 (Bolivian)
7.92mm Mauser M1889/1916 (Belgian)
8mm Mannlicher M1888/1890/1895
8mm Lebel M1886/1893
8mm Berthier M1907/15
8mm Krag-Jorgensen M1889
10.7mm Colt M1883

Commentary

It is almost impossible to establish the exact quantities of each weapon that reached Republican Spain. However, according to the detailed lists prepared by Gerald Howson, in terms of rifles, Poland supplied 25,100 Mauser wz-1929/1930s, 22,519 Berthier M1907/1915s, 12,000 Mannlicher M1888/1890s, 8,000 Lebel M1886/93s, 2,930 old Russian rifles (probably Berdan M1868/

M1870s) and 2,000 Mauser M1889s; and, in terms of machine-guns, 92 Schwarzlose M1912s, 48 Browning wz-30s, 525 Browning wz-28s, 8,690 Chauchat M1915s, 1,481 Bergmann MG15s and 400 Lewis Mark 1s. For Russia, meanwhile, it is hard to be precise as many of the shipments were not listed by type, but known figures are as follows. Rifles: 216,580 Moisin-Nagant M1891s and M1891/1930s, 10,000 Mannlicher M1888/1890s, 9,000 Winchester M1895s, 8,400 Berthier M1907/15s, 1,000 Lee-Enfield M1895/1913s and 900 Lebel M1886/1893s. Machine-guns: 5,146 Degtyarev M1930s, 2,000 Maxim-Tokarev M1926s, 1,982 Maxim M1910s, 1,200 Colt M1895s, 1,172 Chauchat M1915s and 200 Lewis Mark 1s. Also known with some certainty is the total for Czechoslovakia, namely 50,000 Mauser vz-24 rifles and 2,000 ZB vz-26 light machine-guns.[2]

Notes

1   Molina Franco and Manrique García, *Armas y uniformes*, pp. 186–9.
2   For all this, see Howson, *Arms for Spain*, pp.260–303 *passim*.

APPENDIX 10

Foreign aid in the Spanish Civil War

From Appendices 8–9, it is apparent that the Republic was not left entirely defenceless against the rising of July 1936. Using the plentiful credit available to them as a result of the transfer of the Spanish gold reserve to Moscow, Republican agents were able to buy arms and ammunition in a number of countries in both Europe and Latin America, while, setting aside aircraft and armoured vehicles, the Russian government alone dispatched a minimum of 499,000 rifles, 21,000 machine-guns, 667 infantry-support weapons (e.g. anti-tank guns and mine-throwers), sixty-four anti-aircraft guns, 437 pieces of field artillery and sixty pieces of heavy artillery.[1] As has been inferred in the text, however, mere numbers were not everything, the form of military organization adopted by the Republic having the effect of dissipating the impact of even the better material that was dispatched to the latter's assistance. Yet, if the choice of the mixed brigade was spectacularly unhelpful, we must also consider the quality of the weapons that appeared in the hands of the People's Army. At their very best – the DP light machine-gun is a good example – these last were every bit as good as anything in the hands of the Nationalist forces – whilst many weapons, good or bad, appeared in both armies: the notoriously complicated and unreliable Saint Etienne came to Spain from both Russia and Italy, just as the much better MG08 and MG08/15 turned up in shipments from Russia and Poland as well as Germany. At the same time, it should be remembered that a large part of the weaponry supplied came from a similar stable, namely the immense quantities of arms left over from the First World War, and that it was therefore generally comparable in terms of its age and level of performance and sophistication. A few weapons did turn up that belonged to a more modern generation of armaments – here we might cite the German 37mm PAK36, 88mm FLAK18, 105mm leFH18 and 150mm sFH18 – but the last two of these only appeared at the very end of the war and even then in very small numbers. As for the PAK36 and the

FLAK18, whilst both were excellent items of equipment, such were the conditions of the struggle that only the latter made a really significant contribution to the fighting. Nor could even Germany do much more: with re-armament still in its early stages, it is striking that right up till 1989, the 'cutting-edge' anti-tank and anti-aircraft guns could be accompanied by nothing more striking than the hopelessly obsolescent 77mm C96na, the unpleasant but short-ranged M1914 bomb-thrower and a relatively small number of the more effective 77mm FK16.

On the surface, then, there was a certain equity, but careful consideration of the situation suggests that there were a series of factors that combined to tip the balance against the Republicans. In the first place, as mentioned in the text, there was the question of ammunition, spare parts and other necessities. Having all been in service until comparatively recently, and in some cases remaining in service till well into the Second World War, the weapons sent from Germany and Italy could be serviced and re-supplied with comparative ease, but this was in many instances not the case with the arms that were sent to the Republican zone, arms, moreover, that had in many instances been in a very poor state of repair even before they reached Spain; indeed, in some cases they were not even complete – plenty of artillery pieces arrived without proper sights, for example. Given that ammunition was also often only dispatched in the most miserly quantities (something that was never the case on the Nationalist side), the net result was that many of the guns and howitzers sent to the Republicans either never saw action at all or had to be withdrawn after the briefest of periods at the front.

On top of all this, there was also the issue of the actual weapons. Almost nothing that the Nationalists received dated back to the generation of weapons of the period prior to the invention of the magazine rifle, the automatic machine-gun and the hydraulic recoil system first seen in the French 75mm M1897 (the one significant exception was the Canon de 149/35 M1910, an 1895 design of which there appeared some 16 examples). In the Republican camp, by contrast, this was not the case. Thus, the Vetterli, Berdan, Chassepot and Gras rifles that appeared amongst the first consignments of weapons sent to the Republic had to be reloaded manually after every shot and in some cases did not even use smokeless powder, though it has to be said that, as such weapons constituted only some 25,000 out of the 500,000 foreign rifles that appeared in the Republican zone, the importance of the issue has been much exaggerated. That said, the same problem affected the artillery: at least 217 of the guns and howitzers concerned – some eight per cent of the total – represented types that lacked modern recoil mechanisms and could not compete with the weapons that had replaced them in the period leading up to 1914. Matters were particularly serious here in respect of the particularly precious resource represented by heavy artillery (i.e. pieces with calibres of 120mm and above). Here, the proportion of outmoded models shot up to 103 out of 333, while the problem was worsened still further by the fact that another thirty – the 170mm and 250mm Ehrhardts and the Russian 240mm Korokosvolny Minomet – were effectively little more than glorified mortars possessed of a range little more than half that of guns and howitzers of the same calibre.

All this said, the greatest issue facing the Republic was not that of weapons, but rather that of ammunition, for, if the People's Army only received 200 heavy artillery pieces that were of any real worth, the Nationalists only got 112, of which eight arrived so late as to see almost no service whatsoever. In so far as ammunition is concerned, meanwhile, the most important area by far was artillery, in which respect Russia provided the Republic with what at first sight seems the not ungenerous total of 6,616,504 shells, these being joined by 368,638 from Poland. Yet of these 7,000,000 shells, an extraordinary proportion – perhaps 5,500,000 – were for 37mm and 47mm weapons, calibres that together represented just 465 of the Republic's 2,177 artillery pieces of all calibres. As the Italians sent 7,000,000 shells for a range of weapons that, aside from a few anti-tank weapons, had no calibre smaller than 65mm, it follows that the Republicans were never able to compete with the weight of fire that could be delivered by their opponents.[2]

Thus far, nothing has been said about the tanks and aircraft that have tended to monopolize discussions of the weapons and weapons-systems dispatched to the rival contenders. In so far as actual planes and armoured fighting vehicles are concerned, sufficient has been said in the text to render further comment superfluous. It should already be apparent that the Messerschmitt 109 outclassed the I15 and the I16; that the I15 and the I16 outclassed the Fiat Cr32; that the T26 and BT5 outclassed the Panzer I and the L3. What is more important here is analysis. Taking the tanks first of all, the honest truth is that, whilst they could be a useful adjunct to infantry attacks, as deployed in Spain they simply did not have the sort of capacity that was necessary to create a breakthrough, let alone exploit one by driving deep into the enemy rear. Far more important was airpower. Here, much has been made of the Nationalists' use of the SM81s and Ju52s sent them by Mussolini and Hitler at the very beginning of the war to get the Army of Africa across the Straits of Gibraltar, but, important as this service was, what really mattered was the circumvention of the Republican naval blockade: once airpower had been used to drive off the ships sent along the coast from Cartagena, the way was opened for the use of means of transport that were both more conventional and more cost effective. Thereafter, like tanks, aircraft rarely proved capable of dramatic results: in the northern campaigns, certainly, the overwhelming aerial superiority available to the Nationalists proved of enormous assistance – the Basque forces, in particular, were all but broken by the concerted use of tactical bombing – but elsewhere, with the possible exception of Guadalajara, where the Italian columns were caught without any air cover whatsoever on the open plains of the *meseta* by the large force of planes that had been operating from nearby Barajas, there was nothing similar. That the Nationalists had achieved complete air superiority by 1939 cannot be doubted – as in Vizkaya, constant bombing badly disorganised the defence of Catalonia, whilst spreading confusion, fear and demoralization – but, even so, the numbers of planes available to them, and still more so the limitations of bombing's capacities as a weapon of war, meant that their Heinkels and Savoias could in the end never be anything other than an auxiliary: for all its efforts to do so, for example, the Nationalist air force was never able to bomb the vital bridges that kept the Army of the Ebro in operation for so long out of existence. As for the reason why aerial superiority was achieved, this was not so much a question of quality but rather of numbers and organization: not only was the air the one area where the Nationalists really did do better than their opponents in terms of the quantity of material that was sent, but the fact that both the Condor Legion and the Legionary Aviation were air forces that came complete with a full staff of ground crews and other technical staff meant that standards of maintenance were much higher and rates of repair much quicker.

To conclude, then, the Republic received substantial numbers of foreign arms, numbers that in some categories were larger than those received by their opponents. At the same time, with some exceptions, if their negotiators were very often cheated in terms of the value of what was sent, the quality of the actual weapons was comparable, as witness the fact that the Nationalists were in many instances only too willing to make use of the copious material that they captured. Yet too much should not be made of this, a series of factors conspiring to ensure that the impact of the steady flow of arms and munitions to the Republican zone was greatly reduced, the most important of these being the adoption of a system of military organization that not only did not concentrate the resources of the People's Army and the Republican air force but also actively dissipated them.

Notes

1 These figures are the ones given by Howson; see Howson, *Arms for Spain*, pp. 302–3.
2 For details of the ammunition sent to Spain, see Thomas, *Spanish Civil War*, pp. 979–82.

APPENDIX 11

The International Brigades

XI International Brigade (formed at Albacete, October 1936)

Commune-de-Paris Battalion (French)
Edgar André Battalion (German)
Dabrowski Battalion (Polish)
Engineer company
Artillery section
Cavalry squadron

XII International Brigade (formed at Albacete, November 1936)

Garibaldi Battalion (Italian)
Thaelmann Battalion (German)
André Marty Battalion (French)
Engineer company
Artillery battery (three 75mm guns)

XIII International Brigade (formed at Albacete, December 1936)

Chapaev Battalion (Slavic)
Louise Michel Battalion (Franco-Belge)
Henri Vuillemin Battalion (French)
Cavalry squadron
Engineer company
Signals company

XIV International Brigade (formed at Albacete, December, 1936)

Nine-Nations Battalion (Slavic)
Domingo Germinal Battalion (Franco-Belge)
Pierre Brachet Battalion (Anglo-French)[1]
Henri Barbusse Battalion (Franco-Belge)
Cavalry squadron
Engineer company
Artillery battalion (three batteries of two guns)

XV International Brigade (formed at Albacete January 1937)

Dimitrov Battalion (Slavic)
6 February Battalion (Franco-Belge)
Saklatvala Battalion (British)[2]
Abraham Lincoln Battalion (American)
Artillery battalion (two batteries)
Engineer company
Transport company

Commentary

Changes in the order of battle of the International Brigades were frequent. For example, before the end of 1936, the Thaelmann Battalion and the Dabrowski Battalion had changed places, whilst just prior to the battle of Brunete, the XV Brigade was reinforced by the Latin-American Español Battalion, the American Washington Battalion (a formation that lost such heavy casualties in the fighting that it was almost immediately merged with the Abraham Lincoln Battalion), and a British-manned 45mm anti-tank battery, yet another unit – the Canadian Mackenzie-Papineau Battalion – turning up in time for the battle of Belchite. Equally, the XII Brigade was briefly reinforced by a second Italian battalion – the Figlio – whilst, having suffered heavy losses, the XIII Brigade was reformed in the summer of 1937 on the basis of the Dabrowski Battalion (which was replaced in the ranks of the XII Brigade by a Spanish unit), the newly formed Hungarian Rakosi Battalion, the Polish Mickiewicz Battalion and the Hispano-Polish Palafox Battalion. From 1937 onwards, Spanish battalions were a constant feature, at least five such units having been identified as having appeared in the XI-XV Brigades' order of battle at various times (viz. the Asturias-Heredia, Madrid, Prieto, Primera Unidad de Avance and Batallón de Voluntarios No. 24). Meanwhile, troops were always switched the other way, the LXXXVI, CXXIX and CL Mixed Brigades all containing varying numbers of international battalions at different times. Finally, various artillery units were formed at different times that were never part of the structure of the individual brigades: at the Battle of Jarama, for example, there appeared a 'Grupo de Artillería Internacional' consisting of a field-artillery battalion, an anti-aircraft battalion and an anti-tank battalion.[3]

Notes

1 The British company whose inclusion permits the denomination 'Anglo-French' was after a few weeks transferred to the newly formed British Battalion.
2 Shapurji Saklatvala was an Indian Communist resident in London who had died early in 1936. However, the name did not take, and the battalion was therefore invariably known as the British Battalion.
3 By far the best guide to the organization of the International Brigades is that provided in Alcofar Nassaes, *Spansky*, pp. 197–355 *passim*.

APPENDIX 12

Nationalist forces engaged in the assault on Madrid, November 1936[1]

Column No. 1 (Carlos Asensio Cabanillas)

VI Bandera del Tercio
I Tabor de Tetuán
III Tabor de Tetuán
1 battery light artillery

Column No. 2 (Fernando Barrón Ortiz)

I Bandera del Tercio
I Tabor de Melilla
II Tabor de Melilla
1 battery light artillery

Column No. 3 (Francisco Delgado Serrano)

IV Bandera del Tercio
II Tabor de Alhucemas
III Tabor de Alhucemas
1 battery light artillery

Column No. 4 (Antonio Castejón Espinosa)

V Bandera del Tercio
II Tabor de Tetuán
II Tabor de Ceuta
1 battery light artillery

Column No. 5 (Heliodoro Rolando Tella de Campos)

VIII Bandera del Tercio
I Tabor de Alhucemas
1 battalion, Infantry Regiment, No. 27 (Argel)
1 battery light artillery

Column No. 6 (Siro Alonso Alonso)

1 *tabor* Mehall-la de Larache
1 battalion Voluntarios de Sevilla
1 battalion Voluntarios de Canarias
1 battery light artillery
1 company engineers
In support:
2 companies of tanks
1 company of armoured cars
1 battery 20mm FLAK30
5 batteries of 37mm PAK36
5 batteries 65mm C.65/17 M1906
5 batteries 75mm Schneider M06
4 batteries 105mm Vickers M22
4 batteries 155mm Schneider M1917

Commentary

In 1936, the Foreign Legion (Tercio de Extranjeros) was organised into six battalions known as *banderas*, and the Moorish *regulares* into five regiments (viz. Alhucemas, Ceuta, Melilla, Larche, Tetuán), each of which was in turn divided into three *tabores*. A *bandera* numbered about 600 men, a *tabor* about 250. Also present was a battalion of Spanish regular infantry, a *tabor* of the Mehall-la (the army of the Caliph of Morocco), and two unidentified units, namely the Voluntarios de Sevilla and the Voluntarios de Canarias: these are not included in the standard lists of volunteer units raised by the Nationalists, and they may therefore rather have been detachments of volunteers drawn from the Seville and Canarias infantry regiments.

Note

1   Martínez Bande, *Marcha sobre Madrid*, p. 236.

APPENDIX 13

Nationalist order of battle, campaign in Vizkaya, April 1937[1]

First Group, Sixth Division

Commander: José Solchaga Zala
Chief of Staff: Juan Vigón

I Brigada de Navarra (Rafael García Valiño)

First half-brigade:

2/Tercio de Lácar
5/Tercio de San Fermín
2/Mountain Battalion, No. 8 ('Sicilia')
II Bandera de Falange de Navarra

Second half-brigade:

2/Tercio de Navarra
1/Infantry Regiment No. 23 ('América')
2/Infantry Regiment No. 23 ('América')
3/ Infantry Regiment No. 23 ('América')

Reserve:

3/Tercio de Montejurra
Tercio of Roncesvalles
3/Tercio de Zumalacarreguí
2 companies, V Bandera, Falange de Navarra
Artillery: 3 batteries, 105mm Schneider M19
Engineers: 1 company

II Brigada de Navarra (Pablo Cayuela Ferreira)

First half-brigade:

1/Mountain Battalion No. 7 ('Arápiles')
IV Bandera, Falange de Navarra
6/Tercio de Nuestra Señora del Camino
4/ Infantry Regiment No. 23 ('América')

Second half-brigade

I Bandera, Falange de Navarra
II Bandera, Falange de Navarra
Tercio de San Miguel
Tercio de San Ignacio

Reserve:

5/Infantry Regiment No. 23 ('América')
1/Tercio de Oriamendi
'Fronteras' Bandera
2 companies, Mountain Battalion No. 7 ('Arápiles')
Artillery: 3 batteries, 105mm Schneider M19
Engineers: 1 company

III Brigada de Navarra (Rafael Latorre Roca)

First half-brigade

2 companies, 2/Tercio de Nuestra Señora de Begoña
2 companies, VI Bandera, Falange de Navarra
3 companies, 6/Infantry Regiment No. 23 ('América')
8/Infantry Regiment No. 23 ('América')
2/Infantry Regiment No. 22 (San Marcial)

Second half-brigade

Tercio de la Virgen Blanca
9/'Infantry Regiment No. 24 (Bailén)
2 'mixed groups'
Artillery: 1 battery of mountain guns (unspecified); 1 battery 65mm C.65/17
Engineers: 1 company

IV Brigada de Navarra (Camilo Alonso Vega)

First half-brigade

1/Mountain Battalion No. 5 ('Flandés')
2/Mountain Battalion No. 5 ('Flandés')

5/Infantry Regiment No. 28 ('Victoria')
3/Mountain Battalion No. 8 ('Sicilia')

Second half-brigade:

5/Grupo de Regulares No. 2 ('Melilla')
Batallón de Cazadores No. 3 ('Melilla')
C/Batallón de Cazadores No. 2 ('Las Navas de Tolosa')
C/Infantry Regiment No. 25 ('San Quintín')
4/Infantry Regiment No. 25 ('San Quintín')

Reserve

3/Infantry Regiment No. 22 ('San Marcial')
4/Infantry Regiment No. 22 ('San Marcial')
3/Infantry Regiment No. 24 ('Bailén')
3/Infantry Regiment No. 24 ('Bailén')
Artillery: 2 batteries 105mm Schneider M19, 1 battery 65mm C.65/17

V Brigada de Navarra (Juan-Bautista Sánchez González)

2/Infantry Regiment No. 31 ('Burgos')
4/Infantry Regiment No. 29 ('Zamora')
11/Infantry Regiment No. 30 ('Zaragoza')
7/Infantry Regiment No. 29 ('Zamora')
5/Infantry Regiment No. 25 ('San Quintín')
8/Infantry Regiment No. 20 ('Valladolid')
3/Infantry Regiment No. 27 ('Argel')
II Bandera, Falange de Navarra
4/Grupo de Regulares No. 5 (Alhucemas)
1 company, Vizcayan requetés
Machine-gun battalion No.7
Artillery: 2 batteries, 70mm Schneider M08; 1 battery, 105mm Schneider M19
Engineers: 1 company

VI Brigada de Navarra (Maximino Bartomeu González-Longoria)

10/Infantry Regiment No. 29 ('Zamora')
64/Mountain Battalion No. 7 ('Arapiles')
8/Infantry Regiment No. 29 ('Zaragoza')
35/Infantry Regiment No. 35 ('Mérida')
57/Infantry Regiment No. 23 ('América')
D/Batallón de Cazadores No. 1 ('San Fernando')
B/Batallón de Cazadores No. 2 ('Las Navas de Tolosa')
C/Batallón de Cazadores No. 6 ('Ceriñola')
Artillery: 2 batteries, 70mm Schneider M08; 1 battery, 105mm Schneider M19
Engineers: 1 company

Flechas Negras Brigade

Commander: Sandro Piazzoni
First Infantry Regiment (3 battalions; 2 C.65/17)
Second Infantry Regiment (3 battalions; 2 C.65/17)
Assault battalion
Anti-aircraft battery (4 20mm Breda M1935)
Field-gun battalion (12 C.75/27 M1906/M1911)
Howitzer battalion (12 O.100/17 M1914)

Attached

Armour: 1 tank battalion; 1 company of armoured lorries

Artillery: 6 batteries 75mm Schneider M06; 2 batteries 88mm FLAK18, 3 batteries 100mm O.100/17 M1914; 2 batteries 105mm Vickers M1922; 3 batteries 105mm Schneider M19; 2 batteries 105mm C.105/28 M1913; 2 batteries 149mm C.149/35 M1910; 3 batteries 155mm Schneider M1917; 2 batteries 210mm Plasencia M1885/91; 2 batteries 260mm M.260/9 M1916; 1 battery 305mm O.305/17 M1917 (N.B. all batteries consisted of 4 guns).

Commentary

This order of battle provides a useful snapshot of both the evolution of the Nationalist army and the organizational practices that it employed. Let us begin with the issue of institutional evolution. In July 1936, the garrisons in the provinces of Guipúzcoa, Navarre, Logroño, Alava and Burgos had together constituted the Spanish Army's Sixth Division. Despite the formation of ever larger numbers of regular and volunteer battalions, this had survived as a single entity, the problem of how to absorb all the new units being resolved by dividing it into two *agrupaciones* or groups, each of which was sub-divided into a number of brigades. This was still the situation at the start of the campaign in Vizkaya, but, as the table shows, the latter were in reality each the size of divisions and the First Group a veritable army corps. In the course of the campaign, the absurdity of this situation was finally recognized and the Sixth Division split into two as the Sixty-First and Sixty-Second Divisions, but this was still not enough of an adjustment, the situation only catching up with reality in the wake of the fall of Asturias, at which point the Sixty-First Division was reconstituted as the Army Corps of Navarre and the Brigades of Navarre as divisions.

With regard to organizational practice, what shines through is first of all both a continued reluctance to employ Carlist and Falangist militia in the front line and a decline in the importance of the Army of Africa. Of the sixty-six separate infantry units, then, forty-three were composed of regular troops as opposed to only thirteen Carlist battalions (*tercios*) and eight Falangist ones (*banderas*), together with two others that may have had some militia content; meanwhile, of the forty-three regular battalions, thirty-five were drawn from regiments of the metropolitan army as opposed to just eight from Army of Africa (in fairness, the proportion of Moors and Foreign Legionaries in some other formations was much higher – at the battle of Brunete, of 13 Division's fourteen battalions, six were Moorish and one Foreign-Legion). Beyond this, we see the pattern that mobilization and expansion followed in the regular army: rather than new regiments being created, exactly as was the case in the rather similar situation that pertained in Britain in the First World War, additional battalions were added to existing ones on the basis of cadres that were drawn from their ranks (thus, 8/Infantry Regiment No. 29 means the eighth battalion of the Twenty-Ninth Infantry Regiment).[2] Finally, very clear is, first, the Nationalist determination to concentrate all their resources at the decisive point – every single one of 260mm and 305mm weapons received by Franco up until that moment appeared on the Vizkaya front – and, second, the limited importance of foreign aid, only eighty-eight of the 200 guns attached to the Sixth Division and the Flechas Negras being of foreign origin.

Notes

1   Martínez Bande, *Vizkaya*, pp. 166–8; Steer, *Tree of Gernika*, pp. 156–8.
2   Seemingly, the same practice was also employed in the Carlist militia, no fewer than seven of the eleven *tercios* listed here having clearly possessed more than one battalion at this time (by contrast, Falangist battalions were independent units that were simply added to a provincial list, the Falange of Navarre eventually forming seven battalions).

APPENDIX 14

The Republican Army at the Battle of Brunete

V Corps: Juan Modesto

11 Division (Enrique Lister): I, IX, C Mixed Brigades
46 Division (Valentín González): X, CI Mixed Brigades
35 Division (Karol Swierczewski, aka Walter): XI International Brigade, XXXII, CVIII

Mixed Brigades

1 battalion of cavalry
3 batteries 76.2mm Schneider–Saint Chamond M1897/Obujov-Putilov M1902/ Putilov
M1902/1930 (9 guns)
3 batteries 105mm Krupp M1904/Schneider M1913/Krupp lFH16/Vickers M1922 (9 guns)
1 battery Vickers 4.5" M1910 (3 guns)
1 pioneer battalion
1 armoured battalion (30 T26, 10 BA10)

XVIII Corps: Enrique Jurado

10 Division (José-María Enciso Madollel): III, LXVIII, XVI Mixed Brigades
15 Division (Janos Galicz, aka Gal): II, CV Mixed Brigades
34 Division (José María Galán): XIII International Brigade, XV International Brigade

1 battalion of cavalry

1 battery 75mm type unknown (3 guns)

6 batteries 76.2mm Schneider-Saint Chamond M1897/Obujov-Putilov M1902/ Putilov

M1902/1930 (9 guns)

3 batteries 105mm Krupp M1904/Schneider M1913/Krupp lFH16 (7 guns)

1 pioneer battalion

1 armoured battalion (30 T26, 10 BA10)

Reserve:

45 Division (Manfred Stern, aka Kléber): XII International Brigade, CL Mixed Brigade

47 Division (Gustavo Durán): Brigada Marinos-Carabinieros, LXIX Mixed Brigade

2 squadrons of cavalry

2 batteries 155mm De Bange M1877/155mm Perm M1881/Schneider M1917 (4 guns)

8 batteries 107mm Meiji Type 38 M1905 (24 guns)

1 battery 105mm Krupp M1904/Schneider M1913/Krupp lFH16 (2 guns)

2 batteries 75mm type unknown (4 guns)

Commentary

It is instructive to compare this order of battle with that of Nationalist forces that had recently been employed against Vizcaya (Appendix 14). In that operation, the attacking force had been composed of 50,000 men and 200 guns, whereas at Brunete, it was composed of 80,000 men and 72 guns. In short, whereas the Nationalists deployed one gun for every 250 men, the Republicans could only field one gun for every 1,000 men. Meanwhile, the weight of fire available to the Nationalists was much heavier: whereas the Republicans deployed just four guns of 150mm or above, for the Nationalists the total was thirty-two. The Nationalist offensive, of course, was delivered over a much wider front, but even so, the contrast is striking. At Brunete, true, the Republicans had more aircraft – 200 to perhaps 140 – but the figures are nevertheless extremely stark and all too redolent of a situation in which large numbers of guns were left stranded on secondary fronts because of the demands of the mixed-brigade system: according to figures proffered by the Soviet adviser Nicolai Voronov, at this time the Republicans possessed at least 1,681 artillery pieces of all calibres.[1]

Also worth noting is the prominence of Communist brigades and commanders. Along with the Spanish commanders Modesto, Lister, González and Galán, we see the 'Internationals' Swierczsewski, Galiscz and Stern, while the twenty-one mixed brigades who fought in the battle included four of the five International Brigades and several others that were strongly Communist in character. In the Republican zone, then, political distinctiveness was highlighted, whilst in its Nationalist counterpart, it was played down.

Note

1   Molina Franco and Manrique García, *Armas y uniformes*, p. 239.

BIBLIOGRAPHY

Primary sources

Albiñana, J. M., *España bajo la dictadura republicana: crónica de un periodo putrefacto* (Madrid, 1933).

Alcocer, S., *Y Madrid dejó de reir: andanzas de un periodista por la zona roja* (Madrid, 1974).

Alvarez, S. (ed.), *Historia política y militar de las brigadas internacionales: testimonios y documentos* (Madrid, 1996).

Amilibia, M. de, *Los batallones de Euzkadi* (San Sebastián, 1978).

Barea, A., *The Forging of a Rebel* (London, 2001).

Barrio, J. del, *Memorias políticas y militares* (Barcelona, 2013).

Biescas Palacio, E., *Memorias de la Guerra Civil Española* (Montevideo, 2005).

Bolín, L., *Spain: the Vital Years* (London, 1967).

Borkenau, F., *The Spanish Cockpit* (London, 1937).

Bowers, C., *My Mission to Spain: Watching the Rehearsal for World War Two* (London, 1954).

Brenan, G., *Personal Record, 1920–1972* (London, 1974).

Bullón de Mendoza, A., and Diego, A. de (eds.), *Historias orales de la Guerra Civil* (Barcelona, 2000).

Cabezas, J. A., *Asturias: catorce meses de guerra civil* (Madrid, 1975).

Camps, J., and Olcina, E. (eds.), *Les milícies catalanes al front d'Aragó, 1936–1937* (Barcelona, 2006).

Candelas, A., *Adventures of an Innocent in the Spanish Civil War* (Penzance, 1989).

Cardozo, H., *March of a Nation: my Year of Spain's Civil War* (London, 1937).

Carrillo, S., *Dialogue on Spain* (London, 1976).

Casado López, S., *The Last Days of Madrid: the End of the Second Spanish Republic* (Madrid, 1939).

Cebreiros, N., *Las reformas militares: estudio crítico* (Santander, 1931).

Cervera Gil, J., *Ya sabes mi paradero: la guerra civil a través de las cartas de los que la vivieron* (Barcelona, 2005).

Chalmers-Mitchell, P., *My House in Málaga* (London, 1938).

Clark, R., *No Boots to my Feet* (Shelton, 1984).

Cortada, J.W. (ed.), *Modern Warfare in Spain: American Military Observations on the Spanish Civil War* (Washington, 2012).

Cortes Roa, A., *Tanquista desde mi tronera* (Madrid, 1989).

Cox, G., *The Defence of Madrid* (London, 1937).

Díaz Plaja, F., *La historia de España en sus documentos: el siglo XX – dictadura y república* (Madrid, 1964).

Elorza, A., et al. (eds.), 'Quo vadis Hispania? 1917–1936: España entre dos revoluciones – la visión exterior y sus limites', *Estudios de Historia Social*, Nos. 34–35 (July–December, 1985), pp. 323–463.

Etchebehere, M. de, *Mi Guerra de España* (Barcelona, 1977).

Escobar, J. I., *Así empezó* (Madrid, 1974).

Fisher, H., *Comrades: Tales of a Brigadista in the Spanish Civil War* (Lincoln, Nebraska, 1998).

Fraser, R., *Blood of Spain: the Experience of Civil War* (London, 1979).

Gallego, G., *Madrid: corazón que se desangra: memorias de la Guerra Civil* (San Lorenzo del Escorial, 2006).

García Oliver, J., *My Revolutionary Life* (London, 2008).

García Santa Cecilia, C. (ed.), *La matanza de Badajoz: crónica de un testigo de uno de los episodios más trágicos de la guerra civil de España* (Mérida 2007).

Gerahty, C., *The Road to Madrid* (London, 1937).

Gil Robles, J.M., *No fue posible la paz* (Barcelona, 1968).

Grandío Seoane, E. (ed.), *Las columnas gallegas hasta Oviedo: diario bélico de la Guerra Civil Española, 1936–37: Faustino Vázquez Carril* (Pontevedra, 2011).

Gregory, W., *The Shallow Grave: a Memoir of the Spanish Civil War* (London, 1986).

Gurney, J., *Crusade in Spain* (Newton Abbott, 1976).

Heredia, M. de, *Monarquía, república, guerra: memorias* (Madrid, 1976).

Hernaiz Grijalba, V. (ed.), *Memorias de mi padre: Guerra Civil Española, 1937–1938* (Barcelona, 2012).

Herrero Alonso, E., *Los mil días del tercio 'Navarra': biografía de un tercio de requetés* (Madrid, 1974).

Hidalgo de Cisneros, I., *Cambio de rumbo: memorias* (Bucharest, 1964).

H.M.S.O. London (ed.), *Documents on German Foreign Policy, 1918–1945, from the Archives of the German Foreign Ministry. Series D, vol. III: Germany and the Spanish Civil War* (London, 1951).

Hooper, D., *No pasarán! A Memoir of the Spanish Civil War* (London, 1997).

Horn, G. R. (ed.), *Letters from Barcelona: an American Woman in the Spanish Civil War* (Basingstoke, 2009).

Ibarruri, D., *El único camino* (Paris, 1965).

Ibarruri, D., *They Shall Not Pass: the Autobiography of La Pasionaria* (London, 1966).

Inglis, A. (ed.), *Lloyd Edmonds: Letters from Spain* (Sydney, 1985).

Iniesta Cano, C., *Memorias y recuerdos: los años que he vivido en el proces histórico de España* (Barcelona, 1984).

Izcaray, J., *La guerra que yo viví: crónicas de los frentes españoles, 1936–1939* (Madrid, 1978).

Jiménez de Aberásturi, L. M., and Jiménez de Aberásturi, J. C. (eds.), *La guerra en Euzkadi; transcendentales revelaciones de unos testigos de excepción acerca de la guerra del 36 en el País Vasco* (Barcelona, 1978).

Kemp, P., *Mine Were of Trouble* (London, 1957).

Kindelán, A., *Mis cuadernos de guerra* (Madrid, 1982).

Kisch, R., *They Shall Not Pass: the Spanish People at War, 1936–39* (London, 1974).

Knickerbocker, H. R., *The Siege of the Alcázar: a Warlog of the Spanish Revolution* (Philadelphia, 1936).

Knoblaugh, H. E., *Correspondent in Spain* (London, 1937).

Koltsov, M., *Diario de la guerra de España* (Geneva, 1963).

Langdon-Davies, J., *Behind the Spanish Barricades* (London, 1936).

Largo Caballero, F., *Escritos de la república: notas históricas de la guerra en España, 1917–1940*, ed. S. Julia (Madrid, 1985).

Largo Caballero, F., *Mis recuerdos: cartas a un amigo* (Mexico City, 1976).

Larios, J., *Combat over Spain: Memoirs of a Nationalist Fighter Pilot, 1936–1939* (London, 1974).

Lee, L., *A Moment of War* (London, 1991).

Lee, L., *As I Walked Out One Midsummer Morning* (London, 1969).

Lerroux, A., *La pequeña historia: apuntes para la historia grande vividos y redactados por el autor* (Buenos Aires, 1945).

Lister, E., *Memorias de un luchador* (Madrid, 1977).

Low, M., and Brea, J., *Red Spanish Notebook* (London, 1937).

Lunn, A., *Spanish Rehearsal* (London, 1937).

Mackee, S., *I was a Franco Soldier* (London, 1938).

MacMaster, N. (ed.), *Spanish Fighters: an Oral History of Civil War and Exile* (Basingstoke, 1990).

Mangini, S. (ed.), *Memories of Resistance: Women's Views of the Spanish Civil War* (New Haven, Connecticut, 1995).

Manzanera, E., *The Iron Column: Testament of a Revolutionary* (London, 2006).

Marichal, J. (ed.), *Manuel Azaña: obras completas* (México, 1966).

Martín Blásquez, J., *I Helped to Build an Army: Civil-War Memoirs of a Spanish Staff Officer* (London, 1939).

Martínez Barrio, D., *Memorias de Don Diego Martínez Barrio* (Barcelona, 1983).

Maura, M., *Así cayó Alfonso XIII* (Madrid, 1962).

Max, J., *Memorias de un revolucionario* (Barcelona, 1975).

McCullach, F., *In Franco's Spain: being the Experiences of an Irish War Correspondent in the Great Civil War which began in 1936* (London, 1937).

Mera, C., *Guerra, exilio y carcel de un anarquista* (Chatillon-sur-Bagneux, 1977).

Milany, J., *Aviador de la República* (Barcelona, 1971).

Miralles Bravo, R., *Memorias de un comandante rojo* (Madrid, 1975).

Modesto, J., *Soy del Quinto Regimiento* (Barcelona, 1978).

Mola Vidal, E., *El pasado, Azaña y el porvenir: las tragedias de nuestras instituciones militares* (Madrid, 1934).

Mora, C. de la, *In Place of Splendour: the Autobiography of a Spanish Woman* (New York, 1939).

Nelson, C., and Hendricks, J. (eds.), *Madrid, 1937: Letters of the Abraham Lincoln Brigade from the Spanish Civil War* (New York, 1996).

O'Neill, C., *Una mujer en la guerra de España* (Madrid, 2003).

Orwell, G., *Homage to Catalonia* (new edition; London, 1951).

Pamies i Bertran, T., *Quam érem capitans: memories d'aquella guerra* (Barcelona, 1974).

Peers, E. A., *The Spanish Tragedy, 1930–1936: Dictatorship, Republic, Chaos* (London, 1936).

Pettifer, J., (ed.), *Cockburn in Spain: Dispatches from the Spanish Civil War* (London, 1986).

Pons Prades, E., *Un soldado de la República: itinerario ibérico de un joven revolucionario* (Madrid, 1974).

Puig, I. (ed.), *Personal Memories of the Spanish Civil War in Catalan and English* (Lampeter, 1999).

Pulido Mendoza, M. (ed.), *Así fue pasando el tiempo: memorias de una miliciana extremeña* (Seville, 2006).

Revilla Cebrecos, C., *Tercio de Lacar* (Madrid, 1975).

Rivas-Cherif, *Portrait of an Unknown Man: Manuel Azaña and Modern Spain* (Madison, Wisconsin, 1995).

Rojo, V., *Alerta los pueblos! Estudio político-militar del periodo final de la Guerra Española* (Barcelona, 1974).

Rojo, V., *Así fue la defensa de Madrid* (Mexico City, 1967).

Roncuzzi, A., *La otra frontera: un requeté italiano de la España en lucha* (Madrid, 1982).

Rubin, H., *Spain's Cause was Mine: a Memoir of an American Medic in the Spanish Civil War* (Carbondale, Illinois, 1997).

Ruiz Vilaplana, A., *Burgos Justice: a Year's Experience of Nationalist Spain* (London, 1937).

Sandoval, J., and Azcarate, M., *Spain, 1936–1939* (London, 1963).

Sanz, R., *Los que fuimos a Madrid: Columna Durruti, 26 División* (Paris, 1969).

Sender, R., *The War in Spain: a Personal Narrative* (London, 1937).

Sommerfield, J., *Volunteer in Spain* (London, 1997).

Steer, G., *The Tree of Gernika: a Field Study of Modern War* (London, 1938).

Stansky, P., and Abrahams, W. (eds.), *Journey to the Frontier: Julian Bell and John Cornford: their Lives and the 1930s* (London, 1966).

Stradling, R. (ed.), *Brother against Brother: Experiences of a British Volunteer in the Spanish Civil War* (Stroud, 1998).

Tagueña Lacorte, M., *Testimonio de dos guerras* (Barcelona, 2005).

Tarazona Torán, F., *Yo fui piloto de caza rojo* (Madrid, 1974).

Thomas, F., *To Tilt at Windmills: a Memoir of the Spanish Civil War* (East Lansing, Michigan, 1996).

Tisa, J., *Recalling the Good Fight: an Autobiography of the Spanish Civil War* (South Hadley, Massachusetts, 1985).

Toynbee, P. (ed.), *The Distant Drum: Reflections on the Spanish Civil War* (London, 1976).

Urra Lusarreta, J., *En las trincheras del frente de Madrid: memorias de un capellán de requetés herido de guerra* (Madrid, 1967).

Vidal, C. (ed.), *Recuerdo 1936: una historia oral de la Guerra Civil Española* (Barcelona, 2008).

Watson, K. S., *Single to Spain* (London, 1937).

Wet, O. de, *Cardboard Crucifix: the Story of a Pilot in Spain* (London, 1938).

Wintringham, T., *English Captain* (London, 1939).

Woolsey, G., *Death's Other Kingdom* (London, 1988).

Zugazagoitia, J., *Guerra y vicisitudes de los españoles* (Barcelona, 1977).

Secondary sources

Ackelsberg, M., *Free Women of Spain: Anarchism and the Struggle for Women's Liberation* (Bloomington, Indiana, 1991).

Ackelsberg, M., 'Models of revolution: rural women and anarchist collectivisation in Civil-War Spain', *Journal of Peasant Studies*, XX, No. 3 (April, 1993), pp. 367–88.

Alcofar Nassaes, J. L., *Spansky: los extranjeros que lucharon en la Guerra Civil Española* (Barcelona, 1973).

Albert, F. C., *Carros de combate y vehículos blindados de la guerra, 1936–1939* (Barcelona, 1980).

Albert, G. J., '"To help the Republicans not just by donations and rallies but with the rifle": militant solidarity with the Spanish Republic in the Soviet Union, 1936–1937', *European Review of History*, XXI, No. 4 (September, 2014), pp. 501–18.

Alpert, M., 'The clash of Spanish armies: contrasting ways of war in Spain, 1936–1939', *War in History*, VI, No. 3 (July, 1999), pp. 331–51.

Alpert, M., *The Republican Army in the Spanish Civil War, 1936–1939* (Cambridge, 2013).

Alpert, M., 'The Spanish Civil War and the Mediterranean', *Mediterranean Historical Review*, XIII, Nos. 1/2 (June, 1998), pp. 150–67.

Alexander M., and Graham, G. (eds.), *The French and Spanish Popular Fronts: Comparative Perspectives* (Cambridge, 1999).

Alvarez, J. A., *The Betrothed of Death: the Spanish Foreign Legion during the Rif Rebellion, 1920–1927* (Westport, Connecticut, 2003).

Anderson, P., and Arco Blanco, M. A. del (eds.), *Mass Killings and Violence in Spain, 1936–1952* (London, 2014).

Arosteguí Sánchez, J., and Martínez Martín, J. A., *La Junta de Defensa de Madrid, noviembre 1936–abril 1937* (Madrid, 1994).

Balcells, A., *Catalan Autonomy Past and Present* (Basingstoke, 1996).

Balfour, S., *Deadly Embrace: Morocco and the Road to the Spanish Civil War* (Oxford, 2002).

Beevor, A., *The Battle for Spain: the Spanish Civil War, 1936–1939* (London, 2006).

Ben-Ami, S., *Fascism from Above: the Dictatorship of Primo de Rivera in Spain, 1923–1930* (Oxford, 1983).

Ben-Ami, S., 'The dictatorship of Primo de Rivera: a political reassessment', *Journal of Contemporary History*, XII, No. 1 (January, 1977), pp. 65–84.

Ben-Ami, S. *The Origins of the Second Republic in Spain* (Oxford, 1978).

Blanco Escolá, C., *La incompetencia militar de Franco* (Madrid, 2000).

Blanco Escola, C., *Vicente Rojo, el general que humilló a Franco* (Barcelona, 2003).

Blaye, E. de, *Franco and the Politics of Spain* (London, 1974).

Blinkhorn, M., *Carlism and Crisis in Spain, 1931–1939* (Cambridge, 1975).

Blinkhorn, M., 'Carlism and the Spanish crisis of the 1930s', *Journal of Contemporary History*, VIII, No. 3 (July, 1972), pp. 65–88.

Bolloten, B., *The Spanish Civil War: Revolution and Counter-Revolution* (London, 1991).

Brenan, G., *The Spanish Labyrinth* (Cambridge, 1943).

Bueno, J. M., *Uniformes militares de la Guerra Civil Española* (Madrid, 1997).

Cabeza San Deogracias, J., 'Buscando héroes: la historia de Antonio Col como ejemplo del uso de la narrativa como propaganda durante la Guerra Civil Española', *Revista de Historia y Comunicación Social*, X (2005), pp. 37–50.

Campo Rizo, J. M., 'El Mediterráneo: campo de batalla de la Guerra Civil Española: la intervención naval italiana – una primera aproximación documental', *Cuadernos de Historia Contemporánea*, XIX (1997), pp. 55–87.

Cardona, G., *El poder militar en España contemporánea hasta la Guerra Civil* (Madrid, 1983).

Carr, R., *Spain, 1808–1975* (Oxford, 1982).

Carr, R. (ed.), *The Republic and Civil War in Spain* (London, 1971).

Carr, R., *The Spanish Tragedy* (London, 1977).

Carroll, P. N., *The Odyssey of the Abraham Lincoln Brigade: Americans in the Spanish Civil War* (Stanford, California, 1998).

Cerda, N., 'Political ascent and military command: General Franco and the early months of the Spanish Civil War, July–October 1936', *Journal of Military History*, LXXV, No. 4 (October, 2011), pp. 1125–57.

Colodny, R., *The Battle for Madrid: the Central Epic of the Spanish Conflict* (New York, 1958).

Comín Colomer, E., *El quinto regimiento de milicias populares* (Madrid, 1973).

Cores Fernández de Cañete, A., *El sitio de Oviedo* (Madrid, 1975).

Corum, J., 'The Spanish Civil War: lessons learned and not learned by the Great Powers', *Journal of Military History*, LXII, No. 2 (April, 1998), pp. 313–34.

Coverdale, J., *Italian Intervention in the Spanish Civil War* (Princeton, New Jersey, 1975).

Coverdale, J., 'The battle of Guadalajara, 8–22 March, 1937', *Journal of Contemporary History*, IX, No. 1 (January, 1974), pp. 53–75.

Delperrie de Bayas, J., *Las brigadas internacionales* (Madrid, 1980).

Díez, L., *La batalla del Jarama* (Madrid, 2005).

Eby, C., *Comrades and Commissars: the Abraham Lincoln Battalion in the Spanish Civil War* (Harrisburg, Pennsylvania, 2007).

Eby, C., *The Siege of the Alcázar: Toledo, July to September 1936* (London, 1965).

Ellwood, S., 'Falange Española and the creation of the Francoist "new state"', *European History Quarterly*, XX, No. 2 (April, 1990), pp. 209–25.

Emiliani, A., et al., *Spagna,1936–39: l'aviazione legionaria* (Milan, 1976).

Engel, C., *Estrategia y táctica en la Guerra de España, 1936–1939* (Madrid, 2008).

Esdaile, C. J., *Spain in the Liberal Age: from Constitution to Civil War* (Oxford, 1999).

Español Bouché, L., *Madrid, 1939: del golpe de Casado al final de la Guerra Civil* (Madrid, 2004).

Fleming, S., 'Spanish Morocco and the *alzamiento nacional*, 1936–1939: the military, economic and political mobilisation of a protectorate', *Journal of Contemporary History*, XVIII, No. 1 (January, 1983), pp. 27–42.

Flores Pazos, F., and Recio Cardona, R., *Ejército Popular Republicano, 1936–1939: uniformes y pertrechos* (Madrid, 1997).

Frank, W. C., 'Naval Operations in the Spanish Civil War, 1936–1939', *Naval War College Review*, XXXVII, No. 1 (January, 1984), pp. 24–55.

Galey, J., 'Bridegrooms of death: a profile study of the Spanish Foreign Legion', *Journal of Contemporary History*, IV, No. 2 (April, 1969), pp. 47–64.

Garate Córdoba, J. M., *Tenientes en campaña: la improvisación de oficiales en la guerra del 36* (Madrid, 1976).

García Venero, M., *La Falange en la guerra de España: la unificación y Hedilla* (Paris, 1967).

González Alcantud, J. A. (ed.), *Marroquis en la Guerra Civil Española: campos equívocos* (Granada, 2003).

Gibson, I., *Paracuellos: la verdad objétiva sobre la matanza de presos en Madrid en 1936* (Madrid, 2005).

Graham, H., *The Spanish Republic at War, 1936–1939* (Cambridge, 2002).

Harris, W. B., *France, Spain and the Rif* (London, 2014).

Herreros, I., *Mitología de la cruzada de Franco: el alcázar de Toledo* (Madrid, 1995).

Herrmann, G., 'Voices of the vanquished: leftist women and the Spanish Civil War', *Journal of Spanish Cultural Studies*, IV, No. 1 (March, 2003), pp. 11–29.

Hoffmann, G., 'The tactical and strategic use of *attaché* intelligence: the Spanish Civil War and the U.S. army's misguided quest for a modern tank doctrine', *Journal of Military History*, LXII, No. 1 (January, 1998), pp. 101–33.

Hogg, I., *Armour in Conflict: the Design and Tactics of Armoured Fighting Vehicles* (London, 1980).

Holguín, S., 'How did the Spanish Civil War end? Not so well', *American Historical Review*, CXX, No. 5 (July, 2015), pp. 1767–83.

Howard, V., and Reynolds, M., *The Mackenzie-Papineau Battalion: the Canadian Contingent in the Spanish Civil War* (Ottawa, 1986).

Howson, G., *Arms for Spain: the Untold Story of the Spanish Civil War* (London, 1998).

Jensen, R., 'Jose Millán Astray and the Nationalist "crusade" in Spain', *Journal of Contemporary History*, XXVII, No. 3 (July, 1992), pp. 425–48.

Johnston, V., *Legions of Babel: the International Brigades in the Spanish Civil War* (Harrisburg, Pennsylvania, 1967).

Kaplan, T., 'Spanish anarchism and women's liberation', *Journal of Contemporary History*, VI, No. 2 (April, 1971), pp. 101–11.

Keene, J., *Fighting for Franco: International Volunteers in Nationalist Spain during the Spanish Civil War, 1936–1939* (Leicester, 2001).

Kowalsky, D., 'Operation X: Soviet Russia and the Spanish Civil War', *Bulletin of Spanish Studies*, No. 1 (January, 2014), pp. 159–78.

Kowalsky, D., 'The Soviet Union and the International Brigades, 1936–1939', *Journal of Slavic Military Studies*, XIX, No. 4 (December, 2006), pp. 681–704.

La Porte, P., 'Civil–military relations in the Spanish Protectorate in Morocco: the road to the Spanish Civil War, 1912–1936', *Armed Forces and Society*, XXX, No. 2 (Winter, 2004), pp. 203–26.

Landis, A. H., *Death in the Olive Groves: American Volunteers in the Spanish Civil War* (New York, 1989).

Lannon, F., 'Women and images of women in the Spanish Civil War', *Transactions of the Royal Historical Society*, Sixth Series, I (1991), pp. 213–28.

Leguineche, M., *Anual: el desastre de España en el Rif, 1921* (Madrid, 1996).

Lezamiz, J., 'La conección mejicana: armas y alimentos para la República', *Revista electrónica iberoamericana*, IX, No. 1 (January, 2015), pp. 1–18.

Lines, L., 'Female combatants in the Spanish Civil War: *milicianas* in the front lines and in the rearguard', *Journal of International Women's Studies*, X, No. 4 (May, 2009), pp. 168–87.

Lines, L., 'Francisco Franco as warrior: is it time for a reassessment of his military leadership?' *Journal of Military History*, LXXXI, No. 2, pp. 513–34.

Lines, L., *Women in Combat in the Spanish Civil War* (Lanham, Maryland, 2012).

Llarch, J., *La batalla del Ebro* (Barcelona, 1972).

López Fernández, A., *General Miaja, defensor de Madrid* (Madrid, 1975).

Low, R., *The Spanish Firebrand* (London, 1992).

Macksey, K., *Tank Warfare: a History of Tanks in Battle* (London, 1971).

Madariaga, R. M. de, 'The intervention of Moroccan troops in the Spanish Civil War: a reconsideration', *European History Quarterly*, XXII, No. 1 (January, 1992), pp. 67–98.

Malefakis, M., *Agrarian Reform and Peasant Revolution in Spain* (Newhaven, Connecticut, 1970).

Martínez Bande, J. M., *El final del frente norte* (Madrid, 1972).

Martínez Bande, J. M., *La batalla de Teruel* (Madrid, 1974).

Martínez Bande, J. M., *La batalla del Ebro* (Madrid, 1978).

Martínez Bande, J. M., *La campaña de Cataluña* (Madrid, 1979).

Martínez Bande, J. M., *La gran ofensiva sobre Zaragoza* (Madrid, 1973).

Martínez-Bande, J. M., *La llegada al mar* (Madrid, 1975).

Martínez Bande, J. M., *La lucha en torno a Madrid en el invierno de 1936–1937* (Madrid, 1984).

Martínez Bande, J. M., *La marcha sobre Madrid* (Madrid, 1982).

Martínez Bande, J. M., *La ofensiva sobre Segovia y la batalla de Brunete* (Madrid, 1972).

Martínez Bande, J. M., *Vizkaya* (Madrid, 1971).

Matthews, J., '"Our Red soldiers": the Nationalist army's management of its left-wing conscripts in the Spanish Civil War, 1936–1939', *Journal of Contemporary History*, XLV, No. 2 (April, 2010), pp. 344–63.

Matthews, J., *Reluctant Warriors: Republican Popular Army and Nationalist Army Conscripts in the Spanish Civil War, 1936–1939* (Oxford, 2012).

Matthews, J., 'The vanguard of sacrifice? Political commissars in the Republican Popular Army during the Spanish Civil War, 1936–1939', *War in History*, XXI, No. 1 (January, 2014), pp. 82–101.

Massot i Muntaner, J., *El desembarcament de Bayo a Mallorca, agost–septembre, 1937* (Montserrat, 1987).

McCannon, J., 'Soviet military intervention in the Spanish Civil War, 1936–1939: a re-examination', *Russian History*, XXII, No. 2 (Summer, 1995), pp. 154–80.

Merriman, M., and Lerude, W., *American Commander in Spain: Robert Hale Merriman and the Abraham Lincoln Brigade* (Reno, Nevada, 1986).

Mesa, J. L. de, *El regreso de las legiones: voluntarios italianos en la Guerra Civil Española* (Madrid, 1994).

Molina Franco, L., and Manrique García, J. M., *Atlas ilustrado de armas y uniformes de la Guerra Civil Española* (Madrid, 2009).

Moradiellos García, E., *La perfidia de Albión: el gobierno británico y la Guerra Civil Española* (Madrid, 1996).

Mortera Pérez, A., and Iniesta Pérez, J. L., *La artillería en la Guerra Civil: material de origen alemán importado por el bando nacional* (Valladolid, 1996).

Mortera Pérez, A., and Infiesta Pérez, J. L., *La artillería en la Guerra Civil: material de origen italiano importado por el ejército nacional* (Valladolid, 1997).

Mortera Pérez, A., and Infiesta Pérez, J. L., *La artillería en la Guerra Civil: material fuera de servicio incorporado en la campaña* (Valladolid, 2000).

Mortera Pérez, A., and Infiesta Pérez, J. L., *La artillería en la Guerra Civil: material reglamentario en 1936* (Valladolid, 1999).

Nadal, A., *Guerra civil en Málaga* (Málaga, 1984).

Nash, M., *Defying Male Civilisation: Women in the Spanish Civil War* (Denver, Colorado, 1995).

Nash, M., '*Milicianas* and home-front heroines: images of women in revolutionary Spain, 1936–1939', *History of European Ideas*, XI, Nos. 1–6 (n.d.), 1989, pp. 235–44.

Nash, M., 'Women in war: *milicianas* and armed combat in revolutionary Spain, 1936–1939', *International History Review*, XV, No. 2 (May, 1993), pp. 269–82.

Navajas Zubeldia, C., *Ejército, estado y sociedad en España, 1923–1930* (Logroño, 1991).

Navajas Zubeldía, C., *Leales y rebeldes: la tragedia de los militares republicanos* (Madrid, 2011).

O'Connell, J. R., 'The Spanish Republic: further reflections on its anti-clerical policies', *Catholic Historical Review*, LVII, No. 2 (July, 1971), pp. 275–89.

Payne, S. G., *Falange: a History of Spanish Fascism* (Stanford, California, 1961).

Payne, S. G., *Fascism in Spain, 1923–1977* (Madison, Wisconsin, 1999).

Payne, S. G., *Politics and the Military in Modern Spain* (Stanford, California, 1967).

Payne, S. G., *The Franco Régime, 1936–1975* (Madison, Wisconsin, 1987).

Peers, E. A., *The Spanish Tragedy, 1930–1936: Dictatorship, Republic, Chaos* (London, 1936).

Pérez Conde, J. et al., *La guerra civil en Talavera de la Reina: conflicto bélico, represión y vida cotidiana* (Talavera, 2008).

Permuy López, R. A., *Atlas ilustrado de la aviación en la Guerra Civil Española* (Madrid, 2012).

Poulain, D., 'Aircraft and mechanised land warfare, 1937: the battle of Guadalajara', *Journal of the Royal United Service Institution*, LXXXIII, No. 530 (May, 1938), pp. 362–7.

Prazeres Serém, R. E. L., 'Conspiracy, coup d'état and civil war in Seville, 1936–1939: history and myth in Francoist Spain', London School of Economics Ph.D. thesis, 2012.

Preston, P., *Franco: a Biography* (London, 1995).

Preston, P., 'Franco as military leader', *Transactions of the Royal Historical Society*, Sixth Series, IV, pp. 21–42.

Preston, P., 'Great statesman or unscrupulous opportunist? Anglo-Saxon interpretations of Lluis Companys', *Bulletin of Spanish Studies*, XCII, Nos. 8–10 (December, 2015), pp. 493–509.

Preston, P., 'Lights and shadows in George Orwell's *Homage to Catalonia*', *Bulletin of Spanish Studies*, XCV, Nos. 1–2 (October, 2017), pp. 1–29.

Preston, P. (ed.), *Revolution and War in Spain, 1931–1939* (London, 1984).

Preston, P., *The Coming of the Spanish Civil War* (London, 1978).

Preston, P., *The Politics of Revenge: Fascism and the Military in Twentieth-Century Spain* (London, 1995).

Preston, P., *The Spanish Holocaust: Inquisition and Extermination in Twentieth- Century Spain* (London, 2012).

Proctor, R., *Hitler's Luftwaffe in the Spanish Civil War* (Westport, Connecticut, 1983).

Quesada, A., and Walsh, S., *The Spanish Civil War, 1936–1939 (1): Nationalist Forces* (Oxford, 2014).

Quiroga, A., *Making Spaniards: Primo de Rivera and the Nationalization of the Masses, 1923–1930* (Houndmills, 2007).

Rees, T, and Thorpe, A. (eds.), *International Communism and the Communist International, 1919–1943* (Manchester, 1998).

Requena Gallego, M., and Eiroa, M., *Al lado del gobierno republicano: los brigadistas de Europa del este en la Guerra Civil Española* (Cuenca, 2009).

Reverte, J. M., *El arte de matar: cómo se hizo la Guerra Civil Española* (Barcelona, 2009).

Reverte, J. M., *La batalla de Madrid* (Barcelona, 2007).

Richards, V., *Lessons of the Spanish Revolution* (London, 1972).

Richardson, R. D., *Comintern Army: the International Brigades and the Spanish Civil War* (Lexington, Kentucky, 1982).

Richardson, R. D., 'The defence of Madrid: mysterious generals, Red-Front fighters and the International Brigades', *Military Affairs*, XLIII, No. 4 (January, 1979), pp. 178–85.

Romero, L., *El final de la guerra* (Barcelona, 1976).

Rosenstone, R., *Crusade of the Left: the Lincoln Battalion in the Spanish Civil War* (new edition, New Brunswick, New Jersey, 2009).

Ruiz, J., 'Defending the Republic: the García Atadell brigade in Madrid, 1936', *Journal of Contemporary History*, XLII, No. 1 (January, 2007), pp. 97–115.

Ruiz, J., '"Incontrolados" en la España republicana durante la Guerra Civil Española: el caso de Luis Bonilla Echevarría', *Historia y política*, No. 21 (January, 2009), pp. 191–218.

Ruiz, J., *'They have passed!' The Beginning of Francoist Rule in Madrid, April 1939* (Oxford, 2005).

Salas Larrázabal, J., *Air War over Spain* (Shepperton, 1974).

Salas Larrázabal, R., *Historia del Ejército Popular de la Republica* (Madrid, 1963).

Seco Serrano, C., *Alfonso XIII y la crisis de la restauración* (Madrid, 1979).

Seidman, M., 'Agrarian collectives during the Spanish Revolution and Civil War', *European History Quarterly*, XXX, No. 2 (April, 2010), pp. 209–35.

Seidman, M., *Republic of Egos: a Social History of the Spanish Civil War* (Madison, Wisconsin, 2002).

Seidman, M., 'The unorwellian Barcelona', *European History Quarterly*, XX, No. 2 (April, 1990), pp. 163–80.

Seidman, M., 'Work and revolution: workers' control in Barcelona in the Spanish Civil War, 1936–1938', *Journal of Contemporary History*, XVII, No.3 (July, 1982), pp. 409–34.

Shores, C., *Spanish-Civil-War Airforces* (London, 1977).

Sullivan, B., 'Fascist Italy's military involvement in the Spanish Civil War', *Journal of Military History*, LIX, No. 4 (October, 1995), pp. 697–727.

Thomas, G., and Morgan Witts, M., *The Day Guernica Died* (London, 1975).

Thomas, H., 'The hero in the empty room: José Antonio and Spanish fascism', *Journal of Contemporary History*, I, No. 1 (January, 1966), pp. 174–82.

Thomas, H., *The Spanish Civil War* (London, 1977).

Thómas, J. M., *El gran golpe: el caso Hedilla o cómo Franco se quedó con la Falange* (Barcelona, 2014).

Tuma, A. al-, 'Tangier, Spanish Morocco and Spain's civil war in Dutch diplomatic documents', *The Journal of North African Studies*, XVII, No. 3 (June, 2012), pp. 433–53.

Tusell Gómez, J., *Radiografía de un golpe de estado: el ascenso al poder del General Primo de Rivera* (Madrid, 1987).

Vargas Alonso, F. M., 'Voluntarios internacionales y asesores extranjeros en Euzkadi, 1936–1937', *Historia contemporánea*, XXXIV (2007), pp. 323–59.

Vidal, C., *Las brigadas internacionales* (Madrid, 1998).

Viñas, A., 'Playing with history and hiding treason: Colonel Casado's untrustworthy memoirs and the end of the Spanish Civil War', *Bulletin of Spanish Studies*, XCI, Nos. 1–2 (January, 2014), pp. 295–323.

Whealey, R. H., *Hitler and Spain: the Nazi Role in the Spanish Civil War* (Lexington, Kentucky, 1989).

White, B. T., *Tanks and Other AFVs of the Blitzkrieg Era, 1939–1941* (London, 1972).

Wright, P., *Tank: the Progress of a Monstrous War-Machine* (London, 2000).

Willis, L., *Women in the Spanish Revolution* (London, 1975).

Woolman, D., *Rebels in the Rif: Abd-el-Krim and the Rif Rebellion* (Stanford, 1969).

Zaloga, S. J., *Spanish-Civil-War Tanks: the Proving Ground for Blitzkrieg* (Oxford, 2010).

Zaloga, S. J., 'Soviet tank operations in the Spanish Civil War', *Journal of Slavic Military Studies*, XII, No. 3 (December, 2007), pp. 134–62.

INDEX